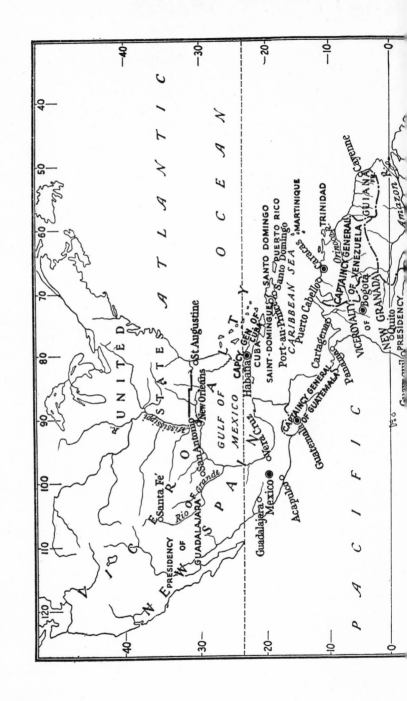

FRANCE AND LATIN–AMERICAN INDEPENDENCE

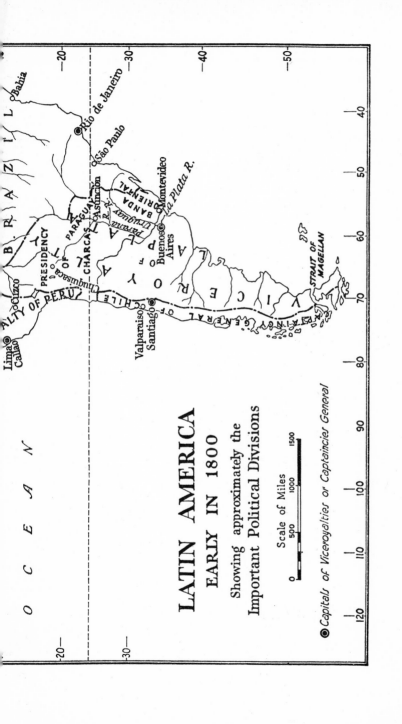

LATIN AMERICA
EARLY IN 1800

Showing approximately the
Important Political Divisions

Scale of Miles

● Capitals of Viceroyalties or Captaincies General

THE ALBERT SHAW LECTURES ON DIPLOMATIC HISTORY, 1939
THE WALTER HINES PAGE SCHOOL OF INTERNATIONAL RELATIONS

FRANCE AND LATIN–AMERICAN INDEPENDENCE

BY

WILLIAM SPENCE ROBERTSON

1967

OCTAGON BOOKS, INC.

New York

Reprinted 1967
by special arrangement with The Johns Hopkins Press

OCTAGON BOOKS, INC.
175 FIFTH AVENUE
NEW YORK, N. Y. 10010

LIBRARY OF CONGRESS CATALOG CARD NUMBER: 67-18782

Printed in U.S.A. by
NOBLE OFFSET PRINTERS, INC.
NEW YORK 3, N. Y.

To

The Memory Of

FREDERICK JACKSON TURNER

PREFACE

The thoughts of publicists and scholars in both the Old World and the New are turning more and more to the vast domain known as Latin America. Indeed it seems that a critical issue in the not distant future may be concerned with the policies of certain European powers toward the southern neighbors of the United States. Though the labors of American scholars have placed in relief salient features of the relations of the United States with Latin America, the foundations for the study of intercourse between powers of continental Europe and Latin nations of the Western Hemisphere have not been laid.

My interest in diplomatic history began while I was studying history under Professor Frederick J. Turner at the University of Wisconsin. Many years ago, while gathering materials in European libraries and archives for a biography of that knight-errant of Spanish-American independence, Francisco de Miranda, I became interested in the attitude of French leaders toward Latin America. Accordingly on two occasions, while on sabbatical leave of absence from the University of Illinois, I carried on a search in European archives and libraries for materials concerning the relations of France with Spanish and Portuguese America. During my sabbatical sojourn in Europe in 1932-33, my work was greatly facilitated by a generous Grant-in-Aid from the Social Science Research Council. After a preliminary survey, I decided that I would lay aside temporarily the alluring topic of the influence of French culture in Latin America and confine my investigations to a fundamental

issue, namely the policy of France toward the nations that
gradually arose in the New World after Napoleon invaded
the Iberian Peninsula. At various points this research involved a consideration of the attitude of Spain, Portugal,
England, Russia, and the United States toward the Indies.
Further, it seemed fitting that some attention should be
paid to unofficial French sentiment regarding Latin-American independence. This study is also concerned with commercial relations between France and the Latin nations of
America; for economic as well as political motives affected
the attitude of French journalists, merchants, and statesmen.

On the other hand, I have excluded from this monograph
a consideration of French intervention in America except
when such intervention was inextricably related to an acknowledgment of the independence of a new American
nation by France. Whenever the policy of armed interposition in Latin America was seriously considered by a
French official in connection with its recognition, I have
noticed proposals for the establishment of a protectorate.

A general acknowledgment is hereby made for the courtesies of officials of libraries in which I sought for materials.
In particular I am under obligations to the staffs of the
Bibliothèque Nationale, the British Museum, the Library of
Congress, and the Library of the University of Illinois. Dr.
Leo S. Rowe, Director of the Pan American Union, kindly
made available to me rare materials in its library. I am
indebted to my colleague, Professor Frederick S. Rodkey,
for undertaking to supplement my researches in the Archives du Ministère des Affaires Étrangères by searching for
manuscripts regarding the policy of Russia toward Spanish
America in the Arkhiv Revoliutsii i Vneshnei Politiki at
Moscow. For aid in securing copies of certain documents

which escaped my attention in English repositories, I am obliged to Dr. Robin A. Humphreys of University College, London. The eminent English historian, Professor Harold Temperley of Peterhouse College, Cambridge, kindly furnished me with a copy of a manuscript from English official archives entitled " Notes on Spain, 1824-25." Helpful suggestions concerning my researches in the Archivo General de Indias were furnished by my friend, Dr. José de la Peña, who is now on the staff of the Instituto Hispano-Cubano de América at Seville. For assistance in securing permission to work in the archives of France and Spain, I am indebted to American embassies in those countries. In particular, I am under obligation to Mr. Hugh Millard, second secretary of the American Legation at Madrid in 1933, who effectively aided me in gaining access to certain papers in the Archivo Histórico Nacional. I cannot omit mentioning the freedom of investigation allowed me by Mr. A. E. Stamp of the Public Record Office, London, and by Herr Lothar Gross of the Haus-, Hof- und Staats-Archiv in Vienna. For useful information about material in the French archives I am thankful to Mr. Waldo G. Leland, now secretary of the American Council of Learned Societies. M. Abel Doysié greatly facilitated my investigations in Parisian libraries and archives. As the most important materials for this monograph were found in the Archives du Ministère des Affaires Étrangères, I acknowledge my special indebtedness to M. Abel Rigault, who was directly in charge of those archives when I gathered material there.

I am indebted to Professor W. Stull Holt for the kind invitation to deliver the Albert Shaw Lectures on Diplomatic History at The Johns Hopkins University in 1939. For courtesies extended to me while the monograph on which those lectures were based was being prepared for the press, I am also under obligation to Mr. Owen Lattimore, director of the Walter Hines Page School of International Relations. Dr. Albert K. Weinberg, also of the Page School of International Relations, gave finishing touches to my manuscript.

My daughter read carefully a draft of this monograph and made critical suggestions. My wife aided me in reading the proof.

WILLIAM SPENCE ROBERTSON.

Urbana, Illinois,
    July, 1939.

CONTENTS

MAPS

Chapter I

THE HISTORICAL BACKGROUND

Through the tangled web of European relations with Latin America runs the golden thread of commerce. From an early period merchants of France took an interest in trade with the colonies of Spain and Portugal. By the middle of the sixteenth century the Portuguese were transporting French cloth and cordage to the Indies to exchange for products of the mines. During the next century, merchants brought into France from the Portuguese possessions sugar, tobacco, hides, gold, silver, precious stones, and Brazil wood. It appears that a French captain could even navigate to Portuguese America under his own flag. After the War of the Spanish Succession broke out, however, those friendly commercial relations were interrupted. A daring commander named Duguay-Trouin led a French squadron to Brazil in 1711, captured the city of Rio de Janeiro, and forced the governor to pay a large ransom in treasure.

During the negotiations that preceded the signing of the peace treaty on April 11, 1713, the Portuguese diplomats seem to have proposed not only an offensive and defensive alliance with France but also a treaty of commerce by which both Portugal and Brazil were to furnish a vent for French manufactures. This treaty would have enabled French merchants to regain the trade which they had lost during the protracted war. Yet the Treaty of Utrecht merely restored the commercial relations between France and Portugal to the condition that had existed before the outbreak of hostilities. As a result, France lost to other European nations a large share of the trade with Brazil. French merchants felt this loss severely.

The instructions to the French ambassador at Lisbon in the autumn of 1713 accordingly directed him to secure from Portugal permission to station some French merchants at the Bay of All Saints on the Brazilian coast. " The commerce of Brazil," continued these instructions, " is an object of infinite consequence to the French because of the gold produced by the mines of Goyaz and the large amount of it that we may obtain in return for the goods which the French will send there. No more essential service can thus be performed for France, nor one more agreeable to the King and advantageous to the State, than the promotion of everything that concerns the maintenance and increase of this commerce." [1]

The author of a memoir concerning the trade of France with Portugal declared in 1723 that the Dutch and the English had become the masters of Portuguese commerce. He complained that French merchantmen had been seized by Brazilian officials on the charge that they were engaged in contraband trade.[2] In consequence consular and diplomatic agents of France at Lisbon repeatedly tried to induce Portuguese diplomats to concede by treaty to Frenchmen trafficking in their dominions all the rights and privileges enjoyed by the subjects of any other nation. Nevertheless, for many years England, the ancient ally of Portugal, re-

[1] " Mémoire concernant le Commerce Maritime, la Navigation de les Colonies pour servir d'instruction au Sr. Abbé de Mornay, ambassadeur extraordinaire de Sa Majesté en Portugal," signed by the King and Phélypeaux, October 23, 1713, A. A. E., Portugal, 45.

[2] " Mémoire sur le commerce de France en Portugal," June 28, 1723, A. N., F^{12}, 644.

mained the most-favored-nation with respect to Portuguese trade.

Stories concerning fabulous riches on the distant shores of Spanish America had meanwhile attracted attention in France. Indeed our first glimpse of Verrazano dimly reveals him as a corsair preying upon galleons carrying treasure from Mexico to Spain. As early as the sixteenth century, French merchants covertly loaded their wares on caravels freighted in Seville for the Indies. A century later, it was estimated that the illicit French trade with Spanish America amounted to ten million francs annually. Louis XIV and Colbert granted to the Company of the East Indies in 1674 the exclusive right to trade in the Indies and the South Sea. Four years later, Colbert directed the commander of an expedition that was sent to salvage wrecks at the Aves Islands to determine secretly the exact routes followed by Spanish fleets to the Indies, the fighting strength of the treasure ships, and the size of the armaments which would be required to overpower them. A memorialist of the French Government stated in 1691 that more than one-quarter of the commerce carried on through Cadiz with the Indies was French. In 1698 the French Government gave the Royal Company of the South Sea a monopoly of commerce not only with the region lying between La Plata River and the Strait of Magellan, but also with those shores of the Pacific Ocean that were not already occupied by Europeans.

When hostilities broke out between France and Spain, buccaneers, who were swarming in the Antilles, were encouraged by the French to make raids upon Spanish settlements. In 1699 an expedition composed of filibusters from Saint-Domingue led by Governor du Casse and of French soldiers commanded by Baron de Pointis sacked Cartagena and quarreled over an immense booty. By a treaty between France and Spain in the autumn of 1701, the French Company of Guinea was authorized to carry on the slave trade with the Indies, to build ships in Spanish ports on the Pacific Ocean, and to dispose of the merchandise which it received in return for Negro slaves. Under cover of this contract, an extensive illicit trade developed between French merchants and Spanish colonists.

Instructions to the French ambassador at Madrid in 1705 declared that commerce with Spain formed a veritable bridge over which precious metals from the Indies were transported to Europe. " It is certain that the more merchandise we take to the Spaniards," ran these instructions, " the more will we bring back of goods and of money in gold and silver." [3] When the galleons arrived from the Indies in that year under an armed escort commanded by Du Casse, a naval agent of France was dispatched from Madrid to the Spanish coast to supervise the unloading of the precious cargoes. In spite of orders which prohibited French subjects from making voyages to the South Sea without passports from the Spanish King, adventurous French traders frequently sailed along the Pacific coast of South America and covertly exchanged goods with Peruvian merchants.[4] As a result of scientific observations made while voyaging around South America and travelling in

[3] " Mémoire du Roy concernant le Commerce et les Colonies pour servir d'instruction au Sr. Amelot, ambassadeur extraordinaire de sa mate. près du Roy Catholique," April 29, 1705, A. N., Marine, B², 173.

[4] Dahlgren, Les relations commerciales et maritimes entre la France et les côtes de l'Océan Pacifique, I, 676-702.

Chile and Peru, a French savant named Feuillée drew in 1714 a surprisingly accurate map of that continent.

As the War of the Spanish Succession did not deprive Philip of Anjou of the Spanish crown, the relations between Spain and France entered upon a new phase. The Treaty of Utrecht not only stipulated that ports in the Spanish colonies were to be closed to the direct commerce of foreign merchants but also transferred to England the lucrative contract to engage in the slave traffic which the French company had enjoyed. In Cadiz, however, there were established French mercantile houses through which illicit traffic with those colonies was carried on. To paraphrase an official report, the commerce of France took the route by way of Cadiz for the disposal of such of her agricultural and manufactured products as found markets in Spanish America.[5] In order to supply French merchants, the Spaniards brought back from the Indies quinine, tobacco, vanilla, cacao, sugar, dyewood, cochineal, gold, silver, and precious stones.

Foreign interest in the Indies early awoke the jealousy of the Spaniards. Even before La Salle planted a colony in the Mississippi Valley, Spanish officials had become alarmed at the proposal of a renegade compatriot to Louis XIV that France establish a colony near the northern frontier of Mexico. In the face of English expansion in America, however, French statesmen developed a singular interest in the conservation of the Spanish dominions. "The Spanish colonies in America are as dear to the French King as his

---

[5] " Rapport sur la législation politique que régit le Commerce de la France, à l'egard de l'Amérique Espagnole et des Colonies Étrangères en général," February 2, 1716, A. A. E., Mémoires et Documents, Amérique, 31.

own American possessions," avowed the astute Duke of
Choiseul, Foreign Minister in 1759, "and, if it should
happen that the English attacked those colonies, aside from
the friendship and union with Spain which would not suffer
Louis XV to allow England to encroach upon the territories
of the King, his cousin, the interest of France and of all
other nations in that domain is such that they would unite
to check English ambition in Spanish America." [6]

On August 15, 1761, Franco-Spanish compacts of 1733
and 1743 were superseded by an agreement which became
known as the Bourbon Family Compact. In its preamble
the parties declared that the intention of the monarchs of
France and Spain in contracting the engagements assumed
by this treaty was to perpetuate the sentiments of their
common ancestor, Louis XIV, "and to establish forever
a solemn monument of the reciprocal interest which should
be the basis of the desires of their hearts and of the prosperity of their royal families." [7]

The fundamental principle of this convention was that
whosoever attacked one crown also attacked the other.
Articles providing for coöperation between the contracting
parties stipulated that, when both powers were at war with
the same enemy, they were to act in concert. When one
party became involved in either an offensive or a defensive
war, it could call upon the other for specific military and
naval aid. Subjects of one party domiciled in the European
dominions of the other party were to be considered with
regard to commerce as subjects of the kingdom within
which they resided. In Spain the French flag was to be

[6] Morel-Fatio, *Recueil des instructions données aux ambassadeurs
et ministres de France*, XII *bis*, 349-50.

[7] Clercq, *Recueil des traités de la France*, I, 81.

treated with the same favor as the Spanish flag. Charles III and Louis XV mutually guaranteed the integrity of each other's dominions.[8]

This "perpetual" family compact was a diplomatic triumph for France. It denoted a much closer intimacy between the contracting parties than did an ordinary treaty of alliance. In conjunction with a secret offensive alliance between the two parties signed on the same day, it constituted an offensive and defensive pact aimed against England. Instructions framed for the French ambassador to Madrid in 1785 began with the following interpretative passage:

The Treaty known as the Family Compact is the basis of the relations existing between France and Spain. That treaty blends the interests of the two monarchies in such a manner that one party cannot be attacked or even entertain offensive policies without the other party being obliged to participate.[9]

Partly because of this treaty, Spain became involved in wars between France and England. In consequence important transfers of territory took place between the Bourbon allies. Furthermore, during the years when members of the elder branch of the Bourbon dynasty sat upon the throne of France, this famous compact was destined to exercise a pervasive influence not only upon the policy which French statesmen pursued toward Spain but also upon their attitude toward her possessions in the New World.

The Duke of Choiseul wished to promote intimate relations between France and the Indies. He was led to formu-

---

[8] *Ibid.*, I, 81-88.
[9] Morel-Fatio, *op. cit.*, XII *bis*, 377.

late such a policy by Abbé Béliardi, who for several years
served as French commercial agent at Madrid. On November 8, 1762, the abbé sent to Choiseul a memorandum
proposing that Louisiana be exchanged for the Spanish portion of the isle of Santo Domingo. Further, he urged that
a strong French colony be built up in Guiana in order that
at the first opportunity France might be able to make herself
the master of southern America.[10] In the following year
Béliardi sent to Choiseul a memorandum with regard to
the condition of the Spanish colonies. Among the reforms
in Spain's colonial policy which this agent proposed was
that the commerce between Europe and the Indies be
relieved of duties. He reasoned that such a reform would
result in a prodigious exportation of European merchandise
to Spanish America from which France would profit
greatly.[11]

After Charles III of Spain had radically changed the
regulations concerning trade with the Indies in 1765,
Choiseul and Béliardi planned to develop a French colonial
empire in America with bases at Guiana, Martinique, and
Saint-Domingue. Béliardi dreamed that in this fashion
France might acquire a strategic position which would
enable her to gain influence in Brazil; she might check the
advance of the English in the Caribbean region, and
organize a Franco-Spanish colony near the mouth of the
Mississippi that would serve as a counterpoise to the English
colonies in North America.[12] In this manner French states-

[10] Villiers du Terrage, *Les dernières années de la Louisiane
française,* p. 154.
[11] " Commerce des Indies Espagnolles actuel et projet d'un nouveau sisteme pour son augmentation," MSS. F., Papiers de l'abbé
de Béliardi, no. 10,768.
[12] Muret, " Les papiers de l'abbé Béliardi et les relations com-

men might have transformed the Gulf of Mexico into a Bourbon sea.

Louis Antoine de Bougainville had meanwhile proposed to the French Government that it recoup its losses in the Seven Years' War by the discovery of lands in the Southern Hemisphere. One result of this proposal was an abortive attempt to plant a French colony in the Falkland Islands.[13]

Soon after the people of the Thirteen Colonies began to struggle against the motherland, the French Minister of Finance prepared a memorial concerning the manner in which the Bourbon Allies should view that quarrel. Turgot was convinced that North American revolutionists would incite Spain's colonists to follow their example.[14] It is scarcely an exaggeration to say that as early as 1775 this eminent financier caught the vision of an emancipated Spanish America.

A year after France intervened in the struggle between England and her colonists by virtue of the Treaty of Alliance of February 6, 1778, Spain, influenced by the Family Compact and by a pledge from France that certain possessions would be restored to her when peace was made, also decided to aid the Americans. This junction of the Bourbon allies affected the policy of France toward the Spanish Indies. About the middle of April, 1779, Count D'Estaing, commander of the French expeditionary forces in the New World, notified Luis de Unzaga, the captain general of Venezuela, that Louis XVI had ordered him, in

---

merciales de la France et de l'Espagne au milieu du XVIIIᵉ siècle," *Revue d'histoire moderne et contemporaine*, IV, 669.

[13] Gœpp and Cordier, *Les grandes hommes de la France*, pp. 38-45.

[14] Turgot, *Œuvres*, II, 564-65.

case of an attack by the English upon the dominions of the
Bourbon powers in America, to use his forces to defend the
Spanish possessions rather than the French.[15] Upon being
notified by a royal order that Spain had entered the war
against England, Unzaga wrote to D'Estaing, who had just
captured the island of Grenada from the English, to express
the hope that French naval forces would protect the Spanish
colonies against the common enemy.[16] Officials of both
France and Spain in the New World thus contemplated
joint action to defend Spanish America against an attack
by the English.

Shortly after England recognized the independence of
the United States, the French Government undertook to
make a scientific, political, and commercial reconnaissance
of the northwest coast of North America. The instructions
prepared in 1786 for Count de la Pérouse, who was made
the commander of an expedition to that region, directed him
to study the character of the Spanish settlements, to determine what articles would be most advantageous for traffic
with the inhabitants, and to consider the possibility of
planting French colonies there.[17]

The Bourbon Family Compact had meanwhile been invoked by Spain in a dispute with England respecting the
title to land in America. Yet, as Louis XV refused to
support by force of arms his ally's claim to the Falkland
Islands,[18] the Spaniards agreed to restore an English settlement which they had seized there to its former condition.

---

[15] D'Estaing to Unzaga, April 17, 1779, A. N., Marine, B⁴, 163.
[16] Unzaga to D'Estaing, July 27, 1779, *ibid*.
[17] Blue, " French Interest in Pacific America in the Eighteenth
Century," *Pacific Historical Review*, IV, 255-59.
[18] Flammeront, *Le chancelier Maupeou et les parlements*, p. 190.

Again, upon the occasion of the controversy between England and Spain in 1790 concerning the title to Nootka Sound, the National Assembly of France decided that it would recognize only the defensive and commercial clauses of the Family Compact, and proposed that this pact be transformed into a national treaty.[19]

During the French Revolution seditious papers from France were secretly circulated in the Indies. In 1792 a French contraband trader called Coste was suspected of conspiring with fellow-countrymen in the island of Santo Domingo to set New Spain adrift from the motherland.[20] During the same year Admiral Kersaint presented a memorandum to the government proposing that France make war on Spain and, by the aid of other nations, liberate the Indies from their Spanish masters.[21] In November, 1792, Brissot and Dumouriez contemplated placing Francisco de Miranda, the Venezuelan apostle of revolution who had been made a general in the French service, in charge of the colony of Saint-Domingue. From this base, by the aid of a strong military and naval force, he was to revolutionize Spanish America.[22] Again, the instructions of the government of France to Citizen Genêt directed that, if he should not succeed in arranging a treaty with the United States which would establish an intimate union between the two countries, he was to undertake to spread the principles of

---

[19] Sorel, *L'Europe et la révolution française*, III, 93-94; Montmorin to Fernán Núñez, September 1, 1790, A. H. N., Estado, 4038.

[20] Rydjord, *Foreign Interest in the Independence of New Spain*, pp. 133-36.

[21] "Mémoire sur la guerre contre l'Espagne," October 1, 1792, A. A. E., Mémoires et Documents, Espagne, 210.

[22] Robertson, *The Life of Miranda*, I, 127-30.

the French Revolution in the Spanish colonies bordering upon the American Republic.[23] In 1794 a French publicist named Flassan composed a suggestive memoir concerning the future relations of the Bourbon allies. He reasoned not only that the Family Compact should be abrogated, but also that it would be inconsistent with her principles for France to support despotic rule in the Spanish Indies, and furthermore that the emancipation of South America would give a great stimulus to French commerce:

As the ingots of Peru and the piastres of Mexico would no longer be in the possession of the indolent Spaniards, those riches would belong to the people most useful to Spanish America because of the amount of their exports. In that respect rejuvenated France could without doubt aspire to the primacy.[24]

At the opening of the nineteenth century the colonies of Spain and Portugal included about sixty-five per cent of the territory in the New World. The Portuguese settlements in Brazil were organized into divisions designated as captaincies under the control of royal officials known as captains general. Though in certain circumstances some of those officials could correspond with the Portuguese Government, in general they had fallen under the control of the viceroy of Brazil, who was seated at Rio de Janeiro. Other institutions for the management of Portuguese America were located at Lisbon under the nominal direction of the monarch.[25]

[23] " Clark-Genêt Correspondence," *American Historical Association Report*, 1896, I, 958.

[24] " Considérations sur la nature de nos relations futures avec l'Espagne," A. A. E., Mémoires et Documents, Espagne, 210.

[25] Pereira da Silva, *Historia da fundação do Imperio Brazileiro*, I, *passim*.

On the eve of the revolutionary struggles which separated the Indies from the motherland, Spain claimed title to territory in the New World which stretched from the sources of the Mississippi to Cape Horn. Comprising almost one-half of the area of the Three Americas, this domain included some seven million square miles. Legally the title to the Indies was vested not in the Spanish people but in the King. In the administration of the colonies, however, he was aided by special institutions. The most important institution in Spain was the Council of the Indies, which exercised executive, legislative, and judicial authority. Some functions of this council had been assumed by the Minister of the Indies, who managed the voluminous correspondence with Spanish America. Important institutions of colonial administration in the New World were the viceroys, the captains general, and the *audiencias*. By 1800 four viceroyalties had been carved out of the Spanish dominions in America: the viceroyalty of New Spain, which included Mexico, Florida, and islands in the West Indies; the viceroyalty of New Granada, which comprised a large part of northern South America; the viceroyalty of Peru, which embraced the territory stretching from Tumbez to the Desert of Atacama; and the viceroyalty of La Plata, which extended from the Andean range to the south Atlantic.

The authority of the viceroys had been gradually curtailed by the appointment of captains general, who were placed in charge of minor divisions carved out of the viceroyalties. In the age of Charles IV there were four captaincies general in the Spanish Indies: Chile, Venezuela, Cuba, and Guatemala or Central America. In many respects a captain general was a viceroy in miniature. By 1800 the captains general of Guatemala, Venezuela, and Chile were virtually independent of the adjacent viceroyalties. While the authority of each viceroy extended over a region in which there were two *audiencias*, the jurisdiction of a captain general did not extend beyond the area controlled by a single *audiencia*.[26]

By 1800 twelve *audiencias* had been established in cities of Spanish America. Each of these tribunals was composed of magistrates who acted as the appelate court of a district which had been roughly delimited by the Council of the Indies. In the New World these courts became advisory councils to the officials who presided over their meetings. In districts where neither a viceroy nor a captain general resided, the *audiencias* also exercised some political authority. As the respective circumjacent areas were under the control of the jurists who presided over the deliberations of the *audiencias*—officials who were styled presidents—such regions were designated as presidencies. Thus to a certain extent the regions controlled by the *audiencias* located at the cities of Quito and Chuquisaca constituted distinct administrative entities. The boundaries of the important divisions known as presidencies, captaincies general, and viceroyalties dimly foreshadowed the limits of certain nations of Spanish America.

Though as a result of the Seven Year's War France had lost her continental domain in North America, and though in 1803 she had transferred the one-time Spanish province of Louisiana to the United States, yet she retained control of outlying portions of the American Continent. Among her insular possessions she still claimed title to the revolted

[26] Robertson, *Rise of the Spanish-American Republics*, pp. 1-7. On the *audiencias*, see further Ruíz Guiñazú, *La magistratura indiana*.

colony of Saint-Domingue in the western part of the island of Santo Domingo. The islands of Guadeloupe and Martinique furnished her with outposts in the Caribbean Sea. At the same time the penal settlement at Cayenne in Guiana enabled officials at Paris to keep in touch with movements in both Spanish and Portuguese America. Furthermore, as papers preserved in the Archives Nationales amply demonstrate, the seas surrounding Middle and South America were being frequently traversed by French frigates, the captains of which composed for the Navy Department instructive reports concerning the Latin colonies in the New World.

French merchants early displayed a keen interest in the commerce of Spanish and Portuguese America. Long before the opening of the nineteenth century, Frenchmen had looked longingly at the rich and extensive domains in the Western Hemisphere which were under the sway of other Latin nations. A desire to conserve the Spanish colonies for their Bourbon ally, the alluring dream of a new French empire in America, and vague speculations concerning the separation of the Indies from the motherland—all occasionally surged through the fertile brains of French statesmen.

CHAPTER II

FRENCH DESIGNS UPON SPAIN AND PORTUGAL

The struggle for supremacy between England and France that began in 1793 led Napoleon to extend his political system to the Iberian Peninsula. Because Portugal refused to accede to his demands, which included the cession of her colony in Guiana, at his instance Spanish soldiers invaded that country. Consequently the Portuguese soon agreed to a treaty which provided that their harbors were to be closed to the English and that French trade with Portugal was to be placed upon a most-favored-nation basis. A supplementary treaty, signed on September 29, 1801, stipulated that no assistance was to be given by Portugal to Napoleon's enemies, that the Portuguese were to pay France a large indemnity, and that the southern boundary of French Guiana was to be extended to the Amazon River. On February 16, 1805, Prince Talleyrand prepared instructions for General Junot, who was sent on a diplomatic mission to Lisbon. Junot was informed that the time had arrived for Portugal to break with the Mistress of the Seas and to adopt a new political system more suitable to the interests of herself and France.[1]

As the nineteenth century opened, the attention of French statesmen was directed more and more to the Spanish Indies. An observer in Mexico informed the French Government that the vicious administration of that country and a weak

---

[1] Sorel, *op. cit.*, VI, 105; Clercq, *Recueil des traités*, I, 435-37, 455-57; Mouy, " L'ambassade de General Junot à Lisbonne d'après des documents inédits," *Revue des deux mondes,* CXXI, 144-45.

defense would render its conquest easy.[2] In 1803 an émigré suggested to Napoleon that in the basin of La Plata there should be founded a French mining colony that might threaten the flanks of both the Portuguese and the Spanish dominions in South America.[3] Three years later an anonymous paper concerning the Indies was laid before General Murat, Duke of Berg. Its author declared that the French Emperor was mentioned with enthusiasm in the South American possessions of Spain. He added:

Humiliated by living under the laws of a government which has neither the skill to govern them nor the power to protect them, the people are in that condition of apathy which almost always precedes a new order of things. The wisdom of Napoleon the Great can determine the destiny of the irresolute Americas.[4]

In 1806 François de Pons, who had served as French commercial agent in the captaincy general of Venezuela, presented to the Ministry of Foreign Affairs a memorandum in which he maintained that only the French could save the Indies from English designs. He suggested that, as a reward for protecting that vast domain, France should be given possession of Venezuela.[5] Shortly afterward Santiago Liniers, who avowed that despite a long absence from France he was still a Frenchman at heart, informed Napoleon of the defeat of invading redcoats in the viceroyalty

[2] Rydjord, *Foreign Interest in the Independence of New Spain*, pp. 195-96.

[3] Lokke, "French Designs on Paraguay in 1803," *Hispanic American Historical Review*, VIII, 397-401.

[4] " Copie d'un Mémoire remis Particulierement à S. A. I. le Grand Duc de Berg à son retour à Paris à la suite de la Paix de Presbourg," A. A. E., Mémoires et Documents, Amérique, 33.

[5] " Mémoire sur la cession de la capitainerie générale de Caracas à la France," 1806, A. A. E., Colombie, 1.

of La Plata by colonial soldiers under his leadership.[6] In 1807 D'Esmenard, who had long resided in Spain, addressed a memorial to the Emperor in which he reasoned that France could easily become mistress of that decrepit country and thus ensure herself control of the rich commerce of the Spanish colonies.[7]

The year 1807 was the date when the Emperor's designs with respect to the Iberian nations took a definite form. As Junot's mission had failed, Napoleon in July made three requests of the Portuguese ambassador at Paris: that Portugal close her ports to English commerce; that she seize all Englishmen residing in that kingdom; and that all English property there be sequestrated. These demands were evidently accompanied by the threat that in case of refusal Portugal would become involved in a war with both France and Spain. The diplomatic representatives of the Emperor's allies at Lisbon were instructed that, if Portugal did not yield, they were to ask for their passports. These requests frightened Regent John, a vacillating young prince who had married Carlota Joaquina, the eldest daughter of Charles IV of Spain, and who was ruling Portugal on behalf of his demented mother, Queen Maria I. This prince feared France and looked upon England as his natural ally.[8]

On August 12, in accordance with urgent instructions from Count Champagny, the Minister of Foreign Affairs, François Rayneval, who was French chargé at Lisbon, notified the Portuguese Government that, if by September

---

[6] Rayneval to Talleyrand, March 3, 1807, A. A. E., Portugal, 126.

[7] Desdevises du Dezert, " De Trafalgar à Aranjuez (1805-1808), *Cultura española*, no. 5, p. 18.

[8] Neves, *Reflexões sobre a invasao dos Franceses em Portugal*, 18-19; Mouy, " L'ambassade de General Junot à Lisbonne d'après des documents inédits," *loc. cit.*, CXXI, 146.

1 the Prince Regent did not yield to these demands and
also unite his naval forces to those of France, the Prince
would be considered to have renounced the cause of the
European Continent. In that case Rayneval was to demand
his passports and to declare war on Portugal in the name of
his Imperial Master.[9] The Portuguese minister Araujo
replied that the Regent was startled at this ultimatum, that
he had scrupulously tried to observe neutrality, and that it
was unjust to require Portugal to declare war upon her
ancient ally against whom she had no complaint.[10] Rayneval became convinced that the Portuguese ministers would
not favor hostilities against France. As an afterthought he
added: ". . . it is impossible for me to determine whether
in the last extremity they will succeed in persuading the
Prince Regent to embark for Brazil." [11] After his efforts at
an adjustment failed, Rayneval on October 1 left Lisbon
en route for Madrid.[12]

Speculation was rife in Lisbon regarding the next move
in Portuguese policy. On October 17, 1807, a memoir concerning the attitude which Portugal should adopt with
respect to France and England was addressed to the Prince
Regent. The anonymous author declared that France, with
a preponderating influence upon the Continent, undoubtedly
aimed at political dominion. On the other hand, England,
by a system antagonistic to that of her rival, had founded
her greatness upon commercial intercourse. The very existence of Portugal, reasoned this adviser, depended upon her

[9] Hauterive to Rayneval, July 30, 1807, A. A. E., Portugal, 126;
Rayneval to Talleyrand, August 12, 1807, *ibid.*

[10] Enclosure in Hauterive to Rayneval, July 30, 1807; Araujo
to Rayneval, August 21, 1807, *ibid.*

[11] Rayneval to Champagny, September 3, 1807, *ibid.*

[12] *Idem* to *idem,* October 2, 1807, *ibid.*

commerce; hence the Portuguese should align themselves with the English rather than with the French. "Not only to promote her future happiness," he continued, "but to ensure her very existence, Portugal should transfer the seat of her government to her transatlantic dominions, where she would not have to dread either Continental influence or invasion by sea." [13]

Aware of the threat to Portuguese autonomy, the English Secretary of State for Foreign Affairs, George Canning, soon undertook negotiations with Souza Coutinho, the Portuguese ambassador in London, with respect to an agreement which would determine afresh the relations between England and her ancient ally. On October 22, 1807, these diplomats signed a secret convention of friendship and alliance. This convention provided that, if the Prince Regent should be forced by the French to sail for Brazil or should send there a prince of the Braganza dynasty, His Britannic Majesty would promote the undertaking. Souza Coutinho agreed that, if the Regent went to Brazil, he was to take with him the navy of Portugal as well as her merchant marine. Once established at Rio de Janeiro, the Portuguese Government should negotiate a further agreement with England concerning aid and commerce.[14] The hesitation of the Regent over the ratification of this treaty was not terminated, however, until he learned that the English had instituted a rigorous blockade of Portuguese ports and that French soldiers had invaded his country.

[13] "Parecer ofrecido á S. A. R. O. Principe Regente Nosso Senhor. En 17 de Outubro de 1807," MSS. B. N. P., 235.

[14] Santarem, *Quadro elementar das relaçoes politicas e diplomaticas de Portugal com as diversas potencias do mundo*, XVIII, 443-48.

He then decided that if need arose he would flee from Lisbon to Rio de Janeiro.[15]

On the other hand, negotiations between France and Spain culminated on October 27, 1807, in the Treaty of Fontainebleau. In that treaty Napoleon declared that, when an auspicious time arrived, he would recognize Charles IV as the " Emperor of the Two Americas." The parties agreed that Portugal was to be dismembered, and they promised to make an equal division of the islands, colonies, and other outlying Portuguese possessions. In a supplementary convention the agreement was reached that a French army of twenty-eight thousand men should be permitted to march through Spain toward Lisbon.

On October 10 a French army corps under General Junot had in fact crossed the river Bidassoa. Incited by orders from Napoleon, Junot proceeded from Salamanca to Alcántara, and down the Tagus River to Abrantes. Thence he marched toward the Portuguese capital. Meanwhile Regent John had become convinced of Napoleon's ulterior designs. Soon there was circulated in Lisbon a copy of the *Moniteur*, dated November 13, 1807, which announced that because of Portugal's subservience to England Napoleon had decided to depose the Portuguese ruler.[16] After news was received that an invading column was rapidly approaching that city, the Regent ceased to hesitate. On November 26 he issued a proclamation announcing that he had decided to avoid the sanguinary war which would be caused by armed resistance, and that he would sail with the entire royal family to his American colony. He ex-

[15] Temperley, *Life of Canning*, pp. 80-81; Oliveira Lima, *Dom João VI no Brazil*, I, 38.

[16] Sorel, *L'Europe et la révolution française*, VII, 219.

pressed his intention to establish himself in Rio de Janeiro until a general peace was made.[17] In a justificatory manifesto the Regent later made a further explanation of his motives by declaring that Brazil was the most important and the most easily defended part of the Portuguese dominions.[18]

On November 27 the Portuguese royal family accordingly proceeded to the Tower of Belem at the mouth of the Tagus River and embarked on the flagship *Principe Real*. Officials, court attendants, and ministers of state took ship on fourteen other vessels, which also bore the royal library and the treasure of the Braganza dynasty. Merchant vessels were crowded with refugees who had decided to take part in the exodus. Two days later the Portuguese fleet left Lisbon harbor for South America. It was promptly supplied with provisions by Sir Sidney Smith, who on November 22 had announced a blockade of the Tagus. Escorted by a fleet commanded by Admiral Smith, the Portuguese vessels reached Bahia in January, 1808. After issuing a decree announcing that the ports of Brazil would be open to foreign trade, Prince John sailed to Rio de Janeiro, where on May 1 he issued a manifesto declaring war against France.[19] As the *Times* stated on December 23, 1807, it was " a singular incident in the history of civilized society, for a Prince to remove the seat of his government, across an almost boundless extent of ocean, to a distant colony of his subjects. . . ."

This memorable event had a lasting influence upon Portuguese history. Royal administrative machinery was transplanted from Lisbon to Rio de Janeiro. The functions of the last viceroy of Brazil, Count Arcos, were taken over by

---

[17] *Correio braziliense ou armazem literario*, I, 5.
[18] *Ibid.*, 264.   [19] *Ibid.*, 267-68.

ministers of the Prince Regent. Brazilian industry and commerce were freed from restrictions which had hampered their development. A stimulus was given to art, letters, and science.

Indeed the flight of the Braganza dynasty from Lisbon to Rio de Janeiro was the first of a series of events that culminated in the separation of Portuguese America from the motherland. Further, the establishment in Brazil of a dynasty which was related by marriage to the King of Spain stimulated the spirit of dissent in neighboring Spanish colonies. A provisional junta which was later established at Buenos Aires even suggested to the government at Rio de Janeiro that all the people of South America should adopt common measures to thwart Napoleon's ambition.[20]

Immediately upon entering Lisbon, General Junot issued a proclamation to the Portuguese stating that he had come to release Regent John from the malign influence of England.[21] In a broadside which he circulated in the capital city on February 1, 1808, the French commander declared that by abandoning Portugal the Regent had renounced all his rights to the sovereignty of that kingdom. Further, Junot announced that the Emperor desired that " this beautiful country should be administered and governed entirely in his name, and by the general in chief of his army." [22] The attitude of France toward Brazil was suggested by a letter from the Minister of Foreign Affairs instructing Junot not to grant passports to any diplomats who might desire to proceed to that colony. Champagny explained that the

[20] Rubio, *La infanta Carlota Joaquina y la política de España en América*, pp. 291-92.

[21] *Correio braziliense*, I, 8.

[22] A. A. E., Portugal et Brésil, 127.

French Government would not facilitate relations between other governments and a power which was at war with it.[23]

The destiny of Brazil was now brought directly to the Emperor's attention. An obscure adventurer who subscribed himself as Mariano Isasbiribil proposed to Napoleon an expedition to that country. He stated that, as the result of a direct order of "Monseigneur," meaning perhaps the Emperor, he had prepared a plan for the invasion of Portuguese borderlands in South America. Isasbiribil declared that supplies could be secured in southern Brazil as well as in the Spanish colonies on the Pacific. The sale of church property, he asserted, would furnish funds for the prosecution of the enterprise. He avowed that he would gladly dedicate himself to any service which would enable him to follow the Napoleonic eagle.[24]

Napoleon did not undertake to carry out the ambitious scheme of this adventurer. In fact, the hostilities which had broken out between France and Portugal actually caused an extension of Portuguese America. As the monarchy seated at Rio de Janeiro claimed to be the legitimate government of the mother country as well as of Brazil, and as Portugal had declared war against France, the Regent soon prepared an expedition against French Guiana. In December, 1808, Brazilian soldiers, aided by a small Portuguese naval squadron and an English corvette, made an attack on that colony. On January 12, 1809, the garrison at Cayenne capitulated to the besiegers. The forts and military stores in French Guiana were promptly relinquished to Regent John. Though no attempt was made to displace

---

[23] February 10, 1808, *ibid.*

[24] Undated but presumably composed late in the autumn of 1808 and addressed to "Monseigneur." *Ibid.*

the Napoleonic Code in the conquered colony, yet French Guiana, as well as Portuguese Guiana, passed under the direct sway of the Braganza dynasty.[25]

While the Regent was busy in Brazil, Talleyrand advised the Emperor to place a prince of the imperial family upon the Spanish throne and thus to secure a splendid portion of the heritage of Louis XIV.[26] The influential Spanish minister, Manuel Godoy, the Prince of the Peace, sedulously fostered an estrangement between King Charles IV and his eldest son, Ferdinand, Prince of Asturias, a superstitious, self-willed youth who was blindly loved by the Spanish people. Napoleon skilfully used the dissensions in the family of Charles IV to strengthen his hold on the Spanish situation. He also took advantage of a clause in the Treaty of Fontainebleau which provided that if the English landed troops in Portugal he might, after notifying Charles IV, dispatch forces to assist Junot. In January, 1808, Napoleon accordingly sent two fresh army corps into Spain. Undismayed by a strange terrain and a hostile populace, the invaders soon seized Burgos, Valladolid, and other cities in Old Castile. Shortly afterward French grenadiers captured the frowning fortress at Pamplona, the medieval capital of the province of Navarre. Barcelona and San Sebastián soon fell into French hands. Haughty Spaniards were astounded to learn that their northern gates were held by foreign garrisons.

The Prince of the Peace now suggested that the Spanish royal family should flee from Madrid to Seville. He con-

[25] Carra de Vaux, " Documents sur la perte et la rétrocession de la Guyane française (1809-1817)," *Revue de l'histoire des colonies françaises*, I, 334-35.

[26] Sorel, *L'Europe et la révolution française*, VII, 220.

ceived of that trip as the prelude to a longer journey. Influenced by the example of the Braganza dynasty, certain
Spaniards even felt that their ruling family should abandon
the motherland and voyage to Vera Cruz or Buenos Aires.
They thought that in a colonial capital Charles IV would be
safe against capture by the French.[27] Whether or not he
had ever dreamed of thus disposing of the Spanish Bourbons, it appears that by February, 1808, the Emperor, anxious to keep the wealth of the Indies from passing beyond
his control, had decided to prevent the Spanish King from
sailing for America. Soon afterward Charles IV was persuaded to sign a paper stating that bodily infirmities made
it impossible for him longer to bear the heavy burden of
administering his kingdom. On March 19 he abdicated in
favor of the Prince of Asturias, who was to be immediately
acknowledged as king throughout the Spanish dominions.[28]
At the instance of that idolized prince, the Council of the
Indies on April 10 addressed to the viceroys, captains general, presidents, governors, *audiencias*, and town councils of
the Spanish Indies a royal order announcing that the crown
of Spain had been transferred from Charles IV to Ferdinand
VII.[29]

The succession to the Spanish throne had meanwhile become a serious issue. General Murat, who had entered
Madrid at the head of a French army on March 23, scrupu-

[27] Fugier, *Napoléon et l'Espagne*, II, 441-42; Cevallos, *Exposición de los hechos y maquinaciones que han preparado la usurpación de la corona de España y los medios que el Emperador de los
Franceses ha puesto en obra para realizarla*, 11, 31, 65-66.

[28] Thiers, *Histoire du consulat et de l'empire*, II, 823; Oman, *A
History of the Peninsular War*, I, 607.

[29] *Documentos relativos á los antecedentes de la independencia
d- -ública argentina*, pp. 14-15.

lously refrained from recognizing Ferdinand VII. Besides, the former King soon regretted his abdication and declared that this act was null because it had been performed to prevent bloodshed among his subjects. Despite the advice of a Spanish nobleman, who warned a companion of Ferdinand VII that precarious conditions in the motherland would incite the Spanish Americans to cast off her heavy yoke, the new king crossed the frontier into France.[30] Napoleon also lured Charles IV to Bayonne, where he arrived in the middle of April. There the patriarchal former king was induced by the Emperor to issue a decree appointing Murat president of a junta which had been set up at Madrid and directing that the Council of Castile, the governors, and the captains general obey his commands.[31] On May 5 Charles IV was forced to renounce to Napoleon by treaty his right to the Spanish throne. This treaty stipulated that the integrity of the Spanish monarchy be preserved, that the prince whom Napoleon would enthrone at Madrid be independent, and that the boundaries of Spain be not altered.[32] The act of renunciation was cited in a decree dated May 8, 1808, by which the former King, speaking for the Bourbon dynasty, announced to his subjects that he had ceded to Napoleon the sovereignty over the Spanish dominions!

By a treaty which has been signed and ratified, I have

[30] Rovigo, *Mémoires*, II, 365-66. On the ambitions of Murat, see Bourgeois, *Manuel historique de politique étrangère*, II, 332-41.

[31] Napoléon I, *Correspondance de Napoléon 1er*, XVII, 59, n. 1.

[32] Clercq, *Recueil des traités*, II, 246-47. In contemporary notes concerning a change of dynasty the interesting analogy was drawn that conditions in Spain under Charles IV were analogous to those which in 1700 facilitated the accession of a French prince to the Spanish throne. See " Espagne. Notes inserrées dans ce Dossier," A. N., A. F., IV, 1610, plaq. I, VI, nos. 195 ff.

ceded to my ally and dear friend, the Emperor of the French, all my rights over Spain and the Indies, with the stipulation that the Spanish Empire in Europe and America shall always remain independent and intact, as it has been under my sovereignty, and that our sacred religion shall not only be the recognized faith in Spain but also the only one to be acknowledged in all the dominions of this monarchy. You shall accordingly communicate this decision to the councils, to the tribunals of my kingdom, to the chiefs of the provinces, whether military, civil, or ecclesiastical, and to all the judges of my people. This last act of sovereignty shall accordingly be made known throughout my provinces of Spain and the Indies, in order that you may help to carry into due effect the measures of my dear friend, Napoleon, Emperor of the French, which are calculated to preserve peace, friendship, and union between France and Spain and to prevent those commotions and popular tumults that always cause havoc, the desolation of families, and the ruin of everything.[33]

Ferdinand VII was soon forced to follow his father's example. On May 10 he agreed to a treaty which declared that he endorsed his father's abdication in favor of Napoleon and renounced his rights as heir to "the crown of Spain and the Indies." [34] Two days later, on their way to exile at Valençay, Ferdinand and his brothers addressed to the Spaniards a proclamation warning them that any attempt to assert their rights would not only cause rivers of blood to flow in Spain but would also ensure the loss of a large number of Peninsular provinces and of all the transatlantic colonies.[35] The Council of the Indies soon sent to the chief civil and ecclesiastical officials in America copies

---

[33] Blanco, *Documentos para la historia de la vida pública del Libertador de Colombia, Perú y Bolivia*, II, 143-44.

[34] Clercq, *op. cit.*, II, 248.

[35] Bonaparte, *Mémoires et correspondance politique et militaire*, IV, 453.

of significant documents containing news of the renunciation of the crown of Spain and the Indies by Charles IV and the Prince of Asturias.[36]

The Emperor's papers show that in the spring of 1808 he was seriously considering the destiny of the Spanish dominions. He wrote to his brother Louis, King of Holland, and stated that he had decided to place a French prince upon the Spanish throne. Assuring him that he would become the sovereign " of a generous nation, of eleven million people, and of important colonies," Napoleon asked Louis whether he would undertake to rule Spain.[37] However, King Louis preferred to remain in Holland. On April 15, 1808, the Emperor directed the Minister of the Interior to take measures to encourage trade between the French dominions and the Spanish Indies.[38] A report of Champagny dated nine days later, which bore corrections in the Master's own hand, expressed the view that Napoleon's position with respect to Spain resembled that of Louis XIV and that the task accomplished by that monarch would have to be performed again.[39]

A project for the mediation of France in Spanish affairs, drafted soon afterward, stated that the Indies were disturbed because of the condition of the motherland. It declared that the Spanish colonists might yield to suggestions by enemies of the Continental powers. This scheme contained a clause which guaranteed the integrity of the Spanish possessions in Asia and America. Napoleon agreed to recognize as the king of Spain and emperor of Mexico a personage who should be selected by the Spanish people, on

[36] Blanco, *op. cit.*, II, 144-45.

[37] Napoléon I, *Correspondance*, XVI, 500.

[38] *Ibid.*, XVII, 1-2, 47.   [39] *Ibid.*, 33-37.

the express condition that this candidate be a member of his family.[40] The Emperor's plan with respect to the Spanish dominions was further unfolded in a letter of May 2 to Murat which made known that he had selected the ruler of Naples to govern Spain.[41] Eight days later Napoleon wrote to his eldest brother Joseph, King of Naples, and, after depicting the condition of Spain in a few graphic sentences, he went on to say:

The nation, through the Supreme Council of Castile, asks me for a king. I destine this crown for you. Spain differs greatly from the kingdom of Naples; the former has eleven million inhabitants and more than one hundred and fifty millions of revenue, without including all the Americas and the immense income to be derived from them.[42]

On May 8 Napoleon had written to Murat to state that, in order to arrange properly the affairs of Spain, he wished to convoke at Bayonne an assembly composed of deputies from all her provinces. Murat was instructed that the governmental junta at Madrid should announce that both Charles and Prince Ferdinand had ceded their rights to Napoleon and that the latter wished to consult the Spanish nation in regard to the choice of a new sovereign, who was to be selected from his family.[43] Four days later Napoleon wrote to Murat to suggest that the Council of Castile ask him to make his brother Joseph the king of Spain. " I would agree to this proposal," continued Napoleon, " and from that moment the King will be acknowledged in Spain, and the Americas will know by whom they are owned." [44] The council responded that the acts of Charles IV and

[40] *Ibid.*, 64-65.
[41] *Ibid.*, 54-55.
[42] *Ibid.*, 87.
[43] *Ibid.*, 76.
[44] *Ibid.*, 111.

Ferdinand VII renouncing the Spanish crown were null and void, for they could not legally transfer their rights to a foreign prince.[45]

Under the influence of Murat, however, the Council of Castile soon waived the question of legality and agreed that the eldest brother of Napoleon, Joseph Bonaparte, King of Naples, should be selected as the Spanish monarch.[46] Murat assured Napoleon that the desire of the Spaniards to conserve their colonies would dispose them to accept the new régime.[47] On May 19 the Emperor's lieutenant issued an ordinance providing for the convocation at Bayonne on June 15 of an Assembly of Notables composed of one hundred and fifty Spaniards. In imitation of the mediaeval Cortes of Spain, this assembly was to contain deputies who would represent the different classes or estates of the kingdom. Altogether without precedent, however, was a provision that six members were to be natives of the Spanish Indies who were to represent Cuba, Mexico, Guatemala, Peru, and La Plata.[48] On May 25 Napoleon issued to the Spaniards a proclamation declaring in optimistic words that he had undertaken to remedy their ills:

Your princes have ceded to me all their rights to the crown of the Spains. I do not wish to rule in your provinces; but I do wish to gain an everlasting right to the love and appreciation of your posterity.

Your monarchy is old. My mission is to rejuvenate it: I shall improve your institutions; and you shall enjoy the

[45] *Historia de la vida y reinado de Fernando VII de España*, I, 171-72.

[46] *Ibid.*, 172.

[47] Conard, *La Constitution de Bayonne*, p. 15, n. 1.

[48] *Actas de la diputación general de Españoles que se juntó en Bayona el 15 de Junio de 1808*, pp. 5-6.

benefits of reform without suffering any dissensions, disorders, or convulsions.[49]

Joseph Bonaparte did not bid farewell to the Bay of
Naples without misgivings. It seems that on his hurried
journey to Bayonne he spoke of his prospective subjects as
a proud and fiery people, who had only participated in wars
for independence. "I see a horizon overcast with dark
clouds," he exclaimed, "which conceal in their breast a
future that frightens me! Will the star of my brother
always shine brilliantly in the heavens?"[50] On June 6,
1808, shortly before the eldest Bonaparte arrived at Bayonne, Napoleon issued a decree which proclaimed that
Joseph was "King of Spain and the Indies." The Emperor
announced that he guaranteed to his beloved brother the
independence and integrity of the Spanish dominions not
only in Europe but also in Africa, Asia, and America.[51] At
Bayonne, on June 10, the new King issued a proclamation
announcing that he had accepted the crown of Spain. Signing this announcement after the time-honored custom of
Spanish monarchs as *Yo el Rey,* he declared that his first
duty would be to conserve the Roman Catholic religion and
the independence and integrity of the monarchy.[52]

When the Assembly of Notables gathered at Bayonne
five days lated, it recognized Joseph as king.[53] In accordance with Napoleon's policy, the junta of government and
Murat had selected from Spanish Americans residing in
Madrid persons who were to represent the Indies. That

[49] Broadside found in A. N., A. F., IV, 1610, plaq. I¹, no. 16.
[50] Bonaparte, *Mémoires et correspondance,* IV, 178.
[51] *Actas de la diputación general de Españoles,* pp. 20-21 n.
[52] *Historia de la vida y reinado de Fernando VII,* I, 372.
[53] *Actas de la diputación general de Españoles,* pp. 20-21 and n.

junta seems to have nominated representatives for Cuba, Mexico, Guatemala, Peru, La Plata, Venezuela, and New Granada, but no deputies for Cuba or Peru attended the assembly.[54]

Upon being presented to the new monarch, Francisco Antonio Zea, deputy for the captaincy general of Guatemala, made an address which expressed appreciation for the recognition that had been given to the Indies. Zea declared that in view of the treatment accorded them by the Emperor the Spanish Americans could not fail to proclaim the new monarch with enthusiasm. In fawning tones he proclaimed that Napoleon had reconciled the Old World with the New:

> The enemies of Your Majesty in vain flatter themselves that they will bring our compatriots back to obedience. We should render ourselves conspirators in their sight; they would unanimously refuse to acknowledge us as brothers and would declare us unworthy of the name American, if we did not solemnly avow before Your Majesty their fidelity, love, and eternal recognition.[55]

A note in Zea's hand records that the representatives of the Indies also indited an address to the Emperor. In it they acknowledged the honor accorded them by the invitation to collaborate with delegates of the mother country in the reorganization of the Spanish monarchy. The American deputies styled that participation as the first act of consideration and justice which Spain had accorded the Indies and declared that the news of this step would be received with enthusiasm by Spanish Americans. They predicted that

[54] Villanueva, "Napoléon et les députés de l'Amérique aux cortès de Bayonne," *Bulletin de la bibliothèque américaine*, pp. 11-12.

[55] *Ibid.*, p. 15, n. 3.

their compatriots would acclaim the Napoleonic dynasty, the child of genius and of victory, and that, despite the attempts of the enemies of two continents, acclamations of gratitude, due to the hero who was the regenerator of the world, would reecho from all the region between the sources of the Mississippi and the Strait of Magellan.[56]

A draft of a monarchical constitution which had been framed by the French Emperor was submitted to Spanish ministers. Some important alterations were made in the proposed frame of government before it was presented to the assembly. Under the presidency of Miguel José de Azanza, the Spanish Minister of Finance, the deputies held twelve meetings. Ten sessions were devoted to the consideration of the fundamental statute for the Spanish monarchy.[57] As a result of the discussions in the assembly, other changes were made in the plan.

A fresh draft was then prepared by Hugues Maret, the accomplished Secretary of State of the Emperor, who had accompanied him to Bayonne. Title IX of the statute, which was devoted to the " Spanish colonies in America and Asia," provided that the colonies were to enjoy the same rights as the motherland. Every province in the Spanish dominions was to be represented at the capital by deputies to the Cortes. Quotas of its members were allotted to particular sections of the Indies. Deputies were to be chosen by the votes of municipal organizations selected by the viceroys or by the captains general of the respective administrative divisions. In case two candidates received an equal number of votes the final choice was to be made by lot.

---

[56] *Ibid.*, p. 17.
[57] *Ibid.*, pp. 19-20.

Each deputy was to serve for eight years or until the arrival of his successor.[58]

In the discussion of this plan, which took place on June 22, the deputy of the viceroyalty of New Granada, Sánchez de Tejada, urged that proper relations be maintained between the colonies and Spain. This deputy praised certain clauses of the statute but drew a melancholy picture of the conditions prevailing in Spanish America. Among the remedial measures which he proposed were the following: the reëstablishment of the Ministry of the Indies; the prompt publication of the constitution in America; the inducing of the colonial clergy to favor that fundamental law; the projection of economic and social reforms; the dispatch of special agents to the colonies with favorable reports about the new régime; and the sending of secret instructions to viceroys and captains general to check any defiance of the Napoleonic system.[59]

The assembly decided to transmit the speech of Sánchez de Tejada to the new government, in order that it might adopt suitable measures to improve the rélations between the Spaniards and the Spanish Americans. José del Moral, the representative of Mexico, also presented his views. Although he lauded the principles of equality embodied in the constitutional project, he suggested that provision be made for certain administrative reforms. Not only did he propose that American deputies share in the administration of the colonies but he also argued that the colonists were not given sufficient representation in the Cortes and

[58] *Ibid.*, pp. 21-22.   On Maret's part see Ernouf, *Maret, Duc de Bassano*, pp. 249-50.

[59] Villanueva, "Napoléon et les députés de l'Amérique aux cortès de Bayonne," *loc. cit.*, pp. 22-27.

suggested that certain classes, such as the clergy, be alloted deputies. In addition, he maintained that the article stipulating that there be only one legal code for the kingdom should be made applicable to the Indies as well as to Spain. Del Moral finished his observations by expressing the most ardent sentiments of gratitude for the Emperor, who "by his benevolence and greatness of soul had formulated the bases of the happiness of two worlds by giving them a constitution as worthy of his great genius as it was beneficent for the people who ought to obey it." [60]

The deputies of the viceroyalty of La Plata presented some unctuous reflections to the Emperor on June 29. They declared that their surprise at his policy was equal to their gratitude:

> Generations of Hispanic Americans will accord the tribute of their respect, their love, and their gratitude to the august name of Napoleon the Great. In the midst of their transports of joy the incomparable generosity of their Liberator will be the eternal theme of their songs.

A memorial of the Platean deputies to Napoleon included three measures: one for the security and independence of the provinces of La Plata; a second designed to promote the public prosperity of those provinces; and a third proposing rewards to those inhabitants who had in 1806 and 1807 repelled the English invaders. In a later statement one of these deputies plausibly explained that his complaisant attitude in the Assembly of Notables was due to the violence in which that meeting had originated; he declared that "it was not possible to denounce the Emperor." [61]

During the debates concerning the constitution, the deputies decided that the extensive provinces of Yucatan and

[60] *Ibid.*, p. 33.   [61] *Ibid.*, pp. 33-37.

Cuzco should each have a delegate in the Spanish Cortes. This increased the number of Spanish-American representatives who were to have seats in that legislature to twenty-two. Further, the fundamental law provided that the American delegates were to have the same qualifications as Spanish deputies.[62] In the end the province of Caracas was deprived of a prospective delegate in order that one might be given to the province of Charcas. The assembly decided that one and the same commercial code should be in force throughout the Spanish dominions. The plan included stipulations to the effect that agriculture and industry in the colonies were to be untrammeled, that reciprocity was to prevail in the commercial relations between them and Spain, and that no special privileges of importation or exportation were to be granted to any party. There was also inserted a clause providing that six Spanish Americans sit in the Council of the Indies and have a voice in all matters concerning the colonies.[63] At the session of July 7 King Joseph presented the final draft of the constitution, which the members of the constituent assembly swore to obey.[64] When he received them, Napoleon expressed the wish that Spain would now recover her ancient glory.[65]

There remain to be noticed some general provisions of the constitution which were of moment to the entire Spanish dominions. It provided that Roman Catholicism be the national religion. It stipulated that there be a perpetual

[62] *Ibid.*, p. 37.

[63] Conard, *La Constitution de Bayonne*, pp. 69-144; Ríos, *Código español del reinado intruso de José Napoleón Bonaparte,* pp. 10-33.

[64] Villanueva, "Napoléon et les députés de l'Amérique aux cortès de Bayonne," *op. cit.,* p. 40.

[65] *9ª, 10ª, 11ª y 12ª sesiones de la junta española.*

alliance, both offensive and defensive, between France and Spain. The Spanish crown was declared to be the patrimony of the male descendants of King Joseph. If the male line of Joseph lapsed, that crown was to pass to the French Emperor, to his male descendants, or to other males of the Napoleonic dynasty. Throughout the Spanish dominions the people were to take an oath of fidelity and obedience to the King, the constitution, and the laws.[66]

On July 8, in the presence of the notables, Joseph solemnly swore to observe the constitution and to preserve the independence and integrity of the Spanish dominions. In his decrees and proclamations the new monarch ordinarily used the title, "King of Spain and the Indies." [67] As his ministers Joseph soon selected officials who had been in the Spanish service. The subservient Azanza became Minister of the Indies; Count Cabarrús became Minister of the Treasury; and Pedro Cevallos, who had been the Secretary of State for Ferdinand VII, became Minister for Foreign Affairs. Evidently Joseph wished to administer his empire through Spaniards who were partial to French interests.

Napoleon and his brother Joseph had meanwhile signed a treaty concerning Spanish affairs. Its first article stated that the Emperor ceded to Joseph the right to the crown of Spain and the Indies which he had acquired from Charles IV and Ferdinand VII. A secret article declared that Napoleon guaranteed to Spain the integrity of those colonies which she actually possessed. In return for this guarantee, Joseph agreed to allow the introduction into the Indies of

[66] Ríos, *op. cit., passim.*

[67] Geoffrey de Grandmaison, *L'Espagne et Napoléon, 1804-1809,* p. 252.

a quantity of French merchandise transported thither upon French ships from Bordeaux or Marseilles. Such ships were to be authorized to exchange their cargoes for colonial products which were to be carried directly to France. The ships and their cargoes were not to pay any heavier charges or duties in American ports than those paid by Spanish vessels.[68] Evidently both Joseph and Napoleon Bonaparte wished to promote French commerce with Spanish America.

The policy pursued by Napoleon toward the Iberian Peninsula caused changes there which radically affected the social and political structure in the extensive dominions of both Spain and Portugal. By the enforced flight of the Braganza dynasty from Lisbon to Rio de Janeiro the Portuguese seat of government was transferred from Lisbon to a distant and aspiring colonial capital. A series of important alterations subsequently took place in Brazil which cleared the way for its separation from the motherland. No evidence has been found, however, to show that Napoleon ever formed a plan to annex that huge colony to his empire. On the other hand, there is ample evidence to prove that for a time he entertained the plan of extending his sway over the magnificent domain of Spain in America. Indeed, it was at the instance of Napoleon that the Assembly of Notables at Bayonne adopted a constitution which declared that Spain's colonies in the Indies were to have the same rights as her provinces in the Peninsula. For the first time in history, Spanish America was viewed as a distinct political entity.

[68] Clercq, *Recueil des traités*, II, 257-61.

CHAPTER III

NAPOLEON THE LIBERATOR

That wise political philosopher, Lord Bryce, not inaptly designated the French Emperor as the Liberator of Spanish America. Sporadic outbursts of discontent with the existing régime were, however, not infrequent in the Indies during the last half of the eighteenth century. Historical research may indeed prove that rebellious uprisings in Latin-American colonies were the logical outcome of a long evolutionary process. Economic and political discontent might finally have provoked a far-flung insurrectionary movement in Spanish America, but it was Napoleon who caused the revolutionary tinder scattered about those dominions to burst into devouring flames. This chapter will indicate how his designs upon the autonomy of Spain incited uprisings in the Indies which developed into a protracted struggle for independence.

On April 13, 1806, François de Pons sent a note to Napoleon suggesting methods by which English intrigue in the New World might be checked. De Pons proposed that French commissioners be dispatched to Spanish America with instructions to enlighten the colonists concerning the advantages which would accrue to them by the regeneration of the motherland.[1] Spanish colonial officials may also have brought the Indies to Napoleon's attention. In a letter to Count Mollien, the French Minister of Finance, Napoleon

---

[1] "Mémoire sur l'Amérique espagnol," June 22, 1806, A. N., A. F., IV, plaq. IV, no. 170.

in May, 1808, mentioned the receipt of a letter from Cuba which expressed sentiments favorable to his rule.[2]

As early as May 10, Champagny addressed letters to viceroys and captains general in the New World making known the renunciation of the Spanish crown by Ferdinand VII and the appointment of Murat as lieutenant general of Spain. Spanish colonial officials were directed to obey Murat's orders. At the same time both the civil and the military authorities in Spanish America were confirmed in their offices.[3] On May 13 Azanza addressed a circular to captains general, intendants, presidents of *audiencias*, and other colonial officials which contained news of the important change in the ruling dynasty. According to the dispatch sent to the intendant of Caracas, such officials were instructed to suspend the execution of a Spanish royal order of April 10 which directed that the elevation of the Prince of Asturias to the throne as Ferdinand VII be publicly celebrated. This intendant was further informed that Ferdinand had abdicated the Spanish throne in favor of his father, and that Charles IV had made Murat the lieutenant general of the kingdom.[4]

On May 15 Minister Azanza addressed to the commandant general of the interior provinces of Mexico a letter notifying him that Charles IV had renounced all his rights to the Spanish throne in favor of the Emperor of the French and that the Prince of Asturias had done likewise. The minister stated that the Emperor had selected as ruler of Spain

[2] Mollien, Mémoires d'un ministre du trésor public, II, 223, n. 1.

[3] " Notes sur les lettres que le nouveau gouvernement d'Espagne envoyé dans les colonies," A. A. E., Espagne, 674.

[4] Pérez de Guzmán, *El dos de Mayo de 1808 en Madrid*, pp. 854-55.

his brother the King of Naples, a monarch whose excellent qualities promised Spain the greatest prosperity. Azanza declared that the Emperor of France and Lieutenant General Murat were considering the reforms which should be made in the administration of that kingdom. " Only the dynasty has changed," ran a summary of this letter, " the nation has preserved the integrity of her dominions and her independence." The résumé added that the Emperor wished to be the protector and the restorer of Spain, that he would energetically aid in maintaining " the tranquillity of distant possessions and their union with the motherland in such a manner as to strengthen the indissoluble bonds resulting from their intimate family relations and from that identity of religion, language, laws, usages, manners, and interests which make of Spain and her colonies a single nation destined by Providence to remain forever one of the leading nations of the world." [5]

The lieutenant general of Spain on May 19 sent to the captain general of Chile a letter stating that the princes of the Bourbon dynasty had renounced their rights to the crown of Spain in favor of an august brother of the Emperor. Murat congratulated the Spanish people upon the good fortune of seeing their government in the hands of a prince who was not only an experienced ruler but also an appreciative judge of the merits of men, a prince who expressed the intention of " reuniting all the Spaniards around a throne which is about to regain in Europe the elevated position that it should never have lost." Declaring that to attain this end he relied upon the zeal of persons holding important offices, he asked the captain general of Chile to

[5] " Notes sur les lettres que le nouveau gouvernement d'Espagne envoyé dans les colonies," A. A. E., Espagne, 674.

acquaint his subordinates with this policy. He affirmed that the benefits of a union between the colonies and Spain would become reciprocal: " Once the perfidious suggestions by which our common enemy will attempt to destroy that union are frustrated, those rich dominions will advance to a condition of prosperity which should satisfy the desires of their inhabitants." [6]

The French Minister of Foreign Affairs tried to link Spain and her colonies in a common cause. From Bayonne, on May 17, 1808, Champagny addressed a dispatch to colonial officials regarding Napoleon's intentions. He declared that the new sovereign of Spain and the Indies confirmed them in their functions and counted upon their loyalty to watch over the respective colonies which they administered:

The dynasty has changed, but the monarchy remains. We should consider it an honor as well as a duty to defend the part of this trust which is confided to you and to ensure that such a splendid monarchy will not lose a single one of its precious possessions. Although the Emperor declared Spain to be independent, he will constantly watch over the prosperity of that kingdom. He has a high esteem for the courage and noble character of its inhabitants: he will extend his protection and support to the Spaniards of the colonies as well as to those on the European Continent; and the bond which will unite France to Spain cannot be otherwise than advantageous to the American colonies in opening a wider field to their commerce. The Emperor will not lose sight of the position and the needs of the country which you govern; he will aid the King his brother to send there all necessary succor, but both those rulers will henceforth place their main confidence in your vigilance and fidelity. The news that I am sending you, Sir, should be brought in Spanish vessels dispatched from Cadiz by the actual government

[6] Pérez de Guzmán, *op. cit.*, p. 855.

of Spain. Napoleon has judged it advisable to make this
known to you also in other ways in order that you may not
be in doubt for a single moment of the course which you
should pursue.[7]

On May 24 Champagny sent to a commissioner at Bordeaux ten packets of papers intended for the Spanish Indies. Officials in charge of French colonies in America were
to transmit those communications to neighboring Spanish
settlements.[8] During the following month French schoon-
ers tried to slip through the enemy's blockade to convey
messages which officials in Guadeloupe and French Guiana
were to distribute in Spanish America.[9]

The Emperor himself had meanwhile taken steps to
transmit to the Indies news of the important changes in
Spain. As early as May 11 he wrote from Bayonne to Vice-
Admiral Decrès, who had served France at Malta and was
now Minister of Marine, to instruct him that a ship which
had been captured from the English was to be dispatched to
the Spanish Indies with one thousand bullets, three hundred
muskets, three hundred pairs of pistols, and three hundred
sabres. A brig which had just been launched was to be
prepared for departure to Spanish America within ten days
with a cargo of one thousand muskets; its ballast was to
consist of four thousand bullets of various calibres. Six war
vessels were to be constructed at Bayonne for use in communicating with the Spanish colonies.[10] Napoleon notified
Minister Decrès on May 15 that he had ordered the equip-
ment at Lisbon of six corvettes for dispatch to Spanish

[7] A. A. E., Espagne, 674.

[8] Bergevin to Champagny, May 26, 1808, A. A. E., États-Unis, 61.

[9] *Idem* to " Monseigneur," June 25, 1808, *ibid.*

[10] Napoléon I, *Correspondance*, XVII, 90.

America, and he believed that other vessels could be sent there from Nantes, Bordeaux, and Rochefort.[11]

On the following day he wrote to Decrès that he was dispatching a small corvette to Venezuela via Cayenne, that he was sending another vessel to Guadeloupe, and that he was instructing the governor of that island to spread the news of what had happened in Spain throughout northern South America.[12] Ten days later the Emperor instructed Murat that the *San Fulgencio*, which was stationed at Cadiz, was to be prepared for a mission to Buenos Aires and was to bear four hundred men and four thousand muskets. About this time Napoleon appointed Gregorio de la Cuesta, captain general of Old Castile, as viceroy of New Spain. The new viceroy was to take with him military officers who were to be placed in charge of Vera Cruz and other important cities. Packet boats were to be prepared in small ports lying between Cadiz and the Portuguese frontier in order that, if the frigate *Flora* should be long delayed in setting sail for America, the prospective viceroy could embark on one of them. There were to be laden on that frigate three thousand muskets and other articles which might be necessary in New Spain. Untoward circumstances evidently foiled this scheme, for a Bonapartist viceroy never reached the city of Mexico. Napoleon also made known his intention to appoint Vicente Emparán captain general of Venezuela. Emparán was to sail at once for his new post on board a brig laden with some two thousand muskets.[13]

Napoleon directed Murat to issue orders that no time should be lost at Ferrol in securing provisions; for it was urgent that aid should be sent to South America. Asserting

[11] *Ibid.*, 129.   [12] *Ibid.*, 139.   [13] *Ibid.*, 212-13.

that by a little activity Murat could have ready at that port four vessels and two frigates which could transport three thousand men, Napoleon sanguinely reasoned that those men, together with the soldiers on board the *San Fulgencio*, would ensure France the possession of part of the Spanish Indies.[14] As his agent to southern South America, the Emperor selected the Marquis de Sassenay. While domiciled in the United States as an émigré, Sassenay had engaged in commercial expeditions to the city of Buenos Aires and had met his compatriot Santiago Liniers, who by 1808 had become viceroy of La Plata. Count Champagny explained to the viceroy that the Marquis was charged with this mission because he had lived in La Plata, because he knew the language of the country, and because he was worthy of esteem and confidence.[15] The emissary's general instructions, signed by Champagny on May 29, 1808, were in part as follows:

M. de Sassenay will present to General de Liniers the dispatches with which he is entrusted. He knows what he is to tell the viceroy about the present condition of Spain, France, and Europe. He will inform that official what he has seen and heard at Bayonne. He cannot but re-echo the language of the Spaniards who congratulate themselves upon a change of dynasty accomplished in so pacific a manner—a change which promises to their country the remedy for the evils that it has so long endured, and which gives them the hope of seeing their ancient glory and prosperity restored. He will announce that an assembly has been convoked at Bayonne to consider the regeneration of the country and will mention the hopes which this assembly

[14] *Ibid.*, 213.

[15] Champagny to Liniers, May 29, 1808, A. A. E., Espagne, 674. See further Sloane, "Napoleon's Plans for a Colonial System," *American Historical Review*, IV, 452; Jurien de la Gravière, *Souvenirs d'un amiral*, II, 132-35.

revived throughout Spain, where the towns and cities cordially welcome the sovereign who has been promised them, namely Joseph Napoleon, King of Naples and Sicily. M. de Sassenay will make known to America what glory envelops France and what influence the powerful genius who governs her exercises upon Europe to which he dictates laws. He will gather all the information that he possibly can regarding the condition of Spanish America, and in particular about the viceroyalty of La Plata. He will observe with special attention the effect produced upon colonial officials by the news of the happy change that has taken place in Spain. If it is possible, he will collect information of the same kind about Chile and Peru. Nevertheless, the importance for Europe of the news that he will gather should cause him to hasten his return. It will be his task to set the date of his departure. He will take charge of the dispatches of General de Liniers and return to France on the *Consolateur*.[16]

Sassenay also carried dispatches of Champagny addressed to captains general and viceroys in other parts of the Spanish Indies. These communications reviewed the events which had occasioned the renunciation of the Spanish crown by Charles IV and Prince Ferdinand. The minister stated that the French Emperor would guarantee the independence of Spain, the integrity of her territory, and the unity of her religion under Joseph. That monarch confirmed the viceroys and captains general in their posts; they were to use the entire influence of their administration to promote the security of the colonies under their respective control. Declaring that after renouncing their rights the members of the Spanish royal family had advised the Spaniards to obey the authority of the new monarch, Champagny exhorted the viceroys and captains general to honor and

[16] Sassenay, *Napoléon 1ᵉʳ et la fondation de la République Argentine*, pp. 132-34.

defend the part of the Spanish dominions entrusted to their care and to guard the monarchy against losing a single one of its precious possessions. He asserted that the bond which united France to Spain would become useful to the Spanish-American colonies after it had opened a more extensive field to their commerce. In conclusion, Champagny assured colonial officials that the Emperor would not lose sight of conditions in the respective regions which they administered and that he would aid King Joseph by sending them all the necessary succor.[17]

In a dispatch dated June 11 addressed directly to Viceroy Liniers, with which he transmitted a collection of published documents concerning the change of dynasty in Spain,[18] the Minister of Foreign Affairs said of the Assembly of Notables at Bayonne:

Everyone shows great devotion to the sovereign who is summoned to restore to Spain her ancient prosperity and who has already declared that he will devote particular attention to the welfare of her colonial possessions. The King proposes to create a Ministry of the Indies, which will be specially charged to watch over the interests of the American colonies. In order that henceforth those affairs may be considered with all the attention which they deserve, several personages of the Two Americas have been named as deputies to the assembly. You will see by their names inserted at the end of official papers that the Spanish colonies, to the preservation and happiness of which both the French Emperor and the King of Spain attach so much interest, will be properly represented.[19]

[17] Villanueva, *Historia y diplomacia; Napoleón y la independencia de América,* pp. 173-75.
[18] A list of these documents is found in the *acuerdo* of the *audiencia* and the *cabildo* of Buenos Aires, August 14, 1808, A. H. N., Junta Central, Estado, 55.
[19] A. A. E., Espagne, 675.

In May, 1808, Champagny also instructed Victor Hugues, the enterprising commissioner of the Emperor in French Guiana, to dispatch vessels to adjacent Spanish-American colonies with news of the changes in Spain. Early in July Commissioner Hugues accordingly dispatched the *Rapide* from Cayenne with documents destined for Vera Cruz. In addition the *Phénix* was sent from Cayenne to Guadeloupe, where the captain was to deliver to General Ernouf who was in charge of that island certain propagandist papers transmitted to Hugues by Champagny, as well as similar papers which were to be forwarded to Puerto Rico, Cuba, and Florida.[20]

Further, when in the midsummer of 1808 Lieutenant Lamanon, in command of the frigate *Serpent*, arrived at Cayenne from a cruise along the African coast, Hugues decided to send him as an agent to neighboring Spanish colonies. Lieutenant Lamanon was a capable and prudent officer who upon his departure from Brest had been instructed by Decrès ultimately to place himself at Hugues' disposal.[21] The orders of Hugues to Lamanon, dated July 5, 1808, directed him to proceed with the *Serpent* successively to La Guaira, Puerto Cabello, Santa Marta, and Cartagena. In accordance with his instructions, Hugues entrusted to Lamanon more than a dozen packets of dispatches and papers for distribution among the Spanish colonists in Venezuela and New Granada. Packets addressed to Venezuela and New Granada contained letters for important civil, ecclesiastical, and military authorities.[22]

[20] Hugues to Champagny, July 24, 1808, A. A. E., États-Unis, 61.
[21] Decrès to Lamanon, February 8, 1808, A. N., Marine, B B⁴, 274.
[22] " Copie des Instructions données à Mʳ Paul de Lamanon, par

Copies of official papers transmitted to Lamanon for distribution included the act of Charles IV by which he ceded all his royal rights to the French Emperor, the act by which the Prince of Asturias relinquished to Napoleon his right to the crown of Spain, and the decree of Charles by which he announced that Murat was lieutenant general of the kingdom. Lamanon was also entrusted with journals in French and in Spanish to which he was to give the utmost publicity. The instructions of Hugues to the emissary proceeded as follows in the third person: "He will also announce the accession of a prince of the imperial house to the crown of Spain, namely the King of Naples, Joseph Napoleon, whose religious beliefs, royal virtues, talents, and courage have won the esteem of all persons who have had the good fortune to know him." In all the Spanish colonies to which the agent was instructed to proceed he was to present himself with amenity and dignity. Lamanon was to deliver to the respective officials the papers with which he was entrusted. Hugues added:

He will engage them to keep the people in obedience and respect, and he will assure them that the sentiments of the Emperor for Spain are not doubtful: he is animated by interest, good will, and a constant solicitude for her glory and prosperity. . . . The Emperor, our August Master, in elevating his beloved brother, the King of Naples, to the throne of Spain, has consecrated the properties, the laws, the customs, and the Catholic religion in their absolute independence and has also conserved the integrity of the Spanish monarchy as well as that of all its colonies beyond the seas.[23]

The activities of the Minister of Foreign Affairs did

le Commissaire de l'Empereur à Cayenne," July 5, 1808, A. A. E., États-Unis, 61.
 [23] *Ibid.*

not cease with the dispatch of Lamanon and Sassenay. Upon sending to Hugues documents manifesting French policy, Champagny on June 25, 1808, asked him to use every opportunity to forward them to Spanish America. That minister also transmitted letters addressed to captains general of the Spanish colonies and to other colonial officials. Then, after stating that King Joseph would proceed to Madrid at once, he declared that the new monarch would take measures to promote the prosperity of Spain and her colonies.[24] Champagny also sent dispatches to Guadeloupe for distribution among the neighboring Spanish settlements.[25] Further, he instructed Governor Villaret of Martinique to transmit to Cumaná, Caracas, Maracaibo, and Bogotá documents containing the news of the far-reaching changes in Spain.[26] Villaret's agent reported that the contents of those papers had been made known to the Venezuelan people, but that they entertained views contrary to the desires of France and cherished the design of establishing their independence.[27]

Subsequently Minister Decrès sent to French officials in Guiana, Guadeloupe, Martinique, and Santo Domingo circulars expressing Napoleon's desire to spread the news of recent events in Spain. On November 14, 1808, Decrès expressed the hope to Commissioner Hugues that the Spanish colonists would perceive the abyss into which the English would try to lead them: " May they instead rally around the sovereign and the laws that guarantee them the

---

[24] A. A. E., Espagne, 675.

[25] Gourhain to Champagny, September 15, 1808, A. A. E., États-Unis, 61.

[26] Villaret to Champagny, August 20, 1808, *ibid.*

[27] *Idem* to *idem*, September 20, 1808, *ibid.*

greatest sum of happiness and prosperity which they have ever enjoyed." [28]

In his American ambitions the Emperor originally had the coöperation of General Murat. On May 18 that commander wrote to Napoleon that the Spaniards realized the necessity of preserving the Indies and of keeping them faithful to Spain. Near the end of May rumors that England contemplated an attack on the viceroyalty of La Plata stimulated Murat to fresh activity; hence he informed Napoleon that he would arrange everything at Ferrol for an expedition to Buenos Aires. Murat added that he considered La Plata most important to the conservation of a large part of the Spanish Indies and that the English would not succeed in their design to separate the Spanish colonies from the mother country.[29]

His dispatch to Liniers dated May 25, which was intercepted by the English, declared that a squadron might appear off the Platean coast and that to enable it to proceed to its destination the crews of the ships might have to be increased by recruits. Murat expressed the hope that the viceroy of La Plata would have ready for the expedition a force of about one thousand sailors and a supply of three hundred thousand rations.[30] The fact that no such force appeared on the South American coast supports the view that a number of the ships dispatched by Napoleon with emissaries and messages for the Spanish Indies were captured by English warships. Some months later exaggerated reports reached Spain from England to the effect that none

[28] A. C., Colonies Occidentales, Correspondance, 56.

[29] Murat, *Murat, lieutenant de l'Empereur en Espagne*, p. 374.

[30] Murat to Liniers (translation), enclosure in Smith to War Office, March 24, 1809, W. O., 1/163.

of the vessels which had been sent by Napoleon to bring Spanish America under his control had reached its destination.[31]

Meanwhile, on May 30, Captain Dauriac had left Bayonne in command of the *Consolateur*, bearing the French agent Sassenay and a cargo of muskets. Sassenay landed at Maldonado on August 9; on the next day that brig was captured by English warships.[32] The French agent, however, proceeded to Montevideo. There he was astounded to learn that the colonists were preparing to swear allegiance to the Prince of Asturias. Upon reaching Buenos Aires he found that, in order to avoid any appearance of connivance with the French, the viceroy chose to receive him in company with the *audiencia* and the *cabildo* of that city. The dispatch box was opened in their presence,[33] and the events which followed are set forth in the words of Sassenay:

When the members of the junta became aware of the contents of the dispatches, I was informed that they had no desire whatever for any other king than Ferdinand VII. Several members were of the opinion that they should take violent measures against me and that I should be detained; but finally the view prevailed that I should be required to embark immediately for Montevideo. . . . I am convinced that, if the viceroy had had the means or perhaps if he had

---

[31] *Gazeta ministerial de Sevilla,* November 11, 1808. Champagny soon informed the French Minister at Washington that the time was not propitious for the settlement of the differences existing between Spain and the United States. Only after the new Spanish Government was well established could an adjustment be reached. Champagny to Turreau, December 10, 1808, A. A. E., États-Unis, 61.

[32] Dauriac to Decrès, July 20, 1810, A. N., Marine, B B⁴, 275.

[33] Groussac, *Santiago de Liniers,* pp. 208-09.

had more audacity, and if I had been able to return to Europe, events might have taken a different course.[34]

This report is supplemented by an account of the junta composed of colonial officials. They felt that the news brought by Sassenay would be apt to produce serious consequences in the Spanish Indies. Besides, as some of the papers transmitted did not seem to be properly authenticated, as other documents had been secured by coercion and violence, and as all of them came through a strange channel, they unanimously decided to carry out their intention to proclaim the Prince of Asturias as their king and to repulse with the utmost energy any soldiers who were not Spanish or who did not intend to maintain the rights of their legitimate sovereign, Ferdinand VII. Those officials also decided that the seditious papers brought by Sassenay should be burned. Furthermore, they took the view that the viceroy should warn not only officials of the viceroyalty of La Plata about the French menace but also the authorities in other sections of South America in order that they might all unite to preserve public order.[35]

Upon arriving at Montevideo, the French emissary found Captain Dauriac guarded by colonial soldiers. The two unfortunate Frenchmen were informed that a sloop from Cadiz had arrived with the news that hostilities had broken out between France and Spain and that consequently they were prisoners of war.[36] After a dire captivity of twenty-one months, Sassenay finally escaped from his Spanish gaolers and made a dolorous report to Champagny.[37]

[34] Sassenay, *Napoléon 1er et la fondation de la République Argentine*, pp. 251-52.

[35] *Acuerdo* of the *audiencia* and the *cabildo* of Buenos Aires, August 14, 1808, A. H. N., Junta Central, Estado, 55.

[36] Dauriac to Decrès, July 20, 1810, A. N., Marine, B B⁴, 275.

[37] Sassenay, *op. cit.*, p. 248.

Lieutenant Lamanon met a similar fate. On July 6, 1808, the *Serpent* sailed from Cayenne bound for Venezuela and New Granada. This frigate reached La Guaira on July 14. There Lamanon disembarked in order to deliver to the captain general of Venezuela the dispatches with which he was entrusted. However, the people of Caracas were much displeased by the news of the dynastic change in Spain. Furthermore, during the forenoon of the following day the English frigate *Acasta*, commanded by Captain Beaver, anchored near La Guaira.[38] Lamanon implored Captain General Casas to give orders that the English flag be not displayed there and that the authority of King Joseph be acknowledged, but to no avail.[39] After Captain Beaver brought to Caracas the news of the Spanish uprising against the French and the assurance of a *rapprochement* between England and the Spanish Patriots, the people proclaimed the rule of Ferdinand VII by heralds throughout the city, placed his portrait in the hall of the *cabildo*, and even menaced the agents of France. When the French frigate weighed anchor on July 17, the *Acasta* gave chase and soon forced Lamanon to surrender. A year later, however, a French council of war declared unanimously that his conduct had been above reproach.[40]

News of Napoleon's usurpations caused a stir in the continental part of the viceroyalty of New Spain. In August, 1808, the *Gazeta de México* published a report that his

[38] "Rapport sur la Prise du brick le Serpent, Capitaine Lamanon, par une frégate Anglaise, le 17 Juillet, 1808," A. N., Marine, B B⁴, 274.

[39] Lamanon to Casas, July 15, 1808, *ibid.*

[40] Smyth, *The Life and Services of Captain Philip Beaver*, pp. 334-39; Minute of the Council of War, July 19, 1809, A. N., Marine, B B⁴, 274.

agents had secured large loans from the Bank of France to
be used in gaining the adherence of Mexican officials. Early
in that month, a French brig reached the fortress of San
Juan de Ulúa bearing dispatches and papers for the viceroy.
The military commander of Vera Cruz ordered these papers
to be secretly transferred immediately to the post-office. In-
furiated citizens soon proceeded to that building, wrote
Faustino Capetilla to his brother, and, " demanding the
delivery of the boxes containing documents and dispatches
which were deposited there, they burned them in the center
of the plaza, while giving voice to the most execrable denunciations of the Emperor of the French." After this
" the mob set a number of tables in the same plaza, where
they made the people swear allegiance to Ferdinand VII
and proclaim him king, whereupon the frightful agitation
began to quiet down." [41]

Napoleon's policy toward the Bourbon dynasty had
meanwhile exercised a far-reaching influence in Spain. As
if by magic, in important Spanish cities juntas sprang up in
1808 which acted as local organs of government and fer-
vently proclaimed their allegiance to Ferdinand VII.
Agents sent by the junta of Oviedo to London won the
support of the English Government for the Spanish Patriots in their struggle against Napoleon. Spanish juntas
soon sent messages to Mexico, New Granada, Peru, and La
Plata to inform the colonists of their bitter opposition to
French policy. Subsequently the Patriots of Spain took steps
to form a central junta to oppose Napoleonic designs.[42]

[41] August 18, 1808, A. H. N., Junta Central, Estado, 57. See
further Rydjord, *Foreign Interest in the Independence of New Spain,*
p. 262; García, *Documentos históricos mexicanos,* II, 343-60.

[42] Robertson, " The Juntas of 1808 and the Spanish Colonies,"
English Historical Review, XXXI, 581-82.

Early in June, 1808, the Central Junta, which was seated at Seville, formally declared war upon the French Emperor.[43] A few days later it addressed to officials in Spanish America a dispatch urging them to maintain inviolable the bonds which united the colonies to the motherland. Those officials were asked to counteract the intriguing dispatches of Napoleon and Murat, who were attempting to deceive the Spanish colonists and to make them disregard their sacred duties.[44] The Central Junta also addressed to colonial officials in May, 1809, a circular which began with these words: " As it is difficult to decide whether the French are more fertile in performing evil acts or in seeking every possible means of seduction and deceit, it will not be strange, if, in pursuit of the iniquitous plan of usurpation which their Emperor has proposed, they undertake to extend their machinations to America as they have extended them throughout Europe." [45]

Meanwhile reports of the startling events which were taking place in Spain had produced a ferment in certain parts of Spanish America. The news of the abdication of Charles IV and the accession of Ferdinand VII evoked many declarations of loyalty to the new monarch. Ferdinand was proclaimed king in such important cities as Bogotá, Caracas, Buenos Aires, and Santiago de Chile. High up on the Andean plateau at Chuquisaca, a silver medal was minted to commemorate the elevation to the throne of Ferdinand VII, King of Spain and the Indies.[46]

---

[43] *Gazeta ministerial de Sevilla,* June 11, 1808.

[44] Miyares to the Central Junta, September 4, 1808, A. H. N., Junta Central, Estado, 57.

[45] " Circular á las autoridades de América," May 10, 1809, *ibid.,* 54.

[46] René-Moreno, *Últimas días coloniales en el Alto Perú,* I, 306-07, and n. 1.

The news of the formation of patriotic juntas in Spain created a desire to imitate that example in Spanish America. In July, 1808, a spasmodic attempt was made to induce the captain general of Venezuela to establish a junta at Caracas.[47] During the same month the *cabildo* of the city of Mexico framed a representation to the viceroy protesting against his holding that colony for Spain while she was under the domination of France.[48] Viceroy Iturrigaray soon issued a proclamation to the Mexicans announcing that a junta at their capital had pledged itself not to obey any commands of the French Emperor. Alarming rumors concerning Napoleon's emissaries soon reached the Mexican capital.[49]

Denunciations of French policy were printed in Spanish-American journals and pamphlets. A pamphlet was circulated in the city of Mexico which harshly criticized Napoleon and declared that the Mexicans would remain faithful to Ferdinand VII: " How is it possible to suffer with patience the haughtiness with which Bonaparte and the presumptuous French try to mock us by regarding us as simpletons without any discretion who are needful of their aid? And, finally, how can we expect guidance and good faith from them? " [50] On September 2, 1808, the president of the *audiencia* of Guadalajara issued a mani-

[47] Blanco, *Documentos para la historia de la vida pública del Libertador*, II, 160-62.

[48] Alamán, *Historia de Méjico*, I, 177.

[49] García, *Documentos históricos mexicanos*, II, 60. On " General Alvina," a supposed emissary of Napoleon who was arrested at Nacogdoches in August, 1808, see Cox, *The West Florida Controversy*, pp. 313-14, 317; and also " El aventurero Conde Octavino d'Alvimar espía de Napoleón," *Boletín del archivo general de la nación*, VII, 161-63.

[50] *Contestación del reino de Nueva España al oficio*, p. 19.

festo in which he announced the measures of the French in order that he might enroll volunteers who would defend that section of Mexico. He stated that, in three days, more than four thousand men had enlisted in the city of Guadalajara, and that those who had volunteered in the rest of the presidency numbered fifty thousand. Among those volunteers were " Indians who offered themselves armed with bows and arrows and even promised that their wives and daughters would sally forth to fight." [51]

The governor of the Venezuelan province of Maracaibo informed the Central Junta that on July 19, 1808, an agent arrived at his capital from Curaçao with the news that hostilities between England and Spain had ceased. " From that moment I redoubled my vigilance in the province under my command," added the governor, " in order not to be surprised by French emissaries entrusted with the task of wresting these dominions of the Indies from the legitimate authority of our beloved sovereign Ferdinand VII by means of dispatches which were at the same time both absurd and null; and, for the same reason, I did not lose an instant in forwarding this news to the vice-royalties of Peru and New Granada. . . . " [52]

On August 28, 1808, the *cabildo* of Buenos Aires sent a letter to the *cabildo* of Lima which denounced Napoleon's execrable conduct and unexampled perfidy. The response from Lima, dated October 26, described the reaction of that capital to his usurpations:

Nothing else is heard in all the streets and plazas but a general murmur, a harmonious voice, and a strong protest

[51] *Manifiesto,* October 30, 1808.
[52] Miyares to the Central Junta, September 11, 1808, A. H. N., Junta Central, Estado, 57.

against the detestable conduct of that tyrant. Patriotism, the enthusiasm of honor, the sacred fire of religion, and an inexplicable love for our sovereign Ferdinand VII produced a ferment and a general agitation in the minds of men. . . . All the people displayed their willingness to shed the last drop of their blood to secure the liberty of their King. At every step they repeated their protests that they would not submit to foreign domination and that they would obey only their esteemed monarch or his legitimate successor.[53]

A most emphatic protest against Napoleon's policy was made by an ecclesiastic of La Plata. On September 4, 1808, Dean Gregorio Funes, acting in place of the bishop of Córdoba, issued an address to the clergy of the diocese. Dean Funes declared that the reports from Spain had disturbed the people greatly: " Everything was in doubt among us, except that Ferdinand VII reigned in our hearts. With regard to France our decision had already been taken: this was no other than that in case of extremity we would place between ourselves and the usurper the stern barrier of death." After mentioning Napoleon's difficulties with the Holy See, Funes, who later became a champion of the revolution against Spanish domination, made this avowal: " We belong to Ferdinand, and not to Napoleon, who, desirous of establishing a universal monarchy, will perhaps bring events to pass which will leave him without any power." Upon forwarding this stirring appeal to the Central Junta, the cleric added that it was necessary to immolate the personage who had profaned the throne and the laws of Spain.[54]

The ferment caused by Napoleonic usurpations in the

[53] *Oficio del excmo. cabildo de Lima al excmo. señor virey,* p. 16.
[54] Funes, *Proclama al clero del obispado de Córdoba de Tucumán por su provisor gobernador,* pp. 2-7.

Iberian Peninsula even spread beyond the limits of the Spanish Indies. Because of the dynastic change in Spain Princess Carlota Joaquina at Rio de Janeiro felt impelled to protect her claim to the Spanish crown. The Princess asked Regent John to induce England to arrange her naval force so that it would not only protect the coast of Brazil against an attack by the French but would also shield the Atlantic shores of Spanish South America. Carlota Joaquina also besought the Regent to place at her disposal means of communicating her views to the civil and ecclesiastical authorities of the Spanish colonies.[55]

In response Regent John suggested that the time might arrive when the ruling dynasties of Spain and Portugal could act together. Further, he expressed the hope that the Spanish Americans would unite their military contingents to his forces for mutual protection against French aggression.[56] Another step of Carlota Joaquina was to address to the American subjects of Ferdinand VII a printed manifesto presenting her views concerning the succession to the Spanish throne.[57] Her propaganda, which developed into an attempt to gain control of that part of the Spanish Indies adjacent to Brazil, stimulated the revolutionary spirit in the viceroyalty of La Plata.

The policy of the Spanish Patriots also caused repercussions in the Indies. On August 20, 1808, the governor of Panama received from Cuba a notice addressed to the authorities of Peru, Chile, and La Plata announcing that

[55] Carlota Joaquina, *Justa reclamación que los representantes de la casa real de España . . . hacen á Su Alteza Real el Principe Real de Portugal.*

[56] João, *Respuesta de S. A. R. el Principe Regente de Portugal.*

[57] Carlota Joaquina, *Manifiesto dirigido á los fieles vasallos de Su Magestad Católica.*

on June 6 the Central Junta had declared war upon the French.[58]   Shortly afterward the *Gazeta de Guatemala* printed this declaration of hostilities.   In the same number of that gazette the captain general of Guatemala announced that a junta assembled in his capital had decided that all property belonging to Frenchmen should be sequestrated and that their persons should be seized.   Further, this junta had resolved that Spanish vessels arriving in Central American ports should be carefully examined while foreign vessels should be completely excluded.[59]   In April, 1809, at the instance of the Central Junta the viceroy of New Spain, anxious to prevent fresh dissensions from disturbing the Mexican people, gave orders that the former king, Charles IV, was not to be allowed to disembark in any port of the viceroyalty to which it was suspected the French Emperor designed to send him.[60]

The efforts of Joseph and Napoleon Bonaparte to secure control of the Spanish Indies did not cease in 1808.   Acts of various Bonapartist officials indicate the scope of this policy.   Decrès continued to send to Cayenne, for distribution in Spain's South American colonies, bulletins and journals containing accounts of the progress of French arms.   On March 13, 1809, he instructed Hugues to use all the means in his power to spread in the adjacent Spanish colonies the news of Napoleonic victories, in order that these reports might induce the colonists freely to espouse the cause of France.[61]   During the same month Azanza gave to the French envoy at Madrid for transmissal to Decrès

---

[58] Juan de la Mata to " M. P. S.", September 1, 1808, A. H. N., Junta Central, Estado, 56.

[59] *Gazeta de Guatemala,* September 19, 1808.

[60] Alamán, *Historia de Méjico,* I, 298.

[61] A. C., Colonies Orientales et Occidentales, Correspondance, 59.

several large packets of letters which were destined for Cuba, Puerto Rico, Mexico, Peru, Venezuela, and New Granada. In the meantime the ministers of Joseph had selected agents who were to go on missions to certain sections of the Spanish Indies. One named Suárez was to sail to Cuba, where he was to gather such information as might tend to keep that island under the rule of the motherland. Thence he was to proceed to Venezuela.[62]

On March 31, 1809, Azanza informed José de Mazarredo, who was serving the intrusive government at Coruña, that in a few days he would send three commissioners to him from Madrid. One known as Colonel Cabello was to bear several packets of papers which would contain, in addition to thirty-six political gazettes and one hundred copies of the Spanish Constitution, correspondence intended for Peru, La Plata, New Granada, Mexico, Cuba, Puerto Rico, and the Philippines. Mazarredo was instructed to give each of those commissioners correspondence designed for the section of Spanish America to which he was dispatched. Azanza suggested that the agent sent to Mexico might well be given the packet of documents intended for the Philippines. Another agent, entrusted not only with papers but also with arms and munitions, was to proceed to Buenos Aires. The packets intended for Cuba and Puerto Rico were to be consigned to any of the agents who might touch at those islands. A certain commissioner was evidently to bear messages intended for Peru. The minister also directed Mazarredo to select another emissary, who was to be dispatched on a mission to Venezuela and New Granada. Each of these men was to be given copies of the Spanish Constitution for distribution in the part of the

[62] La Forest, *Correspondance*, II, 158-59.

Indies to which he had been assigned.[63]   Azanza later
directed Mazarredo to give the commissioners passports
which would merely indicate that they were returning to
their native land.[64]

Declarations by officials and corporations in the Spanish
Indies to the effect that they would remain faithful to their
captive monarch evidently did not disconcert the ministers
either of Joseph or of Napoleon. In December, 1808,
Champagny informed Count La Forest, the French envoy
in Madrid, that official documents concerning the changes
in Spain had been forwarded by the governors of Guadeloupe and Cayenne to Spanish colonies near the Gulf of
Mexico. The minister declared that no desire had been
manifested for separation from Spain either in the West
Indies or in New Granada, but that conditions in Venezuela alarmed him. As yet, he averred, no news had been
received in France from either Mexico or La Plata directly,
but early reports concerning the political condition of those
sections induced him to believe that they were inclined to
follow the fortunes of the mother country. Champagny
believed that, if this view was correct, " every victory won
in Spain would be another victory won in the colonies." [65]

The Patriots of Spain evidently believed that the ministers of Joseph had deliberately preserved certain parts of
the Spanish administrative machinery in order that they
might conveniently use them to promote their designs upon
the Americas. On June 27, 1809, the Central Junta addressed to the captains general of Cuba, Guatemala, Venezuela, and Chile, and to the viceroys of New Spain, New

[63] A. H. N., Junta Central, Estado, 54.

[64] April 11, 1809, *ibid*.

[65] Villanueva, *Historia y diplomacia*, p. 231.

Granada, Peru, and La Plata a circular which declared that the Bonapartist régime had allowed the Council of the Indies to exist in order that through this agency it might conveniently circulate regulations and decrees designed to deceive and subvert the Spanish colonists.[66]

On August 12, 1809, Silvestre Collar, secretary of the Council of the Indies, addressed a note to Ferdinand VII which passed into the hands of the Central Junta. Secretary Collar stated that he had been asked by the Gallic government to relinquish the Great Seal of the Chancellery of the Indies which had been engraved for the use of Ferdinand VII. Collar explained that the government of Joseph wished to destroy the seal and to make a new one bearing the name and the arms of the Napoleonic King. Collar confessed that he had resorted to various artifices in order to retain this seal and ultimately deliver it to his beloved sovereign.[67] At that time the ministers of Joseph evidently wished to replace the Great Seal of the Indies with a new seal which could be used in communications with the Spanish colonists. Obviously it was the sanguine hope of both Napoleon and Joseph Bonaparte that the immense colonial empire stretching from Puget Sound to the Strait of Magellan would ultimately be brought under their sway.

Engrossed with the startling developments in Spain, several months passed before the new king turned his attention seriously to administrative problems of the Indies. As early as July 12, 1808, however, Joseph had issued a decree making certain changes in the royal escutcheon. He announced that the Spanish coat of arms would henceforth

[66] A. H. N., Junta Central, Estado, 54.
[67] *Ibid.*, 22.

consist of a shield composed of six parts: besides one part for each of the ancient kingdoms of Castile, León, Aragon, Navarre, and Granada there was to be another for the Indies, represented, according to ancient custom, by two globes and two columns. Above all these insignia there was to be placed the eagle which was the distinctive symbol of the Napoleonic dynasty.[68]

Evidently Joseph did not always agree with his ministers with regard to the steps to be taken concerning his kingdom's commercial relations. In June, 1809, he refused to sanction a decree framed by Count Cabarrús which proposed that, if certified by customs papers showing that the cargoes came from the Spanish dominions, products of the American colonies as well as of the provinces in Spain under French domination be freely admitted into ports under his control.[69] So far as Spanish trade with the Indies was concerned, Joseph's government evidently did not soon reach a definite decision.

Joseph's ministers carefully considered the problem of Spanish America in the following August. In a report addressed to the King they declared that the weak feature of his policy was its failure to conserve the colonies. Apprehensive of the attitude of England toward Gallic Spain despite the assurances and guarantees of the Emperor, they affirmed that the Indies were lost and reasoned that, after the Spaniards had exerted themselves for three centuries to keep possession of them, their sudden emancipation would perhaps reduce Spain to misery. The ministers took the view that it would be a great advantage for their government to make a separate and permanent peace with Eng-

[68] Cambronero, El rey intruso, pp. 156-57.
[69] La Forest, Correspondance, II, 280.

land. " By ending our disquietude concerning the Indies," they observed, " this peace will suffice to disarm resistance on all sides." Further, they suggested that if the Braganza dynasty was no longer to rule in Portugal the reannexation of that country to Spain, even though it might entail the loss of a small portion of territory in South America, would be very helpful to her interests and would greatly flatter her national dignity.[70]

During the same month, a report that the viceroy of La Plata was maintaining an attitude of neutrality toward Joseph as well as toward the Central Junta induced that monarch to modify his policy. He decided upon the immediate dispatch to the United States of secret agents who were to proceed thence to the Spanish Indies. The King asked La Forest to furnish letters of introduction to General Turreau, who had become the French minister at Washington and who was used by the Bonapartes as a medium of communication with Spanish America.[71] On October 1, 1809, Decrès forwarded to him seven packets of letters presumably intended for distribution in the Spanish colonies extending from Cuba to La Plata.[72] By the end of that year a director of Bonapartist agents called Desmolard, in company with subordinates, had established himself at Baltimore. Early in 1810 the Spanish minister in the United States declared that Desmolard had under his direction in that city fifty minor agents of Joseph who were in touch with Turreau.[73]

[70] Bonaparte, *Mémoires et correspondance*, IV, 467-68.
[71] La Forest, *op. cit.*, III, 169-70.
[72] A. C., Colonies Orientales et Occidentales, Correspondance, 56.
[73] " Noticias sobre el origen de las noticias recibidas del Ministro Español en los Estados Unidos sobre los Emisarios de Bonaparte para revolucionar la América," W. O., 1/104.

On October 2, 1809, Joseph addressed to the Spanish colonists a proclamation which partook of the nature of instructions to the Napoleonic agents who were to foment a revolution in the Spanish Indies. They were to persuade the Creoles that His Imperial Majesty had as his sole object the giving of liberty to a people which had long been enslaved. The Emperor, it was averred, did not expect any other recompense than the friendship of the inhabitants and commerce with the Two Americas. To accomplish this object Napoleon offered to the Creoles all necessary assistance in troops and munitions. Upon becoming acquainted with his particular district, each agent was to select suitable persons who were to sow the seeds of discontent among the colonists. These persons were to describe the manifold advantages that independence would bring to the country by abolishing monopolies, freeing agriculture from restraint, promoting manufactures, and opening ports to commerce. Neither pains nor expense were to be spared to gain the good will of colonial officials. Emissaries of the Emperor were to instill in the minds of the colonists the idea that he had been sent by God to chastise monarchs. Creoles were to be reminded of their shameful treatment by Peninsular Spaniards, while Indians were to be told of the dreadful cruelties of the Spanish conquest. The striking differences between an enslaved Spanish America and the progressive United States were to be set forth with emphasis. Both the emissaries and their subordinates were to prepare lists of the friends of liberty. Spanish colonists were to be informed that their tyrannical monarch did not even rule in his own country but was in the power of Napoleon.

The agents were warned not to declaim against either the Inquisition or the Church. On the insurrectionary banner was to be inscribed this motto—" Long live the Catholic, Apostolic, and Roman Religion, and Perish the Bad Government!" Having made these preparations, the emissaries were to arrange for the insurrection to begin at the very same hour at the different places agreed upon.[74]

This incendiary proclamation angered some colonial officials. By order of the viceroy it was publicly burned by the hangman in the great square in front of the viceregal palace of Mexico. Meanwhile, on October 3, 1809, Joseph, " First King of Spain and of the Continent of America," as he now designated himself, sent a proclamation to the higher clergy in the Indies. He besought them to persuade their communicants to submit to their true monarch, who was destined for them by God. Asserting that Ferdinand VII had freely ceded his sovereign rights to Napoleon, Joseph maintained that the Spanish colonists had been released from their allegiance. The King threatened to punish the archbishops, bishops, and other prelates who did not obey his commands. He declared that a people who persisted in rebellion against their legitimate sovereign would bring upon themselves not only the rigor of the law but also the vengeance of God. In conclusion, he warned the worthy ecclesiastics to beware of the insidious intimations of agents of the English Government.[75]

Napoleon's usurpations in Spain undoubtedly had a disrupting effect upon the ties between the Indies and the mother country. Among the influences which incited the

[74] Villanueva, *Historia y diplomacia,* pp. 242-45. The original is in F. O., 72/104. An English translation is found in Walton, *An Exposé on the Dissensions of Spanish America,* appendix, document B.

[75] Rydjord, *Foreign Interest in the Independence of New Spain,* pp. 299-301.

Spanish Americans to break the bonds that united them to Spain must be reckoned the insidious activity of Bonapartist agents. It would seem that there were few Spanish Americans who wished to acknowledge French sovereignty. Bands of devoted Loyalists, however, followed the standard of Spain on widely separated battlefields in America. Nevertheless, many colonists who seemed loyal to Ferdinand VII were loath to yield allegiance to the changing Patriot governments in the Peninsula. Influential leaders who had long been discontented because of inherent evils in the Spanish colonial system were convinced that the opportune moment had arrived to begin a separatist movement. Certain Creoles, indeed, reasoned that the dethronement of the Spanish King precluded the formation of political relations with either the Patriot régime or the intrusive government of Spain. Here and there a clever leader, accepting the convenient political theory that the Indies were joined with the Spanish King in a personal union, maintained that the deposition of Ferdinand VII had destroyed the link which bound the colonies to the motherland.

Bernardo O'Higgins, the Chilean hero of the struggle for independence, asserted that from a French chateau Ferdinand VII " could not keep in his hand the extremity of the noose, or, speaking more properly, of the chain which fastens America." [76] A Venezuelan leader named Roscio declared that the bull of Pope Alexander VI which conceded the Indies to the Catholic Monarchs and their legitimate successors did not apply to the French usurper or to the Spanish Patriots, for the concession was confined to

[76] Manning, *Diplomatic Correspondence of the United States concerning the Independence of the Latin-American Nations*, II, 910.

those crowned heads. Failing them and their legitimate
heirs and successors, he added, Spanish America was emancipated and restored to its original independence. Roscio
argued that if the papal grant conferred other favors " it
did not extend them to the Peninsular Spaniards but to the
discoverers and settlers now represented by us." [77] A Mexican scholar, one who has made a notable contribution to
our knowledge of the movement that culminated in the
separation of his native land from Spain, apostrophised the
Emperor of the French in these words: " Napoleon Bonaparte! . . . to you, immortal genius, to you Spanish America
owes the liberty and independence which it now enjoys.
Your sword struck the first blow at the chain which bound
the two worlds." [78]

[77] Amunátegui, *Vida de Don Andrés Bello,* p. 83 n.
[78] Bustamante, *Campañas del General D. Félix María Calleja,*
p. 5.

Chapter IV

BONAPARTIST POLICY TOWARD SPANISH-
AMERICAN REVOLUTIONS

The formation of patriotic juntas in Spain created in
Spanish America a desire to imitate that example. In 1808
provisional juntas, which undertook to advise the existing
colonial governments, were set up in Buenos Aires and the
city of Mexico. During the following year revolutionary
conspiracies were formed in the viceroyalty of New Spain,
in the captaincy general of Venezuela, and in the presidencies of Quito and Charcas. The leaven of discontent
spread rapidly among the disaffected Creoles, who had
long aspired to political power.

The relations between Joseph and the French Emperor
with respect to the management of the Spanish dominions
present a tantalizing problem. Though at first Napoleon
apparently made few important decisions concerning those
dominions without consulting Joseph, in time he came to
view that king as an indolent and pleasure-loving monarch
who was scarcely fit to serve as the nominal head of the
French armies in Spain. Presumably *El Rey Intruso*, as
Joseph was styled by the Spaniards, adopted toward the
Indies an attitude which was in harmony with the Emperor's
views, so far as they were known to him. On the other
hand, Napoleon evidently made some important decisions
concerning Spanish America without consulting his brother.
This became increasingly the Emperor's policy as the struggle in Spain developed into a national uprising against his
troops—the beginning of a war of peoples. During the

months when the Emperor was developing a new policy toward the revolutionary communities in Spanish America, agents who had been sent out by his brother continued the activities that they had begun in 1809. To a considerable extent, however, the direction of such agents was taken over by the Imperial Chancellery.[1]

Anticipating far-reaching changes in the Spanish dominions, Napoleon decided to alter the policy which he had been pursuing toward the Spanish colonies. In an address to the Corps Législatif on December 12, 1809, he reviewed the condition of his empire and reformulated the policy which he wished to pursue toward the Indies:

> The Emperor will never oppose the independence of the continental nations of America. That independence is in the natural course of events: this is just and is in the acknowledged interest of all nations. It was France that established the independence of the United States of North America; it was she who aided that country to acquire several provinces; she will always be ready to defend her work. . . . Whether the people of Mexico and of Peru should wish to remain united with the motherland, or whether they should wish to elevate themselves to the height of a noble independence, France will never oppose their desires—provided that these peoples do not form any relations with England.[2]

Napoleon thus announced that he was no longer determined to include the Spanish colonies on the American Continent in his empire and that, on condition that the

[1] Cambronero, *El rey intruso*, pp. 111-14; Geoffroy de Grandmaison, *L'Espagne et Napoléon, 1809-1811*, pp. 262, 269, 274; Thiers, *Histoire du consulat et de l'empire*, III, 563-70; Sorel, *L'Europe et la révolution française*, VII, 339, 390, 477. The instructions to the agent D'Amblimont of September 24, 1810 (*infra*, pp. 79-81) were dated at the Tuileries.

[2] *Le Moniteur Universal*, December 14, 1809.

Spanish-American insurgents form no liaisons with the English, he was willing to see the revolutionary communities become independent of European powers.

His announcement became known in Madrid through Parisian journals which were passed from hand to hand. Surprised at the strange reticence of the official gazette with regard to the government's American policy, La Forest set forth in a note his own interpretation: " I have reason to believe that the good judgment of King Joseph caused him to appreciate the true viewpoint which is contained in the confession of faith of the French Government regarding the continental colonies of Spain in America." La Forest expressed the opinion, however, that the King felt that his ministers should have suggested to him the use of language which would baffle at the same time both insurrectionary discontent and English intrigue in the Spanish Indies. "Nevertheless," continued the ambassador, " I should say that some of his ministers are loath to relinquish narrow and jealous ideas. It is not through them that the King has become aware of the dignity of the question." [3]

Even before Napoleon's declaration to the Corps Législatif, steps had evidently been taken in France to promote the separation of the Spanish colonies from the motherland. In December, 1809, the French warship *Tilsit,* which had sailed from Bayonne, was moored to a wharf at Baltimore. When Luis de Onís, the minister of Spain in the United States, heard that an emissary of *El Rey Intruso* had arrived on this vessel, that minister had its commander, Captain Desmolard, carefully watched. Onís soon reached the conclusion that this commander had disembarked several

[3] La Forest, *Correspondance,* III, 169-70.

persons at Norfolk who were French agents and were furnished with letters and proclamations obtained from Joseph. The minister concluded that these emissaries were destined to proceed from the United States to Habana, Caracas, and other important cities in the Spanish colonies, where they were to intrigue for the separation of those dominions from Spain. Desmolard, who was directing these machinations, had set up his headquarters at Baltimore, where he occupied a fine mansion and maintained a splendid retinue. After allowance for exaggeration due to the excited state of mind of the Spanish minister at Washington, the fact remains that a center of agitation for the revolutionizing of Spanish America by the aid of French agents had thus been established in the United States.[4]

Napoleon's views acquired more significance in the following year, when disaffection in the Spanish Indies took definite form. On April 19, 1810, when commissioners arrived in the captaincy general of Venezuela with orders for the recognition of the Regency which the Central Junta had appointed to succeed itself, a meeting of the town council of Caracas, known as a *cabildo abierto* because other leading citizens were invited to attend, deposed Captain General Emparán and established a junta. The soldiers in that city quietly went over to the revolutionists. The act by which the junta was installed declared that natural right dictated the creation of a system of government that would exercise the sovereign power which had reverted to the people. All officeholders were commanded to take an oath

---

[4] An English translation of the report of Onís to Garay concerning Desmolard, dated December 29, 1809, is found in Rydjord, "Napoleon and the Independence of New Spain," *New Spain and the Anglo-American West,* I, 306-09.

of allegiance to Ferdinand VII.[5] Emparán and other colonial officials were soon deported.

Governor Layard of Curaçao, to whom the junta of Caracas transmitted copies of instructions to French emissaries which were found among the papers of the deposed captain general, was convinced that he was really an agent of Napoleon.[6] Though some Creole leaders of Venezuela still professed allegiance to Ferdinand VII, yet, as subsequent events demonstrated, this uprising of April, 1810, in Caracas was a revolution in disguise.

Similar movements soon took place in other parts of Spanish America. In May, 1810, after the new viceroy of La Plata, Baltasar de Cisneros, had indiscreetly published a manifesto containing news of French victories in Spain, a *cabildo abierto* in Buenos Aires deposed him and established a provisional junta that was ostensibly formed to conserve the authority of the Bourbon King of Spain. At Bogotá, on July 20, a *cabildo abierto* formed a junta for New Granada which issued a manifesto declaring that it would not relinquish the rights of the people of that viceroyalty to any other person than Ferdinand VII. On September 18 of the same year, a junta at Santiago de Chile, which also professed fidelity to the idolized king, deposed Captain General Carrasco. During the same month a seditious curate named Miguel Hidalgo y Costilla started a revolt against the Spanish régime in Mexico. In widely separated sections of the Indies fires were thus lighted which signalized the beginning of a revolution against Spanish rule on the American Continent.

[5] Blanco, *Documentos para la historia de la vida pública del Libertador,* II, 391, 393.

[6] Layard to Liverpool, June 10, 1810, W. O., 1/103.

At the very time when these revolutionary movements were taking place in the Spanish Indies, French designs with respect to that region were being cautiously unfolded. Documents bearing the imperial seal, secured by Luis de Onís, the vigilant envoy of the Spanish court, through the confidant of a French emissary and transmitted by that minister to Cuba and South America in order to put Spanish officials on their guard against Bonapartist intrigues, indicate that by the middle of April, 1810, French agents had been dispatched to various European dependencies in America.[7] To facilitate their operations these colonies had been carved into districts. A principal agent and nine subordinates had been given posts in Mexico. Four agents had been assigned to Central America. Three emissaries had been given charge of districts in Venezuela and New Granada. One emissary-in-chief and five subordinates had been distributed along the coast of South America from Panama to the Río de la Plata. Others had apparently been dispatched to strategic points in Florida, Louisiana, Jamaica, Cuba, Puerto Rico, St. Thomas, Curaçao, and Trinidad. As early as May 15, 1810, the *audiencia* of Guatemala had warned officials in Central America to beware of spies or emissaries of Joseph's government.[8]

On December 27, 1810, Onís wrote to the captain general of Cuba to warn him of the spread of French propaganda in the Spanish colonies: "Napoleon continues his intrigues and machinations against the faithful provinces

[7] Onís to Someruelos, February 7, 1811, A. G. I., Papeles de Cuba, 1708.

[8] Villanueva, *Historia y diplomacia,* pp. 238-41; Rydjord, "Napoleon and the Independence of New Spain," *New Spain and the Anglo-American West,* I, 308-09.

in America of our master, the King, by means of emissaries who are constantly proceeding from France to this country, which is their place of reunion." Onís expressed the opinion that mysterious persons who had recently arrived in the United States from Bordeaux were spies and emissaries of Napoleon who had been dispatched for the purpose of revolutionizing Spanish America.[9]

Attempts were actually made to win over to the French interest some outlying provinces of New Spain. In the summer of 1810 a Bonapartist agent named Alemán arrived at Habana from the United States charged with dispatches from Madrid for certain colonial officials. Among the papers with which he was entrusted were journals describing occurrences in Europe that were favorable to France, the Constitution of Bayonne, an order from *El Rey Intruso* directing colonial officials in Spanish America to continue to exercise their functions, and a manifesto signed by the Minister of the Indies exhorting the colonists to adhere to the cause of his King. After delivering his message to the Cuban *audiencia,* however, the emissary was adjudged guilty of high treason. On the morning of July 30, 1810, he was executed. Shortly afterward Gustav de Witt, who seems to have been in the service of Joseph, reached Yucatan in an American sloop. To the governor of that province the mysterious agent would only declare that his mission was to persuade the Spanish colonists to remain under the control of the motherland. Suspected of being a conspirator and a rebel, the emissary was condemned to death. A historian of Mexico states that on November 12, 1810, the unfortunate De Witt was shot.[10]

[9] A. G. I., Papeles de Cuba, 1708.
[10] Posada, *Apostillas á la historia colombiana,* pp. 184-85; Fabela, *Los precursores de la diplomacia mexicana,* pp. 156-57, 167.

In the meantime, fresh attempts had been made to bring the destiny of the Indies directly to the Emperor's attention. On September 20 Captain Mallard addressed a memoir to Napoleon in which he raised the question whether the Spanish colonies could succeed in separating from the motherland without foreign aid. Mallard also asked what the probable effect of their independence upon Spain and France would be. He even submitted a project for the launching of an armed expedition by France against Spanish colonies in the South Sea.[11]

The policy to be adopted toward Spanish America was also the subject of memoranda submitted to French officials by Jacques d'Amblimont. A letter addressed on September 17 by Councillor of State Fleurieu to Napoleon recommended that D'Amblimont be appointed a secret agent of France and be given full power to act with respect to the Kingdom of Portugal, as well as with regard to the countries of the New World, in whatever manner should seem most advantageous to the interests of the French Empire.[12] Confidential correspondence which fell into the hands of the Spanish minister to the United States shows that Napoleon's instructions for D'Amblimont were signed on September 24, 1810. This agent was directed to take out a passport under a fictitious name and to observe everywhere the strictest incognito. When engaging persons to promote his projects, he was to refrain from informing them of the object of his mission. Should he arrive in the United States in November, 1810, he was to equip suitable vessels for an expedition which was being contemplated against Portugal.

[11] Mallard to Désmarin, September 20, 1810, and enclosures, A. N., F⁷, 6246.

[12] A. G. I., Papeles de Cuba, 1708.

In any case, this special commissioner was eventually to proceed to New Orleans and to undertake through subordinates of French agents to spread in the Spanish-American colonies a desire for liberation from all the governments of Europe. Intelligent persons were to be engaged to map out the shortest and most convenient routes between New Orleans and the city of Mexico. Plans of the roads in Cuba were to be obtained. Article XVIII of the instructions declared that the special commissioner was to increase as much as possible the number of agents who, furnished with American naturalization papers and passports, were to be dispersed as merchants throughout Cuba and Mexico with directions to disseminate ideas of independence. The next article instructed the commissioner to employ other agents who were cleverly to depict to important individuals the licentious horrors to which the idea of absolute independence carried its devotees. These agents were to cause colonists of substance to realize that the nobility of Europe had become convinced of the necessity of seeking the protection of the French Emperor in order to shelter their persons and property from the fury of demagogism. Another article directed the emissaries to use every available means to prejudice the Creoles against Peninsular Spaniards. Article XXVI gave the commissioner discretionary power enabling him in unforeseen contingencies to proceed in the manner most conformable to the intention made known to him by word of mouth.[13]

[13] (Copy), *ibid.* A translation of the instructions from Napoleon to D'Amblimont of September 24, 1810, is given in Rydjord, *op. cit.*, pp. 309-12. A Spanish text of these instructions containing words in cipher is printed in *El movimiento histórico en México*, no. 1, pp. 1-4. With the copy of these instructions in the Spanish archives, the writer found a printed key to a cipher code which was pre-

On September 24, 1810, Decrès addressed to D'Amblimont a letter in which he transmitted these instructions as well as an order for ten thousand francs to pay the expenses of his journey. Besides, the commissioner was given a letter of credit for forty thousand dollars to cover expenditures connected with his special mission. D'Amblimont was informed that, in case his enterprise demanded greater outlays, he was to draw upon Decrès for additional money. He was to inform that minister regularly, however, of the use which he made of the funds thus placed at his disposal.[14]

In a letter of Eusebio Bardaxí, Secretary of State of the Central Junta, transmitting copies of D'Amblimont's instructions and related papers to Henry Wellesley, the English ambassador to Spain, the ambassador was assured that the documents had been obtained by His Catholic Majesty's minister in Washington by means that were secret.[15] It would accordingly seem that D'Amblimont was actually to be engaged in America to revolutionize the Spanish colonies near the United States. Obviously his mission resembled that earlier essayed in America by Citizen Genêt.

Early in 1811 D'Amblimont and another emissary of Napoleon were weaving a net of intrigue in Philadelphia.[16]

---

sumably used by Napoleon in corresponding with his agents in Latin America; another copy of this key was found with Napoleon's letter to Ledreznech of April 12, 1811. French administrative officials who were shown a photograph of this key by the writer saw no reason for doubting its authenticity. Presumably this code was used also in D'Amblimont's correspondence with subordinate agents in Spanish America (see *infra,* p. 82).

[14] A. G. I., Papeles de Cuba, 1708.

[15] March 30, 1811, F. O., 72/110.

[16] Onís to Someruelos, February 1, 1811, A. G. I., Papeles de Cuba, 1708.

In March Onís informed the captain general of Cuba that he had succeeded through a confidant in stealing from D'Amblimont's papers the key to a cipher of his confidential correspondence with the French Government and also the key to his secret correspondence with subordinate agents in Latin America.

Not only had Onís learned the names of certain agents whom D'Amblimont contemplated dispatching to ports in Latin America but he had also ascertained the appellations of some Napoleonic commissioners already located in those dominions.   Onís directed the captain general of Cuba to take steps to intercept a subordinate agent named Mouliat who had recently left the United States in a ship bound for Venezuela.[17]   According to a list found in the Spanish archives, a number of French emissaries had already voyaged via Habana to Puerto Rico, Jamaica, St. Thomas, Curaçao, Trinidad, Venezuela, Mexico, Central America, and the Isthmus of Panama.[18]

By the spring of 1811 D'Amblimont had reached Mexico. On April 14 Hugues Maret, who had been made the Duke of Bassano and was soon to replace Champagny as Napoleon's Minister of Foreign Affairs, complimented that emissary on the success of his mission:

Sir, His Royal and Imperial Majesty has charged me to express to you his great satisfaction at the success of your operations in the viceroyalty of New Granada and at the

[17] Onís to Someruelos, March 10, 1811, *ibid.*

[18] "Lista de los Agentes Franceses que han ido á la Havana," *ibid.* As yet, the activities of these minor French agents are little known. See Caillet Bois, "La misión de Antonini en 1808," *Boletín del instituto de investigaciones históricas,* XV, 203-04. In A. G. M., Correspondencia de Virreyes, 1813-1816, 18/268, are documents of 1815 concerning French designs on Spanish America.

arrangements that you have made with respect to Mexico. He urges you to promote as much as possible the revolution which has been projected in that country and also to continue the measures which you have suggested in regard to the island of Cuba. . . . In addition to the orders that he has given to his ambassador at Washington to furnish you with such sums of money as you may need, he has also directed M. Ledrezenech, one of his special agents, to place at your disposal the sum of two hundred thousand francs, as you can see by the tenor of his general instructions which His Royal and Imperial Majesty has directed me to communicate to you. His Majesty is persuaded that your operations will be crowned with the greatest success, because of the assurances which you have received from the Mexican Metropolitan. The palace of His Excellency is, as you have said, a safe asylum in the shelter of which you can brave the rage of the governor.[19]

On the same day the Duke of Bassano addressed a letter to the Metropolitan of Mexico. Bassano expressed the Emperor's gratification at the rôle which the archbishop was playing in the emancipation of Spanish America from the yoke of England. He declared that the Emperor attributed to English avarice the decline in the morale and power of the Roman Catholic Church in Mexico, as well as the dissensions and bloodshed which prevailed there. In intriguing phrases the ecclesiastic was asked what would become of his holy religion if Napoleon did not build dykes to guard it against the devasting torrents of atheism. Were not all the potentates of the European Continent forced to seek the protection of the all-powerful Emperor? Would there exist in Europe a single Catholic temple if Napoleon the Great had not been animated by the most profound respect for the sanctity of such temples? An intimation was even conveyed that Charles IV was

[19] A. G. I., Papeles de Cuba, 1708.

pitilessly dethroned by an ungrateful son because of seditious ideas adroitly spread by the English. The prosecution of the war in Spain by the French was attributed to political reasons, and especially to the desire gradually to win over to the Gallic cause the victims of English astuteness.[20]

More light on Ledreznech is furnished by his instructions, which were signed by Bassano on April 12, 1811. That agent was ordered to present himself immediately to Count Sérurier, the French minister to the United States. To this minister he was to deliver a packet of papers and to mention a password; he was then to receive the information which Sérurier had been directed to transmit to him concerning his mission. The instructions to Ledreznech provided further that, after the departure of an agent destined for Tangier, he was to search for the means to dispatch to Spanish America subordinate emissaries, munitions, and everything that the insurrection there would need. In conjunction with D'Amblimont and three Portuguese, Ledreznech was authorized to bestow brevets and diplomas of the King upon proselytes to the French cause. He was also authorized to insert in blank forms the names of those persons who rendered service against the government which pretended to rule the Spanish communities in the New World.

Article XI of the instructions stated that an assurance had been given by the President of the United States to the minister of France that he would coöperate indirectly in every way to promote the political independence of the Spanish states in the New World. The fourteenth article ran as follows: " If M. d'Amblimont is not able to under-

[20] *Ibid.*

take the mission to Tangier, and if his zeal should detain him in Mexico, he shall remain entrusted with the promotion of the independence of that country. In those circumstances and for his information, M. Ledreznech shall send him by a trustworthy person a copy of the present instructions, the funds that he may need, and also a number of the brevets and diplomas of His Catholic Majesty which are annexed to packets numbers eight, nine, and ten." The instructions continued thus: "Under conditions assumed in the preceding article, according to which M. d'Amblimont may remain in Mexico to direct the operations there and in neighboring countries, M. Ledreznech shall direct his attention to New Granada and Peru and shall stimulate as much as possible the discontented colonists in Paraguay, in Chile, and particularly in Uruguay by pecuniary rewards, by publications distributed by clever agents, and by the bestowal of brevets and diplomas." In elastic terms this emissary was informed that if unforeseen difficulties should arise the government would depend upon his recognized zeal, devotion, intelligence, ability, and integrity.[21]

The Minister of Foreign Affairs had informed Sérurier, on December 29, 1810, of the attitude of France toward America. Bassano declared that Napoleon would not object to the acquisition of Florida by the United States. With respect to the Spanish Indies the Emperor assumed a more advanced attitude than he had taken a year earlier:

He favors everything that may encourage the independence of Spanish America. France has done nothing but congratulate herself on the independence of the United States; and, like that nation, France does not base her commerce upon exclusive claims. She will behold with pleas-

[21] (Copy), A. G. I., Papeles de Cuba, 1708.

ure the independence of a great state, provided that that state is not under the influence of England.[22]

Soon after his arrival in Washington the French minister entered into correspondence with Ledreznech in regard to his mission. Sérurier asserted that, faithful to engagements with France, the President of the United States would soon send to the governors designated by Ledreznech special agents instructed to influence them in favor of the French emissary. Sérurier expressed the opinion that the enthusiasm of the people of Venezuela for independence was too pronounced for one to dread the possibility of a backward step there: " To me it seems that it would be better instead to send to Cartagena the precious succor which you wish to dispatch to Caracas, in order that the people of New Granada may act in harmony with the measures of other colonists and at the same time." [23] The ramifications of this project are indicated by the fact that in December, 1811, Sérurier invited the French consul general, Baron Lescalier, from New York to Washington for a conference upon matters pertaining to the Emperor's service. Among the problems to be considered was the policy that should be pursued with respect to the revolutionary Spanish colonies.[24]

Meanwhile a congress of delegates from provinces of the captaincy general of Venezuela, which assembled in March, 1811, soon assumed the functions that the governmental

[22] A. A. E., Colombie, 1. In a letter dated St. Cloud, August 9, 1810, Napoleon declared: " L'indépendance de l'Amérique est un des principaux titres de gloire de la France." See Thompson, " Napoléon et l'Amérique," *Franco-American Review,* I, 213.

[23] Sérurier to Ledreznech, July 14, 1811, A. G. I., Papeles de Cuba, 1708.

[24] Lescalier to " Monseigneur," December 31, 1811, A. A. E., États-Unis. 67.

junta had exercised since April 19, 1810. The congress
proceeded to consider the political status of those provinces.
An animated debate took place in its halls over the proposal that the mask of allegiance to Spain be discarded. On
July 5, 1811, on behalf of the United Provinces of Venezuela, the congress voted in favor of a declaration of independence. It also undertook to adopt a design for a national flag and to formulate an oath which would pledge
governmental officials to support the new régime. Venezuela was the first Spanish colony which, through delegates assembled in a congress, formally declared itself independent of the motherland.

Even before adopting a declaration of independence, the
Venezuelans had taken measures to establish relations with
foreign powers. On July 27, 1811, the new government
furnished Telésforo de Orea and José R. Revenga with
credentials as agents to the United States. Sérurier reported to his government on November 10 that Orea had
called at the French legation. " He informed me," continued the envoy, " that the republic of Venezuela ardently
desires to send a minister to the Emperor." [25]   Orea addressed a letter to Sérurier on the following day in which
he pleaded his country's cause as follows:

Venezuela takes pleasure in recalling that two years ago
the French Minister of Foreign Affairs declared that, in
accordance with her former policy, France would have the
glory of contributing to the liberty of all the New World.
The actual situation of Venezuela furnishes the best opportunity that could be offered for such a glorious enterprise.
Union and intimate friendship between her and France

[25] *Ibid.,* 66. The mission of Orea to the United States is described
in Robertson, " The Beginnings of Spanish-American Diplomacy,"
Turner Essays in American History, pp. 248-49, 252-57.

would be very beneficial to the political interests of both countries.

Profoundly convinced of the advantages of this union and friendship, the Venezuelan Government would already have dispatched a mission to the Emperor of the French if the war which unhappily exists in Spain had not forced it to postpone such an important negotiation. In these circumstances, I am fully authorized to express to Your Excellency the desires of the United Provinces of Venezuela and their favorable attitude toward France. May you serve as an agency to reëstablish between the two countries the friendship which has been interrupted only by the violence of those persons who governed Venezuela.[26]

Sérurier evidently informed Orea that direct relations between France and the new republic could not be formed before he received instructions from Bassano. As the result of a conference with the French envoy, however, the Venezuelan agent felt that relations might be established earlier. On December 4, 1811, he accordingly sent another plea to Sérurier. Orea declared that, in order to establish the bases of mutual friendship between Venezuela and France, his government only wished an assurance that its agents sent to the French Emperor would be received by him with the esteem due to friends and the consideration which the representatives of an independent nation might expect. The agent expressed doubt whether in the critical international situation the Venezuelans would be allowed to enjoy their freedom, and he asked whether in case of need France would protect their efforts to preserve independence. " This question will be the subject of direct communications between the agents of Venezuela and ministers of His Majesty the Emperor," he explained, " but I should be happy if Your Excellency would authorize me to announce

[26] November 11, 1811 (Copy), A. A. E., Colombie, 1.

to my government that it may count with certainty not only upon the friendship but also upon the generous protection of the Emperor." [27]

On December 6 the French minister responded in these words:

I am pleased to repeat to you in writing, Sir, what I said to you yesterday, that each day strengthens my conviction of the benevolent and friendly attitude of my sovereign with regard to your State, and that I am assured that your minister will be favorably received in Paris. You desire to know further, Sir, if His Majesty would deign to accord his protection and succor to the new republic in case the establishment of her independence should encounter opposition on the part of enemies of France. Although, because of the inadequacy of our respective powers for such a negotiation, I can in this respect give you no assurance that is absolutely official, I can nevertheless make known to you my firm conviction that in such a state of affairs you would not have recourse in vain to so powerful a monarch, and that your republic would find in his general policy all the support that she could desire. You may, Sir, inform your government that, until it has a minister in France, it may communicate with me in regard to anything it wishes, and that I would take special satisfaction in being the organ through which its dispositions and wishes are made known to the Emperor.[28]

A few days later Orea had a long conference with the French minister. Sérurier informed him of the generous views of the Emperor toward Venezuela. Orea then expressed his gratification at the assurance of Napoleon's favorable disposition. He declared that this attitude would have a strong influence upon Venezuelan policy, but he seemed to fear that in the existing state of affairs England

[27] (Translation), A. A. E., États-Unis, 66.
[28] (Copy), *ibid.*

and the Patriot government of Spain would not allow the Venezuelans peaceably to establish free institutions: "In this condition of uncertainty our attention is first directed toward France. We have believed that perhaps she would today accomplish for the South of America what she did so generously thirty years ago for North America; and I am happy to see that we have not expected too much of the great soul of the Emperor." The agent felt that the projected mediation of England between Spain and her revolted colonies would not be successful. He asserted that "Venezuela would always consider France as the first nation that had deigned to recognize her, that she would be pleased always to favor French commerce in her ports," and that, if his nation became involved in war, as seemed very likely, she "would receive with gratitude the protection and assistance that His Majesty might wish to give her."

Orea displayed an ardent desire to procure from Sérurier a document elucidating the attitude of France toward Venezuelan independence in order that he might transmit it to Caracas. The minister naturally hesitated to do this, but he promised that if the agent would present his plea in written form he would respond in general terms concerning what he believed to be the intention of his government. Sérurier reported that Orea believed that, "upon the arrival of his dispatches in Caracas, the envoy destined to carry to His Majesty the wishes of the republic" would immediately leave for France, if indeed he had not already departed.[29]

The policy of France toward the revolted colonies of Spain had meanwhile become a topic of conversation be-

─────────

[29] ...rier to Bassano, December 9, 1811, *ibid*.

tween the American chargé d'affaires at Paris and Minister
Bassano. On August 20, 1811, that minister confidentially
informed Chargé Russell that with regard to the Spanish
Indies the French Emperor had definitely decided " to
acknowledge and support their independence so far as they
have the spirit and strength to assert it with a reasonable
probability of success." [30]

When he reported this conversation to Washington the
American diplomat stated that the Emperor had resolved to
aid in the establishment of Spanish-American independence.
The chargé added that Bassano had intimated that " the
only mode in which this aid could be efficaciously furnished
was through the concurrence and agency " of the United
States. Bassano had further stated that Sérurier would be
instructed to submit to the American Government specific
propositions concerning such coöperation. Suggestions had
been made that the aid of which the Spanish Americans
" stood most in need was arms—ammunition, and military
skill (officers) to afford which His Majesty was entirely
disposed." Regions which, like the Spanish West Indies,
could not maintain their independence were not to be aided
in any attempt to separate from Spain. Russell then suggested that, as East and West Florida were not capable of
existing in the form of an independent nation, France
should consent to the possession by the United States of
that portion of the Floridas which included Amelia Island.
Whereupon Bassano declared that, in accordance with assurances already given, the annexation of the Floridas to
the North American republic would be in harmony with
French policy.[81]

[30] Russell to Bassano, September 4, 1811, *ibid.*
[81] Manning, *Diplomatic Correspondence of the United States*

On September 16, 1811, Bassano sent Sérurier an important dispatch concerning the Indies. Bassano declared that reports from Spanish America agreed that revolutionary partisans were winning the struggle against the Royalists. He ventured to outline the policy of France:

The intention of His Majesty the Emperor is to favor this general movement and to encourage the independence of all the Americas. You have already been informed of this disposition by the letter of December 29, 1810, but today it has assumed a more positive character. His Majesty does not now confine himself simply to the approval of the principle of independence; he will aid in the establishment of independence by the shipment of arms and by all other succors that may be expected from him, provided that the independence of these colonies be unconditional, and that they do not form any special relations with the English. . . .

The American Government should be disposed to support the principle to which it owes its own existence, and which assures to the entire Continent on which it is established the best and the highest destiny. . . . Maintaining always the necessary reserve, explain the intentions of His Majesty not only to the President but also to the agents or deputies that the Spanish colonies may send to the United States. Seek to form relations with them. Become acquainted with their positive views, learn about the kind and quantity of succor which each particular country needs and the type of commercial and political arrangements which those countries are inclined to make with a power that supports their independence. In addition, make known in every way the views of His Majesty toward the Spanish colonies. Make them known through the Federal Government and through all the agents that it may have in those colonies upon whom dependence can be placed. Should the United States have no agents there who will favor the movement for independence, it would be useful if that government

concerning the Independence of the Latin-American Nations, II, 1371.

could send there other persons who are capable and devoted. You are yourself authorized to dispatch agents into those colonies. Select men in whom you have confidence,— no matter to what nation they belong, whether French, American, or Spanish. You can judge, according to time and circumstance, which persons can best fulfill these delicate missions.

Bassano further informed the minister at Washington that Spanish-American agents in the United States were complaining of England's design to compel the Spanish colonists to demand her protection. Sérurier was warned that, in his discussions with the promoters of independence, he should avoid anything that might injure their feelings or alter their ideas with respect to the generous disposition of the Emperor:

On a former occasion France promoted the independence of the United States; today she will carry on this glorious work, worthy of her power and of the soul of her master. She earnestly desires a success which should further promote the civilization, the commerce, and the prosperity of people.[32]

The American poet, Joel Barlow, who had meanwhile been appointed minister to France, had been instructed by Secretary of State James Monroe that ministers of the United States in Europe were " to avail themselves of suitable opportunities to promote " the recognition of Venezuela by other nations.[33] Shortly after his arrival in Paris, Barlow became acquainted with the views of the French Government concerning the Indies. In a letter to Monroe dated September 20, 1811, he wrote as follows: " The Emperor has determined to declare the Spanish Americans free and independent and to give them arms and ammunition to de-

---

[32] A. A. E., États-Unis, 66.   [33] Monroe, *Writings*, V, 364.

fend themselves; this, however, on condition that they do not connect themselves with England by exclusive privileges of trade." The minister added that Napoleon desired the aid of the United States in the transportation of arms and ammunition to Spanish-American insurgents. Barlow ventured the conjecture that, although Napoleon wished the Spanish colonists to free themselves from the rule of the motherland, he might intend to dictate to them the form of government which they should adopt.[34]

Barlow informed Bassano on January 8, 1812, that a friendly response had been made at Washington to the request of Venezuela for the acknowledgment of her independence. The American minister stated further that the Venezuelans had been notified that the ministers of the United States in Europe would be instructed to promote the recognition of the new republic by other powers. He expressed pleasure at finding that the French Emperor was in harmony with President Madison in the desire to see the independence of the Spanish colonies established.[35] A memorandum filed in the French Ministry of Foreign Affairs which commented on Barlow's views declared that Sérurier had held a long conversation with the President and the Secretary of State, that both of them strongly desired to see the independence of the Spanish-American communities achieved, and that they were pleased to learn that Napoleon cherished the same views.[36] The way was thus prepared for a *rapprochement* between the United States and France with regard to the policy to be pursued toward the Spanish-American republics.

[34] Manning, *op. cit.*, II, 1372-73.   [35] *Ibid.*, 1373.
[36] "Note sur une lettre de M. Barlow relatif à l'independance de Venezuela," A. A. E., Colombie, 1.

Still, Minister Sérurier soon became suspicious that the
Department of State was taking a keener interest in Mexico
than it displayed to him. He expressed to Secretary Monroe
his dissatisfaction with this attitude, and he even intimated
that, if the American Secretary persisted in this policy, it
would be better for France and the United States to act
separately. In a dispatch to Paris the minister added:

But I insinuated to Monroe that, whatever might be the
wish of the republic, I did not think that its own military
and financial embarrassments would at present allow it to
offer very efficient aid to the Patriots of Spanish America,
that it would be better and more convenient for all the
world for us to make known to those peoples the agreement
that we have reached in their favor; and that, if they wish
to liberate themselves without forming relations with England, France would recognize them and would furnish the
arms which the United States would undertake to transport
to them. The Secretary of State asserted that the administration had not yet entered into any arrangement with the
Patriots, that its intention had always been to inform me of
everything that it contemplated in respect to these colonies,
and to reach an agreement with me concerning the support
which was to be given to them. Mere words! [37]

On January 18, 1812, Bassano prepared for Napoleon a
careful report concerning French relations with South
America. After stating that the strongest of the parties
which had appeared in the Spanish Indies since 1808 was
that which favored independence of Spain, the minister
sketched Venezuela's attitude toward France. Then he interpreted French policy generously in these words: " From
the very beginning of the fermentation in the Spanish Indies, Your Majesty had anticipated that it would have inevitable and far-reaching results. You had foreseen that

[37] December 5, 1812, A. A. E., Mexique, 1.

those colonies would some day succeed in elevating themselves to the rank of nations, that it would be advantageous
to prepare long in advance for relations with them, that
their affection should be gained early, that they should be
encouraged by kindly declarations, and that they should be
informed that you would not place any obstacle in the path
of their destiny." Bassano reasoned that Venezuela offered
a vast field for commercial development, but that the Emperor wished to encourage the rivalry of the United States
with England in that country until the establishment of
maritime peace permitted Frenchmen to engage in South
American trade. The minister concluded that the time had
arrived when France should aim to secure commercial privileges and advantages in Venezuela:

> Steps taken by the agent of that government show how
> much he desires the support of Your Majesty and by what
> proofs of deference he wishes to obtain it. The power
> which Miranda enjoys in that section of America, after be-
> ing for a long time in the service of France, gives her a
> special hold upon the Venezuelan Government and permits
> her to acquire a species of personal influence on its opinion.
> I think that the government of Venezuela should not yet
> be acknowledged as independent, but that Your Majesty
> should instruct his minister in the United States to receive
> the agent from that country and to inform him that the
> mission which may be sent from Venezuela to Your Majesty
> will be received with favor. Before this mission departs for
> Europe, it must be furnished with full powers. Then France
> will be able to negotiate with it a treaty of amity and com-
> merce which would recognize the independence of the new
> state.[38]

Thus, shortly after the Venezuelans adopted a declaration
of independence, the French Minister of Foreign Affairs

[38] A. A. E., Colombie, 1.

outlined a policy which, had circumstances been propitious, would have led to an acknowledgment by France of the independence of a revolted Spanish colony. It seems that this was the earliest decision by a world power to adopt a policy of recognition in relation to the new states that were rising in America. In general, the precedent to be followed in this matter was evidently the negotiation which culminated in the Treaty of Alliance of 1778 between France and the Thirteen Colonies. Not only was the independence of Venezuela to be acknowledged by the Emperor, but he made known at Washington that France was ready to support that South American republic by supplying her with arms and ammunition through the coöperation of the United States.

However, untoward events which soon took place in Venezuela completely checked her negotiations with France. In this South American country a counter-revolution made startling progress. In March, 1812, a terrible earthquake devasted insurgent cities and inspirited the Loyalists. A series of misfortunes convinced Miranda, who had became dictator of Venezuela, that the cause of independence was, for the time being, doomed to failure. Accordingly in July, 1812, at La Victoria, the key to the capital city, he arranged a capitulation with the commander of the Royalist forces, General Monteverde. Soon afterward Miranda's discontented compatriots betrayed him to the Spaniards. Monteverde entered the city of Caracas in triumph, ignored the terms of the capitulation, and treated Venezuela as a conquered province. The hope of recognition vanished and with it the dreams of foreign gold, of munitions, of fleets, and of armies.

Another commissioner from northern South America

soon attempted to carry on the negotiations which Orea had
been compelled reluctantly to relinquish. In the city of Cartagena, on November 11, 1811, a revolutionary junta had
adopted a declaration of independence of Spain; and, during the following year, a Venezuelan Patriot named Manuel
Palacio Fajardo was commissioned by that junta to represent the province of Cartagena in the United States. His
credentials further authorized him " to treat with the Emperor of the French " and to make known the desire of the
" the State of Cartagena " to negotiate agreements which
would be mutually advantageous and would assure its independence. This agent proceeded to France via Washington. Soon after his arrival in that capital, he became aware
of Napoleon's favorable attitude toward the insurgent Spanish colonies and consequently held conferences with Sérurier. He informed this minister that Cartagena had been
invaded by Royalists from a neighboring province who had
been reënforced by Spanish soldiers. Consequently Palacio
Fajardo solicited aid from France. Upon being told by
Sérurier that he was not authorized to grant succor to an
insurgent province of Spanish America, the agent decided
to proceed to Paris in order to appeal directly to the Emperor. Palacio Fajardo asserted that the French diplomat
had offered to advance the funds necessary for his journey
and had given him gratifying assurances of the success of
his mission.[39]

Sérurier informed this agent that France favored the independence of the Spanish colonies in America, that he
would find the Emperor's views concerning them to be as

[39] The credentials of Palacio Fajardo, signed by M. R. Torices
on October 5, 1812, are in A. A. E., Colombie 1; Palacio Fajardo
to Sérurier, December 25, 1812 (translation), *ibid.*

liberal as he might desire, and that the French Government would be pleased to enter into arrangements which would promote his mission. Further, Palacio Fajardo was told that Sérurier had made an arrangement with the French consul general in the United States to pay all the expenses of that emissary's proposed journey to France.[40]

The French minister promptly notified his government that Palacio Fajardo desired to be given a supply of arms and the aid of twelve hundred Frenchmen, who might be assembled in the United States. " I replied to him that my powers did not extend so far as to allow me to sign treaties or to grant succor," reported the minister, " but that I could assure him of the all-powerful protection of my sovereign and of his excellent intentions in favor of those Spanish colonies which wished to establish local governments, independent of the motherland, and without liaisons with our enemies." Sérurier added that Palacio Fajardo had stated that his mission had been approved by the Congress of Cundinamarca, the central province of the viceroyalty of New Granada, and that as soon as the enemies of the province had been checked this congress would accede to any arrangement which he might make. " It would appear from the conversation of this agent," concluded Sérurier, " that an expedition comprising some vessels and several thousand men would not alarm the people of Cartagena; but that they even desire such aid as the most prompt and certain means of finishing at one blow the revolution in northern South America." [41]

Palacio Fajardo arrived in Paris in April, 1813. On April 7 he wrote to Bassano that he had recently met Luis

[40] Sérurier to Palacio Fajardo, December 26, 1812, *ibid.*
[41] Sérurier to Bassano, January 1, 1813, *ibid.*

Delpech, a Frenchman who had been in the service of
Venezuela and who alleged that he had been commissioned
by Dictator Miranda to proceed to Paris. The agent of Cartagena further stated that, as their missions had the same
purpose, they were acting together in order to solicit the
support of the French. In a joint note on the same day
Delpech and Palacio Fajardo declared that, in order to re-
sist their enemies and to establish advantageous relations
with France, both Cartagena and Venezuela solicited the
protection of the Emperor.[42]

A report by Bassano to Napoleon, dated April 10, 1813,
represented that, although Venezuela was now under Spanish domination, there would be no inconvenience in allow-
ing her agent to be present at his informal conferences with
Palacio Fajardo. The minister expressed his opinion as follows concerning the policy to be pursued toward the Spanish colonies:

> The decision of Your Majesty to show himself favor-
> able to their independence has become for them a powerful
> encouragement. Further, their first glance has been turned
> toward France and the United States, the emancipation of
> the latter state having been accomplished by the aid of the
> French. It appears that an agent of Buenos Aires will soon
> proceed to France, and that Paraguay, which up to this
> moment has pursued a middle course, is disposed to pro-
> claim her independence in as formal a manner as Cartagena
> and Cundinamarca did, and as Venezuela indeed did before
> her disasters. I have the honor to propose to Your Majesty
> that you continue to encourage this movement and that you
> authorize me to listen to the proposal for an agreement with
> Cartagena which its agent, Palacio Fajardo, can make—a

[42] Palacio Fajardo to Bassano, April 7, 1813; Delpech and Palacio Fajardo to *idem,* April 7, 1813, *ibid.* In May, 1812, Miranda
had evidently commissioned Delpech to proceed to England as
agent of Venezuela. See Robertson, *Life of Miranda,* II, 158-59.

proposition which I shall have the honor of reporting to Your Majesty.[43]

On April 15 Delpech and Palacio Fajardo made another joint appeal to France. After mentioning early assurances of the French Government with regard to Spanish-American independence, they expressed their confidence in Napoleon but complained that he had allowed them to remain in uncertainty. Asserting that Latin Americans were appealing to the Emperor to relieve them from the yoke of the English, the Portuguese, and the Spaniards, they reasoned that their compatriots would form a close union with the French and would favor the founding of a political system which would not only promote the prosperity of South America but also augment the prosperity and glory of France. The petitioners declared that if these observations served to persuade the French Government promptly to aid the Latin Americans they were ready to make suggestions regarding the gradual execution of their plan.[44]

On April 28 Delpech sent a note to Bassano in which he pleaded that immediate succor be sent to South American revolutionists. He requested that there be sent to the Patriots fifty thousand muskets, one hundred bronze cannon, twenty thousand uniforms, thirty thousand hats, and twenty thousand copies of a treatise on infantry tactics. In a supplementary note of the same date Delpech asked not only for military supplies but also for political and spiritual aid; he urged that ecclesiastics devoted to the French interest be

[43] A. A. E., Colombie, 1. The view of an Argentine diplomat in regard to the prospect of the recognition of La Plata by Napoleon before the battle of Waterloo is found in Centeno, *Virutas históricas, 1810-1928,* I, 80.

[44] A. A. E., Colombie, 1.

installed in Spanish America. The Pope should be induced to send bulls there which would inspirit the partisans of independence.[45]

On May 1, after they had been accorded an interview by Bassano, the two agents increased their demands by asking for printers, carpenters, miners, foundrymen, and artillery officers who might be transported to the Spanish Indies under the United States flag.[46] Bassano evidently brought these appeals to the attention of the Duke of Feltre, Minister of War. Subsequently that minister made a report to Bassano concerning the military supplies which he could furnish if the Emperor authorized that step. He confessed that it would be absolutely impossible for him to furnish any muskets, pistols, sabres, or other small arms. Feltre later admitted that it would be difficult to determine the number of artillery officers which his government could allow New Granada. Further, he reported that France did not possess soldiers who were either printers or miners and that she had no coppersmiths. Besides, he declared that only a half dozen military artificers could be furnished to the Spanish Americans. Finally, he stated that workmen for the manufacture of arms and ammunition could only be supplied by diminishing the output of imperial munition factories.[47]

Unable to rally the Spanish colonists to the cause of Joseph, Napoleon had evidently decided that he could seriously harass the Patriots of Spain by promoting the revolutionary movement in the Indies. A strange concatenation of circumstances prevented the acknowledgment by France of

[45] *Ibid.*   [46] *Ibid.*
[47] Feltre to Bassano, May 17 and May 22, 1813, *ibid.*

the independence of a certain Spanish-American people in the early years of the struggle that separated them from Spain. In northern South America, where the revolutionists had made the most notable progress, the surrender of Miranda to the Spaniards in July, 1812, checked the insurrectionary movement. The declining fortunes of Spanish-American Patriots and the pressing military needs of the French Emperor in Europe prevented him from rendering efficacious aid to the revolutionary cause in the Indies. Acclamations of the Grand Army en route to Moscow obliterated the despairing complaints of Joseph as well as the passionate pleas of South American emissaries. Spanish-American agents in Paris did not even find a Beaumarchais.

It appears that ultimately the policy of the Bonapartes toward the revolted Spanish colonies became essentially Napoleonic. Despite the activity of the English navy, however, even in 1812 and 1813 cotton from Brazil and hides from La Plata were brought into French ports in exchange for French silks and bric-a-brac.

Napoleon's downfall occurred at a time when the fortunes of the insurrectionary Spanish colonies were precarious. Although his usurpations in Spain had lighted powder magazines in the Indies, there were certain regions like Peru which were little affected by revolutionary explosions. Unable to induce the colonists to support his brother Joseph, Napoleon decided to acknowledge the independence of the Spanish Americans. Yet, in December, 1813, after the intrusive King had been driven out of Spain and when the Napoleonic régime was tottering, the Emperor acknowledged by a curious treaty the title of the captive Ferdinand VII to the throne of Spain and the Indies. By the triumph of the Allies, France was afforded an opportunity to restore the relations with Spain which had been established by the Bourbon Family Compact of 1761. With respect to Portugal, however, the situation was fundamentally different; for the momentous year 1814 found the Portuguese dominions still distracted because of the residence of the Braganza dynasty in Rio de Janeiro.

CHAPTER V

LEGITIMIST TENDENCIES UNDER LOUIS XVIII

In the spring of 1814, Alexander I of Russia and Frederick William III of Prussia made a triumphal entry into Paris. Prince Talleyrand, who had served as Napoleon's Minister of Foreign Affairs, took an attitude in favor of the restoration of Prince Louis, the brother of Louis XVI, to the throne of France. Hence the Allies announced that they would not treat with Napoleon. The Senate formally deposed the Emperor and released his soldiers from their oath of allegiance. On April 5 it adopted a provisional constitution which declared that the French people freely called Prince Louis to the throne. Napoleon then made his abdication unconditional; he was assigned the isle of Elba as a residence. The tricolor which had been displayed over the Tuileries was replaced by the white flag.

After the arrival of the Bourbon Prince in Paris, a charter was prepared which assured to the people certain rights won during the revolution and provided for a government modelled after that of England. This constitution was promulgated as a grant from the new King. Meanwhile, on May 14, Louis XVIII had selected his cabinet; as Minister of Foreign Affairs he appointed the skillful diplomat Talleyrand.

By the Treaty of Peace signed at Paris on May 30, 1814, between France, on the one hand, and Austria, Prussia, Russia, and England, on the other hand, an attempt was made not only to reconstruct the map of Europe but also to change colonial boundaries in America on the basis of the principle of legitimacy. Though Portugal had no part in framing this treaty, Article X provided that the Portuguese monarch was to return to the King of France the territory known as French Guiana with its boundaries as recognized in 1792. The issue which was thus revived between France and Portugal with regard to the boundary line between their colonies in South America was to be decided by the mediation of the King of England.[1]

Upon learning that hostilities between Napoleon and the Allies had ceased and that a Bourbon prince had been made the French King, Regent John in June, 1814, appointed Marquis Marialva ambassador extraordinary on a special mission to France. Marialva was directed to felicitate Louis XVIII upon his restoration to the throne.[2] The letter of credentials for the Duke of Luxembourg, the first French ambassador to the court at Rio de Janeiro, mentioned Marialva's mission as a gesture which had given much pleasure to the French monarch.[3]

On June 18, 1814, the Prince Regent issued a decree which announced that his country had resumed friendly relations with France.[4] A dispatch was promptly sent to Lisbon stating that in consequence all vessels of France, and those of other nations which had been subject to French domination or influence and which accordingly were considered enemies of Portugal, would henceforth be admitted into the ports of the Regent's dominions.[5] These

---

[1] Clercq, *Recueil des traités*, II, 419.

[2] June 15, 1814 (copy), A. A. E., Portugal et Brésil, 129.

[3] Signed by the King and Richelieu, February 29, 1816, *ibid.*

[4] *Collecção das leis do Brazil*, 1814, p. 14.

[5] Araujo to "Sor. Patriarcha Eleito de Lisboa," June 18, 1814, A. H. C., 216.

measures facilitated the resumption of commercial relations between France and Brazil. Though the ambassador of Regent John signed with plenipotentiaries of the Allies an act declaring that hostilities with France were at an end, the Regent soon announced that he would not ratify the Treaty of Paris because of his objections to Article X concerning the restoration of French Guiana. He considered that article incompatible with his dignity and royal rights.[6]

Meanwhile, however, negotiations in Europe between the Portuguese and the French had borne fruit. In July, 1814, a temporary agreement regarding commercial and diplomatic relations was reached at Paris between Prince Talleyrand and Count Palmella, envoy extraordinary and minister plenipotentiary of the Regent. Commercial intercourse between the two countries was to be upon the basis of perfect reciprocity. Consular agents of each party were to have in the dominions of the other party all the privileges and prerogatives which they had enjoyed in January, 1792. The subjects of one country domiciled in the other country were to enjoy identical advantages upon a reciprocal basis.[7]

The issue of restoration by the Portuguese of the French colony in Guiana was reopened at the Congress of Vienna by Count Palmella, who, with Lobo da Silveira, represented Portugal. On behalf of the Prince Regent, Palmella urged that as an equivalent for the restitution of French Guiana his government should receive the town of Olivença, which in 1801 had been ceded by the Portuguese to Spain. Again, in view of the prospective marriage between the Duke of

[6] Brito to Jaucourt, February 3, 1815, A. A. E., Portugal et Brésil, 128.

[7] "Instructions pour l'ambassadeur de S. M. T. C. au Brésil," A. A. E., Mémoires et Documents, Portugal, 8.

Berri and a Portuguese princess, Palmella suggested that the retrocession of Guiana might be considered as the dowry of that princess. This proposal evoked from Talleyrand the retort that affairs of the heart should not be confused with affairs of state. Moreover, that diplomat declined to sketch the boundaries of the former French colony. Article CVII of the Final Act of the Congress of Vienna stipulated that French Guiana was to be returned to Louis XVIII and that the boundary between that colony and Brazil was to be the river Oyapok. Both the time and the manner of this transfer were to be determined by an arrangement between the courts of Paris and Rio de Janeiro. By an exchange of notes the Portuguese diplomats secured an agreement that France was never to alienate the Guianan colony.[8]

The peculiar status of Portuguese America was soon brought directly to the attention of Louis XVIII. On December 5, 1814, Count Jaucourt, Minister of Foreign Affairs ad interim during Talleyrand's absence at Vienna, addressed to the King a memorandum which raised the pertinent question whether the interests of the European system would be better served by the presence of the Prince Regent in Portugal or by his residing in Portuguese America. The count maintained that French commercial interests in Brazil demanded protection; hence an agent should be selected to represent Louis XVIII at Rio de Janeiro. He suggested that such an agent might properly be designated consul general; for, as Brazil had become the residence of Regent John, it could no longer be considered a colony. Further, the minister reasoned that the appointment of a

[8] Oliveira Lima, *Dom João VI no Brazil,* I, 482, 486-89, 511; Clercq, *Recueil des traités,* II, 610-11.

French consular agent to Rio de Janeiro would be an innovation which would have a good influence upon the Regent. Such an agent might even be given the title of chargé d'affaires; in that case he could exercise political as well as commercial functions. In conclusion Jaucourt recommended that Colonel J. B. Maler, an upright and capable official who had been in the Portuguese service for several years, be appointed the chargé of France in Brazil. This memorandum bears the endorsement, "Approuvé Louis." [9]

Colonel Maler had presented his views concerning Portuguese America to the French Government in October, 1814. At that time he volunteered to gather such information about the new régime in America as might be useful to France. Emphasizing the significance of the opening of Brazil's ports to the world's commerce, he asserted that the Brazilians held out their hands to the French. He reminded them of the fact that the Portuguese of both America and Europe had sent to Paris delegations bearing congratulations on the restoration of Louis XVIII to the throne of his ancestors. Should not France profit by this favorable disposition? Maler expressed his willingness to proceed to Rio de Janeiro to serve in a manner suitable to the French Cabinet.[10]

After Napoleon had been defeated by the Allies at Waterloo, Maler was appointed French consul general to Brazil and was authorized to exercise also the functions of chargé d'affaires. In this dual capacity he was received at Rio de Janeiro in September, 1815.[11] He was instructed to consider seriously the status of the colony which France had

[9] A. A. E., Portugal et Brésil, 128.
[10] October 28, 1814, addressed to "Monseigneur," *ibid.*
[11] Campos, *Relações diplomaticas do Brasil*, p. 163.

formerly held in South America. On December 26, 1815, the Duke of Richelieu, a highminded statesman with moderate views, who had become Minister of Foreign Affairs as well as President of the Council of State, directed Maler to induce the Brazilian Government to favor the return of the Guianan colony to France.[12]

Meanwhile a significant alteration was made in the title accorded to Brazil. While conversing with one of the Portuguese plenipotentiaries at the Congress of Vienna, Prince Talleyrand declared that because of the bad government of Spain the Spanish colonies were almost lost to the motherland, and that the bonds between Portugal and her colony in America should be strengthened in every possible manner. Further, the prince suggested that, in order to flatter the Brazilians " and to destroy the notion of a colony which was distasteful to them," Brazil ought to be designated as a kingdom, and that her sovereign should become the ruler of the United Kingdom of Portugal and Brazil.[13] This suggestion was received with favor at the colonial capital; by a decree of December 16, 1815, Regent John announced that Portuguese America had been elevated to the rank of a kingdom and that his dominions were henceforth to be designated as the United Kingdom of Portugal, Brazil, and the Algarve.[14] He thus placed the Portuguese colony in America on the same constitutional plane as the mother country. Upon the death of the demented Queen Maria, the Regent was formally proclaimed the monarch of the United Kingdom with the title of John VI. In February, 1816, Francisco de Brito, who was acting as the agent of

[12] A. A. E., Portugal et Brésil, 128.

[13] Oliveira Lima, op. cit., I, 520.

[14] Collecção das leis do Brazil, 1815, pp. 62-63.

that monarch at Paris, notified the French Government of the change in Brazil's legal status.[15]

On April 12, 1816, Brito directed the attention of Richelieu to the fact that a tariff bill under discussion in the Chamber of Deputies did not take cognizance of the political union of the Portuguese kingdoms. This bill provided that coffee, cotton, and sugar taken to France from Brazil either in French vessels or in foreign vessels were to pay heavier duties than when transported to France from Portugal in such vessels.[16] In Richelieu's reply he justified this discrimination by taking issue with Brito's contention regarding the existence of a united kingdom of Portugal and Brazil:

> These two countries are united without being coalesced. Each country has the title of kingdom; each has its institutions and laws and a customs system so distinct that one country admits articles of French commerce which the other country excludes.[17]

The Duke of Luxembourg was appointed ambassador extraordinary to the court at Rio de Janeiro in February, 1816, for the express purpose of negotiating for the return of the Guianan colony to France, irrespective of the new adjustments which were being made in Europe concerning the boundaries of states. His instructions expressed the view that the nation seated at Rio de Janeiro desired to elevate Portuguese America to the same plane in South America as that occupied by the United States in North

---

[15] Campos, *op. cit.*, p. 53. As John VI resided in Brazil until 1821, the term Brazilian has been uniformly employed in the text in mentioning the activities of agents or soldiers of the Portuguese-Brazilian kingdom.

[16] A. A. E., Mémoires et Documents, Portugal, 8.

[17] April 22, 1816, *ibid.*

America. Luxembourg was directed to promote the development of commercial intercourse between France and Brazil.[18] Soon after he arrived at Rio de Janeiro, he was informed by Count Barca, the Brazilian Minister of Foreign Relations, that his government did not intend to concede any new commercial favors at that time. Barca also intimated that the Treaty of 1810 between his nation and England rendered trade between Brazil and other foreign countries very difficult. The ambassador reported to Paris that the customs régime which prevailed in Brazil was vexatious and iniquitous for those foreign merchants whose governments did not have treaties with that country. With respect to the chief object of his mission Luxembourg found that, as he was not authorized to determine the boundaries of French Guiana, the Court of Rio de Janeiro preferred not to treat with him. He accordingly took leave of that court on September 18, 1816.[19] Marquis Marialva, as ambassador, and Francisco de Brito, as chargé d'affaires, had meanwhile been empowered by the Prince Regent to negotiate at Paris with regard to the restoration of French Guiana.

The deep interest which France now took in Latin America was indicated by the decision of the Minister of Marine, taken in March, 1815, to send a naval expedition to Brazil.[20] This expedition does not seem to have been undertaken, however, for, in the midsummer of the follow-

[18] A copy of Luxembourg's credentials dated February 29, 1816, signed by the King and Richelieu, is found in A. A. E., Portugal et Brésil, 129. "Instructions pour l'Ambassadeur do S. M. T. C. au Brésil," February, 1816, are also found in A. A. E., Mémoires et Documents, Portugal, 8. Cf. Campos, *op. cit.*, p. 163.

[19] Oliveira Lima, *Dom João VI no Brazil,* I, 85, 396-97, 559-62.

[20] "Mémoire pour servir d'Instructions à Monsieur Baudin," March, 1815, A. N., Marine, B B⁴, 388.

ing year, Chevalier de Villela, commander of the frigate *Hermoine*, was ordered to sail to Rio de Janeiro. Villela was instructed that, during the time when his marines would be almost under the walls of a palace in which a monarch resided who was an ally of Louis XVIII, he scrupulously observe the rules of naval discipline. Thus the first warship in twenty-five years to display the Bourbon flag of France in Brazilian waters would leave a favorable impression of her navy.[21]

In the spring of 1817, because of the departure of Marialva from France, Francisco de Brito was made envoy extraordinary and minister plenipotentiary of the United Kingdom of Portugal and Brazil. At Paris, on August 28, 1817, Brito signed with Richelieu a series of conventions that adjusted the differences which had arisen between France and Brazil concerning the peace negotiated at Vienna. One of those treaties provided that within three months the Brazilians should return to the French the territory stretching from Dutch Guiana to the river Oyapok. Commissioners were to be appointed promptly by both parties to survey the boundary which had been sketched between French Guiana and Portuguese Guiana by the Treaty of Utrecht and by the Final Act of the Vienna Congress. The forts, magazines, and military supplies in the ceded territory were to be returned to France according to the terms of the inventory mentioned in the articles of surrender of 1809. An agreement was reached that the same transports which were to bring French troops to Cayenne should carry the Portuguese garrison and officials back to

[21] " Ordre de Service de M. le Chev. de Villela," June 6, 1816, *ibid.*, 395.

Brazil.[22] Yet the transfer was so long delayed that not until November, 1817, was Cayenne restored to France.[23]

Friendly relations between France and the government seated at Rio de Janeiro were accordingly established after the restoration of a Bourbon Prince to the French throne. French Guiana was returned to its former owner. A provisional, reciprocal agreement was quietly reached with respect to commercial intercourse between France and Portuguese America. Notwithstanding these readjustments, the French Government did not agree with the view of Brazilian authorities that Portugal and Brazil were united in one kingdom. The delicate problem confronting France and other European states with respect to the constitutional relation between the Portuguese junta governing at Lisbon and the Braganza dynasty reigning in Brazil was left unsolved.

Strange as it may seem, the restoration of Ferdinand VII to the Spanish throne in March, 1814, did not recall the American colonists to their allegiance. Sporadic uprisings, precipitated by French usurpations in Spain and stimulated by rumors of Bonapartist designs upon the Indies, had been transformed into separatist movements. In Mexico the warrior-priest Morelos had caught the mantle that fell from Hidalgo's shoulders. Hailed as Liberator by his compatriots, the dauntless revolutionist Simón Bolívar had proclaimed a war to the death against the Spaniards in Venezuela. After decisively checking the Royalists in La Plata, in August, 1814, the great strategist General San Martin had

[22] Clercq, *Recueil des traités,* III, 100-03.

[23] Carra de Vaux, " Documents sur la perte et la rétrocession de la Guyane française (1809-1817)," *Revue de l'histoire des colonies Françaises,* I, 350-54.

decided to prepare an army for the liberation of Chile and Peru. On the other hand, the absolutist King of Spain soon undertook to organize an expedition under General Morillo designed not only to subjugate the revolutionists in northern South America but also to aid in the conquest of the western and southern portions of that continent.

Instructions given to Pedro Gómez Labrador, the Spanish plenipotentiary at the Congress of Vienna, naturally displayed a spirit of apprehension with respect to France. The Council of State of the Regency, which had been acting during the exile of Ferdinand VII, took the view that the Family Compact was abrogated as well as the Treaty of San Ildefonso. In supplementary instructions the Spanish envoy was informed that Spain was fearful that the restoration of Guiana to France might enable French merchants and adventurers to furnish aid to revolutionists in northern South America. If France wished to revive the Treaty of the Family Compact, Gómez Labrador was only to agree to the renewal of certain honorable articles and was to preserve equality between diplomatic agents of both courts. He was to avoid any negotiations concerning commercial relations with the Spanish colonies in America.[24]

Soon after his arrival in Paris, the Spanish plenipotentiary took action concerning the policy which imperial France had pursued toward the Indies. On July 1, 1814, Gómez Labrador addressed a dispatch to Talleyrand, request-

---

[24] Villa Urrutia, "España en el congreso de Viena," *Revista de archivos, bibliotecas y museos,* XV, 178-79, 183-84. On July 5, 1814, Spain agreed to a treaty with England which contained a pledge that the Family Compact would not be renewed. Cantillo, *Tratados,* p. 733. The treaty signed by France and Spain on July 20, 1814, did not mention the Family Compact. See Clercq, *op. cit.,* II, 433-34.

ing that the French Government at once cease to furnish succor of any sort to rebels in the Spanish colonies. Seven days later, Talleyrand replied that the intentions of the Bonapartist government with regard to the American revolutionists were so contrary to the wishes of Louis XVIII that all instructions concerned with succor to them would have been rescinded without a special demand from Spain. Gómez Labrador was assured that directions had been issued to revoke at once any orders found in French ministries which tended either " to foment or to protect the insurrection " in Spanish America.[25]

The peace settlement between France and the Allies contained stipulations in regard to Spain. Article VII of the Treaty of Paris restored to her the eastern part of the island of Santo Domingo, which had been ceded to France by the Treaty of Basel. At Paris, on July 20, 1814, a convention was signed between France and Spain which included pertinent articles of the Treaty of Peace between France and the victorious Allies. Besides, the second article of the Franco-Spanish convention stipulated that, pending the negotiation of a treaty of commerce between the two countries, their commercial relations were to be restored to the conditions which had existed in 1792.[26] This evidently signified that the clauses concerning trade in the Bourbon Family Compact of 1761 and in other treaties between the two neighbors were acknowledged as again having a binding force. It appears, however, that France and Spain did not entirely revive former practices concerning their commercial intercourse.[27]

[25] Decretos del Rey Don Fernando VII, I, 219-20.

[26] Clercq, op. cit., II, 434.

[27] Becker, Relaciones comerciales entre España y Francia durante el siglo XIX, pp. 20-30.

The French Government soon prepared a précis regarding the policy which it intended to pursue toward Spain. On August 9, 1814, Count d'Agoult, an official of the Ministry of Foreign Affairs, framed instructions for the Duke of Laval-Montmorency, an émigré who on his return to France was sent as ambassador to the Court of Madrid to succeed a chargé d'affaires. These instructions, which were approved by the King, began with a résumé of French policy.

D'Agoult declared that the ties of blood existing between France and Spain were given a new strength by the Family Compact. That treaty sheltered Spain from Continental wars, relieved France from apprehensions concerning her southern frontier, and combined the maritime forces of the two nations. The alliance suited their mutual interests; for both nations had colonies to protect, and they had the same rival. In 1793, however, treaties were discarded and force took the place of political calculations. The French minister went on to say:

The return of the Bourbon dynasty to power in Spain induces the hope that all the former relations between the two courts will be reëstablished. This is the end at which the ambassador of His Majesty should aim. Beyond doubt there will be obstacles to overcome: Spain is still full of melancholy recollections and resentment; time alone will soothe the exasperation of the public. The solicitude of the ambassador will also promote this—he will undertake to show the difference between the epochs. Spain had as an enemy not France but a single man. It was the power of one man that covered her with ruins; the army which he forced to obey him was also his victim, and France herself is to demand of him a reckoning for all the evils which she has suffered.

Called upon to heal so many wounds, the King will also consider everything that may be of use to Spain. He desires the prosperity of that country: he wishes to promote this, and the Congress of Vienna may furnish him with the opportunity.

Suggesting that the plenipotentiaries of the Bourbon nations at Vienna should speak the same language, D'Agoult argued that this policy was especially necessary at a time when other powers had acquired a great accendancy over the destinies of Europe. He held that the Spanish colonies were very important to the motherland. After a review of the effects in those colonies of the Napoleonic usurpations in Spain, he admitted that the French Emperor had encouraged the revolutionary party in the Spanish Indies:

After stimulating this revolutionary spirit, however, Napoleon confined himself to vague promises. He did not dispatch to America either men, or subsidies, or arms, or vessels. The wars of Europe engrossed his forces; he sought for other ways of weakening his enemies; and he doubtless hoped to reduce Spain more easily by placing her at odds with her American subjects.

If the disturbances in Europe had a marked influence upon the situation of the Spanish colonies, one is ready to believe that the return of order to Europe will also have some influence upon them. Already the discussions concerning those colonies have become less complicated. . . . Besides we may now expect large defections from the party of independence, as it can no longer expect the support upon which it counted the most. Spain will now be able to employ her forces to subjugate the revolutionaries. The prospect of an attack against which they can scarcely be prepared in advance will help to disarm them.

The King will himself promote this end. He has ordered his minister in the United States not to aid the party of independence in any manner and to deprive it of any hope of succor. Declarations to this effect will be made to the American Government. At Madrid the ambassador of France will express the firm intention of the King to favor as much as possible the reëstablishment of the bonds between the Spanish colonies and the motherland. A dismemberment of her dominions would enervate Spain. Her prosperity is closely bound up with the possession of the New World. Europe itself is interested in a reunion that would facilitate the circulation of specie currency and promote commerce. All these considerations will serve to direct the ambassador with respect to the language which he should use at the Court of Madrid.[28]

These extracts indicate that the French King wished to promote the reunion of the insurgent Spanish colonies to the motherland. Not only did Louis XVIII repudiate the Napoleonic policy of encouraging the revolutionary faction in the Spanish Indies, but he also avowed the intention of rehabilitating the Bourbon Family Compact. Although at the Congress of Vienna Talleyrand suggested to the Spanish plenipotentiary that this pact be reaffirmed, it appears that Gómez Labrador responded by non-committal phrases. Indeed, on October 1, 1815, the Spanish Secretary of State warned him that the Family Compact had been prompted by a spirit of vengeance and that France might eventually renew the war in order to efface her fresh humiliation.[29] Two months later, however, a capable Spanish publicist, García de León y Pizarro, formed a plan for the cession of Spain's colony in Santo Domingo to France in return for the despatch of a French expedition of eighteen ships manned by six thousand French soldiers who were to be disembarked in Mexico. Pizarro, as he was ordinarily called, thought that by such means the remaining Spanish colonies might be saved to the motherland.[30]

An opportunity to elaborate its views concerning the Indies was furnished the French Government in the ap-

[28] A. A. E., Espagne, 694.
[29] Villa-Urrutia, "España en el congreso de Viena," *Revista de archivos, bibliotecas y museos*, XV, 194-195 and n. 5.
[30] García de León y Pizarro, *Memorias de la vida*, III, 222.

pointment of naval officers to positions near the Caribbean Sea. On August 27, 1816, in instructions to Captain Meynard de la Farge of the frigate *Euridice,* who was placed in charge of the naval station near the Windward Islands, Viscount Dubouchage, the Minister of Marine, informed him that he was to watch over the French islands of Guadeloupe and Martinique. He was warned that the stirring events which were taking place in the neighboring Spanish colonies might expose his sailors to dangerous intrigues against which he should use the utmost vigilance.[31] In a confidential letter to Captain la Villegonan of the frigate *Néréide* on December 31, 1816, the Minister of Marine instructed him to watch carefully the activities of a pack of adventurers. His attention was directed to the fact that the West Indies were infested with corsairs, who sometimes under false colors and at other times under the flags of insurgent Spanish-American colonies, preyed upon commerce and often attacked vessels which displayed the Spanish banner.[32]

During the next year privateers which unfurled the flag of an insurgent Spanish-American colony frequently pursued Spanish merchant ships as well as the vessels of England and France. Newspapers of both America and Europe published accounts of the depredations committed by such craft. The *Times* reported that in March, 1817, two privateers, ostensibly hailing from Buenos Aires and burdened

[31] A. N., Marine, B B⁴, 395. Viscount Dubouchage, who became a member of the first cabinet of the Duke of Richelieu in September, 1815, was styled Minister of Marine and the Colonies. In the text the abbreviated title, Minister of Marine, is frequently used.

[32] *Ibid.* On the corsairs, see further the reports from English newspapers printed in *Le Moniteur,* May 14, July 7, 24, 26, and 30, and October 14, 1817.

with treasure which they had captured on the high seas, had cast anchor at Norfolk, Virginia.[33] A letter from Jamaica dated June 19, 1817, complained bitterly that no merchantman could safely navigate Caribbean waters because of corsairs which preyed upon ships of all nations.[34] In the following month advices reached London that pirates were hovering near the Azore Islands, where they had seized richly laden vessels dispatched from Bengal, China, Venezuela, and Puerto Rico.[35] Two months later, a report was published in the United States of the capture near Cuba, by a Spanish-American corsair, of a Spanish brig laden with indigo and specie. Rumors reached New York City that piratical craft had escorted to Amelia Island four caravels heavily freighted with sugar, cochineal, and pieces of eight.[36]

A shrewd commentary in the *Courier* of London on September 9, 1817, concerning the pernicious activity of South American corsairs ostensibly sailing from countries whose insurgent governments had not been recognized, indicates one horn of the dilemma which confronted European nations. This journal reasoned that for a neutral state to request a revolutionary Spanish-American government to disavow piratical acts committed under its flag would be virtually to acknowledge its political existence. In an attempt to find a remedy for this evil, the English Government later brought the depredations of pirates in Latin-

---

[33] *Le Moniteur,* May 14, 1817.

[34] *The Courier,* July 16, 1817.

[35] *Le Moniteur,* July 26, 1817.

[36] *Ibid.,* November 5, 1817. On the privateers, see further Griffin, *The United States and the Disruption of the Spanish Empire,* pp. 105-06 and n.; and Webster, *Britain and the Independence of Latin America, passim.*

American waters to the attention of the Congress of Verona. It appears that careful surveillance by France at this time restricted the equipping of corsairs for La Plata in her ports.[37]

An unsigned memorandum filed in the archives of the Ministry of Marine shows that a careful study had been made by a French official of the activities of piratical craft in America. This memorandum, which was composed early in 1818 after Count Molé, an adaptable publicist who had served under the Empire, had become Minister of Marine, stated that the reports of French naval captains indicated that the number of vessels ostensibly belonging to Spanish-American insurgents was steadily increasing and that they generally respected the French flag, but that corsairs harassed all merchant ships in American seas. Advices had reached Paris that pirates were gathering in divers places with the design of planning the liberation of the restless personage who was confined at St. Helena or of concerting an attack upon the colonial establishments of European powers in the New World. The memorandum raised the question as to what precautionary measures the French Government could take. By way of reply the opinion was hazarded that the naval forces of France in America were too small to afford adequate protection to her commerce, that the French navy could not watch St. Helena, and that England should increase the forces which were guarding Napoleon. This project, which was of interest to all nations, raised the further problem whether irregular privateers should not be confiscated. The rôle of the French naval station in the Antilles was in meeting this problem described as follows:

[37] Bealer, *Los corsarios de Buenos Aires,* pp. 188-89.

For three years France has maintained at Martinique a station which is regularly composed of two frigates and three brigs or corvettes. These vessels patrol the archipelago of the Antilles, communicate with Habana in order to promote the collection of funds which are owing by Spain, and protect French commerce. They are constantly under instructions to protect French navigators against any insults, but to act in such a manner that no one might suppose that France is departing from absolute neutrality in the contest which is raging between Spain and her colonies in America.[38]

On January 8, 1818, the frigate *Zélée* brought to Martinique Governor Donzelot, a capable and prudent general who had been in charge of the Ionian Islands. Molé sent to that governor on February 20 a confidential dispatch containing his instructions. Donzelot was told to gather information concerning the real condition of those countries where a struggle was taking place between Spanish soldiers and insurgent colonists:

Every day it becomes more important for the French Government to learn with exactness the resources of each of the parties and to judge what will be the result of the quarrel that divides them. It is also useful to know the movements, the endeavors, the resources, and the projects of that swarm of adventurers who have gone from various parts of the globe to the United States or to Spanish America in order to cover their depredations with the flag of the revolutionists, and perhaps to be duped in enterprises which they meditate either against the colonies belonging to European nations in the Antilles or even—despite the wildness of the project—against that island for the guardianship of which England is today responsible to all Europe.

Accordingly, General, the intention of the King is that you are to neglect no means of securing as positive in-

---

[38] " Février, 1818," A. N., Marine, B B⁴, 402. On alleged designs of corsairs upon St. Helena, see Hyde de Neuville, *Mémoires,* II, 270.

formation as possible concerning what is happening in the countries adjacent to the Windward Islands. The vessels of the station offer you in this respect great resources; it should be easy for you, without depriving commerce of adequate protection, to detach successively one or two ships from the station in order to send them to places where you may hope to gather useful information.

This kind of investigation should be the object of all your solicitude. The Duke of Richelieu is about to instruct all French consuls in the United States to use every opportunity to inform you of facts that may come to their knowledge. That information, in conjunction with the data which you may gather, will enable you to give instructions to the officers whom you entrust with missions of inquiry. I authorize you, whenever you may judge it convenient, to detach from service a naval officer and to dispatch him on a ship that you send on a mission, or to employ instead, if you judge it necessary, an official who is under your orders at Martinique. All latitude is allowed you in order that you may accomplish the end which is proposed. It is understood that, if you discover any facts of major importance for the interests of France, you are immediately to dispatch a ship in order to advise me.[39]

These confidential instructions, which ordered Governor Donzelot to use Martinique as an observation station for France, not only made that island a coign of vantage against corsairs, but, as time passed, converted it into an outpost from which the governor was able to direct a careful surveillance over neighboring Spanish colonies that were struggling to establish their independence.

Attacks on merchantmen by corsairs in Spanish-American waters provoked France in 1818 to take vigorous measures for the protection of her commerce. On July 14 Count Molé addressed a circular not only to the naval commandants at Cherbourg, Brest, L'Orient, Rochefort, and Toulon but also to the governors or commandants of Senegal,

[39] A. N., Marine, B B⁴, 405 *bis*.

Guadeloupe, Martinique, French Guiana, and the Île de Bourbon concerning the depredations of vessels that apparently did not belong to either belligerent party in Spanish America. The commanders of all the warships of France were to be instructed to protect her merchant ships from insults. Whenever it was positively known that a corsair had committed acts of piracy against a French ship, these commanders were to pursue the offender and, upon capture, to convoy the piratical craft with her captain and crew to a port in France or in the French colonies. There the accusations against the pirate were to be given a judicial examination, and, if proven, the ship and the crew were both to be detained during the King's pleasure. French naval captains were instructed to observe the strictest neutrality in the struggle between colonial insurgents and the Spanish Royalists.[40]

The attitude of France toward the dissensions in Spanish America was further elucidated in a memorandum now lodged in the archives of the Ministry of Marine. Its author evidently belonged to that ministry, if indeed he was not an undersecretary. This paper, which was prepared in the midsummer of 1818, contrasted the policy of France toward the Spanish Indies with the attitude adopted by England and the United States. It assumed that England was animated by a wish to improve her commercial relations with the revolutionary colonies and that the United States was influenced by a desire for territorial expansion. On the other hand, France was deeply interested in seeing that the Spanish colonies remained tranquil and submissive to Spain: " France may some day find in those dominions a useful

[40] " Circulaire à M. M. les commandants de la Marine," July 14, 1818, *ibid.*

auxiliary; it is disquieting for her to see her three western colonies menaced at the same time by the blacks of Saint-Domingue and by Spanish-American revolutionists who could soon make common cause against those weak establishments." The author maintained that because of fiscal and political conditions France was forced to be extremely discreet with regard to the struggle between the Spanish colonies and the motherland. He held that, if France could not at this time plan to secure advantages when that struggle terminated, it was very important that her commerce be protected against depredations by cruisers hailing from revolutionary communities.

This memorandum specified three conditions which would justify the capture and detention of a corsair ostensibly belonging to the Patriots of Spanish America: if the vessel should carry artillery; if the size of its crew should be unduly large in proportion to its tonnage; if three-fourths of the crew should not be composed of mariners belonging to the country where the ship had been fitted out.[41]

Partly because of reports of her colonial administrators and naval captains, France from 1816 to 1818 dispatched officers of the navy on special missions to Spanish and Portuguese America. The purpose of the French Government was expressed in the instructions prepared by Minister Dubouchage on August 1, 1817, for Le Bozée, the commander of the *Flore* stationed at Cayenne, who was to make a cruise of the Caribbean Sea in that frigate, accompanied by three corvettes. This commander was directed to display the utmost deference to any Spanish officials whom he might encounter and to conduct himself in a manner becoming the officer of a nation bound to Spain by ties of blood and

---

[41] " 29 Juin, 1818," A. N., Marine, B B⁴, 402.

by respect for the principle of legitimacy. Still, as his trip had for its prime object the protection of French commerce, he was to decline to accede to requests of Spanish colonial officials that he take an active part in attacks upon the insurgents. All piratical craft which he might encounter were to be warned that he would chastize any of them that either insulted the French flag or interfered with the maritime activities of Frenchmen. The minister continued as follows:

During your cruise you will take care to gather the most exact information possible regarding the situation of the troops that are loyal to the Spanish King and the condition of those colonists who are in arms against their legitimate sovereign. It appears that there reach Europe only inaccurate reports which are equally exaggerated by both parties to the struggle; I attach great importance to learning what the real state of affairs is and what reasonable conjectures this furnishes for the future. You see, Sir, that your mission has a double purpose: to display the royal banner in an imposing manner so as to protect our commerce, and to examine attentively what is going on in the countries which you may visit.[42]

At the end of November, 1817, Commander le Bozée left France with two ships bound for Martinique. He sailed from that island for South America on December 9 and visited successively La Guaira, Santa Marta, Cartagena, Porto Bello, and Habana. After cruising along the coast of Puerto Rico and Santo Domingo, he returned to Martinique on March 30, 1818. Soon after casting anchor at Brest, Le Bozée sent Molé an account of hydrographic, political, and military conditions in each region visited, an account which paid some attention to the status of the insurrection. The Minister of Marine was pleased to learn that this commander had tried to skirt along the coast near enough to

[42] *Ibid.*, 395.

display the French flag and that, when he touched at Habana, Porto Bello, and La Guaira, Spanish colonial officials gave him a flattering reception.[43]

The return of the Bourbon dynasty to the throne was thus followed by a radical change in the policy pursued by France toward Spain and the Indies. Despite the reluctance cf the provisional Council of State, French statesmen soon made known to the Court of Madrid that they considered the Bourbon Family Compact again in force. Though statements made by Spanish diplomats concerning that treaty were not consistent, no evidence has been found that the ministers of Ferdinand VII notified France that the pact was not to be revived. Indeed the following pages will make clear that upon more than one occasion after Napoleon's downfall they mentioned the Family Compact in terms which would indicate that they also considered it as being in force with all its vigor. No longer, as in the time of Napoleon, were French officials in America directed to sympathize with Spanish-American insurgents, to offer them military support, or to assure them that France would soon acknowledge the independence of the nascent commonwealths.

A new phase of French policy is revealed by the fact that naval officers in Latin-American waters were instructed diligently to protect French merchant ships against corsairs that often displayed a revolutionary banner. The early policy of the restored Bourbon monarchy toward the Indies was also marked by an attempt to study conditions in the insurrectionary colonies and to collect data which might enable it to determine whether or not the time had actually arrived to modify its legitimist attitude.

[43] Le Bozée to Molé, May 10, 1818; Molé to Le Bozée, June 1, 1818, *ibid.*, 404.

CHAPTER VI

LATIN AMERICA IN EUROPEAN POLITICS,
1815-1819

The attitude of France toward the insurgent Spanish colonies from 1815 to 1819 can be fully understood only when considered in connection with the international policy of the Continental powers. Preëminent among the reactionary forces that became manifest on the European Continent after the exile of Napoleon was the Holy Alliance. This alliance was the by-product of a war-weary age. At the Congress of Vienna the plenipotentiaries of seven powers had arranged for the reconstruction of Europe according to the principle of legitimacy. While attending this congress certain personages had entertained the idea that the sovereigns there assembled might appropriately terminate its sessions by a proclamation pledging themselves to maintain peace throughout Europe. Such a proclamation was actually framed by the secretary of the congress, Friedrich von Gentz, who was the assistant of the astute, versatile, and influential Austrian diplomat, Prince Metternich. With a measure of truth that prince has often been depicted as the most unrelenting legitimist. Among other dignitaries the Russian autocrat, Alexander I, was very favorably disposed toward proposals for universal peace. After the burning of Moscow, he fell under the influence of evangelical revivalists and his thoughts took on a deeply religious tinge.

In June, 1815, while sojourning at Heilbrunn on his way to France, the Czar met Madame de Krüdener, a religious enchantress who considered herself divinely commissioned to teach him her mystic cult. Madame de Krüdener later asserted that she had been the instrument of God to propose the Holy Alliance to the Czar. Both von Gentz and the English Secretary for Foreign Affairs, Lord Castlereagh, believed that Alexander I had formed the project of that alliance while in her company.[1] Yet the Russian autocrat later asserted that the idea of a sacred league of sovereigns had originated in his own mind; apparently he did not even mention the influence of Madame de Krüdener. It seems, however, that she was partly responsible for the religious tone of the Treaty of the Holy Alliance.[2]

This treaty was signed at Paris, on September 26, 1815, by Alexander I, Emperor of Russia, Francis I, Emperor of Austria, and Frederick William III, King of Prussia. Its preamble declared that those three monarchs, because of the great events which had taken place in Europe and the blessings conferred upon them by Providence, had become convinced that the conduct to be observed by European powers should be based upon the sublime truths of Christianity. The first article declared that the three signatory monarchs would remain united by fraternal bonds; that they would always lend each other aid and assistance; and that they would lead their soldiers " to protect religion, peace, and justice." The second article declared that the three powers would aim to be of reciprocal service to each other and that they would consider themselves as chosen by Providence " to govern three branches of the same family." The

---

[1] Muhlenbeck, *Étude sur les origines de la Saint-Alliance* p. 249; Gentz, *Dépêches inédites*, I, 216.

[2] Cresson, *The Holy Alliance*, pp. 29, 41, n. 1; Capefigue, *Histoire de la restauration*, I, 428.

third article provided that those states which solemnly avowed the sacred principles of the treaty and recognized that its ideals should exercise their proper influence over the destinies of mankind would be "received with as much cordiality as affection into this Holy Alliance." [3]

Contemporary opinion of this Act of Alliance varied greatly. In a dispatch to Lord Liverpool, Castlereagh mentioned it as a "piece of sublime mysticism and nonsense." [4] A little later, in the House of Commons, Brougham referred to it as an extraordinary treaty put forth by the contracting parties as if they were the monopolists of Christianity; but, he added, "their pretension justified serious suspicion that they were leagued against some state not Christian, and that they had something in view, which it was not deemed prudent to avow." [5]

The Act of the Holy Alliance occupies a unique place in diplomatic history. That act can scarcely be considered as a treaty in the ordinary sense. Conceived by an Emperor of the Greek faith, it was also signed promptly by a Protestant king and a Catholic emperor. It was not subscribed by the foreign ministers of those allies. It included no trace of a definite pledge or of a diplomatic concession, which Gentz declared to be the very essence of treaties.[6] In reality the Act of the Holy Alliance was originally little more than a joint declaration of principles by three autocratic monarchs. Indeed it is scarcely an exaggeration to

[3] Martens, *Recueil des traités et conventions conclus par la Russie avec les puissances étrangères*, vol. IV, pt. 1, pp. 4-7.

[4] Wellington, *Supplementary Despatches, Correspondence, and Memoranda*, XI, 176.

[5] Hansard, *Parliamentary Debates*, XXXII, 347.

[6] Gentz, *Schriften*, III, 21.

say that the so-called Treaty of the Holy Alliance was neither a treaty, nor holy, nor an alliance.

Prince Metternich disingenuously described this alliance as a blatant nothing. He maintained that it was not " an instrument to keep down the rights of the people, or to promote absolutism or any other tyranny." [7] From 1815 to 1822 the Holy Alliance was almost inextricably involved with the Quadruple Alliance or, as it is sometimes designated, the Grand Alliance, which was consolidated by the treaty signed at Paris on November 20, 1815, by England, Austria, Prussia, and Russia. At times contemporaries of Alexander I confused the Holy Alliance with the Grand Alliance. This fact helps to explain why historical writers have occasionally tended to fuse the two alliances. There is a measure of justification for this tendency, for some signs suggest that certain powers belonging to the Holy Alliance may occasionally have constituted an inner circle of the Grand Alliance—a species of Continental concert that aimed to maintain the doctrine of legitimacy.

The three monarchs who signed the Treaty of the Holy Alliance soon addressed to the Prince Regent of England a note inviting him to attach his signature to the act. Early in October, he responded that English constitutional custom prevented him from formally acceding to this league.[8] On November 19, 1815, however, Louis XVIII signed an act of accession avowing the sacred principles embodied in the treaty.[9] In May, 1816, at the invitation of Czar Alexander, without the knowledge of his Secretary of State, Ferdinand

[7] Metternich, *Aus Metternich's nachgelassenen Papieren,* vol. I, pt. 1, p. 216.

[8] Wellington, *op. cit.,* XI, 184-85.

[9] Clercq, *Recueil des traités,* II, 630.

VII acceded to the Treaty of the Holy Alliance. He praised the sublime thought which had inspired the league, declared that he would strenuously endeavor to restore order in Spain, and asserted that the situation of her colonies encouraged the hope that their union with the motherland would be reëstablished. " I have given to M. de Tatistcheff my act of accession to this fraternal union," added the King in a letter to the Czar, " and henceforth it is as your ally that I shall claim your advice and support." [10] The Holy Alliance soon came to be viewed as an instrument of legitimacy and reaction in both the Old World and the New. On October 11, 1817, in an article concerning Spain and her colonies, *Niles' Weekly Register* expressed the hope that the " unholy alliance " of European monarchs would soon be broken so that every nation might regulate her own affairs.

Latin America was meanwhile assuming a new and startling aspect. Early in 1816 John VI of Brazil had become the titular King of Portugal, where a regency had been ruling under English protection. On July 9, 1816, a congress of delegates from certain sections of the viceroyalty of La Plata proclaimed the independence of the United Provinces of South America—a state which was ordinarily designated as the " United Provinces of La Plata " or simply " La Plata." By a heroic march over the Andean range General San Martín invaded Chile and de-

---

[10] Villa-Urrutia, " España en el congreso de Viena," *Revista de archivos, bibliotecas y museos,* XVI, 169. Cantillo, *Tratados, convenios y declaraciones de paz y de comercio,* p. 785, erroneously gives the date of Ferdinand VII's accession to the treaty of the Holy Alliance as June 4, 1817. The act of accession is not mentioned in Martens, *Recueil des traités et conventions conclus par la Russie avec les puissances étrangères,* XIV.

feated the Royalists at Chacabuco. The victory of the Patriots at Maipú on April 5, 1819, ensured Chilean independence.

The attitude of the Holy Allies toward the nations that were rising in America was largely determined by the foreign policy of France and Russia. In 1817 General Pozzo di Borgo, the influential Russian ambassador at Paris, was diligently promoting an *entente* between Russia and France. Hence the policy of those powers became involved with the activities of the congresses which were held in Europe from 1815 to 1822. Inedited diplomatic correspondence shows conclusively that in 1817 the Russian Government was carefully studying the relations between Spain and her American colonies.[11]

At that time, Russia's interest was aroused because of the proposed mediation of England in the quarrel. In June, 1817, the sentiments of Alexander I were expressed in a note from Dmitri Tatistcheff, his influential ambassador at Madrid, to the Spanish Secretary of State. Tatistcheff declared that the Czar, as the intimate friend of Ferdinand VII, was considering a problem which involved interests that were dear to that king and to humanity: " The insurrection of a part of the transatlantic dominions of His Catholic Majesty is not simply a Spanish question or an American question. From its outcome the world should gain a new experience in regard to the results of rebellion,

---

[11] At this time Ferdinand VII secured from Russia eight armed ships presumably to be used against the insurgent colonies. Most of these ships were in such poor condition, however, as to be practically useless. See García de León y Pizarro, *Memorias de la vida,* II, 158-60, III, 427-53; Villa-Urrutia, " España en el congreso de Viena," *loc. cit.,* XVI, 179-81. An alleged treaty providing for the transfer of these ships is found in Cantillo, *op. cit.,* pp. 795-97.

of anarchy, and of an attempt against the rights of legitimacy." After suggesting that in place of English mediation, which Russia did not oppose, Spain might grant concessions to her rebellious colonists, Tatistcheff declared that he was following the wishes of a magnanimous monarch who was devoted to his allies and disposed to protect the principles of morality—"the unique guarantee of the sacred bond which unites the people and the kings and assures the general welfare." [12]

Spain tried to interest her Bourbon ally in the fate of the revolted colonies. In the autumn of 1817 the Duke of Fernán Núñez, the Spanish ambassador to France, broached England's proposal for mediation between Spain and her colonies in conferences with Richelieu and Pozzo di Borgo. The Spaniard directed their attention to the fact that the English plan for the reconciliation of the Spanish colonies with the motherland stipulated that armed intervention was not contemplated. Fernán Núñez expressed the conviction that such mediation would be scorned by the insurgents and that, unless the attempt at reconciliation was accompanied by force or by threats of coercion, little or no advantage would be gained by Spain.[13] Shortly afterward, Secretary Pizarro notified Fernán Núñez that Ferdinand VII approved of those sentiments.[14] Pizarro evidently wished that international conferences regarding Spain's insurgent colonies be held in Madrid.[15]

[12] Addressed to "Monsieur," June $\frac{6}{18}$, 1817, A. G. I., Estado, 88.

[13] Fernán Núñez to Pizarro, October 16, 1817, *ibid.* On Pozzo di Borgo's rôle, see Maggiolo, *Pozzo di Borgo,* pp. 250-53, 258.

[14] October 28, 1817, A. G. I., Estado, 88.

[15] Pizarro to Fernán Núñez, October 28 and 31, 1817, *ibid.* On English policy toward the revolted Spanish colonies, see Webster, "Castlereagh and the Spanish Colonies, I," *Eng. Hist. Rev.,* XXVII, 83-88.

Early in 1818 Fernán Núñez sent a note to the Duke of Richelieu regarding the negotiations for a reconciliation between Spain and the Indies. The Spanish ambassador mentioned the pleasure with which Ferdinand VII had heard of the reception of his views concerning the interest of the allied sovereigns in " the pacification of America and the utility of intervention by those sovereigns." Though hoping for a common accord among them on this important matter, the Court of Madrid felt that the events happening in Spanish America made a reconciliation with the colonies difficult and even threatened general subversion of the European political system.[16] In reply the French minister said in part:

His Very Christian Majesty, who considers the cessation of the troubles which harass America as a matter most important to the interest of European politics and to the welfare of humanity, has directed the undersigned to assure His Excellency the Count of Fernán Núñez that he is ready to coöperate in all measures which Spain and the powers that she invites to take part in this mediation may judge adapted to produce so desirable a result. Yet at the same time His Majesty thinks that the most certain and prompt mode of producing that unanimous accord of views and of action which alone can ensure complete success in an affair of this nature would be above all for Spain to make known to France, as well as to the other powers, upon what bases and by what means she believes the pacification of the colonies can be accomplished. Besides, the Cabinet of Madrid, which is directly interested, is the only power that is sufficiently acquainted with the different districts and with the actual condition of affairs in those vast countries to be able to furnish the materials for a general plan which would then receive all the force necessary for its execution from the coöperation of Spain and the mediatory nations.
Louis XVIII flatters himself that His Catholic Majesty

[16] February 28, 1818, A. G. I., Estado, 89.

will be convinced of the necessity of this preliminary step. At the same time the King desires that Ferdinand VII should see in the confidence with which he has discussed with him so delicate a matter a new proof of his friendship and of the constant interest that he takes in the prosperity of the Spanish monarchy.[17]

The government of Spain then formed and proposed to European powers a program, dated June 17, 1818, as a basis for the pacification of the Spanish colonies. Shortly afterward it was presented as a circular note by Fernán Núñez to Richelieu and the ambassadors of Russia, Austria, Prussia, and England at Paris. This plan laid down four bases for an adjustment between Spain and her colonies. 1. A general amnesty was to be assured to the rebels when they submitted to Spanish authority. 2. Offices and honors in the Spanish Indies were to be as open to Creoles as to European Spaniards. 3. Commercial relations between the pacified provinces and foreign countries were to be regulated upon liberal principles suitable to the changed conditions. 4. Besides, Ferdinand VII was disposed to adopt such measures suggested by his allies as would be compatible with his dignity and the preservation of his royal rights. In a conference with Castlereagh concerning the pacification of Spanish America, the Spanish ambassador in London was assured that the Congress of Aix-la-Chapelle would formulate bases for the mediation between Spain and her colonies.[18]

[17] (Copy), undated, *ibid.* Fernán Núñez had been given the title of Duke in August, 1817.

[18] The Spanish circular note is published in *British and Foreign State Papers,* V, 1217-19. It is also printed in Webster, *Britain and the Independence of Latin America,* II, 367-69, with the date June 18. See further Molinari, "Fernando VII y la emancipación de América (1814-1819)," *IIº congreso internacional de historia de América,* IV, 276-80 and footnotes.

The views which Richelieu held in the following August
with regard to Spanish-American affairs were elucidated in
a dispatch explaining the attitude of his government toward
a ship displaying a flag of the Spanish-American insurgents
which had been ordered to leave a French port. Richelieu
declared that this incident showed that the aggrieved tone
of the Spanish minister had little justification:

Our conduct toward the Spanish Ministry is, and always
will be, frank. In stating that the discussions of Spain
with her colonies might reconcile the parties, we have
neither expressed an opinion nor made a decision which
was contrary to her rights and interests or which might give
her offence.[19]

The first move toward another European congress was
made by Alexander I. His government issued a circular in
April, 1818, which praised the results accomplished in
Europe by international action and proposed the convocation
of a new congress composed of representatives of the
nations belonging to the Grand Alliance. Besides, France
was invited to send a representative to the meeting.[20] In
confidential conversations with a colleague, Richelieu intimated that Ferdinand VII should be summoned to appear
before the congress. The head of the French Ministry
hoped that this monarch might thus be induced not only to
recognize the independence of Spanish South America but
also to send the son of the former Queen of Etruria to
Buenos Aires to reign over an American principality.[21]

The attitude of Austria, Prussia, Russia, and England
toward French participation in their councils was indicated

[19] August 24, 1818, A. A. E., Espagne, 702.
[20] Cresson, *The Holy Alliance*, pp. 69-74.
[21] Noailles, *Le Comte Molé*, III, 363.

by their proceedings in regard to the controversy between Spain and Portugal concerning the Banda Oriental del Uruguay. This region had long been claimed by both Spain and Portugal. A rude chieftain named José Artigas had become the leader of a revolt which was directed not only against Spanish sovereignty but also against domination by Brazil. In 1816 Brazilian soldiers under General Lecor overran this debatable land. Lecor was soon appointed the head of a provisional government located at Montevideo. Ferdinand VII accordingly requested the allied powers to mediate in the impending dispute with John VI over the title to the Banda Oriental.

Early in 1817 France was invited to take part in the conferences of the four allies regarding this dispute.[22] Richelieu signed the collective note which on March 16, 1817, they addressed to Brazil in protest against the invasion of the Banda Oriental. The Spanish envoy at Paris represented to Richelieu that the Brazilian invasion was an act of aggression against Spain, that Brazil's allegation that it was necessary to protect her territory against anarchic disturbances in Uruguay was a mere pretext, and that this invasion was contrary to the principles of international comity recognized by European nations.[23]

Accounts of the dispute concerning the title to Uruguay found their way into Parisian newspapers. An editorial printed in the *Journal de Paris* in the autumn of 1817 indicates the manner in which it wished to direct public opinion. This journal asserted that a supposition that Spain had

[22] Polovstoff, *Correspondance diplomatique des ambassadeurs et ministres de Russie en France et de France en Russie avec leurs gouvernements de 1814 à 1830,* II, 85.
[23] Wellington, *Supplementary Despatches,* XI, 670-74.

agreed to allow the Brazilians to occupy the Banda Oriental had been destroyed by the Allied note of March 16. It raised the question whether, in view of the status of the revolutionary movement in other South American provinces, the diplomatic intervention of France, Russia, Austria, and Prussia in the Portuguese-Spanish controversy would produce for Spain the results which that power desired. Could the Continental sovereigns, pertinently inquired this journal, find the remedy for the evils which existed in so distant a region? As for England, her commercial interests were so much interwoven with her political interests that it was impossible to separate them. English trade had nothing to gain either by the annexation of Uruguay to Brazil or by the restoration of the insurgent Spanish colonies to the motherland.[24]

In instructions to Hyde de Neuville, who was serving as French minister at Washington, Richelieu developed his views with respect to the Spanish Indies. On July 20, 1817, the Duke reasoned that Europe could not remain indifferent to the spread of an anarchical system which threatened to affect the entire American Continent. Though agreeing with Hyde de Neuville on "the utility of forming in the New World two monarchies under the sceptre of the Bourbons," he felt that it would be difficult to make Spain realize the wisdom of this policy in time to carry it out.[25]

These instructions were supplemented by a dispatch from Richelieu to Hyde de Neuville dated February 16, 1818, in which the Duke weighed in the balance mediation between

[24] *Journal de Paris,* August 21, 1817. The *Times* replied to this editorial on August 26.

[25] Hyde de Neuville, *Mémoires et souvenirs,* II, 326.

Spain and her colonies and the recognition of their independence. Richelieu maintained that the proposal to acknowledge the independence of the provinces of La Plata should be considered with caution by the United States. When the colonies of a European monarchy were in question, he declared, the attitude which was taken at Washington was necessarily noticed in Europe:

> That liaison of interests has become more apparent since the great powers of Europe have shown themselves disposed to intervene by their mediation in the affairs of America and in its pacification. This pacification, especially that of the Spanish colonies with their motherland, will not be accomplished without difficulty or perhaps without some sacrifice.

Richelieu held that it would be imprudent for the United States to assume an attitude toward the important question of the status of the insurgent colonies and thus to shoulder a responsibility which might compromise her in the eyes of European powers.[26] Accordingly the French envoy, hoping that an acknowledgment of Spanish-American independence by the United States might be delayed or prevented, tried in his conferences with Secretary of State John Quincy Adams to persuade him to adjust his government's dispute with Spain.[27]

On November 17, 1817, the Czar addressed to the mediating powers a précis concerning the controversy over the title to Uruguay and the situation of the Spanish colonies. Alexander I called their attention to the condition of the

[26] *Ibid.,* 335. In October, 1817, Richelieu had discussed mediation between Spain and her colonies with Fernán Núñez. See Molinari, " Fernando Septimo y la emancipación de la América (1814-1819)," *IIº Congreso internacional de historia de América,* IV, 268-69 n.

[27] Adams, *Memoirs,* IV, 87, 162.

vast and fertile regions of the Western Hemisphere which
European nations were deeply interested in preserving from
the horrors of revolution. With regard to the dispute over
the invasion of Uruguay by Brazilian troops, the autocrat
suggested that the application of the principle of legitimacy
would adjust all territorial differences between Spain and
Portugal. He reasoned that, after this controversy was settled, a negotiation concerning the pacification of the Spanish colonies could be undertaken. In a certain passage of
that document the Czar proposed that the Spanish-American
countries be pacified by having the plan for their reconciliation with Spain conform to stipulations of the Congress of
Vienna.[28] However, as von Gentz pointed out to Nesselrode in a commentary on that proposition, there was no
analogy between the transactions of certain sovereigns concerning Europe and the problem of a vast continent in revolt. The Austrian diplomat also expressed the opinion
that Spain expected from Russia not simply mediation but
active intervention by means of thirty or forty thousand
European soldiers who would reduce the Spanish-American
insurgents to the most abject submission. Von Gentz
thought that Russia flattered herself that she would be able
gradually to make other European powers agree to this
scheme.[29]

It is clear that, whatever measures Russia might favor for
the pacification of the Spanish Indies, she expected to secure
the coöperation of France. In a commentary on the policy
of the Russian Cabinet the French envoy at St. Peters-

[28] Polovstoff, *op. cit.*, II, 474-82. See also " Correspondence of
the Russian Ministers in Washington, 1818-1825," *Am. Hist. Rev.*,
XVIII, 312-14.

[29] Nesselrode, *Lettres et papiers*, V, 295; Gentz, *Dépêches inédites*, I, 333.

burg remarked: " I believe that, although recognizing the rights of Spain over her American subjects, it will seek to free the colonists from the monopoly exercised by the motherland." [30] In spite of the endeavors of the powers, however, the attempt at mediation failed. The three chief issues on which an agreement could not be reached were, according to Richelieu, as follows: the occupation of a provisional military line by Brazilian soldiers until the provinces of La Plata were pacified, the payment of an indemnity to Spain by the Brazilians when they relinquished Montevideo, and the demand of Brazil that a clause be inserted in the proposed treaty stipulating that a policy of neutrality with regard to the Uruguayan insurgents be formally adopted by both parties to the dispute.[31]

In June, 1818, Spain addressed to the Allies a circular which aimed to enlist their favor in the struggle which she was waging against the American revolutionists.[32] Shortly afterward, the Spanish minister at St. Petersburg dispatched a communication to the Russian Cabinet in which he requested that, upon the occasion of the proposed conference of European nations at Aix-la-Chapelle, the four Continental allies should, in conjunction with the government of Spain, consider the means of pacifying the revolted colonies. This proposal was made known to the Emperor of Austria and was favorably received by Prince Metternich. The Spanish Government even appointed two plenipotentiaries to attend the proposed congress.[33]

[30] Noailles to Richelieu, November 30, 1817, A. A. E., Russie, 157.

[31] Richelieu to Laval-Montmorency, August 6, 1818, A. A. E., Mémoires et Documents, Amérique, 34.

[32] *British and Foreign State Papers,* V, 1217-20.

[33] De Hudelist to Golowkin, August 18, 1818, H. H. u. S., Con-

Richelieu's views in regard to the Spanish Indies were formulated in a paper dated August 6, 1818, addressed to the French ambassador at Madrid. In this memoir the minister expressed regret at the failure of joint mediation in the dispute concerning Uruguay. He maintained that, because of commercial reasons, England was not averse to the continuance of revolutionary struggles in the Spanish Indies. Richelieu then made some observations to Laval-Montmorency concerning the policy that might be adopted toward the American colonies of Spain:

In such circumstances, not being able to count upon England, attacked and outraged by the United States, without a navy, without money, almost without an administration, should not Spain listen to the advice of her true friends and thwart the plots of all those who wish to enrich themselves at her expense? It is necessary for her to make the important resolution of renouncing with good grace that which she can never regain, of arranging with her rebellious subjects to give a prince to La Plata while that colony will still receive one, and of establishing there a monarchy under her protection. Relieved of this foe, the most powerful and the best organized of all her enemies, after this war of extermination has ended Spain could easily pacify Venezuela by granting some concessions to that country, which, according to conversations that I have had with Baron Humboldt, demands very little and could be satisfied at small cost. When those two great divisions of Spanish America once were pacified, Mexico and Peru would not cause any anxiety if a more liberal system were adopted, especially with respect to commerce and the admission of Creoles into public office.

After suggesting that the revolutionary movements in America would have a disastrous effect upon Europe, the

---

gress zu Aachen, 32; Becker, *Historia de las relaciones exteriores de España durante et siglo XIX*, I, 440-41.

minister expressed the opinion that they could be made less dangerous by establishing monarchical systems in Latin-American states:

A prince of the Spanish dynasty, such as the Prince of Lucca or Prince Francisco, could be offered to Pueyrredón, who, I believe, would accept him with enthusiasm. What would Spain risk by attempting such a move? Can she in good faith flatter herself that she is able to reëstablish her authority in the New World by force of arms? Where are the vessels, the soldiers, and the funds sufficient for the armaments which would be necessary in order to achieve a purpose that would still be very uncertain of attainment? In the declining condition of unhappy Spain how can she so much delude herself as to believe that she can obtain happy results solely by the use of force? However great may be the delusion of Señor Pizarro, he cannot have blinded himself to that extent. It does not, therefore, appear to me to be out of the question to induce him to undertake a policy that would harmonize so well with the true interest of Spain and that would turn aside the dangers with which all Europe is menaced. There is no time to lose. Hyde de Neuville informs me that popular enthusiasm will carry the government of the United States much farther than it wishes to go, that once started it will be unable to stop, and that if Europe does not intervene the recognition of La Plata at the approaching session of Congress is certain. And how can Europe intervene if Spain does not reach a decision?

I regret, I admit to you, that the idea of inviting the King of Spain to Aix-la-Chapelle has been rejected. Once Ferdinand VII had been admitted to the council of sovereigns, it would have been easy to make him adopt a reasonable course. It would not be advisable for us in our position to promote anything which could complicate the matter, so important to us, which is to be considered in this reunion. In view of the fact that the other powers would dislike inviting Ferdinand VII to the congress, and that their decision has been made, it is no longer politic that I express an opinion; but I persist in thinking that the best mode of giving the policy of Spain toward America a wise

direction would have been to bring the King into a fresh
atmosphere. However that may be, as that move is no
longer practicable it is necessary to search for other means.
This, my dear Duke, is what I wish you to undertake with
all the resources at your command.

The Minister of Foreign Affairs instructed Laval-Montmorency to take up if possible the problem of the policy to
be adopted by Spain toward her colonies with Secretary
Pizarro. If this should not be feasible, he was to broach
the problem to the Russian ambassador Tatistcheff. Should
the proposal for the creation of monarchical systems in the
Spanish Indies be agreeable to the mother country, continued Richelieu, it would be easy for him to make the first
overtures to La Plata and thus to prepare the way for the
new régime. He even expressed his willingness to submit
the plan for the establishment of Bourbon monarchies in
La Plata to the Congress of Aix-la-Chapelle. In any case,
the essential point was to overcome the obstinacy of the
Spanish ministers. Believing that France should make every
effort to disillusion the Spanish Cabinet and to avert the
evils which menaced European society, Richelieu maintained
that Spain could not rightly hold that the issue of the Spanish colonies was simply her problem. It was the affair of
every government and of all peoples.[34] Yet, according to
the discerning diplomat Baron Boislecomte, Richelieu's vision of Bourbon monarchies was dimmed when the Spanish Government requested England and France to make

[34] A. A. E., Mémoires et Documents, Amérique, 34. Osmond,
the French ambassador in London, broached the project of enthron-
ing a Spanish prince at Buenos Aires to Castlereagh and believed
that the latter received it favorably because he dreaded the establishment of republics in Spanish America. Osmond to Richelieu,
August 14, 1818, A. A. E., Angleterre, 611.

known by what means they intended to reduce the American insurgents to obedience.[35]

Thus, in the years immediately following the downfall of Napoleon, the Czar evidently wished to consolidate the authority of Ferdinand VII in the New World. It appears that Russia and France were ordinarily in agreement concerning the best policy to pursue in international politics. The view that they were acting conjointly with regard to the Indies is supported by the following explanation given by Richelieu's successor, Baron Dessolle, concerning the problem of Spanish America in world politics:

On the approach of the Congress of Aix-la-Chapelle, Spain conceived the idea of taking part in it and of broaching there the discussion of that great question. France and Russia thought that this view should be accepted; that, if it was possible to lead the Spanish Government to more equitable ideas with respect to its own interests and to reconcile them with those of Europe, this could be done by acting directly and by force upon the King; and that the personal influence of the sovereigns gathered at Aix-la-Chapelle would be of all means the most efficacious. However, England and Austria expressed a contrary opinion, and Prussia seemed to support them. France was forced to realize that it would be dangerous for her to complicate the issues. Russia thought that it was necessary to direct the opinion of other powers at a moment when the future of France depended upon their more or less favorable disposition. Consequently, to serve us, Russia relinquished a project which she had warmly approved and which in any other circumstances she would doubtless have supported in such a manner as to have caused it to be realized. In a sense re-

[35] Boislecomte, "Ambassade de France en Espagne. Études sur les relations politiques et commerciales suivies entre les deux pays depuis l'éstablissement de la maison de Bourbon en Espagne et sur l'État interieure de ce Royaume (1700 à 1827)," A. A. E., Mémoires et Documents, Espagne, 97.

pulsed, Spain made it known that she renounced the idea of having recourse to the intervention of the powers.[86]

The instructions of France to the Duke of Richelieu, who was to represent her at the Congress of Aix-la-Chapelle, were dated September 16, 1818. It is likely that they had been framed by Richelieu himself in collaboration with the King. As the first problem worthy of the attention of the Congress there was mentioned the condition of the insurgent Spanish colonies; for grave dangers, it was declared, would menace European monarchies if republicanism should prevail in the major portion of America. Richelieu was instructed that, as soon as the affairs of France were adjusted at Aix-la-Chapelle, he was to strive to induce the other nations represented there to consider the condition of the Spanish-American colonies and to submit a plan for their pacification founded upon three bases:

(1) The independence of the Platean provinces was to be acknowledged " through the establishment there of a constitutional monarchy with its throne occupied by a Spanish prince." Certain concessions were to be made to Spain on the basis of the reciprocity granted to her commerce " as a common bond and as a memorial of the origin of the two peoples." (2) Political and commercial privileges were to

---

[86] Polovstoff, *Correspondance diplomatique*, III, 204. On the *rapprochement* between Russia and France in September, 1816, see Martens, *Recueil des traités et conventions conclus par la Russie avec les puissances étrangères*, XIV, 368. On the attitude of Russia toward Spanish America, see the communication of the Russian Ministry to Zea Bermúdez, April 20, 1820, *Annual Register*, 1820, p. 723. A copy of this memorial, which was evidently sent to Russian ministers at foreign courts, is found in A. A. E., Espagne, 705. See further Perkins, " Russia and the Spanish Colonies, 1817-1818," *Am. Hist. Rev.*, XXVIII, 663, 664, 666.

be granted to Venezuela and New Granada, which were not entirely detached from Spain. (3) A more liberal system was to be adopted toward Peru and Mexico with regard to commerce and the admission of natives to public office.

In a commentary upon these proposals Richelieu took the view that the establishment of local government and of a reasonable liberty in La Plata would satisfy the Patriots, while the installment of a Bourbon prince there would please the Royalists. The grant of commercial privileges to northern South America was to be coupled with regulations which would encourage the trade and industry of the mother country. Richelieu reasoned that a change in the system of colonial administration would undoubtedly preserve to Spain the two oldest and richest colonies in the Indies. The instructions stated: " His Majesty thinks that these are the true means of preventing the general conflagration with which America is menaced, the reaction of which upon Europe will be terrible. Thus the gradual emancipation of that vast continent, which must be expected because it is in the immutable order of nature, would be retarded and rendered less dangerous for Europe by conserving there the forms of monarchical government." Further, it was observed that, even though England might oppose it, King Louis wished to have present at the congress not only agents of Brazil but also delegates of the United States. Evidently he was persuaded that by admitting these American powers to the conference a satisfactory decision concerning the Spanish colonies might be reached more easily.[37]

[37] Cisternes, *Le Duc de Richelieu*, pp. 25-28. The instructions may also be found in Sbornik, *Imperatorskago Russkago Istoricheskago Obschestvo*, CXIX, 825-27. A part of these instructions was recapitulated in a note of Dessolle to Hulot, May 1, 1819, A. A. E., Russie, 159.

At the end of September, 1818, representatives of the Great Powers began to assemble at Aix-la-Chapelle. Czar Alexander, King Frederick William III, and Emperor Francis I appeared in person, greeted by the acclamations of the people. The diplomatic delegates were the following: for England, Lord Castlereagh and the Duke of Wellington; for Russia, Count Nesselrode and the Greek Capodistrias; for Prussia, Prince Hardenberg and the Chancellor, Count Bernstorff; and for Austria, Prince Metternich. The Duke of Richelieu was present as representative of France.

Not until the decision was reached that the soldiers of the Allies were to evacuate France and that she was to be admitted into the Grand Alliance did the assembled diplomats turn their attention to the Indies. Meanwhile, on October 5, Richelieu had communicated his views concerning the American colonies of Spain to Laval-Montmorency, who was still at Madrid. Richelieu reasoned that before the Allies could concert a general plan for the pacification of Spanish America it was necessary to prevent an acknowledgment by the United States of La Plata's independence. He declared that if this recognition should take place Brazil would soon follow the example of the United States. Further, England might feel that this change in the situation justified her forcing by public opinion some action in favor of Spanish-American independence. In such circumstances, declared the Duke, the revolution in the Spanish Indies might react in the most dangerous manner upon Europe:

One may not consider without apprehension that such important events depend upon the decision of a sovereign who shuts his eyes to the situation and upon ministers whose uncertainty about their own fate prevents them from making the situation clear. It appertains to the ambassador of the Head of the House which governs Spain to render to that monarchy the important service of pointing out the abyss into which it is about to precipitate itself and of indicating the means of safety that exist.[38]

Spanish-American affairs were considered in a session of the congress by the diplomats of Austria, France, England, Prussia, and Russia. The protocol of a meeting which they held on October 23 runs as follows:

Today the plenipotentiaries considered the affair of the Spanish colonies of southern America in respect to which the Court of Madrid has solicited the intervention of the five cabinets. Lord Castlereagh gave an account of the negotiations which have taken place on this subject between the British Cabinet and Spain. He developed his views with respect to the advantages as well as the difficulties of mediation. The plenipotentiaries examined this important question in its various relations with Spain, with America, and with the European powers. Several propositions were made in regard to the means of reaching a satisfactory understanding with the Court of Madrid. After these proposals had been discussed from different points of view, an agreement was reached to postpone a continuation of the deliberations to a later meeting.[39]

Near the end of October, Lord Castlereagh calmly brought before the congress as a practical problem the moot question of mediation between Spain and her American colonies. He stated that the motherland had asked Austria, France, Great Britain, Prussia, and Russia to consider her plight, and that she desired to be represented at Aix-la-Chapelle. It became apparent that Russia not only wished Ferdinand VII to be admitted to the con-

[38] A. A. E., Espagne, 702. The protocols concerning the admission of France into the Quadruple Alliance are found in Lesur, *Annuaire historique,* 1818, pp. 432-41.

[39] " Protocol 18. Aix-la-Chapelle le 23 Octobre 1818. Entre les Cinq Cours," H. H. u. S., Congress zu Aachen, 29.

gress but also that she desired it to decide upon some form
of intervention. Castlereagh proposed that the five states
represented at Aix-la-Chapelle should undertake to mediate
collectively between Spain and her colonies but that this
interposition should be limited to a proffer of good offices.
Early in November, he submitted to Metternich a memorandum concerning the insurgent colonies which expressed
the opinion that " the five Powers understand each other to
the extent that Force is not to be employed, and that this
important fact is to be made clear not only to each other but
to the government of Spain." [40]

As has been indicated, Richelieu favored the admission
of the Spanish King into the Congress. It is to be presumed that he also urged the acceptance of the threefold
scheme of pacification which had been outlined in his instructions. A joint Franco-Russian note concerning the
Spanish Indies, which had been written by Sérurier and
sanctioned by Richelieu and which was presented at Aix-la-
Chapelle in November, indicates that by this time the
French plenipotentiary had modified his views. This note
declared that the most important problem confronting the
powers was to check the progress of the insurrection in
South America and to prevent it from becoming formidable
before a plan of pacification could be matured and carried

[40] " Memorandum: Queries respecting Mediation between Spain
& her Colonies," November 7, 1818, *ibid.*, 31. The *Pamphleteer*,
XVIII, contains a pamphlet entitled " The Declaration of England
against the Acts and Projects of the Holy Alliance," which states
(p. 15) in regard to the Congress of Aix-la-Chapelle that " a
deficiency of power alone prevented at that time an enterprise " for
the subjugation of the Spanish colonies. Cf. on the attitude of
the powers toward intervention the brief statement in Martens,
*Recueil des traités et conventions conclus par la Russie avec les
puissances étrangères*, VII, 297.

out: " The event which would most tend to make the evil irremediable would undoubtedly be the recognition by any state whatever of one of the governments established by the insurgents." Apprehension was expressed that the Democratic party in the United States would exert all its strength in the next session of the federal legislature to secure an acknowledgment of Platean independence. An extensive republican federation headed by the United States might be formed which would become a serious menace to the Old World:

A whole republican world, young, full of ardor, rich in the products of every clime, and with a soil of incomparable fertility, establishing itself in the presence of old Europe, which is entirely monarchical, overpopulated, shaken by thirty years of revolutionary agitation, and scarcely re-established upon its ancient foundations, would certainly present to the eyes of statesmen a spectacle worthy of their most serious meditations and a very real danger. All that remains in Europe of the spirit of discontent, of faction, and of discord would naturally seek a *point d'appui* in America. The consequences of this might be incalculable.[41]

Despite this appeal to the monarchical spirit, Castlereagh expressed his emphatic dissent from the Franco-Russian

[41] Wellington, *Supplementary Despatches,* XII, 806-07. See also Villanueva, *La Monarquía en América; Bolívar y el General San Martín,* pp. 74-78, who ascribes this note to Sérurier; Belgrano, *La Francia y la monarquía en el Plata,* pp. 28-32, follows Villanueva; Cresson, *The Holy Alliance,* pp. 79-80, who saw the memorandum in the Russian archives, ascribes it to Russia rather than to France. At the head of this document, found in the French archives in the handwriting of Sérurier, is the following statement by the chief clerk of the department of foreign affairs: " Cette note était destinée à être communiquée officieusement par Mr. le Duc de Richelieu aux ministres des grandes puissances assemblés en Congrès. C'est dans ce but qu'elle a été conçue et redigée." A. A. E., Mémoires et Documents, Amérique, 34.

plan, which suggested interposition by the powers through
the use of arms or by restraints on commerce to check the
Spanish-American rebellion. He notified the Russian delegation that he considered that project highly objectionable.
In an interview he informed this delegation that reports
were in circulation to the effect that Russia and France were
trying to engage Spain in an offensive and defensive alliance. Further, he expressed the opinion that Spain should
be made fully to realize her precarious situation, that she
should be disillusioned with regard to the hope of forcible
interference in the Indies by European powers, and that she
should depend upon her own efforts for the recovery of her
colonies. As the result of an interview which Castlereagh
had with the Czar, Russia evidently withdrew her support
from Richelieu's proposals.[42] The project of armed intervention by Continental powers or of coercion by the use of
economic sanctions to bring the revolted colonies back under
the sway of Ferdinand VII was thus thwarted by England.

The Duke of Wellington even declined the request of
France and Russia to undertake a delicate mission to Madrid
to offer, on behalf of the nations represented at Aix-la-
Chapelle, mediation in the struggle between Spain and her
colonies. When he refused to serve, Wellington declared
that the disputed points could not be settled without consulting the interests and desires of Spanish America as well
as those of Spain. He thought that adequate representation

[42] Webster, *Britain and the Independence of Latin America,* II,
64-66. See further *idem,* " Castlereagh and the Spanish colonies, I,"
Eng. Hist. Rev., XXX, 633-35; *idem, The Foreign Policy of
Castlereagh,* 418-21; Perkins, " Russia and the Spanish Colonies,
1817-1818," *Am. Hist. Rev.,* XXVIII, 669-70; and Manning,
*Diplomatic Correspondence of the United States concerning the
Independence of the Latin-American Nations,* III, 1859-60.

for the colonists would not be found at Madrid.[43]   The
American minister at Paris reported that Wellington had
insisted that the intention of the Allies not to use force be
stated in the mediatory act, that France and Russia had
then proposed that the Allies bind themselves not to enter
into relations with such insurgent colonies as might reject
the overtures of the mediators, but that England could not
accept this condition.[44]

Portugal evidently made an attempt to bring the long-
standing dispute with Spain concerning the title to Uruguay
to the attention of the Congress of Aix-la-Chapelle. The
Court of Lisbon seems to have directed to the assembled
plenipotentiaries a note embodying a proposal of the government of La Plata to the effect that a solution of the
dispute be reached by the establishment of a monarchy at
Buenos Aires under a prince related to the dynasties of both
Bourbon and Braganza.[45]   However, if this proposal was
actually made to European diplomats, it did not gain their
approval. Instead they decided to advise Spain to accede
to the project of a treaty framed at Paris by the mediatory
powers for the peaceful adjustment of her boundary controversy with the monarchy reigning in Brazil. This adjustment they considered essential to the establishment of
tranquillity in South America.[46]   Presumably at the instance

[43] Wellington, *Supplementary Despatches,* XII, 850-51.

[44] Manning, *op. cit.,* II, 1392. The view of Secretary of State
John Quincy Adams concerning the influence of the United States
on the deliberations of the Congress in regard to mediation between Spain and her colonies is found in Clark, *Memorandum on
the Monroe Doctrine,* pp. 79-80.

[45] C.... de S...., *Les Provinces de la Plata erigées en monarchie,* pp. 11-16.

[46] " Protocol 12. Aix-la-Chapelle le 15 Octobre 1818, entre les
quatre Cabinets," H. H. u. S., Congress zu Aachen, 29.

of the Congress of Aix-la-Chapelle, Richelieu composed a state paper on this subject in which he strongly urged that Spain make sacrifices in order to promote an adjustment with John VI. He reasoned that such a settlement would facilitate the pacification of the Spanish colonies.[47]

None of the distinguished plenipotentiaries who signed the protocols at Aix-la-Chapelle seems to have dreamed that the revolutionary movements against Spain and Portugal which were gaining headway in Latin America were destined to take this dispute entirely out of the hands of European powers.

While the Congress of Aix-la-Chapelle was in session, Spanish diplomats became apprehensive that messengers from insurgent communities in South America might appear in its halls. In September, 1818, the Duke of Fernán Núñez secured an assurance from the French Government that it would not consent to the admission into the congress of any commissioner of American revolutionists. Fernán Núñez was warned, however, that France could not prevent such agents from proceeding to other countries whence they would be able to journey to Aix-la-Chapelle.[48] Alarmed at this contingency, the Spanish minister at Vienna made representations to the Austrian Chancellor. On October 2 Metternich replied that as yet there had not appeared at Aix-la-Chapelle any agent of the insurgent Spanish colonies in America, and that, if any such persons had had " the temerity to present themselves there, all the cabinets would have agreed not to admit them." Further, Metternich

[47] " Note sur la mediation entre l'Espagne et le Portugal. Remis par M. le Duc de Richelieu," *ibid.*, 31.

[48] Fernán Núñez to Pizarro, September 16, 1818, A. G. I., Estado, 89.

expressed regret that the Spanish Government had given credence to the absurd rumor that revolutionary emissaries would be admitted into such an august assemblage.[49]

In sum, neither Ferdinand VII nor Spanish-American agents gained admission to the Congress of Aix-la-Chapelle. The opposition of England and Austria thwarted the joint attempt of France and Russia to have the congress offer advice to Spain and her insurgent colonies. Wellington's polite refusal to undertake a mission to Madrid completely foiled the Franco-Russian attempt to bring collective pressure to bear on Ferdinand VII for the purpose of inducing him to take a realistic view of the colonial issue. Although England was strongly opposed to armed intervention in Spanish America, no decision was reached with regard to collective mediation in Spanish affairs. A proposal of Portugal to place a check on the activity of corsairs in American waters was met by a suggestion on the part of Richelieu that an international league to police the high seas might well be formed which the United States should be invited to join. The French plenipotentiaries felt, however, that " such an invitation could not be well extended until Spanish America was pacified." [50]

As a result of the Congress of Aix-la-Chapelle, Richelieu accordingly modified his views concerning the Spanish Indies. That minister seems to have dismissed the idea that the independence of La Plata should be recognized. Instead of becoming an advocate of the acknowledgment of the independence of the Spanish-American states, he now undertook to oppose such a policy. Early in 1819 Hyde de

[49] Enclosure in Cevallos to Casa Yrujo, October 14, 1818, *ibid.*, 90.

[50] Cresson, *The Holy Alliance*, p. 82.

Neuville read to Secretary Adams passages from certain of Richelieu's dispatches which manifested a desire to dissuade the United States from recognizing the insurgent governments of South America.[51]

While Richelieu was attending the Congress of Aix-la-Chapelle, an agent of the Platean insurgents had actually attempted to enter into negotiations with him. This commissioner was Bernardino Rivadavia, a talented South American of Galician descent. In 1814 he had been sent by the government of La Plata on a mission to European courts, in company with a revolutionary general named Manuel Belgrano, in order to propose the establishment in La Plata of a monarchy with a European prince as its ruler. After a visit to Paris, Rivadavia made an attempt in Madrid to reconcile Spain with the Platean provinces but without avail. Shortly after being invested in February, 1816, with authority to establish relations between La Plata and European powers, Rivadavia undertook to initiate negotiations with France. At the instance of his government, the Spanish envoy made a protest against the sojourn in the French capital of an emissary of Spanish-American rebels.[52]

On October 14, 1818, Rivadavia addressed a note to Richelieu in which he declared that the government of La Plata believed that the foreign policy which it had

---

[51] Adams, *Memoirs*, IV, 216. In the "Mémoire de M. Bechu sur sa mission à Varsovie" (A. A. E., Russie, 161) the allegation is made that Richelieu as well as Capodistrias had contemplated inducing Ferdinand VII at Aix-la-Chapelle "to sign the act of emancipation of his colonies," but that this design was thwarted by the opposition of the Austrians and the English. Cf. Lesur, *Annuaire historique*, 1818, p. 579.

[52] *Comisión de Bernardino Rivadavia ante España y otras potencias de Europa (1814-1820)*, especially I, 146-48; II, 38-42.

adopted would gain the esteem of the leading sovereigns of Europe. Reports about the Congress of Aix-la-Chapelle had encouraged him to hope that "no other object would be so worthy of the attention of the august sovereigns as that of reuniting Spanish America to Europe by other bonds than those of the colonial system."

The Platean agent declared that his desire to enter into negotiations with the French minister was due to a conviction that the nations whose mediation was solicited by Spain could not, without considering all the circumstances, rightly judge a quarrel in which more than twenty million people were interested. Maintaining that his native land had not been able to explain its aspirations in a suitable manner, Rivadavia declared that his mission had been inspired by the belief that "the political existence, the internal organization, and the foreign relations of the most beautiful, the most extensive, and the most fertile part of America are not simply matters of importance to Spain but matters which interest the civilized world." He maintained that the commerce between Europe, on the one hand, and La Plata and Chile, on the other hand, was in a chaotic condition. "Thus everything," he declared, "contributes to make this moment the most opportune to beg Your Excellency to inform your August Master that I am authorized by the government of the United Provinces of South America to manifest their most sincere desire to place upon solid bases the peace of the New World as well as its future relations with the Old World." [53]

[53] A. A. E., Mémoires et Documents, Amérique, 34; Villanueva, *Historia de la república argentina,* I, 152-54. A facsimile of a copy of this note filed in the Argentine archives is found in the appendix of Belgrano, *La Francia y la monarquía en el Plata.* See

It is possible that Rivadavia's mention in this letter of new ties which might bind his country to Spain signified that his harassed compatriots would favor the establishment of a Bourbon monarchy in South America. However, the French minister did not reply to this overture. Nor was any response evoked by a letter of identical tenor addressed by the Platean emissary to Metternich on October 18. For the time being, at least, leading statesmen of Europe evidently felt bound by the decision which had been reached at Aix-la-Chapelle.[54] After inditing these appeals, Rivadavia wrote his government to express the opinion that the intransigent attitude of Ferdinand VII toward the Continental powers had caused a reaction among them in favor of the Spanish-American cause.[55] Upon becoming convinced that his mission was fruitless and upon being superseded by a new commissioner, Rivadavia returned to his native land.

Other steps had meanwhile been taken to develop Franco-Platean relations. On March 4, 1818, Juan Martín de Pueyrredón, a merchant's son proud of his French blood who had been made the chief executive of the United Provinces of La Plata, addressed a significant letter to Richelieu. In this epistle Pueyrredón attempted to interest the minister in establishing commercial relations between his country and France " and any other relations which might be considered of most interest to the powerful French

---

also the minute dated October 15 in *Comisión de Bernardino Rivadavia ante España y otras Potencias de Europa*, II, 64-65.

[54] H. H. u. S., Congress zu Aachen, 32. Apparently Rivadavia sent similar letters to the chancelleries of England and Russia.

[55] Belgrano, *op. cit.*, p. 85 and appendix, citing the Argentine archives.

nation." [56] As the communication was delivered in an undiplomatic manner, however, Richelieu made no reply.

About the same time the Marquis of Osmond, the French ambassador in England, who had become deeply interested in the destinies of South America, directed a French colonel named Le Moyne, who was residing in London, to proceed on a secret and unofficial mission to the city of Buenos Aires, where he was to inform governmental officials that Europe would view the establishment of a republic in South America with displeasure.[57] Colonel le Moyne reported to Osmond on September 2 that after he made representations to Supreme Director Pueyrredón this leader had assured him that he highly esteemed the French. The colonel ventured to urge upon the Platean leader the creation of a monarchy in La Plata under the Duke of Orleans, the very prince who later became King of France. On the eve of his return to Europe, Le Moyne had an interview with Pueyrredón, who apparently assured him that, if France would furnish the people of La Plata with the prince whom they desired, they would not only transfer to him the sovereignty of the United Provinces but would also make any sacrifice necessary to ensure him the possession of that fair land. However, before the French officer embarked

---

[56] Villanueva, *La monarquía en América; Bolívar y el General San Martín*, p. 65 n. This author asserts (p. 80) that Richelieu furnished Rivadavia with a passport so that he might proceed to Aix-la-Chapelle. Villanueva mistakenly declares (p. 67) that in his note of October 14, 1818, Rivadavia informed Richelieu that he was authorized by his government to negotiate for the establishment of a monarchy in La Plata upon the basis of the recognition of its independence.

[57] *Ibid.*, pp. 90-91.

for Europe, Pueyrredón took the precaution of destroying the communications sent to him by that emissary.[58]

Le Moyne's mission evidently incited Pueyrredón to lay his views directly before the French Government. On October 24, 1818, without making public the visit of Le Moyne, he secretly appointed José Valentín Gómez, a canon of the cathedral of Buenos Aires and a loyal supporter of the independent movement, envoy extraordinary to European courts to take the place of Rivadavia. The credentials given to Gómez by Pueyrredón stated that this appointment was made because of political conditions in America and Europe. In a passage addressed to any diplomat whom it might concern but presumably designed for Richelieu, Pueyrredón added in regard to the envoy's mission:

I hope that Your Excellency will show him every consideration, and that for the sake of humanity you will employ every resource of your high diplomacy to put an end to the hostilities which drench with blood these countries which are worthy of a better fate. Desirous of this happy metamorphosis, their citizens and other inhabitants clamor for this outcome as well as I, although they are resolved to maintain their independence at all cost.[59]

Instructed to arrange for a loan from two to four million pesos, the secret agent of Pueyrredón reached France in April, 1818. Six months later Gregorio Tagle, the new Secretary of Foreign Relations of La Plata, praised Gómez for his circumspect conduct in Paris and instructed him to act cautiously in regard to an acknowledgment of the independence of his country by European powers. He was

[58] *Ibid.*, pp. 91-96, 119; Belgrano, *La Francia y la monarquía en el Plata*, p. 61.

[59] A. A. E., Buenos Ayres, 1; Villanueva, *Historia de la república argentina*, I, 155.

warned not to consider as a candidate for a Platean throne any member of the Spanish ruling dynasty or indeed any prince of an inferior grade.[60]

In the meantime, on December 26, 1818, the first Richelieu cabinet had fallen. General Dessolle became President of the Council of State and Minister of Foreign Affairs. On May 1, 1819, in a confidential dispatch to General Hulot, who was sent on a special mission to St. Petersburg and instructed to inform Russia of the Gómez mission, Dessolle declared that France was disposed to favor an adjustment between Spain and her colonies upon three bases. The first was the establishment of a monarchy in La Plata under Spanish protection. The second was the pacification of northern South America by granting commercial and political concessions to the colonists. The third basis was the reunion of Peru and Mexico with the motherland by the adoption of a more considerate administrative system in respect to the aborigines than that which during three centuries had been employed by Spain.

Dessolle made an analysis of international sentiment regarding the rise of new states in the Indies. He declared, on the one hand, that the people of Europe feared the establishment in Spanish America of republican governments whose views would constantly be opposed to the interests of European monarchs. On the other hand, the minister asserted that the statesmen of La Plata despaired of consolidating the political system which had been brought into existence there by the revolution. He held that the monarchical customs of the Platean people formed an insurmountable obstacle to the establishment of a republican

[60] Mitre, *Historia de Belgrano y de la independencia argentina,* III, 714.

régime and that the idea of establishing an independent kingdom was steadily gaining favor among their rulers.[61] In the third person Dessolle described how he cautiously began informal negotiations with the emissary of La Plata:

Señor Gómez has had a conversation with the Minister of Foreign Affairs. Gómez did not conceal that the leading men in his government wish to assure the independence of their country by inviting as sovereign of La Plata a prince belonging to one of the ruling houses of Europe. He intimated that the similarity of manners, the identity of religion, and the old custom of considering the French as their friends had made those leaders cast their eyes upon a prince of the older branch of the house of Bourbon and that they wished to offer the crown to the Duke of Orleans. The minister did not hesitate to reject this proposition. He declared to Gómez that, aside from the political condition of France, the bonds which united the royal families of France and Spain would not permit the execution of this scheme; but at the same time he indicated that he would approve the project for the establishment of a monarchical government at Buenos Aires. He did not, however, conceal the fact that the independence of La Plata was at this moment threatened by the most serious preparations for the subjugation of that country which Spain had yet made.

Upon learning of the overtures of the secret agent, Louis XVIII felt that, in view of the confidence which the Czar had always displayed in him and of that monarch's interest in Spain, he should inform Russia of this mission. The King thought, recorded Dessolle, that the logic of events assured La Plata's independence: "He desires that this independence should neither be dangerous for Spain nor disquieting for Europe; he believes that, if Spain consents

[61] "Note Secrete," A. A. E., Russie, 159. A copy of this important note was also filed in A. A. E., Buenos Ayres, 1. A Spanish version is found in Cané, "La diplomacia de la revolución," *La biblioteca,* V, 100-02.

to this sacrifice, she will put an end to all the embarassment and will assure the tranquillity and prosperity of her other colonial possessions." Dessolle explained that, in order to render the independence of La Plata less objectionable to Spain, the proposal had been made to offer the crown of the prospective kingdom to a Spanish prince. If the people of La Plata were strongly opposed to this proposal, the King of France believed that Prince Louis, the heir presumptive of Parma, should be brought forward as a candidate for the proposed throne at Buenos Aires:

Prince Louis is so closely related to the King of Spain that he might well be regarded by him as a prince of his family, and as in fact he belongs to a different branch of the House of Bourbon, the objections which might still be raised at Buenos Aires against this choice could easily be swept away.

Dessolle added that if the Czar, as he had reason to believe, entertained the same views as Louis XVIII concerning the pacification of the Spanish colonies, that King desired that Alexander I should give to his envoy at Madrid confidential instructions to favor the monarchical project: "The Czar has sufficient influence at the Court of Spain to induce Ferdinand VII to accept a plan which in truth conforms to his interests but which certainly wounds his *amour propre*." [62] In conclusion Dessolle declared that, although the French minister at Madrid had been directed to make known to the Spanish Government this opportunity for an adjustment with the insurgent colonies, Louis XVIII believed that serious negotiations with Gómez could not be undertaken until he learned the attitude of the Russian autocrat toward this project.

[62] Dessolle to Hulot, May 1, 1819, A. A. E., Russie, 159.

On April 25, 1819, Dessolle had written cautiously to the Duke of Laval-Montmorency with regard to the overtures of Gómez. The ambassador was informed that, if the proposal to erect a Bourbon appanage in South America was acceptable to Spain, and if she authorized France to engage in conferences in her name, Dessolle would quietly begin negotiations with Gómez. If, however, Spain declined to authorize France to carry on negotiations in her name, or if she remained long in doubt regarding the action to be taken, Dessolle declared that he would abruptly terminate all relations with the Platean agent. The minister stated that he desired to restore the prosperity of Spain as well as to promote the pacification of Spanish America. He believed that circumstances assured the independence of La Plata, but that his government would act in an impartial and conciliatory manner toward both the mother country and her insurgent colonies. Asserting that France did not aspire to any special favors herself, he argued that she could not approve of any extreme pretension by either party to the struggle.[63]

Shortly after he received this dispatch, Laval-Montmorency reported that he had brought to the consideration of the Marquis of Casa Yrujo, an experienced diplomat who had recently become Secretary of State, the prospect of La Plata " reorganized into a monarchy and that empire governed by a prince of Spanish blood." The new minister maintained, however, that legitimist principles and the hope of subjugating the colonies kept his government from being attracted by proposals like those of Gómez. A monarchy independent of Spain, with its crown placed upon the head

---

[63] Villanueva, *Le monarquía en América; Bolívar y el General San Martín*, pp. 129-33.

of a Spanish prince, wrote Laval-Montmorency, seemed to Casa Yrujo a proposal that could never be accepted by his country: "He assured me that he would never take the liberty of wounding the ears of the King with this proposition and begged me to spare him from emphasizing the consequences which would arise from the founding of a new empire in the midst of the other colonies." Casa Yrujo maintained that the only proposal concerning Spanish America which he could transmit to Ferdinand VII was one which might modify the old monarchical forms but without affecting the sovereignty of Spain. The minister assured Laval-Montmorency of the Spanish Cabinet's belief that the honor of the French Government would prevent it from continuing relations which were prejudicial to Spanish interests, but that it was not equally certain of the disinterestedness of other governments. Still, the Spanish ministers did not insist that France terminate her relations with the emissary of La Plata. They did, however, intimate that those negotiations should not be taken up by others.[64]

Evidently the French Cabinet considered that it was politic to continue informal negotiations with the Platean agent. In his report of a conference held with Dessolle on June 1, 1819, Gómez declared that the French minister had expressed a desire for a happy outcome of the revolt in La Plata. Dessolle had remarked that the proper form of government for that country was a constitutional monarchy. He held that the acceptance of a European prince by La Plata would facilitate the acknowledgment of her

---

[64] Laval-Montmorency to Dessolle, May 11, 1819, A. A. E., Buenos Ayres, 1. A Spanish translation of this dispatch is found in Cané, "La diplomacia de la revolución," *La biblioteca*, V, 265-70.

independence. As a candidate the French minister proposed the Prince of Lucca. This personage would be regarded favorably by Austria and Prussia, could not be opposed with any good reason by England, and would be supported by the King of France. On his part, Gómez expressed surprise that so obscure a prince should be selected to guide the destinies of his promising country. Nevertheless, Dessolle persisted; he mentioned other reasons for favoring the Prince of Lucca's candidacy. This prince, he maintained, might marry a Braganza princess, and Uruguay would then be evacuated by Brazilian soldiers. Further, as this prince was a scion of the Bourbon dynasty, the King of France would furnish him aid of every kind in the enterprise. Gómez then tactfully declared that he was not fully authorized to enter into such a negotiation, but that he would report the proposal to his government and ask for fresh instructions.[65]

In the summer of 1819 a memorial concerning the monarchical scheme came into the hands of the Platean agent. Apparently this was framed by Colonel Le Moyne, but possibly it had been sanctioned by François Rayneval, who was now an influential official in the Ministry of Foreign Affairs.[66] Couched in such terms that it might have been considered as a communication from the French Government, this memorial stated that France desired to promote the liberation of the people of La Plata from Spanish rule

[65] *Proceso original justificativo contra los reos acusados de alta traición en el congreso y directorio,* pp. 7-9.

[66] On the authorship of this memorandum see *ibid.,* p. 9; Cané, " La diplomacia de la revolución," *op. cit.,* pp. 257-59, 262; Villanueva, *op. cit.,* pp. 144-45; Belgrano, *La Francia y la monarquía en el Plata,* pp. 164-65, 219. Cf. Webster, *Britain and the Independence of Latin America,* II, 167, 382.

and the formation there of a constitutional monarchy strong enough to treat with other states. Its author proposed that France take steps to obtain the consent of all the European courts to the establishment of the Prince of Lucca upon a throne at Buenos Aires. According to a copy of this memorial preserved in French archives, the author declared that his government would undertake "to furnish the necessary succor in expeditionary troops and maritime forces in order that this prince may not only be able to make himself respected but that, if necessary, he may also be enabled to struggle successfully against any nation which might wish to oppose his elevation to the throne." [67]

This clever memoir praised the Duke of Lucca as a worthy person with a military education who would enthusiastically embrace the Spanish-American cause. It suggested that, in order to consolidate the position of the proposed monarch, steps should be taken to arrange a matrimonial alliance for him with a princess of the Braganza dynasty. Closing with an argument against English influence in La Plata, it predicted that dire consequences would result both to the Church of Rome and to the civilization of South America should an English prince instead of a Latin prince be enthroned at Buenos Aires. Not without conscientious scruples, but evidently in the belief that this intriguing proposal embodied the views of the French Ministry, Gómez transmitted it to La Plata, where General Rondeau had succeeded Pueyrredón as Supreme Director.

[67] " Mémoire dont il est fait mention dans la dépêche officielle de l'envoyé Gómez," A. A. E., Buenos Ayres, 1. A somewhat different version was published in Parish, *Buenos Ayres and the Provinces of the Rio de la Plata*, pp. 396-99. A Spanish text of this memorandum is found in *Proceso original justificativo contra los reos acusados de alta traición en el congreso y directorio*, pp. 11-14.

However, the French envoy at St. Petersburg had meanwhile sent Dessoles a dispatch in cipher describing an audience with the Russian autocrat. General Hulot had informed Alexander I of the mission of Gómez to Paris and of his first interview with Dessolle. While attempting to discover whether Russia would be willing to sanction joint negotiations with Spain concerning her colonies, Hulot became convinced that the Czar did not favor the scheme to erect monarchical governments in Spanish America:

The Emperor, although agreeing that the principle of the scheme was right, seems to believe that the best means of settling the problem of the Spanish colonies is to abandon them to themselves, to reject all overtures or proposals that they may make, and not to furnish them any sort of succor. He believes that this general neglect would crush them and would soon leave them unsteady and almost defenseless to face the efforts of the mother country. In speaking of the creation of monarchical governments in South America, the Emperor designated them as republics disguised under cover of monarchical forms. He said that to enter into negotiations with Spain on this matter at the very moment when she was about to launch great attacks upon the colonies would cause her injurious delays. Then he added that the invariable rule of his conduct would not allow him to handle this affair by himself, but that, if it was of such a nature that it might be communicated to the Great Powers, he would on his part coöperate in every way to promote the success of whatever might offer real advantages to Spain.[68]

The scheme to pacify the Indies by erecting monarchical governments there continued to meet with formidable obstacles in Madrid. Laval-Montmorency found that the Spanish Government persistently refused to accept the

[68] $\frac{26 \text{ May}}{7 \text{ June,}}$ 1819, A. A. E., Russie, 159. See further La Ferronnays to Pasquier, $\frac{15}{3}$ April, 1820, *ibid.*, 160.

Gómez project as favored by France. Secretary Casa Yrujo absolutely opposed an acknowledgment of the independence of La Plata even under the rule of a Bourbon prince. He insisted that he could transmit to his King only propositions which would serve to modify the old forms of government in the colonies without disturbing the sovereignty over them; that, for example, approval could be given to the idea of a separate kingdom governed under the authority of Ferdinand VII but with different laws and administration from those of motherland.[69]

Early in August, Dessolle informed Hulot that France had decided not to negotiate regarding the Spanish colonies without the support of all the powers which had been united by the declaration of Aix-la-Chapelle. A dispatch was accordingly sent to Madrid to the effect that the mission from La Plata had come to an end.[70]

Utterly ignorant of the attitude assumed by the courts of Madrid and St. Petersburg, on September 6 Gómez ventured to send to Rondeau's Secretary of Foreign Relations his views concerning the policy which was being pursued by France. The Platean agent interpreted the cautious policy of Dessolle to mean that this minister wished to curry favor with the revolutionary colonies as well as to prepare men's minds for the time when Spain would abandon her design to conquer the new states.[71] In a message dated October 26, 1819, Rondeau urged the Congress of the United Provinces to accept Dessolle's proposal. Partly because of the supposed menace of a Spanish attack on La Plata, on November 3 that congress decided to consider the

[69] Dessolle to Hulot, May 22, 1819, *ibid.*, 159.

[70] *Idem* to *idem*, August 6, 1819, *ibid.*

[71] Belgrano, *La Francia y la monarquía en el Plata*, p. 170.

French overtures. During the discussion which took place regarding them in secret session, certain of its members showed a desire to incite England to acknowledge Spanish-American independence, while others evinced a wish to influence France with a view to thwarting the contemplated Spanish expedition against La Plata.[72]

On November 12, 1819, Congress decided by a majority vote to accept the French proposal on nine stipulated conditions : (1) Louis XVIII was to secure the consent to this monarchical plan of five great European powers, including Spain. (2) He was then to facilitate the marriage of the Prince of Lucca to a princess of Brazil; and the Braganza dynasty was to renounce any claim to the former Spanish dominions in America. (3) France was to pledge herself to give the Prince of Lucca all the aid that might be necessary to establish a monarchy in the provinces of La Plata and to make it respected. " This monarchical system should comprise at least all the territory belonging to the former viceroyalty of La Plata," and should hence include within its limits Uruguay, Entre Ríos, Corrientes, and Paraguay. (4) These provinces were to recognize the Prince of Lucca as their sovereign but were to retain their existing constitutions with such changes as would make them harmonize with a hereditary, constitutional monarchy. (5) The project should be carried out as soon as the great European powers had agreed upon the choice of a ruler for La Plata, even though Spain might not wish to renounce her hope of reconquest. (6) In such a case, France was to ensure the execution of this monarchical project by repulsing Spanish attacks and by furnishing La Plata with a loan of three

[72] *Proceso original justificativo contra los reos acusados de alta traición en el congreso y directorio*, pp. 16-18.

million pesos. (7) If there was reason to apprehend that England would forcibly oppose the elevation of the Prince of Lucca to a South American throne, the project should not be carried out. (8) Provision should be made for a treaty between France and La Plata which was to be ratified by the Director with the consent of the Senate. (9) Gómez was to demand that ample time be allowed for the negotiation of an agreement which was fraught with such far-reaching significance.[73]

There are good reasons to believe that because of existing circumstances France would have found it very difficult, if not impossible, to ensure the fulfillment of these conditions. Within the limits of the former viceroyalty of La Plata, Uruguay had asserted its desire to become an independent republic, and Paraguay had undertaken to form an autonomous political organization under José de Francia. Spaniards who advocated the subjugation of the American colonies were typified by the legitimist Ferdinand VII. Gómez had been forced to conclude that it was impossible to arrange a loan with French bankers or with the French Government. France could scarcely be expected both to abrogate the Bourbon Family Compact and to employ arms against her ancient ally, especially in view of the unwillingness of the Czar to favor such a policy. And England had consistently opposed the use of force to bring the colonists back under the rule of their Spanish masters.

[73] Villanueva, *Historia de la república argentina,* I, 161-62. See further Manning, *Diplomatic Correspondence concerning the Independence of the Latin-American Nations,* I, 545-47 n. Documents relating to this affair were printed contemporaneously in *Monarchical Projects or a Plan to Place a Bourbon King on the Throne of Buenos Aires*; later by Parish, *Buenos Ayres and the Provinces of the Río de la Plata,* pp. 399-400; and in *British and Foreign State Papers,* VI, 1099-1100.

Because of attendant circumstances, and in the light of subsequent events, it is probable that the attitude of the Congress of La Plata toward the monarchical project was largely opportunistic. Platean statesmen may have conceived this project in the hope of inducing Pope Pius VII, who was opposed to the separation of the rebellious colonies from Spain, to favor Spanish-American independence. Gómez had, indeed, been entrusted with a mission to the Vatican which he never carried out.[74]

Then, too, the Congress of La Plata might ultimately have rejected the monarchical plan, even though the conditions which it formulated had been fulfilled. In fact, when this project became known in the city of Buenos Aires the opposition party bitterly criticized Pueyrredón. Though Gómez was sympathetic toward the scheme, his support was only lukewarm. It seems that the real stake for which he was playing was the recognition of La Plata's independence by European powers.

Upon hearing of the negotiations between Gómez and Dessolle, the American Secretary of State caustically declared that France had been plotting a monarchy for the Prince of Lucca, "which she seems to have considered as a sort of compromise between political legitimacy and bastardy, to be purified by crossing a breed of the Bourbon and the Braganza blood." [75] When these negotiations became known to Lord Castlereagh, he denounced them to the Russian ambassador in London as an unprecedented perfidy. Castlereagh maintained that France had engaged in them at the very time when her government was stating its views to

[74] Leturia, *La acción diplomática de Bolívar ante Pío VII*, pp. 48-52.

[75] Adams, *Writings*, VII, 453.

the plenipotentiaries of the Allies in terms which were diametrically opposed to its policy in the Gómez intrigue.[76] Pérez de Castro, who became the Spanish Secretary of State in April, 1820, was enraged at the refusal of the French Government to make a public explanation of its attitude toward the creation of a Bourbon monarchy in La Plata. He wrote to the Spanish ambassador at Paris that the refusal demonstrated that such a project existed, and he stigmatized the conduct of France as scandalous.[77]

When the French Government learned that documents concerning this affair had fallen into the hands of Pueyrredón's political enemies and had been published in England as well as in South America, the Minister of Foreign Affairs sent a dispatch to Laval-Montmorency which justified France's conduct as follows:

We shall insist chiefly upon this point, which is very essential and very true, namely that the French Government entered into *pourparlers* with the agent of Buenos Aires only at the express desire of the Spanish Government. We shall add that, after that government had rejected the overtures which you made to it, the relations between Señor Gómez and the French Ministry were terminated.[78]

Despite the *débâcle* of 1819, the idea of founding Bourbon appanages in the New World did not die on either side of the Atlantic. During the following year an indi-

[76] Webster, *The Foreign Policy of Castlereagh,* pp. 566-67.

[77] Belgrano, *La Francia y la monarquía en el Plata,* pp. 211-12. On the reactions of European chancelleries to the monarchical project, see further *idem,* " La Francia y la monarquía en el Plata: actitud de Inglaterra, 1818-1820," *Bol. inst. inves. hist.,* XVIII, 82-113.

[78] July 6, 1820, A. A. E., Buenos Ayres, 2. A defence against the accusation that he had been bought by agents of Spain while he was Supreme Director is found in Pueyrredón, *Documentos del archivo,* II, 207-23.

vidual subscribing himself as " C. . . . de S. . . . ," who was evidently well acquainted with the negotiations between France and La Plata, published in Paris a pamphlet concerning the establishment of a monarchy in La Plata. The pseudonymous author declared that in the existing circumstances the only means of solving certain troublesome problems of Spain, Portugal, and the Platean provinces was to organize those provinces under a monarchical form of government. He alleged that this plan was favored by leading inhabitants of La Plata, that it was agreeable to the government located at Buenos Aires, and that it had actually been suggested several times to the Portuguese King. He reasoned that to transform the republican régime of the United Provinces of La Plata into a monarchical system it would only be necessary to replace the Supreme Director by an hereditary monarch. As a suitable candidate for this throne, the author proposed Prince Sebastian, an offspring of the marriage of the Portuguese Prince Pedro with a daughter of Charles IV of Spain. In this manner there would be formed at Buenos Aires a political organization which would be nominally independent under a prince agreeable to the Braganza dynasty. Peace would thus be assured among the powers that were in dispute over the title to Uruguay.[79]

During the years from 1815 to 1819 France did not formulate a definite policy with respect to the insurgent Spanish colonies. This attitude was due largely to the fact that she was temporarily outside the pale of the European concert. The international situation was not simplified by the desire of England to mediate between Spain and her

[79] C. . . . de S. . . . , *Les Provinces de la Plata érigées en monarchie*, pp. 3-16.

colonies. Nor was a solution promoted by the evident wish of Russia to employ threats or even force to promote a reconciliation. Although loyal to Spain, Richelieu occasionally contemplated attempting to induce Ferdinand VII to acknowledge the independence of La Plata. As the advocate of a recognition policy, however, the French Minister of Foreign Affairs was like a voice crying in the wilderness.

At times that minister also cherished the notion of persuading Spain to make a compromise with her rebellious colonists by favoring the establishment at Buenos Aires of a monarchy under a Spanish prince. Richelieu believed that such a policy would tend to retard a recognition of the independence of insurgent colonies of Spain by the United States. He felt that, if the New World became a congeries of republican nations under the leadership of that republic, the international situation would inevitably become dangerous to monarchical Europe. Besides advocating reforms in the administration of Mexico, New Granada, and Peru, Dessolle sympathized with the scheme to found a Spanish appanage in La Plata as propounded by Gómez. However, as that project was favored neither by Alexander I nor by Ferdinand VII, he eventually relinquished it. Upon hearing of Dessolle's retirement from office, the Argentine emissary wrote to Buenos Aires to declare that this change was a loss to La Plata and to express the opinion that in more favorable circumstances Dessolle's attitude might have led to results acceptable to the United Provinces. Still, as South American leaders had manifested a hankering after foreign fleshpots, the scheme to carve a European principality out of a former Spanish colony was not entirely discarded by either French journalists or French statesmen.

Chapter VII

FRANCE AND THE CHANGING AMERICA

After the Congress of Aix-la-Chapelle, Frenchmen became keenly aware of the need of encouraging trade with Latin America. This conviction was occasionally shown in measures which were primarily of a scientific character. In the autumn of 1818 the Minister of Marine decided to employ a small fleet to make a survey of the Brazilian coast. As the leader of this undertaking he selected Captain Albin Roussin, who had recently directed hydrographic explorations on the western coast of Africa. On September 30 Molé notified Roussin that, early in the following year, with the corvette *Bayadère* and other vessels stationed at Toulon, he was to proceed to the coast of South America.[1]

Molé signed that captain's instructions on November 23, 1818. Roussin was directed to leave Brest about the middle of January and to sail to southern Brazil, where his investigations were to start. He was to reconnoitre that coast from the island of Santa Catharina to Rio de Janeiro, to make surveys at specified points on the route between that capital and Cayenne, and to terminate his investigations at Cape North on the coast of Guiana.[2] Although the collection of hydrographic data was to be his chief object, he was to gather all the information that he possibly could concerning the commerce, industry, population, and maritime strength of the sections where he made surveys. He was also directed to regulate carefully the behavior of his ex-

[1] A. N., Marine, BB⁴, 404.
[2] *Ibid.*; Roussin, *Le Pilote du Brésil*, p. 9.

peditionary force toward the quarrel between Spain and her
colonies.[3] When instructing the captain of the *Favori* with
respect to his conduct in case of separation from the fleet,
Roussin quoted Molé's special instructions regarding the
Indies as follows:

In the quarrels which are raging between Spain and
America France has up to the present observed the most
exact neutrality. You should not allow anything to induce
you to depart from this policy. Consequently you should
refuse every invitation that may be extended to you by the
officials of any power to escort warships or merchant vessels or even to accompany them; you should adduce the
nature of your mission, which demands the employment of
all your resources. In encounters at sea you will carefully
observe the same neutrality; but I have no need to tell you
that, in avoiding any acts which have an aggressive character, you should upon all occasions see that the French
flag is respected and give special protection to all our merchant vessels which seem to need it. I have reason to believe that whenever you come within sight of ships, or of
the coast, or of other vessels, you would do well to display
your colors.[4]

In April, 1821, Roussin sent to Portal a detailed report of
his extensive survey of the coast of South America—an
investigation which furnished the basis for that captain's
useful guide to navigation entitled the *Pilote du Brésil*.

In December, 1818, when Rear Admiral Victor Duperré,
who had distinguished himself during the Napoleonic Era,
was appointed commander of the French naval station in
the Antilles, Molé directed him to act in conjunction with

[3] Molé to Roussin, November 23, 1819, A. N., Marine, B B[4],
404.
[4] January 1, 1819, *ibid.*, 409. In April, 1821, Roussin transmitted to Portal a report concerning navigation on the Brazilian
coast. Portal to Roussin, April 30, 1821, *ibid.*

Governor Donzelot in protecting French commerce. Admiral Duperré was informed that, because of the bloody struggle in Spanish America, West Indian waters were being traversed by ships displaying flags which were not recognized by any European nation. Some of those craft respected the colors of vessels belonging to all nations except Spain. Yet a large number of privateers manned by adventurers from various countries were attacking any vessel that seemed an easy prey. "You will be on guard against one kind of corsair as well as the other," advised the minister, "and, without committing any aggression that may compromise the King's standard in the quarrels in which France up to the present time has not taken any part, you should not suffer French ships to be insulted by these pirates, and you will accord the most complete protection to all our ships that claim it."

With regard to harassed navigators of other nations, the admiral was directed to proceed in a different manner. He could defend foreign ships that might take protection under French guns, but, in such a case, he was to abstain from any hostile demonstration which was not provoked. In respect to Spanish vessels his instructions were more explicit. Duperré was authorized to furnish an escort for such craft as demanded protection when warships under his charge left a port of the Spanish colonies. "It is no less essential," added Molé, "that the government should be accurately informed of everything that happens on the continent of America, in order that it may, with a knowledge of the causes, judge concerning the influence which may be exerted upon the commerce and the tranquillity of our colonies either by the success or by the defeat of the Spanish royalist armies in their contest with the insur-

gents." [5]   In July, 1819, Duperré wrote to the Minister of
Marine that Spain was threatened with the loss of her
colonies one after another.[6]

After a study of the situation, on June 15, 1819, a little-
known nobleman named Portal, who had been appointed
Minister of Marine, addressed a note to Dessolle concerning the depredations perpetrated by South American corsairs.   Portal asserted that insurgent governments whose
flags those piratical craft displayed had been forced to disavow them because they were imitating the fury of the
filibusters.   French merchantmen were often the prey of
pirates, who, not content with pillaging their cargoes, often
treated their crews barbarously.   Insurance companies and
chambers of commerce in all parts of France were making
complaints and asking that the navy adequately protect
trade with the New World.   In particular, they demanded
that agents without a diplomatic character be sent to the
Spanish Indies in order to investigate and report upon the
measures best adapted to promote French commerce.

Besides, Portal urged that the government make a decision concerning the rôle which it wished to play in the
struggle between Spain and her colonies.   Such action was
imperative to spare its naval forces the necessity of engaging in demonstrations from which French commerce would
derive no profit.   He reasoned that the government could
choose one of three possible modes of action.

First, France might acknowledge the independence of
insurgent governments in Spanish America and even assist
them in their struggle against Spain on the express condition of receiving concessions from the new states.   That

[5] December 8, 1818, A. N., Marine, BB⁴, 402.
[6] Duperré to Portal, July 16, 1819, *ibid.*, 408.

action would make France the ally of Spanish-American revolutionists.   Second, France might take part in the struggle as the ally of Spain on condition that the motherland pay for this aid in advance.   Such a proceeding would be more honorable but probably not more advantageous than the first mode of action.   Third, France might maintain " a neutral attitude and await the issue of events in the New World, but with the intention of taking advantage of circumstances which might become favorable to her " before she decided upon the policy to pursue.   This was the mode of action which England had followed.   If France adopted the last mode of procedure she should send more imposing military and naval forces to the Antilles. Designs which England was suspected of entertaining against Puerto Rico should be thwarted.   In that connection Portal even queried whether a secret arrangement might not be made with Spain by which she would allow French soldiers to be stationed in Cuba under pretext of furnishing protection against the insurgents.[7]

Comments written on the margin of this communication record the reactions of the French Ministry of Foreign Affairs.   The first proposal was described as " impossible "; the second was passed over in silence; and the third was designated as " the only practicable " policy.[8]   Obviously this ministry had decided for the time being not to take sides with either party in the internecine struggle which was disrupting the Spanish Empire but to bide its time and, in the light of subsequent events, to make such a decision as would most redound to the advantage of France.

Count Decazes, who had been Minister of the Interior,

[7] A. N., Marine, B B[4], 405 *bis.*
[8] A. A. E., Buenos Ayres, 1.

became President of the Council of Ministers on November 19, 1819.   He chose Baron Pasquier, a wise publicist who had occupied several administrative posts during the Empire and the Restoration, as Minister of Foreign Affairs. Pasquier continued to serve in this post in the second cabinet of the Duke of Richelieu, which held office from February 20, 1820, until December 12, 1821.

Important changes had meanwhile taken place in the Spanish dominions.   Early in 1820 Rafael Riego, the leader of a revolutionary uprising, proclaimed his adhesion to the liberal constitution which had been promulgated at Cadiz in 1812.   Ferdinand VII was compelled to relinquish his absolute authority and reluctantly to sanction a liberal, constitutional régime.   Nevertheless, he clung fanatically to the idea that the rebellious colonists should be brought back under his sovereignty either by negotiations or by military force.   With every passing year, however, it became more evident that he was engaged in a vain effort to set back the clock.

The resentment of Ferdinand VII was presumably not lessened by the fact that at times the Liberals showed a conciliatory disposition toward the insurgent colonies. Martínez de la Rosa, a littérateur who had returned from exile to become a leader of the moderate Spaniards, was appointed Secretary of State.   Convinced that neither the King nor the people favored an acknowledgment of Spanish-American independence, that minister aimed to secure a truce with the revolutionists and reëstablish commercial intercourse with them in the hope that political relations might later be resumed.[9]

[9] Sarrailh, *Un homme d'état espagnol: Martínez de la Rosa,* pp. 125, 154.

While Liberal statesmen at Madrid were seeking a mode of adjustment with Spanish America, the revolutionary cause was making signal progress. Patriots from Venezuela led by Bolívar had surmounted the northern Andes and had at Boyacá decisively defeated the Royalist soldiers of New Granada on August 7, 1819. Aided by revolutionary partisans from that viceroyalty, Bolívar's legions routed the Royalists at Carabobo on June 24, 1821. As a result of these victories, Venezuela and New Granada were welded into the Republic of Colombia. Furthermore, in September, 1820, General San Martín had led a liberating expedition from Chile into the Peruvian viceroyalty—the last bulwark of Spanish power in South America.

On April 26, 1820, Baron Portal informed Real Admiral Jurien de la Gravière, who when a young naval officer had visited Brazil, La Plata, and Saint-Domingue, that he was to skirt along the Brazilian coast southward to the isle of Santa Catharina, and thence to proceed to La Plata River. After threading the Strait of Magellan, he was to sail north along the shores of Chile and Peru. If time allowed he was to ascend the Pacific coast as far as 20° North. Then, after rounding Cape Horn, he was to return to Rio de Janeiro. He was to proceed thence successively to Puerto Rico, Santo Domingo, Jamaica, Cuba, Florida, the Gulf of Mexico, Yucatan, the Mosquito Shore, Panama, Cartagena, and La Guaira. Portal expressed the hope that Jurien might penetrate as far north in the Pacific Ocean as Mexico, because the French flag had not been displayed in that ocean since the Restoration.

The object of this extensive tour was to display French warships at many points, to train cadets and young officers, to gather information useful to navigation, to demonstrate that the royal navy intended to protect French commerce, and to collect data which might be useful to the political and commercial interests of France.   In his reminiscences the admiral recorded that Portal directed him to secure for French commerce the guarantees necessitated by the political instability of the new states and to collect such information as would enlighten his government regarding the future of insurrectionary movements which it did not wish either to discredit or to recognize.[10]

On June 6, 1820, three war vessels under Jurien's orders, the *Echo*, the *Colosse*, and the *Galathée*, sailed from Brest. The admiral sighted Cape Frio on August 1.   His expedition visited successively Rio de Janeiro, Santa Catharina, Maldonado, Montevideo, Buenos Aires, Valdivia, Concepción, Valparaiso, Callao, and Lima.   Then Jurien returned to Rio de Janeiro, and on June 19, 1821, he anchored at Fort Royal.   Five days later he left Martinique en route for Margarita, La Guaira, and Habana.   During this long cruise he gathered information concerning the products and the commerce of the countries visited, the activities of French subjects there, and the progress of revolutionary movements.[11]

The sudden appearance of Jurien's squadron in the Pacific startled the new-fledged statesmen of Chile.   On behalf of Bernardo O'Higgins, who had become the chief executive of that state, Secretary of Foreign Relations Echevarría sent in January, 1821, an inquiry to Admiral Jurien concerning the purpose of his voyage.   Echevarría pro-

[10] A. N., Marine, B B,⁴ 414 *bis*; Jurien de la Gravière, *Souvenirs d'un amiral*, II, 246.

[11] " Rapport du Voyage du Contre Amiral Jurien, 6 Juin, 1820— 6 October, 1821," A. N., Marine, B B⁴, 420.

tested that a French mission to promote amity and commerce with independent Spanish-American states scarcely required the dispatch of a fleet. He suggested that the admiral postpone his visit to Peru until the liberating expedition led by San Martín had expelled the Loyalists from that viceroyalty.[12] Admiral Jurien de la Gravière assured Echevarría, however, that his cruise had no hostile purpose and that the Chileans had no cause for disquietude. Jurien declared that his government sought only the means of opening new markets for French merchants: "Its strict neutrality, its conduct, and its actions ought to be reciprocated; and French mariners should find assistance and protection in foreign ports." [13] In his memoirs the French commander elucidated his attitude as follows: "Our policy was not two-faced—it was expectant. A few words would have explained our policy in all its sincerity, but those words we could not utter." [14]

During the second part of his cruise the admiral had an encounter with both of the contending parties in Spanish America. Upon touching at La Guaira in July, 1821, he found that Royalist soldiers who had taken refuge in that port after the battle of Carabobo were in a desperate plight. Their commander, Colonel Pereyra, was reluctant to accept the terms of capitulation offered by General Bolívar. However, Jurien induced that colonel to agree to those terms, with a modification to the effect that Bolívar would allow the Spanish garrison to sail from the beleaguered city for Puerto Cabello on board French warships. After a capitulation including this proviso had been signed, Jurien

[12] Echevarría to Jurien, January 15, 1821, *ibid.*

[13] January 16, 1821 (copy), *ibid.*

[14] Jurien de la Gravière, *op. cit.*, II, 271.

sent on shore an officer instructed to inform the Patriot commander that French merchant vessels would count upon his justice and protection. In response Bolívar was quoted as saying: "You can assure the admiral that French commerce will nowhere be so well protected as in the Republic of Colombia." [15]

On the alert for any developments which might favor the commercial interests of France, Minister of Marine Portal took action when he heard of the negotiation of an armistice between Bolívar and the Royalist commander Morillo in November, 1820. He wrote to Pasquier to suggest that, if the independence of Colombia should be acknowledged by Spain, French ships might be admitted into Colombian ports on the most-favored-nation basis. Portal proposed that France strengthen her naval squadron in the Caribbean region in order not only to protect her commerce but also to develop friendly relations with South American leaders. In February, 1821, he suggested to the Council of State that France might soon have to send to Colombia agents who were publicly accredited. He held that intercourse between the two countries could be further promoted if the Colombian Government would take measures to check the depredations of privateers cruising under its flag.[16]

[15] *Le Moniteur,* September 16, 1821; Gervain, *Un ministre de la marine et son ministère sous la restauration,* pp. 107-08. Another mention of the activity of French naval commanders in South American waters can be found in *L'Étoile,* April 4, 1826. The Spanish ambassador at Paris informed his court that France had stationed a large number of warships in various seas not only to protect her commerce but also to demonstrate her naval strength. Casa Yrujo to Martínez de la Rosa, April 16, 1822, A. H. N., Estado, 5227.

[16] Gervain, *op. cit.,* pp. 98-100, 104-06.

Privateers that displayed the flags of various insurgent Spanish colonies were indeed plowing the seas as far as the southern coast of Europe. In March, 1821, Portal accordingly instructed the captain of the frigate *Jeanne d'Arc*, who was to make a cruise in the Mediterranean, to keep a watchful eye on such craft and to conduct himself circumspectly with regard to strange flags. The minister declared that the government desired to shield French commerce from anything which might injure or retard its development.[17] Portal warned other naval officers to scrutinize the activities of corsairs ostensibly holding commissions from Spanish-American insurgent communities.

Admiral Jacob, who was directed in 1821 to succeed Duperré in command of the naval station in the Antilles, was informed by Portal that, although France had no consular agents in Spanish America, yet the dissensions between Spain and her colonies had opened new markets to French commerce. Portal reasoned that, if a permanent adjustment between Spain and Colombia followed the recent armistice, European nations could probably make advantageous and lasting commercial arrangements with Spanish-American states. France should accordingly take certain preparatory steps. The minister was convinced that, as yet, his government had not gained every concession which its neutral policy toward the contending parties gave it a right to expect. As privateers equipped in ports of Colombia still traversed the American seas, Portal expressed the hope that her government would take steps to check the activity of those brigands who did not respect the French standard. Insurgent governments in southern America should be in-

[17] Portal to De la Mare de la Mellerie, March 20, 1821, A. N., Marine, B B⁴, 414.

duced to announce that they disavowed all the pirates who infested the adjacent waters. If necessary those marauders should be declared outside the pale of law.[18]

The minister supplemented these instructions in a dispatch to Ducret de Villeneuve, the captain of the frigate *Antigone,* who on April 3, 1821, was directed to proceed, via Madeira and the Canary Islands, to Brazil and La Plata. When explaining to Villeneuve that the government at Buenos Aires was to check the activities of maritime marauders, Portal expressed the following views:

> You will praise the products of our soil and industry as well as the methods of our factories. Above all, you are to make known that France has always observed a strict neutrality in the quarrels which have arisen between the government of Buenos Aires, on the one hand, and both the Spanish and the Portuguese governments on the other hand. France has a right to expect all the consideration due to such a policy. Yet the seas of America and Europe are often infested by privateers who insult and pillage French ships. Such excesses cannot be tolerated. If they continue we shall be forced to treat rigorously the corsairs who engage in them; and besides, such armed vessels can, so to speak, be regarded as pirates.[19]

On April 21, 1821, Admiral Duperré wrote to Portal about the activities of privateers in the Caribbean Sea. The admiral reported that the island of St. Bartholomew, which belonged to Sweden, served as a refuge for piratical craft. In March he had captured a corsair displaying a device attributed to Artigas; that vessel had been taken to Martinique, where it had just been condemned by a prize court. Duperré stated that he had announced his intention to pursue other ships flying the same flag. Further, he declared

---

[18] March 22, 1821, *ibid.*   [19] *Ibid.*

that according to current reports the letters of marque carried by such privateers had been issued illegally at St. Bartholomew by a French creole named Duplessis. He wished Portal to consider two problems: should the banner of Artigas be recognized by France and should her frigates pursue and capture all merchantmen or warships which were engaged in privateering? [20]

Duperré's views perhaps influenced the French Minister of Marine to assign a frigate for special service. On May 8, 1821, Portal framed instructions for Captain Ange Mackau of the frigate *Clorinde,* who had distinguished himself in 1811 and was now to make a South American cruise. That captain was directed to touch at the French West Indies and then to proceed to Brazil, Uruguay, La Plata, Chile, and Peru. Portal said:

> Your mission to those countries has no other object than to display the standard of the King, to give efficacious protection to French vessels that are found in their waters, to observe what conditions may injure or promote our commerce if it is directed toward those countries, to claim upon fitting occasions the justice and protection of local authorities in favor of French navigators and merchants, and to demand for them the consideration and regard due to the subjects of a nation which has maintained and still maintains the most scrupulous neutrality in the quarrel that is raging between Spain and the inhabitants of her dominions in southern America.

Because of the varying conditions in Spanish-American countries Mackau was instructed to exercise care, in any relations that he might form with Spanish commanders or with leaders of the insurgent colonists, that neither party could compromise him in the eyes of the other. On behalf

[20] A. N., Marine, B B⁴, 418.

of his government he was to express loyal and pacific intentions which were not concerned with anything else
than the welfare of French subjects.[21] During that trip
Mackau made reports to his government about conditions
in Peru, Chile, and La Plata.[22]

In pursuance of his orders, Duperré on July 19, 1821,
drew up for his successor in the Antilles a memorandum
concerning the activities of the ships on that station. A
part of this report dealt with privateering. The retiring
naval commander stated that the war between Spain and
her colonists had encouraged the equipping of privateers
furnished with letters of marque of Colombia. He explained that, according to the intentions of his government,
the naval station in the Antilles had always refrained from
interfering with Colombian privateers. Yet, as piratical
ships built at St. Bartholomew that boldly displayed the
colors of Artigas now harassed peaceful navigators, in
accordance with his instructions such craft had been pursued by French warships. Duperré added that claims arising
from insulting attacks upon French ships by corsairs were
still pending against the Colombian government.[23]

On August 8, 1821, an official in the Ministry of Marine
made an investigation of privateering in Latin-American
waters. Referring to the capture of an alleged Uruguayan
privateer, he declared that the papers of that vessel were
questionable. This official reasoned that, as Artigas was

[21] *Ibid.,* 414.

[22] Mackau to Clermont-Tonnerre, December 12, 1821, and January 5, 1822, *ibid.,* 434.

[23] " Mémoire remise en Exécution des Ordres de S. E. le
Ministre de la Marine à mon successeur dans le Commandement,
sur le service et l'emploi des bâtiments de la Station des Antilles
et du Golfe du Mexique," *ibid.,* 418.

now doubtless a prisoner of Dictator Francia in Paraguay, some letters of marque from the Uruguayan chieftain which were carried by corsairs in the Caribbean Sea were evidently spurious. The explanation was given that, in spite of the irregular proceedings of certain armed vessels displaying the Colombian standard, they had been tolerated by France in accordance with her policy of non-interference toward the party which was struggling for independence. With regard to ships flying the flag of La Plata, the statement was made that there were no complaints about the conduct of such ships toward French merchant vessels. It was urged that representations be made to the Swedish authorities requesting that steps be taken to prevent Uruguayan corsairs from receiving protection at St. Bartholomew. The view was presented that France should continue the policy of non-interference which she had adopted toward privateers of Haiti, Colombia, and La Plata who respected the French flag. On the other hand, it was recommended that corsairs displaying the flag of Artigas be henceforth treated as pirates.[24]

In accordance with these recommendations, on September 5, 1821, instructions from the Minister of Marine to the governor of Martinique and to the naval commander on the Antilles station modified French policy toward privateers. Those instructions declared that France would continue to adhere to her policy of strict neutrality toward the parties involved in the Spanish-American Revolution. However, she would insist that her flag and her commerce be respected. Molé's orders of July 14, 1818, concerning privateering were still to be considered in force and should

24 " Rapport," August 8, 1821, A. N., Marine, B B⁴, 418.

be operative with regard to corsairs that had abused the commissions issued by revolutionary authorities of Spanish America. Both Governor Donzelot and Admiral Jacob were to insist that insurgent governments close their ports to unlawful privateers, that the prizes of such pirates should be returned to their legitimate owners, and that proclamations should be directed against any parties furnishing men or supplies to piratical craft.

Portal maintained that the Spanish-American governments ought to follow the rules adopted by European nations with respect to privateers, letters of marque and reprisal, suits concerning sequestrated vessels, and punishments for piracy. The officials of those governments should recognize that France had steadily pursued a loyal policy toward them. Donzelot and Jacob were to announce that French warships would allow the free navigation of all vessels sent out by Spanish-American authorities which exhibited papers showing that their armaments were regular. Commerce between France and the new nations was to be freed immediately from the sea robbers who pillaged peaceful navigators.[25]

Evidently these instructions were largely the outcome of Duperré's report. Their purpose was to enunciate certain general principles on the basis of which a flag like that ascribed to Artigas would not be recognized by French navigators. According to a memorandum preserved in the archives of the Ministry of Marine, between April, 1821, and September, 1822, eleven French vessels had been attacked, pillaged, or captured by corsairs. Most of those depredations had been committed in the Caribbean region.

[25] *Ibid.,* 414.

Four of the pirates bore no distinctive device whatever. One ship had displayed an unknown standard bearing blue and white stripes. Another piratical ship unfurled the ensign of La Plata at the masthead. Two ships bore the Spanish colors. Colombia's pennant had been hoisted by two other vessels. A strange craft flew alternately the Colombian flag and the banner of Artigas.[26]

It was evidently because of Portal's instructions that on January 18, 1822, Captain Roussin, who had anchored at Montevideo with a French squadron, sent to the government at Buenos Aires, through a private channel, a note asking for an explanation of the activity of privateers. In response Bernardino Rivadavia, who was serving as Minister of Foreign Relations for that province, informed Roussin that his government had recently decreed that privateering under its flag was to cease. Further, although professing high esteem for France and for her King, this minister stated that La Plata would never accord either commercial or political recognition to any foreign agent who might present himself at the head of an armed force or without due observance of the formalities prescribed by the law of nations.[27]

France eventually submitted to the government at Bogotá claims for depredations committed by Colombian corsairs during the Spanish-American Revolution. Many years later,

---

[26] "Bâtiments français attaqués, pillés ou capturés par des corsairs (depuis le mois d'Avril, 1821, jusqu'en Septembre, 1822)," *ibid.*, 438.

[27] Núñez, *Noticias históricas, políticas y estadísticas de las Provincias Unidas del Río de la Plata*, pp. 36-37 n.; *Documentos para la historia argentina*, XIV, 75-76. The decree of La Plata concerning corsairs, dated October 6, 1821, is found in *Registro oficial de la república argentina*, I, 591.

when those claims were adjusted by a convention providing for the payment of an indemnity to France, the Secretary of Foreign Relations of New Granada affirmed that some of the spoliations were abusive or wrongful, while others were acts of piracy committed by foreign adventurers who, sailing under the independent flag, had engaged in privateering for their own exclusive benefit.[28]

Evidently neither the prohibitory decree issued by the government at Buenos Aires nor the strict instructions transmitted to French naval commanders checked sufficiently the depredations of corsairs. In April, 1822, Admiral Bergeret, the commander of the naval station in the Antilles, wrote to the Minister of Marine to urge that the naval force there be increased. Bergeret maintained that such a measure was needed to protect adequately the commerce of France, to ensure the safety of her colonies in the Antilles, and to carry out her missions to the Spanish Indies.[29]

Meanwhile French officials took steps to develop commercial relations with Spanish-American countries. In 1819 Captain Drenalt, commanding the frigate *Duchesse de Berri*, made a brief sojourn at Buenos Aires. While there he became acquainted with Antoine Leloir, a Frenchman who at the request of his countrymen had been acting since December, 1817, as the agent for their commerce. Drenalt informed the Minister of Foreign Affairs that French trade with La Plata had not developed because it lacked protection. Stating that several entrepôts had been set up along the banks of La Plata River, he declared that if

[28] Uribe, *Anales diplomáticos y consulares de Colombia*, III, 399, 428; Clercq, *Recueil des traités*, VII, 205-06.

[29] April 30, 1822, A. N., Marine, B B⁴, 428.

protection should be afforded by French warships a profitable trade might be developed between La Plata and France in oil, hides, beef, and mutton. The progress of French commerce would be marked, he added, if the entrepreneurs could count upon a maritime force which would guard their interests. He reasoned that such protection was indispensable in a country where an insurrection was taking place and where regular justice was not yet assured to foreigners.[30] As a result of Drenalt's report, Richelieu sent a note to Leloir to thank him for his zeal in guarding the mercantile interests of Frenchmen in La Plata.[31]

A scientist named Auguste Plée, who had served in the secretariat of the Council of State, was in 1819 directed by the Minister of the Interior to sail for South America as a naturalist of the French Government. To this scientific expedition there were secretly linked various matters of trade and foreign policy. In a report sent from Martinique in May, 1820, Plée transmitted information connected with the secret object of his mission. He stated that at Fort Royal he had received news concerning conditions in northern South America from a French officer named Rieux and a Spanish American named Cortés who asserted that they were emissaries of Colombia. The itinerant scientist reported that these agents had been dispatched to Paris to solicit aid for the insurgent armies but that, although Cortés had been granted an interview with the French Minister of Marine, he had pleaded in vain. While Plée subsequently drew sketches of scenes in the West

---

[30] November 25, 1819, A. A. E., Mémoires et Documents, Amérique, 29; Leloir to Richelieu, April 6, 1818, A. A. E., Buenos Ayres, 1.

[31] May 5, 1820, A. N., Marine, B B⁴, 414 *bis*.

Indies and in North America, it does not appear that he penetrated the South American Continent.[32]

In 1821 the French Government definitely adopted the policy of dispatching agents to the Spanish Indies to inquire into existing conditions. One who played a distinctive rôle in relations with northern South America was Benoît Chasseriau, a Frenchman residing in the West Indies who had been recommended to Governor Donzelot as brave, capable, and reliable.[33]   At this time, Chasseriau visited Paris and presented his views concerning Latin America to certain officials. In a note addressed on May 24, 1821, to François Rayneval, who was now Undersecretary for Foreign Affairs, Chasseriau stated that the mission to be confided to him was designed to gather information about the situation in certain parts of Spanish America and to secure agents for French commerce in those regions. To promote these ends he proposed that the French Government appoint him commercial agent for France in the island of Cuba, that he be instructed to gather information concerning the Spanish Indies, and that, before taking up his residence at Habana, he make a tour of inspection in the part of South America extending from the Isthmus of Panama to the Orinoco River.[34]

On August 20, 1821, Rayneval made the following response:

[32] " Rapport fait à son excellence Monseigneur Le Ministre Sre. d'État de l'Interieure," May 17, 1820, A. A. E., Colombie, 1. On Plée, see further Leland, *Guide to Materials for American History in the Libraries and Archives of Paris,* I, 270.

[33] Mackau to Donzelot, May, 1819 (copy), A. A. E., Mémoires et Documents, Amérique, 34.

[34] A. A. E., Colombie, 1.

I cannot but approve, Sir, of the project of a journey in South America which you have submitted to me. In accordance with your wishes, I authorize you to correspond with me on all subjects that will be of interest to the King's service. At the same time I ask you also to profit by the useful relations which you have formed by your sojourn in the countries that today form the state of Colombia in order to procure for French commerce all desirable facilities and to secure for the subjects of the King the protection which they may need.[35]

This brief statement should be supplemented by the agent's interpretation of his instructions. In an account of his trip sent to the Minister of Foreign Affairs, Chasseriau declared that he had been dispatched to South America without any title but that he was directed to gather reliable information concerning the real condition of affairs, the attitude of insurgent leaders toward France, and anything else which might be of interest to the King's service.[36] Evidently he was not authorized to speak in the name of his government but only as an individual.

Chasseriau left France on October 14, 1821, bound for Fort Royal. Thence he sailed on the corvette *Béarnaise* for South America. He proceeded to the city of Caracas via Cumaná, Barcelona, and La Guaira. In a sketch of conditions in Colombia based upon his trip, the agent urged that measures be taken to promote French commercial intercourse with that young nation. With regard to the acknowlegment of Colombian independence, he expressed the hope that France would not imitate the recognition policy of the United States immediately. Recommending that commis-

[35] *Ibid.*

[36] Chasseriau to Montmorency, August 24, 1822, enclosing "Compte rendu de un voyage d'observation fait dans Colombie de 1821 à 1822," *ibid.*, 2.

sioners be secretly sent to Colombia to watch over French commerce, he suggested that there be a principal agent at Bogotá and two or three subordinate agents in each province of the republic. These agents should promote French commercial intercourse and aid Frenchmen who might wish to settle in northern South America.[37]

The opposition of Ferdinand VII to the proposal of Liberal ministers that negotiations be carried on with the insurgent colonists had disturbed Baron Pasquier. Expressing the opinion that it was not possible for Spain to administer the Indies as provided by the Constitution of 1812, Pasquier declared that, if she insisted upon doing this, the loss of her colonies would be even more inevitable under a constitutional régime than under the absolutist government which had existed before 1820. Sooner or later, he added, it would accordingly be necessary to prepare the way for the emancipation of the Spanish Indies in such a manner that some advantage might be secured for the motherland which would render her losses less disastrous. Pasquier concluded that, because of conditions existing in Spain, the problem of her future relations with the Indies would be decided by other counsels than those of prudence and moderation.[38]

Placed under the tutelage of Liberal ministers, the King of Spain had meanwhile become profoundly dissatisfied. On October 25, 1820, taking advantage of the departure of the Portuguese diplomat Saldanha from Madrid for Paris, Ferdinand VII entrusted him with a confidential letter to Louis XVIII. The Spanish King declared that Sal-

[37] *Ibid.*
[38] Pasquier to Laval-Montmorency, June 25, 1821, A. A. E., Espagne, 713.

danha's journey offered him the only recourse by which he could inform the French monarch of the dangerous situation in Spain: "I beg Your Majesty to believe all that Senhor Saldanha tells you, whether concerning the condition in which I find myself, or with regard to a demand from Your Majesty in conjunction with your allies for the means of liberating me as well as my family and of preserving this kingdom from the condition of anarchy into which it is falling because of the measures of the present régime." [39] Several months later, Ambassador Laval-Montmorency wrote to Pasquier to the effect that Ferdinand VII hoped that the Allies would interfere in the affairs of Spanish America, because such a policy would lead to explanations concerning his peculiar position in the constitutional system.[40]

On July 10, 1821, Ferdinand VII addressed a confidential letter to the King of France in which he expressed full confidence in Laval-Montmorency. The Spanish monarch asserted that, if he should not be released from captivity, the evils which encompassed him would soon threaten Louis XVIII; for the Spanish revolutionary faction was laboring ceaselessly to spread Jacobinical and anti-monarchical flames to the rest of Europe. Spain's nearest neighbor, France, and hence the person of her King, would be the first party affected by such an irreparable disaster. Ferdinand VII therefore conceived that the only real remedy for the situation was for the French King to join the sovereigns of northern Europe, to aid him with an armed force strong enough to pacify his kingdom, and "to carry out in it those reforms and improvements compatible with

[39] Stern, *Geschichte Europas seit den Verträgen von 1815 bis zum Frankfurter Frieden von 1871*, II, 557.

[40] June 11, 1821, A. A. E., Espagne, 713.

the dignity and security of his throne" and the spirit of the age.[41] These pleas imploring the intervention of the Allies in Spanish affairs constituted another factor in the complicated international situation which French statesmen had to consider in formulating their foreign policy.

The attitude of France toward intervention in the Spanish Indies at this time was explained in a confidential dispatch from Minister of Foreign Affairs Pasquier to Count Lagarde, who had succeeded Laval-Montmorency as ambassador to Madrid. After mentioning the proposed sale of two vessels by France to Spain, Pasquier indicated the dilemma which caused his government to hesitate at that transaction:

The condition of the New World should also be taken into consideration. It appears impossible that the insurgent countries should return to the rule of Spain. Not having been able to prevent events from reaching this stage, France should obviously take measures to ensure that the new order which is to prevail in those vast countries may be made useful for the development of her commerce and for the payment of her indemnity. One ought therefore to inquire whether the succor which we could furnish to Spain might not be considered by the emancipated provinces of America as an indirect attack upon their independence. Finally, the impression that might be produced upon different courts of Europe by the condescension of France toward the existing Spanish Government and upon some courts in particular by the very nature of the succor which would be given Spain should likewise be anticipated, as well as all its consequences.[42]

Events had meanwhile occurred in Mexico which were destined to affect French policy. The dissatisfied Royalist officer Iturbide had on February 24, 1821, joined hands with a brave insurgent leader named Guerrero and had pro-

---

[41] *Ibid.*   [42] November 6, 1821, *ibid.*, 714.

claimed the Plan of Iguala, which provided that Mexico should become independent under a prince of the Spanish ruling dynasty. On August 24, 1821, Juan O'Donoju, an official sent by the Liberal government of Spain to take charge of the viceroyalty, signed a treaty with General Iturbide at Córdoba by which he accepted, with a slight modification, the plan proclaimed by revolutionaries at Iguala. The Treaty of Córdoba, which provided for the establishment in Mexico of a constitutional monarchy under the aegis of the Spanish monarch, was transmitted to Madrid for ratification. The prospect of the creation of European appanages in the New World alarmed the Liberator of Colombia. In a letter to San Martín dated November 15, 1821, Bolívar discussed the Treaty of Córdoba. Apprehensive that the establishment of European princes in Spanish America might cause important alterations in the political systems adopted by the new states, he reasoned that it was imperative to complete the expulsion of the Spanish Royalists from the American Continent and to rally the new states against any enemies that might appear.[43]

When he learned of the achievements of revolutionists in Mexico and South America, Pasquier sent suggestive queries to Count Lagarde:

In such a conjuncture of events will not the Spanish Government think of profiting by the door which the revolution in Mexico has still left open? And will it not hasten the departure of a prince of the House of Spain who will proceed to occupy such an important throne as that of the Mexican Empire? What other remedy could one employ which would offer the slightest efficacy? Without doubt, its application presents difficulties; but if one does not venture something, all will be irretrievably lost. Indeed it

[43] O'Leary, *Memorias del General O'Leary*, XVIII, 577.

is evident today that the demand which has been made of us for two vessels of the line to be sent to the succor of Lima is now without purpose. Yet this demand might have an entirely different significance if it were concerned with the transfer of a Spanish prince to Mexico. It appears to me indispensable that you use the first opportunity that presents itself to sound Señor Bardaxí on this question, which I consider vital for the Spanish nation.[44]

Shortly afterward Pasquier reiterated to Lagarde his views regarding the founding in Mexico of a Spanish appanage. He reasoned that all the states of Europe were in the highest degree interested, for it did not suit them that the republican system should be established throughout the American Continent. Lagarde was directed to urge the government of Spain to adopt the only measure which would assure intimate relations with its most important American possession. However, the French envoy soon informed Pasquier that the time was not propitious for the dispatch to Mexico of a Spanish prince. Ferdinand VII was unwilling to be separated from Prince Carlos; he might, however, eventually decide to send the infante Francisco to Mexico.[45]

Moreover, the Liberal government was reluctant to compromise with the Mexicans on the basis of the Treaty of Córdoba. The Secretary for the Colonies on December 7, 1821, addressed to Spanish officials a circular stating that O'Donojú had not been authorized to agree to a convention which recognized the independence of a rebellious colony. On February 13, 1822, the Cortes passed a decree announcing that the acknowledgment of the independence of any

[44] November 19, 1821, A. A. E., Espagne, 714.
[45] Villanueva, *La monarquía en América; Fernando VII y los nuevos estados,* pp. 107-08.

Spanish colony by a foreign state would be considered as an act of hostility toward Spain. Pasquier later expressed the opinion that this was the juncture when the uncompromising attitude of the Cortes ensured the separation of the Spanish colonies from the motherland.[46]

French merchants and publicists were meanwhile developing a keen interest in commercial intercourse with the insurgent colonies. A memorandum composed in the summer of 1821, presumably by an official in the French Ministry of Foreign Affairs, directed special attention to South America. Its author urged that the nations of Europe take definite action in regard to the Spanish-American states. France, in particular, should act because of her commercial interests. " France can, without failing in the respect due to the Spanish Government," he reasoned, " prepare sources of prosperity by beginning under the veil of commerce to establish connections with the independent governments." Declaring that the region which offered most advantages was Colombia, he affirmed that this country would not only furnish French merchants with opportunities for trade but would also offer an outlet for the increasing population of France. Furthermore, when a beginning had been made there, commercial intercourse might be extended to other Spanish-American countries. The author suggested that an agent be sent to Bogotá to form relations with the government there and with influential Colombians.[47]

On November 30, 1821, the Council of Commerce sent a memorial to the Minister of the Interior concerning trade with Spanish-American countries. This council stated that

---

[46] *Mémoires,* vol. V, pt. 2, p. 294.
[47] A. A. E., Colombie, 1.

several cargoes had recently been dispatched from France to the countries where they had found profitable markets. It suggested the scope of French commerce with the western shores of South America as follows:

Seven vessels equipped at Bordeaux and Havre are ready to leave for that destination. Each of them carries merchandise to the amount of at least one million francs. Hence one might value at twelve millions or more the French resources which are about to be employed in this commerce. These developing relations open to our industry a vast continent and furnish it with many consumers in a region which has no manufactures. Further, this intercourse is very precious to us because up to the present day it has been carried on exclusively in French ships and because at the same time it interests our agriculture, our manufactures, and our navigation.[48]

On December 12, because of persistent opposition, the Duke of Richelieu resigned his post. Louis XVIII soon formed a new ministry under Count Villèle, a conservative statesman who took direct charge of the finances. Villèle selected as Minister of Foreign Affairs Viscount Mathieu de Montmorency, a leader of the jingoes.

At a time when, as will be seen in a subsequent chapter, the recognition of the Brazilian Empire was being considered, a debate concerning the budget took place in the Chamber of Deputies which furnished an occasion for a consideration of the intercourse with revolted Spanish colonies. On March 18, 1822, Bignon, who sat on the left, urged that it was necessary for France to form relations with the states which had recently been established

[48] " Le Conseil General du Commerce à son Excellence le Ministre Secretaire d'État de l'Interieure " (copy), A. A. E., Mémoires et Documents, Amérique, 35.

in southern America. He asserted mistakenly that both England and the United States had sent to the Spanish-American countries agents who were authorized to acknowledge their independent status.[49] General Foy directed attention to the Spanish-American people on the following day by declaring that because of their manners and customs they had more affinity for the French than for the English. He inquired what the government had actually done to develop trade with the new nations:

> What consuls have you placed in their ports? How have you replied to their agents? What mention of alliances have you made to them? Quite otherwise—you have displayed more hostility toward them than has even their offended motherland! You have even insulted their leaders in your official journals! You have called them factious and rebellious! Are you ignorant that these men are the arbiters of our commerce and of the fortunes of our merchants in distant countries? . . . Are you ignorant that the name of Bolívar will be revered in coming centuries like that of Washington? [50]

It seems likely that such biting criticisms of French policy induced the ministers to consider the Spanish-American problem anew. The appointment of Viscount Chateaubriand, the distinguished man of letters who had served as minister to the Court of Berlin, as ambasador to England, furnished an occasion for Viscount Montmorency to express his views concerning the Spanish Indies. His instructions to Chateaubriand, dated March 27, 1822, stated that France was vitally interested to learn what the policy of England was toward the Spanish-American provinces which had declared their independence. Further, Montmorency formu-

[49] *Le Moniteur,* March 20, 1822.
[50] *Ibid.,* March 21, 1822.

lated four pertinent queries: Was England disposed to acknowledge that independence openly or would she indeed delay such action until the example should be set by another power, as by the United States? Had England not sent agents to Spanish-American countries to form commercial relations with them? Were such agents avowed by her and recognized by the authorities of those countries? Should they not make known the character with which they were invested at the moment when such recognition took place? [51]

Shortly after he arrived in London, in a conversation with Castlereagh, Chateaubriand mentioned the message of President Monroe to Congress on March 8, 1822, proposing the acknowledgment of Spanish-American independence. The ambassador expressed a fear that the spread of republican ideas in the New World would tend to compromise the fate of European monarchies. Chateaubriand reported that Castlereagh agreed with this view and then surprised him by declaring that the English Cabinet was not disposed to recognize the revolutionary American governments. However, Chateaubriand doubted the sincerity of these words. He expressed the opinion that, sooner or later, influenced by public opinion and by commercial motives, England would acknowledge the independence of the Spanish colonies.[52]

Chateaubriand soon had another conference with Castlereagh in regard to the Indies. On May 5 the English minister expressed the view that both England and France should allow their subjects to trade with Spanish Americans. Asserting that the English Ministry would delay the recognition of the revolutionary governments so long as possible,

[51] A. A. E., Angleterre, 615.
[52] Chateaubriand, *Correspondance générale*, III, 13.

Castlereagh suggested that France act in concert with England " in everything relating to the political and commercial question of the Spanish colonies." Further, he proposed to open a frank and loyal negotiation between France and England concerning the measures which should be pursued under the existing circumstances. Chateaubriand advised Montmorency to make an amicable reply: France had great advantages to gain by acting in concert with England; she should hasten to promote freedom of commerce with Spanish America. " If Europe is obliged to recognize the *de facto* governments in America," said Chateaubriand, " European policy should tend to bring monarchies into existence in the New World instead of republics which will send us their principles with the products of their soil." [53] The association of France with England, he added, would tend to restore his nation to her high place among European powers.

Upon receipt of Chateaubriand's dispatch containing the English proposals, Montmorency considered them so important that he straightway submitted them to the consideration of the Council of State. He declared rightly that the policy to be pursued toward Spanish America presented a different problem to France from that which it presented to England. He explained to Chateaubriand the council's attitude:

We have very many motives for being cautious with Spain. Above all, the loyalty of the King does not allow him to commit himself before he has sounded the Spanish monarch with reference to his attitude. The ties of blood

[53] *Ibid.*, 70, 71. On these conferences, see further Webster, " Castlereagh and the Spanish Colonies, II," *Eng. Hist. Rev.*, XXX, 642-43.

and the misfortune of the situation in which Ferdinand VII is placed impose upon His Majesty the duty of showing the greatest consideration toward that monarch.

At the same time, the situation in Spain disposes her to become irritable with us. She would seize with avidity the first plausible pretext to produce a rupture which is actually contemplated by the very men who have cast her into disorder and anarchy. Her pride would be wounded by any action that we might prematurely take in regard to the colonies. Although not frightened at the irritation which she shows toward us, we should not disdain her too much. A quarrel with Spain would immediately deprive our commerce of a considerable market. The revolutionary spirit would be afforded the joy of beholding discord arise in this House of Bourbon which it wishes to overthrow. . . . Another reason, the most important of all, is that if the King should decide upon the recognition of Spanish-American independence or upon the admission of the independent flag into our ports, the Spanish people would hold Ferdinand VII responsible. They would believe him to be in agreement with France, and the situation of that ruler would become more perilous.

Finally, as up to the present time the King has been in agreement with all his allies regarding the grave questions with which the policy of Europe is concerned, has he not in his continental position special motives for refraining from a decision upon a question which has long held their attention until he has learned the opinions which they may have formed and the views which they may entertain in the common interest? In the light of what I have briefly recounted, the King's Council has decided that we cannot at present agree to what seems to be the preliminary of the negotiations proposed by England by admitting, as does she, the flag of the Spanish colonies into our ports.[54]

The minister further instructed Chateaubriand to inform Castlereagh in a confidential interview that France appreciated his frankness and the implied guarantee of good

[54] Montmorency to Chateaubriand, May 13, 1822, A. A. E., Angleterre, 615.

relations. The ambassador was to explain the French attitude as follows:

We have for some time maturely examined the question of the independence of the Spanish colonies. We know very well that sooner or later it will be necessary for the powers of Europe to recognize them as independent despite the efforts and the protests of Spain. The admission of their flag is a measure which the commercial interests of a nation may well justify at a certain time; and, with respect to the conduct of England, 'such a concession is perhaps determined entirely by special considerations.

Still, although we also have our commercial interests to foster, we are not, like her, in a situation which allows us any latitude in this matter. Our position with regard to Spain is very complicated. It is expedient that the bonds which unite the two sovereigns, as well as the personal position of King Ferdinand, be respected.

The Spanish people are very irascible. They will seize upon the slightest grievance to give rein to their hostile sentiments. A war with a neighboring state which affords our commerce a very large market would be a danger to which we could not expose ourselves. Accordingly we cannot at present enter into the negotiation which the Court of London proposes to us, especially as this probably involves adopting the same policy as that which it has adopted in regard to commercial relations.[55]

On May 18 the French ambassador read to the English minister a part of Montmorency's dispatch. Castlereagh received this communication in diplomatic fashion. He did not seem hurt at the refusal of the French Cabinet to act with him in regard to Spanish America, and he even asked for a copy of a particular paragraph of the dispatch, which Chateaubriand decided to give him after excising some words. Largely because of her peculiar relations with Spain, France thus declined to enter into negotiations with Eng-

[55] *Ibid.*

land for the formulation of a policy toward the insurgent Spanish-American colonies which would be common to both nations.[56] Several days later, Chateaubriand wrote to Montmorency and expressed his views concerning the future of the insurgent colonies. Declaring that the United States feared that an empire might be founded in Mexico, he argued that European powers should direct their efforts toward the establishment of monarchical governments in all the Spanish-American colonies that had declared their independence. "If the New World ever becomes entirely republican," the ambassador added, " the monarchies of the Old World will perish." [57] It would seem that Chateaubriand had already caught a vision of European appanages in the Western Hemisphere.

The attention of European diplomats had meanwhile been directed to the mission of Francisco Antonio Zea, a Colombian botanist and publicist. His credentials authorized him to serve with unlimited powers as envoy extraordinary and minister plenipotentiary of Colombia to European courts.[58] From London this agent proceeded to Paris, where, on April 8, 1822, he addressed to the diplomatic corps an overture for the formation of political and commercial relations with his country. In sum, he maintained that Spanish America had come of age, that Spain would never be able to recover her lost colonies, and that his country was free, sovereign, and independent. With the naiveté of a novice in diplomacy, Zea stated that his government would recognize all existing governments, but that it would not communicate with countries which did not acknowledge its

[56] Chateaubriand, *Correspondance générale,* III, 84-85.
[57] *Ibid.,* 97.
[58] Cadena, *Anales diplomáticos de Colombia,* pp. 45-47.

independence. Furthermore, he declared that commerce with Colombia would be reciprocal for all those nations that acknowledged her independence, that her ports would be closed to the subjects of all states which did not recognize her political existence, that a delay in recognition would cause the opening of Colombian ports to be postponed, and that his country would take steps to exclude from her harbors merchandise from countries which had refused to accord her recognition.[59]

With this circular Zea sent a note to Montmorency in which he stated that Colombia attached much importance to the manner in which her overture was received by the French King. He declared that his government based its chief hope of recognition upon France and England. He asserted further that England had gained by her policy a title to eternal gratitude from his country. Colombia was anxious to establish intimate relations with France, " which, by her brilliant industry, by her happy character, and by the marvellous analogy of her manners, language, and religion with our own thus offers us, so to speak, a natural ally." [60]

Zea's circular also became known to the courts of Berlin, London, and St. Petersburg. To the impassioned plea of the Colombian agent, who declared that his government would resort to commercial retaliation if its independence was not recognized, neither France nor any of her Continental allies seems to have made response.[61] Their silence

[59] *British and Foreign State Papers,* IX, 851-54; Webster, *Britain and the Independence of Latin America,* II, 108-09.

[60] April 8, 1822, A. A. E., Colombie, 2.

[61] On May 19 Martínez de la Rosa wrote to Casa Yrujo that the Spanish chargé in Berlin had reported that Prussia would make no reply to the unseasonable circular of Zea. A. H. N.,

made it plain that the threats of a diplomatic agent would not open the door of the society of nations to Colombia.

On April 18, 1822, the *Journal des Débats* published Zea's appeal. It expressed the opinion that France should carefully consider the status of the Spanish nations which were being formed in America. Though those nations demanded immediate recognition, this journal advised that some preliminary measures should first be taken by the French Government. It added that, although an excellent botanist, Zea was not versed in diplomacy and hence sometimes used language that was inexact and unseasonable. Without denying that commercial intercourse with the Spanish-American nations would be very desirable, the same journal observed on October 31 that, before recognition was accorded to a new state, it was essential to know whether that state had a stable government and whether its political system offered security for those who entered into commercial relations with the inhabitants. "We take the liberty of saying to Señor Zea that, as the old ally and friend of Spain, France would display very poor grace in hastening to recognize the separation of the Spanish colonies from the motherland before she has given her consent or before it is proved by evidence that this separation is irrevocably consummated. We believe that, in order to secure this preliminary information, a prudent government should proceed by sending to those colonies commissioners instructed to make sure of the condition of affairs."

Estado, 6846. Nesselrode, writing to Tuyll on July 13, 1822, declared: "Les ouvertures de M. de Zea prétendu agent de la République de Colombia n'ont été accueillées par aucun des Cours Alliées." A. R. V. P., Washington, 1822. On the neutral attitude of the Hanse towns, see Baumgarten, *Ibero-Amerika und die Hansestädte*, p. 176.

The new Foreign Minister accepted with scarcely any alteration the project of establishing Bourbon monarchies in Spanish America. In a note to Lagarde on May 13, 1822, Montmorency declared that Spain should listen to France when the latter asked her to adopt a policy of reconciliation which was in the interest of Spain. He suggested that the dispatch of an infante to Mexico would probably conserve in that country a monarchical system which would ensure immense advantages to Spain.[62] On June 28 the minister repeated the suggestion with emphasis; as the prince to be sent to Mexico, he proposed a brother or a nephew of Ferdinand VII:

This is the only means that remains to Spain of conserving an influence from which she may draw immense advantages. If she neglects this step, the ordinary revenues will not enable her to retain among the powers of Europe the rank which she ought to occupy and which the Allies desire her to occupy. They see with disquietude the formation in America of powerful republics and will be grateful to King Ferdinand for all that His Majesty can do to check the progress of a system which, in time, could have a dangerous reaction upon Europe. This idea of dispatching an infante to Mexico should, therefore, also be a subject of your conversations with Señor Martínez de la Rosa. It is the most feasible basis for a mediation between the motherland and her colonies that would naturally make the Allied Powers and France, in the first place, interfere in the affairs of the Peninsula. This measure could become a mode of executing the plan which it would be wise for King Ferdinand and his chief minister to adopt at once.[63]

The representations of France, however, did not affect Spanish policy. In fact, on the very day when Montmorency

---

[62] Villanueva, *La monarquía en América; Fernando VII y los nuevos estados,* pp. 136-37.

[63] A. A. E., Espagne, 716.

penned the last-mentioned note, the Cortes of Spain adopted a decree which authorized the dispatch of commissioners who were instructed to treat with *de facto* governments that had been formed in Spanish America. Though the formal reconciliation of the revolutionary communities with the motherland was the avowed object of these missions, yet the agents of the Liberal régime were authorized to negotiate commercial agreements with Spanish-American countries. Startling though it may seem, they were not prohibited from ostensibly considering adjustments that contemplated the separation of the colonies from Spain.[64]

At this time, the policy adopted by the United States toward the Spanish colonies attracted considerable attention in Europe. As already mentioned, on March 8, 1822, President Monroe urged Congress to recognize the *de facto* governments which existed in Mexico, Colombia, Chile, Peru, and La Plata. Eleven days later the Committee on Foreign Relations recommended to the House of Representatives that certain nations of Spanish America be acknowledged as independent. On May 4 Monroe accordingly signed a bill which appropriated one hundred thousand dollars to pay the expenses of diplomatic missions to independent nations of the American Continent.[65]

This decision to acknowledge Spanish-American independence not only provoked protests by Spain but also precipitated reactions in France. As soon as he heard of Monroe's message the Marquis of Casa Yrujo, who was now serving as the Spanish ambassador in Paris, hastened to

[64] Robertson, " The Policy of Spain toward Its Revolted Colonies, 1820-1823," *Hispanic Am. Hist. Rev.*, VI, 37-44.
[65] *Idem*, " The United States and Spain in 1822," *Am. Hist. Rev.*, XX, 781-83.

Montmorency and declared that despite this action Spain would maintain all her rights over her transatlantic possessions. The ambassador also expressed hope that the French Government, which was founded upon the principle of legitimacy, would not be influenced by the action of the United States. Montmorency, wrote Casa Yrujo to his court, responded that France would follow the course which Spain desired.[66] Albert Gallatin, the American minister at Paris, informed Secretary Adams that the sentiments of the French Government were made known in the *Journal des Débats.* The King's brother, continued Gallatin, " who always expresses himself in a very friendly way towards the United States, told me that he apprehended the ' moral ' effect of our recognition on the revolutionary spirit of Europe." [67] Such were the sentiments of Count Artois, a leader of the Ultra-Royalist party, who was destined to become the King of France.

On April 15, 1822, the *Courrier Français* declared that the admission of four or five American members into the family of nations was a very important event for Europe, which had long held a large part of the New World in bondage. Two days later the *Journal des Débats* published a keen commentary on the policy of the United States:

The European nations, and especially France, are in a slightly different position which permits them to have recourse to less decisive measures. We can represent to the Spanish Government that, while still recognizing its rights, we find it impossible to exclude a moiety of the world from commercial relations; that, if those relations should be publicly prohibited, they would be established

[66] Casa Yrujo to Martínez de la Rosa, April 25, 1822, A. G. I., Estado, 90.
[67] Gallatin, *Writings,* II, 240.

in a clandestine manner and would thus become the source
of disorders and perhaps of disasters; that, faced by the
necessity of setting those relations in order, France is obliged
to send consular agents into the different Spanish provinces
of America; and that, in order to make the activities of
those agents possible, it is necessary to enter into *pourparlers*
with the public authorities that are established in those
regions.

There is another circumstance which would furnish the
motive for a useful delay in making these *pourparlers*. No
matter what the President says of them in his message, the
new governments of Spanish America are not yet established upon an entirely solid footing. Each province is independent, but we do not know by what body or by what
personage the public authority is there exercised.

A sharp criticism of the policy of the American Republic
was published on April 27 by the *Gazette de France*. It
declared that the report of the Committee on Foreign Relations concerning the President's message recognized only
facts as a determining principle of government, only American interest as public law, only force as a basis of justice.
The *Gazette* declared that these doctrines, resting upon
sophism and injustice, deserved "the reprobation of all
governments which wished to enjoy a reputation for equity
and morality in the eyes of posterity." Despite the recognition which European public law had solemnly received, the
United States had acted in a manner "destructive of all
public law and of all society." The journal further alleged
that ambassadors of the United States near the courts of the
Allies did not hesitate "to offer toasts in public to the
success of rebellions." It even hinted that, if the cabinets
of Europe should decide to wrest the ruling power from
Spanish-American revolutionists by fire and sword and were
successful in the endeavor, Monroe's declaration would be
sufficient to justify such a legitimist undertaking.

To counteract the evil effects of Monroe's message to Congress proposing the acknowledgment of Spanish-American independence, on April 25 Secretary Martínez de la Rosa forwarded to Casa Yrujo for use in his communications with the French Government an exposé of conditions in Spanish America which was far from favorable to the insurgents.[68] Soon afterward, the Secretary of State sent that minister a manifesto in which Spain vigorously protested to European powers against the recognition policy of the Unite States.[69]

On May 9 Martínez de la Rosa transmitted to Casa Yrujo an important dispatch advising him on the attitude which he should take toward France. The ambassador was to urge that the French Government refrain from recognizing the revolutionary authorities in Spanish America either directly or indirectly, that it neither send to nor receive from the Spanish colonies any public agents, and that it abstain from forming any political relations with Spanish-American governments. Casa Yrujo was to represent that, should the doctrines championed by the United States gain acceptance, France had much to lose, for she still claimed title to a part of the island of Santo Domingo. On the other hand, if the negotiations which the Spaniards were undertaking for the pacification of their colonies should succeed, the French would gain many commercial advantages. Martínez de la Rosa added:

[68] " Estado de los diferentes paises de América segun las ultimas noticias," A. H. N., Estado, 6846.

[69] *Manifiesto del gobierno español á las potencias extrangeras sobre la independencia de las Américas.* An English translation of that manifesto is found in *British and Foreign State Papers,* IX, 889-94.

France, the most natural ally of Spain, has a direct and very immediate interest in avoiding any decrease in her power. In view of the weight which her rights in America give her, and because of the ease with which she can rehabilitate her navy, Spain can not only contribute to the maintenance of the general equilibrium of Europe but in time may aid France in order that the two nations united may check the maritime influence which other powers wish to assert.[70]

On May 9 Martínez de la Rosa sent to Casa Yrujo a dispatch containing further arguments for use in his discussions with French ministers. Casa Yrujo was to explain that his government was opening negotiations with insurgents in the Indies and had frankly communicated its plan to other European governments in the conviction that they would not interpose any obstacle to a transaction which involved the prosperity of a neighboring nation, the tranquillity of America, and the well-being of all the powers. The Spanish Secretary of State maintained that should Spanish-American emancipation be accomplished France might well consider her own colonies as lost. On the other hand, should Spain secure the adjustment with Spanish America which she actually desired, the French would gain more commercial advantages than any other people. A nation like France, which still claimed Haiti, could not approve a doctrine that sanctioned rebellion without placing herself in an absurd position.[71]

Before this dispatch reached Paris, Casa Yrujo had sent to Minister Montmorency a copy of the official exposé of conditions in the Spanish Indies, an exposé which he asserted to be a faithful description of their actual condition based upon the last reports received by the Spanish Govern-

[70] A. H. N., Estado, 6846.   [71] *Ibid.*

ment. " Though the assurances that Your Excellency has
given me," he continued, " with regard to the manner in
which His Very Christian Majesty views this question leave
me nothing to desire, yet I flatter myself that you will find
in this account fresh motives to confirm the French Government in a conduct as agreeable to its character as to its
sentiments of sincere friendship toward the government of
His Catholic Majesty." [72] Casa Yrujo transmitted to the
French envoy on May 20 a copy of Spain's manifesto protesting against Monroe's attitude toward Spanish-American
independence.[73]

The recognition policy of the United States was soon
seriously discussed in an interview between Casa Yrujo and
Montmorency. In accordance with his instructions, Casa
Yrujo emphasized the evil results which would ensue if
European nations followed the example of the American
Republic. Spain's ambassador was pleased to find that
Montmorency confirmed and elaborated his previous declarations. Casa Yrujo reported to his court that, because of
considerations of family, of friendship and neighborliness,
as well as of justice and sane policy, the French Government would not recognize any of the insurgent communities
of Spanish America. Nor would it admit their flags into
French harbors even though the United States admitted
those flags into her ports and England followed her
example.

The French minister took occasion to urge upon Casa
Yrujo that a Spanish prince be sent to Mexico. Viscount
Montmorency conveyed the impression that France would
give all the aid necessary for the execution of this project.

[72] May 8, 1822, *ibid*.   [73] *Ibid*.

An undersecretary of the Ministry of Foreign Affairs named
Hermann then gave the Spaniard to understand that, in addition to refusing to recognize the independence of the new
American governments, France would not receive their
emissaries nor appoint any political agents to those governments. However, Hermann cautiously remarked that this
assurance was not intended to last for an indefinite period.
He further stated that, in view of the contradictory reports
which were received concerning Spanish America, France
would send some persons there without any official character solely for the purpose of securing accurate information
about its real condition. When Casa Yrujo observed that
such a step might give rise to an interpretation prejudicial
to the interests of Spain, the undersecretary replied that the
agents entrusted with this mission would appear to be occupied with their own affairs so that no one could suspect the
origin and purpose of their journeys. Hermann then alluded
to the plan of sending an infante to the Spanish Indies. If
such a project met with approval—so wrote the Spanish
minister to his court—the undersecretary assured him that
France would furnish the funds and the frigates necessary
to carry it out.[74]

Early in June Montmorency replied tentatively to Spain's
representations as follows:

At the moment when His Catholic Majesty announces
that he is attempting to adjust his differences with the dissident provinces, the government of His Very Christian
Majesty can only express its sincere wish that the dispatch
of Spanish commissioners entrusted with that important
mission may have a favorable result. The French Govern-

[74] Casa Yrujo to Martínez de la Rosa, May 24, 1822, A. G. I.,
Estado, 90.

ment will not take any premature step in regard to so grave a problem; and its attitude toward Spain is so amicable that it cannot but desire that this discussion terminate without any injury to the interests and the prosperity of that power.[75]

Less than a year after the departure of Chasseriau, steps were taken by Villèle's Ministry to dispatch four agents to America. On July 26, 1822, the Marquis of Clermont-Tonnerre, a court favorite who had recently become Minister of Marine, sent a dispatch which was endorsed "very secret" to Captain Bégué of the *Tarn* directing him to transport certain persons via the United States to Mexico and South America. Among those passengers were G. T. Mollien, Count Landos, Colonel Schmalz, and Achille de la Motte, who seems to have acted as secretary for Schmalz. The Colonel was eventually to be landed at Vera Cruz, and Landos was to be put ashore at Puerto Bello. Clermont-Tonnerre stated that the object of the journeys of Messrs. Landos and Schmalz was to gather information concerning the commercial relations which France might be able to form in the parts of Spanish America that they were to visit.

The minister then explained that, as the governments recently formed in Spanish America had not yet been recognized by France, it would be advisable for Captain Bégué to make special arrangements concerning the salutes which should be fired by French ships upon their arrival in harbors of the new republics. Still, Bégué was cautioned to observe much care in regard to those salutes because this advice embodied only a provisional rule of conduct, the motive of which it was not convenient to disclose. He was

[75] Montmorency to Casa Yrujo, June 9, 1822, A. H. N., Estado, 6846.

further advised to avoid anything that would tend to encourage on the part of the new governments a pretension to absolute equality and reciprocity with France. According to the general usage, French officers were to salute the forts and towns which they might visit, yet they were to refrain from insisting in the name of Louis XVIII that their salutes be returned by an equal number of guns. From insurgent authorities the respective naval captains of France should obtain assurances that responses would be given to their salutes because of regard for the French flag and for the authority which they exercised. In the capacity of royal commanders who were executing their orders but not citing the King's name, they were to refrain from expressing their views concerning the political events of which Spanish America was the theater.[76]

In September, 1822, a new problem arose because of the commercial intercourse between France and South America. A question of maritime procedure was provoked by the increasing frequency with which vessels from insurgent countries were anchoring in French harbors. An officer commanding a ship stationed at the mouth of the Gironde River inquired of Clermont-Tonnerre what conduct he should follow in regard to vessels displaying the flags of South American governments. The Minister of the Navy confessed to Montmorency that he did not foresee any inconvenience which would arise from the admission of such ships into French ports, provided that they were engaged in regular traffic, and on condition that they should under no circumstances hoist their flags. Before issuing orders to that effect, however, Clermont-Tonnerre asked Montmo-

[76] A. N., Marine, B B⁴, 414.

rency to inform him what conditions he thought proper to prescribe.[77]

Montmorency replied on September 10, 1822, that he had laid this inquiry before the Council of State. " It thought as do you," he declared, " that those ships could be admitted into our ports whenever they were engaged in regular traffic, and whenever the nature of their cargoes proved that they were not intended for use as privateers; but it insisted that they should refrain from unfurling their flags. . . ." [78]

Thus, notwithstanding the conservative attitude of the Ministry of Foreign Affairs with respect to an acknowledgment of the independence of the new states of America, in order to promote the development of commerce the Council of State was now willing formally to admit merchantmen from Spanish-American countries into French ports, provided that they did not openly display their flags. Yet this step was scarcely as liberal as that taken by the United States as early as 1815, when she freely admitted vessels from insurgent Spanish colonies into her ports regardless of the flag flying from the masthead.

The attitude of France toward Latin America from 1819 to 1822 was largely opportunistic. Though ostensibly following a policy of neutrality, she aimed to take advantage of circumstances which promised the development of commercial intercourse with the revolutionary communities. Further, she adopted measures designed to protect this trade from the ravages of pirates. Pasquier was convinced that Spain should modify her antiquated colonial system. He reasoned rightly that any succor which might be furnished

[77] September 5, 1822, A. A. E., Colombie, 2.
[78] *Ibid.*

by France to Spain for the subjugation of her colonists would be considered by them an attack upon their independence. Both Pasquier and Montmorency wished Spain to promote the founding of European appanages in Spanish America.

The Council of State took the attitude that, mainly because of her close relations with Spain, France could not openly admit into her ports vessels flying the pennants of insurgent colonies. At the same time, through special agents dispatched to various sections of Spanish America, the French Government tried to gather data concerning the actual condition of the new American nations. Certain French journals sharply criticized the acknowledgment of Spanish-American independence by the United States. Despite Montmorency's adherence to his decision not to recognize any of the nations rising in the New World, Spain was informed that this conservative policy would not be continued indefinitely. The attitude of France toward Latin America during the ministries of Pasquier and Montmorency was thus largely determined by commercial and political opportunism, a spirit which indeed was seldom absent from the deliberations of French statesmen.

CHAPTER VIII

LATIN-AMERICAN ISSUES AT THE CONGRESS OF VERONA

Even before Richelieu resigned his ministry, the stage was being prepared for the Congress of Verona. Revolutionary changes in Europe had furnished occasion for a congress that met in October, 1820, at Troppau. A preliminary protocol signed there on November 19 by ministers of Austria, Prussia, and Russia declared that states belonging to the "European Alliance" which suffered changes in their internal organization that threatened other nations would cease to belong to the alliance. The three powers agreed to refuse to recognize political alterations accomplished by illicit means. The Allies agreed that, when states that had been illegally altered threatened the peace of their neighbors, they if possible would bring such states back to the concert by amicable means or by coercion. As the Kingdom of Naples was in disorder, the contracting parties agreed to put these principles in force there in order to give liberty to the King and the nation.

In a meeting held at Laibach in January, 1821, Austria, Prussia, and Russia sanctioned armed intervention in Naples. An Austrian army of sixty thousand men soon marched into that kingdom, overthrew the revolutionary government, and restored Ferdinand IV to his throne.[1] At

---

[1] In contrast with this policy it should be noticed that, when an agent named Boyé appeared at St. Petersburg and urged Russia to acknowledge the independence of Haiti, the Czar, who was at Laibach, suggested to the French plenipotentiary there that it would

Laibach the powers decided that another meeting should be held in the following year. Metternich prophesied that the congress which Austria wished to have assemble at Verona would mark an epoch in history.

Prominent among the issues confronting European statesmen was the disturbed condition of the Spanish Empire. Ferdinand VII and his adherents hoped that France would intervene in Spain to end the rule of the detested Liberals. A successful outcome of the efforts of liberal Spanish statesmen for reconciliation with the colonies was considered doubtful. In fact, some European publicists were convinced that any attempt on the part of Spain to recover the Indies would be hopeless. On the other hand, Spanish statesmen, apprehensive that France or some other nation would advocate interference in Spain, were determined to resent any national humiliation even at the cost of war. Evaristo San Miguel, who in July, 1822, had become Secretary of State, wrote to the Spanish envoy at Paris that the love of liberty, " which destroyed the throne of Napoleon that was supposed to be omnipotent, will spoil the plans of the Holy Alliance." [2]

With regard to intervention by force of arms in Spain to put down the revolutionists, as also with regard to the policy to be pursued toward the rebellious colonies, the attitude of France was most important. An inkling of her

---

be politic for France to recognize Haiti in return for commercial advantages. La Ferronnays to Rayneval, March 1, 1821, A. A. E., Mémoires et Documents, Amérique, 15. See further *infra,* p. 452.

[2] San Miguel to San Lorenzo, September 3, 1822, A. H. N., Estado, 6849. The English historian Temperley designates the " union " of Prussia, Austria, and Russia against revolutions after 1820 as the " Neo-Holy Alliance." See *The Foreign Policy of Canning, 1822-1827,* pp. 16-17.

views is afforded by an account which Sir Charles Stuart, the capable English ambassador at Paris, gives of an interview that he had with Villèle. That statesman defended to Stuart the policy of French ministers toward Spanish America by declaring that, if they had had any intention to obtain a footing there, "nothing would have been easier than to procure a request in writing from the King of Spain for the departure of a joint French and Spanish expedition from Cadiz for Vera Cruz." Villèle "admitted that he had listened to visionary schemes for sending the Junior Branches of the Spanish Royal Family to South America," but that the "utter incapacity of all the persons placed about Them had shown such a measure to be impracticable, and had compelled him rather to place all his reliance upon the efforts of a Congress to settle the mode" of establishing Spanish-American independence. He further confessed that France could not "look forward to any reasonable suggestions on the part of the Spanish Ministers upon this subject, and that a premature acknowledgment of the independence of the Colonies . . ." would not remove the difficulties to which the prejudices of those ministers would give rise.[3]

Instructions for the French plenipotentiaries at the Congress of Verona were framed by Villèle on August 30, 1822. Villèle declared that for France the situation of Spain doubtless constituted the most delicate topic which would be considered by the congress. The French diplomats were advised that they should not pose as authorities on Spanish affairs. However, their instructions implied that France might find it necessary to wage war upon her south-

---

[3] Stuart to Canning, November 3, 1822 (no. 562), F. O., 27/296.

ern neighbor. With respect to the policy which the congress ought to adopt toward Spain, the view was presented that, as France was the only power which should act through her soldiers, she should be the only judge of the necessity for armed interference. Although intervention in Spain should not be solicited by the French delegates as indispensable to their country, yet such action was to be mentioned as the policy which they considered most politic.

The instructions then turned to the issue raised by insurrectionary movements in Latin America—an issue which Villèle evidently considered no less important to France than intervention in Spain:

If the dispositions of the sovereigns are such that the French plenipotentiaries believe that it would be useful to have the Congress consider the question of the recognition of the governments established in Brazil and Spanish America, it would be helpful to have the assembly of sovereigns request Spain and Portugal to make known their intentions concerning their American colonies, as well as the means which they have at hand for the reëstablishment of security for European navigation and for the restoration of peace and order in that part of the world. It would be helpful if the assembly of sovereigns would offer to Spain and Portugal the means of concurring with them by mediation in this restoration and, in the probable case of a refusal on the part of the motherlands, if they would state through a treaty framed by the great powers that they consider this refusal and the actual situation of the Spanish and the Portuguese colonies as sufficient to induce them to acknowledge as independent states the communities which are regularly constituted on the American Continent. It would also be helpful if the sovereigns pledged themselves that no power was to claim any special advantages in the commercial relations to which the act of recognition of these new states may give rise.

In fine, the French plenipotentiaries ought not to consent to the Congress prescribing the policy of France with regard to Spain. They ought not to accept succor purchased either by pecuniary sacrifices on our part or by the passage of foreign soldiers across our territory. They should aim to have the question of Spain considered in its general relations and to secure from the Congress a contingent treaty, honorable and useful to France, either in case of war between herself and Spain or in case the powers should decide to recognize the independence of Spanish and Portuguese America.[4]

A discerning commentary upon the passages of Villèle's instructions concerning the Spanish Indies is furnished by Baron Boislecomte, who acted as secretary for the French delegation to the Congress of Verona. In his account of its proceedings Boislecomte took the view that Villèle wished it to offer to mediate in the dispute between the Iberian nations and their American colonies, and that, if this attempt failed, he wished it to recognize the independence of the colonies. Boislecomte further declared that Villèle was animated by the desire that England should not desert the other powers while they were considering the Spanish problem. Nor should she be allowed to take advantage of the embarrassment of France in this issue by negotiating favorable treaties with new American states.[5]

This contemporary interpretation is supported by a letter written by Villèle to Viscount Montmorency in which the head of the Cabinet suggested that it would be advantageous to agree with England that, until the end of the antici-

---

[4] " Instructions pour les Plénipotentiaires françaises au congrès de Vérone du 30 Aôut 1822," endorsed "minute de la main de M. le cte. de Villèle," A. A. E., France, 721. In part in Chateaubriand, *Congrès de Vérone,* I, 102-04; see also Nettement, *Histoire de la restauration,* VI, 233-34.

[5] " Résumé historique du Congrès de Vérone, 1822," A. A. E., France, 721.

pated war, no nation should undertake any special measures with regard to the Spanish colonies. Villèle further suggested that the policy to be pursued toward them be formulated at the same time as the policy concerning the pacification of Spain.[6] Evidently he felt that the great powers should reach a common decision which might perhaps involve an acknowledgment of Spanish-American independence. As the delegates of France to the Congress of Verona, Villèle originally selected Montmorency, Caraman, who was ambassador at Vienna, and La Ferronnays, ambassador at St. Petersburg, who had attended the Congress of Laibach.

As Montmorency had expressed his intention to return to Paris whenever the allied sovereigns left the congress, Villèle decided to instruct Chateaubriand to proceed there in order to take charge of the negotiations upon Montmorency's departure.[7] Even before this littérateur was appointed to represent his nation at Verona, he had been meditating about the discordant condition of Spain and her colonies.[8] Chateaubriand told the English ambassador at the French capital that he had tried to induce his government to give a suitable trend to the instructions which were to be prepared for the guidance of the French negotiators after Montmorency left Verona.[9] Boislecomte intimated that Chateaubriand had been dispatched to the congress as the real interpreter of Villèle's opinions.[10]

[6] October 17, 1822 (copy), *ibid.*

[7] Stuart to Bathurst, September 19, 1822, F. O., 146/48.

[8] Chateaubriand, *Correspondance générale,* III, 69; *idem, Mémoires d'outre-tombe,* IV, 261, 263; *supra,* pp. 207-11.

[9] Stuart to Bathurst, September 19, 1822, F. O., 146/48.

[10] " Résumé historique du Congrès de Vérone, 1822," A. A. E., France, 721.

On October 4 Villèle addressed a confidential letter to Montmorency to advise him that he was sending Chateaubriand to Verona with directions for the French delegates which had been approved by Louis XVIII.[11] The part of those instructions that was concerned with Spanish and Portuguese America presented, in fine, a view similar to that given in Villèle's instructions to Montmorency. If circumstances seemed auspicious, the French plenipotentiaries at the congress were to propose the mediation of the assembled powers in the disputes between the Iberian nations and their American colonies. Should this proposal be rejected by Spain and Portugal, the powers might then take steps preparatory to an acknowledgment of the independence of those new American states that were properly organized.[12] The French Ministry evidently considered that the recognition of Latin-American nations was on the agenda.

The instructions to the French diplomats were supplemented by letters from Villèle to Montmorency. On September 23, 1822, Villèle expressed the opinion that the aims of the French Government could be accomplished by a simple and loyal act of intervention by the Allies in respect to the colonies of Spain and Portugal. He maintained that none of the Allies should gain control of any territory in Latin America; nor should any power secure there special commercial advantages. Further, Villèle reasoned that there was no obstacle in the way of recognizing the monarchical government of Brazil, provided that favorable terms were conceded by it to the mother country.

Villèle believed that Spain should be encouraged to furnish a prince to be placed at the head of the independent

[11] Nettement, *Histoire de la restauration*, VI, 259.
[12] *Ibid.*, 261.

Mexican Government. Spain should be aided to do this, he continued, "because it is probable that, by means of the mediation of the powers and perhaps by their intervention, they could at the present moment induce that country to agree to this transaction which the Mexicans at first desired." He recommended that means should also be sought to pacify Colombia and other countries of South America by consenting to recognize their independent governments "so far as their organization and their progress appear to offer sufficient guarantees that they will maintain themselves without dissensions and without compromising the general peace." [13] When he mentioned intervention by the Allies in Spain, Villèle hinted that, if this should take place, certain members of the Spanish royal family might be embarked on a French squadron and sent to Mexico. If, however, the Spanish Bourbons refused to encourage a scheme for such interference in their affairs, the Allies could then act together in regard to the insurgent colonies.

In a letter to Montmorency on October 12, Villèle again mentioned the Latin-American issue. The New World, he asserted, was in a chaotic condition because of the follies committed by Spain and Portugal. He suggested that either the diplomats assembled at Verona should initiate negotiations with the courts of Lisbon and Madrid concerning the status of their colonial possessions or the Great Powers should agree to acknowledge successively the independence of all the states which were organized in those domains. He even stated that, on her part, France would consider acknowledging conditionally the independence of her revolted colony of Saint-Domingue.[14] In thus proposing that

[13] Villèle, *Mémoires et correspondance*, III, 70-71.
[14] *Ibid.*, 115-16.

the Congress of Verona recognize the independence of Latin-American nations, Villèle evidently wished to anticipate the recognition of those nations by England.

Three days later he wrote another suggestive letter to Montmorency concerning the relations between Latin America and the Iberian states. Villèle declared that European powers could scarcely intervene usefully in the affairs of Spain without also adopting a uniform and definite policy with regard to her colonies and those of Portugal. The Allies might offer to mediate in order to terminate the troubles of those states with their colonies by assuring to the motherlands all that they could hope to conserve. If Peninsular demagogues refused such intervention or hindered it, continued Villèle, then the Holy Alliance would feel called upon to declare itself the sponsor of the reëstablishment of order in Latin America:

Each of the powers belonging to the Alliance should interdict any annexation of territory as well as the acquisition of any special advantage of commerce or intercourse by one ally to the exclusion of the others. All the Allies would employ their ships of war to clear the seas of the pirates that infest them. Finally, they would protect and favor all the countries and all the governments which would organize themselves successively under the aegis of this powerful guardianship.[15]

Villèle later confessed that his purpose in suggesting a constructive policy which involved the recognition of both monarchical Brazil and the Spanish-American republics was to prevent England from devouring the Latin-American oyster and leaving to France only the shell which she had opened.[16]

[15] *Ibid.*, 122-23.　　　　　[16] *Ibid.*, 190.

In the autumn of 1822, from widely separated European capitals, diplomats and monarchs wended their way to Italy. Czar Alexander journeyed there in company with his diplomatic advisers. Among them was the Secretary of State for Foreign Affairs, Count Nesselrode. Emperor Francis arrived with a suite that included von Gentz as well as Prince Metternich. With King Frederick William there came his chief diplomatic advisers, Prince Hardenberg and Count Bernstorff. To quote a contemporary chronicler, " rejoicings and splendid illuminations signalized the arrival of these august potentates." [17] The Duke of Wellington was sent as the plenipotentiary of England; for on August 12 Castlereagh, who planned to attend the congress, had committed suicide. There also appeared at Verona a large number of lesser dignitaries. As has been aptly said, this congress convoked " to decide the fate of two worlds " was one which " recalled by the splendour of its concourse the glories of the Congress of Vienna." [18] Careful of this splendor, Austrian police took steps to prevent suspicious foreigners from making a long sojourn at Verona.[19]

Soon after the diplomats of Austria, Prussia, Russia, France, and England assembled, it became evident that Spanish affairs would be in the focus of attention. The Duke of Wellington had been instructed to oppose intervention in Spain and to favor the acknowledgment of Span-

[17] Lesur, *Annuaire historique,* 1822, p. 397.

[18] Phillips, *The Confederation of Europe,* pp. 266-67. A long list of dignitaries attending the congress and of their attendants is found in " Verzeichnisse des Gefolges des Monarchen auf dem Congress zu Verona," H. H. u. S., Congress zu Verona, 45.

[19] *Le Moniteur,* December 18, 1822; Lesur, *Annuaire historique,* 1822, p. 398.

ish-American independence.[20]   On October 20 Montmorency held a confidential conference with representatives of England, Austria, Prussia, and Russia concerning Spanish affairs. According to a précis preserved among the papers of the Verona Congress in the Haus-, Hof- und Staats-Archiv at Vienna, the leading French plenipotentiary presented the view that the revolutionary spirit in Spain threatened the rest of Europe with moral contagion. He confessed that, on the one hand, despite her plans, France might not be able to prevent a rupture with her southern neighbor; and, on the other hand, the Spanish Government might suddenly decide upon aggressive measures toward France.[21] Montmorency accordingly submitted three hypothetical questions to the consideration of the plenipotentiaries of the four powers:

(1) In case France should find herself forced to recall her minister from Madrid and to sever all diplomatic relations with Spain, would the High Courts be disposed to adopt a similar measure and to recall their respective legations?

(2) If war should break out between France and Spain, under what form and by what acts would the High Powers accord to France the moral support which would give to her measures the force of the Alliance and inspire a salutary dread in the revolutionists of all countries?

(3) What, in fine, is the intention of the High Powers concerning the extent and the form of the material assist-

---

[20] Wellington, *Despatches, Correspondence, and Memoranda*, I. 284-88.

[21] " Précis des communications verbales faites par Mʳ le Vicomte de Montmorency dans la reunion confidentielle de Mrs. Les Ministres d'Autriche, du Grand Bretagne, de Prusse et de Russie, à Verone le 20 Octobre 1822," H. H. u. S., Congress zu Verona, 43.

ance which they would be disposed to give France in case their active intervention at her demand should become necessary? . . . [22]

On October 30, in confidential answers to those questions which implied the outbreak of war between France and Spain, the four allies reached conclusions that were not identical. In the first hypothetical case, both Austria and Prussia agreed that, if France should be compelled to recall her minister from Madrid, they would break off diplomatic relations with that court. In the second case, those powers promised only their moral support to France should hostilities take place between her and Spain. In the third case, they stated that if war broke out they could give France armed assistance only in case the allies had decided upon the nature of that aid.[23] Russia responded that, if the contingency mentioned came to pass, she would withdraw her ambassador from Madrid and give France all the moral and material support which she needed. By means of Wellington the English Government dropped a bombshell on the council table in the form of a statement that such

[22] *Ibid.*; Lesur, *Annuaire historique,* 1822, pp. 399-400. This précis was published in part by Chateaubriand, *Congrès de Vérone,* I, 105-10. The originals of some papers printed in that work by Chateaubriand in 1838 are not found in A. A. E., France, 721, but merely copies made from his *Congrès de Vérone.* Evidently Chateaubriand obtained the official documents from the Ministry of Foreign Affairs and used them in the preparation of his work. Marcellus declared that, because of protests made to Chateaubriand, the latter suppressed about one-half of the material which he had originally planned to publish concerning the Congress of Verona. *Chateaubriand et son temps,* pp. 224-26. See further Thomas, " Supplément au Congrès de Vérone," *Revue politique et littéraire,* vol. L, pt. 2, p. 513.

[23] Chateaubriand, *op. cit.,* I, 117-20.

interference seemed to be an unnecessary assumption of authority. This pronouncement caused a rift in the congress.

Finally, on November 15, Austria, Prussia, and Russia signed a procès-verbal that mentioned four contingencies in which they agreed to furnish succor to France: the dissemination of revolutionary propaganda in Europe by a Spanish official, the deposition or trial of any member of the Spanish royal family by the Liberals, an act extinguishing the legitimate right of succession to the Spanish throne, and an attack by Spain upon France.[24] Meanwhile Villèle meditated about the influence of French intervention in Spain upon the fortunes of the Indies. He feared that the English would use the opportunity afforded by such interposition to secure a monopoly of trade with the insurrectionary colonies, and he even thought of forming an alliance with Russia and the United States in order to check the supposed designs of England upon Spanish America.[25]

Notwithstanding Villèle's view that the affairs of Spain and Portugal could not well be separated from the problem of their colonies, Montmorency felt that it would not be

[24] "Reponse confidentielle" of Austria, Prussia, and Russia, H. H. u. S., Congress zu Verona, 43; Chateaubriand, *Congrès de Vérone*, I, 112. See further Temperley, *The Foreign Policy of Canning*, pp. 67-68.

[25] Villèle, *Mémoires et correspondance*, III, 240-43. At Paris Wellington accorded an interview to the Duke of San Lorenzo, the Spanish ambassador at the French capital, as well as to Count Toreno, with regard to the threatened intervention in Spain. From his interview Toreno drew the conclusion that England would support Spain, provided that the latter took pains not to provoke a war with the Allies and made clear to them that she intended to undertake an adjustment with her colonies. "Conferencias con Wellington," enclosure in San Lorenzo to San Miguel, December 19, 1822, A. H. N., Estado, 6849.

politic for France to initiate a discussion of Latin-American affairs in the congress. In the belief that Austria, Prussia, and Russia, unlike France, had no commercial relations with the Indies, he felt that those allies were scarcely in a mood to consider impartially the policy of friendly mediation between Spain and her insurrectionary colonies. Besides, Montmorency believed that should an offer of mediation by the Allies be refused by Spain there would be only one recourse left to these powers, namely to acknowledge the independence of the Spanish-American states—a step which three of the five allies would consider an abandonment of principle. Accordingly, at a council of the plenipotentiaries of France, the decision was reached that they would not raise the issue of mediation by the Allies between Spain and her colonies in the discussions of the congress.

To ease his conscience, however, Montmorency broached this problem in a private conversation with Metternich. The Austrian Chancellor promptly responded that it was not possible for the Allies to give countenance, by a move in favor of mediation in the quarrel between the colonies and Spain, to a European government which it would soon be necessary to place under the ban of the Alliance.[26]

Montmorency wrote to Villèle on October 29, 1822, to declare that he looked upon the plan to mediate between

[26] Nettement, *Histoire de la restauration,* VI, 265. This historian evidently drew his information from a memorandum written by Montmorency shortly after his return to Paris from Verona and entitled " Ecrit sur le congrès de Vérone." See *ibid.,* 249 n. and ff. At the end of November the Duke of San Lorenzo had an interview with Villèle in which the latter conveyed the impression that the powers represented at Verona were hostile to Spain but that France could protect her from the wrath of the northern powers. San Lorenzo to San Miguel, November 28, 1822, A. H. N., Estado, 6844.

Spain and her colonies as a very delicate proposal and one which could not be broached at Verona at that time. The plenipotentiary added that he had already expressed his opinion concerning the inconveniences which would arise if in the discussions of the congress the issue of the colonies were linked to the affairs of Spain.[27]

A debate concerning the policy to be adopted in respect to Spanish America was precipitated on November 24 by a " memorandum on the necessity of some further recognition of the independence of the Spanish colonies " which was presented to the congress by the Duke of Wellington. This memorandum mentioned the policy of the United States in acknowledging the independence of Spanish-American republics. Further, it suggested that the depredations of pirates who lurked in the harbors of Spanish America might provoke England to promote in the interest of her trade " recognition of the existence *de facto* of some one or more of these self-erected governments." [28] In the ensuing discussion Wellington did not deny that the relations which his government contemplated forming with Spanish America might hinder the success of Spain's attempts to pacify the insurgent colonies.[29]

[27] A. A. E., France, 721.

[28] Wellington, *Despatches, Correspondence, and Memoranda*, I, 388. The original is found in H. H. u. S., Congress zu Verona, 44. On November 28, 1822, Wellington sent Metternich this " Mémoire upon the Spanish Colonies." *Ibid.* Green, in his " Wellington, Boislecomte and the Congress of Verona, 1822," presents the view that in reality Metternich and Wellington were working together at the Congress of Verona and that Wellington was not always acting in accordance with Canning's instructions, which disapproved the contemplated invasion of Spain by France. *Transactions of the Royal Historical Society*, 4th series, I, 71-76.

[29] " Procès-Verbaux de la Conférence du 28 Novembre, 1822," A. A. E., France, 721.

The responses made by the Allies to Wellington's communication concerning the Spanish Indies were naturally affected by the policies of their respective cabinets. On behalf of Austria Metternich stated that, although because of the geographical position of his country Francis I had no relations with the Spanish colonies, he respected the motives which impelled the English Government to furnish the navigation and commerce of its subjects with the protection which Spain was not able to guarantee. With regard to the *de facto* recognition of the new governments established in Spanish America the Chancellor explained:

1. That His Imperial Majesty, invariably faithful to the great principles upon which depend the social order and the support of legitimate governments, will never recognize the independence of the Spanish provinces in America as long as His Catholic Majesty shall not have freely and formally renounced the rights of sovereignty which he has exercised over these provinces. 2. That His Imperial Majesty has further decided not to depart from this line of conduct. Still, in the actual state of affairs and as long as Spain finds herself under a régime which revolutionary chiefs have in fact imposed upon the King and his country, the Emperor feels at liberty to adopt toward the Spanish colonies such an attitude in fact as considerations of interest or of general utility may suggest to him. His Imperial Majesty, however, will always observe the express reservation that, whatever this attitude may be, it shall not work any permanent prejudice to the imprescriptible rights of the Spanish King and the Spanish crown.[30]

In response to Wellington's announcement, the representatives of Prussia expressed their monarch's repugnance to any attempt to disparage " the principle of justice and conservation that forms the basis of the great European

[30] Webster, *Britain and the Independence of Latin America*, II, 80.

Alliance by recognizing, to the prejudice of the legitimate rights of His Catholic Majesty, governments which derive their existence from the sole fact of revolt and anarchy and do not have for the authority that they exercise any other title or guarantee than the force of the moment." The Prussian plenipotentiaries, however, did not conceal the fact that the impotence of Spain, which that country ascribed to a revolutionary régime, rendered her at that time unable to subjugate the Indies, and that the existence of *de facto* governments there would create embarrassments for European powers. The plenipotentiaries concluded that the least propitious moment to recognize Spanish-American governments was that at which Spanish affairs were approaching a crisis that might furnish a new opportunity to terminate the bitter quarrel between the motherland and her colonies.[31]

The Russian plenipotentiaries declared that, though their flag rarely appeared in the American seas which were infested by corsairs, they hoped that the English navy would soon put an end to piratical raids. With regard to the recognition of the Spanish nations of the New World, the envoys repeated the views which Count Nesselrode had already formulated on behalf of their master. They declared that the Czar was pleased to learn that certain measures offered to His Catholic Majesty the hope of restoring his authority in the Spanish Indies:

Faithful to the conservative principles which his policy has always observed, persuaded that upon these principles there even depend the maintenance of legitimate governments and the rights which they possess, His Imperial Majesty is inclined to make any decision that would tend to

[31] *Ibid.,* 81.

prejudge the question of the independence of the southern part of America. He will continue to cherish the wish that Spain will have the good fortune to reëstablish her relations with the colonies upon bases that are solid and mutually advantageous.[32]

On November 26 the plenipotentiaries of France replied to the Iron Duke. Chateaubriand, who because of the departure of Montmorency was now acting as the head of the French delegation, stated that France, like England, hoped that Spain would adopt measures which would bring peace and prosperity to the American Continent. He declared that, animated by this hope, the Cabinet of the Tuileries had declined to accept certain advantages which were offered to it and made this further explanation:

Besides, a motive of more general importance regulates the conduct of France with regard to *de facto* governments. She thinks that the principles of justice upon which society reposes cannot be lightly sacrificed to secondary interests. It appears to her that these principles become more grave when one considers the recognition of a political order which is virtually an enemy of that which prevails in Europe. France also thinks that on this great question Spain ought to be previously consulted as the legal sovereign of her colonies.

Nevertheless, France avows with England that, at a time when the troubles in America are being prolonged, and when, because of the impotence of one of the belligerent parties, the right of nations can no longer be exercised, natural law resumes its sway. She agrees that there are inevitable prescriptions; that a government, after having for a long time resisted the force of events, is sometimes obliged to yield, in order to put an end to many evils and not to deprive one state of the advantages from which other states would be able to derive the sole benefit.

In order to avoid arousing rivalries and commercial emulations which might involve governments in precipitate steps

[32] *Ibid.*, 83.

despite their wishes, a general measure taken in common
by divers cabinets of Europe would be the most desirable
solution. It would be worthy of the powers composing the
Grand Alliance to consider whether it would not be possible to adjust at the same time the interests of Spain, those
of her colonies, and those of other European nations by
adopting as a basis of negotiation the principle of generous
reciprocity and perfect equality. Perhaps one would find in
concert with His Catholic Majesty that it is not altogether
impossible, for the common welfare of governments, to
reconcile the rights of legitimacy with the necessities of
politics.[33]

This cautious declaration of the French delegation to
the Congress of Verona lent itself to interesting interpretation. It not only demonstrated that for the time being
France had adopted a policy of compromise and delay with
regard to the status of the Spanish colonies, but it also foreshadowed her course for the immediate future. Chateaubriand subsequently asserted that in the exposé presented to
this congress he had expressed the views entertained by the
French people. In May, 1824, he wrote to Prince Polignac,
the French ambassador at the Court of London: "Our
policy with respect to the Spanish colonies is fully expressed
in our declaration at Verona." [34]

Baron Boislecomte was more explicit in his contemporary
interpretation of this declaration: "France seemed to anticipate that some day she would herself be forced to acknowledge the independence of Spanish America, and she desired
to safeguard that contingency by referring to the inevitable

---

[33] " Litt. G, au protocol du 28 Novembre," H. H. u. S., Congress
zu Verona, 44, published with different paragraphing in Chateaubriand, Congrès de Vérone, I, 93-94. The protocol with annexes is
also found in A. A. E., France, 721.

[34] Chateaubriand, Correspondance générale, V, 224. See also
ibid., 145, 189-90.

prescription which time imposes in such cases." [35]   Indeed,
France did convey the implication that the lapse of a reasonable time after revolutionary changes had occurred in a
country could be held to justify the recognition of a new
and disputed sovereignty.[36]

In sum, the replies of the Allies to Wellington's propositions not only made known their resolution to consider the
rights of Ferdinand VII inviolable but also their determination to refrain from reaching any decision in regard to the
insurgent colonies except in accord with him.[37] The Duke's
announcement concerning English policy toward Spanish
America raised the delicate question of recognition *de facto*
and recognition *de jure*. Boislecomte declared that, after the
four responses to this announcement had been made, a lively
debate took place in the congress between Wellington and
the plenipotentiaries of Austria, Prussia, and Russia. "I
have too much respect for the navy of England," exclaimed
Prince Hatzfeld, a member of the Prussian delegation,
"to accept the view advanced by the noble Duke that she
will be compelled to conclude agreements with the insurgents and that she will not be able by her own force to
exterminate the pirates who ravage the seas!" Wellington
was visibly embarrassed by the criticisms of his adversaries.
"The assembly concluded," reported Boislecomte, "by
taking notice of the contradiction between the professed

[35] Boislecomte, "Congrès de Troppau, de Laybach, et de Vérone,
1820 à 1822," December 15, 1822, A. A. E., France, 720.

[36] See *infra,* pp. 352-54, for the views of Baron Damas in December, 1824, in regard to the recognition of a new state; these show
the influence of the doctrine formulated by Chateaubriand at
Verona.

[37] La Ferronnays to Montmorency, December 1, 1822, A. A. E.,
France, 721.

desire of favoring the reconciliation of Spain with her colonies and the adoption of a measure that would evidently be prejudicial to the steps which she might take in regard to an adjustment." [38]

The delegates of Austria, Prussia, and Russia reached the conclusion that it was England's intention to send commercial agents to Spanish-American states. Yet the French plenipotentiaries did not express their views on that phase of the international situation. In a dispatch to Montmorency Count La Ferronnays explained this silence as follows: " Our peculiar position and a knowledge of the measures which our government may feel obliged to take from one moment to another constrained us to remain silent spectators of this discussion." [39] A circular dispatch sent out by Austria, Prussia, and Russia from Verona on December 14, 1822, however, contained a provocative statement to the effect that rich colonies were justifying their separation from Spain by the same maxims as those upon which the mother country had built her public rights, but which she nevertheless wished to condemn in another hemisphere. [40]

In his account of the international congresses which met in Europe from 1820 to 1822, Boislecomte made this comment on the proceedings of the Congress of Verona:

We see the emancipation of the Spanish colonies more assured than ever and in a manner even legitimized by the revolution in Spain. We are astonished at the error, committed by so many Spaniards, of believing that they could induce the American insurgents to obey by offering to share with them the liberty which the revolution had brought to the motherland, without discerning that, as the sovereignty

---

[38] " Résumé historique du Congrès de Vérone, 1822," *ibid.*
[39] La Ferronnays to Montmorency, December 1, 1822, *ibid.*
[40] Metternich, *Nachgelassenen Papieren*, II, 583.

of the people was the basis of the Spanish Constitution, this principle would give to the Spanish-Americans the same right to free themselves from Spain as that which the Spaniards had invoked to liberate themselves from absolute power." [41]

Prominent Continental publicists were evidently of the opinion that with respect to the insurgent colonies in America the Liberal government of Spain was openly pursuing a policy which was not consistent with its acknowledged attitude toward absolute rule at home.

The deliberations of the assembled diplomats were disturbed by the arrival of Manoel Rodrigues Gameiro Pessoa, an envoy of Brazil. Peculiar though it may seem, this agent had been allowed to proceed to Verona by Metternich, to whom he had been referred by the Austrian ambassador at Paris. Gameiro Pessoa's object was apparently to solicit on behalf of the Brazilian Government the moral support of the sovereigns who had gathered at the Congress and even to secure from the Allies an acknowledgment of the independence of his country. Metternich maintained that, as Brazil had constituted herself not as a republic but as an empire, a conference should be held at London to consider what action might properly be taken by the Allies with respect to that new state. On the other hand, Wellington pointed out that such a step would be inconsistent with the attitude of the Allies toward the Spanish-American republics and that England had never gone so far as to receive officially an accredited agent of Latin-American insurgents.[42]

[41] " Congrès de Troppau, de Laybach, et de Vérone, 1820 à 1822," December 15, 1822, A. A. E., France, 720.

[42] Vincent to Metternich, October 28, 1822, H. H. u. S., Berichte aus Frankreich, 349; Wellington, *Despatches, Correspondence, and Memoranda,* I, 642-43.

According to Boislecomte, Metternich without replying to the Duke asked La Ferronnays what his opinion was with regard to the dilemma. That plenipotentiary said in answer: " This is a great and difficult question, which demands months of reflection, and one scarcely knows how to improvise a response. . . . It seems to me, however, that the noble Duke has rightly declared that the Congress would seem to contradict itself if, proclaiming the principles which it professed yesterday, it should today recognize the independence of Brazil." Besides, he went on to say, " an act of mediation cannot well be performed except at the wish of both parties. Further, one does not yet know the opinion of Portugal on this matter." Upon being asked by Metternich what should be done with the Brazilian agent, La Ferronnays replied that he would simply send Gameiro Pessoa away from Verona. Chateaubriand supported this view, arguing that the acknowledgment of Brazil's independence at that time would be extremely inconvenient. According to Boislecomte, the discussion ended in the following manner: " The motion of the Austrian Chancellor was accordingly rejected by a unanimous vote; the plenipotentiaries agreed that Gameiro Pessoa should be informed that the Congress would not consider his request, and that there was nothing he could do but to retire." [43] Thus, contrary to the desire of Metternich, and in accordance with the views of La Ferronnays, the Congress refused to receive an agent of the huge colony which had just proclaimed its independence.

Months after the Congress adjourned there was published in the *Morning Chronicle* of London a treaty which pur-

[43] " Résumé historique du Congrès de Vérone, 1822," A. A. E., France, 721.

ported to have been signed at Verona on November 22, 1822, by Metternich for Austria, by Nesselrode for Russia, by Bernstorff for Prussia, and by Chateaubriand for France. The preamble of this convention declared that the signatories had been specially authorized by their sovereigns "to make some additions" to the Treaty of the Holy Alliance. In the first three articles of this so-called " Secret Treaty of Verona " the signatory powers agreed to prevent the extension of the system of representative government, to suppress the liberty of the press, and to sustain the measures of the clergy who acted as a conservative force in their respective countries. By the fourth article the parties entrusted to France the task of suppressing the Spanish Revolution by force of arms.[44]

This alleged treaty has been used not only to indicate the intentions of the Allies at Verona with respect to Spain but also to lend support to the notion that they contemplated armed intervention in Spanish America. After the " treaty " became known in France a debate broke out among leading Parisian journals concerning its authenticity. Some years afterward, when Count Marcellus, who had served France in several diplomatic posts, brought this curious document to the attention of Chateaubriand, the retired diplomat declared that it had been fabricated in the Strand and first

[44] *Niles' Weekly Register,* XXIV, 347. This alleged treaty was later reprinted in the United States in Snow, *Treaties and Topics in American Diplomacy,* pp. 245-46, in somewhat different language. It was translated into Spanish in *Historia de la vida y reinado de Fernando VII de España,* III, 21-23. Though Schaumann published an English text of the treaty in 1855 (" Geschichte des Congresses von Verona," *Historisches Taschenbuch,* 3rd series, VI, 95-97), he regarded it as spurious. It was published in *El Argos,* Buenos Aires, on January 24, 1824.

published in London in 1823. Though Marcellus cannot always be trusted implicitly—for he sometimes printed spurious or apocryphal documents—yet in his account of this interview there is a passage which at least points the moral. According to that diplomat, Chateaubriand said:

There are many people who will read nothing in history but what they wish to see there! . . . Without doubt, the discovery of this Secret Treaty of Verona is an event. Another pearl for future historians! . . . There is in it neither a word nor even the semblance of truth. . . . Two years ago, someone spoke to me about this treaty, . . . and I wrote, it seems to me, to the *National* that the allegation that a secret treaty had been signed by me at Verona was absolutely false. . . . November 22 was the day of the departure of M. de Montmorency; nothing either official or secret could have been signed by me at Verona on that day. Up to that date it was M. de Montmorency alone who had the right to sign; and, after his departure, my colleagues and myself together.[45]

Important though it was, the Congress of Verona did not determine the fate of two worlds. A decision was indeed reached by the Continental allies that pressure should be brought to bear on Spain to induce her to alter her

[45] Marcellus, *Politique de la restauration en 1822 et 1823*, pp. 61-72. See further Perkins, *The Monroe Doctrine, 1823-1826*, pp. 52-53. There is no mention of the treaty in question in Chateaubriand, *Correspondance générale*, in Gentz, *Dépêches inédites*, or in Lesur, *Annuaire historique*, 1822. The treaty is not found among the documents in the French archives relating to the Congress of Verona. Nor is it found among the protocols in the Austrian archives. As is shown in the text, the problem of the Spanish colonies was not seriously considered by the Congress of Verona until November 24. Since the above passages were written, there has come to hand the article by Schellenberg entitled "The Secret Treaty of Verona: A Newspaper Forgery," *Journal of Modern History*, VII, 180-91.

political system. From this decision England sharply dissented. The policy to be pursued by the Allies toward Spain was occasionally mentioned at Verona in connection with the attitude to be adopted toward her revolutionary colonies. Indeed, the French plenipotentiaries scarcely hoped to keep the two matters separate and distinct.

The attitude assumed by those plenipotentiaries at the congress shows that in 1822 France was willing to consider an acknowledgment of Spanish-American independence. At the same time, the head of the French Ministry dreamed that the Allies might use their good offices to promote a reconciliation between the Iberian nations and their rebellious colonies. Still, with seeming inconsistency, Villèle suggested that the Allies recognize the independence of monarchical Brazil. With respect to Mexico, he thought that the Allies should favor the enthronement there of a Spanish prince. He even invoked the Holy Alliance by name as the force that as a last resort could reëstablish order in both Spanish and Portuguese America.

The reactions of the Continental powers to Wellington's memorandum, hinting at the acknowledgment of the independence of the Spanish colonies by his government, indicate the attitude of those powers toward the Spanish Indies. Austria did not wish to take such a momentous step until the King of Spain had renounced his sovereign rights over those dominions. Prussia did not deem 1822 a propitious time to depart from her policy of the non-recognition of governments which had been formed to the prejudice of the legitimate rights of Spain. Russia wished to reëstablish the sovereignty of Ferdinand VII over the Indies.

To an appreciable extent France agreed with England. Both Chateaubriand and Montmorency expressed the hope that Spain would adopt a policy which might assure tranquillity to Spanish America. Though avowing their faith in the principle of legitimacy, the French plenipotentiaries believed that the time was approaching when European powers might well promote such an adjustment between Spain and her colonies as would reconcile legitimacy with political necessity.

Lastly, the so-called Secret Treaty of Verona, which purported to contain additions to the Treaty of the Holy Alliance, should be dismissed from consideration by students of history and diplomacy, except as an indication of contemporary sentiment with respect to designs occasionally entertained by one or another of the Continental powers. It has never been demonstrated that in 1822 the Holy Allies entered into an agreement to restore the rule of Ferdinand VII over his insurgent colonies in the New World. It remains, however, to consider the attitude of those allies, especially of France and Russia, toward Spanish America during the years between 1822 and 1830.

Chapter IX

FRANCE CONSIDERS INTERVENTION

On November 30, 1822, Viscount Montmorency arrived in Paris with the agreement by which Austria, Prussia, and Russia undertook to make common cause with France in case she became involved in war with her southern neighbor and England aided Spain. He wished the King to sanction another measure, namely the dispatch by each of the four courts of an identical note to Spain couched in such terms that it would inevitably lead to a rupture with her Liberal government. This proposal provoked criticism in Parisian journals. It caused a clash in the Council of State between Montmorency and Count Villèle, who had meanwhile been accorded the title of president of that council. As the King decided to refrain for a time from withdrawing his minister from the Court of Madrid, Montmorency promptly resigned.

At the instance of Louis XVIII, Villèle offered the vacant post to Chateaubriand, who at first declined to accept it. However, on the evening of December 28, after a long interview with the King, the author of *The Genius of Christianity* signified to Villèle that he would join the Cabinet. The littérateur wrote to Madame Récamier on January 2, 1823, that he was about to cross the Seine in order to recline in a ministerial bed which had not been made for him—a bed in which one slept very little and where one remained a very short time.

Shortly before Chateaubriand accepted a portfolio, the prospect of interference in the Spanish Indies had been mentioned in both Paris and London. The English Secretary of State for Foreign Affairs, George Canning, a firm believer in the policy of non-intervention in the internal affairs of other nations, informed Villèle that England was opposed to the acquisition of any part of Spanish America by any nation.[1] Nevertheless, that French statesman did not make a similar disclaimer on behalf of his government. On the contrary, he intimated to Wellington that France, desirous of restoring the authority of Spain, was willing to transport to the Indies an infante accompanied by Spanish soldiers.[2] A sentiment in favor of intervention was manifested even in a Parisian newspaper. The *Journal des Débats* printed on December 13, 1822, an article which proposed the transfer of Spanish infantes to Mexico and Peru. This journal declared that naval succor would be furnished to the motherland for the execution of the monarchical design and intimated that, if Spain would not favor the scheme, her coasts would be blockaded by France. Shortly afterward Chateaubriand explained to the Austrian minister in Paris that maritime aid was to be placed at the disposal of Ferdinand VII to enable him, if possible, to retain certain colonies which were not entirely detached from the mother country.[3]

The decision of the Allies at Verona to interfere in Spain naturally lent color to a belief that they also contemplated the restoration by armed force of the rule of Ferdinand VII over the Indies. It is, accordingly, pertinent to consider the relation between the intervention of France in Peninsular

---

[1] Webster, *Britain and the Independence of Latin America,* II, 110.

[2] Wellington, *Despatches, Correspondence, and Memoranda,* I, 639.

[3] Temperley, " French Designs on Spanish America in 1820-5," *Eng. Hist. Rev.,* XL, 40.

affairs and her attitude toward the insurgent Spanish colonies. Eighteen hundred and twenty-three was the year when European interposition in Spanish America seemed most imminent.

First to be considered are certain measures taken by the Minister of Marine before French soldiers marched beyond the Pyrenees. On January 20, 1823, the Marquis of Clermont-Tonnerre sent a dispatch to Captain Grivel, who had been made commander of the naval station on the Brazilian coast, to suggest that hostilities might break out between France and Spain and to urge him to watch carefully French commercial interests.[4] Identical advice was forwarded to Captain Roussin, who was now cruising along the Pacific coast of South America.[5] Chateaubriand soon advised Clermont-Tonnerre that, although France had not recognized the independence of the Spanish colonies, she did not confuse their interests with those of Spain. He felt that it was improbable that those colonies would aid the mother country if a rupture should take place between Spain and France. In case hostilities broke out between the Bourbon powers, French naval commanders were not to treat vessels of the dissident colonies in the same manner as Spanish ships.[6] On January 29 the Minister of Marine instructed Grivel to resort to reprisals on Spanish ships as soon as he learned that war had begun. To supplement these instructions Clermont-Tonnerre sent to Grivel a few days later a dispatch which contained the following passage:

I have already notified you that France has constantly observed and will continue to observe the strictest neu-

---

[4] A. A. E., Brésil, 2.
[5] Clermont-Tonnerre to Chateaubriand, January 20, 1823, *ibid.*
[6] January 31, 1823, *ibid.*

trality toward Spain and her South American colonies. At the same time, I have recommended that when occasion offers you form with the actual chiefs of Buenos Aires all the relations necessary to assure our navigators the regard which is due them. The same instructions regulate the conduct to be followed by the officers of our ships that are cruising in the Pacific Ocean in their relations with the new authorities of Chile and Peru.

The Minister of Marine expressed the opinion that if war actually broke out the insurgent colonies would not take part in the hostilities waged against France by the mother country. He maintained that Spanish-American ships deserved different treatment by French cruisers from that which would be accorded to the vessels of Spain. " You should, accordingly," added Clermont-Tonnerre, " seize vessels under the Spanish flag which have been armed in the ports of European Spain or in the ports of colonies still belonging to her; but you should treat in friendly fashion the ships of insurgent Spanish colonies and maintain the relations that have been established with the new governments of southern America in such a manner as to prepare for us, whatever may be their future, relations which will be favorable to our commerce." [7] In a later dispatch announcing the invasion of Spain by French soldiers, the minister further explained that France was merely waging war upon those Spaniards who had been armed by the Cortes against her and in favor of the revolutionists of all countries. He declared that it would therefore be proper for French forces to take hostile measures only against partisans of the Spanish revolutionaries. [8]

[7] Clermont-Tonnerre to Grivel, February 1, 1823, A. N., Marine, B B⁴, 447.
[8] *Idem* to *idem*, April 15, 1823, *ibid.*

Instructions which contemplated war between France and Spain had also been sent by Clermont-Tonnerre to Governor Donzelot. His attention was directed to the strict neutrality which had been observed by France toward the struggle for independence that was being waged by the Spanish and the Portuguese colonists. He was informed that identical directions had been sent to Admiral Bergeret, the commander of the French naval station at the Antilles. Clermont-Tonnerre surmised that if war with Spain actually took place her colonies would not join her against France. Hence he reasoned that the new governments deserved special consideration by French cruisers. The armaments of Spanish-American states, he observed, were not to be confounded with Spanish armaments. French warships should accordingly seize armed vessels flying the flag of Spain, but they should treat the ships of her insurgent colonies as friendly craft.

Governor Donzelot was directed to pursue a cautious policy with respect to privateering in Spanish-American waters:

I urge you, as well as Rear Admiral Bergeret, to carry out, when occasion arises, the measures undertaken a long time ago for the purpose of ensuring that privateers equipped in the insurgent Spanish colonies are subjected to such positive and severe regulations that they can easily be identified. If war with Spain breaks out, the necessity of recognizing by certain devices the armaments prepared in the ports of those colonies and at the expense of their inhabitants will become still more imperative. Otherwise, in such a case, we should have to fear the double danger of treating as our enemies those vessels which are fitted out against the mother country by the colonies and of seeing ships that are really Spanish evade our cruisers by simulating the colors of the new states of southern America. In the absence of Rear Admiral Bergeret, after this reaches you

I ask you to give orders to the effect of the present dispatch to the commanders of the King's ships that are near Fort Royal.[9]

In response to Clermont-Tonnerre's directions, Rear Admiral Bergeret stated that the prospect of a rupture between France and Spain had caused him to concentrate the naval forces under his command. Further, in case it became necessary to make war upon the Spaniards, he had arranged with Governor Donzelot to undertake a *rapprochement* with Spanish-American revolutionists. He agreed with the Minister of Marine that the colonists would not join the Spaniards in order to wage hostilities against France, but he believed that at the instance of his government they would be disposed to take steps against the Spanish armaments in America. He asserted that the French naval forces in the West Indies could maintain a useful surveillance of Puerto Rico and that, by obstructing its revictualling, they could effectively contribute to the capitulation of that island to the insurgents. Finally, Bergeret reasoned that it would be easy to distinguish between Spanish vessels and ships belonging to the Republic of Colombia.[10]

It is accordingly clear that, although in the early months of 1823 France was preparing to take hostile steps against Spain, she was directing her naval commanders to discriminate carefully between Spanish vessels and ships belonging to the insurgent colonies. Undoubtedly she desired to avoid any clash with the revolutionists that would injure their cause and complicate her impending war with Spain. Furthermore, although France was anxious to exterminate the

[9] February 5, 1823, *ibid.*, 446.
[10] Bergeret to Clermont-Tonnerre, May 18, 1823, A. N., Marine, B B⁴, 446.

troublesome pirates who infested Latin-American seas, she also wished to improve her commercial relations with the new states. Bergeret was even planning to employ French naval forces in conjunction with Spanish-American insurgents against Spanish Royalists in the West Indies.

French officials in Europe did not always make the objectives of their government clear. When the ministers of Austria, France, Prussia, and Russia presented identic notes to the Spanish Government requesting that Ferdinand VII be restored to absolute power, their demand was refused. In consequence those ministers promptly demanded their passports. On April 2, 1823, at the head of a French army, the Duke of Angoulême crossed the river Bidassoa. Upon entering Spanish territory he issued a proclamation announcing that one purpose of his invasion was to put an end to the anarchy which was destroying Spain and depriving her " of the power to pacify her colonies." [11]

Rumors of French designs upon the Spanish dominions added a new whirl of color to the kaleidoscope. As Angoulême's forces gained success after success, apprehensions arose in the minds of Spanish-American insurgents that France might also contemplate an attack upon the nations that were rising in the New World. In consequence some of those Patriots even displayed their sympathy with Spain. A significant proposal for a *rapprochement* between South American revolutionists and Spanish Liberals at this critical time may indeed be found in the annals of Argentina. Because of the hostilities undertaken by France against the Spanish people the insurgent government at Buenos Aires, in the same month that it sanctioned a preliminary treaty

[11] Lesur, *Annuaire historique,* 1823, p. 717.

of peace with the liberal government of Spain, placed itself on record as favoring the appropriation of twenty million pesos by Spanish-American republics for the defense of the mother country against French aggression.[12] When Chateaubriand heard of this proposed appropriation, he intimated to Polignac that France might rightly consider it equivalent to a declaration of war against her by the Platean republic.[13]

In June, 1823, Louis XVIII, anticipating the speedy restoration of Ferdinand VII to the throne and the reëstablishment of the friendly relations which had so long existed between France and Spain, decided to send a diplomatic mission to Madrid in the person of an ambassador. In communicating this decision to the Marquis of Talaru, who was accredited to that court, Chateaubriand sent him a comprehensive summary of the Cabinet's policy toward Spain. He explained that the French had not intervened in that country either to increase their territory or to gain any special advantage. France had been animated neither by a fear of constitutional institutions nor by a desire to reëstablish Ferdinand's absolute authority. Instead her object was to destroy a military revolution which was founded upon the sovereignty of the people, " thus menacing the existence of all the monarchies of Europe." Anticipating that Ferdinand VII would soon be clothed with his former authority, Chateaubriand analyzed the colonial problem of Spain as follows:

[12] *Convención preliminar acordada entre el gobierno de Buenos Aires y los comisionados de S. M. C.* See also Lesur, *op. cit.*, 1823, p. 651.

[13] Chateaubriand, *Correspondance générale*, V, 39. The unfavorable reaction of Mexico's Secretary of Foreign Relations to the Argentine proposal is found in *La diplomacia mexicana*, III, 34-35.

If we consider the condition of the Spanish colonies whose separation from the motherland is feared, we see that there are some colonies, like Cuba and Puerto Rico, which ask only to be protected by the mother country in preserving the advantages that time and circumstance have given them. Peru could easily be brought back and retained under the domination of the King, for only the towns along the coast have declared themselves independent. The interior of that country has remained loyal. As yet, Mexico is only imperfectly separated from Spain. By the exercise of care, reason, and skill, it would perhaps be possible to establish in America great monarchies governed by princes of the House of Bourbon. In this manner we could combat the waxing system of republics, while Spain would retain the sovereign power as well as immense advantages in those fine colonies which are about to escape from her control.

When it becomes necessary to deal with this question, the King's ambassador will receive special instructions; but he already knows the direction in which France wishes to act and he can prepare the spirit of the Spanish ministers.

The actual condition of our commercial relations with Spain should receive the special attention of the ambassador of France. By virtue of the treaties of 1814 those relations should be reëstablished upon the same terms as those upon which they stood in 1792. The basis had been laid in earlier treaties, particularly in the Treaty of August 15, 1761. . . .[14]

It is significant that in this important communication to Talaru the Minister of Foreign Affairs made no mention of the use of armed force by France in Spanish America. However, that recourse was soon to be proposed by the head of the Cabinet. On July 3, in a dispatch to the Duke of Angoulême, Villèle suggested that the Latin princes, Francisco, Lucca, and Sebastian, be placed at the head of

---

[14] Instructions pour Monsieur le Marquis de Talaru, Ambassadeur du Roi en Espagne," June 9, 1823, A. A. E., Espagne, 722.

hereditary appanages in the Spanish Indies.[15] Two days later, in more ample detail, Villèle urged that Angoulême propose to the Spaniards the pacification of their colonies by the adoption of a plan for the creation of three Spanish dependencies in America. One appanage should be established in Mexico, another in Peru and Chile, and a third in Paraguay and La Plata. With respect to each of those sections there should be an understanding that the customs duties were to be reduced ten per cent in favor of the commerce of the mother country. Villèle continued in these words:

France would furnish to Spain the maritime force necessary for the transportation and admission to the colonies of the infantes as well as a few soldiers and funds sufficient to guarantee the success of the operations thus conceived. It seems to us very proper that these operations should be favored by the different cabinets of Europe in order to reëstablish peace and order in the New World, to honor by a useful conclusion our intervention in Spain, and to make more tolerable to France by this consideration and by the new markets furnished to our products the extraordinary expense which we have incurred and which we should have to incur for Spain. Finally, these measures would promote the credit and the financial reconstruction of that country; for, if they could be carried out, if peace were established between the motherland and the colonies, the commercial favors reserved to Spain would more than compensate her for what she would have lost in respect to her sovereignty. Our ambassador who goes to Lisbon will favor with all his influence a similar arrangement between Portugal and Brazil.[16]

In a letter to Angoulême on July 18, Villèle elaborated certain details of this plan. He took the view that only

---

[15] Villèle, *Mémoires et correspondance,* IV, 188.
[16] *Ibid.,* 200-01.

Cuba, Puerto Rico, and the Philippines could still be retained in the Spanish colonial system. As for Spain's continental colonies in America, he maintained that it would be
vain to attempt to bring them back under the yoke of the
motherland and to oblige them to renounce the commercial
relations which they had formed with other states. He
believed, however, that the project of hereditary appanages
which he had sketched would not only satisfy the reasonable
wishes of the continental colonists and the pretensions of
foreign nations but would also assure to Spain large profits
and commercial advantages. With regard to the reception
of the infantes Villèle added:

> In all those countries armed parties exist which favor the
> motherland. If the infantes should not find in Spanish
> America submissive realms, they would at least find realms
> which could easily be subjugated by the aid of our navy and
> our credit. Their use for this purpose would be approved
> by France because of her anticipation of the commercial
> advantages which those sacrifices would assure her in the
> future.[17]

In November, 1823, Villèle informed Stuart that it would
have been easy for France to secure a written request from
Ferdinand VII for the dispatch of a joint French and
Spanish expedition against Mexico, but he admitted that
such a proceeding would have led to a war between England
and the Bourbon powers.[18]

The policy envisaged by Villèle in 1823 thus not only
contemplated a loan to Spain but also the use of French
military and naval forces to ensure the establishment of

---

[17] *Ibid.*, 239-40.
[18] Temperley, "French Designs on Spanish America in 1820-5,"
Eng. Hist. Rev., XL, 42-43.

Bourbon monarchies in Spanish America. He sanguinely thought that a war with England might nevertheless be avoided. Chateaubriand perhaps had a better understanding of the English attitude toward French intervention in Spain than did the head of the Cabinet. On August 23 the former wrote to La Ferronnays that England viewed with extreme jealousy a garrison stationed in Cadiz and that she would like to compel the French to withdraw from a stronghold so near Gibraltar:

> England knows well that we neither intend to occupy this place much longer nor to take possession of some Spanish colonies, but she pretends to fear this and proposes to enter into negotiation with us concerning the colonies. She feels chagrined when we frankly respond to her: " The Spanish colonies are not for us; we cannot undertake to consider their fate except in conjunction with the King of Spain, their legitimate sovereign, and with the Alliance." [19]

Chateaubriand evidently meant that he could treat concerning the insurgent colonies only with the King of Spain acting as a free agent. It does not appear that at this time France actually made an offer of armed aid to Spain to promote the recovery of her continental colonies. Yet a suspicion that the French Government entertained such a design lingered in the minds of Englishmen. The proposal which Canning made at this time to Richard Rush, the American minister at London, for a joint understanding between England and the United States with respect to the independence of the Spanish-American colonists shows that he feared forcible intervention by France in Spanish America.[20] In November, 1823, Sir Robert Wilson, a

[19] Chateaubriand, *Correspondance générale*, IV, 379.
[20] Rush, *A Residence at the Court of London*, II, 11, 24-25.

soldier of fortune who had unsheathed his sword on the side of the Spanish Liberals, wrote from Spain that, unless England either repealed an act prohibiting foreign enlistments or protected South America, the New World would again be inhabited by slaves! He asserted that the French were fortifying Cadiz and that an armament in Spanish vessels was being prepared for the West Indies.[21]

Meanwhile Ferdinand VII had been set at liberty by French soldiers. On October 1 he published a decree which announced that all acts of the so-called constitutional government of Spain were null and void. This iconoclastic measure was presumably framed by an ultra-conservative Spaniard named Victor Saez, who had served as Minister of State ad interim of the absolutist Spanish Regency at Urgel and had now become the chief minister as well as the confessor of the restored King. Talaru characterized this influential ecclesiastic as false, obstinate, and intriguing.[22] As early as July 30, Saez had informed the French ambassador and the envoys of other powers at Madrid that Spanish-American affairs could not be handled with the promptness which the Regency desired and that his government would not spare any pains to make the colonists return to their allegiance.[23]

On October 8, 1823, Ambassador Talaru advised Chateaubriand that it would be wise to send a French frigate to the Spanish colonies.[24] In another letter of the same date he sketched the measures which he was proposing to the Spanish Government:

[21] Temperley, *Life of Canning,* p. 180 n.
[22] Talaru to Chateaubriand, August 17, 1823, A. A. E., Espagne, 723.
[23] (Translation), *ibid.,* 722.   [24] *Ibid.,* 724.

I am constantly urging the dispatch of commissioners and of the requisite orders for the island of Cuba, but officials move so slowly in this country that it is necessary to return often to the charge. I am about to speak of the dispatch of infantes to Spanish America, but this measure will meet with obstacles higher up. Nevertheless, it is the only mode by which Spain can preserve some ties with America, if indeed there still is time.[25]

On October 20 Talaru reported to Paris an interview with Saez concerning the preliminary treaty of peace which Spanish commissioners had signed with the government of La Plata. The ambassador advised Chateaubriand that he should cease to be anxious about this treaty, for he had been given assurances by Secretary Saez that unless forced to do so King Ferdinand VII would sanction no measure that the Liberal Cortes had authorized. " ' Besides,' " said the legitimist ecclesiastic to the French diplomat, " ' it would be very difficult to destroy at once in the minds of Spaniards the hope of some day regaining Spanish America. The recollection of the immense riches which they have drawn from there during several centuries will always prevent them from voluntarily renouncing those possessions.' " [26] Four days later Talaru declared that, even if Spaniards should find a minister clear-sighted enough to realize that their colonies were lost and that Spain could only try to secure a species of compensation by an acknowledgment of their independence, he doubted whether such a minister would be courageous enough to sign a formal act of separation.[27] Early in 1824, after Chateaubriand had instructed the French ambassador to urge upon the Court of Madrid the dispatch of an infante to Mexico, Ferdinand VII made

[25] *Ibid.* [26] *Ibid.* [27] *Ibid.*

known his unshaken opposition to the establishment of Spanish appanages in America. He maintained that such a step would virtually constitute an acknowledgment of Spanish-American autonomy.[28] It accordingly became clear to French statesmen that no proposition which even squinted at the independence of the insurgent colonies would be seriously considered by the Spanish King.

In the autumn of 1823 the English Foreign Office became a storm center in Latin-American affairs. Prince Polignac, a conservative publicist who occasionally followed his own impulses in diplomacy, had become the French ambassador in London. Rumors concerning promises of French aid to Spain in the Indies and statements in the *Journal des Débats* about the founding of a Bourbon principality in Mexico had made Canning anxious to learn the real intentions of France.[29]

During an interview on October 1, 1823, Canning asked Polignac some pointed questions concerning the purpose of French foreign policy. Among these was an inquiry about the intentions of France with regard to the Spanish Indies in case of her success in Spain. Canning seemed alarmed at a rumor that a French fleet from the Antilles was approaching Spanish America with hostile intent. In asking for instructions to guide him in this matter, Polignac took the view that the apprehensions of Canning sprang from a belief that the government of Ferdinand VII would induce France to terminate in its name the insurrection which was raging in the Spanish colonies. From this conference Polignac drew the conclusion that England would not op-

[28] Chateaubriand to Talaru, January 3, 1824, *ibid.*, 726; Villanueva, *La monarquía en América; la Santa Alianza*, pp. 73-74.
[29] Temperley, *Life of Canning*, pp. 105-09.

pose amicable intervention in Spanish America by France acting in concert with herself.[30]

A few days later, Chateaubriand sent fresh instructions to Polignac. The Foreign Minister asserted that his government had not intervened in Spain either to satisfy its ambition or to influence the fortunes of Ferdinand VII. Emphatically he disclaimed for France any designs upon the Spanish colonies: "It is so far from true that our fleet threatens those colonies, that we have recalled, the *Jean Bart,* the only ship of the line that we had in the waters of the Antilles." Although France wished to gain no special advantage in the Spanish Indies herself, she would consider it her duty to oppose the acquisition of such an advantage by another nation. Chateaubriand reasoned that Frenchmen could not, at the very time when they were removing the odious yoke which had been forced upon King Ferdinand by rebellious Spaniards, think of placing upon his neck another yoke formed by them in conjunction with revolutionary colonists. As soon as that monarch was free to act, France was ready to discuss the moot question; her wishes and her interests in that matter, he added, were similar to those of England. He desired to learn whether Canning proposed to pursue the same policy with respect to Portuguese America as that which he wished to follow with regard to Spanish America.[31] In a letter to Polignac on October 6 Chateaubriand expressed his opposition to any agreement with England to deprive Spain of her colonial possessions at a time when French soldiers were

[30] Polignac to Chateaubriand, October 1, 1823, A. A. E., Angleterre, 617.

[31] Chateaubriand, *Correspondance général,* V, 28-30.

fighting for the liberation of Ferdinand VII. France would not assume such a Machiavellian rôle.[32]

Meanwhile Canning was so suspicious of French designs that he contemplated sending a confidential note to Polignac to warn him that Britain was determined not to allow France to use force against the Spanish colonies. At Wellington's suggestion and by choice of Polignac, however, the English minister decided to express his views in an interview with that prince. Of the interchange of views that took place there are two accounts: one, the paper prepared by Canning which he induced the French ambassador to sign in the form of the so-called "Polignac Memorandum"; and the other, a dispatch of Polignac to Chateaubriand from London, dated October 10, 1823. Here we are primarily concerned with Polignac's avowals concerning the policy of France toward Spanish America.

In the Polignac Memorandum, the prince was recorded as stating that France believed that any attempt to reduce the Indies to its former dependence on Spain would be "utterly hopeless." He was quoted as disavowing an intention on the part of his government to appropriate any portion of Spanish America or to secure "any exclusive advantages." The ambassador evidently declared that France disclaimed any design of acting against the Spanish-American colonies "by force of arms"; like England, she was willing to see the motherland enjoy special commercial advantages in Spanish America. He further stated that France wished to postpone negotiations concerning the Spanish colonies until Ferdinand VII was set free. After this event took place she would discuss that problem with England and her allies.

[32] *Ibid.*, 32.

Because of the distracted condition of the insurgent communities, Polignac argued that the acknowledgment of their independence would be " nothing less than a real sanction of anarchy." Accordingly it would be worthy of European governments to concert a means of soothing party passions and of unifying views with regard to the system of government to be adopted in the insurgent colonies.[33]

On October 10 the French ambassador declared that Chateaubriand's views concerning the Indies agreed perfectly with his own. In his account of the conferences with Canning, the prince stressed more than did the English minister in the Polignac Memorandum the intention of France not to intervene in Spanish America. Polignac reported himself as repeating Chateaubriand's instructions in saying " that the noble disinterestedness which France had manifested in the affairs of Spain would furnish an index to the conduct which she would later follow in regard to the Spanish colonies, against which she would not claim the right to act with armed force in any way." He further reasoned that the purity of the intentions of France and " her entire abnegation in this grave question gave her the right and imposed upon her the obligation of opposing all enterprises on the part of other governments which

[33] Temperley, *The Foreign Policy of Canning,* pp. 115-17. An official French version of the Polignac Memorandum is found in A. A. E., Mémoires et Documents, Amérique, 35. The memorandum was published in French in 1824. See Lesur, *Annuaire historique* for that year, pp. 655-57. Extracts from an English text of the memorandum were published in *Communications with France and Spain relating to the Spanish-American Provinces presented to both Houses of Parliament by Command of His Majesty, March, 1824.* The suppressed parts of the English version of the memorandum are to be found in Ward and Gooch, *The Cambridge History of British Foreign Policy,* II, 633-37.

would have as an object to obtain an advantage that she believed both her duty and her dignity required her to oppose." Polignac thought Canning far from reaching a decision to treat the problem of the Spanish colonies in conjunction with the Continental powers.

Another moot issue mentioned in the Polignac Memorandum, the attitude of France toward Brazil, will also be clarified by a quotation from the ambassador's report to Chateaubriand. "I added finally," said Polignac, "that in the interest of humanity, and more particularly in the interest of the Spanish and the Portuguese colonies, it would be worthy of the European governments to strive to calm irritated passions, to regulate misguided spirits, and to direct toward a principle of unity in matters of government those people among whom the spread of absurd theories has encouraged trouble and discord." [34]

Upon receipt from Canning of his account of the conferences, Polignac seems to have felt that a slight misunderstanding had arisen with respect to their nature. He wrote to Canning to repeat what he claimed to have stated during the meetings—that the memorandum could be considered only as "an aid afforded to the memory of Mr. Canning in order that he might recall the substance of two conversations which they had held and not as a document clothed with an official character." [35] In his reply Canning reminded Polignac that before the conferences he had a communication to make to the French Government con-

[34] Polignac to Chateaubriand, October 10, 1823, A. A. E., Angleterre, 617. Polignac's copy of the memorandum, made on October 21, 1823, is in *ibid.*

[35] Webster, *Britain and the Independence of Latin America,* II, 121.

cerning Spanish America which had to be made in some
form or other. Canning declared that as possible modes
of procedure he had suggested that he might simply address an official note to Polignac, that he might authorize
Stuart officially to communicate his views to Chateaubriand,
or that he and Polignac might meet in conference and
afterwards place on record the substance of what happened
in that conference, authenticated in the usual way. The
English diplomat stated that Polignac had preferred the
last of the three modes, and that the memorandum was the
fruit of the resulting conferences.[36] In conclusion, Canning
offered to reconsider any part of the memorandum which
Polignac considered inaccurate.

After a further exchange of notes between the two diplomats, slight alterations in the language of the document
were adopted in order to still Polignac's qualms. On November 9 Canning sent to Stuart " an amended copy of the
Memorandum of the Conference . . . such as the Prince
de Polignac has finally consented to certify as authentick,
and to transmit as an official document to his Court." [37]

When Villèle and Stuart undertook to compare the two
versions of the memorandum which transformed a frank
exchange of views into a state document, the French minister
seemed disturbed because they contained a declaration to
the effect that the acknowledgment of Spanish-American
independence by England was not dependent upon recognition by Spain. Yet Villèle declared to Stuart that many
advantages flowed from " the mutual understanding established by the Memorandum, since, by giving a full and free

[36] Canning to Polignac, October 19, 1823 (copy), *ibid.*
[37] Webster, *op. cit.,* II, 125.

explanation of the views of both Courts, and by showing the lengths " to which the English Government was determined to go, a guide was furnished for the conduct of the French Cabinet on this important issue. Villèle further informed the English ambassador that he had recently ascertained that the views of the Allies concerning the Spanish Indies more closely resembled those of France and Great Britain than he had had reason to suppose. However, the French statesman maintained that because of political reasons it would be inexpedient to admit a delegate from the United States to a European conference on Spanish-American affairs.

Stuart accordingly reported to Canning that Villèle had acknowledged by his citations that the Polignac Memorandum was an official document in which the views of the two courts had been " recorded by mutual consent." [38] Chateaubriand was scarcely as well satisfied with this memorandum as Villèle. In a dispatch to Talaru the Foreign Minister declared that nothing which Polignac had said should wound Spain or any other European nation. Nevertheless, Chateaubriand asserted that as the memorandum had been penned by Canning its language was perhaps neither as frank nor as clear as the words of Polignac.[39]

Meanwhile, on October 15, Chateaubriand had instructed Talaru to urge the King to retrace the steps which had been taken by the Liberal government with respect to the acknowledgment of the independence of certain insurgent

[38] *Ibid.*, 124. On November 15, 1823, Stuart stated that he had given Chateaubriand a copy of the amended Polignac Memorandum which the latter had been willing to recognize " as an official document in its former shape." *Ibid.*, 127.

[39] November 27, 1823, A. A. E., Espagne, 724.

colonies, such as La Plata. He declared that otherwise those colonies might be thrown into the arms of England.[40] Fifteen days later, after mentioning the disinclination of King Ferdinand to grant concessions to Spanish-American revolutionists, Chateaubriand directed Talaru to find out what kind of succor that monarch expected to receive for the reconquest of his American dominions:

> Without doubt Ferdinand VII believes that only France will furnish him with money, soldiers, and ships for such an enterprise. In truth, the new rulers of those colonies are not seated upon solid bases; they will for a long time be the playthings of revolutions. Yet are not the people very averse to placing themselves again under the yoke of the motherland? What can they hope or fear from a government so feeble, so uncertain, and so easily disturbed? The King of Spain cannot be ignorant of the fact that commercial nations are not disposed to postpone establishing political and mercantile intercourse with the new states which he cannot subjugate. In this important matter France herself has never renounced the right to consult the interests of her commerce.[41]

Scarcely had Chateaubriand been informed of the Polignac Memorandum than he sent word of it to the Allies. He seems to have mentioned to the Duke of San Carlos, who had recently been appointed Spanish ambassador to France, his hope that in a conference at Paris the Allies would decide to aid Ferdinand VII to sustain his rights over the American colonies as far as possible. Chateaubriand further assured San Carlos that France would use all her influence to induce the Allies to join her in order to support Spain in the most efficient manner. San Carlos

---

[40] Chateaubriand, *Congrès de Vérone,* II, 273-74.
[41] A. A. E., Espagne, 724.

transmitted to Madrid an intimation that, if commercial concessions were made to European nations trading with Spanish America, its affairs could be more easily adjusted.[42]

On November 1, 1823, Chateaubriand expounded his ideas concerning the insurgent colonies in a dispatch sent to the French envoys at Berlin, Vienna, and St. Petersburg. He stated that it had always been the intention of his government to consider the issue of Spanish-American independence in common with the cabinets of Austria, Prussia, and Russia, as well as with the Cabinet of Spain, but that the precipitate action of England had put a new face on the affair. Hence he directed each of those envoys to request the court at which he resided " to send to its ambassador at Paris the authority to treat concerning the problem of the Spanish colonies in a conference with the French Government and the ambassador of Spain."

Chateaubriand believed that the proposed conference should consider four questions: (1) If England should acknowledge the independence of the Spanish colonies without the consent of Ferdinand VII, would any of the allied governments also recognize those colonies? (2) Had any nation determined to make common cause with France if she felt obliged to take the part of Spain in refusing to acknowledge the independence of those colonies recognized by England? (3) Would any state that did not possess a colony leave the Spanish colonial problem entirely to France and England for adjustment? (4) If Spain refused to make an arrangement with her colonies, and if she claimed rights over them without any means of establishing her authority, would a particular government judge that it was free to

[42] San Carlos to Saez, November 1, 1823, A. G. I., Estado, 90.

act toward the Spanish colonies as its interests dictated? [43]
A note scrawled on the margin of this circular queried
whether in the contingency mentioned in the second question the respective government would unite its forces with
those of Spain in order to oppose the recognition by
England of the independence of Spanish America.[44]

On the same day Chateaubriand transmitted a copy of
this circular note to Talaru. Besides, the minister directed
the ambassador to inform Saez that the policy of England
toward the insurgent colonies compelled France to assume
a position. He suggested four possible modes of action by
the Spanish Government: to recognize the independence
of the colonies on certain conditions; to dispatch commissioners to deal with independent Spanish-American governments; to send to the Indies infantes accompanied by
soldiers in order to establish there monarchies linked to
the mother country by bonds of interest and love; or to
acknowledge its inability to conquer the insurgents and
allow European nations to act as they should judge best.
A hint was conveyed that, if none of these solutions was
agreeable to Spain, France might herself be compelled by
the need of protecting her commerce to make a decision in

[43] Chateaubriand, *Congrès de Vérone,* II, 307-08; "Copie d'une
dépêche de M.ᵣ le V.ᵗᵉ de Chateaubriand à M.ᵣ le Marquis de
Caraman," November 3, 1823, enclosure in Metternich to Vincent,
November 26, 1823, H. H. u. S., Weisungen nach Frankreich, 355.

[44] Villanueva, *La monarquía en América; Fernando VII y los
nuevos estados,* pp. 192-93. On January 17, 1824, Galabert sent
from Madrid to Paris a paper entitled "État des forces de Terre
et de Mer que le Gouvernement Britannique a echelonnées et dis-
posées en Europe et en Amérique pour operer l'Independance et
s'assurer la possession exclusive du commerce et des productions
de l'Amérique Espagnole." A. A. E., Mémoires et Documents,
Amérique, 35.

regard to Spanish-American independence. In a postscript Chateaubriand added that Talaru was to induce Spain to ask that the Allies mediate in her struggle with the colonists.[45]

In a dispatch of the same date to La Ferronnays the minister explained how another solution might be reached concerning the status of the insurgent Spanish colonies:

Could not this great question be treated in a European congress to which the King of Spain would be invited? There that monarch, in the midst of his peers, might receive useful instructions and might learn by counsel and by example how to govern his dominions. This is my idea. I mention it to you with diffidence, not having thoroughly examined the subject.[46]

Thus a European congress including Ferdinand VII, like that which Montmorency had contemplated in 1822, was Chateaubriand's favorite plan in November, 1823, for a solution of the vexatious colonial problem. Not altogether disassociated from this scheme, it would seem, was the old design of transplanting the Bourbon monarchical system to the Indies. During the same month of November Chateaubriand decided to send new commissioners to Mexico and Colombia and also to reënforce French garrisons at Guadeloupe and Martinique.[47] Louis XVIII, as

[45] Villanueva, *op. cit.*, pp. 196-97. On November 1, 1823, San Carlos informed Saez of a conference with Chateaubriand: " Segun se me ha explicado, . . . la Francia hará todos sus refuerzos para que las demas potencias . . . se reuna á ella para sostenernos del modo mas eficaz." A. G. I., Estado, 90.

[46] Chateaubriand, *Congrès de Vérone*, II, 299.

[47] *Idem, Correspondance générale*, V, 74. On October 14, 1823, Ambassador Vincent informed Metternich of a conversation with Louis XVIII concerning Spanish affairs in which the King expressed himself in favor of a conference at Paris to consider inter-

well as the minister, hoped to induce Spain to accept the
mediation of the Alliance in order to adjust her relations
with the revolted colonies.   However, as will be shown
later, Chateaubriand did not rightly forecast Canning's attitude.   Chateaubriand gave Stuart an interesting exposition
of his government's views concerning the Spanish colonial
problem.   In recapitulating statements which he had made
during one of their conferences, Chateaubriand said that
French ministers had declared their intention not to accept
any territorial advantages in America.   He attributed to
them further the statement " that they will certainly observe
a strict neutrality in the quarrel between Spain and her
Colonies and that, upon this principle they will neither
grant the assistance of French troops to bring about the
submission of those Colonies to the Mother Country, nor
will they furnish French vessels to convey the Spanish
troops destined to be employed in that service."   He explained that France would advise Spain to acknowledge
Spanish-American independence in an advantageous manner, and that representatives of European courts should
deliberate concerning this object; but that, if Spain should
persist in her intention to recover her American colonies by
force of arms, the members of the congress would feel
free to act as they saw fit.   To one aspect of the proposed
congress Chateaubriand did not allude, namely the re-
straining influence which he assumed it would have upon
England's policy toward the insurgent communities.[48]

The *Constitutionnel* analyzed the problem of the Spanish

---

vention by the Allies in the Spanish colonies. H. H. u. S., Berichte
aus Frankreich, 353.

[48] Webster, *Britain and the Independence of Latin America*, II,
129.

colonies in a suggestive fashion on November 19, 1823. It declared that England wished to exploit their independence, that Spain wished to draw subsidies from them, and that France wished to gain advantages which would compensate her for the expense of her war in Spain. It declared that the European Continent could choose between two solutions of this tantalizing problem: either suddenly to attack the Spanish colonies, or immediately to acknowledge their independence. The journal then avowed that " to subjugate Spanish America by force and in spite of the English is impossible." On the other hand, " to recognize it is a mortal sin that the Holy Alliance would never commit." The conclusion was pessimistic: " The Continent will therefore engage in useless proposals for an adjustment and will lose in fruitless parleys the time that England will employ in useful negotiations."

On November 1, 1823, Villèle directed Polignac to inquire whether Canning expected to apply to Brazil the same principle which he intended to follow in regard to the Spanish colonies. The head of the Cabinet asserted that the relations of France with that country were more useful than those which she could establish with the Spanish Indies. Further, he maintained that, in contrast with the republican systems which were being established in Spanish America, the monarchical form of her government should bind Brazil closely to France. Such considerations induced French statesmen " to desire that the recognition of the independence of the Spanish colonies should be the result of the mediation of the Holy Alliance between the motherland and her colonies and that their emancipation should take place on the condition of the establishment overseas of Spanish princes whose position should resemble

that of the Prince of Portugal in Brazil." Villèle concluded that the commercial advantages which European
nations could draw from this independence would be more
fruitful if those countries were tranquil than if they were
harassed by civil war for an indefinite period.[49]   The
French Premier had thus become an advocate of the erection of European principalities throughout Latin America.

The unflinching opposition of England to intervention
by force in the Spanish Indies was made known by Chateaubriand to French legations on the Continent.   Canning
read the Polignac Memorandum to the ministers of Austria, Prussia, and Russia.   A copy of it was furnished to the
American minister at London.[50]   In time its substance became known even in certain sections of South America.[51]
Notwithstanding this fact, Ferdinand VII and his ministers
persisted in their design to subjugate the rebellious colonists.   Early in November, 1823, the English envoy to
Madrid wrote to Canning as follows:

The Government Gazette teems with Articles all indicating the firm resolution of attempting the recovery of the
lost Colonies.   If France be determined to act up to the
language held by Prince de Polignac in his conversation
with you, Sir, I cannot imagine [upon] what grounds any
hopes of success can be founded." [52]

Upon making known to Saez the tenor of the Polignac
Memorandum and its bearing upon European policy, Talaru

[49] Villèle, *Mémoires et correspondance,* IV, 489.
[50] San Carlos to Saez, November 1, 1823, A. G. I., Estado, 90.
Bagehot, *George Canning and His Friends,* II, 208-09; Rush, *Residence,* II, 65 n.
[51] Temperley, " French Designs on Spanish America in 1820-5,"
Eng. Hist. Rev., XL, 46.
[52] À Court to Canning, November 8, 1823, F. O., 72/273.

convinced the Spanish minister that the hope which the latter had fondly cherished that European powers would intervene in Spanish America was perhaps unfounded. Saez was much irritated at the evident intention of England to acknowledge Spanish-American independence. Loath to relinquish the hope of reconquest, he reluctantly reached the conclusion that perhaps the most feasible solution of Spain's colonial problem was to be found, as Talaru had suggested, in a European congress.[53]

Yet there were scheming individuals who did not despair of restoring the authority of Ferdinand VII on the American Continent. On November 15, 1823, a French official named Guillemin, who had resided for some years in the Spanish Indies, addressed a note to Chateaubriand. This official maintained that in order to conquer New Spain Ferdinand VII needed the aid of a strong maritime nation. Guillemin reasoned that this task naturally devolved upon France, who had delivered Old Spain from factious hands. In conjunction with her allies France should proceed in Mexico according to the same principle of legitimacy which she had pursued in Spain. She should move toward a similar end, namely that of reëstablishing the authority of the legitimate sovereign over a portion of his dominions which had been torn from him by revolutionists. Such a policy could be defended successfully against the English Government because it was in harmony with the principles for which that government had contended for a quarter of a century. Guillemin argued that France under the Bourbons had become strong enough to maintain those principles by force of arms. Still, he warned Chateaubriand that if

[53] Talaru to Chateaubriand, November 13, 1823, A. A. E., Espagne, 724.

France engaged in so delicate a project as intervention in Mexico she would need to proceed circumspectly.[54]   This champion of interposition forgot, however, to estimate the strength of the armament which would be necessary to restore the authority of Ferdinand VII in Mexico.

Shortly afterward Gregor McGregor, a soldier of fortune who had fought under Miranda in Venezuela, laid an intriguing proposition before Chateaubriand. McGregor reasoned that Spain could never subjugate her American colonies. Accordingly he proposed that, on the one hand, she refrain from all acts of hostility toward the insurgents. Instead she should carve Spanish America into four principalities and give them princes of the Bourbon dynasty as rulers. Spain should also undertake to promote the formation in the projected kingdoms of strong parties in favor of those princes, so that upon arrival at their respective capitals they would be received with acclamation. Nevertheless, each of those personages ought to be furnished with a bodyguard as well as with a squadron of warships. In the household of each of the sovereigns there should be placed natives of the Indies who were known to be strongly attached to monarchical principles. Military and naval officers of the existing revolutionary governments should be confirmed in their respective positions. Titles and honors ought to be liberally distributed. Not only should the clergy be treated with marked consideration, but new benefices should be created in Spanish America. Commerce with the new kingdoms should be placed upon a basis of equality for all nations.

McGregor further suggested that it might be wise for

[54] November 15, 1823, A. A. E., Mexique, 2.

His Catholic Majesty to assume the title of " Emperor of the Indies " or " Sovereign Protector of the Indies." By such measures, he concluded, Spain might be able to retain the title to that vast domain. She might also be able to relieve herself of financial embarrassments; for a stipulation could be made that for a term of years the ruling princes should pay an annual subsidy to the Spanish crown. On this variation of the old proposal to establish Bourbon monarchies in the Spanish Indies, a discerning official in the Ministry of Foreign Affairs inscribed the following comment: " The plan is certainly very good, but its execution is difficult." [55]

Early in the next year, when Talaru made fresh representations to the Spanish Government in favor of the founding of Bourbon monarchies in America, he found that circumstances were not auspicious. The controversy which had broken out between John VI and his son Pedro I with regard to their respective authority over Brazil had convinced Ferdinand VII that the dispatch to Spanish America of princes who were his relatives, " and hence less dependent than a son, would be equivalent to as formal a declaration of independence as one might dread." [56]

It was at this critical time, when France was being urged to intervene on one side or another of the struggle in Spanish America, that Talaru and Saez held conferences concerning the insurgent colonists. By November 17 these diplomats had progressed so far that a circular note from Spain to the European Allies was being prepared in the Spanish Chancellery. Talaru described this note to Chateau-

[55] November 25, 1823, A. A. E., Mémoires et Documents, Amérique, 35.
[56] Talaru to Chateaubriand, January 11, 1824, A. A. E., Espagne, 726.

briand as follows: it will declare that Ferdinand VII,
" being restored to the plenitude of his power, after having
turned his attention to the interests of his European subjects, wishes now to promote peace and happiness in his
American colonies; that, in order to attain this end, he
hopes that the Allied Powers, who have so nobly concurred
in the establishment of order in Spain, will also contribute
to the restoration of tranquillity in America; and that Spain
invokes their mediation in order to adjust the differences
existing between herself and her colonies." [57]

Two days later, Talaru assured Chateaubriand that a
memorandum concerning the proposed circular note which
that minister had transmitted to him had been carefully
considered in his conferences with the Spanish Secretary of
State. The ambassador added that he had insisted with
Saez that the demand for mediation should appear to come
from the Spaniards and should be based upon the fact that,
" as France and the Allied Powers had contributed to the
restoration of European Spain, Ferdinand VII also solicited
their good offices and mediation to arrange the affairs of
America." [58] Upon becoming acquainted with a draft of
this circular, Chateaubriand protested that the copy intended for the Continental allies was not couched in precisely the same terms as the version intended for the Court
of London.[59] The procedure followed in the framing of
this note makes plain that, although the French Government exerted considerable influence in its preparation, that
government was anxious to convey the impression that the
pronunciamento had emanated entirely from the Court of
Madrid.

[57] *Ibid.*, 724.   [58] *Ibid.*
[59] Chateaubriand to Talaru, December 11, 1823, *ibid.*

However, the wishes of the French Government with regard to the terms of the circular were not strictly followed. Its content, if not its exact tenor, is undoubtedly found in a note dated November 29, 1823, intended by Secretary Saez for the Spanish ambassadors at Paris, Vienna, and St. Petersburg, a copy of which is still preserved in the Archivo General de Indias. Ambassador San Carlos was directed to transmit this letter to the French Ministry of Foreign Affairs. After a detailed analysis of the conditions prevailing in Spanish America Saez mentioned the unyielding attitude of Ferdinand VII, who wished a conference of European nations to be summoned to consider the issue of the insurgent colonies. Expressing the King's belief that those colonies could undoubtedly be pacified if the Royalist soldiers there were aided by the forces which the Allies could employ to support the cause of order and legitimacy, Saez concluded with the following exhortation:

His Majesty, who has seen with the utmost gratitude the forces of the sovereigns united in the Holy Alliance—to which he is proud to belong—employed to preserve the principles of legitimacy in Europe, cannot avoid hoping that they will equally contribute to the same worthy object in those vast regions and conserve in them his sovereignty. The noble and generous sentiments which animated those monarchs inspire the greatest confidence in the King, our Master. At the same time he flatters himself that such illustrious princes cannot fail to realize that the prolongation of the condition of affairs existing in Spanish America is bound to produce fatal results in Europe; for it will perpetuate the spirit of revolution and will steadily undermine the most conservative elements in the social structure.[60]

[60] A. G. I., Estado 90. On December 1, 1823, Saez enclosed a copy of this circular with a dispatch to the Spanish ambassadors at Paris, Vienna, and St. Petersburg. *Ibid.*

The phraseology of this note almost justified the view of the English ambassador at Paris, who declared that the Spanish minister solicited " the assistance of the several allied Governments in Troops, Ships, and Money, to enable the King of Spain to recover his sovereignty over the States in South America, who have thrown off the yoke of the Mother Country." [61]   The purpose of the proposed circular was unmistakable. Spain's Chancellery wished to appeal to the Holy Alliance to restore her authority over the rebellious colonies in America by force of arms.

There is little doubt that Saez viewed France and Russia as constituting the forefront of the Holy Allies. Though it is clear that at this time the French Minister of Foreign Affairs cherished the hope that the Czar would aid him to create Bourbon monarchies in the New World, yet, upon receiving a copy of Saez's circular, Chateaubriand sent to Ambassador Talaru a dispatch stating that France disapproved of it, that she could not risk a war with England to sustain in principle the pretensions of Spain, that such a war would afford the Spanish colonies the safest means of consolidating their independence, and that, as the commercial nations of Europe would support England, Spain would lose everything.[62] The ambassador had in the meantime returned the proposed communication to Saez and had informed him that the use of force to restore Spain's authority over her colonies was incompatible with the pacific nature of the proposed mediation. Ambassador Pozzo di Borgo, who was supervising Russian legations in Western Europe and had been sent by the Czar on a special mission from

[61] Stuart to Canning, December 4, 1823 (no. 629), F. O., 27/297; see further Barante, *Souvenirs*, III, 155.

[62] *Idem, Correspondance générale*, V, 96.

Paris to Madrid, also disapproved of the circular and declined to transmit it by his courier to San Carlos.[63]

On December 11, 1823, in a dispatch to Talaru, Chateaubriand explained the rôle which he conceived France should
play in world politics. Asserting that he stood at the center
of the international circle, the minister declared: " I see all
the radii and the divers parts of the circumference. Our
true policy is to act with Russia—a policy by which we can
set off against each other two inveterate enemies, Austria
and England. If Russia wishes to become too prepon-
derant, a slight inclination on our part toward England
will soon readjust the balance." [64]   In fact, there is no evidence to prove that France and Russia—both of whom took
a deep interest in the fortunes of the insurgent colonies—
ever reached an agreement to engage in armed intervention
in the New World.

Among the papers which touch upon the moot issue of
French intervention in the Spanish colonies, the most emphatic and interpretative statement by the French Ministry
of Foreign Affairs is found in a dispatch dated March 31,
1824. After declaring that his insistence upon England's
participation in the proposed mediation was due to a desire
to check Canning's intention of acknowledging the independence of Spanish America, Chateaubriand instructed
Talaru to explain the reluctant attitude of France to Ofalia
as follows:

[63] Talaru to Chateaubriand, December 5, 1823, A. A. E., Espagne,
724. See also Villanueva, *La monarquía en América; Fernando
VII y los nuevos estados,* pp. 198-200, 205; Nesselrode to Bulgari,
January 9, 1824, A. R. V. P., Madrid, 1824, no. 9027.

[64] Chateaubriand, *Congrès de Vérone,* II, 322.

The Alliance insists upon special conferences regarding the colonies. We have embarrassed it by inquiring specifically whether we would be supported by the Allies in case a rupture with England should be the outcome of those conferences. You are aware that neither Austria nor Russia wishes to take up arms or to close their ports to the English, and that Russia would consider the matter very carefully if it should actually be necessary to unsheath the sword. It is easy to declaim, to enunciate legitimist principles, and to formulate theories in a conference, but when it is a matter of equipping vessels and of spending two hundred millions, as we did, in order to send one hundred thousand soldiers into action, very little ardor is displayed. It is obvious that, after we had been compelled to adopt extreme measures, the Allies would leave us alone on the field of battle, and we would lose our treasure, our fleets, and our colonies without any recourse.[65]

By this time the United States had unwittingly furnished conservative European statesmen with another argument against admitting her into the proposed conference on Spanish-American affairs. In the words of the American minister at Paris, President Monroe's message to Congress on December 2, 1823, surprised many Frenchmen. The Liberals " seized upon it with avidity; the 'royalists' treated it as an effusion of personal sentiment which would not necessarily direct the policy of the United States; the 'fanatics' viewed it with resentment." [66] The ministers of Louis XVIII read the message with much interest. Neither the principle of non-colonization nor the principle of non-intervention by European nations in America pleased Chateaubriand. He at once suggested to Stuart that a joint

[65] A. A. E., Espagne, 724. For less emphatic statements of Chateaubriand's attitude, see his *Congrès de Vérone,* II, 328; *Correspondance générale,* V, 74-75, 88.

[66] Monroe, *Writings,* VI, 432.

representation be made to the United States by England and France against " the prohibition of future colonization on the Continents of America." [67]

A few days later, the French minister even intimated to Stuart that the resemblance of the language of Monroe's message to the communications between the English Government and Prince Polignac regarding the affairs of the colonies " almost justified in his mind the supposition that these doctrines were now set forth for the first time by the President, in virtue of an understanding " between the English and the American governments. Furthermore, Chateaubriand thought that this declaration of the principles which President Monroe undertook to pronounce for the New World should be resisted by all the nations possessing interests in that hemisphere, " and more especially by Great Britain and France, inasmuch as it strikes at the principle of Mediation brought forward by them both, by peremptorily deciding the question of South American Independence " without listening to the concessions which either of the contending parties might be willing to make.[68]   In a letter to Polignac on January 4, 1824, the minister declared that the establishment in the Spanish Indies of limited monarchies attached to the motherland would be a happy outcome for both France and England. Chateaubriand thought that Canning was no more interested than he in favoring armed rebellions, popular sovereignty, and other condi-

[67] Robertson, " The Monroe Doctrine Abroad in 1823-4," *American Political Science Review,* VI, 551. Cf. Temperley, " Documents illustrating the Reception and Interpretation of the Monroe Doctrine in Europe, 1823-4," *Eng. Hist. Rev.,* XXXIX, 591.

[68] Webster, *Britain and the Independence of Latin America,* II, 131.

tions mentioned by Monroe as traits of *de facto* governments.[69]

Chateaubriand wrote to the French ambassador in St.
Petersburg that the trenchant language and the bold decisions in Monroe's message could be explained only
by either of two hypotheses: that the United States hoped
by such declarations to secure the support of England, or
that the message was inspired by the latter nation.[70] Still,
upon learning of a dispatch from Canning to Stuart which
aimed to remove the suspicion that had been aroused in the
minds of French ministers by the resemblance they had
noticed between the language of Monroe's message and
that of the Polignac Memorandum, Chateaubriand did not
hesitate to admit that this dispatch was a conclusive answer
to the reflections in which he had indulged upon first hearing of the Monroe Doctrine. The French minister added
that his remarks ought not to be considered beyond the
scope of private conversation since no proof of an agreement with England appeared on the face of the message.[71]

Leading journals of Paris furnished their readers with
various comments on the message of December 2. On
January 1 *L'Étoile* discussed the message under the rubric
" Mélanges Politiques." This journal maintained that there

[69] Chateaubriand, *Correspondance générale*, V, 114. In the postscript of a letter of January 12, 1825, to Polignac, Chateaubriand
informed the ambassador that Stuart, on behalf of Canning, had
disclaimed entertaining views identical with those announced by
President Monroe. *Ibid.*, 129-30.

[70] Chateaubriand to La Ferronnays. January 13, 1824, A. A. E.,
Russie, 166.

[71] Webster, *op. cit.*, II, 136. Cf. " A tribute of patriotic gratitude to the happy message of his old friend and companion in
arms " paid by Lafayette in Philadelphia in 1825. *Niles' Weekly
Register*, XXVIII, 340.

was no design in Europe to oppress the Spanish colonists but rather a desire to release them as their brothers in Spain had been released, from " the yoke of ambitious and greedy revolutionists." It strongly objected to the part of the message concerning the *de facto* governments and averred that such a doctrine would disturb the European political system. Three days later the journal severely criticized Monroe as having assumed the tone of a powerful monarch whose armies and fleets were " ready to move at the first signal," and it wrongly interpreted the message to mean that under Monroe's political system Ferdinand VII could not attempt to reconquer his colonial dominions. The *Times* promptly sprang to the defense of the original Monroe Doctrine and declared that the editors of *L'Étoile* were writhing " under the lash thus inflicted on the plots of their masters against human freedom." [72]

On January 2 an article in the *Constitutionnel,* which was perhaps written by the deputy Girardin, defended Monroe in brilliant fashion. This comment declared that in his message the wise President had traced the limits of the New World, had " put into practice all the principles which we proclaim," and had given an impression of " serenity and good will." The author reasoned further that, if European powers proposed to take up arms against an insurgent Latin-American colony, the neutrality of the United States would be at an end. The struggle would no longer be the contest of a colony with a mother country but would become the quarrel of a continent with a continent:

The United States would see her independence compromised; she could not remain a peaceable spectator of

[72] January 6, 1824.

such subversion of all rights. . . .   The anti-revolutionary system has traversed all Europe; it has broken down the Alps and the Pyrenees in the two peninsulas; it has touched the Columns of Hercules; and it now needs only to cross the ocean to accomplish the reconstruction of the past and to revoke all enfranchisements.   However, the freedmen are members of a nation, and they declare to Old Europe that she shall not cross the sea to replace the yoke of former domination.

Seven days later the *Journal des Débats* declared in a bantering tone that it was certain that no Continental power was dreaming of war.   The fleets of the United States might triumphantly plow the seas, where they would behold only friendly flags.[73]

Rumors concerning French intervention in Spain, however, caused a stir in certain parts of America.   In June, 1823, a special agent of the United States wrote from Bogotá to Washington that Vice-President Santander had expressed the fear that after the Holy Allies had regulated the affairs of Spain they would aid the motherland to subjugate Colombia, and that France would attack Cuba and Puerto Rico.[74]   On February 5, 1824, after reports reached Buenos Aires that French soldiers had overthrown the constitutional government of Spain and that an expedition was being prepared there against Spanish America, Bernardino Rivadavia, who was still serving as Minister of Foreign Relations for the province of Buenos Aires, addressed a circular to Spanish-American states.

This circular declared that, when the government of

---

[73] See further Robertson, "The Monroe Doctrine Abroad in 1823-4," *Am. Pol. Sci. Rev.*, VI, 553-56.

[74] Manning, *Diplomatic Correspondence of the United States concerning the Independence of the Latin-American Nations*, II, 1262.

Buenos Aires began " to perceive more clearly the manner in which the powers of the European Continent displayed their intention to interfere directly in the politics of America, it decided that the hour had come in which it should take action." That government accordingly began by making known its views not only to the provincial authorities of La Plata but also to independent Spanish-American states. Rivadavia urged that, upon the first warning from Cadiz that European powers would interfere with their progress, the nations of Spanish America should take every possible precaution against any foreign attack upon their liberty or independence.[75]

This significant manifesto to Spanish-American statesmen, exhorting them to act together in opposition to a European attack, has been said by a scholar belonging to the new school of history in Argentina to constitute the aegis of his country's independence.[76]   The truth, however, seems to be rather that the supposed menace of intervention by the Holy Allies provoked a spirited plea to sister republics from a distinguished founder of Argentine nationality. Rivadavia's appeal, which was made before news of the Monroe Doctrine reached Buenos Aires, can be regarded not only as an early expression of what may be styled Latin-Americanism but also as the first move by a statesman of Argentina to assert a hegemony for his nation in South America.

Rumors of French interposition in the Spanish Indies were prevalent in European diplomatic circles especially at

[75] *Correspondencias generales de la provincia de Buenos Aires relativas á relaciones exteriores*, pp. 437-38.

[76] Molinari, " Mito Canning y Doctrina Monroe," *Nosotros*, XVII, 94.

the time when French soldiers invaded Spain.   Instructions
sent out by the French Ministry of Marine to naval officers,
however, show that, in spite of its policy of intervention
in Spain, the French Government was anxious to maintain its neutrality in the struggle between the motherland
and her revolted colonies.   Though Chateaubriand evidently dreamed at times of furnishing armed assistance to
Ferdinand VII for the restoration of his authority over certain colonies, yet the chief mode of action which that minister contemplated was the creation of Bourbon monarchies in
Spanish America. It is evident that Chateaubriand was not
always in agreement with the head of the Cabinet.   In fact
the most ardent and persistent French advocate of armed
intervention in the Indies was Villèle, who proposed to
employ both men and money to ensure the firm establishment there of monarchical governments which would be
recognized by the Allies.   However, he realized with much
chagrin that his hands were tied.   On February 10, 1824,
he wrote to Polignac that it was impossible for France to
gain concessions for the Spanish colonies from the Court of
Madrid: "Spain is a dead body to which we are attached;
God grant that the dead may not injure the living." [77]

Ferdinand VII did not feel in the least inclined, however, to relinquish his intention of subjugating the Indies.
Chateaubriand believed that a solution for the vexatious
problem should be sought in a European congress which
might possibly furnish the Spanish King with armed forces
for the conquest of his refractory colonists. In the conferences between Canning and Polignac the French ambassador
gave a pledge that his government would not intervene in

[77] Villèle, *Mémoires et correspondance*, IV, 531.

Spanish America. Yet the reactions of French journalists and statesmen to Monroe's message of 1823 demonstrated that some of them disliked intensely the principle of non-intervention in America by European nations. The sequel will show that certain statesmen of France did not find it easy to dismiss from their minds the prospect of interference by force in the struggle between the Spanish monarchy and its colonists. A most significant reaction to the policy of French intervention in Spain was Rivadavia's circular, one of the earliest attempts by a Latin-American statesman to rally the new nations of America in defense of their common interests or ideals.

CHAPTER X

CHATEAUBRIAND'S CONSTRUCTIVE POLICY

Chateaubriand not only had important views with respect to French interference in Spanish America but also adopted an attitude which was pregnant with consequences with regard to the acknowledgment of Spanish-American independence by England, the reform of Spanish colonial policy, and the dispatch of French commissioners to the Indies. At times even those issues involved a consideration of intervention.

Chateaubriand did not readily relinquish the plan of holding a European congress, as outlined in his circular of November 1, 1823. On November 23 he wrote to Talaru and expressed his pleasure at the information that Ferdinand VII had decided to demand the mediation of the Great Powers in colonial affairs. Yet he advised the ambassador that, as England was still a member of the Grand Alliance, she must be invited to attend the meeting. He therefore instructed Talaru that the Spanish Government should be induced to direct its ambassador at London to urge that England send a delegate to the conference. If she did so France would be placed between England, which wished to sacrifice the rights of Spain, and the other powers, which perhaps anticipated in the conference only a discussion of principles. In a postscript written in his own sprawling handwriting, Chateaubriand explained his views concerning the proposed congress:

If England accepts the invitation to the conference, she will find herself involved in a negotiation which will prevent her, at least for some time, from declaring herself in favor of the colonies. If she does not accept, then she can have no reproach to make to Spain and the Continental powers, and she will be embarrassed in her rôle. It is probable that England will agree to take part in the conference with the reservation that she would not consent to any arrangement injurious to her interests. We should freely concede her that prerogative which we could not withhold, especially as we should not wish any more than she to submit to the decision which it might please Spain or the Allies of the Continent to make if our interests should be injured. Still, such an open negotiation offers us a thousand happy chances. The object for the entire world lies in inducing Great Britain to enter the congress or in forcing her to refuse to attend.[1]

In dispatches to the French envoys in Prussia and Russia, Chateaubriand supplemented this analysis. He described his plan to La Ferronnays in these words:

Our desire is that the plenipotentiaries accredited here should be authorized by their courts to attend the congress, and that so grave a problem as that of the Spanish colonies should be discussed in common. We hope thus to strengthen the bonds of the Alliance, to eliminate the chances of a rupture, and to create for Spain better means than she can have on hand of securing in the present state of affairs some advantage from those colonies. . . . In effect, without antagonizing the Court of Spain, we can let it do with its colonies what it judges suitable; and, without ourselves interfering in any of its quarrels beyond the sea, we can devote our efforts to the promotion of our commercial relations with Spanish America.[2]

Talaru's refusal to approve the draft of a circular inviting the Allies to a conference on Spanish-American affairs prompted the Spanish minister to frame another appeal,

[1] A. A. E., Espagne, 724.
[2] Chateaubriand to La Ferronnays and Rayneval, December 7, 1823, A. A. E., Russie, 165.

the terms of which still left it doubtful whether armed intervention was intended. Thereupon the ambassador referred the matter to his court, which evidently instructed him to return the second draft to Saez with a statement that the French Ministry could not entertain " any proposition implying the reëstablishment of the sovereignty of Spain over the colonies by force." [3]

Because of the obstacles encountered in formulating a plan for the mediation of the Allies in the struggle between Spain and her colonies, early in December, 1823, Chateaubriand sent word to Talaru of another possible solution of that issue. The minister now suggested that Ferdinand VII might at one stroke remove an obstacle to a prompt solution by a decree announcing that all nations would be permitted to trade freely with the colonies on the basis of complete equality. Chateaubriand declared that by such a measure Spain would not lose anything; for, though the commerce with her American colonies was not legally free, it was actually free. He reasoned that the step proposed would cause England to lose interest in the independence of the Spanish-American countries, because she wished merely to improve her commercial relations with them:

We should be placed in a position to reply to the industrial interests of our nation which accuse us of throwing the Spanish colonies into the arms of England. Europe would feel relieved to see an issue removed which threatens to produce trouble in the bosom of the Alliance and to kindle a war which would be at the same time both continental and maritime. Lastly, the Spanish colonies would regard this measure as a long step toward the amelioration of their fate and would favor a *rapprochement* with the mother country. . . .

[3] Stuart to Canning, December 8, 1823 (no. 629), F. O., 27/297.

In case the King of Spain should consent to issue such a decree, Marquis, you may announce that, on his part, the King, your Master, would consent by a special convention to prolong the sojourn of his soldiers in the Peninsula, and, further, that we should leave in our provinces adjacent to the Pyrenees a considerable body of troops which, in case of need, could reënforce those that we should leave in Spain.[4]

Early in December, insistent pressure from France and Russia induced Ferdinand VII to remove Saez from office and to replace him by the Marquis of Casa Yrujo.[5] That diplomat died soon afterwards. The King appointed as his successor Narcisco de Hereida, who had negotiated the Treaty of 1819 with the United States. He was known in diplomatic circles as Count Ofalia.

One of the new minister's first steps was taken in response to persistent representations of the French ambassador. On December 26, 1823, Ofalia transmitted through the Spanish envoys in France, Austria, Russia, and England a modified invitation to those nations to participate in a conference at Paris where they might aid Spain to adjust affairs in her revolted colonies. The Spanish minister declared that his Master wished to adopt measures which would reconcile the interests of other nations. Asserting that Ferdinand VII hoped that his dear and intimate allies would aid him to restore peace between Spain and her colonies by upholding the principles of order and legitimacy, the minister argued that, if these principles should be subverted in America, the revolutionary taint would be

[4] December 9, 1823, A. A. E., Espagne, 724.
[5] Nelson to Adams, December 18, 1823, D. S., Despatches from Spain, 22; "Papeles de Ugarte," *Boletín de la biblioteca de Menéndez Pelayo,* vol. XVI, no. 3, pp. 219-20.

transmitted to Europe. At the instance of Talaru, the appeal
to the Holy Alliance to restore the sovereignty of Ferdinand
VII over his insurgent colonies was omitted from this
circular.[6]

Chateaubriand soon assured Stuart in plausible words
that the Spanish ministers had promised that, after the
negotiations actually began, they would sanction the commercial intercourse which had developed between European
countries and Spanish South America; that Spain would
demand only an acknowledgment of her sovereignty by
those colonies which had not completely separated from
her; and that the independent status of other communities
would be recognized by Spain upon the payment of a mone-
tary indemnity.[7] The French minister's optimistic assurances with respect to Spain's colonial policy, however, must
have seemed to English diplomats like an attempt to obscure
the real issue.

In response to Ofalia's invitation, Secretary Canning
maintained that England did not need to participate in a
conference in order to make known her opinions about
the status of the Spanish colonies. Declaring that his
government could not delay much longer the recognition
of the Spanish-American nations, Canning intimated that
any mediation which was not based upon their independence
would be unsuccessful. He declared emphatically that armed
force should not be used against the colonies by any
mediatory power. After Canning's refusal to attend the

[6] *British and Foreign State Papers*, XI, 54-57. On the framing
of this circular, see Talaru to Chateaubriand, December 26, 1823,
A. A. E., Espagne, 724.

[7] Webster, *Britain and the Independence of Latin America*, II,
138.

conference the ambassadors of the Allies at Paris, in conjunction with Chateaubriand, decided at the instance of Emperor Alexander that England should again be invited to participate in a conference. But Canning refused the second invitation, which on April 20 was sent to À Court by Ofalia.[8] It appears that at this time the Spanish minister had no intention of seriously proposing an acknowledgment of the new states in an international conference, but merely contemplated conceding certain privileges to the Spanish Americans which would leave the sovereignty of Ferdinand VII intact.[9] In the face of English opposition to a conference, however, the hope that such an assemblage could adjust the relations between Spain and her insurgent colonies faded from the minds of Continental statesmen.

In January, 1824, Chateaubriand still hesitated to acknowledge the independence of the Spanish colonies. Writing to Polignac, he said that, although recognition might not provoke war between the two Bourbon powers, it might nevertheless contribute to the loss of a rich colonial empire by Spain. He seriously doubted whether the Spanish states in America were sufficiently tranquil to warrant recognition by France. He confessed that his country had paid by thirty years of bloody slavery for the independence of the United States, where conditions were radically different from those prevailing in the Spanish Indies. He took the view that certain colonies still acknowledged Spanish sovereignty, that others were yet being torn by the struggle between Loyalists and revolutionists, and that still others had completely separated from the mother country. Fearing that decades might elapse before the Spanish-American

[8] *British and Foreign State Papers,* XI, 59-62; XII, 958-62.
[9] Ofalia, *Escritos,* pp. 578-79.

countries became stable enough to negotiate and observe treaties, he asked whether the envoys of foreign nations to those countries would be furnished with " blank credentials which they will fill out at pleasure whenever one commander drives out another commander and whenever a military tyranny replaces a republic? " Yet he felt that even the passive opposition of Spain to the recognition of the Spanish-American republics would exert a malignant influence upon their fortunes. In sum, he maintained that England would not be justified in refusing to accede to a congress. Chateaubriand informed Polignac that Canning might have a copy of this dispatch. Though the English minister made no reply, he sent copies of it to the English ambassadors at Berlin, Vienna, and St. Petersburg and suggested to these envoys answers to its main arguments in case these views were put forth at the courts to which they were respectively accredited.[10]

Early in March, 1824, the French minister undertook to elucidate to Stuart his views concerning the effect of the military occupation of Spain by France upon her American policy. Insisting that the French Government had carefully refrained from taking advantage of the presence of its army in Spain to support her in the maintenance of her old colonial system, Chateaubriand declared that his views on the question of South America remained unchanged and were the same which had been clearly explained in his note to the allied cabinets at Verona.[11] Soon afterward, the Russian ambassador in Paris apparently received an

---

[10] Chateaubriand, *Correspondance générale*, V, 147-49; Canning, *Some Official Correspondence*, I, 136-38; Temperley, *The Foreign Policy of Canning, 1822-1827*, 543-54.

[11] Webster, *op. cit.*, II, 149.

avowal from Chateaubriand that France had decided not to acknowledge the independence of the Spanish colonies at that time.[12] On the other hand, Bolívar, in a remote hamlet in Peru, became apprehensive with respect to French designs. The Liberator occasionally feared that France might furnish the King of Spain maritime aid for the subjugation of the new nations of Middle and South America.[13]

The most illuminating statement of Chateaubriand's reasons for wishing a congress of European nations to consider the status of the Spanish colonies was made in the spring of 1824.   On March 29 the minister wrote to Ambassador Polignac that a motive of his refusal to take part in a congress if England was not represented was his belief that to assemble a conference composed solely of the four Continental allies would be to force Canning immediately to recognize the independence of the insurgent colonies. He confessed to Polignac, however, that the real reason for his refusal was a desire to prevent France from being compelled to give a pledge to the Allies that she would not acknowledge Spanish-American independence. Chateaubriand asked: " Can we recognize the independence of the Spanish colonies before England does so? No, we Bourbons, we, a legitimate monarchy, cannot set the example! " In the following passage the minister further explained his policy:

All that we can do is, as far as possible, to direct events. We have already accomplished a great deal. England has not recognized Spanish-American independence, and dissensions in the Americas will further delay her decision; we have had the courage to inform the Continental allies

[12] Temperley, " Canning and the Conferences of the Four Allied Governments at Paris, 1823-1826," *Am. Hist. Rev.*, XXX, 23.

[13] Bolívar, *Cartas del Libertador*, IV, 39.

that we cannot take sides with them in regard to the colonies; we invite Spain to negotiate; we are about to send a consul to Habana, consuls to Puerto Rico, and consular agents wherever we can. This is all that our present position permits. We shall go farther as rapidly as the progress of events will allow. Meanwhile you can no longer complain of being kept in the dark. You know all our secrets.[14]

A distinctive feature of Chateaubriand's policy was his desire to improve the commercial relations of France with the Indies. By December, 1823, he had decided that Spain ought to modify her policy in regard to commerce with her colonies. He reached this decision partly because he wished to place French intercourse with Latin America upon a better footing, and partly because he wished to check English aspirations. His justification was that during the struggles for independence in Spanish America the restrictive laws of Spain had been waived with respect to English trade. In a letter to Talaru in December, 1823, Chateaubriand urged that Spain establish free trade between the Indies and European nations. However, after presenting this view to Ofalia, Talaru learned that the majority of the Spanish Council of State felt that the regulations concerning commerce with the Indies should not be modified before the conference of the powers assembled, for such a concession might then be used to gain from them a recognition of Spanish sovereignty over the insurgent communities.[15]

---

[14] Chateaubriand, op. cit., V, 199-201. See further Chateaubriand to Polignac, April 1, 1824, A. A. E., Angleterre, 618; Temperley, " Canning and the Conferences of the Four Allied Governments at Paris, 1823-1826," loc. cit., XXX, 23.

[15] Chateaubriand to Talaru, December 9, 1823, A. A. E., Espagne, 726; Talaru to Chateaubriand, January 8, 1824, ibid.

Still, on January 24, 1824, Chateaubriand directed Talaru to urge upon the Spanish Government the pressing need of action concerning commercial intercourse between the Indies and foreign countries. An announcement by Spain that the commerce of her colonies would be free, argued Chateaubriand, would present Villèle's Cabinet in a favorable light to the French public. It would oblige England to become openly the champion of insurrection, for there would be no other way in which she could increase her trade with Spanish America. The minister promised that, if the Spaniards demanded in return certain concessions regarding prisoners of war or the sojourn of French soldiers in Spain, he would fulfill any pledge that Talaru might make.[16] He even dispatched Count Marcellus to Spain as a special commissioner with a model of the desired decree stipulating freedom of commerce between foreign countries and the Spanish Indies. This draft was to be presented to the Court of Madrid as a species of ultimatum.[17]

On January 29 Chateaubriand sent to Talaru another dispatch in which he declared that Spain should formally open commercial intercourse with her colonies to foreign nations. The minister maintained emphatically that the Spanish Court would have to do more than to announce quietly to England and France that it would make such a concession. For herself and for all the other nations of Europe, France desired a royal decree. Chateaubriand maintained that such a measure would gain partisans for Spain in the Indies, would retard the acknowledgment of the independence of Spanish America by England, and would silence those Frenchmen who had decried the Franco-Spanish war. A

[16] Chateaubriand, *Congrès de Vérone,* II, 337.
[17] *Idem, Correspondance générale,* V, 151.

decree legally opening the Spanish colonies to European commerce would be a concession that no other nation had yet secured from the mother country. The French minister continued:

We know well that perhaps this decree will not prevent England from recognizing Spanish-American independence, and it will not open another port to our vessels in either Peru or Mexico. Still, it would ensure us an excellent footing. On the other hand, it would place England in a slippery position. It would reënforce us and would, above all, be of the utmost utility to Spain.[18]

On the very day that Talaru wrote to Paris to state that the desired decree would not be promulgated until it had been approved by the Council of the Indies, Chateaubriand sent to that ambassador an urgent dispatch which began by declaring that, if Ferdinand VII would concede the freedom of colonial commerce, Louis XVIII would consent that the departure of French soldiers from Spain be postponed. It was accordingly by strong and insistent pressure from the Tuileries that the Court of Madrid was induced to favor an important modification of its restrictive colonial system.[19]

On February 9, 1824, Count Ofalia, who had proposed such a reform as early as 1818, promulgated a decree concerning the trade of foreigners with Spanish America. This decree announced that Ferdinand VII had instructed colonial officials to make no changes in existing practices of trade and navigation in the Indies. Further, they were to sanction those direct commercial relations with foreign

---

[18] *Idem, Congrès de Vérone,* II, 341-42.

[19] February, 1824, A. A. E., Espagne, 726. See further Beau de Loménie, *La carrière politique de Chateaubriand de 1814 à 1830,* II, 90-93.

countries which had been permitted in certain colonies by local authorities and which had been authorized in other colonies by the Spanish Government. Throughout the American dominions direct commerce was to be allowed with foreigners who were subjects of nations that were friends or allies of Spain.[20] This evidently signified that the illicit trade which had been developing between certain foreign countries and Spanish America would not be interrupted.

The commercial concession of February 9, 1824, gratified Chateaubriand. Upon receipt of the news he wrote to Talaru, " I am as much pleased as you are." [21] Though he criticized the verbose language of the decree, he expressed the view that, if anything could save the Spanish colonies for the mother country, it was certainly this measure.[22] Several days later, the Foreign Minister said of the reform that one of its good effects would be to take away from any nation the pretext of hastening an acknowledgment of the independence of those colonies: " England, for instance, acknowledges that to accord such recognition is to give a sort of stability to the commercial relations which have been formed with the countries that are moving toward independence." [23] Writing to Polignac two days later, Chateaubriand expressed the view that premature recognition by England would spoil any negotiations tending to lead Spain to a reasonable decision respecting the status of her

[20] *Gaceta de Madrid,* February 12, 1824.

[21] February 14, 1824, A. A. E., Espagne, 726. See further Ofalia, *Escritos,* p. 706.

[22] February 16, 1824, A. A. E., Espagne, 726.

[23] Chateaubriand to La Ferronnays, February 17, 1824, A. A. E., Russie, 165.

colonies.[24] A commander of French naval forces named
Rosamel, who was at Toulon, was instructed to transmit
news of the decree of February 9 to Brazil, La Plata, Chile,
and Peru.[25] Two weeks later, Minister of Marine Clermont-Tonnerre instructed Governor Donzelot to make
known in the Caribbean region that Spain had reformed
her monopolistic commercial system:

> You will realize fully the importance which this decision
> should have for the success of the adjustments that France
> wishes to arrange between Spain and her former colonies.
> In this manner France ought to begin the rôle of mediator
> which she has taken upon herself. The new governments of
> America should discern in this action only a guarantee of
> the intentions of the King and the most positive proof that
> in recent times English journals have calumniated the pow-
> ers of continental Europe by attempting to spread the belief
> that they would lend their support to King Ferdinand in
> order to aid him to reconquer his possessions beyond the
> seas.[26]

The motives which impelled Chateaubriand to advocate
such a reform in the Spanish colonial system are not far to
seek. It is clear that he wished not only to promote French
commerce but also to embarrass the English Government,
which was contemplating an acknowledgment of Spanish-
American independence. Further, the minister hoped that
the French Cabinet would gain prestige at home by this
stroke. In all likelihood he thought that the legalization of
the existing commercial intercourse with the Indies might
be an entering wedge which would promote the acceptance

---

[24] A. A. E., Angleterre, 618.

[25] Rosamel to Clermont-Tonnerre, February 20, 1824, A. N.,
Marine, B B⁴, 459.

[26] Villanueva, *La monarquía en América; la Santa Alianza*, p. 77,
n. 1.

by Spain of his cherished plan of checking democratic tendencies in the New World by the founding of Bourbon monarchies in Mexico and South America.[27]

On February 17 the *Journal des Débats* noticed Spain's decision concerning foreign trade with the Indies. This ministerial journal praised the decree which separated the commercial issue from the political issue of recognition. It interpreted the measure to signify that ships of the European allies would be admitted into Spanish-American ports upon an equal basis. In over-sanguine words it declared that a law opening insular and continental Spanish America to the vessels of all nations was " a great and memorable revolution in the commercial and political world." Obviously this journal wished the French people to believe that the policy of their government would promote commercial intercourse with Spanish nations of the New World.

Two days later the same journal complacently praised the reform decree because Spain, avoiding mention of either her sovereignty or her subjects, did not employ language in it which might offend the pretensions of any state. This journal reasoned that Spain's commercial concession would induce the leading nations of Europe to become interested in an adjustment between Spain and her colonies. It declared:

With regard to France, certain of having nobly executed her task toward Spain and the other European powers, she will tranquilly await the outcome of events and of the general dispositions of good will which animate all the powers. France will thus obtain the most worthy recompense for her expedition against the Spanish revolutionists; she will prove

[27] See further on this matter Rousseau, " L'Ambassade du Marquis de Talaru en Espagne, Juillet, 1823—Août 1824," *Revue des questions historiques,* XC, 102-04.

doubly that she made war only for the welfare of society and the peace of the world.

Whether intended to satisfy eager French merchants or to check the insurrectionary spirit in the Indies, this trade decree was defective because it lacked provisions for enforcement. Moreover, it had been too long delayed. By the time that Spanish statesmen took the hated step of authorizing foreign commerce with their cherished colonial dominions, the partisans struggling for independence there had made startling progress. Besides Mexico, Colombia, Chile, and La Plata, which were outlined upon the map by 1822, other states had meanwhile been carved from the Spanish Empire. In the heart of South America, José de Francia had become the chief executive of Paraguay. On May 24, 1822, General Antonio de Sucre, the able and loyal lieutenant of Bolívar, had decisively defeated Royalist soldiers upon the slopes of Mount Pichincha and had thus assured the independence of the presidency of Quito, which was soon annexed to Colombia. In July, 1823, the provinces of the one-time captaincy general of Guatemala had proclaimed their independence of both Spain and Mexico. Thus by December, 1823, Spain's banner of crimson and gold was displayed upon the continent of America only in beleaguered seaports and in remote Andean highlands.

Unaware of the large measure of success of the Patriot party, Chateaubriand undertook to develop the practice of dispatching missions to the Indies. Not only were existing agents given fresh instructions and new duties, but additional commissioners were appointed. In accordance with the wishes of Governor Donzelot, Minister Clermont-Tonnerre recommended to Chateaubriand on July 23, 1823, that Chasseriau, who was highly esteemed by Colombian lead-

ers, be invited to Paris in order that he might be instructed
with regard to another mission to South America.[28] Some
months later Chateaubriand informed Talaru that Louis
XVIII had decided to send agents to Colombia and Mexico
with directions to discover the disposition of the people, to
seek for personages to whom the French Government might
propose an adjustment with the mother country, and to
offer them the mediation of France.[29] It does not appear,
however, that the Court of Madrid was informed of this
decision.

On November 29, 1823, general instructions were framed
in the Ministry of Foreign Affairs for agents to Spanish
America. A trusted naval officer named Samouel, who was
destined for Mexico, was told that he should stoutly deny
the rumors that France had engaged to aid Ferdinand VII
" with her vessels and her soldiers to subjugate all the
provinces which had withdrawn from Spanish domination."
Lieutenant Samouel was informed that the solicitude of
France for the welfare of Spain extended to her colonies.
The view was presented that, with the aid of France, Spain
could keep Mexico in a condition of dissension and decay.
It was to promote a reconciliation between the motherland
and the Spanish-American countries, stated these instructions, that France proffered them her good offices. France
was " interested to see that tranquillity reigns in these beautiful countries which furnish her with very profitable relations for her commerce."

Samouel was assured that France had everything to gain
by the development of Spanish America. She would not
deprive the Mexicans of any of the advantages which they

---

[28] A. A. E., Espagne, 722.
[29] November 12, 1823, *ibid.,* 724.

had gained by the war for independence: " If her counsels
can be heard, the Mexicans will profit by the mediation
which France offers them; under her guarantee, they will
become reconciled with the mother country and be assured
by a treaty of the continuation of all the positive advantages
upon which their prosperity depends and which they
already enjoy." Once such a treaty was negotiated, Spain
would be strong enough to protect the Mexicans but too
weak to deceive them or to abuse their confidence:
" Thenceforth they would prosper under the aegis of peace
in complete security for the future against any external attack and even against any internal discord." The French
Government was ready to receive their propositions and to
promote them at the Spanish court. A propitious disposition on the part of the Mexicans would facilitate an attempt
by the Allies to induce Spain to favor an adjustment with
her insurgent colonists. France disclaimed any ambitious
designs with regard to Spanish America; she did not desire
any selfish advantage. However, Samouel was advised that
Mexico should refrain from forming political or commercial relations with other powers.[30] Besides emphasizing the
essentials in the directions of November 29, special instructions prepared for Samouel in December, 1823, presented
the view that a stable government had not yet been estab-

[30] " Instructions données aux personnes envoyées au Mexique,"
A. A. E., Mexique, 2. A Spanish translation of a copy of these
instructions, dated December 17, 1823, is found in Villanueva,
La monarquía en América; la Santa Alianza, pp. 38-43. In a
" Note sur les relations de la France avec la Colombie depuis 1821 "
(A. A. E., Mémoires et Documents, Amérique, 31), the statement
is made that the two main objects of the missions of Samouel and
Chasseriau were to allay the apprehensions in Spanish America
concerning French designs and to propose the mediation of France
between Spain and her colonies.

lished in Mexico. As the colony which had presumably suffered the least from Spanish rule, it was suggested that Mexico might be the most easily persuaded to offer to the motherland advantages which would compensate her for her loss of absolute sovereignty:

Perhaps she might consent to receive a viceroy who would direct a strictly Mexican administration that would manage all the internal affairs of the colony. Thus, by paying some subsidies to Spain, by assuring her special advantages for her commerce, and by leaving her the honor of sovereignty, the Mexicans would assure themselves a real independence and would secure protection from any external attack as well as from all internal dissensions. If it should be possible to induce the head of the Mexican Government to accept the bases of such an arrangement, this would be a great advantage not only in itself but also for the negotiations which we would open with the other colonies.[31]

This clever variant of the scheme for planting Bourbon appanages in Spanish America embodied the most practical proposal for a reconciliation between Spain and her colonies which was propounded by France at this time. There is good reason to doubt, however, whether this plan would have been entirely satisfactory to the motherland, which was very jealous of her sovereignty over the Indies. If such a project had been submitted to Mexican revolutionary chieftains shortly after the proclamation of the Plan of Iguala, it would probably have appealed to many of them. However, this compromise measure was formulated too late; for by the end of 1823 influential Mexicans had decided to pattern their political system after that of the United States.

Chateaubriand's instructions to Benoît Chasseriau stated that recent events had encouraged the development of

[31] Chateaubriand to Samouel, December 7, 1823, A. N., Marine, B B⁴, 446.

French trade with Colombia. To promote this commerce the agent was directed to communicate with Colombian authorities and to correspond with French officials in the Antilles. Chasseriau was to make known the desire of his government to see its merchants honorably treated; he was assured that the naval forces of France would always be ready to punish persons who inflicted injuries on her subjects. He was to explain the events which had just taken place in Spain in a manner that was favorable to France: the Spaniards were to be represented as a people who had solicited French intervention and protection; Louis XVIII was to be depicted as a mediator between the Spanish King and his people. " Instead of alarming the Spanish Americans," the instructions averred, " such a representation should make them realize what they can expect from the good will of a government which knows how to make such use of its power." [32]

Shortly before his departure from France the agent was summoned to a conference with the Duke of Rauzan, who held a responsible post in the Ministry of Foreign Affairs. Rauzan informed Chasseriau that an important object of his new mission was to relieve the Colombians of any fears which they might have harbored with regard to the intentions of France after the war with Spain terminated. The agent was to explain to them that his government had engaged in this war solely to check the progress of a revolution which threatened to subvert all Europe. He was to destroy the false impressions spread by Americans and English regarding designs which the French Government entertained upon Spanish America. To cite Chasseriau's re-

[32] December 1, 1823 (copy), A. A. E., Mémoires et Documents, Amérique, 39.

capitulation of these verbal directions: he was to make known to the Colombians that France "was far from dreaming of any enterprise having as its object the appropriation of any part of their territory; that she did not ask for herself any exclusive advantage; that the new states would, on the contrary, find very great advantages in their alliance with France, a nation which would be able to protect them effectively; and that the only favor to which she aspired was that of being treated in her commercial relations with Colombia upon the same footing as that of the most-favored-nations." [33]

Supplementary directions, dated December 1, 1823, informed Chasseriau that he was to gather information concerning conditions in Colombia. In the main this advice followed Samouel's special instructions with regard to the rôle of France toward Spain and her colonies. Chasseriau was directed to work in concert with Mollien; but that agent, who reached Bogotá in February, 1823, had been suspected of spying out the land and was now en route for Paris.[34] Again, Chasseriau was asked to find out whether it would be expedient and practicable for France to have suitable persons designated to serve her commercial interests in the principal Colombian ports instead of consuls. He was also directed to establish contact with Schmalz, who had

[33] "Comte Rendu d'une Mission remplie à Colombie, par ordre de M. le Vicomte de Chateaubriand, alors Ministre des Affaires Étrangères, le 20 Octobre, 1820," *ibid.*

[34] Manning, *Diplomatic Correspondence of the United States concerning the Independence of the Latin-American Nations*, II, 1244-45. See further Mollien, *Voyage dans la République de Columbia en 1823*; "Notes recueillés sur Columbia pendant un voyage fait dans cette République en 1823, par Ordre du Gouvernement française, par G. Mollien" (undated), A. A. E., Mémoires et Documents, Amérique, 28.

fallen under the suspicion of Mexican officials apparently fearful of French projects for a monarchy in Spanish America.[35]

Upon being released from prison, Schmalz sent from New Orleans to the Ministry of Foreign Affairs a careful report on conditions in Mexico. He stated that news of the invasion of Spain by French troops had inflamed many Mexicans. Further, he declared that " letters and newspapers received from Habana and from various parts of the Peninsula announce that, as soon as the affairs of Spain are arranged in Europe, the Holy Alliance, and more particularly France, are to furnish to His Catholic Majesty the means of preparing the expeditions necessary to subjugate the rebels in his American possessions and to reëstablish

[35] " Copie No. 1," presumably by Chateaubriand, A. A. E., Colombie, 2. Under the heading " Extract of the Instructions given by the Duke of Rauzan to M. Chasseriau, sent on a Secret Mission to Colombia," the *Morning Chronicle* printed on September 1, 1824, an inexact and misleading article which conveyed the impression that the recognition of Colombian independence by France was altogether impossible and that, if reconciliation with Spain could not be secured by negotiations, "there will only remain as a last resource to obtain that by force of arms. . . ." Consequently, when Chasseriau returned to France in 1824 he was in disrepute, but Damas was convinced that the statements published in English newspapers about Chasseriau's mission were " not authentic" and "wholly false." Stuart to Canning, September 23, and October 11, 1824, F. O., 27/315. In the " Compte Rendu d'un Mission remplie à Colombie, par order de M. le Vicomte de Chateaubriand, alors Ministre des Affaires Étrangères " by Chasseriau, dated October 20, 1824, the agent did not mention that the use of force against Spanish America had been suggested to him by Rauzan in their conferences just before his departure for America. A. A. E., Mémoires et Documents, Amérique, 39. On the publication by the *Morning Chronicle* of the spurious Secret Treaty of Verona, see *supra,* pp. 248-50.

his domination there. The news of this project, which is reported to be actually arranged, alarms all minds and provokes the Republican party to the highest degree of exasperation." [36]

These missions of inquiry to the Indies were not kept secret. In 1823 the budget presented to the French legislature contained an item of a hundred thousand francs providing for missions to southern America. The legislators were informed that the commissioners had not been accredited to any authorities whatsoever of the new states. Chateaubriand plausibly explained that they were mere travelers with no secret intentions, who were instructed to visit Spanish-American countries only in order to observe a state of affairs concerning which there were many varying accounts, and to furnish such reports as might put the French Government in a position rightly to judge the situation.[37]

From time to time the French Cabinet received from special agents and naval officers detailed reports about the insurgent colonies. On May 22, 1823, Captain Bégué sent to the Minister of Marine a description of his cruise to Colombia on the frigate *Tarn*, in the course of which he had disembarked five agents destined for towns in Spanish America.[38] As Count Landos, the head of the mission to the Pacific coast of South America, died shortly after his arrival there,[39] his aide, Rattier de Sauvignan, sent from

[36] Schmalz to Fleury, February 18, 1824, A. A. E., Mexique, 2. On Schmalz and Motte, see further Bancroft, *History of Mexico*, V, 52.

[37] *Archives parlementaires*, 2d series, XXXIX, 198; Chateaubriand, *Correspondance générale*, V, 205.

[38] A. N., Marine, B B⁴, 446.

[39] "Note pour le Ministre sur les Missions dans l'Amérique

Lima in December, 1823, an instructive report on the condition of Peru which included a list of French manufactures that could be advantageously marketed in that country.[40] In August of the same year, Auguste Plée, " the travelling naturalist of the King in America," as he styled himself, made a report concerning military and political affairs in Colombia. Plée stated that Angoulême's proclamation mentioning the pacification of the Spanish colonies had caused great alarm in Venezuela: " It did not appear to leave any doubt that France, after having pacified Spain, would aid King Ferdinand to bring his former colonies in America again under his authority." [41] Mollien eventually sent to Paris observations made during his sojourn in Colombia in which, emphasizing the danger menacing French commercial interests by English activities in Spanish America, he suggested that the number of French warships in Latin-American waters be increased.[42]

There is little doubt that the information contained in such reports concerning the scope and persistence of the revolutionary movements in South America eventually af-

---

Espagnol " (undated), A. A. E., Mémoires et Documents, Amérique, 35. On these missions, see further Manning, *Diplomatic Correspondence of the United States concerning the Independence of the Latin-American Nations*, II, 1235, 1244, 1272-77.

[40] " Rapport sur la situation de la République du Pérou et de son Gouvernment, en mois de Décembre, 1823," A. A. E., Pérou, 15.

[41] " Extrait d'un Rapport de Mr Plée, naturaliste voyageur du Roi, concernant les affaires politiques et militaires de la Terre Firme Espagnole, datée à bord de la Frégate de S. M. La Thetis, le 31 août 1823," A. A. E., Colombie, 2.

[42] " Notes recueillés sur Columbie pendant un voyage fait dans cette République en 1823, par Ordre du Governement français, par G. Mollien," A. A. E., Mémoires et Documents, Amérique, 28.

fected the attitude of French ministers.[43] Certain it is that by the end of 1823 the Minister of Marine had modified his attitude toward Spanish America. Instructions framed by Clermont-Tonnerre and entrusted to Chasseriau for delivery to Governor Donzelot enable one more fully to understand French policy at this time. That minister expressed the view that Spain could not reconquer her former colonies. Donzelot was informed that France would treat with the rising states on condition that she be accorded the privileges of the most-favored-nation, and that, if Spain did not like these proposals, French statesmen would act independently:

We declare to the Spanish colonies that, as long as your motherland does not recognize you, you have only a precarious existence. The greatest achievement to which you can aspire is to legitimize your independence in the eyes of the world. France is the only nation which is in a position to procure this for you; we are negotiating in that manner with the King of Spain. What do you wish to offer, what can you offer him, which, because of the benefits that his country would gain from new relations with you, will influence Ferdinand VII to renounce his sovereign rights? We are ready to transmit your views to him and ask of you no more than that you concede to us in commercial relations a complete equality with the most-favored-nations, with the sole exception of your ancient Mistress, in the belief that she has a right to special advantages because of

[43] After his return, Alphonse de Moges forwarded to the Minister of Marine an account of his trip to Cuzco (September 10, 1825, A. N., Marine, B B⁴, 470). A description of his visit to Peru, Chile, and La Plata was sent by De la Susse to the Minister of Marine two years after his departure from Toulon: "Rapport général addressé au Ministre de la Marine pour le Capitaine de frégate, De la Susse, sur une mission au Chile, &c.," June, 1826 (copy), A. A. E., Mémoires et Documents, Espagne, 214.

the acknowledgment that she will accord to you—an acknowledgment which for you is politically priceless.

Such, Count Donzelot, is the line of frank, noble, and wise policy that France wishes to follow. It is in this manner that Messrs. Chasseriau and Samouel should speak to the heads of the Colombian and Mexican governments but without assuming any political character until the new order is assured.[44]

Donzelot was warned to keep the missions to Colombia and Mexico secret, lest the rivals of France injure her prospects. He was to send his government exact information concerning English armaments in the New World and the schemes which England might contemplate in regard to Spanish America. Further, Clermont-Tonnerre said:

If a rebellion should break out against the Spanish governors of Cuba or Puerto Rico, and if those governors should ask you for aid, you are to furnish them with it but with such prudence that neither England nor any other power can maintain that we wish to gain control of those colonies. In consequence the succor should be given at the moment of danger; it should be temporary and limited. All your acts should be based upon the principle that we will aid our allies but without wishing to seize or to hold anything for ourselves.[45]

The instructions to Donzelot dated December 17, 1823, are very important. They show that, before the news of the President's message of December 2, 1823, reached Europe, the French Government had authorized the use of its military and naval forces by the governor of Martinique to aid Spanish officials in Cuba and Puerto Rico against revolutionists. This authorization was contrary to the pledge which had been given by Chateaubriand that France would

---

[44] Temperley, " The Instructions to Donzelot, Governor of Martinique, 17 December 1823," *Eng. Hist. Rev.*, XLI, 586.

[45] *Ibid.*, 587.

remain neutral. Further, Clermont-Tonnerre's instructions are important because they draw aside the curtain that frequently conceals the real intentions of French statesmen toward the new American nations. The instructions disclose that Samouel and Chasseriau were authorized to suggest to the Patriot authorities in Mexico and Colombia that France would act as an intermediary between those countries and Spain to arrange peace on the basis of a treaty which, on the one hand, would acknowledge their independence and, on the other hand, would assure commercial advantages to the motherland. As the price for this service, France desired most-favored-nation treatment for her commerce. Upon that condition she now wished to undertake the rôle of mediator which England had fruitlessly essayed in the early years of the Spanish-American Revolution.

A letter to Donzelot in February, 1824, in which Clermont-Tonnerre notified him of Spain's decree permitting foreign commerce with her colonies, reënforced these instructions. Donzelot was directed to make this decree known in Mexico and northern South America:

You will realize fully the influence which this action should have upon the success of the arrangements that France wishes to bring about between Spain and her former colonies. France ought to begin by carrying out the rôle of mediator which she has assumed. The new governments of America should see in this only a guarantee of the King's good intentions toward them and the most positive proof that in recent times English newspapers have calumniated the powers of the Continent by attempting to foster the notion that they would aid King Ferdinand to reconquer his possessions beyond the sea.[46]

When Chasseriau and Samouel arrived at Martinique on

[46] February 23, 1824, A. N., Marine, B B⁴, 405 *bis*.

February 5, 1824, the governor prudently decided to modify their instructions. Donzelot furnished Samouel with letters to Spanish-American Patriots and directed him to proceed on the brig *Seine* to Mexico, where he was to protest against Schmalz's arrest. Further, Samouel was to persuade the Mexican authorities to request that France mediate between them and Spain.[47] On March 26 this agent sailed from Fort Royal for Mexico via New Orleans. In that city he met Schmalz, who was convinced that it would be unwise for him to return to Mexico without a character openly acknowledged by France and without a title that would ensure him respect.[48]

From New Orleans Samouel proceeded to the island of Sacrificios, where he arrived on May 23. He was informed by General Rincón, the Mexican commander at Vera Cruz, that rumors had been circulated in his country that a French army would gather at Martinique to aid Spain to reconquer Mexico. " I have undeceived him," reported Samouel, " and have given him the assurance that, on the contrary, the King wishes to maintain relations of amity and commerce with Mexico." [49]

Upon arriving at the Mexican capital, Samouel found that the Spanish decree concerning foreign trade had provoked fresh apprehensions with respect to the intentions of France. Rival nations, he asserted, had represented her as employing this commercial reform to prevent the acknowledgment of the independence of the Spanish-American

[47] Donzelot to Chateaubriand, February 15, 1824, A. A. E., Colombie, 2.

[48] Villanueva, *La monarquía en América; la Santa Alianza*, pp. 56-58.

[49] *Ibid.*, 60; Samouel to Donzelot, September 15, 1824, A. A. E., Mexique, 2.

states. He reported in addition that the Mexicans did not see any real advantage in this concession, because they had for some time enjoyed free commerce with all countries. As fear prevailed in Mexico that France would aid Ferdinand VII to subjugate Spanish America, Samouel transmitted to Lucas Alamán, Mexico's Secretary of Foreign Relations, an exposition of French foreign policy.[50] In a note addressed to Donzelot that minister expressed the pleasure of the Mexican President at the view presented by Samouel, namely that the King of France, instead of wishing to intervene by force in the struggle raging between Spain and the American countries which were formerly her possessions, would employ his influence to terminate the hostilities that had had such disastrous effects upon the commerce of all nations.[51]

The second mission of Chasseriau aroused grave suspicion in South America. It appears that, after his instructions had been framed, the Duke of Rauzan prohibited him from following them except in so far as Governor Donzelot might consider opportune.[52] The governor's instructions to the agent laid stress on the policy of strict neutrality which France had pursued and intended to pursue toward the Spanish Indies. Donzelot declared that the French Government desired to see the quarrel between Spain and her colonies terminated by a durable peace which would be

[50] *Idem* to *idem*, September 15, 1824 (copy), A. A. E., Mexique, 2. See further Samouel's letter to Clermont-Tonnerre, August 13, 1824, in Villanueva, *op. cit.*, pp. 60-72.

[51] Alamán to Donzelot, June 30, 1824 (copy), A. A. E., Mexique, 2. Certain phases of Samouel's mission are treated in Fabela, *Los precursores de la diplomacia mexicana*, pp. 198-206.

[52] " 8 bre 1824. Extrait des pièces ci-joint," A. A. E., Mémoires et Documents, Amérique, 39.

satisfactory to both parties. Chasseriau was to discredit all rumors implying that France intended to aid Spain to reconquer her insurgent colonies. If necessary, he was to afford aid and protection to French citizens in Colombia. Should need arise, he was authorized to employ the title of " French commercial and maritime agent." He was to explain to the Colombians that Donzelot was anxious to promote commercial intercourse between their country and Martinique; he was also to make clear that the soldiers who had recently arrived at that island were intended to relieve French garrisons in the Antilles and that the naval forces stationed there were designed to protect French commerce against pirates.[53] Chasseriau's trip was thus to be not only a mission of inquiry to Colombia but also a visit designed to remove from the minds of her citizens the fear that France intended to assist Spain against the American insurgents.

Furnished by Donzelot with letters to publicists of Colombia, Chasseriau undertook to visit certain towns in Venezuela and then to proceed to Bogotá via Santa Marta and Cartagena. The governor subsequently transmitted to this agent a species of passport as well as dispatches to Vice-President Francisco de Paula Santander of Colombia and to Manuel Gual, the Colombian Secretary of Foreign Relations.[54] In a letter of May 26 Donzelot suggested to Chasseriau that France was in a position to mediate between Spain and her colonies and further that she would like to arrange a commercial treaty with Colombia on the most-

[53] Donzelot's instructions to Chasseriau, March 18, 1824 (copy), *ibid.*

[54] Donzelot to Chasseriau, March 18 and May 26, 1824 (copies), *ibid.* A copy of Chasseriau's passport, dated May 25, is found in *ibid.*; see also Santander, *Archivo,* XII, 21.

favored-nation basis.[55] Yet, to a greater extent than Samouel, Chasseriau proved to be an *agent provocateur.*

After visiting Cumaná and La Guaira, Chasseriau sailed on a French frigate to Cartagena, where he found that almost all his former acquaintances shunned him. He sought an explanation of this strange conduct from General Soublette. This Patriot general declared that the Colombians were fond of the French but that they now felt justified in considering them hostile to Spanish-American liberty. Among other justifications for this sentiment Soublette adduced the proclamation of Angoulême upon entering Spain, which, he thought, "announced that France would not only employ her armies and her fleets to reëstablish the King of Spain in the Peninsula but also to bring the insurgent colonies back under his domination."[56] Apprehensive that he could not overcome the prejudice against the French due largely to their invasion of Spain, and convinced that a trip to Bogotá would be useless, Chasseriau decided to leave Colombian soil.

Indeed, so intense was the prejudice against France in South America that the governor of Santa Marta informed a naval commander that he considered all the French agents to be nothing else than spies.[57] During a brief sojourn in Colombia, Count Landos had aroused the suspicion that he wished to sound the leading inhabitants with respect to the erection in South America of a nominally independent political system which in reality would be an appanage to the Spanish crown.[58] Upon becoming aware of the movements

[55] (Copy), A. A. E., Mémoires et Documents, Amérique, 39.
[56] Chasseriau to Donzelot, July 15, 1824, *ibid.*
[57] *Ibid.*
[58] Manning, *Diplomatic Correspondence of the United States*

of French emissaries, Secretary Gual tried to discover what aid might be expected from the English Government in case hostilities broke out between Colombia and France. In fact, reports concerning Chasseriau made certain Spanish Americans suspect that he was the precursor of a French army of invasion. At the instance of his government, and on behalf of the new republics of America, the Colombian minister at Washington appealed to the Monroe Doctrine for protection against the Holy Alliance.[59] During the funeral services for Pope Pius VII in Santiago de Chile in April, 1824, a clerical orator described the Holy Allies as instruments of legitimacy chosen by the Almighty to suppress revolutions in both the Old World and the New.[60]

In a letter to the Minister of Marine, Admiral Jurièn quoted a journal of Caracas which intimated that the French Government might even harbor a design to found a monarchy in northern South America. " Take care, patriots," exclaimed the editor of this journal in warning tones, " be free or die! " Jurien gave his own impressions of Chasseriau's trip as follows:

His presence served to incite everywhere a general apprehension of France, and, by combining this fear with absurd rumors, our rivals have succeeded in casting suspicions upon the intentions of the French Government. They have disseminated the notion that the object of France is to join Spain in order to reëstablish the old order in America. By

concerning the Independence of the Latin-American Nations, II, 1272-77.

[59] Webster, Britain and the Independence of Latin America, I, 395-96; Robertson, " South America and the Monroe Doctrine, 1824-1828," Political Science Quarterly, XXX, 88; Bolívar, Cartas, IV, 256.

[60] Barros Borgoño, La misión del vicario apostólico Don Juan Muzi, p. 119.

greatly exaggerating the number of warships and soldiers gathered at Martinique, they have depicted those forces to the people of Colombia as armaments ready to fall upon them. Our rivals make comments about our journals and ascribe interpretations to them which further increase the distrust. Finally, they affirm that, if France really entertained favorable intentions in regard to the Colombians, she would not use as an intermediary the governor of Martinique, whose honesty and character are fully recognized, but who is not vested with sufficient authority to treat directly with their government.[61]

Erroneous views regarding the dispatch of French missions to Mexico and South America were even disseminated in La Plata. On August 28, 1824, the *Argos* of Buenos Aires published a critical editorial entitled " France and America." The *Argos* reasoned that France, which had taken upon herself the reëstablishment of absolutism in Spain, appeared desirous also of exercising her influence in America as the representative of the Holy Alliance. The journal conceded that the French Government had neglected to send agents to La Plata, but it interpreted the omission as signifying France's conviction that this section was not adapted to maneuvers aiming to establish the monarchical principles of the Holy Alliance there. At the same time it asserted that the French emissaries dispatched to Colombia, Peru, and Chile were really spies.[62]

When Captain Mogel, who was well acquainted with conditions prevailing on the Pacific shores of South America, sent a report to the Minister of Marine, he declared that stories were in circulation there that Chasseriau

[61] July 21, 1824, A. N., Marine, B B⁴, 457. See further the *Gaceta de Colombia,* quoted in Villanueva, *La monarquía en América; la Santa Alianza,* p. 35.

[62] " Traduction," A. N., Marine, B B⁴, 459.

had been secretly instructed by the Duke of Rauzan to criticize the independent governments. This captain stated that alleged instructions to that agent implying the use of force by France against the new American states had served as a text for caustic articles in some journals on the Pacific coast. On March 10, 1825, the official journal of Peru made " a veritable appeal to arms against the French." Further, Mogel reported that in Chile anonymous letters had threatened the captain of a French frigate with death. When the alleged instructions of France were made known by a flaming orator to the Congress of Chile, the rage of the people was aroused to such a pitch that they " forced the retirement of French officers from the command of Chilean regiments." [63]

On October 14, 1824, the *Liberal* of Santiago de Chile published an editorial entitled " Monarchists," in which truth and error were curiously mingled. This journal declared that Polignac's associates had asserted that to acknowledge the independence of Chile would be to recognize anarchy. " Should any of them have the hardihood to introduce themselves among us in order to preach their new doctrines," it continued, " the arm of the government or the dagger of patriots will teach them to respect our rights and to abstain from such interference in the affairs of Spanish America as they have undertaken in the affairs of Spain." The Chilean Secretary of Foreign Relations promptly informed a French naval officer that he considered this article as misleading and impudent, that it expressed views inconsistent with those which his government

[63] September 10, 1825, A. A. E., Pérou, 16. A Spanish translation of alleged instructions to " Colonel Galabert " was published in *El indicador,* January 10, 1827.

entertained, and that the authorities would take steps to punish its author.[64]

Upon his arrival on the coast of Peru in October, 1824, Commander Rosamel, who was making a cruise on the *Maria Thérèse*, addressed a letter to Bolívar to inform him of the purpose of his trip. The admiral declared that his King had sent him into those waters in order to cause the flag of France to be respected and to protect her commerce. Rosamel added that the instruction of his government was that he observe the strictest neutrality toward the warring parties:

It has ordered a denial of reports spread by enemies of France or by persons jealous of her prosperity who have ascribed to her government intentions hostile to the new states of South America at a time when she entertains only friendly feelings toward them. France will never intervene in their quarrel with Spain except by her good offices and as a mutual friend, in the interest of the peace and prosperity of both parties, without any selfish motive.[65]

Secretary Carrion, who responded on behalf of Bolívar, declared that the Peruvian Government had paid little attention to reports that France had assumed a hostile attitude toward the new states, and that instead it expected from her government the good offices of a mutual friend who desired the peace and prosperity of both parties to the quarrel. Carrion assured Rosamel of the Liberator's desire to promote friendly intercourse with France.[66]

[64] Pinto to Rosamel, October 14, 1824 (copy), A. N., Marine, B B⁴, 469.

[65] Rosamel to Bolívar, October 9, 1824 (copy), enclosure in Chabrol to Damas, July 28, 1825, A. A. E., Pérou, 16.

[66] Enclosure (translation) in Rosamel to Chabrol, February 20, 1825, A. N., Marine, B B⁴, 469.

Though Bolívar entertained doubts concerning alleged instructions to Chasseriau which were being criticized in South America, he was inclined to consider them authentic. He wrote to Santander that they depicted the aspirations of France correctly and that spies should be sent to observe the armaments in the French Antilles. Bolívar even proposed that steps be taken to prepare the Colombians for a sanguinary war against the French.[67] Nevertheless, in a conversation with an English naval captain, he declared that neither France nor Spain could secure a permanent foothold in his country.[68] In an interview with Rosamel near Lima Bolívar conceded that many advantages would accrue to his countrymen through the development of intercourse with the French, but he expressed much chagrin at the views of Parisian journals which had published articles hostile to Spanish-American independence. However, the French naval commander succeeded in stilling the Liberator's fears.[69] Shortly afterward, he wrote to the Peruvian general, José de la Mar, that Rosamel's positive assurance with respect to the neutrality of his government in the struggle between Spain and her colonies had calmed the agitation aroused by alarming news about the French mission to Colombia.[70]

[67] Bolívar, *Cartas,* IV, 280, 287-90.

[68] Malling to Melville, March 18-20, 1825 (copy), F. O., 61/6. On Bolívar's attitude toward England, see Robertson, *Rise of the Spanish-American Republics,* p. 300.

[69] Rosamel to Chabrol, June 4, 1825, A. N., Marine, B B⁴, 469; Villanueva, *La monarquía en América; el imperio de los Andes,* pp. 72-74.

[70] Bolívar, *op. cit.,* IV, 299. John Quincy Adams was also disturbed by reports of French missions to Spanish America. On July 8, 1824, he wrote to Minister Anderson at Bogotá " that they were missions of inquiry to ascertain what might be done with those

Prophetic thoughts of Chateaubriand concerning the rebellious colonies were expressed on March 16, 1824, in a letter to the French minister at Naples:

You are right with respect to the colonies. They will not lead to a war because we do not desire war and because the Continent, which makes so much noise about its theories, would not support us if we wished to sustain those theories by armed force against England. The Spanish colonies will therefore leave the motherland; and our declaration at Verona has placed us in the best position to profit by this separation. We have foreseen the event, and we have made it understood that we do not sacrifice our interests to political theories. The important thing is that the recognition of Spanish-American independence should not come too soon and that we should be certain whether or not there exist in America governments capable of making and executing treaties.[71]

At the same time, it is clear that Chateaubriand desired, if possible, to secure advantages for the motherland from the Spanish-American states. Upon learning that the Colombian minister at Washington had declared that his government was willing to concede special privileges to Spain on the basis of the acknowledgment of its independence, the French minister wrote to Talaru to ask that he make known this attitude to the Court of Madrid. Chateaubriand suggested that this knowledge might prove useful to the Spanish Government when it essayed the onerous task of pacification.[72] Nevertheless, Talaru was soon forced to realize that Spain was even reluctant to grant exequaturs to French consuls destined for Cuba and Puerto Rico.[73]

---

countries, and that the purposes in contemplation were of a character altogether inadmissible." D. S., Instructions to Ministers, 10.

[71] Chateaubriand, *Congrès de Vérone,* II, 351.

[72] March 29, 1824, A. A. E., Espagne, 726.

[73] Talaru to Chateaubriand, April 7, 1824, *ibid.,* 727. In 1826

Unfortunately for the unfolding of French policy toward Spanish America at this time, Chasseriau and Samouel did not gain the confidence of Patriot officials in Mexico or Colombia. The hesitant policy of France did not foreshadow an attitude which aimed at an early acknowledgment of the independence of those countries in return for commercial concessions. Nor did it insure a decision which contemplated the recognition of those countries by Spain in conjunction with France.

The prospect of joint action by France and England in respect to the Indies had by 1825 completely vanished. Though both Canning and Chateaubriand dreamed of founding monarchies in Spanish America, their minds did not meet. Canning stood staunchly for a policy of nonintervention in the Spanish Indies, a policy to which Chateaubriand had in the main agreed by the Polignac Memorandum. The French minister was not willing to join with Canning, however, in acknowledging the independence of the Spanish-American states. On the other hand, soon after the visit of Chasseriau to Paris Canning was warned by a mysterious go-between that France had decided to forestall England in forming commercial relations with Colombia.[74]

It is clear that Chateaubriand was not yet completely thwarted in his attempt to find a practical solution for the troublesome problem of Spanish America. A memorandum drawn up in his name in 1824 indicates that he was contemplating a comprehensive inquiry. This paper was a form of appointment providing for a commission to study all the

---

the *Almanach royal,* p. 148, included in the list of French consular agents two consuls in Cuba and one in Puerto Rico.

[74] " Extracts from Spain, 1824-5," F. O., 360.

French official documents concerning Spanish-American countries and to prepare three reports. The first report was to be a brief account of the events which had brought the Spanish colonies into their existing condition. The second report was to describe exactly the military, political, and social condition of every one of those colonies and to make inferences with regard to their respective destinies. The third report was to formulate the rules of conduct that might well be adopted by France with regard not only to the communities which the commission felt had irrevocably separated from Spain but also those colonies which in its judgment might still be induced to acknowledge the authority of the mother country. Apparently as an afterthought, a clause was added to the effect that these reports were also to consider the status of Brazil.[75]

This proposal for the appointment, presumably by the sanction of Louis XVIII, of a committee to formulate a well-founded Latin-American policy was wise. It might have resulted in the formulation of more consistent and farsighted measures on the part of France than had yet been adopted. However, the appointment form was left unfinished. The names of the persons who were to formulate the policy that France should adopt in regard to the insurgent Latin colonies in the New World were not inserted in the paper. Probably it was prepared shortly before Chateaubriand relinquished his portfolio.

Just after Canning's death, Chateaubriand published in his *Voyage en Amérique* a suggestive account of his diplomatic rôle with respect to the Spanish Indies. In the prologue the former minister declared that in this work he had

---

[75] This document was merely dated " 1824." A. A. E., Mémoires et Documents, Amérique, 36.

disclosed all that he was permitted to tell concerning his policy toward the insurgent colonies.[76] Chateaubriand declared that, upon the restoration of Ferdinand VII to absolute power, he had conceived a project which he believed would be useful to both America and Europe. He had flattered himself that he had a plan which would reconcile the rights of other nations with the interests of France. His cardinal aim had been the erection of Bourbon monarchies in liberated Spanish America:

I was deluded by the idea of attaching my name to the liberty of the Second America, without compromising this freedom in the emancipated colonies, and without endangering the monarchical principle of European states.

Assured of the favorable attitude of various cabinets of the Continent with only one exception, I did not despair of overcoming the resistance offered me in England by the statesman who has just died. . . . I thought that the administration of which I was a member would allow me to construct an edifice which could only reflect honor upon it; I had the naïveté to believe that the affairs of my Ministry in carrying me afield would not thrust me in the way of anyone. Like the astrologer, I gazed at the heavens, and I tumbled into a pit. England rejoiced at my downfall; it is true that we had stationed a garrison in Cadiz under the white flag, and that the monarchical emancipation of the Spanish colonies by the generous influence of the eldest son of the Bourbons would have raised France to the pinnacle of prosperity and glory. Such was the last dream of my mature years; I believed myself in America, and I awoke in Europe.[77]

It is significant that the tentative policy envisaged by Chateaubriand was evidently formed without the concurrence of the Czar, with whom France had at times been in

[76] Chateaubriand, *Œuvres complètes,* VI, 3.
[77] *Ibid.,* 220-21.

agreement concerning the Spanish colonies. Two letters of the French ambassador, who was high in favor at the Russian court, illustrate the Czar's viewpoint. On November 28, 1823, Count la Ferronnays reported to Chateaubriand that he had just had an audience with Alexander I. During this interview the Czar, who had recently notified the United States of his intention not to acknowledge the independence of the Spanish-American nations, declared that he was in perfect agreement with France concerning the Indies. He maintained that a revolution should be no more sanctioned in America than in Europe. Only Ferdinand VII could decide upon his rights. In challenging words the Russian autocrat ridiculed the idea of acknowledging the independence of Spanish America where everything was in frightful chaos:

> To acknowledge the independence of what? Of whom? Where are the chieftains? Where are the governments? Which is the party that dominates? With whom should we treat? For the result of recognizing a country is the negotiation of treaties. Does one wish to compare the actual situation of southern America with the revolution in North America against England? There is no analogy between them. . . . Where are the Franklins, the Washingtons, and the Jeffersons of southern America? [78]

The positive side of Russia's policy toward Spanish America was made known to La Ferronnays by Count Nesselrode, who had become Minister of Foreign Affairs. In December, 1823, that minister praised the policy of the

[78] A. A. E., Russie, 165. A communication of Russia to the United States in October, 1823, in regard to the recognition of the Spanish-American states is found in Ford and Adams, *John Quincy Adams: His Connection with the Monroe Doctrine* (1823) *and with Emancipation under Martial Law*, p. 32.

Allies, who had refrained from acting with respect to the
rebellious Spanish colonies without the consent of Ferdinand VII. Nesselrode even suggested that those powers
intervene in the quarrel between Spain and her colonies as
mediators and guarantors of the rights of His Catholic
Majesty.[79] Early in the next year the Russian envoy at
Madrid was directed to insist that Spain refrain from acknowledging the independence of her colonies; he was to
arrange in concert with her Cabinet the means of preparing
a Spanish armament to support the Royalists in the Indies.[80]
Nor was this all that Russia proposed. After news of the
Monroe Doctrine reached St. Petersburg, La Ferronnays
informed Chateaubriand on May 14, 1824, of an interview
which he had just had with Nesselrode. In response to the
French ambassador, who expressed regret that the deplorable condition of Spain had unfortunately placed great obstacles in the way of the reconquest of her colonies,
Nesselrode smilingly inquired why the Allies should not
assist the Spaniards: "And what could England say, or
rather what could she do, if an army composed of Spaniards, Frenchmen, Russians, Prussians, and Austrians should
embark upon a fleet equipped and financed by all the allies
of the Spanish King and should proceed to America in
order to regain his lost rights for that monarch?"

Suspecting that this scheme had been unfolded in order
to ascertain his views, La Ferronnays promptly responded
that the proposed concert seemed very finely conceived but
that its execution would not be easy. Further, he informed

[79] La Ferronnays to Chateaubriand, December 6, 1823, A. A. E.,
Russie, 165.

[80] Talaru to Chateaubriand, February 23, 1824, A. A. E., Espagne,
726.

the Russian Chancellor that, as the ambassador of France, he could not favor a project for forcible interposition by the Allies in Spanish America.[81] Russia's half-hearted overture proposing armed aid by the Holy Allies to enable Ferdinand VII to restore his sovereignty over his former colonies in America was thus immediately thwarted by France. La Ferronnays was presumably animated by a feeling like that which had determined Chateaubriand's attitude toward similar proposals, namely that if such intervention should be undertaken, France would eventually be deserted by her allies and be forced to bear the brunt of Anglo-Saxon displeasure alone.

Another indication of the intentions of France toward the new American nations is found in the instructions prepared by Clermont-Tonnerre for naval officers who were sent as agents to the west coast of South America. This minister declared that conditions in Chile and Peru would not yet permit France to dispatch consular or diplomatic agents to those countries. The Council of State had decided, however, that French interests made it advisable to employ naval captains to fulfill temporarily the functions of consular agents. Hence Captains de la Susse and de Moges had been selected for a mission to ports on the Pacific Ocean: " It is accordingly in the honorable uniform of the royal marine and in all French loyalty that they should profit by the sojourn which they will make in the ports of Chile and Peru, in order to give impressions favorable to France, and in order to collect information that will be useful to commerce, to the government, and to the royal navy."

[81] A. A. E., Russie, 166.

Those captains were to destroy any notions prejudicial to their country by pointing out that the French Government had preserved a strict neutrality in the protracted quarrel between Spain and her colonies and that, until a reconciliation took place, France desired only that the commerce of her subjects should be respected. De Moges and De la Susse were informed that an explanation of the intentions of their government would suffice to destroy any harmful reports which foreigners might have attempted to spread. France was " the power that would be most suitable for the governments of Chile and Peru to select as a mediator in any arrangement which would have as its object to induce Spain to recognize the independence of those countries," especially if their rulers should offer to the Spaniards certain commercial advantages. Affixed to these instructions was a long list of topics touching the economic, social, political, and military condition of Pacific coast countries which the agents were to investigate.[82]   Evidently the French Government not only desired to gather useful information concerning the actual condition of the Pacific shores of South America but also wished its agents to make known that it would use its good offices to promote a reconciliation between the colonies and the motherland.

Furthermore, on January 27, 1824, Commander Rosamel, who was in charge of the French naval station in the Pacific Ocean, had been directed by Clermont-Tonnerre to

[82] Clermont-Tonnerre to De la Susse and De Moges, December 29, 1823, A. N., Marine, B B⁴, 447. On certain activities of these captains, see Webster, *Britain and the Independence of Latin America*, I, 356, 358. A report of De la Susse from Valparaiso, dated January 1, 1825, concerning San Martín's campaigns in Chile is printed in Otero, *Historia del Libertador Don José de San Martín*, II, 753-60.

collect such data concerning the places which he might visit as would be of aid to France, if unforeseen events should induce her " to prosecute a war against the new governments of southern America," or if other equally un-foreseen circumstances should compel her " to support those governments against the projects of another power." Rosamel was further instructed that he might extend his conjectures as far as he wished, " in order to multiply the hypotheses and to have a large field in which to sketch a plan of campaign." He was not only to describe the places which appeared most favorable to an attack by sea or by land but also " to indicate the kind and the number of ships that would be needed, the force of soldiers that it would be necessary to disembark, the probability of suc-cess, the means of retaining posts captured by force, and the resources which would be available in case of a re-verse." [83]   On the same day similar instructions were ad-dressed to Commander Grivel on the Brazilian coast. The Minister of Marine declared that it was advisable that Grivel examine attentively what, " in case of war, would be the resources which Portuguese America would offer us, if we were allied with that country, or what would be the means of attacking Brazil, if we had to fight against her government." [84]

On March 1, 1824, Clermont-Tonnerre sent similar in-structions to Admiral Jurien de la Gravière, who had be-come the commander of the naval station in the Antilles. With these instructions were sent copies of the minister's letters to Donzelot dated December 17, 1823, and February 23, 1824, which set forth the policy of France toward the

[83] A. N., Marine, 405 *bis*.
[84] *Ibid.*, 457.

former possessions of Spain in America. Jurien was directed to gather secretly information about the resources
and the means of defence which the French colonies near
the Caribbean Sea could offer to the maritime powers of
Europe that might be allied either with France or with the
governments established in the former Spanish colonies.
The minister declared that unexpected circumstances might
force France to wage war: " In order to have a larger field
in which to arrange our plans of campaign, you can multiply conjectures and can suppose, for example, that France
might be allied with Great Britain against the other maritime powers, or that allied with those powers she might
struggle against England."   Haiti, the former colony of
France in the island of Santo Domingo, was to be included
within the sphere of Jurien's observations. " Our actual
alliance with Spain," added the minister, " is also a motive
for making hypothetical calculations concerning the dangers
which might menace the colonies of Cuba and Puerto Rico
in case a war broke out in Europe, and regarding the best
decision that France could make in such contingency with
respect to these two islands which would offer excellent
bases for her maritime operations."   Jurien was to take
counsel with Governor Donzelot about the protection of
Guadeloupe and Martinique and about measures which
might some day extend the influence of France in other
islands of the West Indies and " upon the continent of
America." [85]

[85] *Ibid.*, 405 *bis*. See further Clermont-Tonnerre to Bougainville,
February 17, 1824, *ibid.* In respect to the rôle of Villèle regarding
intervention in the Spanish colonies and the relations of France
and England, see Temperley, " Canning and the Conferences of
the Four Allied Governments at Paris, 1823-1826," *Am. Hist.
Rev.*, XXX, 23.

French naval officials were thus instructed to gather data for a plan of campaign involving the Spanish colonies from Cuba to the Philippines and possibly including Brazil.   In case war broke out in Europe, this plan was apparently to be executed in America by French armaments either in conjunction with England or, more probably, in opposition to her. The expected contingency, however, did not arise. France was not compelled to attack certain vulnerable dependencies of the British Empire from bases in the West Indies.   She neither tried to rally to her support the distracted colonies of Spain nor to undertake hostilities against them and in favor of the motherland.   Clermont-Tonnerre was presumably acting under directions from the head of the Cabinet.   No evidence has been found, however, to show that Chateaubriand approved the radical steps taken by the Minister of Marine.

Chateaubriand's policy toward Spanish America was many-faceted.   One phase of it was a successful attempt to compel Spain to reform her colonial system in order to permit freedom of commerce with the Indies.   Another was a fruitless endeavor to induce Canning to participate in a European congress which would consider the policy to be followed toward the insurgent colonies.   Both these efforts were mainly designed to hinder the recognition of Spanish-American independence by England.   Chateaubriand felt that the time was not quite ripe for the admission of the new states into the society of nations.   Well realizing, however, that England was the great commercial rival of France in the impending struggle for Spanish-American markets, he did not wish to see his country placed at a disadvantage.   He even indulged in the hope that mercantile concessions by Spain would satisfy England and retard recognition, and that at the same time such concessions would aid French merchants. Consequently Chateaubriand could not coöperate with Canning in an acknowledgment of the independence of the Spanish-American nations.

On the other hand, France could not encourage Russia in the adoption of a coercive policy toward the Spanish-American insurgents. It is evident that in the spring of 1824 Russian statesmen still dreamed that the Holy Allies might aid Spain by armed force to recover her colonies. Notwithstanding the Czar's attitude, however, French diplomats were extremely skeptical at that time of the wisdom of forcible interposition. Indeed, before Chateaubriand left office he had practically dismissed the thought of intervening by force of arms to restore the Spanish continental colonies in America to Ferdinand VII. Still, there is no doubt that occasionally there still flitted through his mind the alluring vision of Bourbon monarchies in the Spanish Indies.

His policy did represent considerable progress. He dispatched commissioners to Mexico and South America with more elastic powers than such agents had hitherto been accorded. These emissaries were not only to garner information about the insurgent communities but were also to explain the neutral yet sympathetic attitude of France toward those personages who had tasted of the fruits of the tree of emancipation. In spite of the legitimist sentiments of the Russian court Chateaubriand, animated by the spirit of his declaration at the Congress of Verona, prepared instructions for agents to Spanish-American countries which contemplated the ultimate acknowledgment of their independence by France. All in all, despite seeming inconsistencies, his policy signalized the most distinctive advance yet made by France in her attitude toward the Spanish nations of the New World.

Though their policies were somewhat interwoven, Chateaubriand and Villèle did not always work in harmony. Perhaps it was Villèle who incited Clermont-Tonnerre to direct French naval officials to collect data which would either have enabled France to prosecute hostilities against the nations that were emerging in Spanish and Portuguese America or which would have aided her to spring to their defence in case they were menaced by a European power. The last contingency possibly contemplated an attack on the insurgent colonies by a Spanish expedition aided by Russian soldiers.

CHAPTER XI

THE FAGGOT OF THORNS

Although Villèle's Cabinet remained in office until December, 1827, certain changes took place in it in 1824. The most important change was that involving the Minister of Foreign Affairs. Louis XVIII evidently became dissatisfied with him because of his attitude toward a legislative debate with regard to the finances. Early in June Chateaubriand received a curt note which contained a royal ordinance providing that, for the time being, Villèle was to serve in his place. The head of the Cabinet was thus given an opportunity to develop his policy toward Spanish America without being hampered by an ambitious Foreign Minister.

To the English ambassador at Paris, Villèle stated that this change affected merely the internal politics of his Cabinet and would have no effect upon its foreign policy. He declared that the only question which was apt to arise between England and France was in regard to the course to be pursued toward the South American states. Villèle explained that, as long as England did not alter her policy, she could depend upon France refraining from all interference with those states and opposing " the execution of any plans combined by other Powers to reëstablish by force of arms the dominion of Spain over Her revolted Colonies." [1] Yet the French minister soon secured the approval of representatives of the Holy Allies of the instructions to Governor Donzelot authorizing him to protect the Spanish

[1] Stuart to Canning, June 8, 1824 (no. 390), F. O., 27/310.

colonies in the West Indies against external attacks or revolutionary uprisings.[2]

The attitude of France toward England remained unchanged. In order to induce Canning to refrain from recognizing Spanish-American independence, the French chargé d'affaires in London continued the measures designed to prevent England from separating from the Allies on the issue of the insurgent colonies.[3] Villèle informed the English ambassador at Paris that reports from Spanish America showed that no uniform political system would suit the various states; republican government was supported in Colombia but detested in Mexico, where there was no hope of improvement " until a Younger Branch of the Spanish Royal Family should be established on the throne." Consequently he believed that, if Ferdinand VII could be persuaded to allow the Prince of Lucca to sail for Vera Cruz, that step would offer the most certain means of pacifying Mexico. At this time, however, Canning was convinced that nothing could come of the project for the creation of a Spanish appanage in Mexico unless it emanated from Madrid.[4] Yet to the chargé at St. Petersburg Villèle wrote that Canning's declarations to Parliament concerning the Indies left room for hope that England would postpone the recognition of the Spanish-American states.[5]

Villèle's policy was also indicated by the informal relations which he had with Spanish-American agents. In

[2] Temperley, " Canning and the Conferences of the Four Allied Governments at Paris, 1823-1826," Am. Hist. Rev., XXX, 23.

[3] Villèle to Talaru, June 15, 1824, A. A. E., Espagne, 727.

[4] Webster, Britain and the Independence of Latin America, II, 158. The views of Canning are indicated in Canning, Some Official Correspondence, I, 247-48.

[5] July 3, 1824, A. A. E., Russie, 166.

July, 1824, José R. Revenga, who had been sent by Colombia on a mission to Spain, had an interview with the French Premier. Villèle informed him that France intended to established direct commercial intercourse with Colombia and that Chasseriau had been directed to deny rumors that his government intended to aid Spain against her colonies. Further, Villèle assured Revenga that France would not help Spain with ships or soldiers, that Spain's other allies would not furnish such aid, and that, if those powers did not take immediate steps in regard to Colombia, it was because they desired proof that she had established the order and tranquillity necessary for civilized states.[6] To a friar named Tomás Murphy, who was serving as confidential agent of Mexico in Europe, Villèle declared that his Cabinet would never interpose in Spain's quarrel with her colonies, but that, if the motherland declined to accept the good offices of France, she would then be free to make a decision.[7] To judge by these secret interviews, Villèle had now discarded the notion of intervening to restore the authority of Ferdinand VII in Middle and South America by force of arms.

On August 4 Louis XVIII shifted to the post of Minister of Foreign Affairs Baron Damas, an experienced publicist, who left the Ministry of War with some trepidation. Though ignorant of diplomacy, Damas was flattered by this appointment, and Villèle secured a Foreign Minister who evidently would be more complaisant than Chateaubriand. A clever comparison attributed to the head of the Cabinet suggests his attitude concerning Spanish affairs.

[6] Zubieta, *Apuntaciones sobre las primeras misiones diplomáticas de Colombia*, p. 404.

[7] *La diplomacia mexicana*, II, 249-51; III, 250, 251, 253, 265.

When Marquis Moustier was appointed ambassador to Madrid, Villèle advised him " to talk little, and to do less, observing that he looked upon Spain as a Faggot of Thorns, which could not be handled without pricking the person who endeavored to lay hold of it." [8]

Manuel Hurtado, whom the Colombian Government had appointed its minister to European courts, was soon induced to cross the Channel from England. Hurtado had scarcely reached Paris, however, when the Spanish ambassador, Francisco de Zea Bermúdez, called upon Villèle and expressed surprise that, in view of her alliance with Spain, France should initiate intercourse with the agent of an insurgent Spanish colony. Villèle explained that his communications with Hurtado had been entirely concerned with the interests of Spain. Modifying his views as a chameleon changes its color, the French minister even declared that, if the presence of a Colombian agent in France gave umbrage to the Court of Madrid, he would direct Hurtado to leave the country.[9]

Colombia's agent informed Stuart that, although Villèle had assured him that all citizens of Colombia who conducted themselves properly in France would be protected, that minister declined to give him an assurance that his government would observe a strict neutrality in the dispute between Spain and her colonies, or that it would admit into French harbors vessels sailing under the flag of a Spanish-American state upon the same basis which had been judged

[8] Granville to Canning, September 29, 1825, F. O., 27/332.
[9] Stuart to Canning, August 30, 1824 (no. 445), F. O., 27/313. On June 29, 1824, Canning informed Stuart that Villèle had sent Hurtado an urgent invitation to visit Paris. Webster, op. cit., p. 155.

advisable in English ports.[10] Hurtado was convinced that France wished commercial concessions from the new American states like those which they had granted to England. Notwithstanding this, he concluded that the object of the French negotiations was to restore Spain's sovereignty over her former colonies.[11] He succinctly reported to Bogotá that the Liberals and the merchants of France favored Spanish-American independence, that the government was neutral because it could not assume a hostile attitude, but that its views were contrary to the interests of Spanish America.[12]

The resentful attitude of the Court of Madrid with regard to the reception of the Colombian agent by Villèle was suggested in an anonymous pamphlet printed under the auspices of the Spanish ambassador shortly after Hurtado reached Paris. After a survey of the rebellion in the Indies and of the relations of England and France with the revolting communities, the author expressed the hope that the great powers of Europe would interfere to hasten the subjugation of the Spanish colonies. A special appeal was made to France to promote intervention there in favor of Ferdinand VII.[13]

That Damas was reluctant to favor the insurgent peoples was soon shown by the suspicions which he entertained concerning the conduct of a Colombian envoy to the Holy See who, while sojourning in Paris in the autumn of 1824,

---

[10] Stuart to Canning, September 9, 1824 (no. 461), F. O., 27/314.

[11] Stuart to Canning, September 23, 1824, *ibid.*

[12] Cadena, *Anales diplomáticos de Colombia,* pp. 517-18.

[13] *Considérations sur l'état présent de l'Amérique du Sud et sur l'arrivée à Paris de M. Hurtado,* p. 47; Stuart to Canning, September 2, 1824 (no. 451), F. O., 27/314.

had consorted with revolutionaries.[14] Colombia's informal negotiations with France were soon renewed by Colonel José M. Lanz. In November, 1824, Lanz was instructed to obtain explanations from the French Government on two matters of policy. If Colombia and her American allies should undertake to liberate Cuba and Puerto Rico from Spanish rule, would France take an active part against them? If French soldiers should take possession of certain Spanish colonies to preserve them from anarchy, would those soldiers join the Royalist forces against the liberating armies of Spanish-American republics?[15] These inquiries indicate the forebodings of some South American leaders who wished their nations to make a common cause against Spain but who were apprehensive concerning the attitude of France toward such an aggressive policy.

Lanz did not obtain direct answers to his queries. As the result of interviews with Villèle and Damas, however, this Colombian agent reached certain conclusions. France professed a desire to enter into relations with Colombia in order to promote commerce and industry. The French Government aimed to terminate the hostilities between Spain and her colonies by acting as a mediator either alone or in conjunction with England. Though that government planned to dispatch commercial agents to Colombia, it would not recognize that nation until her independence was acknowledged by the Spanish Government. It appreciated an invitation by Colombia to send representatives to the congress of Latin-American states which Bolívar had con-

[14] Leturia, *Bolívar y León XII,* pp. 75-76.

[15] Zubieta, *op. cit.,* pp. 474-75; Lanz's credentials signed by P. Gual and dated November 9, 1824, are found in A. A. E., Colombie, 2.

voked at Panama, but it would not send a commissioner there because it desired to lull the suspicions and jealousies of European governments.[16]

In his message to the Congress of Colombia on January 2, 1826, Francisco de Paula Santander, Bolívar's rival who was Acting President of that state, explained that he had striven to secure from the French Government an explicit declaration in favor of his country. Expressing the opinion that the congress would approve the circumspection with which Lanz had proceeded and the firmness with which he had pleaded the cause of the Colombian people, Santander diplomatically concluded that "the French Government, supported by national opinion, will finally recognize our sovereignty in imitation of other great powers and will be inclined to establish relations friendly and useful to both nations." [17]

The conservative attitude of Damas toward the Spanish colonies was shown also by his correspondence with the French ambassador at Madrid. Upon taking leave of Ferdinand VII on August 9, 1824, Talaru mentioned certain legislative measures which were indispensable to the execution of the decree of February 9 concerning commercial relations with the Spanish Indies.[18] Damas accordingly instructed Baron Boislecomte, who succeeded Talaru, to use every opportunity to urge the need of such measures. European governments, he reasoned, no longer had the same interest in separating the Indies from Spain, for free commerce was the chief advantage which they had expected

---

[16] Zubieta, *op. cit.*, p. 476.

[17] Uribe, *Anales diplomáticos y consulares de Colombia,* III, 27.

[18] Talaru to Damas, August 11, 1824, A. A. E., Espagne, 727.

from Spanish-American emancipation.[19] Writing to Boislecomte on October 13, 1824, Damas declared that his
government desired that Spain, strong and happy, should
be able to regain all her possessions; he affirmed that
France did not seek any special advantages at the expense
of her southern neighbor.[20] Two weeks later, in explaining to that ambassador his attitude toward Spanish-American revolutionaries, he asserted that the agents of the
Spanish possessions in America had not even been allowed
to prolong their sojourn in France.[21]

A good opportunity to formulate his views concerning
the colonies was afforded Damas by six queries addressed
to him in December, 1824, by La Ferronnays: (1) If England should recognize the independence of the Spanish
colonies, what action would France take? (2) What were
the actual views of France with respect to them? (3)
Would she still admit, as she did at Verona, a law of necessity and of nature by which nations could acquire their
independence as individuals acquired their properties? (4)
Did she acknowledge a recognition of fact independent of
law, and did her government contemplate applying such a
type of recognition before the other? (5) Was France
inclined to loan the Spanish King vessels, money, or soldiers to aid him to restore his authority over the Spanish-
American colonies? (6) If, after England alone had recognized those colonies as independent states, Spain undertook
to subjugate them by force of arms with the aid of Russia,
and if England made common cause with the new states,
would France decide in favor of Spain, would she support

[19] August 18, 1824, *ibid.*
[20] *Ibid.*, 729.   [21] *Ibid.*

those states, or would she remain neutral? [22]   There is little reason to doubt that the Russian Government had prompted the French ambassador at St. Petersburg to raise these tantalizing questions. Hence their special significance.

The Foreign Minister began his reply by observing that the affairs of Spain were still very complicated. However, experience had shown that it was not imprudent to leave something to time. Important events in Europe which demanded all the attention of the great powers might further retard a decision concerning Spanish America. La Ferronnays' queries were answered consecutively in the following paragraphs:

1. France cannot yet decide what she would do if England should recognize the independence of the Spanish colonies. The example of that nation would soon be followed by several maritime states. This consideration ought to influence the decision which France takes, for it is her duty to watch over the commercial interests of her subjects. A formal protest against recognition by England would be a step which might lead to a rupture with that power; France does not foresee the necessity of making such a protest. To refrain from recognizing the independence of those colonies if England believed it her duty to take such action would be tacitly to protest against the decision which that power had made and at the same time to follow a policy necessary to the maintenance of peace.

2 and 3. France does not retract what she said at Verona. It is certain that we cannot avoid noticing the existence of a sort of prescription for changes in the political order which often result from movements that follow revolutions. In practice it is difficult to fix the term of this prescription; for the term depends less upon time than upon the general condition of affairs, upon the particular situation of a

[22] " Questions adressées au Ministre par M. Cte. de la Ferronnays," December, 1824, A. A. E., Russie, 167.

country that wishes to claim the prescription, or upon the disposition of those powers among which the country in question aspires to be ranked. All these factors were operative with respect to the destinies of The Netherlands and the United States. But in reality the political existence of those nations dates only from the moment when formal treaties recognized it and, so to speak, guaranteed it.

4. There cannot be a recognition *de facto* independent of recognition *de jure*. A nation can admit as a fact that a state exists and may even enter into relations of commerce or other relations with it which do not necessitate arranging political transactions. From the moment, however, that by a formal and explicit act a nation recognizes the existence of another state, the right is joined to the fact which has been acknowledged. The nation recognizing the existence of a new state has undertaken to admit it into the membership of the political society the prerogatives of which it is ready to share.

5. France has had occasion to make known that she was not disposed to aid, either by land and naval forces or by her treasure, the efforts which Spain might make to reconquer her colonies.

6. The hypothesis formulated in this question is highly improbable; and, if it should be realized, the circumstances which would accompany a rupture between England and Russia would also determine the conduct of France.[23]

Damas' doctrine of recognition was the most explicit statement made by a French minister during the emergence of the Latin-American nations with respect to the principles that should determine an acknowledgment of the independence of a new state. It is worthy of notice that his answer to the fourth query formulated a doctrine re-

[23] "Réponse aux questions de M. le Cte. de la Ferronnays," December, 1824, *ibid.*; printed inexactly in Villanueva, "La diplomatie française dans l'Amérique latine," *Bull. bib. am.,* October, 1916, pp. 7-8.

sembling that set forth in 1818 by the capable American
Secretary of State, John Quincy Adams, who in a notable
letter to President Monroe maintained that the fact and
the right combined could alone justify a neutral nation in
acknowledging a new and disputed sovereignty.[24] Unlike
England and the United States, France was loath to admit
that certain Spanish-American nations were in the enjoyment of independence *de facto*. Damas even took the view
that France might admit the *de facto* independence of a
state without acknowledging its independence *de jure*—
a doctrine with which Villèle was presumably in agreement.
In formulating his views Damas scouted the notion that,
on the issue of the independence of the Spanish Indies,
France would ever be compelled to choose between align-
ing herself in militant fashion on the side of England and
taking the side of Spain and Russia.

Shortly after Damas formulated his doctrine of recognition, Secretary Canning reached a decision concerning the
status of the Spanish Indies. On December 31, 1824, he
sent a dispatch to Bosanquet, the English chargé at Madrid,
which was read to Secretary Ofalia. This dispatch announced a new step by England toward certain Spanish-
American provinces which had separated from the motherland. Declaring that the struggle of Spain to reconquer
her colonies was hopeless, Canning served notice that England intended to negotiate commercial treaties with Mexico,
Colombia, and La Plata. Further, he made the interpretative statement that when those treaties were ratified the

---

[24] *Memorandum upon the Power to Recognize the Independence
of a New Foreign State*, Senate Documents, 54th Cong., 2d sess.,
no. 56, pp. 52-53.

effect would be the recognition of the *de facto* governments of those states.[25]

When, early in 1825, he was told of Canning's decision to negotiate treaties of commerce with Spanish-American states, Villèle professed to receive this news on behalf of France with "much indifference."[26] Yet Damas declared to the Austrian ambassador at Paris that the powers of continental Europe should regard the progress of revolutionary principles in America as inimical to their interests.[27] Nevertheless, the new English policy regarding commercial intercourse with Spanish America probably helped to convince Damas that it was necessary for his country to take definite steps to promote trade with the Latin nations of the New World.

In a dispatch to Boislecomte, Damas stated that England was negotiating treaties of commerce with the new states, while Holland and Sweden were imitating her in the hope of gaining commercial advantages. Reasoning that at a time when foreign agents were being stationed in Spanish-American countries French consuls should likewise be sent there, Damas held that they might be able to promote a *rapprochement* between those countries and Spain. He declared that the French Government desired to reconcile its services to Spain with the mercantile interests of its subjects but explained that, after the decree of 1824 opened the Spanish colonies to the commerce of foreigners, numerous interests had demanded special protection there and

[25] Webster, *Britain and the Independence of Latin America,* II, 430-31.

[26] *Ibid.,* 162.

[27] Vincent to Metternich, January 10, 1825, H. H. u. S., Berichte aus Frankreich, 362.

had made the need of French agents more keenly felt. Bois-lecomte was directed not to give umbrage to the Spanish Government by an abrupt demand that it authorize France to send missions to Spanish America. Still, he was to emphasize the advantage of checking the influence of the commissioners of other nations by the presence of agents of " a friendly power that did not separate its interests from those of Spain, and that still sought every occasion to serve her." [28]

Meanwhile French journalists had prepared their countrymen for the change in English policy. On January 9, 1825, the *Journal des Débats* stated that England was about to negotiate treaties of commerce with Colombia and Mexico based upon the acknowledgment of their independence. The journal then declared that the consequences of that measure to the world would be very grave. In conclusion it pertinently inquired what the reaction of continental Europe would be: "What decision will France take? . . . And what has M. de Villèle done?"

On the following day *L'Étoile* took up the theme in a skeptical strain, which may have reflected Villèle's views.[29] Though asserting that by her decision England had virtually released the American subjects of Spain from their allegiance, this journal nevertheless intimated that such

[28] January 10, 1825, A. A. E., Espagne, 731.

[29] In a secret dispatch to Zea Bermúdez on October 22, 1825, Villahermosa, Spain's ambassador at Paris, stated that he had been informed that Villèle had asked the editors of *L'Étoile* to prepare an article dealing with a reconciliation between Spain and her colonies. A. H. N., Estado, 5230. News of the decisive defeat of the Royalist soldiers in Peru at the battle of Ayacucho on December 9, 1824, had not reached Paris on January 10, 1825. See *infra*, pp. 364-65.

declarations meant nothing as long as they were not supported by fleets and armies: " Can one suppose that the
royal troops of Spain, who still occupy the fairest portions
of Peru and Chile, will suddenly withdraw overcome with
terror because some English consuls arrive upon the soil
of the vaguely delineated republics of Mexico and
Colombia? "

The *Courrier Français*, an organ of the Left, complained
on January 10 that neither the legislators nor the people of
France were aware what policy the Ministry of Foreign
Affairs would adopt toward the new American states. On
the same day the editor of the *Constitutionnel* observed
that the destinies of America and Europe were developing:
" Supported by the trident of Neptune, England braves the
Holy Alliance and defies the tempests which may be aroused
against her." The *Quotidienne*, which was not a ministerial
organ, commented on English policy as follows: " The insufficient motives adduced by the Cabinet of St. James give
rise to the thought that it wishes to seek a tardy and cruel
revenge for the rôle which Spain, drawn into the American
Revolution by France, played in the emancipation of the
United States of America." [30] On January 14 the *Courrier Français* characterized Canning's decision as a great act
pregnant with the future, an act " which sets into movement all the couriers and is the subject of a thousand interpretations." In a spirit that was critical of French foreign policy it added: " England has been right to assume
the magnificent rôle which has been neglected by France,
that of placing herself at the head of human societies."

[30] January 11, 1825. A further analysis of the views of Parisian
journals on English recognition of Spanish-American independence
is to be found in *L'Étoile*, February 4, 1825.

When Lord Granville, the new English ambassador at Paris, made known to Baron Damas the intention of his government to acknowledge the independence of Mexico, Colombia, and La Plata, the French minister was tempted to ask England to reconsider so grave an act. He soon sent to Polignac a dispatch which contained the following passages:

Yet, England's decision having been made, we can only express regret, in the interest of the principles of order and legitimacy which Europe is rightly pleased to have reëstablished. We entertain the wish that this step may not lead to new complications in politics by giving to the principles of revolution a false support. We see that England has allowed herself to be dominated by commercial necessity. Still, is it really prudent for her to follow exclusively the impulse of a certain class of individuals and to prefer their interests to those of the entire social order?

What we ought further to conclude from her conduct is that, although she seems to deny it, she has completely left the Alliance. We may well be astonished at this, for it is she who nobly laid down the foundations of the Alliance and gave it so powerful an impulse that it has overcome the formidable obstacles which hindered the reëstablishment of a political equilibrium in Europe. May some circumstance not arise which will make her regret having isolated herself? Is it not in the nature of things today that the nation which remains outside this European association, whose care has thus far maintained the general peace, runs the risk of provoking distrust, of giving umbrage, and also of furnishing the occasion for a new conflict? [81]

Such was the commentary, declared Damas, which he had addressed to Granville on being formally notified of

[81] Damas to Polignac, January 14, 1825, A. A. E., Angleterre, 619. For Spain's protest of January 21, 1825, against England's policy of recognition, see Webster, *Britain and the Independence of Latin America*, II, 433-37.

the momentous decision that England had taken concerning Spanish-American independence, and such was the view which he wished Prince Polignac to express to Canning. In a conference with that minister on January 24, the Prince accordingly expressed regret that the English Cabinet had adopted a new policy without consulting the Allies. On the other hand, Canning maintained that the decision of his government might be useful to the interests of France by tracing a route which she could follow. Polignac responded that one might with equal reason hold the contrary view; for an ignorance prevailed with respect to English treaties with the new states, which might conceivably contain stipulations injurious to French commerce. Canning retorted with some warmth that a fear of injuring French merchants would not prevent England from fostering her own mercantile interests. According to the report of Polignac to his government, he ended the interview by expressing the opinion that England had deceived herself in regard to the advantages to be derived from an acknowledgment of Spanish-American independence.[32] Sir Robert Wilson, however, informed a correspondent that Canning's policy had " set the Continent quite wild with rage and joy, hope and fear." Wilson asserted that France and Russia would be revenged " for the blowing up of the Holy Alliance mine." [33]

In a letter to Ambassador Moustier summarizing the results of certain conferences attended by diplomats representing the members of the Holy Alliance, Damas declared that those powers considered it beneath the dignity

[32] Polignac to Damas, January 26, 1825, A. A. E., Angleterre, 619.

[33] Temperley, *Life of Canning,* p. 189.

of Spain to accept the mediation of England alone and
that the decree modifying the Spanish commercial system
should be followed by other decrees reforming the administration of the colonies which remained loyal. Besides,
Damas again mentioned the need which France felt of
having commercial agents in Spanish America.[34] Count
Puebla, who had become Spain's ambassador at Paris, was
much pleased with the critical attitude which Damas displayed toward England's recognition policy at a conference
of representatives of the Holy Allies held in January, 1825,
at the home of that minister. Consequently Puebla assured
Damas of the keen appreciation of his Royal Master for the
interest which the French King took in the cause of Spain,
and the Spanish ambassador asked that minister, in the
name of His Catholic Majesty, to continue to exercise the
good offices which he had employed up to that time.[35] A
mysterious go-between who had visited Paris now informed
Canning that both the French Ultras and the Liberals were
much exasperated at England's recognition of Spanish-
American independence and that this sentiment had been
stimulated by the intrigues of Pozzo di Borgo.[36]

There is no doubt that Russia as well as France took the
English acknowledgment of Spanish-American independence seriously. Chargé Fontenay reported to Paris that the
Russian Government felt that Spain should act in a calm
and dignified fashion and avoid a rupture: "It thinks that
His Catholic Majesty should content himself with sending
a formal protest to the courts of Europe."[37] On February

[34] January 25, 1825, A. A. E., Espagne, 731.

[35] Puebla to Zea Bermúdez, January 29, 1825, A. H. N., Estado,
6861.

[36] "Extracts from Spain, 1824-5," F. O., 360.

[37] Fontenay to Damas, February 8, 1825, A. A. E., Russie, 167.

16 Ambassador la Ferronnays had an audience with the Czar in which the latter stated that he considered the recognition accorded by England to be a precipitate step taken in order to promote her mercantile interests. Alexander I frankly declared: " The communications which I have directed my ambassador to make to M. de Villèle and M. de Damas will have proved to the King that his manner and my manner of contemplating this question are identical." The autocrat declared that in the protocols of the conferences held at Paris he found the French ministers repeating almost literally the instructions which he had sent to his envoys as soon as he heard of England's decision in respect to Spanish America. He explained: " It will be easy to convince you that in content as well as in form I find myself upon all points in accord with your government, that is to say, unshakeable in respect to the principle but realizing the need of employing calm language without any show of irritation." [38]

A most emphatic protest against English recognition of Spanish-American independence was made by Metternich. On March 2, 1825, the Austrian ambassador at London, Prince Esterhazy, announced to Canning that his government would not relinquish the principle of legitimacy which had guided the Continental allies since Napoleon's downfall.[39] During the same month, at a conference in Paris

[38] " Relation de l'audience solemnelle de son Excellence le Comte de La Ferronnays, Ambassadeur de sa Majesté Très Chrétienne près Sa Majesté L'Empereur de toutes les Russies," *ibid*. On the Russian reaction to England's step, see further Villanueva, " La diplomatie française et la reconnaissance de l'indépendance de Buenos-Aires, de la Colombie et du Mexique par l'Angleterre," *Bull. bib. am.*, October, 1912, pp. 7-8.

[39] Paxson, *The Independence of the South-American Republics*, pp. 247-50; Temperley, *The Foreign Policy of Canning*, pp. 152-53.

attended by Damas and the envoys of Austria, Prussia, and Russia, the Russian ambassador read to them a dispatch from his court which contained a homily on the principle of legitimacy. Pozzo di Borgo made known the Czar's advice: the Allies should not only refrain from acknowledging the independence of the insurgent governments formed in the Indies but should also continue to give Spain their moral support in the endeavor to reëstablish her sovereignty over the revolutionary communities. The members of the conference agreed that the doctrine of legitimacy was in harmony with the law of nations and with the treaties which had furnished the bases for the reconstruction of Europe. With reference to certain remarks which a Dutch diplomat had made concerning the Spanish colonies, Pozzo di Borgo stated that Russia had tried to dissuade The Netherlands from acknowledging the revolutionary Spanish-American communities as independent. Damas revealed that his government had expressed similar views to the Dutch Government, which seemed to have disavowed the project of recognizing the new states immediately.[40]

France and Russia accordingly took a more conciliatory attitude toward England's recognition policy than did Austria. There is no evidence at hand to show, however, as the Venezuelan historian Villanueva seems to have asserted, that it was only the attitude of France which prevented the outbreak of hostilities between England and the Allies as

---

[40] "Résumé de la conference du $\frac{17 \text{ Février}}{1 \text{ Mars}}$, 1825," A. A. E., Espagne, 731; "Protocols of Conferences of Representatives of the Allied Powers respecting Spanish America, 1824-1825," *Am. Hist. Rev.*, XXII, 606-08.

the result of Canning's decision to recognize certain Spanish nations of America.[41]

After Nicholas I became Czar in December, 1825, he expressed pleasure at the harmonious relations which had existed for several years between Russia and France with respect to Spanish affairs.[42]   In response the reactionary Charles X, who had become king upon the death of Louis XVIII in September, 1825, sent a letter to the new Czar expressing his ardent desire to have the policy of his Cabinet concerning international problems harmonize with the policy of Russia.   " I am convinced that our intimate union is the most efficacious means of assuring the tranquillity of Europe," wrote the French King, " and that if, despite our efforts, it should be disturbed, this union will alone be sufficient to reëstablish it upon solid bases." [43] Thus, with regard to the status of Spanish America, there appeared small chance that during the reign of Charles X France would relinquish the policy favored by Russia, the foremost champion of the doctrine of legitimacy.

French policy was, however, affected by kaleidoscopic changes in Spanish America.   Early in October, 1824, a congress in the capital of Mexico promulgated a republican constitution for that country.   During the next month an assembly at Guatemala City adopted a confederate constitution for the provinces of Central America.   High up on the Peruvian plateau, on August 6, 1824, a Patriot army led

[41] Villanueva, " French Diplomacy in Latin America," *Inter-America*, I, 160. This article was translated from the Portuguese version in the *Revista americana* of Rio de Janeiro.

[42] Schiemann, *Geschichte Russlands unter Kaiser Nikolaus I*, II, 436.

[43] *Ibid.*, 438.

by Bolívar and Sucre triumphed over the Royalists at Junín. On December 9 following, under the command of General Sucre, the army of liberation decisively defeated the Royalist soldiers under Viceroy La Serna on an Inca battlefield at Ayacucho. Although Spain did not realize the import of that defeat, it virtually signalized the end of her rule on the American Continent. In August, 1825, a declaration of independence was adopted by an assembly in the presidency of Charcas, the upland region that became known as Bolivia. The broad arch of the Spanish Empire had fallen.

Reports of the battle of Ayacucho reached France early in the following year. Parisian journalists informed their readers of the significance of Spain's Armageddon. On March 14, 1825, the *Constitutionnel* announced the news under the rubric " End of the American War. A Battle of Pharsalus or of Actium has just Taken Place in America." After paying a tribute to Bolívar, the journal reasoned that the blow which had been struck in Peru would be felt in the Old World. Europeans were warned to relinquish hopes full of vanity, to abandon attacks without any object, and to renounce human sacrifices the uselessness of which made them horrible. Further, it declared that this Armageddon should make the Continental powers realize the wisdom of the policy which England had adopted toward the Spanish Indies and the necessity of abandoning a position which injured all interests: " A new era commences for the world with the consolidation of Spanish-American independence."

The *Journal des Débats* declared on March 27 that it was the New World which at the moment furnished " the most news and the most important news." On April 11 this journal printed a critical commentary on French foreign policy which argued that the time had arrived for the government to adopt decisive measures:

We have often insisted upon the need in which France finds herself of assuming a more decided attitude with respect to the new American states; we have described the inconveniences and dangers due to the precarious condition of the interests of our commercial towns, which cannot get along without relations with the ports of La Plata, Venezuela, and Mexico. The Ministry, embarrassed by its incoherent principles, has not taken a single step adapted to a withdrawal from this position: it has seemed to await developments; in particular it has entrenched itself behind the uncertainties involved in the outcome of the war in Peru. Today, all is over—America is completely separated from the motherland; the last detachment of the Spanish army is obliged to evacuate the New World. Ought we to remain longer in fatal irresolution? Should our commerce with a half of the universe remain without protection?

In the spring of 1825 Damas, seeking for a solution of the vexatious problem of the Spanish colonies, was even disposed to listen to Gregor McGregor, a Scotchman who had played a dramatic rôle in the South American wars for independence. McGregor now presented to that minister a project for the reconquest of Mexico by an expedition of five thousand men accompanied by an infante.[44] Boislecomte reported, however, that the Spanish ministers lacked confidence in this adventurer who had no affection for Spain and sought only money and booty.[45] Several months later, in response to suggestions from Madrid, Damas expressed the opinion that even a Spanish prince endowed with rare qualities would run grave risks in at-

[44] Damas to Boislecomte, April 22, 1825, A. A. E., Espagne, 732.
[45] May 5, 1825, *ibid.*

tempting to establish his rule in Spanish America unless he were supported by a considerable force.[46]   At St. Petersburg La Ferronnays, using expressions culled from dispatches of Damas, sent a note to Nesselrode to communicate the view of his government that all that could now be done for Spain was to adopt a policy which might salvage some valuable fragments from the shipwreck of her colonial empire.[47] There is no doubt that Damas had decided that the time was opportune for the adoption by Continental powers of a new policy toward the rising American states.

In addition to the English policy of recognition and the battle of Ayacucho, tue insistent representations of French merchants undoubtedly influenced Villèle's Cabinet.   On January 30, 1825, the *Constitutionnel* printed a letter from a correspondent which directed attention to the immense mercantile interest that France had at stake in the Western Hemisphere.   Among articles of French commerce with La Plata, Peru, Colombia, and Mexico mentioned in an editorial note concerning this letter were cotton cloth, canvas, draperies, velours, laces, ribbons, paper, hardware, porcelain, and jewelry.   The total value of those articles annually exported from France to Spanish America was estimated at one million francs.

In April, 1825, a group of Parisian merchants addressed a petition to the King.   They declared that Spanish-American markets were now open to all countries and that France should participate in relations which were rich with promise.   It was their contention that the religion, the cus-

---

[46] Damas to Moustier, March 17, 1826, *ibid.,* 735.

[47] La Ferronnays to Damas and enclosure, April 9, 1826, A. A. E., Russie, 170.

toms, and the language of the Spanish Americans singularly attached them to the French. Furthermore, they appealed to national pride: "While a rival nation by her policy, her navy, her agents, her aid, and her treaties has undertaken to form the closest relations with Spanish America, it is only at rare intervals that a French frigate is seen in Spanish-American harbors, and when Frenchmen arrive in such ports they find themselves without any consular protection." The petition then stated its objects:

Indeed, Sire, we beseech Your Majesty to direct that official agents, worthy in every respect of such an important mission, be sent wherever French commerce is free to enter, and particularly to the continent of America, in order to legalize and protect our commercial relations. Finally, treaties of commerce should ensure to France all the guarantees and advantages which a great nation can rightly claim for her interests. . . . [48]

Meanwhile Villèle had notified Lord Granville that Commander Rosamel, who was to be sent on another trip to South America, had been directed to take on board his warships certain naval officers of ability and integrity, and that one of these was to be left at any American port where his services would be useful to French commerce. Further, Villèle stated that Rosamel had been instructed to assure Spanish-American governments that "France would not only take no part in the War between those States and Old Spain, but was ready to mediate between them, and would convey any proposal respecting their claims for Independence to the Court of Madrid." [49]

The representations of France to Spain concerning trade

[48] *Journal des débats*, April 11, 1825.
[49] Granville to Canning, March 5, 1825, F. O., 27/329.

were not altogether without effect. Count Chabrol, who in August, 1824, had been shifted from a minor administrative post to become Minister of Marine, informed Damas on April 16, 1825, that the *Circe* would be sent from Rochefort to Cadiz in order to receive dispatches containing the exequaturs for French consuls in Cuba.[50] On May 8 Boislecomte wrote to Damas and stated that he had received from the government of Spain exequaturs for French consuls in the Philippines as well as in the Spanish Antilles. The ambassador expressed the hope that the official recognition of those public agents would calm the growing impatience of French merchants.[51] Granville was told by Villèle in June, 1825, that, as the coronation of Charles X was now over, he expected that the policy to be adopted toward Haiti and South America would soon be considered by the Cabinet. By emphasizing the importance of preserving Cuba and Puerto Rico for Spain, he hoped to prevail upon the Allies to join in a representation to Madrid on the necessity of acknowledging the independence of those colonies which had emancipated themselves.[52]

Shortly afterward, however, Governor Donzelot convoyed Spanish soldiers from Martinique to Cuba. In response to England's protest, Villèle admitted that Donzelot had been authorized to intervene with armed force in that island to support the legitimate government against revolutionists. As such intervention would have been a violation of the agreement reached with England in 1823, Can-

[50] A. A. E., Espagne, 732.

[51] *Ibid.* Cf. Webster, *Britain and the Independence of Latin America,* I, 480-85.

[52] Granville to Canning, June 6, 1825, F. O., 27/330. On the Ordinance of April 17, 1825 concerning Haiti, see *infra,* pp. 462-63.

ning secured a pledge from Villèle that French soldiers would not land there.[53] The United States subsequently became alarmed at the French menace to that island; and Secretary of State Clay instructed Minister Brown at Paris that his government opposed the occupation of Cuba and Puerto Rico by any other European power than Spain. In consequence Brown presented to Damas a pert remonstrance embodying this view.[54] If Villèle had actually planned armed interference in Cuba on behalf of Ferdinand VII, the English protest, reënforced by that of the United States, thwarted this scheme. It seems unlikely, however, that he had contemplated the annexation of Cuba by France.

In the meantime the French ambassador at Madrid had suggested to his government another factor in the Spanish-American problem by expressing the view that the reluctance of the Spanish Government to take action in relation to it was largely due to the King's inertia. In April, 1825, Moustier wrote to Villèle to explain that nothing could be accomplished at Madrid with respect to the rebellious colonies because of the disposition of Ferdinand VII, who did not wish to be troubled with cares of state and would not even think about the evils which menaced him or posterity. " If they speak to the King about the condition of Europe, of the Peninsula, or of America," said the Marquis, " he responds that they should leave him alone so that he can make arrangements for a trip to one of his country houses. He only likes to lend his ear to domestic intrigues, to reports of the police, or to anything which can feed his appetite for gossip and malice." [55]

[53] Temperley, *The Foreign Policy of Canning*, pp. 171-72.
[54] Moore, *A Digest of International Law*, VI, 447; *British and Foreign State Papers*, XIII, 444-45.
[55] Villèle, *Mémoires et correspondance*, V, 195.

There was, indeed, little reason to hope that Spain's ministers would yield to the representations of her allies. On November 18 the Spanish ambassador, the Duke of Villahermosa, transmitted to Damas an explanation of his government's foreign policy that was designed to strengthen the loyalty of its allies. He declared that Ferdinand VII was animated by sentiments of sincere friendship toward his august allies and that he did not entertain the slightest doubt that these sentiments were reciprocal. The ambassador then spoke of his monarch's steadfastness in his policy:

The King, who is placed by God at the head of that great family which makes up the Spanish empire, in a position which enables him to know better than anyone else its wishes, its real interests, and the remedies for the evils which have long tormented that monarchy, considers it useless to give an assurance that in the administration of his kingdom he will never turn aside from the path determined by considerations which are today and will constantly be the sole guide of his conduct.[56]

Despite this position of Spain, some Frenchmen were now inclined to adopt an aggressive policy with respect to Spanish America. Thus the *Journal des Débats* expressed the opinion on November 20, 1825, that the Foreign Minister should represent his country at the international American congress which was about to assemble on the Isthmus of Panama. A petition signed by a large number of merchants was presented to Damas on the same day by the Duke of Aumont. It was addressed to the new king, Charles X, a lover of the old régime who affirmed that he would rather be a woodchopper than rule after the fashion of the King of England. The merchants appealed to the

---

[56] Villahermosa to Infantado, November 19, 1825, *A. H. N.*, Estado, 5230.

King to remedy their plight: " France, Sire, again beseeches free access to those seas in which her ships have appeared not without glory at other epochs; she invokes your royal protection in those countries whose inhabitants are particularly attached to the French by bonds of religion, custom, and mutual needs." In the interest of foreign trade these merchants asked not only that their government negotiate treaties of commerce with Spanish-American countries but also that it send commercial agents to any country where they might be needed. Implied in their petition was a request that a sufficient naval force be sent to American waters to protect French trade with the new nations. On November 30, 1825, at the end of his endorsement of this plan, Damas wrote that the King had approved it.[57]

An incident which occurred at this time illustrates how that minister sought to trim his sails to the breeze. In November, 1825, *L'Étoile* published an article concerning " Spain and Spanish America" which expressed grave doubts whether the motherland had the military force necessary for the gigantic task of subjugating her American colonists. The journal declared that for Spain this was a national question in which she could no longer pursue a waiting policy, but that for other European powers as well it was a political and commercial question. It suggested that the proper step at this time was a long truce between Spain and the new states of America:

France, the government of which finds itself, on the one hand, obliged to guard the interests of industry and commerce and which, on the other hand, is under the influence of the dogma of legitimacy, which is the vital principle of

[57] November 20, 1825, A. A. E., Mémoires et Documents, Amérique, 36.

her existence and the bond that unites her with the other Continental powers, would find in this decision the easiest mode of leaving a delicate position without affecting in any way either her doctrines or her interests. Whether she evacuates the Iberian Peninsula or continues to occupy it, her relations with Spain would be notably improved.[58]

The Spanish ambassador at Paris naturally took notice of this article; for it suggested a truce which, if favored by France, might lead her to acknowledge the independence of Spanish America. A belief that *L'Étoile* was a semi-official organ also incited Villahermosa to solicit Pozzo di Borgo to sound the French Cabinet with respect to this proposal. The Spanish ambassador soon reported to the Court of Madrid as follows: " The reply of Baron Damas was that the ideas of *L'Étoile* scarcely emanated from the French Government, which contemplates neither modifying in any manner its policy with regard to the grave question of America, nor adopting any measure that might be contrary to the rights of the King our Master to those countries or that might in any way weaken those rights." [59]

An event which occurred on the Pacific shores of South America further indicates how France viewed the international dilemma. At Callao a forlorn band of Spanish Royalists had been besieged by soldiers of the independent government of Peru. That government appealed to Rosamel, who had been made a rear admiral, to negotiate with the Spanish commander, General Rodil, for the surrender of that port, which was the last important refuge of the Loyalists on the American Continent. Upon being informed of Rosamel's refusal to engage in such negotiations, Count

[58] November 25, 1825.
[59] Villahermosa to Infantado, November 28, 1825, A. H. N., Estado, 5230.

Chabrol commended this decision.[60] Obviously the French Government did not wish its naval officers to serve as mediators between defeated Royalists and triumphant revolutionists in Spanish America.

With regard to the three special agents of France in that vast region, Damas maintained that their functions should be mainly commercial. He informed Polignac confidentially that these agents were instructed merely to point out the advantages to be gained by the Spanish colonies through a *rapprochement* with the mother country. They were to make it known at the same time, however, that France would not support by armed force any expedition which Spain might launch to bring the colonists back to their allegiance.[61]

In the autumn of 1825 the French Cabinet, disregarding the protests of Spain against the dispatch of agents of European governments to the Spanish Indies, but without altogether relinquishing the dream of transforming viceroyalties into appanages, decided to establish new commercial agencies in Spanish-American countries.[62] On Septem-

[60] Chabrol to Rosamel, June 19, 1826, A. N., Marine, B B⁴, 480.

[61] Damas to Polignac, August 12, 1824, A. A. E., Angleterre, 618.

[62] Granville, describing in a letter to Canning of December 15, 1825, a conversation with Damas concerning the dispatch of an infante to Mexico, reported that France was " still disposed to listen to projects which, if adopted some years ago, might have possibly secured to the Royal Family of Spain a continued dominion over that country." Webster, *Britain and the Independence of Latin America*, II, 204. On December 26 Granville explained to Canning as follows the problem which confronted France: " The connection between the Royal Families of France and Spain, the actual occupation of the Spanish Fortresses, the sentiments of the other Members of the Holy Alliance, are all obstacles to France recognizing the new Governments so long as His Catholic Majesty withholds his Recognition. On the other hand, the Members of the French Government are not insensible to the Danger of sacri-

ber 26 the Minister of Marine informed Admiral Rosamel, who was now on the eastern coast of South America, that the government felt the need of an agent at Buenos Aires:

On the other hand, our intimate relations with Spain prescribe to us the duty of avoiding any step which in any way would imply the recognition on our part of the new state of La Plata. It is accordingly necessary to renounce the dispatch of any diplomatic agent whatever and even the dispatch of a consul, because such agents should only reside near a government which has been recognized. In this condition of affairs, and at the proposal of Baron Damas, the Minister of Foreign Affairs, the King has decided that there should be established at Buenos Aires an inspector general of French commerce. This title, which is novel in diplomatic usage, should not prejudice in the least the nature of our relations with the country.

The inspector in question is commissioned by the Ministry of Foreign Affairs only in order to give to his mission the necessary public character. Nevertheless, according to the authorization of His Majesty, in order that the character may be sufficiently established, and in order also to attribute to this agent the indispensable authority over French subjects, without indicating in any way the title of the government which is located at Buenos Aires, his commission fixes his residence in that city and even vaguely recommends him to the good offices and aid of the local authorities. Finally, Admiral, His Majesty has ordered that, because of the lack of a diplomatic agent at Buenos Aires, this inspector general should be presented and in some manner accredited by you.[63]

Favorable reports by naval officers had influenced the

---

ficing the important commercial Interests of France to a rigid adherence to the principles of Legitimacy, and they are indisposed to abandon as hopeless any proposition by which at the same time that they appear to act consistently with their professed principles, they may enjoy the advantages of a free trade with the South-American Continent." No. 293, F. O., 27/333.

[63] A. N., Marine, B B⁴, 469.

King to appoint as inspector general of French commerce at Buenos Aires a Frenchman named Washington de Mendeville who resided in that city. One Despallières, who had served as student vice-consul in Rio de Janeiro, was named sub-inspector-general of French commerce at the Platean metropolis. Admiral Rosamel was asked to use his influence to secure a favorable reception for those officials.

Shortly afterward the French Government decided to appoint commercial agents to Mexico and Colombia. Claude Buchet de Martigny was selected as agent to Colombia; and Alexandre Martin was assigned to a similar post in Mexico. Chabrol's instructions to Martin directed him to animadvert to the Mexicans upon the notion concerning the hostile designs of France toward the new American states, which had been disseminated in Mexico after the Duke of Angoulême invaded Spain. This agent was to uphold the principle that the flags of neutral vessels cover their cargoes. He was to gather information which would be useful for French merchants concerning such matters as Mexican navigation, products, exports, imports, and customs duties.[64]

These instructions were sent to Duperré, who because of his services at the siege of Cadiz had been made vice-admiral. In December, 1823, he was again placed in charge of the naval station in the Antilles. Count Chabrol explained that Martin had been sent to Mexico in place of a consul general, who could not be appointed to the new nation as long as her independence had not been acknowledged. Duperré, who was now clothed with diplomatic as well as military authority, was directed to detach ships from

[64] Instructions pour M. Martin, agent français à Mexique," December 22, 1825, *ibid.*, 424.

his squadron to transport Martin to Mexico and Buchet de Martigny to Colombia. Other instructions were as follows:

> You will give them letters of credence for the heads of the governments in the respective countries. . . . Besides, you will also give them letters of introduction to the ministers of these governments. . . . Other commercial agents in each port of Colombia and Mexico should be directed to look after the interests of our shipowners and to perform with respect to French ships the functions which devolve upon the consuls of France in foreign ports. You should choose those agents from merchants in certain towns who will be designated to you as being habitually in correspondence with commercial houses in our ports and employed by them as consignees of their shipments.[65]

The credentials furnished Martin by Duperré directed him to act as the "chief agent of French commerce in Mexico." In that capacity he was to solicit recognition from the Mexican Government and was authorized to select merchants in leading Mexican ports who as subordinate agents would execute with respect to French subjects the functions ordinarily performed by consuls. He was directed to communicate frequently with the Minister of Marine as well as with the commander of the French naval forces in the Antilles. Duperré asserted that Martin was the only French official in America who was at that time fully authorized to execute the policy of France toward the new states of America.[66]

In the spring of 1826 this official sailed from Fort Royal in the frigate *Nymphe*, commanded by Captain Cuvillier. At Vera Cruz on April 17 that captain wrote a note to

---

[65] December 22, 1825, *ibid.*

[66] Duperré to Martin, March 14, 1826, and credentials of the same date, *ibid.* See further *idem* to Buchet de Martigny, March 28, 1826, *ibid.*

Sebastián Camacho, Mexican Secretary of Foreign Relations, to announce that Martin had been appointed a principal agent of commerce. Cuvillier enclosed a letter from
Duperré concerning this mission. The admiral explained
that, at the request of Murphy, Charles X had authorized
the establishment of commercial agencies of Mexico in
French ports. As the King thought that the adoption of a
similar measure with respect to ports of Mexico would promote trade between that country and France, he wished an
agent of French commerce to be stationed in the Mexican
capital. This agent was to promote profitable commercial
intercourse between the two countries and was to act as the
sole intermediary for subordinate agents who were to be
appointed by the coöperation of Duperré and the Mexican
Government.[67]

Camacho informed Cuvillier, however, that the reception
accorded to this official would depend entirely upon the
nature of his credentials. Still, in a note to Martin the
minister stated that, as reciprocity was the basis of international relations, and as Murphy had been treated only as a
confidential agent of his country in France, he would merely
be allowed to remain in Mexico with the same title.
Though the Mexican Government thus refused to acknowledge Martin as a superior commercial agent of France, it
accorded to him the authority of such an agent. Consequently he decided to remain in the capital city.[68]

[67] *British and Foreign State Papers*, XIII, 1100-01.
[68] *Ibid.*, 1102-03; Martin to Duperré, May 9, 1826, A. N.,
Marine, B B⁴, 478. On November 20, 1826, Secretary Camacho
wrote to Damas to inform him that Murphy had been given the
title of " general agent of commerce " of the Mexican states, which
was to be effective from the moment Martin presented himself to
the Mexican Government with the same title. A. A. E., Mexique, 2.

Instructions to the agent destined for Bogotá were signed by Chabrol on December 22, 1825. In particular, he was to serve as an intermediary who would remove obstacles that hindered the development of trade between Colombia and France.[69] On March 28, 1826, Admiral Duperré addressed a letter from Fort Royal to the Colombian Secretary of Foreign Relations to introduce Buchet de Martigny, whom he described as a "chief commercial agent delegated by the admiral who was the commander in chief of the naval forces of His Majesty in the Sea of the Antilles."[70] *Mutatis mutandis*, this agent's instructions were identical with Martin's. In addition, Duperré informed Buchet de Martigny that his functions were virtually to be those of a consul general, and that he was to select subordinate commercial agents who were to serve France in important Colombian towns and cities.[71] Buchet de Martigny landed at Cartagena from a French frigate on April 7, 1826. Soon after reaching Bogotá, he sent reports to his government concerning Colombia. On September 28 he wrote to Damas and declared that, if he could serve France, he would not be frightened away from Bogotá by earthquakes, revolts, or civil war. At a dinner given by Bolívar to the English chargé at Bogotá, Buchet de Martigny reminded the Liberator that it was France that had originally ensured the establishment of liberty in the New World.[72]

On August 7, 1826, Chabrol wrote to Damas to urge

[69] Instructions pour M. Buchet de Martigny, agent français à Santa Fé de Bogotá (Colombie)," December 22, 1825, A. N., Marine, B B⁴, 424.

[70] *Ibid.*   [71] December 22, 1825, *ibid.*

[72] A. A. E., Colombie, 3; Webster, *Britain and the Independence of Latin America*, I, 426.

that, instead of being mere delegates of French commanders in the Antilles, Martin and Buchet de Martigny should
be accorded titles identical with those of the agents located
in Lima, Buenos Aires, and Santiago de Chile.[73] Charles X
decided to act on this advice. Hence, on November 23,
1826, Chabrol notified Admiral Bergeret that both Martin
and Buchet de Martigny were to be designated inspectors
of French commerce, a title which corresponded informally
to that of consul.[74]

Articles in Parisian journals stating that France had appointed agents to insurgent Spanish colonies attracted Villahermosa's attention. As *L'Étoile* printed this news without contradicting it, the irate ambassador presented an emphatic protest to the French Ministry. However, Damas
apparently informed him that France had not appointed
any agents to Spanish America, and that the report which
had provoked him did not deserve any more credit than
that which should ordinarily be given to articles in periodicals. Villahermosa was further assured that the French
Government contemplated neither the acknowledgment of
Spanish-American independence nor the sanctioning of any
act contrary to the rights of Ferdinand VII.[75] With this
response, misleading and contrary to the facts, Villahermosa
was disposed to be content.

In the spring of 1826, both Damas and Villèle were
inclined to favor definite action by Continental powers with
regard to the relations between Spain and her colonies.
Early in March the English ambassador at Paris asked

[73] A. A. E., Mémoires et Documents, Amérique, 39.
[74] A. N., Marine, B B⁴, 478.
[75] Villahermosa to Infantado, February 2, 1826, A. H. N., Estado,
6867.

Count Villèle whether, if every effort to induce Spain to acknowledge the independence of the Spanish-American republics should be unsuccessful, he was prepared to recommend to Charles X to withdraw French soldiers from the Peninsula and to recognize those republics. Villèle's reply to this question was indirect. Granville wrote to Canning that, if the Spanish Government should persist in its present policy, Villèle might mention to the Allies the fruitless attempts which had been made to induce it to adopt a more rational policy and declare that, unless their influence could be used more successfully, " France could no longer delay her acknowledgment of the Independence of South America, and must leave the Spanish Government to extricate itself as it could from its Embarrassments." [76] A few days later, at a dinner party in the English embassy, Villèle remarked that, until the colonial problem was settled, Spain was bound to be a subject of serious concern for Europe. " ' All the great powers should unite to intervene,' " added the French minister, " 'in order to make effective their joint mediation and to induce Spain to recognize the independence of those colonies which she cannot now reconquer and to enable her to secure at the same time all the advantages that she can possibly obtain from her concession.' " [77]

About the same time Damas avowed to Count Apponyi, the Austrian ambassador in Paris, that it was urgently necessary for Spain to reach a decision which would offer guarantees for the conservation of the colonies that still belonged to her and which would end the distressing condition pre-

[76] Webster, *Britain and the Independence of Latin America,* II, 209.

[77] Apponyi to Metternich, March 9, 1826, H. H. u. S., Berichte aus Frankreich, 367.

vailing in that unhappy country.[78] On March 2, 1826, Damas informed Granville that France wished to determine in concert with England the means of arranging a peace between Spain and the South American nations. In response to the ambassador's remark that a basis of adjustment which might earlier have been acceptable to the new states would no longer be satisfactory, Damas asked whether, as a preliminary measure, an armistice might not be proposed to the contending parties—an armistice which would lead to recognition.[79]

Two weeks later Granville informed Damas that his government had received favorably the proposal of joint action with France in respect to Spanish America.[80] Though at this time an indirect overture for Anglo-French mediation to end the hostilities between Spain and her former colonies was actually received by Villèle from Hurtado,[81] and though the former had apparently obtained the approval of the Allies to a change in French policy toward the rising states, yet, influenced presumably by reports from South America, Damas became dubious about the stability of the new governments. Shortly afterward, Granville informed Villèle that England wished to coöperate with France, that such action must depend upon circumstances, but that existing conditions were not propitious to joint mediation as the language of the Spanish Secretary of State held out no hope of success.[82] In a conversation with the Austrian ambassador, Villèle explained the situation as follows:

[78] *Idem* to *idem,* March 3, 1826, *ibid.*

[79] Webster, *op. cit.,* II, 208.

[80] Granville to Canning, March 17, 1826, F. O., 27/348.

[81] Webster, *op. cit.,* II, 212.

[82] *Ibid.,* 214-15; Granville to Canning, June 12, 1826 (no. 182), F. O., 27/350.

For a long time we have been in agreement with England in regard to the urgent necessity of inducing Spain to make a definitive decision in the matter of her colonies. We are sincerely disposed to join the Cabinet of St. James and to act in concert with it in order to promote a decision by the Court of Madrid in this matter, so that we may offer that court our joint intervention and aid it by our counsels. But up to the present time, nothing has been done and nothing can yet be undertaken.[83]

Soon afterward, however, in a letter to Ferdinand VII concerning the withdrawal of French soldiers from the Iberian Peninsula, Charles X expressed the opinion that Spain had irrevocably lost her colonies, that only immediate action could save anything from the wreck, and that, if the Spanish monarch obstinately refused all efforts at an adjustment, " the time was not far distant " when France would be compelled to consider the interests of her own subjects.[84]

A littérateur and publicist named José Fernández Madrid had meanwhile been appointed by Colombia to succeed Lanz as agent to France. Early in September, 1826, Fernández Madrid had a significant conference with Damas. The French minister frankly expressed his opinion that the Spanish Americans had not accorded generous treatment to Spain; he asked whether Colombia would not concede commercial privileges or pay an indemnity to the motherland in return for recognition. The agent of Colombia responded negatively. He declared that his country was *de facto* independent and also that the Spanish-American republics were pledged by solemn treaties not to obtain recognition from Spain by purchase.[85]

[83] Apponyi to Metternich, June 13, 1826, H. H. u. S., Berichte aus Frankreich, 368.

[84] George IV, *The Letters of King George IV*, III, 167.

[85] Martínez Silva, *Biografía de D. José Fernández Madrid*, pp. 197-99.

In a contemporary memorandum Damas recorded his answer to Fernández Madrid's inquiry concerning the acknowledgment of the independence of Spanish America, namely that the agent much deceived himself by imagining that France wished to envelop her policy in mystery, but that her relations with Spain obliged her to act with a decorum from which nothing would make her deviate: " Beyond doubt the government of Colombia is a fact, but it is not a right; the French Government therefore recognizes the Colombian Government for what it actually is and nothing more." [86] Thus did Damas apply strictly the doctrine of recognition which he had recently formulated in reply to the queries of La Ferronnays. To the government at Bogotá Fernàndez Madrid expressed the opinion that, if Damas had the sole right to make decisions in regard to the foreign policy of France, Colombia could hope for nothing, but that fortunately other French ministers were favorably inclined.[87]

An issue had meanwhile arisen with Spain concerning the trade between France and Colombia. In the summer of 1825 the admission of a Colombian ship into a French port evoked a fresh protest from Villahermosa. Damas replied that it was impossible to sever the commercial relations which France had formed with Colombia with the consent of the Spanish King. Responding to this, the Spanish Council of State directed the ambassador to repeat his protest and to inform Damas that Ferdinand VII had never given his consent to the admission into French ports of ships from Colombia or from any other revolted colony of

[86] " Minute d'un memorandum dicté par le ministre Bon. de Damas, le 4 Sept. 1826," A. A. E., Colombie, 3.
[87] Martínez Silva, op. cit., p. 200.

Spanish America. Further, Villahermosa was instructed to point out that such a measure would be inconsistent not only with the indisputable sovereign rights of Ferdinand VII but also with the vital principle of legitimacy which had often been solemnly enunciated by France herself.[88] Yet, despite this emphatic protest, merchantmen from Colombia were henceforth admitted into French ports.

The treatment to be accorded to merchant vessels of Spanish-American countries was further considered in 1826 by French ministers. On April 7 the Minister of the Marine wrote to Damas and recapitulated a statement made by that minister in July, 1825, to the effect that Colombian ships might be allowed to enter French ports on condition that they lower their flags before being admitted and refrain from hoisting them again during their visits. Chabrol now expressed the opinion that the vessels of other Spanish-American nations which had declared their independence might be similarly received.[89] Damas replied on April 10 to the effect that there was no reason for refusing to admit the vessels of Mexico and other newly established American states into French harbors on the same condition as the ships of Colombia. He explained that this uniform treatment should be adopted in order to prevent discussion and, further, that nothing would induce France to concede to the vessels of Mexico what she had thus far refused to Colombian merchantmen.[90]

A fresh problem arose in the following autumn when the *Ayacucho*, a Colombian merchant ship laden with cotton, hides, quinine, and vanilla, arrived in France. In accord-

[88] Infantado to Villahermosa, December 19, 1825, A. H. N., Estado, 6861.

[89] A. A. E., Mexique, 2.   [90] *Ibid.*

ance with the prevailing regulations, upon entering the
harbor of Havre that ship was compelled to haul down her
colors. As a result of the protest of Fernández Madrid,
who stated that the Colombian flag had been admitted into
ports of French colonies in the Antilles, and in consequence
also of a communication from Buchet de Martigny concerning the treatment he was receiving in Bogotá, Damas
gave the Colombian agent the confidential assurance that
the *Ayacucho* would be allowed to unfurl her flag.[91]

On September 13, 1826, Chabrol issued instructions to
the naval commissioner at Havre which stated that, as a
French agent had entered upon the full exercise of his functions in Mexico, and as agents of that nation had for some
time watched over her commercial interests in France,
Charles X had decided that Mexican ships should henceforth be permitted to enter French harbors under their own
flags. Suitable orders were accordingly to be issued to
French officials. Chabrol added:

In his solicitude for everything that might be advantageous to French commerce the King has directed the commanders of his naval forces to install in the various countries of Spanish America principal agents whose functions
will be the same as those of the agent actually installed in
Mexico. As soon as official reports make it certain that
these agents have entered upon their duties, the ships of
those nations whose governments have recognized them in
their rôles as commercial agents will enjoy in the ports of
the kingdom the privilege which has just been granted to
Mexican ships; and I shall take care to give you fresh orders
in this matter when the proper time arrives.[92]

L'Étoile shrewdly declared on September 19 that in providing for the security of French commerce, which was

[91] Martínez Silva, *op. cit.*, pp. 200-03.
[92] *Journal des débats*, September 21, 1826.

what the development of intercourse with the new states demanded, the government had wisely distinguished between the commercial problem and the political problem. Besides, it had at the same time displayed respect for the legitimate rights of Spain. That journal not unwarrantedly concluded that in this manner a species of commercial recognition was being accorded to certain Spanish-American nations.

Having been informed that Buchet de Martigny had begun to exercise his functions at Bogotá as agent of French commerce, Chabrol on September 28, 1826, issued supplementary instructions to the general commissioner of the navy at Havre to the effect that Colombian ships were henceforth to be accorded the same treatment as that which had been conceded to Mexican vessels by the order of September 13. Shortly afterward the *Ayacucho* hoisted the Colombian banner to her masthead.[93] On October 10 the director general of customs issued a circular stating that, as superior agents of French commerce were about to exercise their functions in Colombia and Mexico, ships of those countries displaying their respective flags were henceforth to be admitted into the ports of France.[94]

Evidently assuming, as did *L'Étoile*, that this concession by the Minister of the Navy was a species of commercial recognition, the *Journal des Débats* declared on October 16, 1826, that it would not undertake to explain the inconsistencies which seemed to exist between the measures that had been taken by Chabrol and the principles that Damas had enunciated to French ambassadors. Two days later the

[93] *Ibid.,* October 5, 1826.
[94] *Tratados y convenciones celebrados y no ratificados por la república mexicana,* p. 267.

ministerial organ, the *Moniteur*, published an interpretative article on French foreign policy. It undertook to explain to its readers the special considerations which affected the policy of France toward Spain and Spanish America:

The bonds which attach us to Spain and the presence of our soldiers in the heart of her provinces would have imposed upon France a special duty of circumspection, even if the ties of blood that join the two royal houses had not made this a necessity. The journal which declared that these royal family relations are not matters which should embarrass the nations displays little knowledge or a short memory. During the last century our country has derived memorable advantages from the consanguinity of the two dynasties. . . .

The time is still far distant when the commercial relations of Spanish America will assume their full importance. . . . Nevertheless, the whole world recognizes that at last it is time to adopt a policy. All thoughts of decisions common to the great powers have vanished. . . . Besides, it is not for France to erect a Chinese wall beyond the Atlantic and to conceal the Spanish republics from the eyes of her people.

In an editorial comment upon this article, the *Constitutionnel* presented the other side of the case to its readers. It asked what advantages France had derived from her alliance with Spain during the reign of Charles X. It maintained that, in return for benefits conferred, Ferdinand VII had shown ingratitude and had rejected wise advice. It declared that the most remarkable avowal in the profession of faith of the ministerial organ was that all efforts at a common decision by the great powers with respect to Spanish America had ceased: " A long time ago we announced the dissolution of the Holy Alliance; now, after many denials of that fact, the Ministry has finally acknowledged it." [95]

[95] October 20, 1826.

Chabrol's instructions to Admiral Lemarant, who was cruising on the coast of Brazil, show that French statesmen keenly realized their peculiar position. Lemarant was instructed to use much caution in regard to the delicate question of the official recognition of the Spanish-American states. He was informed that, though his government had just taken an important step in its relations with those states, it maintained liaisons with Spain which prevented it from going further, and that the date at which France would view them as independent nations could not be set precisely. Still, he was to let it be understood that the intentions of the French King toward them were entirely friendly and that he would be pleased " to contribute by his counsels to the removal of those obstacles which up to the present time have prevented all Europe from sanctioning their liberation."[96]

A report which Buchet de Martigny sent to Damas in November, 1826, of an interview with General Bolívar, who had just made the toilsome trip from Lima to Bogotá, must have stimulated that minister's interest in Colombia's fortunes. Bolívar, who at heart was a great admirer of Napoleon, had avowed his pleasure at seeing a French agent in Colombia. He expressed the hope that France would not delay any longer an acknowledgment of the independence of the new American nations. " ' When you write to your government,' he added, ' be so good as to say on my behalf that Colombia and all the other states of America will have great satisfaction in entering into relations of every kind with France, and that they particularly wish to form with her liaisons of friendship.' Then he paid a very flattering

---

[96] December 6, 1826, A. N., Marine, B B⁴, 479.

encomium to our country." [97] In his message to the Congress of Colombia on January 2, 1827, Acting President Santander expressed regret that the title of superior agent of commerce was not recognized by international law but stated that Buchet de Martigny had nevertheless been granted an exequatur. Santander expressed the hope that France would take advantage of every opportunity to develop her industry by intercourse with Colombia and that she would not postpone her recognition of the independence of his country.[98]

To promote its relations with the new states the French Government early in 1826 took the important step of appointing agents to Chile and Peru. Damas signed credentials on February 22 for Jean Chaumette des Fossés, former French consul general in Sweden, as " inspector general of French commerce in the city of Lima and its dependencies." He was directed to watch over the persons and property of Frenchmen in that region.[99] On July 29 Admiral Rosamel, who while cruising in the Pacific Ocean had cast anchor in the harbor of Valparaiso, addressed to the Peruvian Secretary of Foreign Relations a letter to inform him of this appointment. Rosamel expressed the hope that Peru would consider that France had no other object in the inspector general's mission than " to establish between the two countries relations based upon reciprocal good will." [100]

The admiral ventured to outline in a letter to Bolívar what he considered the American policy of his government.

[97] November 20, 1826, A. A. E., Colombie, 3.
[98] Uribe, *Anales diplomáticos y consulares de Colombia,* III, 35.
[99] *Suplemento al Peruano,* December 30, 1826.
[100] (Copy), A. A. E., Mémoires et Documents, Amérique, 31.

Reasoning that, because of the obstinacy of Spain, the time was approaching when family ties would no longer determine the policy of France toward the former Spanish colonies, Rosamel asserted that the appointment by France of inspectors general of commerce to Mexico, Colombia, Chile, Peru, and La Plata was a step in the direction of a most important act which he considered close at hand. He assured Bolívar optimistically that the French Government was prepared to recognize the Spanish-American states as independent.[101]

In a letter to Captain de Rossi, the commander of a division of the French naval squadron in the Pacific Ocean who was directed to see Chaumette des Fossés installed in his post, Rosamel declared that this agent had been accorded the functions of a consul general.[102] On November 3 Rosamel requested a passport from José M. Pando, Secretary of Foreign Relations of Peru, in order that Des Fossés, an inspector general of French commerce who was to exercise the functions of consul in that country, might proceed from Callao to Lima. In reply Secretary Pando expressed regret that, as the French agent did not have a title which conformed to international law and custom, he could be treated only as a private individual. Upon receipt of the agent's credentials, which were not signed by the French King, Pando promptly returned them and stated that he could neither receive him in " any public character nor treat him in any other manner than as a gentleman worthy of appreciation and consideration because of his personal qualities." [103] Though Chaumette des Fossés justified his peculiar status as being in accordance with a custom which

---

[101] July 29, 1826, *ibid.* [102] July 29, 1826, *ibid.*
[103] Aranda, *Colección de los tratados,* VII, 524.

France had occasionally employed in dealing with European nations, yet the Peruvian Secretary did not relent, and the discomfited inspector general withdrew to Valparaiso.

Shortly afterward, however, a change of government took place in Lima, and Manuel Vidaurre became Foreign Secretary. In April, 1827, Secretary Vidaurre, declaring that he had learned that the French Cabinet was preparing to acknowledge the independence of Spanish America, wrote to Chaumette des Fossés to state that he would receive him in his public character exactly as indicated by his credentials.[104] Vidaurre explained his decision by asserting that the preceding administration had disseminated the notion that France and Spain entertained plans that were hostile to his country. What does it matter to us, he asked, whether the French commercial agent to Peru is designated consul or inspector. Subsequently the Peruvian Congress voted to admit the French inspector general in his public capacity. Accordingly on July 14, 1827, Francisco J. Mariátegui, the new Secretary of Foreign Affairs, addressed a note to Chaumette des Fossés to notify him of this action.[105]

The new Peruvian Government had meanwhile tried to make an *amende honorable.* It appointed José J. Olmedo as commissioner to France with power to negotiate with regard to his country's commercial intercourse. On June 4, 1827, this commissioner had an interview with Damas in which he explained that, despite the refusal of Peru to recognize the title of inspector general of commerce, she had been plased to concede the French agent permission to live in or near Lima. Olmedo reasoned that the treatment accorded

---

[104] April 23, 1827, A. N., Marine, B B⁴, 494.

[105] Aranda, *op. cit.,* VII, 532-35; Chaumette des Fossés to Damas, June 29, 1827, A. A. E., Pérou, 17.

Chaumette des Fossés was not exceptional, for Peru would not dispense with the regular diplomatic formalities even in her relations with sister American states.[106]

Peru's attitude toward this inspector general was noticed by a leading French journal. On May 31, 1827, the *Journal des Débats* asked its readers whether the policy followed by the Ministry of Foreign Affairs toward Peru was worthy of the French nation. It inquired why France should sacrifice her interests to Spain as the price of her docility. It justified the demands made by Peru of the oldest monarchy in the world by stating that France had consuls general at Algiers, Tunis, and Tangier. It maintained that the Spanish-American nations merely demanded of the French Ministry that they be treated as were the Barbary States. "In truth," it concluded, "we cannot accuse them of very haughty pretensions."

Admiral Rosamel had meanwhile addressed a letter to the Chilean Government to inform it that Charles de la Forest, who had served as French consul at Philadelphia, had been appointed to act as inspector general of French commerce at Santiago. In a note to General Freire, who had become the chief executive after the abdication of Supreme Director O'Higgins, Rosamel declared that this appointment was the augury of a recognition which he desired, and which he had solicited in the common interest of Chile and France.[107] The task of installing this inspector general devolved upon Captain Dumanoir. It was, however, not without some difficulty, arising from the unusual title accorded to La Forest, that the captain succeeded in his negotiations

[106] Olmedo to Damas, June 5, 1827, A. A. E., Pérou, 17.
[107] July 29, 1826, A. A. E., Chili, 1.

with the Chilean authorities.[108] Besides his own zeal, Dumanoir was aided by the fact that the Chilean Government hoped that France would soon acknowledge its independence. Rosamel accordingly warned the Minister of Marine that, by delaying recognition of the Spanish-American states, France risked being deprived of their favor by intriguing and powerful rivals.[109]

On October 19, 1826, the Chilean Government granted an exequatur to La Forest as inspector general of French commerce in the capital city. In enigmatic fashion it declared that the inspector general was to enjoy all the rights and prerogatives which appertained to him by public law.[110] President Pinto, in his message to Congress on February 25, 1828, disregarded the fact that rumors of legitimist instructions to such agents as Chasseriau had reached Chile and had provoked press comment unfavorable to France.[111] He declared that Charles X had demonstrated his favorable attitude toward the independence of Chile by appointing a commercial agent to reside at her capital and that the sentiments of the French Cabinet were favorable to the new American states.[112] In his report to Congress in 1829, the Chilean Secretary of Foreign Relations mentioned favorably the step recently taken by France to promote her commercial intercourse with the nations of Spanish America. He expressed the opinion that her Cabinet would soon yield

[108] La Forest to Zegers, October 19, 1826, *ibid.*

[109] Rosamel to Chabrol, March 7, 1827, A. N., Marine, B B⁴, 494.

[110] *Registro de documentos del gobierno,* no. 44, p. 223.

[111] *El indicador,* January 10, 1827.

[112] *Correo politico y mercantil de las Provincias Unidas del Río de la Plata,* March 26, 1828.

to public opinion and acknowledge their independence.[113]

Meanwhile French trade with the Pacific shores of South America had been developing. The available statistics, which are incomplete, indicate that in 1825 France exported to Bolivia, Peru, and Chile merchandise valued at more than fourteen million francs.[114] According to a contemporary memorandum on commerce with those countries, in August, 1826, there were no less than six French merchant ships anchored in the harbor of Valparaiso. Their cargoes included wines and liquors, olive oil, dried fruit, salt meat, butter, sugar, perfumes, toilet articles, arms, ammunition, boots and shoes, saddlery, hats, silks, furniture, watches, paper, books, pictures, engravings, and music. In order not to compete with each other in the disposal of their merchandise the captains of those vessels had undertaken to proceed to different parts of the Pacific coast.[115]

Tentative measures taken by French officials show that they wished to encourage trade with Spanish America. In October, 1826, the director general of the French customs formulated regulations which made a concession with respect to cotton imported into France from Mexico in either French or Mexican ships. In addition to stipulations regarding certificates of origin for goods sent from one country to the other, the regulations contained a proviso that Mexican ships entering French ports were not to pay any other taxes or navigation duties than those levied upon vessels arriving from the United States.[116] During the next

[113] *Memoria del ministerio de relaciones exteriores presentada al congreso constitucional del año de 1829*, pp. 2-3.

[114] *Statistique du France, commerce exterieur*, pp. 146-59.

[115] Gourbeyre, " Du Commerce Français au Chili & au Pérou en 1826," A. N., Marine, B B⁴, 482.

[116] Clercq, *Recueil des traités*, III, 452-54; *L'Étoile*, June 22, 1827.

spring the arrival in Paris of the Mexican diplomat Sebastián Camacho, who had just negotiated a commercial
treaty with England, set the stage for a new act in Franco-
Mexican intercourse. Damas explained his government's
attitude in a letter to Martin:

Señor Camacho has received from his government the
powers necessary to enter into negotiations with the government of the King on the subject of the recognition of
Mexico. The King's intentions in this matter are not much
different from the desires of the Mexican minister. Nevertheless, Sir, His Majesty thinks that it is still necessary to
allow some time for this affair to mature and to remove the
obstacles which even now hinder the adoption of a definitive policy. Our relations with Spain and those which we
maintain with America are gradually bringing us to that
point; but it accords neither with our dignity nor with our
interest to take any hasty action in a question so grave and
so delicate. Until the moment of announcing our resolution has arrived, Señor Camacho will find us disposed to
converse confidentially with him about the principal bases
upon which we shall be able to establish with Mexico in a
most positive fashion those commercial relations which
would, as a natural consequence, lead later to political relations between the two governments.[117]

It is clear that Damas wished to make an arrangement
with Camacho which would improve commercial intercourse between Mexico and France without implying an
acknowledgment of Mexican independence. Before these
informal negotiations culminated in a definite agreement,
Count Ofalia, who had recently been appointed the Spanish
ambassador at Paris, represented to Damas that the recog-

[117] April 6, 1827, A. A. E., Mexique, 3. It appears that Camacho
ceased to exercise his functions as Secretary of Foreign Relations
on July 5, 1826, when his place was filled by a subordinate official.
*Personas que han tenido á su cargo la secretaría de relaciones
exteriores desde 1821 hasta 1824,* pp. 10-11.

nition of Spanish-American independence was an issue important to all the nations of Europe. Ofalia further maintained that it was unjust to expect Spain to acknowledge the independence of insurgent colonies which offered no guarantee of political stability and which had not even suggested a plan of compensation for the enormous loss that recognition would entail to the mother country.[118] This despairing plea did not have much influence, however, for on May 8, 1827, Camacho and Damas signed a document which became known as " The Declarations."

Article I of this agreement declared that friendship and reciprocal liberty of commerce were henceforth to prevail between France and the United Mexican States. In general, the merchants of each party were to enjoy in the territory of the other party liberty and protection. The subjects of each state were to have in the territory of the other state all the advantages in commerce and navigation which were accorded by the respective state to other foreigners. Duties levied upon the products of the one country entering the ports of the other country were to be no greater than those laid upon products of the most-favored-nation. French goods were to be subject to identical duties upon entering the ports of Mexico whether they were laden on French ships or on Mexican ships, and reciprocally. Another reciprocal provision was embodied in Article VIII, which provided that all French subjects in Mexico were to be at liberty to carry on their own affairs either personally or through agents. The ninth article stipulated that subjects of either nation residing in the dominions of the other nation were to be exempt from all forced con-

[118] Ofalia, *Escritos*, p. 509.

tributions or enforced service by land or sea. Consuls might be sent by either party into the territories of the other party. Those officers were to enjoy in each country the ordinary privileges and exemptions of consuls, as long as they did not become citizens or landowners of the nation to which they were accredited.[119]

This agreement contained no mention of its political import. Though a difference later developed between the parties with respect to the political effects of the agreement, yet, in view of the explanation given by Damas before signing it, one cannot avoid the conclusion that he deliberately aimed to avoid including any clause which would imply the acknowledgment of Mexican independence. In a contemporary memorandum Boislecomte explained why the French minister did not negotiate a treaty like the Anglo-Mexican Treaty of 1826 that consummated recognition. He pointed out that proper consideration for a country which was still occupied by French soldiers restrained Damas from signing with Camacho a political treaty.[120] French diplomats made this caveat even though they had engaged in negotiations with a duly accredited agent of the Mexican repub-

---

[119] Clercq, *op. cit.*, III, 439-46.

[120] " Note sur l'état des rapports de la France avec Mexique et les nouveaux États de l'Amérique du Sud," November, 1837, A. A. E., Quito, 1; Boislecomte, " Ambassade de France en Espagne. Études sur les relations politiques et commerciales suivies entre les deux pays, depuis l'établissement de la maison de Bourbon en Espagne et sur L'État interieur de ce Royaume (1700 à 1827)," A. A. E., Espagne, 97. On June 2, 1828, La Ferronnays instructed Bresson as follows: " Ces Articles, connus sous le nom de *déclarations*, avaient pour object de régler entre la France et le Mexique leurs rapports mutuels de commerce et de navigation, en attendant le moment ou le Roi pourrait reconnaitre par un Traité formel l'independance de cette République." A. A. E., Colombie, 5.

lic—a proceeding which might have been considered an act of recognition. Probably Damas was influenced also by the fact that, if he had formally acknowledged the independence of Mexico, he would have precipitated a serious issue with other Spanish-American republics. The ice in a frozen stream would have been broken.

Damas did not escape criticism at home. In printing the Declarations, which had been made public by the Mexican agent at Havre, the *Journal des Débats* declared that the Minister of Foreign Affairs was trying to reform the language of diplomacy and that he was sending commercial agents to South America instead of consuls. It implied that, by the use of a novel terminology, Damas wished to persuade the Court of Madrid that France had not acknowledged the independence of a single Spanish-American nation.[121]

While Damas was Foreign Minister, France became deeply interested in the policy which the Papacy wished to pursue toward the Church in Spanish America. Bishoprics which had fallen vacant there during the struggles for independence had often not been filled because the right to name candidates was vested in the Spanish crown. The papal nuncio at Madrid blamed the Holy Alliance for the failure of Spain to become reconciled with the insurgents.[122] Hence the Vatican tried to influence France to induce Spain to adopt such a conciliatory attitude toward the revolutionary communities as would allow it to reëstablish spiritual relations with the faithful in the Indies. At the instance of Damas, in January, 1825, the French ambas-

---

[121] June 16, 1827.
[122] Leturia, *La acción diplomática de Bolívar ante Pío VII*, p. 7.

sador at Madrid brought to the attention of Francisco de
Zea Bermúdez, the Spanish Secretary of State, the lack of
bishops in Spanish-American countries. Boislecomte represented to him that the French Government could make an
arrangement with Pope Leo XII by which he would name
for the vacant sees personages whose attachment to Ferdinand VII was beyond doubt and who would become cham-
pions of legitimacy as well as of Roman Catholicism.

Boislecomte recorded the reaction of the Spanish minister
as follows:

Without an instant's hesitation, Señor Zea Bermúdez said
to me: " the idea which you propose is absolutely inadmissible; for it could not be carried out without an understanding with the rebellious communities which we absolutely do not wish. No matter under what terms one disguised the execution of that plan, it would still be necessary that the Holy Father enter into an arrangement with
the upstart governments, and this is what we will never
consent to; we do not wish any nuance, any middle term,
any evasive expedient. Anything that is not the open and
absolute opposition which we maintain and which our
allies maintain toward the rebels is an abandonment of the
principle of legitimacy." [123]

Evidently Spain feared that any exercise of the papal
right of patronage in the revolted Spanish colonies might
prepare the way for an acknowledgment of their independence by the Vatican. On her part, France was naturally
willing to intercede between the Court of Rome and the
Spanish Government—a rôle which would increase her
prestige in the New World.

Despite the rebuff given to Boislecomte, the Papacy did

[123] Boislecomte to Damas, January 26, 1825, A. A. E., Espagne,
731.

not relinquish its efforts to secure the intercession of France with Spain in the interest of the Roman Catholic Church in new American states. In October, 1825, a conference was held at Paris which was attended by Damas, the papal nuncio, and the envoys of Austria, Prussia, and Russia. The nuncio asked the diplomats of the Allies to induce Ferdinand VII to cease his opposition to the reception of agents of the Mexican Government by the Pope in his capacity as Head of the Church. Those diplomats approved the contention of the papal agent that the Holy Father might well confer with agents of revolutionary Spanish-American governments concerning spiritual matters. However, the resulting recommendations of representatives of the Holy Allies at the Court of Madrid were in vain.[124]

On the other hand, in an audience accorded the French envoy at Rome in November, 1825, the Pope expressed his appreciation of the support given to his efforts by France.[125] A few months later, upon notifying that envoy of an agreement reached with an agent of Colombia concerning the appointment of bishops to vacant sees in that country, the Papal Secretary of State expressed his high appreciation of the attempt of France to coöperate with the Vatican in negotiations with Spain for an arrangement by which it might provide for the spiritual needs of Roman Catholics in Spanish America.[126]

[124] Villanueva, *La monarquía en América: la Santa Alianza*, pp. 203-06.

[125] *Ibid.*, p. 206.

[126] Leturia, *Bolívar y León XII*, pp. 129, 139. It was not until after the death of Ferdinand VII that the Papacy undertook to recognize the independence of the republics of Spanish America. On November 26, 1835, Pope Gregory XVI formally acknowledged the independence of New Granada; on December 16 following, Ignacio

The French Government was still feeling its way with regard to Spanish America during the years from 1824 to 1827. While the head of the Cabinet was acting as Minister of Foreign Affairs, he made no advance beyond Chateaubriand's policy. Villèle aimed to restrain England from acknowledging the independence of Spanish America; he dreamed of founding Bourbon monarchies there and wanted his country to develop commercial relations with that part of the world. Waiving the belligerent instructions to Donzelot, Villèle finally put himself on record as opposing armed intervention in the Spanish Indies on behalf of Ferdinand VII.

There was no clash between Villèle and Damas. While the latter was in office, the Ministry of Foreign Affairs continued to gather information concerning conditions in Spanish-American countries. In December, 1824, Damas clearly formulated his doctrine with respect to recognition: in fine, that only the fact of independence and the right combined could justify a neutral government in admitting a new state to the society of nations. As will be shown in a later chapter, the acknowledgment of Haitian independ-

---

Tejada was received in a papal audience as the chargé of that country. See Uribe, *Anales diplomáticos y consulares de Colombia,* III, 90-96; Zubieta, *Apuntaciones sobre las primeras misiones diplomáticas de Colombia,* pp. 596-97. The account of the session of the *sacra congregazione degli affari ecclesiastici straordinari* dated October 11, 1835, which favored the recognition of New Granada and other Spanish-American states by the Vatican on certain conditions, and also the qualified approval given by the Pope to their decision on October 14, 1835, are printed in Leturia, " El reconocimiento de la emancipación hispanoamericana et la ' sacra congregazione degli affari ecclesiastici straordinari,' " *IIº congreso internacional de historia de América,* IV, 245-55.

ence by a royal ordinance in 1825 seemed to certain statesmen a harbinger of the acknowledgment of Spanish-American independence.

News of Canning's recognition of certain Spanish-American states prompted Parisian journalists to assert that France
was dilatory in her foreign policy. Tidings of the decisive
battle of Ayacucho were a further stimulus to those Frenchmen who thought that the time had come for their government to abandon its conservative policy. French mercantile
interests undertook to advocate vigorously not only the
dispatch of commercial agents to Spanish-American countries but also the negotiation of commercial treaties with
them. Special agents of French commerce styled inspectors general were stationed in Mexico, Colombia, Peru,
Chile, and La Plata. Although in 1826 Colombian and
Mexican ships were accorded permission to unfurl their
flags in French ports, the family bonds that joined France
to Spain still restrained Villèle's Cabinet from boldly taking
the decisive step of acknowledging Spanish-American independence. In fact, the Franco-Mexican Declarations were
significant as constituting an attempt on the part of France
to regulate her commercial intercourse with an important
Spanish-American country without according formal recognition. Further, in regard to the delicate problem of patronage in Spanish America, France interceded with Spain in
the vain hope of promoting an agreement by which the
Pope might participate in the choice of personages to fill
vacant sees in the Church of Spanish-American nations.

Lastly, it is clear that the occasional mention by French
publicists of the King's reluctance to act in a liberal fashion
toward the Indies was fully justified. An official memorandum filed in the archives at the Quai d'Orsay furnishes

the following explanation of the relations of France with Spanish America: " The Ministry which M. de Villèle then headed could not misunderstand the importance of these relations, and it would probably have yielded to the almost unanimous wish of French tradesmen if the personal sentiments of Charles X had not formed an insuperable obstacle to any negotiation with the former Spanish colonies, as long as their independence had not received the sanction of the Cabinet of Madrid." [127]

[127] " Note sur l'état des rapports de la France avec Mexique et les nouveau États de l'Amérique du Sud," November, 1837, A. A. E., Quito, 1.

CHAPTER XII

RECOGNITION OF THE BRAZILIAN EMPIRE

As the years passed after the Congress of Vienna, Frenchmen showed increasing awareness that steps were called for to improve their relations with the colonial dominions of the Portuguese. In December, 1819, one Delaroche addressed a representation to his government pointing out the special benefits which France would derive from the development of commercial relations with Portuguese America. He urged it to dispatch missions to outlying sections of Latin America in the interest of commerce and politics.[1] Minister of Marine Portal directed the attention of Baron Pasquier to the need of making satisfactory arrangements with the monarchy seated at Rio de Janeiro concerning the privileges to be enjoyed in Brazil by French navigators and merchants.[2] The intercourse of France with that country was complicated, however, by the residence of the Braganza dynasty in Rio de Janeiro and by the precarious relations existing between Brazil and Portugal. Further, the proceedings of a Cortes which met in Lisbon early in 1821 stimulated the revolutionary spirit that had been developing in Brazil. The situation was further complicated when, in April, 1821, King John VI appointed his son Pedro as regent and took ship for Lisbon.

In April, 1821, Minister Clermont-Tonnerre had notified Colonel Maler, who was still serving as chargé d'affaires

[1] December 18, 1819, A. A. E., Mémoires et Documents, Amérique, 35.

[2] Gervain, *Un ministre de la marine et son ministère sous la restauration*, pp. 103-04.

404

and consul general of France at Rio de Janeiro, that a naval station under Captain Mackau was soon to be established near the Brazilian coast. The minister explained that the ships assigned to this station were to watch the neighboring banks which were frequented by French whaling vessels. This naval station was to guard French interests on the eastern coast of South America from Cape St. Augustin to La Plata River, while the French naval station in the South Sea was to perform the same service on the Pacific shores of that continent and might even extend its surveillance as far as the Philippine Islands.[3]

A month later, Minister of Foreign Affairs Pasquier wrote to Maler directing him to take charge of French interests in Portuguese America. The French agent was instructed that whenever occasion offered he should remind the Prince Regent of the real affection which Louis XVIII cherished for him. Though this agent was to watch carefully the political developments in Brazil, he was warned to refrain from meddling in its affairs.[4] These views were stressed in directions addressed to Captain Mackau on June 5 by the Minister of Marine. Clermont-Tonnerre mentioned recent revolutionary disturbances in South America. He expressed the hope that Brazilian officials would give French navigators support and protection. He instructed Mackau to direct the officers under his command " to refrain from making any reflections upon the institutions which had recently been adopted in Brazil." Mackau was to make the authorities and influential persons understand

---

[3] Maler to Pasquier, September 20, 1821, A. A. E., Brésil, 1; Grivel to " Monseigneur," January 20, 1825, A. N., Marine, B B[4], 468.

[4] Pasquier to Maler, May 28, 1821, A. A. E., Brésil, 1.

that France wished her navigators to be well treated and the commercial operations of her merchants to be facilitated in that country.[5]

In September, 1821, Clermont-Tonnerre directed Captain Roussin, whose hydrographic survey of the eastern coast of South America has already been noticed, to take charge of a naval squadron which was to be dispatched to that continent to protect French commerce and to observe conditions in Brazil. Consequently, on February 1, 1822, Roussin addressed to that minister from Montevideo a report concerning the state of the countries in La Plata basin. Eight months later, he sent to Paris an account of revolutionary discontent in Brazil that touched especially on the rôle which was being played in Rio de Janeiro by the Prince Regent and by José Bonifacio, the scholarly Minister of the Interior and Foreign Affairs.[6] Upon his return from this reconnaissance, in recognition of his services to navigation Roussin was made a peer of France and accorded the grade of rear admiral.

After the insurrectionary disturbances in Portuguese America had developed into a movement for independence, Portal sent special instructions to the naval commander on the Brazilian coast. The minister directed Grivel to take no steps which would display partiality toward the political fermentation that was going on in Brazil or toward the relations to be formed between that country and Portugal. Portal also called Grivel's attention to the fact that an important object of the establishment of a naval station near Brazil was to afford protection to French navigators and French commerce.[7]

[5] A. N., Marine, B B⁴, 414.
[6] *Ibid.*, 433.   [7] July 1, 1822, *ibid.*, 414.

Pasquier had sent significant instructions to Colonel Maler on August 18, 1821. "So long as the Prince Royal, to whom the authority of His Very Faithful Majesty has been transferred, continues to be at the head of the government," said Pasquier, "you may perform the functions of chargé d'affaires which you have always exercised; but if he should lose this preëminence and this authority, if it should happen that the disturbances in Brazil weaken the bonds of that country with Portugal, and tend to create for that Prince special interests and a distinct existence, you will then, Sir, confine yourself to the exercise of the functions of consul general, and you will avoid displaying a political character near an authority whose acts would no longer be recognized by the Portuguese Government." [8] In case Brazil should display a tendency to assume a political existence independent of Portugal, the French agent was accordingly to cease exercising his diplomatic functions near the Prince Regent's Government. The recognition by France of the Brazilian State as an independent political entity was thus to be held in abeyance.

On February 27, 1822, Minister Montmorency addressed a letter of advice to Maler. He expressed fear that the agitation which was taking place in Portuguese America might further weaken the last bonds which connected that colony with the motherland. The separation of Brazil from Portugal, he went on to say, "would be a great element of weakness for the Portuguese monarchy, but, if one may judge by the general tendency of the colonies of the New World, everything seems to point in that direction. Without any wish to favor this tendency, it is prudent to antici-

[8] A. A. E., Brésil, 1.

pate such a trend and to preserve with Brazil our customary relations, from which our commerce may continue to gain advantage." Montmorency, who anticipated the departure of the Prince Regent from the country, declared that if this took place the agent of France could leave Rio de Janeiro, but that he should previously turn over his consular functions to Count Gestas, who had been selected to represent France in that city, and present him to the Brazilian court.[9] In June Montmorency instructed Maler to leave the Brazilian capital even though the Regent was still in Brazil, and he informed Maler that Gestas would eventually take his place.[10]

By October, 1822, consequently, the diplomatic and consular agent of France in Rio de Janeiro felt that the time had arrived to alter his dual status. Since Maler realized the delicacy of the situation as well as the irritable spirit of the Brazilians, he planned to proceed tactfully so as not to prejudice French interests. Early in October, he informed José Bonifacio of his decision with reference to a change in his status.[11] This decision was reached at a critical stage in Portuguese-Brazilian relations. As was noted in an earlier chapter, at this time the Congress of Verona refused to admit to its councils an agent of the Brazilian Empire.

Provoked by reactionary measures of the Cortes at Lisbon and influenced by the revolutionary sentiments of many Brazilians, Regent Pedro, on September 7, 1822, on the banks of the rivulet Ypiranga, near São Paulo, proclaimed that Brazil was independent. Soldiers in the capital city

[9] *Ibid.*
[10] June 10, 1822, *ibid.*, 2.
[11] Maler to Montmorency, October 13, 1822, *ibid.*

speedily discarded the Portuguese cockade.[12]   The town
council of Rio de Janeiro held a special meeting to consider
proclaiming Prince Pedro emperor of the new nation.   On
October 12 this council adopted an act by which it acclaimed him as the " First Constitutional Emperor of Brazil
and Her Perpetual Defender." [13]   At Rio de Janiero, on December 1, 1822, Pedro I was solemnly crowned Emperor.

This important change in the status of Regent Pedro
naturally affected the attitude of foreign nations toward his
government.   Upon becoming aware that the Prince had
decided to assume the title of Emperor, a capacity in which
he had not been authorized to recognize him, Maler told
Minister Bonifacio that his functions as chargé d'affaires
had temporarily ceased.[14]   Soon afterward the French agent
sent Bonifacio the following note:

I had the honor to declare to Your Excellency confidentially on the fourth, the eighth, and the eleventh of this
month that, without previously receiving instructions from
the Court of France, I should not be able to recognize on
my own authority any change whatever that His Royal
Highness the Prince Regent might consider it his duty to
make in his actual title, and, as Your Excellency has been
so good as to inform me on the eleventh instant that His
Royal Highness had adopted in effect the title of Emperor of Brazil, it is my duty temporarily to suspend the
exercise of the functions of chargé d'affaires with which the
King, my Master, has been so good as to honor me at this
court since 1815, and which I was authorized to continue
near His Royal Highness, the Prince Regent of Brazil.

[12] Roussin to Portal, October 1, 1822, A. N., Marine, B B⁴, 433,
gives an account of this revolution in Brazil.

[13] *Centenario da independencia do Brasil: acclamacão e côroção
do Principe D. Pedro, primeiro imperador constitucional do Brasil,*
I, 50.

[14] Maler to Montmorency, October 13, 1822, A. A. E., Brésil, 2.

Although my political character has thus been suspended until the arrival of orders and instructions which the French Ministry will transmit to me, I shall nevertheless continue to fulfill in this capital the functions of consul general of France, and I beg Your Excellency to believe that I shall exercise the same zeal and loyalty as heretofore to preserve and to promote the relations of friendship and commerce which happily link the two nations.[15]

On October 11, 1822, by the act of Chargé and Consul General Maler, who ceased to exercise his diplomatic functions on that day, France thus withheld her recognition of the Brazilian Empire. This decision was commended by Montmorency, who took the view that Maler could not properly continue to exercise the functions of chargé d'affaires to the new, independent government of Brazil because it did not have the same character as the former régime.[16] Soon after he became Minister of Foreign Affairs, Chateaubriand wrote to Maler to express his views about the American situation:

We cannot shut our eyes to the trend of events in various sections of America. A new life seems to be reserved for the New World: great maritime nations dream of favoring this movement for independence, of making Latin America incline to their views, of engrossing the commerce of that vast region, of seeking new possessions there, and of profiting by the differences which exist between the motherlands and the colonies, in order to make them purchase aid and to enrich themselves at the expense of those colonies.

France has not followed such an example. For a long time she has sought to end the dissensions which rage between Europe and America; she has been impelled to this alike by her policy, by the ties of blood, and by her spirit of moderation and justice. In the midst of those differ-

---

[15] Maler to Bonifacio, October 13, 1822 (copy), *ibid*.
[16] December 23, 1822, *ibid*.

ences, she has preserved a wise neutrality; the King has undertaken to protect everywhere the person and the interests of his subjects; and, though he has frequently dispatched his squadrons into American seas, and particularly into Brazilian waters, the use of his forces has never been hostile; their presence has often prevented misfortunes and assured to the weak a place of refuge.[17]

After French soldiers set foot on Spanish soil, Chateaubriand felt that special attention should be paid to the American possessions of both Spain and Portugal. He took pains to make French officials in America acquainted with recent developments in Europe. On October 11, 1823, in a dispatch to Count Gestas, who had been notified that on the departure of Maler from Rio de Janeiro he was to serve as " chargé d'affaires and consul general of France ad interim," [18] the Minister of Foreign Affairs declared that, although the reunion of Brazil and Portugal was desirable, if Brazil was to remain independent it was important that she preserve the monarchical form of government without which the nation would have neither force nor stability, and that she be saved from the encroachments of democracy. " Although your instructions, Count, have already directed you to act in this manner," he added, " I again insist upon this point; in order to show you how much we desire that monarchical institutions be not altered in Brazil if it should happen that that country remains independent." [19]

Seven days later, Chateaubriand disclosed more fully to Consul General Gestas his views concerning Brazil. He declared that, whatever it might be, Portugal's policy toward Brazil would not alter the friendly attitude of France:

[17] January 15, 1823, *ibid.*
[18] Montmorency to Gestas, June 10, 1822, *ibid.*
[19] *Ibid.*

We shall always try as much as possible to induce the Portuguese Government to offer that colony propositions which it can accept and which may thus prevent the dissensions with which it is threatened. Indeed, false measures taken in the situation in which Brazil is supposed to be would easily plunge that country into new revolutions which would wrest that important possession from the house of Braganza. . . .

The intervention of France in the affairs of Spain will lend color to rumors which malevolence is pleased to spread concerning the succor that the King's government may be able to offer to the powers of the Iberian Peninsula for the purpose of reconquering their revolted colonies. Those rumors, which you can declare to be unwarranted, may have caused some anxiety in Rio de Janeiro. In that case, Sir, you should pronounce them to be baseless. You should assure the Brazilian Government that, far from entertaining any hostility toward it, France desires only to strengthen the bonds which have already begun to form between the two countries and to ensure to their commercial relations the greatest possible development. This is the important matter to which you are to devote all your attention. In the execution of the Brazilian customs laws there are still practices burdensome to our commerce which you should undertake to have modified and reformed.[20]

Chateaubriand's advice to the consular agent of France concerning the improvement of relations with Brazil was rendered less effective by the attitude of Hyde de Neuville, who in April, 1821, had been appointed ambassador to the Court of Lisbon. His instructions directed him to undertake the difficult task of cleverly withdrawing Portugal from English influence.[21] Hyde de Neuville apparently interpreted these instructions in an indiscreet manner. The English minister at Lisbon informed his court that in the

[20] *Ibid.*

[21] Hyde de Neuville, *Mémoires et souvenirs,* III, 116; see further *ibid.,* 129-30.

autumn of 1823 the French ambassador formally proposed to the King of Portugal an alliance with France and other Continental powers, " promising a complete guarantee to this Country of its present Form of Government under the House of Braganza, engaging the exertion of all the means in the Power of the Allies for bringing the Brazilian Dominions into a proper Dependence upon this Country, and deprecating any Attempt to introduce a System of representative Government." [22]

When, in accordance with Canning's instructions, the English envoy at Paris brought this report—one which Hyde de Neuville later stigmatized as quite absurd— [23] to the attention of Chateaubriand, that minister declared to Stuart that it was calumnious. Chateaubriand further maintained that the policy of France toward Portugal and Portuguese America was based upon the same motive which guided her conduct toward Spain and Spanish America, that is, a desire to submit the issue to a European congress " which shall decide upon the best mode of offering the joint mediation of the Allied Sovereigns to settle the differences between the Mother Countries and their Colonies, and in which the French Government will take the same part as Great Britain and the other Powers interested in the question." [24]

Though the French Premier did not display as deep an interest in Portugal as did Chateaubriand, yet in July, 1823, he emphatically disclaimed any intention on the part of his

[22] Thornton to Canning, October 31, 1823 (extract), enclosure in Canning to Stuart, F. O., 63/270.

[23] *Op. cit.*, II, 124.

[24] Stuart to Canning, November 15, 1823, F. O., 27/296. See further Chateaubriand, *Correspondance générale*, V, 72-73.

government to interfere in the affairs of that country. Yet he felt that French intervention in Spain would have a salutary effect upon the Portuguese political régime.[25] As has been indicated, Villèle believed that the relations existing between his country and the Empire of Brazil were more useful and salutary than those which might develop between France and the Spanish-American republics. To him this was another reason for indulging in the hope that these republics would eventually invite Spanish princes, like the Prince of Portugal in Brazil, to rule over them. Villèle even declared that, with some limitations, France would eventually not oppose the application to her insurgent colony in Santo Domingo of principles which would promote the peace and prosperity of the world.[26]

Meanwhile imperial soldiers under General Labatut who were besieging Bahia had been aided by maritime forces under Lord Cochrane, who in March, 1823, had been appointed commander of the Brazilian navy. On July 2 following, the soldiers of Portugal evacuated that city, and other cities soon fell into the hands of the Patriots. Thus, after a struggle which lasted scarcely as many months as the Spanish-American Revolution lasted years, the vast colony of Brazil achieved its independence. On November 17, 1823, after Regent Pedro had been crowned Emperor of Brazil, the Minister of Marine informed Grivel that, in view of the return of Ferdinand VII to absolute power and the restoration of King John VI in Portugal, his government did not yet know what relations might be established between Brazil and the motherland, but that it was the intention of Louis XVIII to adhere for the time

[25] Villèle, *Mémoires et correspondance*, IV, 244.
[26] *Ibid.*, 489-90.

being to the strict and useful neutrality which he had observed up to that date. Clermont-Tonnerre added:

> By separating from Portugal the Prince of Brazil has conserved and consecrated the monarchical principle. We see by your letters and by every report which comes from Brazil that he may be endangered by the conduct of numerous partisans of opposing principles. In this situation we owe him the support of our forces in case of need; on this account the government of the King has judged it useful and suitable to strengthen the station which you command. Of course it is understood that in no case will you take part in any struggle in which Brazil finds herself ranged against Portugal. . . . You should reach an understanding with Count Gestas, in order that you may render to the Prince who governs Brazil all the service that you can within the limits which I have outlined to you. It is scarcely necessary to inform you that in this delicate conjuncture you should conduct yourself with firmness and prudence.[27]

In accordance with these instructions, Gestas gave the Brazilian Government assurances that it could count upon the French squadron in the harbor of Rio de Janeiro to support its authority. Writing to Clermont-Tonnerre, Commander Grivel interpreted his special instructions as follows: "Your Excellency directs me, above all, to preserve peace and to maintain the monarchical principle. On the other hand, you inform me that we owe the sovereign of this country the support of our forces in case he is faced by dangers from the Democrats." [28] To Polignac the Minister of Foreign Affairs interpreted Grivel's instructions to mean that, although French naval officers should avoid becoming involved in the controversy between father and son, yet, if measures of the revolutionary and democratic faction at Rio

---

[27] A. N., Marine, B B⁴, 405 *bis.*
[28] Grivel to Clermont-Tonnerre, April 10, 1824, *ibid.,* 458.

de Janeiro should actually endanger the life of Emperor Pedro, French naval officers were not only to give him succor but were also to furnish him with an asylum on board their vessels.[29]   Further, in a letter to Hyde de Neuville, Chateaubriand confessed that France could not view without regret the overthrow of the only monarchical government which up to this time had been established in South America.[30]

The policy to be pursued toward the Brazilian monarchy was unfolded in detail in a letter from the Minister of Foreign Affairs to Gestas on November 27, 1823.   Chateaubriand declared that, although the offer which England had made in the previous autumn to mediate between Brazil and Portugal had been accepted, he was apprehensive with regard to the condition of the former colony.   He felt that the very existence of the government which was attempting to establish its independence was at times menaced.   That precarious condition seemed to him to call for immediate remedy:

> It is important for the present Prince of Brazil to maintain the existing government there, whatever the nature of the arrangements which may be made concerning the question of independence.   You ought therefore, Count, to use every occasion that is offered to rally all spirits to the support of the Prince and to make sure that he does not become involved in proceedings which might compromise him and put his power at hazard.

The government of the King has ordered that the naval squadron at this station be reënforced, and that the officer who commands it be directed to defend the Prince, whenever he shall require aid, against any attacks which may aim to overthrow the monarchical régime.   The squadron will

[29] Chateaubriand, *Correspondance générale*, V, 223.
[30] *Ibid.*, 165.

refrain, however, from interfering in anything that concerns the relations of Portugal with Brazil; it should neither meddle with that question nor take any part in the differences existing between father and son.

Chateaubriand stated that Louis XVIII had noticed with displeasure the violent course pursued in Brazil toward certain commissioners of Portugal who had the right to expect an honorable reception. He declared that the Court of Lisbon was inclined to favor a peaceful adjustment with Brazil. The instructions which he had addressed to the French ambassador at Lisbon were animated by a spirit of moderation. Hyde de Neuville had been directed to keep that court in a conciliatory mood and to make it realize that the first interest of Portugal was not to weaken in Brazil the authority of a prince of the Braganza dynasty.[31] Shortly afterward Chateaubriand supplemented these instructions by a dispatch to Gestas in which he emphasized the need of promoting French commerce and declared that it was necessary to improve the relations of France with Brazil by facilitating communications between the two countries, by establishing Frenchmen in Brazil, and by sending young Brazilians to France for their education.[32]

Early in the following year Chateaubriand elaborated a special mode of adjusting the Portuguese-Brazilian problem. The minister informed Polignac that he was contemplating the admission of a delegation from Portugal as well as from Spain into the proposed European congress. Chateaubriand believed that the Portuguese Government comprehended

[31] A. A. E., Brésil, 2. See Stuart to Canning, February 26, 1824, F. O., 27/306, for a summary of Chateaubriand's views as communicated to Stuart.

[32] December 20, 1823, A. A. E., Brésil, 2.

better than the Spanish Government the difficulty of bringing the Latin-American colonies back under the sovereignty
of the motherlands. Hence he thought that the admission
of Portuguese delegates into the congress would make the
proposed mediation with the revolted Spanish colonies
easier. He explained carefully that his government did not
contemplate the restoration of Portuguese severeignty over
Brazil: " . . . the only thing that it believes possible and
that it wishes for is that the Prince Regent should preserve
there a monarchical government and prevent fresh revolutions which would disturb that country for an indefinite
period." [33] However, as England persistently refused to be
represented in the proposed conference, Polignac did not
have an occasion to broach to Canning the views of
Chateaubriand concerning Portuguese participation in its
meetings.

On January 31, 1824, Chateaubriand directed Consul General Gestas to take advantage of existing conditions to promote the most important matter with which he was entrusted,
namely the development of commercial intercourse between
France and Brazil. The minister reasoned that, upon achiev-
ing independence, Portuguese America would become a
great consumer of manufactured articles which it would pay
for with natural products. He maintained that, without pre-
tending to supplant the English, the French were in a position to offer commercial advantages to the Brazilians if
Brazil should concede special privileges to French products.
Further, Chateaubriand suggested that either the Empire
should be induced not to renew the commercial treaty which
had been negotiated by England in 1810 or it should con-

[33] January 8, 1824, A. A. E., Angleterre, 618.

cede to France the same privileges which English subjects enjoyed in Brazil by virtue of that treaty. Should Gestas secure this concession, he was at once to inform the Brazilian Government that as a recompense France would reduce the import duties on certain Brazilian cottons, and that she would cease to accord special concessions to Haitian coffee. At least, he should aim to secure a modification of the Anglo-Portuguese Treaty of 1810. French commerce was not to be sacrificed.[34]

Disturbing rumors which reached Brazil in regard to the attitude of France toward Latin America soon evoked from Chateaubriand a comprehensive exposition of his policy. He wrote as follows to Count Gestas on April 5, 1824:

You have rightly striven to destroy the false rumors which have been circulated about the supposed project of an expedition prepared by France against Brazil. Such a design has never been formed. France carries on her commercial relations with Brazil peacefully: she wishes to see them favored by the local authorities; she believes them useful to both countries. It is certainly not at a time when she has sent a consul general to Rio de Janeiro with a view to making commercial relations more certain and more numerous that she has suddenly adopted hostile measures which would cause her to lose all the fruit of this system of amity and prudence.

Yet in reassuring the Brazilian Government upon this point, Count, you should carefully refrain from making explanations about the question of recognition. That question is premature. We must also guard our interests in Portugal, and we should not take any step in America which might embarrass us in Europe.[35]

The issue of the recognition of Brazil had meanwhile

[34] A. A. E., Brésil, 3.
[35] Ibid.

been broached at Paris. In May, 1823, the very agent who had visited Verona had an interview with a member of the Ministry of Foreign Affairs on behalf of " the magnanimous Prince to whom Providence had confided the defense and preservation of monarchy in the New World." [36] But in November, 1823, Gameïro Pessoa was succeeded by Borges de Barros, a liberal Brazilian who had served in a minor rôle at the Congress of Vienna and had recently been appointed by Luiz de Carvalho e Mello, the Brazilian Minister of Foreign Affairs, as chargé d'affaires to France. Early in the next year, when Borges de Barros had a conference with Chateaubriand, who was suspected of yielding to Russian influence, the latter intimated that the Brazilians should omit from their proposed constitution certain ultrademocratic clauses. The Brazilian diplomat retorted with spirit that Emperor Pedro was attempting to utilize revolutionary and republican ideas while serving as a champion of monarchical institutions.

In an interview with Villèle, Borges de Barros insisted upon France's recognition that Brazil had separated from Portugal. The chargé argued that the enemies of his country's independence had been vanquished, that the Emperor of Brazil had sworn to support the Constitution, and that the United States had acknowledged Brazil's independence. Borges de Barros maintained that hence the diplomats of the new empire had a right to solicit with more emphasis and to claim with more energy than ever before the recognition by European powers of an accomplished fact. An intimation was also conveyed that, because the English were displaying more interest in Brazil than the French, they

[36] Gameiro Pessoa to Rauzan, May 13, 1823, *ibid.*, 1.

might be accorded special privileges when once the status of that empire was definitely determined.[37]

Meanwhile Gameiro Pessoa had turned up in Paris again. On January 8, 1824, after having been admitted to an interview with Chateaubriand, he addressed a memorandum to that minister expounding his views with regard to the former Latin colonies in America. The Brazilian diplomat expressed the opinion that the conferences which representatives of the Five Powers had recently held in Paris could scarcely have led to the conclusion that the insurgent colonies of Spain should be brought back to dependence upon the motherland. He hoped that instead those powers had decided to end the protracted war for independence by introducing into Spanish America the monarchical system, which was well suited to the character and manners of its inhabitants and which would place at the head of their governments princes of the same dynasty that reigned at Madrid. "This great project is the only one that can be executed," he continued, "and the only one that would justify before the world the intervention of those powers in the affairs of the New World."

The envoy argued that the retention of the monarchical system by his country entitled it to the esteem of European sovereigns. As the circumstances in which Brazil was placed were essentially different from those which confronted the new republics of America, he expressed the

[37] Loreto, "Reconnaissance de l'Empire du Brésil par les puissances européennes," *Revue d'histoire diplomatique*, III, 512, citing the Brazilian archives. The independence of Brazil was recognized by the United States on May 22, 1824, when José S. Rebello was received by President Monroe as chargé d'affaires of that nation. See Robertson, "The Recognition of the Hispanic American Nations by the United States," *Hispanic Am. Hist. Rev.*, I, 265-67.

hope that the mediatory powers "would realize that their own dignity requires they should not confuse Brazil with those republics and that they should not delay the formal acknowledgment of her new political status; for they could scarcely refuse to Brazil what it was generally believed they were disposed to concede to the Spanish-American states on condition that they adopt the monarchical form of government demanded by their own interests." Such an acknowledgment, added Gameiro Pessoa, would not only serve to dissipate the fears entertained in the New World that the Allies would actually intervene in Latin America, but it would also promote the success of their negotiations with the new republics.[38]

A new Brazilian commissioner named Felïsberto Caldeira Brant arrived in London in April, 1824. Joined by Gameiro Pessoa, he undertook to negotiate with the Portuguese minister in London, Count Villa Real, for an adjustment with the motherland. In the discussions which ensued, the resourceful Secretary of Foreign Affairs Canning was present on behalf of the English Government, while Prince Esterhazy and Baron Neumann represented Austria, whose coöperation in the proposed mediation England was willing to accept.[39] When he learned of the presence of the Brazilian commissioners in London, Villèle became anxious to know what was taking place in the conferences. To a dispatch addressed to Prince Polignac that minister added certain phrases with his own pen. He declared that it was very important that the ambassador keep informed of whatever was happening in London with respect to Portuguese America. Polignac was directed to discover, if pos-

[38] A. A. E., Espagne, 726.
[39] Oliveira Lima, *Historia diplomatica do Brazil,* pp. 313-49.

sible, whether the negotiators had succeeded in reconciling Brazil with Portugal or whether they were arranging for the separation of that colony from the motherland. The diplomatic problem which confronted Europe was formulated in these words: " If England should recognize the Republic of Colombia, could not the Continental powers recognize the Emperor of Brazil, and what would come of all this? " [40] However, after a series of Portuguese-Brazilian conferences had been held without any definite result, Canning early in 1825 decided to send Sir Charles Stuart on a mission to Rio de Janeiro via Lisbon.

Relations between France and Brazil were further complicated by the fact that ships displaying the flag of the new empire were casting anchor in French ports. Francisco de Brito, who was now serving as the Portuguese chargé at Paris, addressed a protest to Chateaubriand to complain of the decision of the French Government to admit into its harbors vessels flying the Brazilian colors. Chateaubriand evidently responded that, as there was a consul stationed in Brazil for the protection of French commerce, his government " could not be expected to take any measure, which might compromise the interests of French subjects in that part of the world; and that therefore the same treatment must be extended in France to all ships under the Brazilian flag" which in similar circumstances she claimed for her own vessels from the authorities of Brazil.[41] In the autumn of 1824 Stuart asked Damas whether Brazilian consuls were recognized and allowed to perform their functions in France. Damas replied that his government had refused to grant them exequaturs but had never-

[40] July 26, 1824, A. A. E., Angleterre, 618.
[41] Stuart to Canning, August 10, 1824, F. O., 27/312.

theless declared that such consuls would be allowed in France in order to watch over the commercial interests of their countrymen and that every advantage except public recognition would be accorded them which was enjoyed by French consuls in Brazilian ports.[42]

The peculiar status of the Brazilian Empire was also brought to the attention of the Ministry of Foreign Affairs in May, 1824, by Commander Grivel, who sent a special report from Bahia concerning the relations of that empire with France. Because of Monroe's message to Congress of December 2, 1823, this commander declared that America and Europe were now brought face to face. Grivel maintained that it would be wise to recognize the republican tendency in Latin America; for monarchy might thus be saved from total shipwreck in the New World. He was convinced that the Royalist party would not prevail in Spanish America and that a *point d'appui* for the monarchical system could not be found there. "If we accept the principle that a great monarchy strongly organized in America involves the future tranquillity of Europe," he continued, "we should cast our eyes upon Brazil." He reasoned that the promotion of the development of that country demanded the acknowledgment of its independence, especially by Portugal:

France is thus doubly interested in the immediate recognition and consolidation of the Brazilian Empire. Primarily as a monarchy but also as a naval power, France ought not to miss the opportunity of removing this extensive and rich country from the influence as well as from the commerce of her rival, or at least she should partake of the advantages offered by that country and prepare there asylums for her squadrons. She cannot, as do the other

[42] *Idem* to *idem*, August 10, 1824, F. O., 27/312.

European states, hesitate with impunity and await whatever may suit the Cabinet of Lisbon to decide; for to France this is an important interest, perhaps no less important than that which decided her policy in the American Revolution.[43]

The French people were not left in ignorance of the stake involved in the Portuguese-Brazilian problem.   In June, 1824, Alphonse de Beauchamp, who had written a history of Brazil, published in Paris a volume addressed to European monarchs in which he pleaded for the recognition of Brazilian independence. Beauchamp argued that the liberation of Portuguese America was decreed by Providence and that this emancipated country would furnish a great outlet for the products of European industry. He directed the attention of French merchants to the extensive markets in Brazil for such products as wines, glassware, clocks, hosiery, and draperies.[44]

Upon receipt of a letter from the consul general at Rio de Janeiro stating that that court was not disposed to make any commercial concessions to France unless she acknowledged the independence of Brazil from Portugal, Damas sent a note to Count Gestas explaining the French attitude toward the rising nation. The minister declared that France did not wish to speak upon the questions in dispute between Portugal and Brazil: "Our most constant desire has been to see a reconciliation brought about between the two countries. Your instructions and those of the King's ambassador at Lisbon have been prepared with this object in view; and we have judged that this reconciliation would be

[43] " De l'Europe et de l'Amérique et Specialement de la France et du Brésil," May 20, 1824, A. A. E., Brésil, 3.

[44] *Indépendance de l'Empire du Brésil présentée aux monarques européens,* pp. xii-xiii, 98.

useful without ourselves undertaking to establish its bases and conditions." Damas added that the cautious policy which his government had followed in this delicate question was imperative at that time because of the difficult situation in which the Portuguese Government was placed.

It is not at a time when the very existence of that régime is menaced, when Portugal is obliged to assemble all her forces in order to reëstablish the government, to strengthen her legal authority, and to prevent fresh troubles, that we can venture to declare that we no longer recognize her right to Brazil, that we consider that country independent, and that we sever all the old bonds connecting the two parts of the Portuguese monarchy. . . . We have refrained from passing judgment upon the question of independence; and, at a time when we have also refrained from furnishing to Portugal any succor which she might use against Brazil, the same motives of equity should prompt us to avoid encouraging Brazil in her hostility toward Portugal.[45]

Shortly afterward, Gestas assured Damas that Frenchmen in Brazil had given their support to monarchical principles there. Yet he warned the minister that France would not secure a reward for this valuable service because she could not take the initiative in acknowledging the independence of that country. He predicted that Brazil would pay dearly for the mediation of England between father and son.[46]

Early in 1825 Minister Damas felt that the time had at last arrived for his government to recognize Brazil. His first important step was to instruct the consul general at the

[45] July 1, 1824, A. A. E., Brésil, 3.

[46] August 25, 1824, *ibid.* Cf. the statement which an English agent at Rio de Janeiro made to Pedro I concerning the alleged opposition of France to the recognition of the independence of Brazil by Portugal. Webster, *Britain and the Independence of Latin America,* I, 243-45.

Court of Rio de Janeiro to initiate negotiations for a grant of commercial concessions like that which in 1810 it had included in its treaty with England. On April 18, 1825, Damas directed Gestas to make three requests of the Imperial Government: that Brazilian duties on French merchandise be reduced to fifteen per cent; that the Brazilian authorities determine the value of enumerated products of France in the manner fixed by Article IV of the Anglo-Brazilian treaty; and that in the valuation of non-enumerated articles the same method be followed. Damas reasoned that in commercial intercourse between Brazil and France such arrangements would be of reciprocal advantage. His government wished to be placed on the most-favored-nation basis; it would be willing to allow Brazilian exporters an entrepôt for their sugar, and even offered to admit Brazilian coffee into French ports at one-half of the regular tariff rate. Gestas was instructed to endeavor to secure a treaty of commerce upon the same basis as that negotiated by England: " In this particular it is convenient to imitate her, for her situation with respect to Portugal is perfectly regular; there is nothing contrary to our principles in the course which England is pursuing, and it is proper that we should not do any more than she is doing." The minister enclosed the full powers which were necessary in order that Gestas might negotiate and conclude a treaty with the Imperial Government.[47]

In a separate dispatch Damas informed the consul general that the question of the boundaries of the French colony in South America could not be linked to a discussion of the political existence of Brazil. It was necessary

[47] A. A. E., Brésil, 3.

first to decide to what nation the territory adjoining French Guiana belonged. The minister explained that the Treaty of Utrecht undertook to fix the limits of the French colony by establishing as the line of demarcation the river Oyapok or Vicente Pinzón, but that geographers did not agree upon the location of that river. Two rivers had in fact received the same name. The agreement reached when the colony was returned to France in 1817, that a joint commission determine the boundary between French Guiana and Portuguese Guiana, had never been carried out.[48]

On April 25 Damas explained to Gestas the manner in which he was to proceed with regard to an acknowledgment of the title of Emperor Pedro:

Count, the full powers which I had the honor to send you authorized you to treat with the Brazilian Government without mentioning the title of Emperor borne by Dom Pedro. I ought to explain to you the motives for this reticence. Today Brazil is ruled by a government distinct from that of Portugal. The needs arising from the new situation of Brazil are generally realized; and, inasmuch as one may look for the causes of this separation in the acts of His Very Faithful Majesty, one may induce that King to acknowledge the separation in a manner which does not wound his dignity. Such seems to be the object of the mission that Sir Charles Stuart is carrying out today at Lisbon. The instructions which I am sending to the embassy of France at that capital present the same view. We merely seek to secure, without trouble and without a rupture between Portugal and Brazil, a result which their respective situations seem to render inevitable.

We are so fully convinced that the two countries can no longer have a common government that we are today disposed to negotiate with the government of Brazil. This is evidently to recognize the existence of that nation, and that is the matter which ought at the present moment to have

[48] April 19, 1825, *ibid.*

the most importance for her. With respect to the title which should be accorded to the head of that government, we have thought, Count, that it would be convenient to allow this to be determined first in the negotiations which are now going on at Lisbon. If, as we have reason to believe will happen, the title of Emperor is accorded to Dom Pedro as a concession from the King his father, it will have all the traits of legitimacy: it will perhaps be recognized by the other powers—it will not leave them any longer hesitating painfully between the rights of the father and the power of the son.

Count, you will be informed as promptly as possible of the result of those negotiations; and, if it is such as one has reason to expect, you may then accord to the Prince, in the treaty which you will sign with his plenipoteniaries, a title that has not been conferred upon him in your full powers. You will easily appreciate all the motives which prevent us from according this title from today forth and from taking the initiative in a decision that time will bring about, but which the feelings of the King and his regard for His Very Faithful Majesty do not permit him to promote.

Damas further instructed the consul general that, whether or not Stuart proceeded at once from Lisbon on a mission to Rio de Janeiro, the same title should be used in addressing Dom Pedro as that accorded him in the proposed Anglo-Brazilian convention. The negotiations between Gestas and the Brazilian Government were thus not to terminate before Stuart's arrival in Rio de Janeiro. With this dispatch the minister transmitted the drafts of two treaties. A proposed Franco-Brazilian boundary convention provided that the natural boundary between French Guiana and Portuguese Guiana was to be the river Oyapok, the mouth of which was supposed to be located between two degrees and three degrees, north latitude. The minister was careful to state, however, that definite arrangements with regard to the limits between the possessions of France and Brazil in Guiana were to be reserved for a separate agreement.

The draft of a treaty of commerce which Damas sent to Gestas stipulated that the citizens of one party in the dominions of the other were to enjoy in respect to the payment of imposts or taxes the same treatment as that accorded to citizens of the most-favored-nation. It also provided that, in general, French products were to be admitted into Brazilian ports on the payment of duties amounting to fifteen per cent of their value. The duty laid by France upon cotton imported from Brazil was to be reduced one-half. Each party agreed that the subjects of the other party were to enjoy in its ports all the advantages of its own subjects; while the consuls of both parties were to enjoy most-favored-nation treatment.[49] In the projects of both the Franco-Brazilian treaties transmitted by Damas the title of the Brazilian ruler was left blank to be filled in by Gestas.

Meanwhile the mission of Stuart to Lisbon had borne good fruit. Stuart was accepted by the Portuguese Government as its representative in the negotiations for a treaty with the former colony. On May 13 King John VI of Portugal signed a diploma by which he transferred to his son Pedro the sovereignty over that country and acknowledged him as the Emperor of Brazil.[50] Entrusted with this

[49] A. A. E., Brésil, 3. Both the draft conventions were dated April 25, 1825. On June 30 Consul General Chamberlain wrote from Rio de Janeiro to Canning and reported that Gestas had had an interview with the Emperor concerning the negotiation of a treaty with France. Although the full instructions of Gestas even authorized " the acknowledgment of Independence and the Empire," Pedro I responded that he had determined not to enter into any treaty discussions before the arrival of Stuart. F. O., 13/9.

[50] Oliveira Lima, *Historia diplomatica do Brazil*, pp. 360-63.

concession, Stuart reached Rio de Janeiro in July. After holding conferences with diplomats representing Brazil, Stuart on August 29, 1825, signed with them on behalf of Portugal a treaty of peace and alliance. By Article I of that treaty John VI recognized Portuguese America as an empire independent of Portugal; the Portuguese King also acknowledged Pedro as the Brazilian Emperor. Article IV provided for peace and an alliance between Brazil and Portugal. On the following day Emperor Pedro I ratified this treaty of reconciliation and recognition.[51]

Commenting upon the separation of Brazil from Portugal, the *Constitutionnel* declared that a long chapter in international relations had been closed and called upon the ministers of France to rise to the occasion by erecting a new science of diplomacy:

> Turn your eyes to America. She has no need of us, but we do not know how to get along without her. In former times, while in the colonial status, she was oppressed by us; today, when she is free, the rôles are changed. It is necessary for us to demand concessions of her; for the people that she favors will soon become rich and powerful. . . . It is necessary that we merit a treaty of commerce by good offices.[52]

Consul General Gestas promptly felicitated Emperor Pedro I upon the establishment of an independent régime. The consul general expressed his desire to consecrate the prospective new order in Brazil by negotiating a convention which would determine her relations with France.[53] In a

---

[51] *Ibid.,* pp. 233-45, 352-57; Temperley, *The Foreign Policy of Canning,* pp. 221-22.

[52] November 9, 1825.

[53] Gestas to Carvalho e Mello, September 2, 1825 (copy), A. A. E., Brésil, 3.

note to Minister Carvalho e Mello on September 5, Gestas stated that the Emperor had on that day assured him that it was his intention to treat with all nations on the same basis and that conferences regarding a treaty between France and Brazil should be resumed.[54] Twelve days later that minister replied that the Imperial Government, animated by a keen desire to show the importance which it attached to the relations between Brazil and France, was considering his proposals.[55]

Yet, when Gestas began his conferences with Carvalho e Mello, he encountered two difficulties which were increased by the Brazilian's *amour propre*. The first difficulty was caused by the omission of the title " Emperor " in the consul general's credentials. The second difficulty arose from a notion of the Brazilian diplomat that the French wished to restrict the treaty to commercial matters. However, in transmitting to Carvalho e Mello a copy of his powers, Gestas made a skillful effort to remove the feeling of injured dignity which had affected the Brazilian minister. With regard to the first difficulty, the consul general pointed out that his credentials had been prepared at a time when it was still uncertain what title would be accorded to the Brazilian ruler: " Would it be simply Emperor of Brazil, or would it be Emperor of Brazil, of Africa, and of the possessions in India? Should this title be followed by another designation, such as Hereditary Prince of Portugal? " Such questions could not be settled in the credentials. With re-

---

[54] (Copy), *ibid.* Campos, *Relações diplomaticas do Brasil*, p. 54, incorrectly sets the date of the beginning of negotiations for a commercial treaty between France and Brazil as October 24, 1825. He takes the view that French recognition of Brazilian independence dates from that time.

[55] A. A. E., Brésil, 3.

spect to the second difficulty, Gestas maintained that it was by treating matters of common interest to nations in an official manner that recognition was accorded, and further that the framing of the protocol of a treaty would furnish an opportunity to fill in omissions in his powers. Then he made this tactful explanation:

> The undersigned will terminate these observations by stating that when a nation with thirty million inhabitants, a member of the Holy Alliance, having as king a Bourbon, asks to negotiate—this alone is equivalent to formal recognition. For the rank which France occupies, the influence which she exercises, and her well-understood policy do not justify the idea that she would take such a step lightly. Still less do they warrant the thought that she would so decide without the certainty that propositions agreeable to both countries will be accepted. It would accordingly seem that the plenipotentiaries, thoroughly convinced of the honorable object of their mission and of the intentions of their respective sovereigns, instead of raising difficulties with regard to expressions in full powers which are secret documents, ought to devote their zeal and their talents to removing every obstacle that might delay a conclusion which is mutually desired.[56]

The pressing duties of Brazilian statesmen caused several days to elapse between their meetings with Gestas. At a conference held on November 11 with the Brazilian diplomats, Viscounts Paranaguá and Santo-Amaro, who were now entrusted with the negotiations on behalf of Brazil, the consul general promised that he would later present fresh credentials, mentioning the title of the Emperor. He agreed that the issue concerning the boundaries of French Guiana should be considered after the treaty of commerce was

[56] October 26, 1825 (copy), *ibid.* Accioly, *O reconhecimento da independencia do Brasil*, p. 249, considers October 26 as the date when France acknowledged Brazilian independence.

framed; a French draft of such a treaty was left with the Brazilian diplomats.[57] Near the end of December Gestas informed his government that the negotiations were almost concluded. However, he declared that, in order to overcome objections raised by the Brazilians, he might have to depart from the bases which the French Government had laid down, for the Brazilians not only wished to be assured that, if they reduced the duties laid on French imports into Brazil, the duties levied on Brazilian goods imported into France would not be increased, but also desired that the life of the Franco-Brazilian treaty be limited to one-half of the term that had been specified in the Anglo-Brazilian convention.[58]

On January 8, 1826, Gestas and the Brazilian viscounts signed a treaty of amity, navigation, and commerce. The preamble of this treaty declared that the King of France and the Emperor of Brazil wished " to establish and to consolidate the political relations between the two crowns as well as the relations of navigation and commerce " between the two countries. Further, the French King declared that on behalf of himself and his successors he " recognized the independence of the Empire of Brazil and the imperial dignity in the person of Emperor Pedro I and his legitimate heirs and successors." Gestas signed this treaty not only as consul general but, as he had already begun to style himself, also as chargé d'affaires of France.

The treaty further provided that the subjects of one party in the dominions of the other party were to enjoy all the privileges and exemptions granted to citizens of the

[57] " Conférence du 11 Novembre, 1825," Gestas to Damas, November 19, 1825, A. A. E., Brésil, 3.

[58] Gestas to Damas, December 24, 1825, *ibid.*

most-favored-nation. Products of France imported into Brazil would pay only such duties as were levied on most-favored-nation products. This stipulation virtually reduced Brazilian import duties on French merchandise from twenty-four per cent to fifteen per cent, the rate conceded to England by the Treaty of 1810. Reciprocal freedom of commerce and navigation was to prevail between the two contracting parties. If one of the parties to this treaty became involved in hostilities, the other party was not to trade with the enemies of the nation at war in certain articles designated as contraband.[59] Article IV of the treaty accorded to French consuls the same privileges in respect to the protection of their compatriots as might thereafter be granted to consuls of most-favored-nations. As the Anglo-Brazilian commercial treaty negotiated in 1827 granted to English consuls the right to administer the estates of English subjects who died without testament in Brazil, the fourth article of the Franco-Brazilian Treaty of 1826 secured for consuls of France the right to look after the estates of French subjects who died in Brazil intestate after her treaty with England was ratified.[60]

Upon receiving a copy of the proposed treaty, which did not conform to the draft sent from Paris to Rio de Janeiro, Damas informed the consul general that perhaps some of its provisions might be susceptible of modification but that it would be examined in a conciliatory spirit. The minister promised that new credentials would be sent to Gestas with the ratification of the treaty, if the King approved. Damas added that the problem of " the recognition of the independence of Brazil and of the imperial title of her sov-

[59] Clercq, *Recueil des traités,* III, 402-08.
[60] Manchester, *British Preëminence in Brazil,* pp. 298-99.

ereign " would soon be settled by notes which would be exchanged between himself and Borges de Barros, who had been made Viscount Pedra Branca. " You can," Damas declared, " accordingly announce this as an accomplished fact, and you may add that the King intends immediately to accredit a minister plenipotentiary to the Court of Rio de Janeiro, who will be able to depart from France in a very short time." [61]

Negotiations concerning the acknowledgment of Brazilian independence had in the meantime been initiated at Paris. On February 3, 1826, Pedra Branca asked Damas for a statement concerning the attitude of his government toward the recognition of the Brazilian Empire, in order that he could send word to Rio de Janeiro by the next courier.[62] Ten days later Pedra Branca sent a formal note to Damas to inform him that he had received news of the signing by Portugal and Brazil of the Treaty of August 29, 1825, which would henceforth regulate the relations between those countries. The Brazilian diplomat continued as follows in the third person: " He is at the same time instructed to invite, in the name of his court, the government of His Very Christian Majesty to recognize the independence of Brazil and the imperial title with which His August Master and his heirs are invested." Pedra Branca added that the interest which Louis XVIII had on various occasions displayed in Pedro I had led the latter to believe that the King of France would accept this invitation.[63]

On February 28, 1826, Damas made a formal reply. He declared that he had laid the note of Pedra Branca before Charles X, who had been pleased to learn of the negotiation

---

[61] February 2, 1826, A. A. E., Brésil, 4.
[62] *Ibid.*   [63] *Ibid.*

of a treaty which defined relations between Brazil and Portugal and who did not hesitate to accept the new order that had resulted. In conclusion, Damas made the following announcement: " The undersigned is accordingly authorized to declare that His Very Christian Majesty recognizes the independence of the Empire of Brazil and the title of Emperor which devolves upon Prince Dom Pedro de Alcántara and his descendants, with the understanding that by this title there shall not flow, through the ties of blood, any change to the prejudice of the powers of Europe." [64] It was perhaps not altogether without design that the clause in this announcement safeguarding the European powers was almost identical with the clause that had been employed by Metternich on December 30, 1825, when by a formal note to the Portuguese diplomat Baron Villa-Secca he had recognized the independence of Brazil on behalf of the Austrian Empire.[65]

In fact the action taken in Paris merely followed a significant step already taken in Lisbon. The Portuguese Government had issued on November 15, 1825, a circular announcing to foreign powers the negotiation of the Portuguese-Brazilian treaty of reconciliation. On February 20, 1826, the French chargé at Lisbon addressed to the Portuguese Government a note stating that he had brought the circular of November 15 to the attention of his Court, and that, in deference to the wishes of the Portuguese King, Charles X recognized the independence of Brazil. This note declared further that the sovereignty of that country, as well as the title of Emperor, had been transferred by the

[64] *Ibid.*

[65] Metternich to Villa-Secca, December 30, 1825 (copy), H. H. u. S., Portugal, Varia, 8.

Portuguese monarch to his son Pedro. A saving clause was also added here that by virtue of this action no prejudice should come to the powers of Europe.[66] On March 7, 1826, Baron Pedra Branca was formally presented to Charles X as chargé d'affaires of the Brazilian Empire.[67]

The Brazilians did not display much gratitude at the French decision. Emperor Pedro I asserted in an address to the General Assembly that the acknowledgment of Brazil's independence by France occurred after recognition had been successively accorded by the United States, Portugal, Austria, England, and Sweden.[68] It is noteworthy that, as in the case of the acknowledgment of Spanish-American independence, this important step was taken by France only after both the Anglo-Saxon nations had so acted. With respect to the Brazilian Empire, however, largely because that country had retained monarchical institutions, the recognition of independence by France speedily followed recognition by the United States. The fact that the new state was a monarchy—the very condition which had restrained some statesmen at Washington from promptly recognizing its independence—incited French publicists to action.

On June 7, 1826, four articles explanatory of certain provisions of the Franco-Brazilian Treaty were signed at Rio de Janeiro. When Charles X declared this treaty to be

[66] Merona to Porto-Santo, February 20, 1826 (copy), enclosure in Pflügel to Metternich, February 28, 1826, H. H. u. S., Staatskanzlei, Portugal, 10.

[67] Apponyi to Metternich, March 9, 1826 (no. 3, E), H. H. u. S., Berichte aus Frankreich, 367; Manning, *Diplomatic Correspondence of the United States concerning the Independence of the Latin-American Nations,* II, 1421.

[68] Loreto, "Reconnaissance de l'Empire du Brésil par les puissances européennes," *Rev. d'hist. dip.,* III, 521.

in force, he issued an interpretative ordinance based upon a report of his council to the effect that Brazilian ships entering French harbors were henceforth to pay only the pilot's fees and the port dues levied upon French ships. Products of the soil or industry of Brazil brought from her ports into French harbors in Brazilian ships were to pay no higher duties than those imposed upon such products when imported in French ships, always provided that they were furnished with duly certified papers. For the time being, all vessels owned by citizens of Brazil and commanded by Brazilian captains were to be considered entitled to these special privileges. Long-fibre cotton brought directly from Brazil to France on either Brazilian or French ships was henceforth to pay no higher duties than those levied on short-fibre cotton.[69]

Even before the Franco-Brazilian treaty was formally proclaimed, it had become a topic of discussion in the Parisian press. The *Journal du Commerce* expressed its disapproval of the stipulation that a party to the treaty was to expel on demand a criminal of state who was a citizen of the other contracting party. This journal also objected to a provision for the reciprocal extradition of deserters and to the article which excepted contraband of war from the general liberty of commerce recognized by other articles of the treaty. In reply the *Journal de Paris* defended the convention. It declared that the other journal had not appreciated the real aim of the treaty with Brazil, which was to promote in the two governments that feeling of "security and profound confidence without which commerce cannot flourish." [70]

[69] *Le Moniteur,* October 6, 1826.
[70] *Journal de Paris,* September 13, 1826. See further *Le Moniteur,* September 14, 1826.

Similarly an article printed in the *Journal de Paris* on November 4 lauded the recent achievements of the Ministry of Foreign Affairs. It declared that the treaty with Brazil had been cordially welcomed in both the ports and factories of France and that the appointment of French commercial agents to new states of Spanish America foreshadowed the negotiation of treaties which would be no less advantageous to national industry than the Franco-Brazilian treaty.

On October 18, 1826, the *Moniteur* made interesting observations concerning the Latin-American policy of France. This ministerial organ declared that merchants had not laid their pleas at the foot of the throne in vain: the government had recognized Brazil and the flags of Colombia and Mexico were now displayed in French ports. It explained that, because of events over which France had no control, " a barrier had been raised around America: this barrier now falls; national genius can now take a new flight." The same note was struck by Count Chabrol on November 4 in an address on the opening of the new Bourse. Chabrol congratulated the merchants of Paris upon having completed this structure at a time when " memorable acts prepared for them a future full of hope and prosperity." [71] By the end of 1826 France had stationed five consular agents in the Brazilian Empire.[72]

The acknowledgment by France of Brazilian independence constitutes in certain particulars a step distinct from her policy toward Spanish America. In the case of Brazil, France was neither hampered by any such treaty as the Bourbon Family Compact nor was she restrained by the consideration that her soldiers occupied important posts in

[71] *Journal de Paris,* November 5, 1826.

[72] *Almanach royal,* 1826, p. 148; one of these agents was located at Montevideo.

the motherland. France was undoubtedly much influenced by the fact that, unlike Spanish-American peoples, the Brazilians had retained a monarchical form of government—a conservatism which seemed to French statesmen an assurance that the spread of republican institutions in the New World would be checked. Most important of all perhaps was the fact that the separation of the imperial colony from Portugal had indisputably been accomplished and that the Portuguese King had agreed to sanction this independence. Further, a scion of the very dynasty which was governing Portugal was serving as the ruler of the emancipated colony.

During these negotiations France displayed a tendency to adhere to the principle of legitimacy. In arranging with the Brazilian Empire a treaty of navigation and commerce— the first treaty negotiated by France with a Latin-American nation—French statesmen were animated by an ardent desire to improve commercial relations with that empire. Although the political situation of Portuguese America at this time differed in some particulars from the political condition of Spanish America, the acknowledgment of the independence of Brazil by France constituted a precedent that was not without influence upon the attitude of French journalists and politicians toward the Spanish states of America. Because of the close relations existing between France and Russia, it is to be presumed that the acknowledgment of Brazilian independence by France had some effect upon the foreign policy of the Czar. In December, 1827, Count Nesselrode notified the diplomatic representatives of Russia that their government had recognized the independence of the Brazilian Empire. In an address to the legislature on May 3, 1828, Emperor Pedro I announced that the independent status of his country had been recognized by every European government except that of Spain.

CHAPTER XIII

FRENCH ACKNOWLEDGMENT OF HAITIAN INDEPENDENCE

For several years the Haitian Government exercised authority over that portion of the island of Santo Domingo which had been colonized by Spain. The attitude of France toward her insurgent colony of Saint-Domingue, which was in the western part of that island, thus occasionally involved a part of the former Spanish Empire. Further, some Frenchmen occasionally associated the attitude of their government toward Saint-Domingue with the policy which it was trying to formulate concerning the insurgent colonies of Spain on the American Continent. For these reasons the subject of French policy toward the Latin-American states must include consideration of the Negro Republic which arose upon French foundations in the West Indies.

Although the entire island of Santo Domingo originally belonged to the Spanish Empire, the annals of Haiti differ from those of the Indies. In 1697 Spain ceded the western part of Santo Domingo to France. To furnish the servile labor for their plantations those Frenchmen who became landowners in Saint-Domingue had to employ large numbers of Negroes. Slavery was thus fastened upon the colony.

During the eighteenth century many emigrants proceeded from France to Saint-Domingue. Proud of their origin, whether living on estates or in towns, its landowners formed a flourishing aristocracy. In 1789 there were in the western part of the island of Santo Domingo about 8,000 plantations, which were devoted largely to the cultivation of coffee, cotton, indigo, and sugar-cane. It has been estimated that the population of this colony was composed of some 42,000 whites, 38,000 free colored persons, and 500,000 Negro slaves.[1] The combined import and export trade in 1789 amounted to 716,715,962 livres, which constituted a large part of the foreign trade of France.[2] Saint-Domingue was appropriately designated " the Queen of the Antilles."

The French Revolution precipitated important changes in that colony. When reports of the establishment of the National Assembly reached Saint-Domingue, colonists of all ages and classes adorned themselves with the tricolored cockade. In the spring of 1790 a General Assembly of white delegates from the French portion of Santo Domingo met at St. Marc. Step by step they assumed power which infringed upon the authority of France. They declared that no act of the French legislature relating to the internal régime of the colony was to be considered a law unless approved by its freely elected representatives.[3] On October 12, 1790, the National Assembly accordingly decreed that the actions of the Assembly of St. Marc were destructive of public tranquillity, anti-constitutional, and null.[4]

During the following year menacing insurrections of Negro slaves broke out which resulted in a war to the death between the blacks and the whites. In vain did commissioners from France strive to terminate the sanguinary strug-

[1] Castonnet des Fosses, *La Révolution de Saint-Domingue*, pp. 7-8.

[2] Lacroix, *Mémoires pour servir à l'histoire de la révolution de Saint-Domingue*, II, 277.

[3] Garrett, *The French Colonial Question, 1789-1791*, pp. 60-61.

[4] Schœlcher, *Vie de Toussaint-Louverture*, p. 24.

gles of contending factions. A decree of the National Convention announcing that slaves in the French colonies were free did little more than sanction conditions which had already come to pass in Saint-Domingue.[5] White settlers were driven out and their property was seized by black men.

Led by a remarkable Negro known as Toussaint Louverture, delegates from both the Spanish and the French sections of the island framed a constitution which declared that Santo Domingo was a part of the French Empire but subject to special laws. When, however, Toussaint's agent submitted this fundamental law to Napoleon for sanction, the First Consul declared that it contained stipulations contrary to the dignity of the French people, who possessed sovereign rights over Saint-Domingue.[6] The " First of the Blacks," as Louverture was designated, consequently became involved in a fierce struggle with General Leclerc, who in 1802 was sent by Napoleon at the head of a strong expedition to conquer the refractory colonists and was directed forcibly to seize both the mulatto and the black leaders of the insurrection and to send them into exile.[7] Louverture fell into the hands of Leclerc, was transported to France, and pined his life away in a prison high up in the mountains of the Jura.

Harried by revolutionists and scourged by yellow fever, French soldiers were compelled in December, 1804, to withdraw completely from Saint-Domingue. On January 1 of that year the revolutionists framed a declaration of independence, and they designated the state which they had

[5] *Ibid.*, pp. 28-67.

[6] Janvier, *Les Constitutions d'Haïti*, pp. 7-24.

[7] Adams, " Napoléon I et Saint-Domingue," *Revue historique*, XXIV, 101-11.

founded as " Haiti." An aspiring leader named Dessalines soon assumed the title of Emperor. In May, 1805, Negro leaders framed a new constitution for the " Empire of Haiti " which declared that slavery was abolished forever.[8] The remaining whites were ruthlessly expelled or massacred and their property was confiscated by the state. By 1807 the English Government had issued Orders in Council conceding to Haiti what has been termed " limited recognition." [9]

After the assassination of Dessalines by dissatisfied compatriots, a constitution was framed for the " Republic of Haiti." [10] A black leader named Henri Christophe became president. Meanwhile Alexandre Pétion, a mulatto patriot, extended his sway over the western and southern parts of the island, where he was proclaimed president. Though the authority of Christophe was thus gradually restricted to the North, the titles of President and Generalissimo accorded to him seemed inadequate to his admiring partisans. On April 4, 1811, the Council of State presented a monarchical constitution to Christophe which styled him King of Haiti. His Black Majesty soon surrounded himself with the trappings of a royal court.[11] A revolt against French domination had meanwhile begun in the East. On July 9, 1809, by the aid of an English squadron, revolutionists captured the city of Santo Domingo. French soldiers then evacuated the former Spanish colony. As the title of Spain to the eastern part of the island was reëstablished by the Treaty of Paris, from 1814 to 1821 that section of Santo Domingo again belonged to the Spanish Empire.

[8] Janvier, *op. cit.,* pp. 30-41.
[9] Gibbs, *Recognition,* pp. 42-43. [10] Janvier, *op. cit.,* pp. 49-73.
[11] Leconte, *Henri Christophe dans l'histoire d'Haïti,* pp. 247-87.

The claims of French citizens who had been injured in person and estate by the Haitian revolution early confronted statesmen of the restoration. Frenchmen who held titles to plantations in Saint-Domingue soon solicited the government to restore the sovereignty of France over it. A petition describing the distress of the former colonists was referred to a committee of the Chamber of Deputies headed by General Desfourneaux. This committee naturally took the view of the dispossessed landowners and reported that the revolutionists should acknowledge the French King as their sovereign. Further, it urged the government to support the claims of Frenchmen against the Haitians by a combined land and naval force.[12]

Nevertheless, Baron Malouet, Minister of Marine in the cabinet organized by Louis XVIII, did not think the time opportune for an invasion of Haiti. Instead he decided to appoint agents to negotiate with her rulers. Influence or unhappy chance induced Malouet to select as his commissioners Colonel Dauxion-Lavaysse, a Frenchman who had been driven from Saint-Domingue by the black revolution, an obscure person named Dravermann, and an individual of Spanish descent, Medina.[13] Dauxion-Lavaysse and Dravermann proceeded to Jamaica on an English vessel, while Medina quietly disembarked in the Spanish part of the island.

As King Henry soon became aware of the arrival of Medina, he had the hapless emissary seized at the frontier. The Haitians found upon him the instructions of Malouet;

[12] *Le Moniteur,* September 17, 1814.
[13] Wallez, *Précis historique des négociations entre la France et Saint-Domingue,* pp. 12-13; "Note sur St. Domingue," A. A. E., Haïti, 2.

these were of such a nature that the mission was now doomed to failure. In the words of an unsigned memorandum in the archives of the French Government: " Among other provisions they directed him to attempt by negotiations to win over the leaders, who were mulattoes, and, in fine, by means of them to reëstablish slavery." [14]

Meanwhile Dauxion-Lavaysse had proceeded from Kingston to Port-au-Prince, where he seems to have been favorably received. He soon denounced Napoleon to President Pétion as a despot and praised Louis XVIII as a philosophical king. In a note dated November 9, 1814, Dauxion-Lavaysse described himself as the principal agent of the Minister of Marine and the Colonies for the restoration of the French colony in the island of Haiti. This agent proposed to the President that he recognize the sovereignty of Louis XVIII, as soon as he should judge that the Haitians were suitably prepared for that important event. Dauxion-Lavaysse further suggested that Pétion and his chief advisers form a provisional government in the name of the King of France.[15]

On November 10, 1814, Pétion issued a proclamation in which he announced the arrival of a French commissioner. He declared that he was aware of all the obligations imposed upon himself.[16] Meanwhile papers taken from Medina passed into the hands of Pétion, who could scarcely believe that the alleged instructions were au-

[14] " Note sur St. Domingue," A. A. E., Haïti, 2; for Malouet's instructions, see Wallez, *op. cit.*, pp. 174-89. An account of Medina's examination is found in *ibid.*, pp. 190-204.

[15] *Pièces relatives aux communications faites au nom du gouvernement français au président d'Haytï par M. le Général Dauxion-Lavaysse,* pp. 11-13.

[16] *Le Télégraphe,* November 20, 1814.

thentic.[17] In his response to the commissioner on November 27, 1814, the President expressed the view that the French proposals were prompted less by the King's personal convictions than by the clamors of a group of Frenchmen who wished the old régime restored in Haiti. He declared that it would be an everlasting glory for Louis XVIII to acknowledge the independence of Haiti and to secure for France such a participation in her commerce as would be mutually advantageous. " I propose to Your Excellency," added Pétion, " to establish the bases of a stipulated indemnity which we shall solemnly engage to pay, accompanied by any just guarantee that may be required of us." [18]

On December 3, 1814, the Haitian President published an address to the people and the army. He declared that France's proposal to use conciliatory measures was designed to regain control of Haiti. Explaining that, as the French propositions were incompatible with Haitian principles and institutions, they had been unanimously rejected, Pétion declared that although his people did not fear war they desired peace. They had offered to make pecuniary sacrifices in order to impose silence upon their persecutors, whose importunate pleas for the restoration of their property had reached the French throne.[19]

Pétion allowed Dauxion-Lavaysse to sail for Jamaica, but Medina perished miserably in a Haitian dungeon. When the French Minister of Marine became aware of the nature of Dauxion-Lavaysse's correspondence with the Haitian President, he published a justificatory statement to the effect

[17] " Note sur St. Domingue," A. A. E., Haïti, 2.

[18] *Pièces relatives au communications faites au nom du gouvernement français au président d'Haïti*, p. 27.

[19] *Ibid.*, pp. 4-5.

that that commissioner had not been authorized to make communications so contrary to the object of the mission, which was designed to gather data concerning the actual condition of Haiti.[20]

The first cabinet of Richelieu made an attempt in 1816 to reconcile France and her insurgent colony. Minister of Marine Dubouchage sent six commissioners to Haiti. Although the titular head of this commission was Viscount Fontanges, who had served in Saint-Domingue, its leading spirit was Charles Esmangart, a Councillor of State who had been a landowner in that colony. In the ordinance appointing the Haitian commission, the King declared that its purpose was " to calm the anxiety which the inhabitants of that island might have concerning their situation, to put an end to their uncertainty, to determine their future, and to legitimize the changes which events may have rendered necessary, especially those changes which tend to improve the lot of our subjects." [21]

Upon their arrival at Port-au-Prince in October, 1816, Esmangart and Fontanges sent a letter regarding their mission to King Henry. They also had an interview with President Pétion. Because of Pétion's complaints, they disavowed on behalf of their government the acts of Dauxion-Lavaysse. A memorandum in the French archives indicates the problems which confronted the commissioners of France:

From the first moment Pétion made it clear that he would reject any proposition which would not result in the recognition of Haitian independence. In none of his letters did he indicate the compensation which would be given to

[20] *Le Moniteur,* January 19, 1815.
[21] Wallez, *Précis historique,* pp. 220-21.

France, but in his conversations, and particularly in the conversation of General Boyer, who commanded the army, the conditions were left to the commissioners. Pétion often repeated to Esmangart: " Concede independence; stipulate in this concession the conditions, and I shall sign." [22]

Liberal Frenchmen soon began to consider seriously the acknowledgment of Haiti's independence. Early in 1821 Councillor Esmangart presented to the Ministry of Foreign Affairs an interesting exposé of his views. He expressed the opinion that the Haitian problem had often been viewed from a provincial standpoint. Further, he declared that certain persons considered only Saint-Domingue, whereas the question of this country was related to the policy to be adopted toward the insurgent communities of South America.[23] Esmangart enclosed the draft of a letter which he thought should be sent to General Boyer, a capable mulatto with both civil and military experience who had become president of both Northern and Southern Haiti. In this letter the writer declared that he was awaiting a suitable opportunity to propose to his government that Haiti's independence be acknowledged on conditions which would ensure harmony between that country and France.[24] On

---

[22] " Note sur St. Domingue," A. A. E., Haïti, 2. Pétion promptly printed the correspondence between himself and the second French mission in *Pièces relatives à la correspondance de M. M. les commissaires de S. M. Très-Chrétienne et du président d'Haïti.* An unsigned and undated " Rapport " by a member of this mission stated that their correspondance had been " assez fidèlement imprimée " in Haiti (A. A. E., Mémoires et Documents, Amérique, 15). Wallez (*op. cit.,* pp. 172-89), reprinted this correspondence in France. The views of Pétion in regard to the independence of Haiti are found in *ibid.,* p. 237.

[23] Addressed to " Monseigneur," January 2, 1821, A. A. E., Haïti, 2.

[24] " Projet de Lettre au Général Boyer," *ibid.*

January 6, 1821, Esmangart made a careful analysis of the Haitian problem in a letter addressed to Minister Pasquier. He declared that people everywhere expected to see the government reach a decision which would revive commerce and prepare the way for negotiations with the Spanish-American states:

The word independence seems, in general, to have frightened the Council of State more than independence itself; for those persons who show the greatest reluctance to pronounce that word favor concessions which would at least have the same result. . . .

We can negotiate a treaty with Haiti which will be more or less advantageous to France according to the skill of the negotiator. But the essential thing would be to give up this false position in which we find ourselves as a nation. . . . Upon being restored to his throne the King did not claim that he was obligated to repossess himself of all the dominions which previously belonged to him. The treaty of commerce which we could negotiate would leave matters in the condition in which they were placed by the revolution and would enable us to carry on openly what we now do clandestinely and, I would say almost with shame, under foreign flags.[25]

President Boyer soon ordered his soldiers into the eastern part of the island of Santo Domingo, which in 1821 had declared its independence of Spain. In 1822 Haitian soldiers captured Santo Domingo City. For more than twenty years the Haitians tried to weld the French and the Spanish sections of the island into a unified state. Consequently the fortunes of the former Spanish colony became involved in the negotiations between Haiti and France.

Meanwhile, having failed to reach a satisfactory adjustment in direct negotiations with agents of France, the

[25] *Ibid.*

Haitians resolved to appeal to Czar Alexander I. On August 4, 1820, President Boyer accredited General Boyé as the agent of Haiti to Russia. This general was authorized to promote such commercial relations between the two countries as would be reciprocally advantageous.[26] Early in the following year Boyé reached St. Petersburg and presented his credentials to the Imperial Government. As Czar Alexander I and his Foreign Minister, Count Capodistrias, were attending the Congress of Laibach, Boyé presented his plea for the development of commercial intercourse between Haiti and Russia to Divoff, who was acting as Minister of Foreign Affairs ad interim. In his interview with this minister, Boyé maintained that it would be impossible for France ever to reëstablish her domination over Haiti.[27]

Divoff reported this interview to Capodistrias, who soon informed him of the Czar's views. Alexander I declared that Russia could neither enter into negotiations with the Black Republic nor treat with the agent of a government which was not recognized by the sovereign upon whom Haiti should necessarily depend.[28] Still, in a conversation which Count la Ferronnays had with the Czar, the latter expressed the opinion that the only decision which the French Cabinet could take was "that of acknowledging the complete independence of the Republic of Haiti"; but the Czar held that France should avail herself of this negotiation, upon which depended the acknowledgment of Haiti's independence by other powers, to obtain commercial advantages.[29]

[26] A copy of Boyé's credentials is found in A. A. E., Mémoires et Documents, Amérique, 15.

[27] La Ferronnays to Rayneval, March 1, 1821, *ibid.*

[28] Capodistrias to Divoff, $\frac{15}{27}$ February, 1821 (copy), *ibid.*

[29] La Ferronnays to Rayneval, March 1, 1821, *ibid.*

Shortly after Boyé's mission had been frustrated the French Government sent to Haiti an aspiring naval lieutenant named Dupetit-Thouars, who had been a member of the Franco-Haitian commission of 1816. On May 8 he addressed a note to President Boyer stating that Louis XVIII had " decided to consecrate the independence of the Republic of Haiti " but that the King expected the Haitians to acknowledge his suzerainty, that is, a right of protection similar to that which England was exercising over the Ionian Isles. Commercial relations between Haiti and France, he declared, should be placed reciprocally upon a most-favored-nation basis. The insular republic should indemnify French proprietors for losses caused by the revolution.[30]

On May 10 Boyer replied by reminding Dupetit-Thouars of the negotiations of 1816, during which he had made known the wishes of his compatriots for the acknowledgment by France of Haiti's independence. National honor, added the President, would not permit the slightest restriction upon that independence, either the concession of direct or indirect suzerainty or the placing of the country under the protection of any power whatsoever.[31] Such an emphatic dissent from the French proposals put an end to the negotiations.

Two years later President Boyer again took the initiative by instructing General Boyé to proceed to France and to engage in negotiations for " the solemn recognition of the national independence of the Haitian people." The President continued:

[30] *Pièces officielles relatives aux négociations du gouvernement français avec le gouvernement haïtien pour traiter de la formalité de la reconaissance de l'indépendance d'Haïti*, p. 16.

[31] *Ibid.*, pp. 17-18.

You are too well acquainted with the situation in which the republic finds herself to need details concerning the rights which the Haitians should enjoy in order to obtain the formality of that recognition, because they have been in absolute possession of their independence for twenty years. You should be animated by the idea that it is altogether impossible to take a single backward step from the position in which the favor of the Almighty has placed this island. You should also bear in mind that it will not be possible to have any other kind of relations with France than those of a commercial nature, which will procure the utmost advantages for that kingdom.

Boyer accordingly directed Boyé to propose the negotiation of a commercial treaty with France which would have as a basis the acknowledgment of Haiti's independence.[32]

General Boyé soon proceeded to Holland. On July 4 he wrote to Clermont-Tonnerre and proposed treating with France at a convenient place. The Minister of Marine responded by selecting Brussels as the site of the negotiations. Early in the following month Esmangart was sent to that city to serve as the French agent. His instructions were to the effect that France was disposed to recognize the Haitian nation as free and independent in consideration of the payment of a reasonable indemnity, as Boyer had proposed in 1821. However, the Haitian commissioner made it known that he was authorized to treat only on commercial matters and that he had been expressly prohibited from discussing an indemnity. As a result the conferences quickly terminated; the French commissioner did not reveal in detail the proposals of his government.[33]

[32] *Ibid.*, p. 22.
[33] *Ibid.*, pp. 23-27; Villèle, *Mémoires et correspondance,* **IV,** 326-27.

Shortly afterward Boyé proceeded to Paris. In December, 1823, upon informing the French Ministry of Foreign Affairs that he was ready to renew the negotiations which had been broken off at Brussels, the agent made a series of observations that suggested the Haitian standpoint. Not without justification, he maintained that the acknowledgment of his country's independence was implied in the negotiations which had been initiated:

In demanding anew the recognition of the Republic of Haiti, we are demanding something which we can consider as having been implicitly conceded from the moment when the French Government recognized my powers and appointed an agent to negotiate with me. By that act alone France admitted the principle.[34]

An obstacle to the success of the negotiations, however, was the demand of France that Haiti pay to her millions of francs to indemnify the former landowners of Saint-Domingue. Boyé stated to the French Ministry of Foreign Affairs that conditions in the island of Santo Domingo had changed since the President expressed his willingness to pay an indemnity. That magistrate was no longer struggling with a rival potentate for supremacy. Explaining that Boyer now proposed only the concession of reducing the duties payable on French goods imported into Haiti from twelve per cent to six per cent, the agent admitted that Haiti offered less to France than upon an earlier occasion but reasoned that, as the existence of the insular republic was now better established, France in turn had less to offer Haiti. Boyé predicted that by aid of the proposed tariff

[34] " Pièce annexée au mémoire remis au departement des affaires étrangères le 28 Xbre 1823," A. A. E., Mémoires et Documents, Amérique, 15.

concession, and by virtue of such existing advantages as a common language, France in three years could gain control of Haiti's commerce.[35]

Early in 1824, the Secretary General of the Haitian Government wrote a letter to a correspondent in London asserting that his countrymen had now " nothing to fear from the injustice of those who hitherto have not acknowledged us as a free and independent nation." [36] Yielding to suggestions made by France, President Boyer again decided to dispatch a mission to Paris to treat concerning the status of his country. As agents he now selected Senator Larose and an attorney named Rouanez. He furnished them with secret instructions to negotiate for an ordinance by which the French King would recognize that the Haitian people were free and independent. Should this ordinance be granted, they were authorized to agree that Haiti would pay France an indemnity; they were also to negotiate a commercial treaty which would give to French merchandise entering Haitian ports most-favored-nation privileges.[37] Clermont-Tonnerre again asked Councillor Esmangart to treat for France. In the ensuing conferences the Haitian commissioners at once invited Esmangart to propose to his government the recognition of Haiti by a royal ordinance, " as the only method which could fully inspire the Haitian people with entire confidence in the future." [38]

[35] *Ibid.*

[36] January 3, 1824, in the *Morning Chronicle,* May 14, 1824.

[37] *Pièces officielles relatives aux négociations du gouvernement français avec le gouvernement haïtien,* pp. 51-54.

[38] Wallez, *Précis historique,* p. 393. Correspondence between Haitian commissioners and agents of France from 1821 to 1824 is found in translation in *British and Foreign State Papers,* XII, 688-742.

Larose and Rouanez proposed also to negotiate a treaty with France on three bases: the irrevocable acknowledgment of Haitian independence; the concession of commercial advantages by each party; and the payment of a pecuniary indemnity to France by Haiti.[39] At the end of June the English ambassador at Paris informed his government that the Haitian commissioners had indicated their willingness to concede, in return for recognition, greater commercial advantages to French subjects than to those of any other nation, in addition to a " pecuniary compensation to the amount of One Hundred and Fifty Millions of francs." [40]

The report made to their government by Larose and Rouanez stated that the most difficult matter to adjust was the amount of the indemnity. They further declared that, when an agreement had almost been reached, Esmangart raised a serious question by maintaining that the treaty should be concerned only with that part of the island which had formerly belonged to France. On the other hand, the Haitians declared that they were not free to exclude Spanish Santo Domingo from their negotiations because such a distinction had not been suggested in the overtures made to their government. Furthermore, according to a dispatch of Stuart to Canning, the former proprietors of Saint-Domingue made every effort to prevent the acceptance by the French ministers of the conditions proposed by Boyer's agents.[41]

[39] Wallez, *op. cit.*, pp. 394-95.

[40] Stuart to Canning, June 28, 1824 (no. 322), F. O., 27/310.

[41] Stuart to Canning, July 15, 1824, F. O., 27/312. On March 22, 1824, Stuart had informed Canning that " several meetings of the ancient proprietors in St. Domingo have been lately held at

Influenced presumably by representations of dispossessed Frenchmen, the Minister of Marine told Larose and Rouanez that he wished to inform them of the plan of a royal ordinance which would consecrate the independence of Haiti and which would reserve to His Majesty only external sovereignty. Astounded at the proposal that they thus acknowledge French suzerainty, the commissioners declared that this idea had already been rejected by their government. The result was that, on August 3, 1824, Esmangart notified them that negotiations were broken off because they had insufficient powers to accept the conditions formulated in the proposed ordinance. Count Villèle made a similar explanation of the failure of the mission: he declared it unfortunate that the Haitian commissioners should have come to Paris without power to make the concessions that France was entitled to demand. He felt that their journey only furnished a fresh proof of the difficulty of reaching an understanding with the authorities of Haiti.[42]

A week later, Stuart informed Canning that the Haitian commissioners had expressed to Esmangart their willingness to insert an article in a treaty of recognition acknowledging the suzerainty of the King of France, " provided that no right be founded upon this concession, which shall justify the interference of the French Government in the internal administration of the Island." [43] Yet Villèle soon viewed

Paris, for the purpose of concerting the means of inducing the great capitalists to contract for a loan to be employed in the recovery of their possessions in that Colony." F. O., 27/307.

[42] Wallez, *op. cit.*, pp. 396-98; Stuart to Canning, July 15, 1824, F. O., 27/312. See further Manning, *Diplomatic Correspondence of the United States concerning the Independence of the Latin-American Nations,* II, 1407.

[43] Stuart to Canning, July 26, 1824 (no. 379), F. O., 27/312.

the problem from another standpoint, for early in the next year he declared to the English ambassador at Paris that the " recognition of a Black Empire founded upon Insurrection, and upon the Massacre of the White Population would have a most pernicious moral Effect, and the French Government had been content to sacrifice its own partial Interests rather than lend itself to the establishment of such a dangerous Example." [44]

When he was informed that the negotiations with France had again failed, President Boyer addressed a circular to the commanders of the insular arrondissements. Boyer stated that the French Government still claimed sovereignty over the former colony, a pretension which would never be admissible. He presented this claim as a fresh proof that Haitian distrust of the French propositions concerning recognition was justified.[45]

Boyer accordingly urged his compatriots to neglect no measure which would put them in a good condition of military preparation. A documentary collection concerning the mission of 1824 which he soon published in Haiti contained the following résumé of Franco-Haitian negotiations: " In 1814 the French wished to impose upon us the absolute sovereignty of France; in 1816 they were satisfied with a constitutional sovereignty; in 1821 they demanded only a simple suzerainty; in 1823, at the time of the negotiation of General Boyé, they were satisfied to claim as a *sine qua non* the indemnity which we had previously offered. By what return to a spirit of domination did they in 1824 wish to subject us to an external sovereignty? " [46]   The view

[44] Granville to Canning, January 13, 1825, F. O., 27/329.
[45] *Le Télégraphe,* October 9, 1824.
[46] *Pièces officielles relatives aux négociations du gouvernement français avec le gouvernement haïtien,* pp. 83-84.

rightly suggested in this summary was that the species of sovereignty over Haiti which French publicists proposed to retain in 1824 implied the establishment of a protectorate.

At a meeting of diplomats in Paris, Damas explained to Lord Granville that France had declined advantageous overtures made by Haiti and had insisted upon her right of sovereignty in order not to weaken the principles which she had to observe with respect to Spain.[47] When the negotiations of 1824 became known in Paris, they provoked diverse comments. On January 18, 1825, the *Constitutionnel* published an article which took the view that France was to blame for the failure of the Haitian mission. This journal maintained that Saint-Domingue was more independent in 1825 than the United States had been in 1783 and urged that France not only treat with Saint-Domingue but also recognize the independence of Spanish America. On the following day the *Gazette de France* presented the Ministry's side of the case: " That recognition of suzerainty which has been so much discussed was not intruded into the negotiations as a new right or as a sudden exigency. The offer to recognize the suzerainty of France was indeed made several years ago by the government of Saint-Domingue." However, as that proposal was not in harmony with the revolutionary doctrine of the sovereignty of the people, the Haitians had undertaken to modify their views. The *Gazette de France* further maintained that the allegations of French writers to the effect that there was no danger of an armed attack by France on the insular republic were partly responsible for the changed attitude of the Haitians.

[47] Vincent to Metternich, January 10, 1825, H. H. u. S., Berichte aus Frankreich, 362.

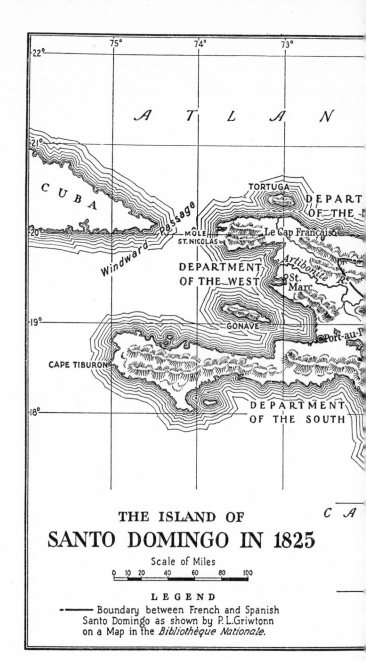

THE ISLAND OF
SANTO DOMINGO IN 1825

Scale of Miles

0   10 20   40   60   80   100

LEGEND

‑‑‑‑‑‑ Boundary between French and Spanish
Santo Domingo as shown by P. L. Griwtonn
on a Map in the *Bibliothèque Nationale*.

The accession of Charles X to the throne afforded the Ministry of Foreign Affairs a convenient opportunity to reconsider the Haitian case. In a discussion between Granville and Villèle in April, 1825, the latter, after alluding to the precarious relations between Spain and Spanish America, declared that in dealing with her own rebellious colony France would never submit to "such degradation as Spain had experienced." With regard to French negotiations with Haiti Villèle said that, because of the color of the inhabitants as well as the massacre of the white population, Charles X could not sign a treaty with the Black Republic. Yet the inclination of the French Government to cut the knot was indicated by Villèle in the following statement of its position:

That His Most Christian Majesty was, however, willing to grant by edict an entire exterior Independence;—that every regulation of internal Government, every thing which related to Customs and Foreign Trade should be uncontrolled by France, that the Haitian Government might make their own commercial arrangements with Foreign Powers, reserving only to France a certain percentage in their Custom Duties more favorable to French commerce than to that of any other Power, but that the King of France would not abandon his Right to the exterior Sovereignty of the Island; —in the first place because His subjects in Martinique and Guadeloupe felt strongly upon this point,—and, secondly, because the reserve of the exterior Sovereignty gave to the Court of France the right to oppose the views of any other State to appropriate to itself that important possession.[48]

After a careful consideration both of the ability of the island to pay an indemnity to the dispossessed colonists and of the inclination of its government to accede to certain conditions, the Council of State recommended to Charles X

[48] Granville to Canning, April 11, 1825 (no. 88), F. O., 27/330.

that he prepare an ordinance acknowledging the independence of Saint-Domingue. In the official journal Minister of Marine Chabrol explained to the public that the King wished to open an advantageous market to French commerce, to assure an indemnity to the former planters of Saint-Domingue, and to terminate the precarious condition in which the inhabitants of Haiti found themselves.[49]

Chabrol was requested to bring this ordinance to the attention of the Haitian Government as the final condition upon which France was willing to renounce her right of sovereignty and to recognize the complete independence of the colony. In accordance with the orders of the King, after the ministers had formulated the terms of the offer Baron Mackau, who was a member of the Council of State, was appointed as commissioner to lay the royal ordinance before the Haitian authorities. In his official report Mackau stated that he received his final instructions on April 20 and that two days earlier the King had summoned him to an audience and explained how he wished his orders carried out.[50]

The royal ordinance dated April 17, 1825, and countersigned by Chabrol and Villèle, was entrusted to Mackau. Citing two articles of the Charter, Charles X declared that he had formulated the terms of recognition. Harbors in the French section of Santo Domingo were henceforth to be open to ships of all nations; import and export taxes, as well as port dues, were to be equal and uniform for all

[49] Granville to Canning, July 18, 1825, F. O., 27/331; *Le Moniteur*, September 2, 1825.

[50] " Rapport à S. E. le Ministre de la Marine et des Colonies de la mission à St. Domingue de M. le Bon. de Mackau " (copy), A. A. E., Haïti, 2. Cf. the explanation attributed to Villèle by the Haitian agent Arduin, quoted in Chancy, *L'indépendance nationale d'Haïti*, pp. 89-90.

vessels except those of France, which were to pay only one-half of the regular charges. Beginning December 31, 1825, the inhabitants of the former colony of Saint-Domingue were to pay France one hundred and fifty million francs in five equal annual payments to remunerate the ejected proprietors who claimed indemnities. "On these conditions"—so ran the edict—"we concede by this ordinance to the present inhabitants of the French portion of Santo Domingo the full and complete independence of their government." [51]

When he heard of this ordinance, Prince Esterhazy, who was on a visit to Paris, made the following observations in a letter to Metternich: "To me the question of the Spanish colonies seems prejudged; for how can France ever lend her assistance to Spain to enable her to establish her rights by force? Is it not more likely that France will follow her own example?" [52] Baron Vincent, the Austrian minister at Paris, asserted that the decision of France to recognize Haiti had been due in large part to the influence exerted by England and to the fact that The Netherlands had recently appointed consuls to that country. He warned Metternich that the Liberal party in France would cause "this act to be considered as the acknowledgment pure and simple of the independence of the nation established in Santo Domingo; the Spanish colonies will see in this recognition the legitimization of the principle of their insurrection; finally, all the partisans of new ideas will find in it a triumph for the cause of independence." [53] Upon receipt of the news that France was acknowledging the independent status of

[51] *Le Moniteur*, August 12, 1825.
[52] June 22, 1825, H. H. u. S., Berichte aus Frankreich, 363.
[53] Vincent to Metternich, June 22, 1825, *ibid.*

Haiti, Metternich confessed that, if the French Government had asked his advice before taking this irrevocable step, he would have remonstrated against its execution at a very inopportune time.[54]

Villèle expressed to the English ambassador at Paris a sanguine hope that the Haitian Government would accept the conditions laid down by Charles X. Although these conditions had not been expressly proposed by Boyer, the French minister was convinced that, if his government had not been earlier influenced by considerations which were no longer applicable, " such as that of France not choosing to take the lead in the recognition of new States on the other side of the Atlantic," an arrangement might have been concluded then on the terms proposed now. Villèle explained, however, that if Haiti should reject the King's terms a blockade of her ports would be declared and enforced immediately. At the same time he remarked that the adoption of hostile measures would not prevent his government from considering a modification of the proposed terms. Granville added the following observations concerning the reception of the royal ordinance:

M. de Villèle is prepared to encounter clamour and personal attack for having advised this measure.

The Ultras will exclaim at the encouragement given to the Principle of Revolt, and the Colonists will be dissatisfied at the Resources of France not being squandered to reinstate them in possession of their Estates.

Austria and Prussia have intimated regret, and the Emperor of Russia has echoed the observations of His Ambassador at Paris, on the abandonment of principle, and the probable failure of the negotiation.

[54] Metternich to Vincent, June 26, 1825, H. H. u. S., Weisungen nach Frankreich, 365.

In Spain, where it might naturally be supposed that such a measure would have provoked complaint and remonstrance, scarcely any sensation seems to have been excited.[55]

Baron Mackau, who was placed in charge of the negotiations with Haiti, was directed to sail to Martinique, where he was to concert the proper measures for the execution of the King's wishes with Governor Donzelot and Admiral Jurien. At the same time Jurien was directed to assemble all the ships of his station at Fort Royal. Grivel, who had meanwhile become a rear admiral, was to proceed from the Brazilian station to the Antilles. By June 20 more than a dozen armed vessels were thus placed at Jurien's disposal; this squadron was not to leave Fort Royal, however, until after Mackau sailed from France for Haiti. He left Rochefort on the frigate *Circe* on May 3 and reached Martinique a month later. At midday of July 3 that frigate, accompanied by two brigs, quietly cast anchor in the harbor of Port-au-Prince.[56]

The Haitians were much surprised at this sudden appearance. However, as a sign of truce their flag was hoisted at the mizzen mast of the *Circe*. Mackau at once sent a naval officer to Boyer with a letter containing this message:

I have arrived from France bearing orders which direct me to enter into relations with Your Excellency; and I believe that I have the right to announce to you now that the communications which I have to make are of such a nature as to be very agreeable, for they can definitely and irrevocably establish the happiness of the country that Your Excellency administers.[57]

[55] Granville to Canning, July 25, 1825 (no. 153), F. O., 27/ 331.

[56] Wallez, *Précis historique,* pp. 447-48.

[57] " Rapport à S. E. le Ministre de la Marine et des Colonies de

President Boyer sent a prompt reply to the effect that the French agent could safely step ashore to execute his mission. Upon landing at Port-au-Prince on the morning of July 4, Mackau beheld Haitians whose faces expressed curiosity mingled with fear. He was escorted to the house of Secretary General Inginac, a venerable colored gentleman who was attired like an English admiral. When Mackau intimated to Inginac that the conditions on which Charles X would grant the complete independence of Haiti were certain commercial concessions to France and the payment of an indemnity of one hundred and fifty million francs, he was surprised to find that, although the indemnity seemed heavy to the Secretary General, the latter felt that the conditions would be acceptable to his government.[58]

On the evening of July 4, Baron Mackau held a conference with Secretary Inginac, Colonel Fremont, and Senator Rouanez, who composed a commission selected by President Boyer. Employing phrases used in the ordinance, the Baron had prepared a written statement of the conditions formulated by Charles X as a basis for the acknowledgment of Haiti's independence. Mackau explained to the commissioners that he was not a negotiator, but that he had been ordered " to explain the only conditions to which His Majesty would deign to agree in conceding independence." He showed them a statement of those conditions, which made a very unfavorable impression. In his report to the Minister of Marine the agent of France declared:

The figures grieved them, and, after an interval of

---

la mission à St. Domingue de M. le Bon. de Mackau " (copy), A. A. E., Haïti, 2.

[58] *Ibid.*

silence, the commissioners repeated all the objections which had been made in the course of the preceding negotiations and others in addition:

An indemnity of 150,000,000 was in excess of all their calculations up to that date; this first condition was inadmissible.

The provision which would open the ports of St. Domingue to all flags was an infringement upon their rights as a free and independent nation.

Finally, they asked why the eastern part of the island, the former colony of Spain, was excluded from the recognition which His Very Christian Majesty was pleased to concede.[59]

At a conference on July 5, when the commissioners would discuss only their duty to Haiti, the French agent explained his mission fully and showed them documents relating to it. Baron Mackau described the result as follows:

They were astonished and touched at this frankness. I expressed myself with warmth, I believe, and, after they had gone over all the official papers which constituted my orders, I showed them the royal ordinance and said that either under its aegis a new life of repose and happiness would begin for them, or the large squadron which their lookouts would soon warn them about would commence its military operations, which could no longer be checked. I owe them in justice to say this—that the fear of war affected them less than the proof of confidence which I had just given them. Indeed this is so true that I am certain that I would have succeeded better if I had refrained from talking to them about the squadron; but the ships were approaching, and it was of the highest importance that I prove myself loyal on every point.[60]

Shortly afterward, the Baron was admitted to interviews with the President, who brought up objections to the procedure of the French Government. He asked why the agent

[59] *Ibid.*   [60] *Ibid.*

had mentioned a warlike squadron. He maintained that the phraseology of Article I of the ordinance wounded the honor of Haiti, which, as an independent nation had the right to grant or to deny commercial favors. In particular, he protested that the amount of indemnity prescribed was enormous, as it exceeded the Haitian estimates by a considerable sum. Hence Boyer proposed to send an extraordinary mission to Charles X in order to suggest certain modifications of the ordinance.

In reply Mackau declared that he had been directed what to do in the case of the rejection as well as in the case of the acceptance of his proposals. On the forenoon of July 7 the President conferred with leading governmental officials. In the evening of that day Mackau read to Boyer an interpretative note in which he maintained that, although Article I of the ordinance was an act of sovereignty by Charles X, that monarch did not expect to retain the right to intervene in Haitian affairs. The agent explained that this article was intended to show that France had remained faithful to the agreements which she had entered into at the Congress of Verona concerning measures of reconciliation between a motherland and an insurgent colony. He justified the ordinance to Boyer in these words:

" France furnishes the first example of a reconciliation, which, upon being imitated by her ancient ally, will concede to all the Americas the tranquillity and the liberty which they have so long desired. It is during the months just after the accession to the throne of the Very Christian King that His Majesty has wished to perform this great act. In proclaiming the independence of Haiti, France wishes to keep her promises made at the Congress of Verona. Her object in the first article of the ordinance, which has awakened so much suspicion, is above all to prove that she has not secured special advantages for any of her Allies. . . ."

" By proclaiming the independence of Haiti, the King has renounced all participation in the exercise of sovereignty over the new state. . . . The King of France has never dreamed of using means of interference in Haitian affairs. His Majesty deigned to state this to me positively; and his thoughts are so well known to me that I do not fear to give an assurance that, if it were demanded, a formal declaration of his Cabinet could be obtained on this point. . . ."

I noticed that emotion was displayed by the President at various statements; after I had concluded, he rose and extended his hand [He then said]: " All is settled between us; Baron, I am convinced. No, France does not wish to deceive us, and, if she had indulged in that thought, she would not have selected you as her agent! In my name, and in the name of the Haitian people, I accept the ordinance of His Very Christian Majesty."

Boyer explained that at a meeting of the chief functionaries of the state he had been fully authorized to make a decision. Then, leading Mackau into an adjacent room, where his guards and certain officers were assembled, the President announced that the King of France had deigned to recognize the independence of Haiti. Boyer asked the assembled personages to acclaim with him: " Long live France! Long live Haiti! " In response many voices repeated exultantly: " Long live His Majesty Charles X! Long live the Dauphin of France! Long live Boyer! " [61]

On July 11, in accordance with the constitution, the Senate of Haiti was convoked at Port-au-Prince to consider the royal ordinance. It was promptly ratified by that body in the presence of Baron Mackau and Admirals Jurien and Grivel. Haitian senators then acclaimed Charles X. At the national palace Boyer made a speech in praise of France

[61] " Rapport à S. E. le Ministre de la Marine et des Colonies de la mission à St. Domingue de M. le Bon. de Mackau " (copy), A. A. E., Haïti, 2.

but stated that for twenty-two years the Haitians had each year renewed their vows to remain independent or to perish. Mackau responded by declaring that Haiti had taken her place among independent nations. The French squadron which was now anchored in the harbor fired a salute to the Haitian colors; the forts of Port-au-Prince then saluted the white flag. In the evening a banquet was held where toasts were offered to the dignitaries of both contracting nations. The President addressed a proclamation to his compatriots announcing the acknowledgment of their independence by France: " By investing the political existence which you have already acquired with the formality of law, this authentic act will legalize in the eyes of the world the rank in which you have been placed and to which Providence calls you." [62]

On July 16, 1825—in the twenty-second year of the independence of Haiti, as her citizens styled it—Boyer addressed a letter to the King of France. The President declared that Mackau's explanations had satisfied his countrymen that it was wrong to interpret Article I of the royal ordinance so as to give umbrage to the republic. Full of confidence in the magnanimity of Charles X, Boyer stated that he was sending a mission composed of Senators Daumec and Rouanez and Colonel Frémont, his aide-de-camp, to Paris to negotiate a treaty of commerce based upon reciprocal advantages: " Sire, I hope that Your Majesty will receive with good will the representations which those envoys are also charged to make concerning the indemnity required by Article II of the ordinance, the heavy burden of which exceeds a just amount." [63] Notice should here be taken,

[62] *Le Télégraphe,* July 17, 1825.

[63] A. A. E., Haïti, 2. The credentials of the agents were signed by Boyer on July 10, 1825. *Ibid.,* 1.

however, of the fact that in an official French report the conclusion had been reached that, on the basis of conditions existing in 1789, an indemnity of one hundred and fifty million francs would assure to the former proprietors of Saint-Domingue little more than the equivalent of one year's income on their properties, or ten per cent of their capital.[64]

The commissioners were instructed to negotiate a commercial treaty with France, to contract a loan on behalf of Haiti, and to secure concessions with regard to the execution of the ordinance. However, Damas declared that the interests of the subjects for whom the indemnity was intended made it impossible to reduce the amount; but he explained that the negotiation of a treaty with Haiti had given the King an opportunity to display his good will.[65] This treaty provided that the ordinance was not to be interpreted as affecting the right of Haiti to treat concerning foreign vessels in her character as an independent state. Products of French soil or industry imported into Haiti were to be admitted upon the payment of one-half of the duties collected upon imports from most-favored-nations. With the exception of sugar, Haitian products imported into France in French vessels were to pay only one-half of the differential duties imposed upon such products imported from other countries.[66] Though this treaty was not ratified, it is worthy of notice as embodying the terms upon which the parties seemed willing to adjust their relations in 1825.[67]

[64] " État général et Récapitulatif des Pertes éprouvées par les anciens Colons, Proprietaires de Saint-Domingue," A. A. E., Haïti, 1.

[65] Damas to Boyer, December 20, 1825, *ibid.*, 2.

[66] Léger, *Recueil des traités et conventions da la République d'Haïti,* pp. 2-6; Clercq, *Recueil des traités,* III, 392-96.

[67] In the " Extrait d'une Résumé sur la Négociation avec Haïti,"

News of the recognition of Haiti by a royal ordinance caused a sensation in Paris.[68] On August 13, 1825, the *Drapeau Blanc* declared that this measure was not a treaty but an act of sovereign power proffered as a benefit and dictated as an order. Maintaining that the commercial advantage granted to France constituted a permanent right of which she could not be deprived without nullifying the recognition conceded to the colony, this journal reasoned that, properly speaking, the sovereignty of France was only suspended: " Suzerainty, in fact, exists by virtue of a clause which constitutes a privilege and which admits, if necessary, succor and protection."

Two weeks later *L'Étoile* declared that, in recognizing the insurgent French colony as independent, Charles X had acted within his prerogative. Haiti belonged to a different category from the Spanish-American states, and should he recognize their independence the King of France " would perform an act contrary to his principles, to his duties, and to his policy—an act beyond the scope of his rights." On the other hand, the *Journal du Commerce* asserted on September 4 that the concession to Haiti had undoubtedly caused French merchants to hope " that something analogous would soon be done for the other new nations of America." It stated that not only were there ships in French ports preparing to sail for Haiti but that ships were also being laden there with cargoes for Mexico, Colombia, Chile, and La Plata: " In fact one should believe that the government will not long delay in taking measures to protect effectively such important interests." [69]

A. A. E., Haïti, 2, the statement is made that this treaty was not ratified because of defects in the protocol.

[68] Barante, *Souvenirs,* III, 266.

[69] See further the views of Guizot in Barante, *op. cit.,* III, 269-70.

On September 8 the *Moniteur* declared that the act of authority which emancipated Saint-Domingue could by that time be judged properly. It analyzed two serious objections of the opposition: first, that the Ordinance of April 17, 1825, was unusual and unconstitutional; and, second, that Charles X addressed the Haitians as their master. It argued that the allegation of illegality was not justified. By using the language of a sovereign the ordinance did not alter the actual condition of affairs: sovereignty *de jure* held by France; *de facto* sovereignty possessed by Haiti. In the protocol which she had formulated France made use of her nominal right, but she could not expect obedience: " She ceded only that right—the sole remnant which remained to her of the ownership of Saint-Domingue." The ministerial journal maintained that the royal ordinance was an act justified by the existence of a state of war between France and Haiti. Mackau was in reality a messenger who bore a flag of truce to the enemy: " The ratification of the ordinance by the Haitian Senate was an act by which a besieged stronghold signed a capitulation that was dictated by the beleaguers."

In their policy toward Haiti French statesmen were desirous of promoting French commerce. They also felt that it was their duty to secure indemnities for Frenchmen who had been driven from Saint-Domingue by the storm of revolution. To save the feelings of the French people, they wished to make an adjustment which would appear as a concession to a colony rather than as a treaty with an independent republic. It seems that the ordinance acknowledging Haitian independence was an act of the royal prerogative in harmony with the traditions and practices of the French Government under the Bourbons. An explanation attributed to Villèle justified the ordinance not as an act of recognition but as a concession: " Royalty imposed its conditions; Haiti accepted them. . . . Liberty was conceded to Saint-Domingue as it had been granted to the French people by the Charter. . . ." [70]

By imposing a heavy financial burden upon Haiti in return for formal recognition, however, French statesmen sowed the seeds of discord between their monarchy and the insular republic. Moreover, a study of the subsequent relations between those nations shows that not all French publicists had relinquished the hope of regaining ownership of the former colony. Of particular significance were the views of Baron Pichon; in a memorandum later presented to the Ministry of Foreign Affairs, he reasoned as follows concerning the bargain which France had struck with Haiti:

The ordinance of emancipation places us in a position to choose between the different methods which are open to us of regaining this possession so unfortunately lost. It excuses us from having recourse to violent means. It permits us to wait, to exercise our influence, and to prepare the spirits of men for a submission which would be only a substitution of one government for another. By setting a price upon independence, and by evaluating that independence at a sum which the Haitians are not able to pay, it still leaves us at liberty to collect by force of arms if the day arrives when this will serve us advantageously. All the treaties which will follow this ordinance will allow us the same recourse, for they will all depend upon the same system as the ordinance—a price set upon independence— and, however moderate this price may be, it is quite doubtful in the present condition of Haiti's finances whether the irregularity of her payments might not soon warrant hostilities on our part if it should suit us to employ them. [71]

[70] Chancy, L'Indépendance nationale d'Haïti, p. 90.
[71] " Haïti," March 8, 1831, A. A. E., Haïti, 5.

With respect to the Haitians, there is reason to believe that some of them were dubious, if not actually suspicious, with regard to French policy. In November, 1825, the *Télégraphe* of Port-au-Prince published a letter from a correspondent which mentioned the ambiguities, the contradictions, and the reservations of the royal ordinance.[72] In fact, when Haitian leaders became fully aware of the crushing weight of the financial burden imposed upon them as the price of recognition, they became bitterly dissatisfied.

On the other hand, Bolívar the Liberator viewed the acknowledgment of Haiti's independence by France as a step favorable to the fortunes of Spanish America.[73] Some French statesmen believed that the recognition as an independent nation of the one-time colony which held sway over the former Spanish dependency in Santo Domingo would influence favorably the attitude of Spanish-American Patriots toward France. Count Chabrol sent a dispatch to Admiral Duperré on December 22, 1825, in which he linked the important step taken by Charles X in regard to Haiti with the destiny of the Spanish Indies:

The emancipation of Haiti should cause a notable change in the opinions of the chiefs of the new governments of America concerning the intentions of the King with respect to them. Today, when His Majesty has himself consented to the independence of an island of which France still possessed the better part, no one can seriously believe that he entertains the project of aiding Spain to recover her former colonies. It is therefore probable that in Colombia and Mexico you will find the Patriots entirely disposed to banish the injurious doubts which they have entertained concerning the sincerity of our assurances of neutrality.[74]

[72] *Le Télégraphe,* November 20, 1825.
[73] Bolívar, *Cartas,* V, 204.
[74] A. N., Marine, B B⁴, 424.

In his address upon the opening of the legislature in January, 1826, Charles X mentioned the ordinance of recognition. Declaring that the time had arrived to heal a painful sore and to determine the destiny of Saint-Domingue, he maintained that a definitive separation from that colony, which had been lost to France for thirty years, would not in the least disturb the security of those colonies which she still retained.[75] On February 11, upon introducing a bill for the indemnification of the dispossessed proprietors of Saint-Domingue, Count Villèle stated that in the negotiations with Haiti the King had used the right which belonged to him of making treaties and ordinances necessary to the welfare of the state. The minister explained that the conditions embodied in the Act of April 17 constituted the price of the concessions made to the Haitians.[76]

Members of the Left in the Chamber of Deputies expressed regret that Charles X had not asked for legislative approval before issuing the ordinance. Enemies of the administration opposed a measure making concessions to a revolution conducted by Negroes. Orators declaimed against the action of the King in alienating a portion of national territory without the consent of the legislature. On the other hand, Villèle argued that the Ordinance of April 17, 1825, was a legal and constitutional exercise of the royal prerogative, in accordance with historic right and certain articles of the Charter.[77]

More than one speaker mentioned the Spanish colonies in a suggestive fashion. Arguing against the proposed indemnity law, a deputy named Agier stated on March 8

[75] *Le Moniteur,* February 1, 1826.
[76] *Ibid.,* February 12, 1826.
[77] *Ibid.,* March 8, 1826.

that he could not help being startled upon reading the view of a Mexican publicist who declared that by acknowledging Haiti's independence the French Government had justified the right of insurrection in all colonies.[78] Alexis de Noailles made a survey of the revolution in the Spanish Indies and concluded that Europe was losing her supremacy in America. Former subjects of European monarchs were everywhere conspiring to found independent governments. Seven Spanish-American nations with a total population of thirty million people were discussing problems of the New World in the Congress of Panama. "In view of this series of events," he asked, "what does the King of France propose to do?" Noailles expressed the opinion that Charles X had manifested his sentiments and his desires by public acts. "The Ordinance of April 17," he declared, "is for the New World a species of charter, a solemn act—the only legal diploma that America possesses."[79]

General Sébastiani argued in favor of the indemnity law. On March 10 he made significant comments on the new Haitian policy of France. "The recognition of the new republics of South America ought, therefore, in our own interest to follow soon after the recognition of Haiti. May our ministers prepare to secure for commerce and industry this immense benefit which is everywhere demanded...."[80] As a result of the debate over the Haitian indemnity bill, the American minister in Paris was convinced that an acknowledgment of the independence of Spanish America would be "as agreeable to the majority in the chamber as it

[78] *Ibid.,* March 9, 1826.
[79] *Ibid.,* March 10, 1826.
[80] *Ibid.,* March 11, 1826.

certainly would be to the French people generally." [81] By a
large majority the Chamber of Deputies finally passed a bill
which apportioned the indemnity among the proprietors
who had been dispossessed in Saint-Domingue. This
measure became a law on April 30, 1826.[82]

Besides the negotiation of a treaty of commerce with
France, the instructions of Daumec, Fremont, and Rouanez
included the arrangement of a loan for their government.
President Boyer seemed to believe that the resources of his
country would enable it to pay the interest on the French
debt and to extinguish the indebtedness in twenty-five years.
In order, however, to enable Haiti to meet the first payment,
due on December 31, 1825, Boyer had decided to borrow
30,000,000 francs in Europe. On October 10, 1825, the
Haitian commissioners issued a prospectus regarding this
loan.[83] The bonds were floated in November, 1825, through
Jacques Laffitte, an optimistic banker and publicist.

This loan was composed of 30,000 bonds of 1,000 francs
apiece, bearing interest at 6% which was to be payable every
six months. The debt was to be extinguished in twenty-five
years. As the loan brought only 80% of its face value to
Haiti, it enabled that government to pay merely 24,000,000
francs on the first indemnity payment of 30,000,000 due to
France. In addition the Haitian agents paid 5,300,000
francs, which still left their government in arrears on the

[81] Manning, *Diplomatic Correspondence of the United States
concerning the Independence of the Latin-American Nations*, II,
1422.

[82] *Recueil général des lois et des arrêts en matière civil, criminelle,
commerciale et de droit public depuis l'avenèment de Napoléon*,
XXVI, 334-35.

[83] *Le Moniteur*, October 13, 1825.

initial payment of the indemnity.[84] At once, therefore, Haiti failed to meet the terms of the agreement by which her independence had been recognized.

In the autumn of 1825 Damas appointed Colonel Maler as chargé d'affaires and consul general at Port-au-Prince.[85] Shortly afterward, an exequatur was issued to him by the Haitian Government. Upon being presented to President Boyer in the national palace on November 13, 1825, the former agent of France in Brazil delivered an address in which he declared that his mission was to encourage the new relations which the emancipation ordinance had established between France and Haiti and to promote the prosperity of both countries. In response Boyer stated that both nations had undertaken to observe religiously all the obligations arising from their reciprocal rights and advantages.[86] Nevertheless, in order to secure the execution of the commercial clauses of the ordinance Chabrol soon directed a naval squadron to proceed to Haitian waters.[87]

At the instance of President Boyer, the Haitian Congress enacted in 1826 a law declaring that the obligation to pay France 150,000,00 francs was recognized as a national debt.[88] Still, Haiti failed to remit the balance due on the first installment of the indemnity. Further, when the second fifth of the indemnity fell due, the Haitian Secretary of the Treasury merely sent to Paris an acknowledgment that his

[84] Roy to Charles X, August 27, 1828, A. A. E., Haïti, 3. See further Esmangart, *La verité sur les affaires d'Haïti*, p. 4.

[85] Damas to Maler, September 2, 1825, A. N., Marine, B B⁴, 466.

[86] *Le Télégraphe,* November 20, 1825.

[87] Chabrol to Demelay, December 22, 1825, A. N., Marine, B B⁴, 466.

[88] *Le Télégraphe,* March 5, 1826.

government owed France 30,000,000 francs.[89] In a message
to Congress on June 10, 1828, Boyer plausibly explained
that he had constantly championed the principle that a
people which was truly independent should not be constrained against its will to recognize forever exclusive
privileges that accrued solely to the benefit of a foreign
power.[90]

Still, both parties repeatedly displayed their willingness
to consider an adjustment of the differences that had developed concerning commercial intercourse and the amount
of the indemnity. When a Haitian agent named Saint
Macary arrived in Paris, the King promptly asked Esmangart and Baron Pichon to negotiate with him. Though
these commissioners considered Saint Macary's propositions
strange, they were convinced that conditions were ripe for a
new arrangement.[91] However, largely because of the reluctance of France to reduce the amount of the indemnity,
attempts to arrange a settlement failed.

In December, 1828, an official at Paris undertook to
consider the effect of Haiti's default upon her political
status. An unsigned précis filed in the Ministry of Foreign
Affairs recorded the legal opinion that, although in civil
transactions the failure to execute a contract would annul the
agreement, yet in international politics such a failure would
not have that effect. Further, the King could not revoke the
ordinance acknowledging the independent status of Haiti
without causing inconvenience and complications. " The
independence of that country is now an accomplished fact,"

[89] Esmangart, *op. cit.*, pp. 4-5.

[90] Lesur, *Annuaire historique*, 1828, *appendice*, p. 184.

[91] Pichon and Esmangart to La Ferronnays, October 30, 1828,
A. A. E., Haïti, 3.

remarked this authority, " and, because of that, it is indeed irrevocable." He reasoned that for France to disavow that recognition would be not only to relinquish the advantages promised by the ordinance but also to injure those nations which subsequently established intercourse with the new State. He added that " in and of itself the independence of a country is not among those material things which one can take back or reclaim after they have been granted." [92] It is to be presumed that whatever notions French diplomats or financiers may have entertained with regard to rescinding the Ordinance of April 17, 1825, were now summarily dismissed.

A fresh report to the Minister of Foreign Affairs in the midsummer of 1830 gave an illuminating interpretation of the ordinance. This account presented the view that the fiscal stipulations in the Haitian charter of independence were entirely out of proportion to the resources of the republic and, further, that the Haitians themselves were partly responsible for the resulting disagreement, for they had exaggerated the means which were at their disposal: " Always influenced by their vanity, the Haitians, by equivocal promises which they were consequently obliged to retract or to explain, gave the impression of bad faith and bad will, although they merely bowed to necessity." [93]

The policy pursued by France toward her former colony naturally followed a different course from her policy toward either Brazil or Spanish America. Because Frenchmen had been driven out of Saint-Domingue and dispossessed of their valuable holdings, France insisted, as the price of the

[92] " Notes sur Haïty, 21 Decembre, 1828," *ibid.*
[93] " Rapport au Ministre," 1830, *ibid.*, 4.

coveted acknowledgment of Haitian independence, upon the payment of an indemnity to those proprietors—an indemnity which may not inaccurately be said to have constituted a lien upon Haiti's sovereignty. Fiscal obligations arising out of the payment of this indemnity caused a heavy drain upon the slender resources of Haiti and were partly responsible for her later financial embarrassments. Further, when the Dominicans undertook later to cast off the hated rule of the Black Republic, this fiscal issue threatened to rise like a wraith to affect the policy of France toward both republics on the island of Santo Domingo.

The acknowledgment of Haitian independence by France was praised by prominent French statesmen and journalists. It was rightly hailed as a favorable augury for Spanish America by the Great Liberator. Canning was quick to point out that the acknowledgment of Haitian independence by the French Government was inconsistent with its reluctance to recognize the Spanish-American nations. He declared that the French transaction with Haiti furnished a practical example how a colony, when its recovery became hopeless, might be used to the advantage of the motherland. Nevertheless, although the Royal Ordinance of 1825 was a precedent which smoothed the way for Spanish-American recognition, the sequel was to demonstrate that a dynastic change was necessary before French statesmen would so far depart from their traditional policy as to discard the Bourbon Family Compact and formally acknowledge the political independence of the former Spanish colonies in America. Furthermore, not until after that change took place was a successful attempt made to adjust the differences between France and Haiti concerning their commercial intercourse and the amount of the indemnity.

Chapter XIV

THE LAST CABINETS OF CHARLES X AND SPANISH AMERICA

Villèle finally lost favor. Although a careful administrator who husbanded the resources of the state, he did not understand the mood of his countrymen. As Lucas-Dubreton has said, the French were less concerned with ensuring a good administration and with tangible realities than with thoughts of liberty and glory. In the spring of 1827 Count Peyronnet, Minister of Justice, tried to force through the chambers an unpopular law concerning the press. The Ordinance of April 29 disbanding the national guard also caused dissatisfaction. Another distasteful ordinance provided for the reëstablishment of censorship. The elections held on November 17 were won by the Opposition, which two days later celebrated its victory at Paris in riotous fashion. Elections held shortly afterward were also unfavorable to the government. On December 6, 1827, King Charles reluctantly notified Villèle that he had decided to form an entirely new ministry.

Early in the following year a cabinet was constituted under Viscount Martignac, an eloquent and courageous lawyer, who became Minister of the Interior. Count Chabrol was retained in the Navy Department, but Baron Damas was replaced in the Foreign Office by the experienced diplomat, Count La Ferronnays, who served until April 24, 1829. In January, 1828, the English ambassador at Paris expressed his opinion concerning the new Cabinet: " This Ministry will be disposed, I doubt not, in questions of Foreign Politics, to follow the policy of M. de Villèle's Government." [1]

The first analysis under the Martignac Cabinet of French relations with Spanish America was a memorandum dated February 5, 1828, which was evidently composed by a government official. Its author asserted that the policy of France toward the Indies had been formed in the light of her interests and of political expediency. In words that may have been inspired he declared:

As soon as circumstances permit, the government of the King will strengthen by political relations the commercial intercourse which it has established with Spanish America, but any precipitancy in this matter would be rightly blamable. No other attitude could have been taken by France; for the people would have been astonished to learn that, at a time when the most important towns in Spain were in the possession of our soldiers, the government of His Majesty had chosen to recognize the countries which not long before had been under the authority of His Catholic Majesty. The motives for such reserve will be readily appreciated; and the King, who in this grave question ought to reconcile the interests of France with the preservation of her dignity and with the consideration which he owes to a monarch who is his relative and his ally, has without doubt the right to expect that we will leave to his wisdom the decisions which still have to be made in order to complete at the opportune time our relations with the new states formed in America. [2]

Charles X's address upon the opening of the legislature in 1828 displeased both the Mexicans and the Spaniards. The Duke of San Carlos, who was again serving as the Spanish ambassador at Paris, was alarmed at certain allusions to foreign affairs and sought an explanation from La Ferronnays. That minister advised him not to be over-

[1] Granville to Dudley, January 4, 1828, F. O., 27/375.
[2] " Note sur l'Amérique Espagnole," A. A. E., Mémoires et Documents, Amérique, 36.

sensitive and assured him that the French King entertained the most cordial feelings for Spain.[3]

As the King's discourse contained no mention of the Franco-Mexican Declarations, Tomás Murphy, who was still acting as agent for Mexico, filed a protest in terms which the Minister of Foreign Affairs considered improper. In consequence the minister asked Murphy to withdraw his note, under pain of a rupture of the relations existing between France and Mexico. The French diplomat explained that, as the Mexican Government had not been recognized by France in the Declarations, the King had not mentioned that agreement in his address. Murphy acknowledged the justice of this explanation and expressed regret at his indiscreet protest. La Ferronnays then directed the French agent in Mexico to inform Camacho confidentially of this incident and to repeat the observations which had been made to Murphy. Martignac's Cabinet thus formally put itself on record to the effect that the Declarations did not constitutue an acknowledgment of Mexican independence by France.[4]

Early in 1828 European statesmen were still jockeying for a position in the race for Spanish-American favor. German merchants and principalities had become deeply interested in the fortunes of the rising states. In June, 1827, the Hanse towns had begun to appoint consular agents to ports in Spanish America.[5] Prussia became concerned about the policy of France toward the Spanish nations of the New World. The attitude of the French Cabinet was demon-

[3] San Carlos to González Salmón, February 22, 1828, A. H. N., Estado, 5233. The King's discourse is found in the *Moniteur,* February 6, 1828.

[4] La Ferronnays to Martin, April 18, 1828, A. A. E., Mexique, 3.

[5] Baumgarten, *Ibero-Amerika und die Hansestädte,* p. 189.

strated by its answers to inquiries made in February, 1828, by the Prussian minister at Paris. He asked the Ministry of Foreign Affairs four searching questions that involved the issue of recognition. Had France concluded treaties or conventions with the new American states? Had her government sent accredited agents to Spanish-American republics? Had those men been dispatched as commercial agents or as consuls? Had the credentials of such agents been signed by a minister or by the King? [6]

On February 26 those questions were answered by an illuminating summary prepared by the Ministry of Foreign Affairs. France had not concluded either treaties or conventions with the new states; the Franco-Mexican Declarations were merely provisional articles intended to regulate certain relations reciprocally. The French Government had accredited agents to the new states of Spanish America. These agents had at first been given the title of inspectors general of commerce; after 1827 they had been designated by the regular title of consul or consul general. Inspectors of commerce were given commissions signed by the Minister of Foreign Affairs; and the consuls were accredited by virtue of certificates signed by the King. When those consuls were selected the government wished to avoid the use of terms in their diplomas which would imply the recognition of the new republics, and consequently considered it necessary to use a special form of appointment couched in these words: ". . . having judged suitable to establish the post of consul general of France at . . . and for the country and government of. . . ." [7]

---

[6] "Note remit par le Mte. de Prusse," February, 1828, A. A. E., Mémoires et Documents, Amérique, 36.

[7] "Communiqué au Mtre. de Prusse le 26 février 1828," *ibid.*

The English Government also asked for information concerning French agents in Latin-American countries. On February 26 the French Government accordingly sent to Lord Granville a list of consular agents who had been selected for the new states of Spanish America. A consul general and a vice-consul had been appointed to reside in the city of Buenos Aires, and consuls general had been sent to Lima and Santiago de Chile. Consuls were to be stationed at Jalapa, Vera Cruz, Bogotá, and Cartagena; for the time being, the consuls at Cartagena and Vera Cruz were to exercise the functions of consul general. Besides an envoy extraordinary, a French consul general was stationed at Rio de Janeiro; consuls were located at Bahia and Pernambuco, and vice-consuls had been placed at Maranhão and Montevideo. It was explained that the salaries paid by France to her consular agents in Latin America depended upon local circumstances.

This response also contained information about the consular representation in France from Latin America. There was a consul general from Brazil at Paris, a consul at Havre, and eleven vice-consuls located at other French cities. The only Spanish-American nation that had commercial agents in France was Mexico. That country was represented at Paris by Murphy, who had been acknowledged by virtue of an exequatur of the King and was styled a general agent of commerce. In addition, Mexico had in France four subordinate commercial agents.[8]

---

[8] " Communiqué à l'Ambor. d'Angleterre (26 février, 1828)," *ibid.*; the *Almanach royal,* 1828 (p. 149), gives the number of French consular agents in Brazil as five. On the flattering reception accorded the French consul general at Buenos Aires, see Villanueva, *Historia de la república argentina,* II, 16-17.

An extraordinary measure adopted by France to obtain advice concerning the policy which she should pursue toward Spanish America at this time was to send Delpech to Brussels to interview the famous revolutionary leader, General San Martín, who in a spirit of self-abnegation had in 1824 withdrawn from La Plata to Europe. In the report of his mission Delpech stated that he had asked this general certain questions in the interest of French foreign policy. Among these questions was an inquiry concerning the steps which would not only promote closer relations between France and South America but also prevent that continent from falling further under the influence of England. San Martín responded that this could best be accomplished through an acknowledgment by France of the independence of the Spanish-American nations.

Besides, he made some interesting suggestions concerning Franco-American intercourse. The commerce of France should be handled so that it could compete with English trade. Frenchmen should form a project for the planting of settlements in Spanish America. They should attempt to profit by the tendency, which according to San Martín prevailed there, in favor of the establishment of monarchical systems. France should display the utmost care in the selection of her agents to the new states. The French Ministry of Marine should increase as much as possible the number of ships that were cruising in Latin-American waters.[9]

Meanwhile Delpech had laid a questionnaire before the French Government concerning the wisdom of recognizing all the new American republics. In a memorandum answering this inquiry, an official in the Ministry of Foreign Af-

[9] Delpech to La Ferronnays, May 25, 1828, A. A. E., Mémoires et Documents, Amérique, 36.

fairs analyzed the situation and reached the conclusion that France should not hesitate to take such a forward step. This official maintained that nothing could prevent the emancipation of the Spanish colonies.

France can no longer struggle against her recognized interests. She should undertake to solve this important question today and should exploit for her special profit that vast field of prosperity which the fortune of events offers her. Every delay will tend to decrease these advantages and to aid her competitors, particularly England, whose timid and vacillating policy makes it impossible for her at present to oppose such an undertaking. Well governed, France can profit by the mistakes of England so as to make almost incurable the severe wounds which British cupidity has given to her commerce and finance; but France should act without delay, since for her to remain stationary any longer would be irreparable and criminal blindness.[10]

An editorial on South America in the *Journal des Débats* on September 21, 1828, indicated the drift of enlightened French opinion. This journal declared that all the political systems established in South America were completely free from Spanish domination, but that much progress had yet to be made:

Mexico, Colombia, La Plata, and Peru will have agents at all the courts of Europe, while the government at Madrid will appoint viceroys for these provinces. . . . In Spanish America there still remain some things to be overcome; these are rivalries, jealousies, and passions. . . . The old edifice has crumbled; it is necessary to construct a new one. In place of slavery, ignorance, anarchy, and corruption, we expect laws, enlightenment, order, and public virtue. Without doubt great advances have been made; but the end has not yet been attained—this is merely the eve of the future.

[10] " Question dans l'intérêt de la France et des Amériques," May 25, 1828, *ibid*. On June 28, 1828, Delpech addressed to La Ferronnays a scheme proposing the partition of Spanish America among European powers. A. A. E., Mémoires et Documents, Espagne, 214.

At the instance of Bolívar, Fernández Madrid, who was now in London, renewed his attempt to enter into negotiations with France. He induced Marquis de Lafayette to write to the Minister of Foreign Affairs in favor of the negotiation of a treaty with Colombia. Taking his cue from a speech which the minister had delivered at the last session of the French legislature, the Colombian agent declared that the time had come which had been set by Damas for the framing of a Franco-Colombian treaty. He assured La Ferronnays that the Colombians were enjoying complete tranquillity and that they had perfect confidence in Bolívar.[11] On October 25, 1828, the minister informed Fernández Madrid that his government was glad to hear of Colombia's progress. He explained that Charles X was not unmindful of that country's desires: " As soon as circumstances permit, His Majesty will use the occasion to make regular and to consolidate his relations with the Colombian Government; his decision in this matter will naturally be based upon the guarantees of order and stability which the condition of the republic presents." [12] La Ferronnays assured Lafayette that the government was considering Colombia's overture but that immediate action would be premature. The minister sent copies of his correspondence with Fernández Madrid to Buchet de Martigny for guidance in his dealings with Colombian statesmen.[13]

Unknown to Parisian journalists or to American agents,

[11] Fernández Madrid to Lafayette, October 6, 1828 (copy); *idem* to La Ferronnays, October 12, 1828; Lafayette to La Ferronnays, October 21, 1828; La Ferronnays to Lafayette, November 1, 1828, A. A. E., Colombie, 4.

[12] *Ibid.*

[13] La Ferronnays to Lafayette, November 1, 1828; *idem* to Buchet de Martigny, December 15, 1828, *ibid.*

the Ministry of Foreign Affairs had meanwhile initiated a measure that seemed fraught with significance for the New World. In May, 1828, La Ferronnays addressed to Charles X an analysis of the political and military situation of Spain. The minister declared that the withdrawal of the remaining French soldiers from that country, the occupation of which had been extended by a treaty in December, 1824, would leave the King free to take a new step in regard to the Indies. La Ferronnays felt that the immediate acknowledgment of the independence of the Spanish-American countries would perhaps be premature, especially as Ferdinand VII was preparing for a last effort to restore his authority over them. A delay in the recognition of the new states would accordingly be a generous gesture by the French King to a prince of his own dynasty. Still, La Ferronnays held that France should use the interval profitably by gathering information about the real condition of the new American republics. He reasoned that the dispatch of an intelligent agent for this purpose would have great advantages and elaborated his views as follows:

It was in this manner that England proceeded before recognizing these new states; and a similar mission is to be sent in the name of His Majesty the King of The Netherlands. This measure, the execution of which will not take more than one year, would place the government of Your Majesty in a position not only to act with full knowledge of the circumstances but also to prepare suitable measures for treating with the American republics, if their situation should permit. As a mission of this nature should be confided to a clever agent who is zealous for the good of the service, I have the honor to propose to Your Majesty to entrust it to Charles Bresson, who has served as second secretary of the French legation at Washington.[14]

[14] La Ferronnays to Charles X, May 7, 1828, *ibid.*, 5. At this

This recommendation of a step which seemed preliminary to the recognition of Spanish-American independence bears the royal indorsement under date of May 7, " Approuvé, Charles." Bresson was soon notified of the contemplated mission. On May 30 he accordingly submitted to the Ministry of Foreign Affairs alternative itineraries for the proposed tour of Spanish America. He calculated that by taking one route he would arrive in Lima about April, 1829, and that by taking the other he would reach that capital in the following September.[15]

On June 2, 1828, Charles X approved two sets of instructions for Bresson. One set explained that the year 1823, when French soldiers had delivered Spain from a revolutionary government, was not a time when Louis XVIII could negotiate in America with insurrectionary provinces. Nor could the independence of the Spanish colonies be recognized while French garrisons held the principal cities of Spain. However, the King, animated by a desire to promote the interests of his subjects, had now provisionally decided to accredit consuls to the new states. The number of consuls would be increased as circumstances permitted France to develop commercial relations with Spanish America. Though the full development of intercourse with the new republics would necessarily follow the acknowledgment of their independence, yet at this time when French troops were actually evacuating Spain the King felt disposed to take definitive action. However, be-

---

very time, however, the envoy of Colombia in London was negotiating with the ambassador of The Netherlands for a treaty which was actually signed in May, 1829. See Martínez Silva, *Biografía de D. José Fernández Madrid,* p. 273; Cadena, *Anales diplomáticos de Colombia,* pp. 524-33.

[15] A. A. E., Colombie, 5.

fore deciding to recognize the new governments in the Spanish Indies, he wished to be informed concerning their real condition and the guarantees of order and stability which they could present: " It is to acquire positive notions with respect to these particulars that His Majesty has judged it necessary to send to America an intelligent agent instructed carefully to observe the state of affairs." [16]

The itinerary mapped out for Bresson was an adaptation of a route which he had proposed. First, he was to sail to Mexico. Thence, by way of Central America, he was to journey to South America, where he was to visit successively Colombia, Peru, Chile, La Plata, and Brazil. A passage from the supplementary instructions to this special agent, which were also written in the third person, will suggest the broad scope of his inquiry:

He shall observe and note with care everything which, in rising states and in countries where men and institutions display themselves under aspects as novel as they are interesting, should naturally attract the attention of an enlightened traveler. He shall undertake to gather as many facts as possible about the governments and the men who are administering them, about the condition and the principles of parties, about the various sources of public wealth, about agriculture and commerce, about the operation of mines and their actual production, and about the condition of those foreign companies which have undertaken to exploit mineral resources. The condition of the people under the existing régime, the state of society, the classes which compose it, and the manners and opinions which the people display because of the diversity of their interests and needs—all these are subjects that lie naturally within the circle of investigation which M. Bresson is called upon to survey.

[16] " Instructions pour Monsieur Charles Bresson, chargé par le Roi d'une mission en Amérique," A. A. E., Mémoires et Documents, Amérique, 36.

Besides, the commissioner was directed to investigate special topics in certain countries. In Mexico he was to examine the influence which the expulsion of the Spaniards would exert upon agricultural, commercial, and political conditions. In Colombia he was to observe not only the proceedings of the Constitutional Convention which had met at Ocaña but also the conduct of Bolívar. In the former Peruvian viceroyalty he was to compare the relative strength of the two republics, Peru and Bolivia, that had emerged in its territory. In Chile he was to discover whether, because of foreign influence, the government was actually contemplating the substitution of Protestantism for Catholicism. In the basin of La Plata he was to examine the condition of the Argentine republic and to study her relations with Brazil. He was also to seek precise information concerning supposed English designs on Uruguay. By no means least in importance was the following instruction:

The attitude of the Spanish-American republics toward France will be another important subject of investigation for M. Bresson. This disposition, which our intimate relations with Spain have kept from becoming very friendly, now appears more satisfying. The new governments should in fact be convinced that France did not entertain any hostile views with regard to them, that she dreamed only of forming with them relations which would be reciprocally useful, and that if up to the present time she has not given to that intercourse more serious consideration, it is because complications of a very special nature did not permit this.

Bresson was directed to hold interviews with leaders of the new nations. He was to inform them that Charles X sincerely desired their prosperity, that he was carefully watching events in Spanish-American countries, and that

" the moment when he will be able to recognize their independence is not far distant." Further, the commissioner was instructed to tell the Spanish-American governments that, before recognizing them as independent, he wished to be certain of the manner in which they intended to treat with France. "The King," it was stated, "has beyond doubt the right to ask for his subjects the treatment and the advantages accorded to the most-favored-nations; he does not suppose that this point can be placed in question, and it is in this sense that M. Bresson shall make explanations."

Furthermore, Bresson was instructed that in every country visited he was to study the actual condition of French commerce and the measures which were necessary to promote its development. Besides, he was to investigate the commercial relations of both England and the United States with Spanish America. He was to carry on with La Ferronnays as active and regular a correspondence as possible; if necessary, in his dispatches to Paris he was to use a cipher.[17]

On June 5, 1828, La Ferronnays signed Bresson's credentials addressed to the foreign secretaries of Central America, Peru, Bolivia, Chile, and Argentina.[18] The commissioner was also furnished with letters to French consuls in Mexico, Colombia, Peru, Chile, and Argentina which directed them to promote the success of his mission. It was described as having a twofold object, namely to gather information concerning the actual condition of the new states and also regarding the attitude of their respective governments to-

[17] A. A. E., Mémoires et Documents, Amérique, 36. Both instructions bear the same title and are endorsed "Approuvé par le Roi, le 2 Juin 1828."
[18] A. A. E., Colombie, 5.

ward France.[19]   Count Saint Cricq, the Minister of Commerce and Manufactures, sent a note to Bresson in which he emphasized the need of gathering data respecting commercial conditions in Spanish America.   Saint Cricq declared that this was necessary for two reasons: to make clear the real importance of the advantages which France might expect from her intercourse with Spanish-American countries, and to ascertain the means by which those advantages might be secured promptly and easily.   The Minister of Commerce asked Bresson to discover whether it was true that the new states would give identical commercial facilities to all countries that would acknowledge their political existence.   This minister also wished to be informed whether it was likely that those states would refuse to extend certain commercial privileges to nations that delayed recognizing their independent status.[20]

A heavy handicap was imposed on the young diplomat. The term assigned for his extensive trip of inquiry was much too short.   No one well acquainted with Latin America would have expected the commissioner in one short year to travel the immense distance involved and to investigate conditions in Mexico, Central America, Colombia, Peru, Chile, Argentina, and Brazil with thoroughness.   An additional handicap lay in the fact that, despite the need for prompt action, Bresson's mission to the new states was considerably delayed.

Accompanied by the young Duke of Montebello, who was lured by a love of travel, and by an attaché named

[19] Copies of letters intended for Martin, Buchet de Martigny, La Forest, Chaumette des Fossés, and Mendeville were sent by La Ferronnays to Bresson on June 12, 1828. *Ibid.*

[20] Saint Cricq to Bresson, July 6, 1828, *ibid.*

Henri Ternaux, who later gained fame as a scholar, Bresson reached the United States in the autumn of 1828. Rumors of anarchic conditions prevailing in Mexico induced him to alter his itinerary. Instead of proceeding to that country he took ship for Colombia, which seemed more tranquil.[21] Early in April, 1829, he reached Honda on the banks of the river Magdalena; shortly afterward he arrived at Bogotá.

On April 18 " the commissioner of France," as Colombians styled him, was formally received by the Council of Ministers. In the address which he delivered on that occasion Bresson, besides praising Bolívar, expressed on behalf of his country the desire that Colombia should become tranquil and prosperous, develop her immense resources, and consolidate strong and liberal institutions.[22] In replying to this speech, the president of the council expressed gratification that France, which had generously promoted the independence of the first republic created in the New World, was now directing her attention to the Spanish nations of America. He hoped that by such an act of justice as the recognition of Colombia the name of Charles X might be rendered glorious and be added to the roll of just and philosophic princes.[23] Evidently the commissioner soon assured Estanislao de Vergara, the Colombian Secretary of Foreign Relations, that France had irrevocably decided to acknowledge Colombian independence.[24] As a Venezuelan

[21] Le Moyne, *La Nouvelle-Grenade,* II, 66; González Salmón to Ofalia, November 24, 1828, A. H. N., Estado, 6876.

[22] Bresson to La Ferronnays, May 3, 1829, and enclosure, A. A. E., Colombie, 5.

[23] Enclosure in *idem* to *idem,* May 3, 1829, *ibid.*

[24] Vergara to Bresson, April 25, 1829, A. A. E., Colombie, 5.

littérateur has aptly said, Bresson enjoyed in Bogotá the attributes, if not the title, of diplomatic agent.[25]

This agent soon held a number of interesting conferences with Vergara concerning the acknowledgment of Colombian independence and the negotiation of a Franco-Colombian commercial treaty. In a *note verbale* embodying the conclusions reached at the conference of April 25, Bresson was cited as having made the following pertinent statement concerning the policy of Charles X:

> The moment when His Majesty will recognize the independence of Colombia cannot be far distant. . . . His Majesty has reached a decision; definite action awaits only assurances of the internal condition of the Spanish-American countries which he wishes to recognize. Naturally he desires to secure there guarantees for his future relations with them.[26]

Bogotá had meanwhile become the theater of transactions which contemplated the enthronement of a European prince in Colombia. A letter from Bolívar to the Council of Ministers urged it to consider the means of securing for his country the protection of one or more of the world powers in order to check the torrent of anarchy which was surging through Spanish America. The members of this council unanimously took the view that a constitutional monarchy possessed the vigor and stability which a well-established government should have. At the same time they believed that a monarchical régime would ensure the guarantees necessary for their prosperity. They accordingly decided that Secretary Vergara should negotiate with the

[25] Gil Fortoul, "Relaciones exteriores de Venezuela," *El cojo ilustrado,* XII, 266.

[26] Enclosure in Bresson to La Ferronnays, May 3, 1829, A. A. E., Colombie, 5.

diplomatic agents of England and France at Bogotá and make known to them that it was necessary for Colombia to adopt a monarchical form of government; that the title of king was to be assumed for the first time by the successor of Bolívar; and that England and France were to be asked whether they would recognize Colombia's right to select as his successor the prince that best suited her interests, and whether, in case other American republics became alarmed at the action of Colombia, she could request the intervention of England and France. Bresson was to be informed that it would be suitable for Colombia to select for her monarch a prince of the French dynasty who professed the Catholic faith and would please her citizens because of many political considerations.[27]

Because Bolívar, actually the uncrowned king of northern South America, entertained monarchical views—views which were approved by the Colombian council—Vergara soon took a significant step. On September 5 he addressed a note to Bresson in which he confessed that for some time lovers of Colombia's welfare had felt that a republican régime did not suit their country. He reasoned that, though neither the ministers, nor Congress, nor the people could forget the illustrious services which had been performed by Bolívar, yet after he had passed from the scene a constitutional monarchy would be the form of government best suited to his country. " His successor will be able to assume the title of monarch," wrote Vergara, " and this successor, if events do not throw obstacles in the way, would be sought in one of the royal families of Europe,

[27] Santander, *Archivo*, XVIII, 136-38. On Bolívar's views concerning a monarchy in South America, see Robertson, *Rise of the Spanish-American Republics,* pp. 300-02.

and probably in that of France—a nation with which, for a thousand reasons, it is proper for Colombia to improve her relations." Vergara declared categorically that his colleagues wished to learn whether the French Government would give its consent to the founding in Colombia of such a political system; he also asked whether it would intervene effectively to make possible the maintenance of monarchical institutions there. With the significant omission of the clause that mentioned the favored candidacy of a French prince, this note was also sent by the Colombian minister to Colonel Campbell, the English chargé at Bogotá.[28]

Bresson replied that he would immediately transmit this note to Paris by the Duke of Montebello and that he had postponed his own departure from Cartagena until the receipt of fresh instructions. Chargé Campbell responded that he had forwarded the Minister's note to his government, which would give it careful consideration.[29]

On September 8 Vergara directed Leandro Palacios, who had become the Colombian agent in Paris, to approach the French Minister of Foreign Affairs with respect to the monarchical project. Palacios was told to suggest that upon the death of Bolívar a prince of a European dynasty might be selected to rule as king of Colombia. The French Government was asked to acknowledge that nation as independent, to induce Spain to recognize that status, and to support with all its influence the new régime projected for the Colombians. At the same time Fernández Madrid, who was now in London, was instructed to sound the English Government concerning the proposed change in the political system of northern South America.[30]

[28] Santander, *op. cit.*, XVIII, 138-43.
[29] *Ibid.*, 144-45.   [30] *Ibid.*, 145-54.

Although the commissioner of France had behaved circumspectly in Bogota, yet the project of establishing a monarchy became known.   Rumors were circulated in that capital concerning a conspiracy against the existing régime in which certain foreign agents were involved.   Buchet de Martigny reported to his government that an ill-informed populace entertained the idea that the object of " Bresson's mission was to ensure that the successor of Bolivar should be a prince royal of France," and consequently they thought that Bresson " was the author of the project of a monarchy for Colombia."   Placards attributing monarchical designs to the French commissioner were posted on street corners in Bogotá.   Anonymous pamphlets were circulated warning Colombians to guard against such attacks on their liberty.[31]

Meanwhile the Court of Madrid, having been warned of Bresson's trip to the New World by its envoy at Washington, was much disturbed.   Count Ofalia, who was again serving as Spanish ambassador at Paris, was instructed to ascertain the real purpose of the mission.   The apprehensions of the Spaniards were increased when Parisian journals reprinted from the *Morning Post* of London a garbled version of the address which the commissioner had delivered in Bogotá.[32]   Dissatisfied with France because she had not aided Spain to subjugate the American insurgents, the Count was not in a mood to dismiss this matter lightly.

When Ofalia brought Bresson's speech to the attention of Count Portalis, who in May, 1829, had become the Minister of Foreign Affairs, the latter did not deny that it had

[31] Buchet de Martigny to La Ferronnays, October 13, 1829, A. A. E., Colombie, 4.
[32] González Salmón to Ofalia, November 24, 1828, A. H. N., Estado, 6876; Ofalia to González Salmón, July 29, 1829, *ibid.*, 5334.

been delivered but extenuated the incident because the commissioner was a fiery youth with little experience. Portalis plausibly explained to Ofalia that Bresson's instructions merely directed him to travel in Middle and South America in order to study the situation in a commercial rather than in a political aspect and to send his observations to Paris. The minister emphatically asserted that Bresson was in no manner auhorized to speak in the name of his sovereign, who had not invested him either with consular authority or with a diplomatic character. Yet, when the ambassador requested him to publish a formal disavowal of the agent's address, Portalis demurred and declared that his government was pleased to see the Spanish-American question for the time being at rest.[33]

This disingenuous response did not please the Spanish Government. A commentary upon French foreign policy which was soon filed in the Ministry of State in Madrid recorded that the explanation of Portalis was unsatisfactory but that, if it was certain that France would instruct her commissioner to act more circumspectly, it would not be politic for Spain to insist upon her protest.[34] After being warned that he should in no circumstances invoke the Bourbon Family Compact, Ofalia informed González Salmón that to solicit from France a declaration that the pact was entirely abrogated would be hazardous and might even antagonize Charles X, for the French Government evidently still considered that compact as being in force. Consequently the Spanish Council of State undertook to consider

[33] Ofalia to González Salmón, August 3, 1829, A. H. N., Estado, 5334.
[34] Memorandum, "Madrid, 12 de Agosto 1829," endorsed on Ofalia's note to González Salmón of August 3, 1829, *ibid.*

measures preliminary to the modification of treaty relations with France.[35]

Shortly after Ofalia made his protest, Portalis wrote to Bresson to inform him that he had learned with regret of the ceremonious fashion in which he had been received at Bogotá, that he had made a mistake by presenting in written form the views of his government concerning the acknowledgment of Spanish-American independence, and that the execution of the project for the establishment of a monarchy in Colombia would be extremely difficult. "We shall leave the new states of America to their own devices," continued the minister; "we shall form good and frank relations with them when they have attained a more tranquil condition, and we shall keep away from their markets whenever they are tormented by revolutions and anarchy, but, I repeat, we shall not attempt to play any rôle in those events, whatever part we may take afterwards." As the proposal for founding a South American monarchy might have placed him in an embarrassing position, Bresson was instructed that, after making some vague expressions of good wishes for Colombia, and after declaring that France seemed determined not to interfere in that nation's internal affairs, he was to leave Bogotá. His mission to Mexico was to be contingent upon the fortunes of an expedition which Spain was preparing against the country.[36]

[35] Becker, *Relaciones comerciales entre España y Francia durante el siglo XIX*, p. 38, quotes Ofalia to González Salmón, October 13, 1829, as follows: "la tecla de la total anulación del *Pacto de Familia* es muy difícil de tocar aquí de una manera oportuna, porque hay peligro de que el rey de Francia se ofenda personalmente de ello y porque aquí . . . dan siempre en sus conversaciones que le considerán vigente."

[36] "Août, 1829," A. A. E., Colombie, 6. Bolívar's interest in

The Ultra leader, Prince Polignac, an unpopular adviser of the King, who in August, 1829, became the head of a new cabinet, was more emphatic than Portalis in his disapproval of Bresson's mission to Latin America. It was presumably at the instance of Polignac that, on November 18, 1829, Baron Deffaudis, a diplomat who had served as head of the commercial division of the Ministry of Foreign Affairs, prepared a report concerning that mission. This official declared that there were inherent difficulties involved in it, that the time allotted for the trip was too short, that Bresson had been mistakenly received as a commissioner of France in Colombia, that very grave proposals had been made to him in Bogotá, and that in consequence he had been placed in a false position. Deffaudis was convinced that the Mexicans viewed this tour of inquiry with disfavor and that recent revolutions in Spanish America had demonstrated that only the Colombian Government had stability. He reached the following conclusion:

The mission of Bresson is today almost without point. Indeed it causes only inconvenience. Impressed by the disorder that prevails in La Plata, Chile, Peru, Bolivia, and Guatemala, the King's Government has already felt it necessary to direct him to leave Colombia without delay and to limit himself to a visit to Mexico, if indeed the risk of a Spanish expedition against that country does not render the trip inopportune. Information received in the last reports concerning the vexatious measures which have been taken in regard to his arrival in Mexico leave no doubt concerning the absolute uselessness of any sojourn that he might make there. The dignity of France might even be compromised. I therefore propose to the minister that, if

this plan for the founding of a monarchy in Colombia supported by England and France is shown by his letter of August 5, 1829, to Campbell. Bolívar, *op. cit.,* IX, 68-70.

M. Bresson has not already proceeded to Mexico, he be ordered immediately to return to France.[37]

Deffaudis' recommendation that Bresson be recalled was approved by the head of the Cabinet. On November 21 he accordingly sent word to this agent to return to Europe without visiting Mexico. Polignac asserted that the Mexicans were disturbed by rumors that Bresson was the bearer of monarchical propositions. If he was still at Cartagena he was to consider that his mission had terminated.[38]

Although conceived by the French Ministry of Foreign Affairs in a broad and far-sighted spirit, Bresson's ambitious trip did not accomplish much. His inquiry began and ended in Colombia. Polignac's conservative policy, which was doubtless strongly favored by Charles X, shattered the hope that France might secure from leading nations of Latin America commitments indicating appreciation of the acknowledgment of their independence by Spain's intimate ally. The absence of pledges implying that the new nations would concede to France special mercantile favors in commercial treaties was deeply felt when a dynastic change in France made feasible the immediate recognition of the Spanish-American republics and when French diplomats undertook to negotiate conventions with them.

Aside from this negative consequence, the most important result of Bresson's journey was a revival of the old project to found Bourbon monarchies in South America. Though in distracted Colombia the scheme now had influential advocates, in Downing Street there was a significant

---

[37] " Rapport au Ministre," A. A. E., Colombie, 6. On Deffaudis, see Damas, *Mémoires,* II, 50 n.

[38] Polignac to Bresson, November 21, 1829, A. A. E., Colombie, 6; Buchet de Martigny to Polignac, April 2, 1830, *ibid.,* 7.

reaction against it. When he became aware of this proposal Lord Aberdeen, the idealistic English Secretary of Foreign Affairs, emphatically warned Fernández Madrid that
his government would never allow a prince of the dynasty
which was ruling France to cross the Atlantic in order to
be crowned as a monarch in any section of the New
World.[39] Thus at this time England, as well as France, set
a seal of disapproval on the monarchical project which
prominent Colombians had cherished.

Early in December, 1829, the Colombian Council of
Ministers asserted that the adoption of this project had depended upon its approval by Congress.[40] Convinced that
public opinion in Bogotá was opposed to the plan, on December 31 Vergara indited a note to Bresson containing
the artful explanation that Bolívar was not disposed to
support a scheme which contrary to his principles would increase his personal prestige, and that consequently the proposal for a monarchy in Colombia was withdrawn. Besides,
Vergara declared that the new administration which would
soon come into power in his country would reach an understanding with France.[41]

After Bresson's instructions had been penned, certain
issues arose in the Chamber of Deputies which involved the
status of the new American republics. On July 4, 1828, in

[39] Zubieta, *Apuntaciones sobre las primeras misiones diplomáticas
de Colombia,* p. 525. See further Gil Fortoul, *Historia constitucional de Venezuela,* I, 465-67.

[40] Santander, *Archivo,* XVIII, 188.

[41] A. A. E., Colombie, 6. The view of a Peruvian scholar concerning the attitude of Bolívar toward the establishment of monarchies in Spanish America can be found in Belaunde, *Bolívar and
the Political Thought of the Spanish-American Revolution,* pp.
280-91.

a debate concerning proposed reductions in the budget of the Ministry of Foreign Affairs, Jacques Lefebvre expressed regret that a certain item had not been included in its expenditures. " Gentlemen," he inquired, " why do we postpone accrediting diplomatic agents to the new states of the American Continent? Has the time not finally arrived to imitate the example which we should have furnished? " Lefebvre declared that the dilatory policy of the government was diametrically opposed to the sentiments of his fellow-citizens, who had beheld with pleasure the achievement of independence by the Spanish Americans. He informed his colleagues that commercial agents bearing commissions from the commander of a naval station had been spurned by certain Spanish-American governments because their credentials were irregular. " France," he said, " admitted into her ports the ships of the new states and permitted them to display their flags there. This implicitly recognized their independence." He argued that the time had come for the dispatch of regularly accredited missions to Spanish-American countries. He declared that, though he was aware that the initiative in this matter did not belong to the Chamber of Deputies, if the legislature did not receive an assurance that France would soon acknowledge the independence of the new American states he would refuse to approve the budget of the Ministry of Foreign Affairs.

In response La Ferronnays stated that he was not ignorant of the argument in favor of the acknowledgment of Spanish-American independence. Explaining that the Ministry was gathering data concerning the actual condition of the new communities, he declared that urgent invitations to recognize the young American states had been neither neglected nor rejected by the Cabinet, and asked whether the news from Colombia and Mexico was such as to encourage Lefebvre to urge immediate action in regard to those countries. The minister admitted that the question which had been raised was worthy of serious attention but reasoned that it could not be separated from considerations of prudence and security which alone could induce his government to reach a definite decision. The commercial interests of France, as well as the Chamber of Deputies, should take this policy in good part.[42] French policy toward Spanish America was still like a lamp flickering in the wind.

Another indication of the views of French publicists was furnished on January 27, 1829, in the King's address to the chambers. After praising the conduct of the navy in certain difficulties which had arisen between France and Brazil, Charles X turned his attention to Spanish America in these words:

The successive shocks which have disturbed some of the new states of South America have produced uncertainty concerning the political situation of those states and have rendered difficult the regular establishment of our relations with them. Doubtless the time is not distant when I shall be able to give to those relations a stability which will be useful to my subjects; meanwhile I have directed consuls to watch over their interests.[43]

The misleading comment of the *Journal des Débats* on this discourse was to the effect that the existence of the Spanish nations of America had been recognized by France without any restriction.[44] In response to the King, the Chamber of Peers framed an address which declared that the dispatch of consuls to South American countries had given to the commercial interests of Frenchmen an imme-

[42] *Le Moniteur*, July 5, 1828.
[43] *Ibid.*, January 28, 1829.   [44] *Ibid.*

diate protection; this measure properly made known that, at the time when the condition of the new states permitted French relations with them to assume " a character of more complete stability, the government of Your Majesty will not neglect to make use of the opportunity." [45] Both houses commended the prudence which the government had displayed in this phase of its foreign policy.

On June 9, 1829, during a discussion of the budget of the Ministry of Foreign Affairs in the Chamber of Deputies, the status of the Spanish-American states again came up for consideration. Chevalier Dubourg criticized a proposal that France form alliances with those states. Victor de Tracy laid the blame for the anarchy existing among them upon the motherland which would not renounce her lost supremacy. Gautier argued that there was not sufficient justification for the delay in placing French relations with Spanish America upon a regular basis. He believed that, in addition to the dispatch of consular agents, further action was imperative because of the industrial and commercial interests of France. Characterizing as inaccurate statements that French merchants would only suffer losses in Spanish America, he declared: " Commercial exchanges which employ fifty million francs and a navigation which utilizes thirty-six to forty large merchant ships should not be treated with this indifference; and those persons who consider commerce worth something cannot despise a resource of such importance." [46]

The attitude of the French Government toward the new American states was also tested by a fresh inquiry concerning the use of a Spanish-American flag. On July 2,

[45] *Le Moniteur,* February 8, 1829.
[46] *Ibid.,* June 11, 1829.

1829, Martignac, as Minister of the Interior, asked La Ferronnays whether he might properly authorize the display of the Colombian colors on a ship anchored in the river Seine near a Parisian wharf. La Ferronnays replied on the following day that, as the government allowed Colombian merchantmen to unfurl their flags in French ports, if one of those ships was so constructed that it could ascend the Seine, French officials could not prevent it from displaying its flag within the walls of Paris. As in the moot case, however, the question was that of hoisting the Colombian ensign on a vessel already moored to a Parisian quay, and as there was nothing to justify the sudden appearance of that flag in the capital, he believed that it would not be politic to allow this. The Minister of Foreign Affairs maintained that it was contrary to French custom to permit a foreign flag to be displayed in a public place; hence he reasoned that a refusal to grant this request should not injure the commercial intercourse of France with Colombia.[47]

During 1829 the relations of France with Mexico received fresh consideration from the Ministry of Foreign Affairs. Its attitude toward that country is made clear by the instructions of La Ferronnays to Cochelot, who had been appointed consul general in the city of Mexico. After mentioning the historic bonds between France and Spain which restrained his country from hasty action with respect to the Spanish-American states, the minister declared that commercial necessity demanded that France should not be outstripped by other powers. He explained that the bonds of religion and of taste which existed between the French and the Spanish Americans would no longer permit the

[47] A. A. E., Colombie, 4.

Cabinet to neglect encouraging the favorable disposition of the new republics. Besides, it had to protect those subjects whose business enterprises led them into Spanish America. Cochelot was sent a copy of the Declarations of May, 1827, which were the avowed bases of Franco-Mexican intercourse. He was informed that France was anxious to promote a *rapprochement* between Mexico and the Papacy. French policy concerning recognition was cautiously reformulated in these words:

With regard to political relations your mission is extremely simple. You are to encourage the Mexican Government to maintain a favorable attitude toward us, to signify to it the interest which we take in the prosperity of Mexico and the desire which we have of extending and completing our relations with her, but you should, Sir, refrain from giving to that government the hope of immediate recognition by France. It is doubtless to be desired that this acknowledgment take place, but it is necessary that such an important measure still be examined with care and that it be justified by an improvement in the political condition of that country. The Mexican Government has announced its intention to establish a legation in France; but we have been forced to observe how premature this decision would be and how it would involve embarrassment and unpleasantness for that legation, for the Spanish embassy, and even for the government of the King. This project can be taken up again later; it ought to be concerted between the two governments, and we have reason to believe that at present it has been relinquished in Mexico.[48]

In spite of opposition by Mexican politicians, their government finally recognized that the Declarations did not have the force of a convention. Further, it took the view that they did not need to be ratified by Congress. " The

[48] January 15, 1829, A. A. E., Mexique, 4.

Mexican Government carried them out to the extent of its ability," read an official French memorandum, "but as it did not have the power to modify the customs tariff, the result was that in spite of the arrangements made by Señor Camacho the products of France were not treated as those of the most-favored-nation." This memorandum added that the agreement had been faithfully executed by France.[49]

About two months after the instructions had been drawn for Cochelot, and soon after the war between Argentina and Brazil over the Banda Oriental had ended in the defeat of the latter, the French Minister of Foreign Affairs sent instructions to Mendeville, who had been made consul general at Buenos Aires. La Ferronnays expressed the hope that tranquillity would soon reign in Argentina so that foreign commerce might flourish there. Apprehensive, however, that Uruguay would find the task of maintaining her independence very difficult, he urged the consul general to send to Paris all the information that he could gather about the countries in the Platean basin. Further, Mendeville was instructed with regard to certain principles of conduct which he was to observe in respect to internal affairs:

I consider it useless, Sir, to recommend you not to display any predilection for the men who have influence upon parties; you know too well the country where you reside not to direct all your movements with due circumspection. You can repeat that the King's Government wishes to refrain in all circumstances from meddling in the internal affairs of the provinces of La Plata and that it desires only the establishment of a firm and durable government which will inspire confidence in trade—a government which will reassure investors with regard to loans as well as with respect to those acts of violence and denials of justice to

[49] "Questions," March, 1829, *ibid*.

which troublesome conditions and internal dissensions would expose them. . . . [50]

Shortly afterward, because of Colombia's proposals, Baron Deffaudis made a careful analysis of French relations with the Spanish-American states. The Baron took the view that his government would scarcely find it convenient unqualifiedly to reject Vergara's monarchical propositions. He raised the question whether France exercised due influence in Spanish America. Affirming that a change in policy would enable France to strengthen her prestige in the New World in various ways, Deffaudis maintained that a single act would produce good effects:

That act would be to acknowledge the independence of Colombia, or, to speak more exactly, to establish with the government of that country diplomatic relations which would assume that recognition had been granted. . . . For a long period we have responded to the appeals of the Americans by saying that the proprieties would not permit us to recognize them while we held Spain under military occupation. They seemed to feel the force of this objection. When we withdrew our soldiers from the Peninsula, we expressed the intention of soon making our relations with Spanish American regular. Recognition was decided upon in principle: the only thing left to do was to determine the time, which in no sense would be very distant, but which would be closer at hand for those new states that presented more proof than others of order and stability. . . . In vain our consuls and commissioners try by the doctrines of a sane political economy to convince the Colombians of the advantages of reciprocity. They respond smilingly that all they desire is to consecrate those doctrines in a formal treaty.

Deffaudis emphasized the advantages which would flow from the adoption of a new policy by the Cabinet. The in-

[50] Villanueva, *Historia de la república argentina,* II, 36-37.

fluence of France in Spanish America would be much increased. Her consuls, placed in false positions there, would be superseded by real diplomats. Well-selected agents would give France a great superiority over both England and the United States. French diplomats would have a natural sympathy for the Spanish-American people. Treaties between France and the new republic would promote commercial intercourse.

This diplomat reasoned that by such a policy his country would exert a good influence upon Spanish America and would check the tendency there toward disintegration. Though wounding Spain for an instant, France would hasten the day when her ally would acquiesce in the work of necessity " at a time when her former colonies might still attach a certain price to such consent." Colombia had declared that she might be able to purchase this consent by granting commercial favors, " and perhaps this would not be her last word." By virtue of the position which France could assume, she would be able to promote such transactions and thus to acquire a claim to the favor of both parties. Deffaudis suggested, however, that Spain be given a hint of the intentions of the French Cabinet in order to preclude a protest on her part. He concluded: " Without pledging ourselves to anything, we should manage in the future to have greater liberty of action, and this would perhaps render Spain more conciliatory by making her fear to see France, and, after her, all of Europe, soon follow the example set by the United States and Great Britain." [51]

Meanwhile controversies which had arisen between French agents and Spanish-American governments brought

[51] " Rapport au Ministre," February 21, 1830, A. A. E., Colombie, 7.

sharply to the attention of the Ministry of Foreign Affairs the problem of the political future of the new states. An acrimonious dispute had broken out between Consul General Mendeville and the government seated at Buenos Aires concerning the enforced military service which it was demanding from foreigners domiciled in Argentina. That government took the view not only that French subjects who were enjoying the protection of its laws must submit to the obligations imposed by those laws but also that the consul general did not have the right to make diplomatic protests against such a policy. In April, 1829, the discomfited consul general, who argued that in the absence of a French chargé he had the right to present protests on behalf of his compatriots, demanded his passports and withdrew to Montevideo.[52]

From his refuge in the Uruguayan capital, the irate consul general sent a dispatch to Paris in which he assumed that this rupture might make it necessary for France to resort to coercion. To counterbalance the expense of an armed expedition against Argentina, Mendeville suggested that his government demand as an indemnity a concession in that country useful to the French navy and to French commerce. He reasoned that the outrage to France had been so public and so flagrant that no nation could deny her the right to demand reparation. Stating that England possessed harbors in many parts of the world which afforded advantages to her commerce and her navy, he pointed out that as yet she did not possess any ports in the southern part of South America. Mendeville argued as follows for France's possession of strategic posts in that region:

[52] *British and Foreign State Papers*, XVI, 917-28.

We are almost completely deprived of the maritime and commercial advantages furnished by these points of contact. It seems to me that a more favorable occasion to secure such a coign of vantage in this region will never be presented to France. Nothing would be easier than to take possession of the province of Patagonia, which is a dependency of the province of Buenos Aires, and which is separated from it by one hundred leagues of desert occupied by savage Indians.[53]

This attractive proposal was elaborated by Viscount Venancourt, commander of the French naval forces in La Plata River, in a letter from Montevideo to the Minister of Marine dated July 4, 1829. Venancourt sketched a project for the planting of a French colony in Patagonia. He urged that an expedition of four thousand soldiers be sent against that province, that French garrisons be stationed there, and that grants of land be made to entrepreneurs of colonization.[54]

As a result of the controversy between Mendeville and the Argentine Government, on the night of May 21 Venancourt seized some war vessels belonging to that government. However, conferences were held between him and Secretary of Foreign Relations Gelly at which an adjustment was reached regarding the seizure.[55] In reply to a protest by Juan Larrea, who had been made Argentine consul general at Paris, concerning the actions of Mendeville and Venancourt, Prince Polignac stated that Charles X fully approved their proceedings, which had terminated a condition of affairs that might have gravely compromised Argentina.

[53] May 20, 1829, A. A. E., Buenos Ayres, 4.

[54] A. N., Marine, B B⁴, 519.

[55] *Correspondencia entre el gobierno de Buenos Aires y el Sr. Visconde de Venancourt,* pp. 17-18.

Polignac further maintained that the right of French consuls to make representations on behalf of their compatriots had never before been contested and was absolutely indispensable in a country where France had no diplomatic representative. The minister reasoned that military service was a peculiar obligation which could be required by a government only from its own citizens. He declared that so completely was this view accepted in France that a foreigner could not be drafted into the ranks of the national guard.[56]

Shortly after the war cloud which had been hanging over La Plata was dispersed, the idea of planting Bourbon monarchies in America was revived by agents of France. On November 11, 1829, La Forest, the French consul general at Santiago, told his government that because of the anarchy which prevailed in Chile the people sighed for the calm which followed a tempest and that they did not confine themselves to vague aspirations. " They offer the aid and influence of their respective parties," he continued, " in order to receive as the liberator of Chile a prince who would be sent to them from Europe. No matter under what title he may present himself, they will all submit to his domination provided that he be the bearer of an act which will consecrate the recognition by Europe of Chile as an independent state." He added that, at a time when it seemed that Spain might reconquer Mexico, Chile under the rule of a European prince would offer the most certain means of pacifying all of South America and of establishing there strong, monarchical, and constitutional governments. The consul even ventured the opinion that, if a prince belonging to the

[56] October 9, 1829, A. A. E., Buenos Ayres, 4. On the dispute concerning the military service required from French citizens in Argentina, see *British and Foreign State Papers,* XVI, 928-37.

Spanish ruling dynasty or to the house of Orleans, bringing with him an acknowledgment of Chilean independence by France and accompanied by an escort of three or four thousand men, should arrive in Chile, he would be received as a "tutelary god and that by the planting of European colonies in the southern part of the country, his power would be as firmly assured as that of other princes of Europe." [57]

Again, during the last months of the Polignac Cabinet Viscount Saint Priest, who had become the French ambassador at Madrid, undertook to revive the project of creating a European appanage in the New World. On February 22, 1830, in a letter to Minister Polignac, the Viscount declared that the best solution for the problems of the Spanish Americans was to send an infante with any sort of a title to rule over them. Saint Priest reported that he had sounded the English ambassador at Madrid in regard to this project and found that he did not favor it. Yet the French ambassador at Madrid proposed to Polignac that Prince Carlos be sent to Mexico. Saint Priest reasoned that "a prince of her house at the head of the vast empire which by its position commands in a fashion the destinies of southern America" would be an advantage to Spain.

Polignac's comments pencilled on Saint Priest's letter record his views concerning this proposition. On the page outlining the general project, Polignac recorded a doubt whether the proposal for the enthronement of an infante in Mexico would be received with favor in that country: "I do not say that this plan would remain forever impossible of execution. Still, considerable time would have to be

[57] A. A. E., Chili, 3.

taken to prepare for it, and it would need propitious circumstances that one cannot anticipate at the present moment." In the margin of the passage suggesting the dispatch of Prince Carlos to Mexico, the minister wrote the discerning comment: "All this would assuredly be very wise for Spain—but for Mexico!" [58]

The prospect for the erection of European principalities in the New World was soon made more alluring, however, by a proposal emanating from southern Spanish America. On March 8, 1830, Ambassador Ofalia informed the Court of Madrid that Bernardino Rivadavia, who had served for a short time as president of the Argentine Republic, had now returned to Paris at the head of a mission for the purpose of soliciting the French Government to place a European prince upon a throne at Buenos Aires. [59] In a dispatch to Saint Priest on March 30, Polignac showed that he was attracted by this proposal. After mentioning the possibility of establishing European princes in Argentina, Colombia, Central America, and Mexico, Polignac asserted that conditions in Spanish America had changed since the revolution had terminated. He argued that the uprising against Spanish rule in America had been inspired more by passion than by proper motives and that considerate conduct by Spain might eventually overcome the sentiments of hatred which had been engendered by the revolutionary struggles. Then he added:

[58] A. A. E., Espagne, 752. An extract from St. Priest's dispatch is printed in Villanueva, "La diplomatie française dans l'Amérique latine," *Bull. bib. am.*, October, 1916, pp. 12-14. See further Webster, *Britain and the Independence of Latin America*, II, 475.

[59] Ofalia to González Salmón, March 8, 1830, A. H. N., Estado, 6892.

It seems possible that circumstances may arise in which the founding of an American monarchy in favor of a younger branch of the Spanish dynasty would become practicable if, after having been adroitly prepared through liaisons with influential men of America, it was frankly declared to be the condition of independence and supported by a suitable display of military force. Certainly this result, if it is still possible with the consent of His Catholic Majesty, would fulfill all the desires of our government; for it would reconcile the real interests of two hemispheres with the sacred rights of legitimacy and with the maintenance of those monarchical principles which are so essential to the repose of the world. France would seize with much alacrity an opportunity to promote this project.

Saint Priest was to unfold this scheme cautiously and hypothetically to Manuel González Salmón, who had become the Spanish Secretary of State. The French minister averred that, having desired to make evasive responses to proposals from Spanish America, his government had not undertaken any negotiations upon this grave matter, and that it had no desire at that time to adopt any other policy. In conclusion Polignac hinted that, even if Spain should make no reply to these overtures, possibly she might modify her colonial policy, and thus France would be enabled to act more freely toward the Spanish-American states.[60] This project, which apparently aimed at the enthronement of a Spanish prince in Mexico or South America as an independent sovereign, was soon cast into the shade, however, by startling events in Paris.

During the last years of the reign of Charles X public opinion in France showed a marked trend in favor of the

---

[60] A. A. E., Espagne, 752. An English translation of this dispatch is found in Villanueva, "French Diplomacy in Latin America," *Inter-America,* I, 164-66.

acknowledgment of the independence of the new American states. Commercial agents of France in Spanish-American countries were now accorded the regular title of consul or consul general, a step which in the opinion of some Frenchmen conceded to those nations what might be styled recognition. The withdrawal by France in 1828 of her soldiers from the Iberian Peninsula freed the minds of French ministers from the fear of linking their attitude toward Spain with their policy toward her former colonies.

The mission on which La Ferronnays dispatched Bresson seemed like the last step preparatory to the recognition of the nations of Spanish America by France. In fact, Bresson was instructed to assure the chiefs of the new governments in Mexico, Colombia, Peru, and Bolivia that France would soon acknowledge those nations as independent. Upon becoming Minister of Foreign Affairs, however, Polignac strongly disapproved of Bresson's mission. Because of the disorder prevailing in certain Spanish-American countries, this minister felt that only Colombia had sufficient stability to warrant the acknowledgment by France of her independence. Thus it was that Bresson caught only a glimpse of the slanting beacon of the Southern Cross.

Contemporaneously, however, debates in the Chamber of Deputies demonstrated that there was a strong feeling there in favor of a recognition policy. In his speech to the legislature early in 1829, Charles X declared that the time was not far distant when France would be able to give more stability to her relations with the Spanish states in America. Furthermore, French commercial interests continued to exert a steady pressure in favor of Spanish-American recognition. Though Deffaudis reasoned that France should feel free to establish diplomatic relations with the new states, yet Polignac's tentative solution of this thorny problem was a fresh consideration of the scheme to plant Bourbon monarchies in the New World—a project which by this time had evidently become impracticable. It seems, however, that in the spring of 1830 even the ultra-conservative Polignac was of the opinion that France should alter her policy toward the Spanish-American nations.

Chapter XV

LOUIS PHILIPPE AND RECOGNITION

The reign of Charles X culminated in a conflict between parliamentary authority and the royal prerogative. In his address at the opening of the legislature in 1830, the King declared that the Charter of 1814 had placed public liberty under the protection of his royal rights and that, if political motives raised obstacles to his rule, he would overcome them by his determination to maintain the public peace. On May 15 he promulgated an ordinance which dissolved the Chamber of Deputies. After the election returned members of the Opposition to that chamber, the King revived the censorship of the press, dissolved the newly elected chambers of deputies in the departments, and altered the régime of the electoral colleges. These autocratic ordinances provoked so much discontent that in certain sections of Paris students and laborers constructed barricades over which they hoisted the tricolor. By July 29 the insurgents had become masters of the capital city.

After an attempt to save his crown by the choice of a new cabinet, Charles X was forced to abdicate and soon went into exile. Power now passed from the elder branch of the Bourbon dynasty to the younger branch. On August 7 the Chamber of Deputies announced that it had invited to the throne the democratic son of Philippe Egalité, Louis Philippe d'Orléans. Louis Philippe acknowledged the parliamentary character of his title under the revised charter. He became known as the Bourgeois King. The new King organized his first Cabinet by an ordinance of August 11, 1830. Count Molé, who had served Louis XVIII as the head of the Naval Department, became Minister of Foreign Affairs. General Sébastiani was appointed Minister of Marine, a post which he occupied until he succeeded Molé.

The accession of Louis Philippe to the throne of France was not well received by European powers. Metternich likened the July Revolution to the bursting of a dyke. Declaring that he would never relinquish the doctrine of legitimacy, Czar Nicholas intimated that he might declare war on France; he later informed the French chargé at St. Petersburg that in no case would he recognize the Orleanist King until he had conferred with his allies. King Louis Philippe soon sent Prince Talleyrand to London as ambassador in order that he might establish relations with England, that had cautiously made known that she might recognize the monarchy which had been born of revolution.

By the July Revolution France was released from fetters of diplomatic precedent. Obviously the Czar's attitude would no longer necessarily affect her foreign relations. Nor would the Bourbon Family Compact henceforth determine her policy toward the Spanish monarchy. Again, the deposition of Charles X encouraged French partisans of Spanish-American independence. Furthermore, the government of the Bourgeois King was itself a suppliant for recognition by the powers of Europe. As a French diplomat later inquired, how could a government which had been created by the insurrectionary principle delay a day or even an hour in acknowledging the independence of American governments which had been brought into existence by virtue of that principle. If Louis Philippe's government followed Restoration cabinets in refusing to recognize the

Spanish-American states, by what right could it claim admission to a place among other nations? [1]

Two memoranda composed while the chancelleries of Europe were considering what policy to pursue toward the Orleanist monarchy show that certain French publicists were contemplating the immediate acknowledgment of Spanish-American independence. A memorandum dated August, 1830, presented to the Ministry of Foreign Affairs by Varaigne, who was later attached to the French legation at Washington, weighed the reasons which should impel France to acknowledge the independence of the South American republics. Varaigne rightly declared that the battle of Ayacucho had shattered Spain's dream of restoring her colonial empire in the New World. Only the United States, he observed, had as yet acknowledged the independence of Spanish America: England had recognized only Mexico, Colombia, and Argentina. Stating that the motives which had deterred previous French cabinets from taking decisive action no longer existed, he maintained that a step worthy of the new régime would be irrevocably to recognize that the new American states were independent.

Varaigne declared that the South Americans did not love the English, that they feared and despised the North Americans, but that they cherished a keen sympathy for the French and desired to cultivate good relations with them. He believed that those relations would become permanent if, to the admiration that they would naturally feel for the July Revolution, they could link a sentiment of gratitude for the important benefits which France could confer upon them

---

[1] Brossard, *Considérations historiques et politiques sur les républiques de la Plata dans leurs rapports avec la France et l'Angleterre*, p. 145.

and which her interests solicited as much as theirs. Admiting that the South American countries were in a deplorable condition, he argued that their independence was beyond cavil and urged that France acknowledge their independent status at once:

By recognizing them we shall allay the evils of those countries or at least the chief causes of those evils. We shall render them productive for the entire world and chiefly for ourselves; a brilliant future will be opened to our foreign commerce, while the development of all branches of our industry will be more and more assured. Time presses, for another month of disorder may bring to pass innumerable consequences in the midst of the distress existing in the New World. . . . [2]

Baron Deffaudis made a fresh analysis of the policy of France toward Spanish America which began with these words: " All good spirits have for a long time been in accord concerning the interest that France has in the recognition of the new states of America." Then he mentioned the bonds of affinity which, in his opinion, caused the Spanish Americans to prefer the French to all other people. He declared that, despite heavy imposts due to the absence of commercial treaties, the total exchange between France and Spanish-American countries amounted to fifty million francs annually. Deffaudis asserted that the relations between France and Spain—especially the occupation of Spain by French troops—had for a time placed a moral restraint upon the recognition of the new American states by France but that conditions had now changed:

Today the occasion for a hesitation so injurious and so ill-founded seems to have entirely passed away. Our princi-

[2] " Mémoire de M. Varaigne, Août, 1830," A. A. E., Mémoires et Documents, Amérique, 36.

ples of government are no longer in any way opposed to the
recognition of the new states of America; and the relations
which we should henceforth maintain with Spain ought no
longer to present an obstacle to that policy. Instead of resting, as has too often been noticed before today, upon sacrifices made on our part without any compensation, the
amicable intercourse which would naturally exist between
two governments united by family bonds and by common
national interests will be regulated only by the equitable
combination of their interests. Therefore I believe that we
ought to propose the immediate recognition of the new
states of America in principle.

With regard to the actual method to be followed, it is
evident that we cannot and should not proceed in any other
manner than by treaties which would ensure us in the different countries not merely certain privileges but the certainty that no other nation will under any consideration be
favored by them to our detriment. It is evident that in
order to frame such treaties we must enter into communication with governments for purposes of negotiation. There
do not at present exist in the former Spanish Indies any
stable governments which are uncontested except those of
Mexico, Peru, Bolivia, and La Plata. . . .

In this condition of affairs, it seems convenient to limit
ourselves to writing to the agents of the King in America,
as well as to the agents of the new American governments
who are actually in France, to the effect that we are disposed to recognize those governments and to negotiate with
them. We should at the same time invite them to send to
Paris agents instructed to give us all the necessary explanations and furnished with full power to negotiate.

Once this decision is adopted and carried out, we shall
inform the motherland. It should be easy for us, after the
many phases through which this affair has passed during the
negotiations between France and Spain, to demonstrate to
her that she cannot find in our present conduct any cause
for surprise or complaint. Besides, we should be able to
offer her as a new proof of our old friendship our good
offices with the American governments, in the event that,
listening at last to the voice of reason and to that of self-

interest, she might herself wish to enter into arrangements with them.[3]

Upon reading this report, Minister of Foreign Affairs Molé promptly decided to make it the basis of a recommendation to the King. In some particulars Molé accepted not only Deffaudis' reasoning but also his very words. Certain passages concerning the Spanish-American states were incorporated by him in full:

The identity of our religion, the affinity of our language, and the ease of our manners have long won for us in the esteem of the different states an affectionate preference over all other people. This preference is primarily an undeniable evidence of the political influence which we are destined to exert in Spanish America and it is no less favorable to the development of commercial relations of prime importance.

The minister affirmed that, while the Bourbon Government of France had not closed its eyes to such facts, it had naturally been averse to forming relations with revolutionary colonies. It had been restrained by its liaison with the Spanish monarchy and by the fact that the presence of French troops in Spain constituted a moral impediment to the acknowledgment of the independence of her colonies by France. Molé accepted Deffaudis' view that the principles of the French Government were no longer opposed to the recognition of the Spanish-American nations.

Still, he foresaw certain practical difficulties. In a passage concerning the need of selecting governments with which to treat, the minister adapted phrases which Deffaudis had stricken out of his report. Molé declared that Colombia had broken into three fragments, dominated by Mosquera, Flores, and Páez. Further, he maintained that it was impos-

[3] " 24 Août, 1830, Rapport," A. A. E., Colombie, 7.

sible to determine which of the contending parties had been victorious in Chile. He admitted that he was imperfectly acquainted with conditions existing in Central America. But he adopted Deffaudis' view that only Mexico, Peru, Bolivia, and La Plata had erected political systems which had a reasonable degree of stability. Molé concluded:

In this condition of affairs, I shall limit myself to proposing to Your Majesty that I be authorized to write to the agents of new American governments who are in France (those of Mexico, Colombia, and La Plata), as well as to the French agents in America (the consuls general in Mexico, Peru, Chile, La Plata, and Colombia), that we are ready to recognize those governments and to treat with them. Besides, I should arrange to have the same notice reach Guatemala and Bolivia through our naval station at Habana and the one near Chile. At the same time, all those governments should be invited to send to Paris agents who will be furnished with the necessary full powers and instructed to negotiate with us.

The original of this plenary instrument, which reposes in the archives of the Ministry of Foreign Affairs at the Quai d'Orsay, bears the endorsement, " Approuvé Louis Philippe, Paris, le   Août, 1830." [4] Thus, at a critical juncture, when it had not been recognized by Austria, Russia, and Spain, the government of the Bourgeois King decided that the independence of the new nations which had arisen on the ruins of the Spanish colonial system should be acknowledged in principle.

Recognition did not spring full-panoplied from the brain of Molé. French statesmen had often considered the admis-

[4] A. A. E., Mémoires et Documents, Amérique, 36. Molé's report is printed in Villanueva, " La diplomatie française dans l'Amérique latin," *Bull. bib. am.*, October, 1815, pp. 18-21, from a copy in A. A. E., Espagne, 753.

sion of the insurrectionary Spanish-American communities into the society of nations. Richelieu had seriously contemplated that momentous step on the eve of the Congress of Aix-la-Chapelle. In 1822 Villèle had proposed that the Continental allies acknowledge the independence of Latin-American nations. French diplomats had dreamed of Bourbon monarchs ruling over Spanish-American states that were attached only by a tenuous bond to the motherland. Both Chateaubriand and Villèle had beheld this alluring vision, but they had been reluctant to promote its realization. They had been restrained not only by the disinclination of Ferdinand VII to accept that solution of the vexatious colonial problem but also by the family ties which linked France to Spain. La Ferronnays had based Bresson's ambitious mission to Spanish-American nations upon the premise that France was on the point of according them recognition. The purpose of that comprehensive survey was thwarted, however, not only by fortuitous circumstances which occurred in Colombia but also by the ultra-conservative policy of Portalis and Polignac.

Just as circumstances were different from those that existed when France acknowledged the independence of the United States, so the justification for Molé's step differed from the doctrine which was enunciated by France during the American Revolution. In March, 1778, the French Government maintained that the Thirteen Colonies were really in the full enjoyment of the independence proclaimed on July 4, 1776, and that this political situation justified it in regarding their independence as established.[5] In contrast

[5] Flassan, *Histoire générale et raisonnée de la diplomatie française,* VII, 167. See further Williams, *La doctrine de la reconnaissance en droit international et ses développements récents,* pp. 20-22.

with that situation, though commercial and political motives were not without influence, yet the important step taken by the Bourgeois King was due mainly to a radical change in the character of the French Government. The actual trigger that exploded the policy of neutrality which France had pursued toward the Spanish-American insurgents was the July Revolution.

French procedure in 1830 with respect to the independence of Spanish America was in one respect more analogous to the policy followed by the United States toward that part of the world than to the policy adopted by England. The French Government decided outright upon an acknowledgment of independence in principle, which was the policy pursued by the United States. Molé announced that recognition was accorded to certain new states and besides that this step was to be followed by the negotiation with them of treaties of amity, navigation, and commerce. In both England and France the decision in favor of a policy of recognition was made by the executive authority; in the United States the decision was reached by the joint action of the President and Congress. Despite the policy tentatively formulated by La Ferronnays, France, unlike her rival across the Channel, did not couple inextricably her recognition of the Spanish nations of the New World with the negotiation of satisfactory commercial treaties with them. The tantalizing delay of France in the adoption of a recognition policy, however, evidently dampened the ardor of certain Spanish-American statesmen for intimate relations with that country.

Though certain difficulties inherent in treaty negotiations with the new nations had been dimly foreseen by French statesmen, it does not appear likely that they anticipated the variety of delicate and complex problems which were destined to arise from time to time in regard to their inter-course with Spanish-American countries—problems which ran almost the entire gamut of international relations. French diplomats were soon troubled by questions concern-ing commercial treaties with those countries. Among other problems that arose was not only the manner in which the *amour propre* of inexperienced Spanish-American diplomats was to be appeased but also the crucial issue respecting the attitude which should be assumed with regard to intriguing suggestions or downright proposals that France establish a protectorate over certain nations of the Western World. More or less vaguely attached to such proposals were occa-sional suggestions that recalled the protean project of creat-ing Bourbon monarchies in the Spanish Indies.

The prospect that the accession of Louis Philippe would precipitate a change in French foreign policy did not escape Ofalia, who in the midsummer of 1829 had been notified that his government did not wish to consider the Family Compact as being any longer in force.[6] On the very day that Deffaudis made his analysis of the relations between France and Spanish America, the observant ambassador warned his court that an agent was expected soon to arrive in Paris to solicit the recognition of Mexico by the new government. Ofalia included in his dispatch a short clip-ping from the *Messager des Chambres* of August 24, which asserted that at the end of that month the independence of the Spanish-American nations would be acknowledged by France. " I do not know the basis for this statement," com-mented Ofalia, " but, in the present condition of France, I suspect that it is correct, and further that there is no way to

[6] Becker, *Relaciones comerciales entre España y Francia,* pp. 37-38.

prevent such a step. I shall speak to the Russian ambassador, who is accustomed to conversing confidentially with the Foreign Minister, to find out whether there is any way to prevent or at least to delay action." [7]

After the Russian ambassador at Paris, who profoundly regretted the *débâcle* of the Bourbon monarchy, had an interview with Molé, Ofalia warned his court that it should not entertain any illusions with respect to the acknowledgment of Spanish-American independence by France. Ofalia reported that, although the King and his ministers wished to avoid that step, they would not be able to restrain the Liberal party which favored immediate recognition. Notwithstanding this fact Pozzo di Borgo had assured him that the Orleanist Government would delay action for some time because there were no authorized envoys of Spanish-American states in Paris with whom an understanding could be reached.[8]

In the Chamber of Deputies, on September 4, 1830, Marquis de Lafayette interpellated the Minister of Foreign Affairs concerning the recognition of the republics of Spanish America, a measure which the Marquis declared to be very important to French commerce. The minister responded in terms similar to those which he had used in the interview with Pozzo di Borgo. Molé took occasion to announce that his government was ready to acknowledge the existence of the Spanish nations of the New World and to treat regarding commercial matters with the properly authorized agents whom they might send to Paris.[9] In a later

[7] Ofalia to González Salmón, August 24, 1830, A. H. N., Estado, 6893.
[8] *Idem* to *idem*, August 28, 1830, *ibid.*
[9] *Le Moniteur*, September 5, 1830.

commentary upon French foreign policy, Deffaudis explained that in 1830 there were in the French legislature ardent and influential friends of Spanish America whose support was needed by the new government—friends who maintained that political principles would allow neither a postponement of the acknowledgment of Spanish-American independence nor the formulation of any conditions prerequisite to recognition.[10] Thus it is clear that the recognition of the Spanish-American nations by the Bourgeois King was a politic measure.

Several days after the announcement concerning foreign policy was made in the Chamber of Deputies, Ofalia had a confidential interview with Molé in which a significant exchange of views took place. The Spanish ambassador stated that the future relations between his country and France would depend upon international law, friendship, harmony, and the neighborliness which had long prevailed between them. Molé assented to Ofalia's view that the Family Compact, which had so often exercised a potent influence upon the policies of the Bourbon monarchies, was no longer in force.[11]

[10] Deffaudis, *Questions diplomatiques et particulièrement des travaux et de l'organization du ministère des affaires étrangères*, p. 77.

[11] An extract from Ofalia to González Salmón, September 14, 1830, concerning the ambassador's interview with Molé reads as follows: " Que la España conforme en su sentimtos. con toda la Europa estaba muy distante de mesclarse ni intervenir en los negocias interiores de francia, y no exigen otra cosa qe. una justa reciprocidad y la estricta observancia no ya de pacto de fama. y estipulaciones antiguas é qe. S. E. acaso podría conceptuan caducados (me interrumpio pa. decirme qe así lo creia) po. si las del dro. de gentes y las de amistad, buen harmonía y vecinidad qe. spre. esteban vigentes." A. H. N., Estado, 6894.

Indeed the impending recognition of Spanish-American independence by France may have influenced the Court of Madrid to delay in accrediting Ofalia as ambassador to the King of France.[12] Evidently it did not accept as the verdict of an impartial observer Molé's dictum that the time had arrived for the mother country to retire from a hopeless contest.

News of the discussion of recognition in the Chamber of Deputies possibly occasioned the publication in the *Gaceta de Madrid* of an article which bitterly deplored the fate that had befallen the Indies. This lamentation over the lost dominions indicates that the faint hope entertained by Spaniards that France might further delay the recognition of the former colonies was now relinquished. The article declared that neither " the revolutionary, nor the anarchist, nor the philosopher, nor the statesman " could have imagined that the rebellion which started in 1810 would by 1830 have accomplished " no other result than the destruction of those countries where it began." This swan song then bewailed the fact that Spanish America, " once rich, populous, flourishing, and coveted by all the nations," was now impoverished, depopulated, and devastated,—a domain " causing sorrow to certain persons, provoking the contempt of others, and offering booty to those who, preaching in favor of its separation from the mother country, have no other object than to despoil her by exhausting all her riches." [13]

[12] It appears that letters of September, 1830, accrediting Ofalia to the government of Louis Philippe, were not presented until near the end of October. Guizot, *Mémoires pour servir à l'histoire de mon temps*, II, 95 n.

[13] September 14, 1830. Upon printing reports of revolutionary disturbances in Colombia and Mexico, on May 5, 1831, the *Gaceta*

During the bustling days which followed the accession of the Bourgeois King, the important news concerning the Spanish-American republics which slowly filtered into the columns of French journals occasioned little comment. Parisian newspapers were largely occupied with congratulatory addresses to the King, with royal ordinances reforming the public administration, and with lists of appointees who displaced the henchmen of Charles X. Such comment on the recognition of Spanish-American independence by France as was published in Paris was mainly concerned with the influence of the new policy upon French commerce. Journalists occasionally linked that policy with the attitude that France had assumed toward the Belgian Revolution, which had evoked from her the doctrine of non-intervention in the affairs of other states.

On October 15, 1830, the *Constitutionnel* stated that the King's decision to acknowledge in principle the independence of the new states and to negotiate commercial treaties with them had been announced by the Minister of Foreign Affairs to the consuls general in France from Mexico, Colombia, Chile, and Argentina. It also declared that similar announcements had been forwarded to Peru, Uruguay, Bolivia, and Central America either by French consuls or by officers of the royal navy. Several months later, in an editorial concerning the recognition by France of the revolutionary government in Belgium, this journal explained that that step was taken in accordance with the same principle of *de facto* recognition which had been operative in regard to Spanish America:

de Madrid made this comment: " Que lección presenta la América Española á los liberales de Europa que han elevado á aquellos paises sur filantrópicas ideas!"

To us Mexico, Colombia, Bolivia, and La Plata seemed to possess, to an extent which would ensure the stability of our commercial transactions, the conditions of guarantee necessary to our treating with them in security. Without disturbing ourselves because of the diversity of political forms through which they might have to pass, without occupying ourselves with the quarrels between province and province or with their discussions with the motherland, we declared that we would negotiate with them as with any other nation which was morally organized.[14]

When news reached Paris that commercial treaties were being negotiated by France with Haiti and Mexico, the *Constitutionnel* made favorable comment: " We have at last forsaken the system of legitimacy which subjected the colonies to the motherlands. . . . " This journal severely criticized the policy which France had followed since 1823 toward the Spanish-American republics: the entrusting of missions to agents without a definite character, resulting in the necessity of protecting French commerce by the dispatch of cruisers to Spanish-American waters. Though the *Constitutionnel* professed ignorance of the proposed treaty, it beheld in the Franco-Mexican negotiations the consecration of a principle which was pregnant with useful and honorable consequences: " In spite of the pretensions of the Spanish Government, France has acknowledged the independence of the American republics. . . . Her policy is more advanced in the New World than in Europe." [15]

It would seem that the recognition policy of Louis Philippe was not altogether without influence upon the Court of Madrid. From San Ildefonso on August 15, 1831, Ambassador Billing wrote to the Minister of Foreign Affairs that Spain had sent an agent to London

[14] August 8, 1831.   [15] April 3, 1831.

and Paris, to initiate negotiations for a reconciliation with her former colonists. Billing expressed the opinion that the ministers of Ferdinand VII were at last ready to favor the scheme of establishing appanages in Spanish America.[16] But despite the example set by their former ally, not until after the death of Ferdinand VII did Castilian statesmen reluctantly undertake to acknowledge the independence of their former colonies on the American Continent.

With respect to relations with France, an agent of a Spanish-American state had meanwhile taken advantage of the opportune moment. On August 26, 1830, Leandro Palacios addressed a note to Molé stating that Colombia had furnished him with full powers to treat with France concerning political and commercial relations between the two countries. The minister replied to him on September 30 that France, " recognizing in principle the independence of Colombia," was " ready to conclude with her a treaty of friendship, commerce, and navigation," based upon the principle of the most exact reciprocity and capable of becoming a pledge of both intimate and durable relations. Molé was asked to interest the Colombian Government in sending to Paris a negotiator.[17]   On September 30, Molé

[16] A. A. E., Espagne, 754.

[17] A. A. E., Colombie, 7. A translation of a letter from Molé to the agent of a Spanish-American state in Paris on September 30 was printed in the *Times* on October 11, 1830. Cf. Gil Fortoul, *Historia constitucional de Venezuela*, I, 381. The republic of Colombia, which from 1822 to 1830 included present Ecuador and Venezuela as well as present Colombia has often been called " Great Colombia" to distinguish it from the nation now designated " Colombia," which includes merely the section styled " New Granada " from 1831 to 1861. Molé's note to Palacios announcing recognition embodied the terms of a dispatch sent on that day to consuls of France in Spanish-American states. See *infra*, pp. 543, 545-46, 548, 553.

also addressed a note to Buchet de Martigny to inform him
of the decision of Louis Philippe concerning the new states
of America. The minister enclosed a copy of his letter to
Palacios and directed Buchet de Martigny to notify Colombia's Secretary of Foreign Relations of the important action
taken by France.[18] This important move by France came
at the very time, however, when " Great Colombia," which
since 1822 had included all of northern South America,
was breaking into three fragments.[19]

News of the acknowledgment of Colombia's independence by France did not attract much attention in Bogotá.
Buchet de Martigny wrote to Molé as follows: " Your
Excellency will not be astonished that at a moment when
the very existence of the country is at stake this news does
not create the sensation that it would have produced some
years ago. In itself, as the declaration of a principle, the
measure cannot but have happy effects and should dispose
the minds of Colombians in our favor, but evidently it
should be followed by a treaty of amity and commerce
between the two countries." [20] Juan García del Río, who
had become the Colombian Secretary of Foreign Relations,
sent an appreciative note to Buchet de Martigny in which
he declared that the act of recognition was worthy of King
Louis Philippe and that nothing would be more agreeable
to his government than to send to Paris a minister authorized to negotiate a treaty with France. Yet the conditions in
northern South America were such that García del Río
wished to postpone the negotiation of a Franco-Colombian

[18] A. A. E., Colombie, 7.

[19] An interesting description of the disruption of " Great
Colombia " is given by Le Moyne, *La Nouvelle-Grenade,* II, 69-92.

[20] January 19, 1831, A. A. E., Colombie, 8.

convention to a more propitious time. The Council of Ministers decided, however, that it was not just that pending the negotiation of a treaty Frenchmen in Colombia should be deprived of commercial advantages.[21]

In accordance with this decision, and mentioning the recognition of Colombia's independent status by Louis Philippe, Dictator Urdaneta on March 7, 1831, issued a decree announcing that French subjects in Colombia were to be accorded rights and exemptions equal to those of the most-favored-nations with which his nation had treaties and that this concession should remain operative until a treaty was in force between her and France.[22] Secretary García del Río stated in his report to Congress in 1831 that until recently the relations of Colombia with France had remained in an uncertain condition but that the July Revolution, which gave the French nation a government more suitable to the exigencies of politics and to her own interests, had facilitated the establishment of closer bonds between the two nations.[23]

In 1831 the advancing disruption of Colombia into Venezuela, New Granada, and Ecuador convinced General Sébastiani, who had become the French Minister of Foreign Affairs in November, 1830, that the negotiation of a commercial treaty with Colombia should be postponed. But he felt that the intention of her statesmen to reimpose the differential duty which had been levied upon French products should be abandoned. Pending the arrival of Count Estournel, who had been appointed minister plenipotentiary at Bogotá, Chevalier le Moyne, who had been serving

[21] February 12, 1831 (translation), *ibid.*

[22] (Copy), *ibid.*

[23] Uribe, *Anales diplomáticos y consulares de Colombia,* III, 58.

France there since 1829 as commercial agent,[24] was appointed chargé d'affaires. Sébastiani mentioned to him the appointment of diplomatic agents to Spanish-American nations: "The establishment of those divers missions completes the measure which His Majesty has taken in recognizing the new states of America; it will not be our fault if there are not established between France and those republics relations as amicable and as satisfying as one could desire." [25]

On October 4, 1831, the French chargé was formally presented to Vice-President Caicedo. Le Moyne declared in a speech that by her recent and glorious revolution France had wished to give a striking proof of her love for liberty. He added that the Bourgeois King, who had been called to watch over the destinies of the French, could only applaud the noble efforts made by the people of Colombia to give her institutions based upon laws. There was nothing that France desired more ardently than to see that nation, "which had so valiantly won her independence and her rights, tranquilly enjoying the spirit of peace." [26] In his response Caicedo expressed pleasure that France had appointed a chargé to Bogotá. He declared that his country ardently wished "to establish and to cultivate the most frank and cordial relations of amity and commerce with one of the most illustrious powers of Europe, because from

[24] Le Moyne reached Santa Marta on October 22, 1828. Le Moyne to La Ferronnays, October 24, 1828, A. A. E., Colombie, 4; see further Le Moyne, *La Nouvelle-Grenade,* II, 175.

[25] Sébastiani to Le Moyne, May 24, 1831, A. A. E., Colombie, 8. On the withdrawal of the commercial concession from France by Colombia, see Uribe, *op. cit.,* III, 58.

[26] Le Moyne to Sébastiani, and enclosure, October 6, 1831, A. A. E., Colombie, 8.

those relations great advantages would flow both to France and to Colombia." [27]

Le Moyne was informed by Minister Sébastiani on October 25, 1831, that the establishment of a French legation at Bogotá had been postponed because of the pending political reorganization of northern South America. The chargé was instructed that he was to represent France in that capital whether Colombia should become a federal state or should break into three independent nations. The minister informed Le Moyne that, in limiting to six months the operation of a decree dated March 7 granting privileges to French commerce, New Granada—the central nucleus of Colombia—had made a treaty with that new nation indispensable. Accordingly Sébastiani furnished him with power to negotiate a provisional convention with New Granada which should serve until the definite organization of that state might permit France to regularize the arrangement and to extend it to the entire federal republic, if such a republic should actually be formed.[28]

Just before the decision concerning Spanish-American recognition was reached at Paris the agent of Mexico had made an appeal on behalf of his country. On August 24, 1830, Tomás Murphy had an interview with Molé in which the minister evidently gave him reason to hope for the negotiation of a treaty of amity and commerce with France. Murphy expressed an ardent desire to reassure his government concerning the good disposition shown by Molé; he hoped that in this way the disquietude in Mexico at the delay in establishing stable relations with France might be stilled.[29]

[27] *Idem* to *idem* and enclosure, October 14, 1831, *ibid.*
[28] *Ibid.*
[29] Murphy to Molé, August 24, 1830, A. A. E., Mexique, 5.

In response to a note from Molé announcing the recognition in principle of Mexican independence, Murphy sent an acknowledgment declaring that this decision would be received in Mexico with much satisfaction, as " a measure which equity and the interest of both countries had demanded for a long time." With charming naïveté he added that he did not hesitate to recognize the government of Louis Philippe in the name of his own state. He expressed the conviction that, upon the receipt of the letter announcing Mexico's recognition by France, his government would send to Paris an agent furnished with the powers necessary for the negotiation of a treaty based upon the principle of exact reciprocity and upon arrangements advantageous to both countries. With respect to pending claims of French subjects against Mexico, he gave an assurance that his government would do all that the honor of the republic and principles of justice demanded.[30]

On September 30 Molé sent a dispatch to Consul General Cochelot to inform him of the decision of Louis Philippe to recognize in principle the independence of the Spanish-American states. Molé reasoned that this announcement would serve as a reply to a note of the Mexican Secretary of Foreign Relations, Lucas Alamán, concerning the appointment of an envoy authorized to negotiate with France. Cochelot was, however, to insist upon the binding force of the Declarations. Further, the consul general was to secure indemnities for injuries suffered by French citizens in Mexico. He was also to attend to the claims of various Frenchmen which were presented in the interest of commerce and navigation.[31]

---

[30] October 5, 1830, *ibid.*, 6.   [31] *Ibid.*

Cochelot informed Molé that news of the acknowledgment of Mexico's independence by France was coldly received in the capital city. Though an account of this event had reached that city on November 29, not until December 4 was a brief, colorless mention of Molé's announcement to Murphy published in the official journal, coupled with a statement that France wished Mexico to appoint an agent authorized to negotiate a commercial treaty at Paris. On the next day an extract from Molé's letter was printed in this journal but, in the words of the French consul, " without a single comment, without any sign of gratitude, and without mentioning to the Mexicans the future which so prompt and spontaneous a decision of the French Cabinet had opened." The conclusion which the consul general accordingly reached was that the July Revolution had disappointed calculations and hopes in Mexico, " that is, that the generous and prompt decision of His Majesty in favor of Mexican independence has probably upset the foreign policy of Señor Alamán. I say of Señor Alamán because that policy depends upon him alone." When Cochelot was accorded an interview with General Anastasio Bustamante, who had usurped the presidential authority, he congratulated the opportunistic chief executive on the policy toward Spanish-America which Louis Philippe had adopted. Cochelot declared chauvinistically that recognition by France was the most important event in the history of Mexico, for it would promote the acknowledgment of her independence by other nations of Europe. The consul general reported that Bustamante displayed much gratitude at the decision of the new French Government and asked him to communicate to it his wishes for the prosperity of France.

Certain Mexican deputies inquired on December 6, 1830,

whether Congress wished to celebrate Mexico's recognition by France as it had celebrated the acknowledgment of her independence by England. When called upon to state his views, Alamán read Murphy's letter containing Molé's announcement and expressed the opinion that, if the government wished to celebrate this event, any action should be postponed until a treaty was negotiated with France, without which the recognition of Mexico by that government could not be regarded as certain. The deputies then decided to refer the matter to the ordinary session of the next legislature.[32]

France took a further step in regard to Mexican recognition on August 21, 1831. On that day Count Molé notified Cochelot that the French King, wishing to give Mexico new evidence of his friendly disposition, had appointed Martin as minister plenipotentiary to that country.[33] Pending his arrival, the consul general was also to serve as chargé d'affaires. Upon being told by Cochelot of his new appointment, Secretary Alamán informed him that Acting President Bustamante had received the news with great satisfaction. In the main hall of the national palace, on December 22, the consul general was formally introduced to Bustamante as French chargé. Then Cochelot delivered an address in which he declared that by his recognition policy and by his attitude toward a treaty with Mexico Louis Philippe had given the most striking proof of the

[32] Cochelot to Molé, December 8, 1830, and enclosure entitled "Chambre des Députés du Congres Grl de la République Mexicaine," December 6, 1830, A. A. E., Mexique, 6. On the Mexican attitude toward recognition by France, see further Estrada, *Un siglo de relaciones internacionales de México*, p. 33.

[33] A. A. E., Mexique, 6.

interest which he took in the future of that country. Bustamante responded in terms that displayed his interest in the Bourgeois King.[34]

On September 30, 1830, Molé notified Pérez Mascayano, the Chilean consul general at Paris, of the King's decision that, recognizing in principle the independence of Chile, " the French Government was ready to negotiate with her a treaty of amity, commerce, and navigation." [35] On the same day a notification of the policy adopted toward Spanish America by France was sent by Molé to La Forest, who for a time remained consul general at Santiago.[36] Relations with Chile were complicated, however, by the fact that the French consulate had been sacked by a Chilean mob on December 14, 1829. For this insult the consul promptly demanded reparation and punishment.[37] On May 27, 1830, Polignac notified Consul General la Forest that, although the Chilean Government had taken severe measures against the principal rioters, he must in addition insist upon the payment of a pecuniary indemnity proportionate to the damage caused by the pillage of the consulate. Polignac further stated that a French naval force had been directed to proceed to Valparaiso.[38] Captain Ducamper, commander of the naval station in the southern Pacific, was directed, if necessary, to support the demands of La Forest " by demonstrations of force." [39] In August, 1831, however, the Chilean Government gave a pledge that it would pay France

[34] Cochelot to Molé, December 22, 1831, and enclosure, *ibid.*
[35] A. A. E., Chili, 14.
[36] *Ibid.*
[37] Barros Arana, *Historia jeneral de Chile,* XV, 463-68 and n. 6.
[38] A. A. E., Chili, 4.
[39] D'Haussez to Polignac, May 21, 1830, enclosing a copy of his letter to Ducamper, May 21, 1830, *ibid.*

twenty-five thousand pesos as an indemnity. Upon leaving Chile, La Forest apparently declared that the dispute was entirely settled.[40] This unpleasant incident not only rendered French relations with Chile delicate but later proved to be a source of embarrassment to La Forest in Argentina.

A lucid interpretation of French policy toward Spanish America was contained in a dispatch sent by Minister Molé to La Forest on November 27, 1830. Molé expressed regret at the notion which prevailed in Chile that France was seeking to intervene by force in the internal affairs of the new American states. After reproving the consul general for views which he had recently expressed concerning the necessity for European interference in South America, the minister stated that the principles of the new French Government were absolutely opposed to " any intervention in the internal affairs of other nations." The decision of Louis Philippe to acknowledge the independence of all the new republics of America should put an end to any doubt concerning French policy: " We earnestly desire that the recognition accorded by us to those new governments should give them a moral force sufficient to repress anarchy and to found a constitutional and legal régime adequate to ensure the tranquillity and prosperity of their respective countries; but, in order to attain this end, they need not expect from us support of another sort." [41]

Early in 1831 the Chilean public was informed by the *Araucano* of the acknowledgment of Spanish-American independence by the French Government.[42] In spite of the

---

[40] *Memoria que el ministro de estado en el departamento de relaciones esteriores presenta al congreso nacional año de 1834,* pp. 3-4.

[41] A. A. E., Chili, 14.

[42] Barros Arana, *op. cit.,* XVI, 162-63, n. 6.

strained relations existing between his country and France, Vice-President Errázuriz in June, 1831, praised the act of the illustrious Prince who occupied the French throne in formally recognizing the independence of Chile and other new American republics.[43]

On September 30, 1830, Molé addressed a dispatch concerning the recognition of the Spanish-American states by France to Consul General Barrère, who had succeeded Chaumette des Fossés at Lima. As Peru had no agent at Paris, the minister sent to Barrère a draft of a communication which he was to transmit to her Secretary of Foreign Relations. Couched in almost identical terms with the announcement of recognition sent to Spanish-American agents at Paris, it expressed Molé's hope that Peru would be animated by reciprocal sentiments. The Peruvian minister was asked to forward this note to the President or to the Council of State and to send to Paris a negotiator vested with the authority necessary to treat with France upon reciprocal bases.[44] In a subsequent dispatch to the consul general, Molé expressed the hope that the governments of the new nations would secure at home the force necessary " to put an end to anarchy and to found constitutional and legal régimes which can guarantee at once the independence and the prosperity of their countries. The suspicion with which French agents have hitherto been viewed ought to be replaced by sentiments of good will which should render easy the accomplishment of their mission." [45]

Early in 1831 the new policy of France toward the Spanish-American nations was announced informally by

[43] *Discurso,* June 1, 1831.
[44] A. A. E., Pérou, 18.
[45] November 25, 1830, *ibid.*

Barrère to the Peruvian Government.[46] On March 12 the *Monitor Peruano* contained an editorial entitled " The Recognition of Our Independence." That journal described French policy as frank and liberal and urged that an agent be sent to Paris to acknowledge this noble conduct. Nevertheless, with respect to the negotiation of a Franco-Peruvian treaty the editor was in doubt; he expressed fear that France might flood Peru with her goods, and he asserted that there could be no reciprocity between the two countries. He reasoned that even a treaty of alliance would be unimportant for France as well as for Peru: " From this we should conclude that the time has not arrived for the negotiation of treaties with France or with any other nation which like her exceeds us in wealth, industry, and power. . . . The mission of our agent should accordingly be reduced to a simple act of courtesy." [47]

On March 28, 1831, Barrère formally notified Carlos Pedemonte, the Peruvian Secretary of Foreign Relations, that France had recognized in principle the independence of his nation and was ready to negotiate with her a treaty of amity, commerce, and navigation which would inevitably become " a guarantee of friendly and enduring relations." The consul general expressed the hope that Peru would send to Paris a diplomat authorized to negotiate such a convention.[48] On August 21 Molé addressed a dispatch to Barrère to inform him that the title of chargé d'affaires to Peru had been added to his designation as consul general. " His Majesty judged that this new title," explained the minister,

[46] Aranda, *Colección de los tratados,* VII, 537.

[47] *El conciliador,* May 19, 1830, prints a translation of Barrère's credentials dated September 25, 1829, and signed by Polignac.

[48] Aranda, *op. cit.,* VII, 539.

" which should render your mission even more important by giving it a political character, is a natural consequence of the recognition which we have given of the independence of Peru." [49] Several months later, in response to Barrère's inquiries, Sébastiani assured him that the appointment as chargé d'affaires conferred upon him all the rights, prerogatives, and immunities stipulated for such diplomatic agents in the *réglement de Vienne*.[50]

On October 18, 1830, Molé informed the Minister of Marine that, as France did not have an agent in either Central America or Bolivia, a notification of the acknowledgment of Spanish-American independence by Louis Philippe would have to be forwarded to those countries by the French navy. Molé transmitted models of the letters of notification which naval officers were to address to the foreign secretaries of Bolivia and Central America. He suggested that, if it did not unduly delay the naval service, the officers entrusted with such announcements should await on shipboard the replies from those secretaries and that they might even consent to transport the agents of the new republics to France.[51]

In his speech to the legislature of the Central American Federation in the autumn of 1831, President Barrundia mentioned with appreciation " the generous example of France in regard to the recognition of our independence." [52] On October 28 of that year, Minister of Foreign Affairs

[49] A. A. E., Pérou, 18.

[50] September 26, 1832, *ibid.*, 19.

[51] A. A. E., Guatemala, 1.

[52] " Discours prononcé par le Président de la République du Centre Amérique, à la cloture des Sessions du Congrès Federal," enclosure in Vinchon de Quemont to Maison, October 1, 1831, *ibid.*

Sébastiani wrote to Cochelot to inform him of his new duties as consul general and chargé d'affaires to the Central American Federation: " It is through you that our relations are to be formed with Central America; it is consequently your duty to indicate to us the means of making those new relations as advantageous as possible to the interests of our commerce and industry."[53] Meanwhile two persons who had been successively appointed as envoys from the Federation of Central America to France declined to serve.[54]

A formal letter from Molé, notifying the Central American Secretary of Foreign Relations of Louis Philippe's decision to acknowledge in principle the independence of the federation and stating that France was disposed to negotiate with it a treaty of amity, commerce, and navigation, was prepared for transmission to Guatemala City by an officer of the French navy. The Secretary of Foreign Relations was asked to bring this note to the attention of the President.[55]

Apparently unaware of the comprehensive character of French acknowledgment of Spanish-American independence, Mariano Calvo, the Secretary of Foreign Relations of Bolivia, had addressed a letter to General Sébastiani through Lafayette declaring that nothing would better promote good relations between Bolivia and France than the recognition of the new republic. Calvo maintained that this step would encourage commerce, consolidate his country's institutions, promote tranquillity and the enjoyment of true liberty, and lead to the appointment of consuls and ministers to Bolivia by foreign nations. His country, added Calvo, would know

---

[53] *Ibid.*
[54] Vinchon de Quemont to Maison, March 20, 1831, *ibid.*
[55] Molé to Sébastiani, October 18, 1830, A. A. E., Bolivie, 1.

how to appreciate such an "act of justice and noble generosity." [56] The announcement to Bolivia of the decision of Louis Philippe to recognize the Spanish-American states and to negotiate treaties with them was made in the same manner as that to Central America. Orders were issued that a formal letter mentioning this decision be transmitted to the Bolivian Government by the commander of a French ship dispatched for that purpose.[57] This announcement, which was forwarded via Cobija to La Paz, reached that capital in June, 1831. Bolivia's Secretary of the Interior soon issued a circular instructing the prefects to announce in their respective departments the news of the recognition of Bolivia by France.[58] On June 23 the progressive publicist, Andrés Santa Cruz, who had earlier tried to interest La Forest in French intercourse with Bolivia and had now become the president of this agitated republic, addressed to him an appreciative letter of which the following words are noteworthy:

The recognition by the French Government during my administration of the independence of Bolivia has filled my heart with content and has satisfied my pride as the head of this republic. An act so noble and generous will have important consequences both for French commerce and for the stability of our institutions. . . . I shall soon designate the person who is to proceed to Paris to thank the King of France for his kindness and to negotiate a treaty of amity, commerce, and navigation which should determine our mutual relations and which, I hope, will be of some advantage to French commerce.[59]

[56] Calvo to Sébastiani, April 13, 1831 (copy), *ibid.*

[57] Sébastiani to Villeneuve Bargemont, December 15, 1830, A. N., Marine, B B⁴, 526.

[58] *Colección oficial de leyes, decretos, ordenes, resoluciones &c. que se han expedido para el régimen de la república boliviana,* 1829-31, pp. 427-28.

[59] (Translation), A. A. E., Bolivie, 1.

President Santa Cruz informed Congress on the following day of the visit to Bolivia of Captain Villeneuve Bargemont with the news that the French Government had recognized her independence. Stating that France desired to negotiate a treaty of friendship, commerce, and navigation with the republic, the President declared that this acknowledgment of Bolivian independence was truly satisfactory. It had awakened gratitude in his country for France, the first European nation to recognize the political existence of Bolivia. He accordingly took the view that the French were entitled to preferential treatment in her markets.[60]

On September 30, 1830, Molé addressed a note to Consul General Larrea to inform him that the King of France, having decided to recognize in principle the independence of Argentina, was ready to negotiate with her a treaty of amity, commerce, and navigation.[61] A notification that the French Government had recognized Argentine independence in principle was on the same day sent by Molé to Mendeville, who had recently been appointed France's consul general at Buenos Aires. This news was communicated by him to the Argentine Government in a letter dated December 20, 1830.[62] Whereas the executive triumvirate of the province of Buenos Ayres made only brief mention of this important event to the legislature, the consul general promptly described at some length the reception of that announcement with ceremonies and festivities.[63] Juan

[60] Santa-Cruz, *El General Andrés de Santa-Cruz,* p. 219.

[61] A. A. E., Buenos Ayres, 20. Larrea had been appointed consul general on October 8, 1828. *Registro oficial de la república argentina,* II, 229.

[62] A. A. E., Buenos Ayres, 20; " Francia; relaciones diplomáticas," *La nación,* July 9, 1916, p. 505.

[63] Mendeville to Molé, December 31, 1830, A. A. E., Buenos Ayres, 20; cf. Mabragaña, *Los Mensajes,* I, 251.

Manuel de Rosas, a forceful gaucho who had recently been appointed by the legislature of the province of Buenos Aires as governor and captain general for three years, asked Mendeville on December 23 to transmit to Paris an acknowledgment of the Argentine provinces for the act of recognition.[64] At a later time, when strained relations had developed between France and Dictator Rosas, Felipe Arana, his Minister of Foreign Relations, declared that this act was both agreeable and flattering to the Argentine Republic.[65]

Another nation had meanwhile emerged within the limits of the former viceroyalty of La Plata. This state was seated in the debatable land often designated as the Banda Oriental del Uruguay. The people of that region claimed title to territory which, after Artigas had been driven into exile, had fallen under the domination of Brazil. During the night of April 19, 1825, led by Juan Antonio Lavalleja, a band of Uruguayan patriots who became known in song and story as the Thirty-three Immortals crossed the Paraná River from Argentina to Uruguay, where they began to struggle for separation from the government at Rio de Janeiro.

This movement soon attracted the attention of French officials, who had a keen scent for revolutionary breezes. On July 29, 1825, Roux de Rochelle, head of the Division of the South in the Ministry of Foreign Affairs, prepared a report concerning the situation of Uruguay. Roux reasoned that, whatever might be the result of the hostilities between that country and Brazil, " it seemed to be in the interest and policy of France not to take any part." He maintained that, as France had commercial relations with Brazil as well as with Uruguay, she should follow the same

[64] Villanueva, *Historia de la república argentina,* II, 82.
[65] *British and Foreign State Papers,* XXVI, 991.

policy in struggles between two states of Latin America as that which she had pursued in the struggles between the Iberian nations and their colonies. Believing that if a war broke out between Brazil and Argentina it would in reality be a contest for the possession of the Banda Oriental, this official urged that France adopt a policy of neutrality toward the Uruguayan struggle for independence. He sagely declared that it would be prudent for European nations to refrain from interfering in quarrels between Latin-American states.[66]

On August 25, 1825, Uruguayan leaders framed a declaration of independence which contained a pledge of adherence to their southern neighbor. As the Congress at Buenos Aires welcomed this pledge, Brazil declared war on Argentina. A frigate was soon dispatched from the French naval station on the Brazilian coast to gather information concerning the hostilities that broke out in the basin of La Plata. The captain of that frigate was warned to maintain a neutral attitude toward the contending parties; he was reminded that Lavalleja's banner was not recognized by France.[67]

The climax of a series of military and naval engagements came on February 20, 1827, when Uruguayan soldiers, effectively aided by Argentine legions, decisively defeated the Brazilian troops at Ituzaingó. In May following, a preliminary treaty of peace was signed between Argentina and Brazil which stipulated that Uruguay was to be free and independent. On September 10, 1829, a Constituent Assem-

[66] " Amérique du Sud: Rapport sur la Situation de Montevideo," A. A. E., Montevideo, 1. On Roux see Damas, *Mémoires,* II, 49-50.

[67] Gauthier to " Monsieur le Capitaine " (undated), A. N., Marine, B. B.⁴ 468.

bly at Montevideo approved a constitution for the new nation.

A notification of the acknowledgment of the independence of Uruguay by France was dispatched by Molé to Vice-Consul Cavaillon at Montevideo. As Uruguay had not yet sent an agent to France, the minister also transmitted to Cavaillon the draft of an announcement which he was to give to the Uruguayan Secretary of Foreign Relations. Molé further requested the vice-consul to communicate to Paris his views respecting the provisions which should be included in a treaty between France and Uruguay.[68]

Immediately on receipt of Molé's dispatch notifying him that the French Government had acknowledged the independence of Uruguay, Cavaillon sent a note containing this news to José Ellauri, her Secretary of Foreign Relations. In reply Ellauri indicated his pleasure at the generous sentiment which had been expressed in connection with French recognition. Ellauri declared that this feeling had excited enthusiasm and gratitude among his countrymen:

The glorious events of July had made them anticipate the possibility of this result which they very much desired; yet they were so much of the opinion that they would have to solicit this favor that, a few days before the receipt of the communication from Your Excellency, the President confided to me not only that he had intended to send an agent to Paris in order to treat concerning the conditions of this recognition, but also that he had already selected the person whom he believed fitted to fulfill that mission.[69]

The acknowledgment of the independence of the Spanish-

[68] September 30, 1830, A. A. E., Montevido, 2.

[69] Cavaillon to Sébastiani, January 11, 1831, enclosing copy of Ellauri to Cavaillon, December 24, 1830, *ibid.*

American nations by France stands out against the hazy background of Restoration policies like a framed picture. Still, as has been noticed, contemporary commentaries on her recognition of Spanish-American independence were not very striking. Subsequently certain commentators pointed out the significance of that tardy decision. To paraphrase the views of a discerning writer in the *Revue de Deux Mondes,* a certain repugnance for the republican institutions of the new states, a lack of confidence in the stability of their institutions and their people, and, above all, a desire to keep faith with Spain were the factors that restrained the government of the Restoration from acknowledging Spanish-American independence. When the July Revolution took place, however, there was only one step left to take. France had already established commercial relations with independent states of Spanish America: in the first place, by the dispatch of inspectors general of French commerce; and, in the second place, by the appointment of consuls regularly accredited to the new governments. What remained to be done was to clothe those relations with a political character.

Not without some justification did this writer maintain that it was French public opinion, which was not fully informed concerning the condition of the new republics, that had induced the government of Louis Philippe to recognize the Spanish-American states and to form the same political relations with them that it enjoyed with some other nations.[70] Certain French diplomats were later convinced that it was a mistake on the part of their govern-

---

[70] C. L. B., " Des rapports de la France et de l'Europe avec l'Amérique du Sud," *Revue des deux mondes,* 4th series, XXXI, 54.

ment to acknowledge the independence of the Spanish-American republics unconditionally. The moral is pointed in Deffaudis' critical commentary on the policy of his country. After stating that France recognized the independence of Latin America gratuitously, he said: " In consequence, and as the Minister of Foreign Affairs had predicted, we were not able to secure any of the diplomatic stipulations which we demanded." [71]

It was because of the deposition of Charles X—that sharp break with the past—that the government of France in August, 1830, decided to alter radically its attitude toward Spanish America. "With the change of dynasty and of councils," said the *Times* on October 11, 1830, " the feelings of the French Government on this subject were instantly changed. Philip I, himself looking for recognition to the despotic governments of the Continent, could not long refuse to acknowledge governments as legitimate as his own." A family bond between France and Spain, the outcome of the Peace of the Pyrenees, was at last severed by mutual consent. Significant though this change was in international politics, some historians have not noticed that in 1830 the Family Compact of the two Bourbon powers was abrogated.

A project for the creation of Spanish appanages in America which had won the support of Polignac was not even considered. In spite of the dissensions which still raged in certain countries, Molé recommended that Mexico, Central America, Colombia, Peru, Bolivia, and Argentina be informed that France was ready to recognize their governments and to negotiate treaties with them. Agents

[71] Deffaudis, *Questions diplomatiques,* p. 77.

of those countries in Europe and French journalists interpreted the decision as the harbinger of commercial treaties between France and the new states. Before a treaty could be negotiated between France and Colombia, however, that state split into three fragments: Ecuador, Venezuela, and New Granada took their places on the map of South America. Perhaps because the formal recognition by France of the independence of the Spanish-American nations had been so long delayed, the announcement of that step did not always receive in their capital cities the measure of appreciation which French statesmen anticipated.

Chapter XVI

COMPLETION OF THE RECOGNITION POLICY

Upon being informed that France was contemplating a treaty with Mexico, Manuel González Salmón, the Spanish Secretary for Foreign Affairs, was much incensed. On June 22, 1831, he sent a letter to Count Ofalia, the Spanish ambassador at Paris, directing him to lodge a complaint against the negotiation by France of a treaty with "the rebel government of Mexico." A formal remonstrance against the recognition of Spanish-American independence which had been framed by the Spanish Chancellery in 1828 was transmitted to Paris for use by the ambassador as a pattern in his representations to the French Government. When he sent this protest, González Salmón instructed Ofalia in no manner to appeal to the old treaties between Spain and France. In particular, he was to refrain from invoking the Bourbon Family Compact of 1761.

According to the model forwarded to Ofalia, he was to declare that the acknowledgment of the independence of the provinces of Spanish America was contrary to the doctrine of legitimacy accepted by the sovereigns of Europe. In this protest it was said further that Ferdinand VII observed with keen regret that the French Government had, without occasion, decided to recognize certain governments founded upon rebellion against their sovereign.[1] Accordingly, on July 31 Ofalia addressed a strong remonstrance to Sébastiani. He asserted that the Spanish King had hoped that the melancholy experiences of years of revolution

[1] A. H. N., Estado, 6909.

would have induced European powers to coöperate with his country in the reëstablishment of order in the Indies. In these circumstances, he continued, Ferdinand VII had been deeply grieved to learn that, without receiving important advantages, and regardless of the treaties which bound friendly nations to the Spanish monarch, certain powers had decided to recognize ephemeral governments founded upon rebellion. Emphatically the ambassador declared that such acts would neither alter nor destroy the rights of Spain over those provinces.[2]

The negotiation of treaties between France and the Spanish-American nations followed slowly on the heels of recognition in principle. From 1830 to 1848 treaties containing provisions regarding commercial intercourse were arranged between France, on the one hand, and New Granada, Mexico, Venezuela, Bolivia, Uruguay, Argentina, Ecuador, Guatemala, and Costa Rica, on the other hand. With the exception of the Franco-Argentine Treaty, in which the stipulations concerning commerce formed part of a claims convention, these treaties were concerned exclusively with amity, navigation, and commerce. They contained most-favored-nation clauses. In that respect and in the stipulations concerning the rights of neutrals, they often followed the precedents set by treaties which had been arranged between Spanish-American nations and the United States. The treaties with Colombia, Guatemala, and Uruguay expressly stated that they gave the finishing touches to the formal process of the acknowledgment of Spanish-American independence by France. In the preamble of the Franco-Uruguayan treaty signed on April 8, 1836, the

[2] A. A. E., Espagne, 754.

parties declared that they wished to promote their commercial relations as well as solemnly to consecrate the acknowledgment of Uruguay's independence by France.[3]

The Revolution of 1848, which made a nephew of Napoleon I president of the Second French Republic, gave fresh courage to statesmen of those Spanish-American nations that had not yet been formally accorded recognition by France. Between 1848 and 1861 the French Government negotiated conventions with Honduras, Nicaragua, Chile, Salvador, and Peru. Among the early treaties negotiated by France with Spanish-American republics, the Franco-Bolivian convention of 1834 may be considered as the model. A decade later French diplomats occasionally took the view that their treaty with Ecuador should be considered as the norm. In the autumn of 1848 Minister of Foreign Affairs Bastide was of the opinion that a treaty which had been concluded with the Dominican Republic should be used as the model in arranging treaties of amity and commerce with the nations of Central America. In general, the treaties negotiated by France with the new states failed to secure for her the special commercial favors which some of her statesmen had fondly anticipated when Louis Philippe decided upon a policy of recognition.

In official interpretations of the Bourgeois King's policy toward the Spanish-American communities Paraguay had not been mentioned. Yet naturally it was included in the scope of French recognition policy. Shortly after the revolt against Spain began at Buenos Aires, certain leaders of the province of Paraguay, dissatisfied with Spanish rule and

[3] Clercq, *Recueil des traités,* IV, 332. Other treaties of France with Spanish-American republics are found in this collection of treaties.

apprehensive of the expansionist designs of the Portuguese, deprived Governor Velasco of his authority and installed a provisional government at Asunción. It does not appear that at this time a formal declaration of independence from Spain was made. The insurgent province gradually fell under the rule of a bizarre leader named José de Francia, who became the dominant personality of a hermit nation. Although the roving French naturalist, Aimé Bonpland, was detained in Paraguay for several years, it does not appear that his government made any attempt to facilitate intercourse with that country. However, from the Argentine capital Consul Roger sent to Paris an account of the Paraguayan Dictator based upon the reports of refugees.[4]

The death of Francia, on September 20, 1840, seemed to augur a change in Paraguayan policy. Accordingly, on February 10, 1842, François Guizot, who had become Minister of Foreign Affairs, addressed to King Louis Philippe a report recommending that France dispatch an agent to Paraguay to study the condition of that country. Although the King approved this recommendation, shortly afterward Guizot decided to postpone the mission.[5]

Leaders of Paraguay did not long delay communicating with Count Lurde, who in May, 1843, was instructed to proceed to Buenos Aires as the diplomatic agent of France. On August 28 of that year Carlos A. López and Mariano Roque Alonso, who had been named consuls and placed at the head of the Paraguayan Government, addressed a note to Lurde in which they informed him of the Declaration of Independence which had been adopted by Congress on

[4] Roger to Thiers, August 10, 1836, A. A. E., Buenos Ayres, 22.
[5] "Rapport au Roi," February 10, 1842; Guizot to Duperré, May 23, 1842; *idem* to Archiac (undated), A. A. E., Paraguay, 1.

November 25, 1842. Further, they expressed hope that they would obtain from King Louis Philippe an acknowledgment of their independence. In reply on November 1, 1843, Lurde expressed the opinion that, as soon as regular relations were established between France and Paraguay, their inhabitants would enjoy reciprocal advantages by the exchange of their products.[6] In November, 1843, an envoy named Peña, who had been quietly sent from Asunción to Buenos Aires, transmitted to Lurde a request that he try to secure from his government " the formal recognition of the Republic of Paraguay." [7] On December 6, 1843, Lurde sent a confidential note to Peña which declared that the liberal policy pursued by his government in respect to the acknowledgment of Spanish-American independence should assure a favorable reception at Paris for Paraguay's demand.[8]

On March 28, 1844, Carlos A. López sent to Lurde a formal announcement that he had become the president of Paraguay. Juan Gelly, the Paraguayan envoy at Rio de Janeiro, made overtures to Chevalier Saint-Georges, who was acting as French chargé there, concerning Paraguayan independence: " On parting, Señor Gelly expressed to me confidentially his desire and that of his country that France, even without according formal recognition, would become interested in the future of Paraguay and would aid her to maintain her freedom. He said to me that the dispatch of some French officers suitable for the instruction of her army and of some marines to organize a naval force for her . . . would be a service highly appreciated." In trans-

[6] A. A. E., Buenos Ayres, 38.
[7] Lurde to Guizot, November 6, 1843, A. A. E., Buenos Ayres, 31.
[8] December 6, 1843, *ibid.*

mitting this request to his government Saint-Georges declared that it merited serious attention.[9]

On December 25, 1850, López addressed a letter to the President of the French Republic in which he repeated the request for recognition. The Dictator confessed that the time had arrived for his country to change her policy of isolation and to develop intercourse with the nations of America and Europe:

The Republic of Paraguay, ambitious to cultivate relations with the illustrious government of France, had the honor to announce to it, in a note of August 28, 1843, the important event of the acclamation and solemn ratification of her Fundamental Act of Independence. Annexed to this note was a legalized copy of that declaration and also of the act which designated the flag and the seals of the nation. Recognition of her independence and national sovereignty was solicited. The Paraguayan Government has not even received a simple acknowledgment of the receipt of that note and of the documents annexed to it.[10]

The Dictator explained that various reasons had prevented his government from sending a minister to Paris. Further, he stated that Austria and the Holy See, as well as Brazil, Chile, Bolivia, Uruguay, and Venezuela, had already recognized Paraguayan independence. With emphasis López repeated the request that the French Republic acknowledge the independence of Paraguay.

Several months after this plea reached Paris, the French Minister of Foreign Affairs notified Saint-Georges that the Prince President had appointed him envoy extraordinary and minister plenipotentiary on a special mission to the

[9] Saint-Georges to Guizot, July 12, 1847, A. A. E., Paraguay, 1.
[10] A. A. E., Paraguay, 1; *El Paraguayo independiente,* December 28, 1850.

countries in the Platean basin. The instructions prepared for
the envoy on May 1, 1852, by Minister of Foreign Affairs
Drouyn de Lhuys declared that, as the free navigation of
the tributaries of La Plata River would favor the development of commerce and the progress of civilization in the
countries which bordered those rivers, he was to undertake negotiations with Brazil and Argentina concerning
riverine navigation—negotiations which might involve Paraguay. In the discussions he was to be guided by the principles adopted by European states regarding the navigation
of rivers as formulated in the Treaty of Vienna and in
the Treaty of 1831 concerning the river Rhine.

With regard to recognition Saint-Georges was to make
López acquainted with the object of his mission, which
was of particular interest to Paraguay: " If he shows himself disposed to support your measures designed to obtain
at Buenos Aires a concession which can give value to the independence of Paraguay by affording that country the possibility—which without this action would be out of the question—of entering into direct relations with leading maritime
powers, you may acknowledge that independence by a
separate act or, what would be better, by the conclusion
of a treaty of commerce conceding implicitly the recognition desired by President López." [11]

The French envoy found the Dictator's son, General
Francisco Solano López, to be a young man of intelligence
and spirit but very sensitive and vain. This ambitious youth,
who was acting as Secretary of Foreign Affairs, seemed
to favor French views.[12] Saint-Georges soon submitted to

---

[11] A. A. E., Buenos Ayres, 28.
[12] Saint-Georges to Drouyn de Lhuys, January 23, 1853, *ibid.*

Dictator López a project of a Franco-Paraguayan treaty which was based on a draft entrusted to him by his government. The Dictator soon presented a counter-project. In addition to other modifications, he proposed to suppress an article in the French draft concerning the acknowledgment of Paraguayan independence; for he wished this recognition to be accomplished by a special ceremony. López maintained that he was unable to accede to the French proposal concerning the free navigation of the Bermejo and Pilcomayo rivers as this was involved in pending negotiations with Argentina and Bolivia. Nor did he wish to admit French warships into the Paraguay River. A proposal that French citizens in Paraguay should be given most-favored-nation privileges seemed to him to have a mysterious meaning.[13]

With respect to an acknowledgment of Paraguayan independence, Saint-Georges soon decided to satisfy the wishes of Dictator López. The French envoy prepared a declaration in which, " by virtue of the full powers conferred upon him by the Prince President of the French Republic and in his name, he recognized by this solemn act the independence and sovereignty of the Republic of Paraguay." In this act Saint-Georges expressed the view that Paraguay had the right " to exercise all the important prerogatives which pertain to her independence and to her national sovereignty." On February 28, 1853, at the palace of government in Asunción, the French envoy solemnly presented to the Dictator the French " Act of Recognition " of Paraguayan independence, and the agents of Sardinia and the United States read similar acts on behalf of their respective govern-

[13] *Idem* to *idem,* February 4, 1855, *ibid.*

ments. During these proceedings a French frigate which was anchored in the harbor saluted the Paraguayan flag with twenty-one guns.[14]

Meanwhile, the French diplomat had decided to carry on his negotiations for a convention in conjunction with diplomatic agents of England, Sardinia, and the United States. On March 4, 1853, Saint-Georges and General Francisco López signed a treaty of commerce and navigation. They declared that they wished to improve the good relations existing between the states which they represented and also to develop their commercial intercourse. Paraguay conceded to French merchant vessels the free navigation of the Paraguay River as far as Asunción and the navigation of the Paraná up to Encarnación. This treaty contained a most-favored-nation article regarding commerce.[15]

Before this agreement had been concluded, differences had arisen between France and Haiti concerning the indemnity stipulated in the Ordinance of April 17, 1825. On June 5, 1831, the Haitian Government cleverly explained that the indemnity stipulated in the Ordinance of 1825 signified the ransom of Haiti and that a government born of the July Revolution could not demand the payment of that ransom without contradicting the very principles which justified its own existence. In a reply dated September 23, 1831, however, General Sébastiani maintained that the indemnity of 150,000,000 francs was simply an inadequate

[14] Saint-Georges to Drouyn de Lhuys, March 1, 1853 (copy); " Acte de Reconnaissance," February 28, 1853, *ibid.* The " Act of Recognition" of the United States is found in Manning, *Diplomatic Correspondence of the United States; Inter-American Affairs, 1831-1860,* X, 102 n.

[15] Clercq, *Recueil des traités,* VI, 303-08.

recompense for damages caused to Frenchmen who had been dispossessed of their properties in Saint-Domingue. The Haitian Government responded by renewing its protest with regard to the debt owing to the former proprietors and by claiming that its failure to ratify the commercial treaty was due to its infringement of the laws and the constitution of the country. A summary of Haiti's fresh proposals made by Count Rigny, the French Minister of Foreign Affairs, ran as follows:

In fine, the government of Haiti demanded that the Ordinance of 1825 be annulled because it offered the Haitians only a purely nominal acknowledgment of their independence; that this independence be recognized by a treaty of peace, amity, and commerce destined to ensure for the inhabitants of both countries most-favored-nation treatment; that by another special treaty the indemnity of 150,000,000 mentioned in the Ordinance of April 17, 1825, be reduced to 75,000,000; and that a deduction be made of some 30,000,000 already paid, which is to say, in reality, that the indemnity be cut down to 45,000,000, for the liquidation of which the Haitian Government would undertake to pay 1,000,000 annually for forty-five years, reserving to herself the right to apply another annuity of 1,000,000 to the service of the loan and to the repayment of advances from the treasury of France.

Such propositions lay bare all the bad faith of the government of Haiti. In effect, this is nothing less than the repudiation of one-half of the debt owed the former proprietors, while the men who are best acquainted with Haiti's financial position agree that this position makes possible the payment of all of that debt.[16]

Years passed before French statesmen would yield to Haiti's demands. In 1837 the Ministry of Foreign Affairs decided that, because of the difficulties which Haiti had

[16] Rigny to Jacob, September 18, 1834, A. A. E., Haïti, 6.

encountered in paying the sums due on account of the
indemnity, it would reduce that debt to 70,000,000 francs.
A draft treaty was entrusted to Captain Baudin and Emmanuel de las Casas, who were sent on a mission to Santo
Domingo accompanied by a small squadron which, if necessary, was to blockade the ports of that island.[17]

The French agents arrived in the harbor of Port-au-Prince,
on the frigate *Néréide,* on March 28, 1838. A few days
later they began conferences with five commissioners of
Haiti. Upon being told of the clause in the proposed treaty
concerning the status of their nation, the Haitian commissioners expressed the opinion that the language employed
was not sufficiently explicit, that the treaty should contain
an emphatic enunciation of the acknowledgment of Haiti's
independence, and that it should include a declaration that
not only the French King but also his heirs and successors
renounced all pretensions to sovereignty over Haiti. With
regard to the indemnity, they protested that their government had fixed the sum which it could pay at 45,000,000
francs, and that a larger amount would provoke difficulties
with the Senate. Secretary General Inginac avowed that
the utmost concession which Haiti could make on that score
would be to set the indemnity at 60,000,000 francs payable
in thirty years. The Haitians strongly objected to a proposed
secret article providing that, in case of the non-execution
of this treaty, France would insist upon the fulfillment of
her rights under the Ordinance of 1825. At a conference
held on February 9, Las Casas announced that the French
commissioners had assumed the responsibility of omitting
the secret article and of agreeing to the amount of the

---

[17] " Instruction pour M. Emmanuel de las Casas et Capt. Baudin,"
October 19, 1837, A. A. E., Haïti, 7.

indemnity proposed by Haiti. An agreement was reached, however, only after a conference with President Boyer. The latter now expressed the view that France had not pursued a frank policy in framing the ordinance which acknowledged Haitian independence, but that Haiti was willing to meet the latest French offer in regard to the amount of the indemnity.[18]

Two Franco-Haitian treaties were accordingly signed on February 12, 1838. Article I of the treaty of amity stated that the King of France " recognized for himself, his heirs and successors, the Republic of Haiti as a free, sovereign, and independent State." Article II provided that peace and friendship were to prevail between the contracting parties. Article III declared that as soon as possible they would conclude a treaty of commerce and navigation. In the meantime the citizens and the products of each party were to enjoy in the dominions of the other party the most-favored-nation treatment. The treaty concerning the indemnity stipulated that the amount due to France by Haiti was to be reduced to the sum of sixty million francs, which was to be payable in annual installments from 1838 to 1867.[19] As that republic still owed the loan floated in Paris, amounting to 30,000,000 francs, her indebtedness to France and French bankers now aggregated 90,000,000 francs.

Las Casas reported to his government that, upon signing the treaty of friendship, he had said to Boyer that it constituted the complete and unconditional recognition of the Republic of Haiti.[20] On February 18, 1838, after giving

[18] Memoranda of the conferences, February 1–February 13, 1838, enclosure in Las Casas to Molé, February 17, 1838, *ibid*.

[19] *Clercq, Recueil des traités,* IV, 397-99.

[20] Las Casas to Molé, February 17, 1838, A. A. E., Haïti, 7.

a summary of the two treaties, the *Télégraphe*, which was published at the Haitian capital, made this comment: " It is doubtless honorable for France to show herself so just and generous; but it is more creditable for Haiti to have crowned the work of her political emancipation by such a result." On the morning of February 27 the forts at Port-au-Prince fired a salute to France, and French frigates anchored in the harbor returned this greeting. At a banquet on the following day Haitian dignitaries, French diplomats and naval officers, and the consular agents of foreign nations that had recognized the independence of Haiti celebrated the signing of the treaties which made regular the political relations between France and Haiti.[21]

Five years later, the wheel of revolution moved again. In 1843 the growing discontent with the despotic rule of President Boyer caused a revolt in the northern part of the former French colony. Under a mulatto leader named Charles Hérard, Haitian soldiers marched upon Port-au-Prince. On March 13, 1843, Boyer resigned and went into exile. A few days later Hérard led his army into the capital city, where a provisional government was soon set up. On September 13, 1843, a Constituent Assembly framed a new constitution for Haiti. A supplementary article of this fundamental law proclaimed that, in accordance with its provisions, Hérard had been elected president of the Haitian Republic.

This revolution provoked differences between that republic and France concerning the payment of the sums due on the indemnity acknowledged by the Franco-Haitian Treaty of 1838. Even before a new constitution had been framed,

[21] *Le Moniteur,* April 1, 1838.

Hérard and other Haitian leaders sent a note to Consul Levasseur asking that a delay be allowed in meeting this fiscal obligation.[22] When he granted this request, however, Guizot declared that his government did not intend to abandon its right to the stipulated indemnity.[23]

That minister soon selected a special agent to watch over French interests. On September 25 he instructed Adolphe Barrot to proceed to Port-au-Prince and to inform the Haitian Government that, although France was again disposed to make a concession to it, she would not agree to any sacrifice of the rights of the former proprietors. Guizot even suggested that Haiti should furnish a guarantee for the faithful performance of her financial obligations. He proposed that the Black Republic might offer as a territorial guarantee the peninsula of Samaná, which could be occupied by the French without coming into immediate contact with the Haitians. " It offers varied resources," said Guizot, " which are precious enough to make it a pledge of undoubted value." [24]

On December 15, 1843, a prominent leader in the eastern part of Santo Domingo named Bonaventura Báez and six of his compatriots addressed a communication to Levasseur in which they denounced the hated rule of Boyer. They solicited French protection on the following conditions: that the eastern part of the island should be independent; that France should agree to favor the emancipation of that region and to ensure the establishment of a stable government there by the grant of subsidies; that she should furnish arms and munitions in sufficient quantities

[22] April 12, 1843, A. A. E., Haïti, 10.
[23] Guizot to Levasseur, June 16, 1843, *ibid*.
[24] September 25, 1843, *ibid*.

to equip their compatriots; and that she should appoint a governor for the new state who was to serve for at least ten years. Further, the ports of the new republic were to be open to immigrants from all countries; and in recognition of the protection of France, that republic was to cede to her the peninsula of Samaná.[25] When he transmitted to Guizot this proposal for a thinly veiled protectorate, Levasseur declared that it merited the serious attention of the French Government. He added: " I know that this agrees perfectly with the view which Your Excellency expressed to me. Consequently I shall watch the proposal with the most careful solicitude during my sojourn at Port-au-Prince. But I shall in no manner compromise the interests or the honor of my government; I shall leave it free on my return to act as it desires." [26]

In December, 1843, secret conferences were attended by Barrot, Levasseur, and emissaries of discontented inhabitants of the eastern part of the island. About the middle of that month Báez and Levasseur seem to have reached an agreement in respect to the revolutionizing of that section. The conspirators apparently gained the impression that France would be ready effectively to promote their designs, if not indeed to establish a protectorate over one-time Spanish Santo Domingo. In return they evidently promised that, if their independence should be assured, they would cede to France the peninsula of Samaná. Shortly afterward Barrot informed Guizot that the situation in Haiti was such that he had considered it imprudent to state the conditions on which France would grant that

[25] " No. 1," *ibid.*, 11.

[26] December 20, 1843, *ibid.* Cf. Tansill, *The United States and Santo Domingo*, p. 124, n. 34.

country a delay in making the payments stipulated in the Treaty of 1838. Yet he had secured assurances from the new government of Haiti that it recognized the binding force of that treaty. It had consequently acknowledged the Haitian debt to France as a national obligation.[27]

At a preconcerted signal on the night of February 27, 1844, revolutionists seized the chief gate of Santo Domingo City. Its military guard promptly went over to the revolutionists. A provisional junta was soon set up. Through the good offices of Juchereau de Saint-Denis, the French consul at the city of Santo Domingo, articles of capitulation were signed between revolutionary leaders and the Haitian commander. On February 29 that city was given up to the Patriots; it soon became the capital of the Dominican Republic. In a report to his government the French consul asserted that, because of the rôle which he had played during this revolution, both parties blessed the name of France.[28]

On March 9, 1844, the Dominican junta addressed a significant note to Consul Saint-Denis to propose the negotiation of a treaty with France on condition that the integrity and independence of their republic should be ensured, and that the individual liberty of the former Negro slaves residing in that country should be respected. Article IV proceeded in this wise: " In the event that France should become involved in hostilities with Haiti, the Dominican Republic will supply her with whatever aid she may need.

[27] January 16, 1844, A. A. E., Haïti, 12.
[28] Saint-Denis to Guizot, March 3, 1844, A. A. E., St. Domingue, 1. See further D'Alaux, *L'Empereur Soulouque et son empire*, pp. 273-75; Manning, *Diplomatic Correspondence of the United States; Inter-American Affairs, 1831-1860*, VI, 28.

Under the existing circumstances, France will furnish that republic with muskets, munitions of war, ships, and the money necessary to place her in a state of defence, as well as with the soldiers that she may need." Article VI read as follows: " In remuneration the Dominican Republic will cede to France in perpetuity the peninsula of Samaná with the boundaries set by nature for that peninsula—this cession being an exception to Article I—and with the express stipulation that slavery shall never exist on that peninsula." [29]

After the Dominican revolution had been consummated, Guizot acknowledged Levasseur's note containing the propositions formulated in December, 1843. The minister stated that his government was attracted by the proposal but feared that the inconveniences and dangers of establishing a protectorate over the Dominican Republic would outweigh the advantages. Guizot expressed the opinion that the adoption of such a policy might precipitate a dispute between France and England. The English might even undertake to secure control of Môle St. Nicolas. Again the French Government could not ignore the fact that Spain had not renounced the titular sovereignty over the eastern part of Santo Domingo. Further, at a moment when France was busily engaged in consolidating at great expense her colonies in Africa and the South Sea, a wise and far-sighted ministry should put nothing at hazard by engaging in adventurous enterprises. Such were the motives which influenced the Council of State not to accept the offer of a protectorate made by Dominican leaders.[30]

Despite the views transmitted by the Minister of Foreign

[29] A. A. E., St. Domingue, 1.
[30] March 19, 1844, A. A. E., Haïti, 12.

Affairs to Levasseur, Saint-Denis soon wrote to Guizot to recommend that France advance credit to the Dominicans with Samaná as a guarantee, and that it also furnish them with arms, field artillery, and one thousand officers. "All that part of the island of Santo Domingo which formerly belonged to Spain is today," he reasoned, "at the mercy and discretion of France." [31] Shortly after this dispatch was penned, the Dominican junta published a broadside which denounced the policy pursued by President Hérard and declared war upon Haiti by land and sea.

By a dispatch dated May 30, 1844, Guizot further dampened the ardor of the consul at Santo Domingo City in regard to French influence in the Dominican Republic. Although the minister approved the measures taken by Saint-Denis to prevent bloodshed and to promote an adjustment between the black garrison of the capital city and its white inhabitants, yet he did not favor the establishment of a protectorate over the new nation: "Our well-founded intention is to respect and, if need be, to cause to be respected, the integrity of Haitian territory, and to intervene in those fatal quarrels only to fulfill our customary mission of conciliation and humanity." [32]

Because of the appeals of the Dominicans, and because of his ardent desire to extend French influence in the West Indies, Saint-Denis persisted in lending an ear to proposals for the establishment of a French protectorate over the infant republic. He also entertained the notion that France might secure possession of Môle St. Nicolas as a pledge that the Haitian obligations to France would be met. In response to these propositions, on July 20,

[31] April 23, 1844, A. A. E., St. Domingue, 1.
[32] *Ibid.*

1844, Guizot informed Saint-Denis that they had been carefully considered by the Council of State:

> Today, as formerly, after balancing the advantages and disadvantages of the occupation of territory in Haiti, the government of the King has come to realize that the disadvantages far outweigh the advantages and that it would not be wise for France again to set foot upon the soil of that island. . . . If, on our own initiative, and without a previous understanding with the government of Haiti, we were to take possession of Môle St. Nicolas, we should make an attack on the independence of that state which would have most disastrous effects upon the spirit of the black population. They would attribute to us a design to subjugate the entire island and to reëstablish slavery. . . . We have acknowledged the independence of Haiti and we intend to respect it, whether Haiti continues to exist as a unified State or becomes divided into several states—no matter what facilities circumstances may seem to offer us for the recovery of this or that part of its territory. . . . The independence of the Haitian state or of the Haitian states ought to be respected by all other powers as well as by France.[33]

However, the French Government did not oppose an increase of its influence in the island of Santo Domingo. On November 22, 1844, Guizot wrote to Saint-Denis to repeat his unfavorable view of the design of establishing formally a French protectorate there. However, he added an interpretative passage indicating that he would, in order to bind the new state to France, be willing to use his good offices to bring about Haiti's recognition of the independence of the Dominican Republic.[34]

[33] A. A. E., Haïti, 13. Cf. the statement of Minister Baroche in 1851 with respect to French policy toward revolutionary movements in Ettinger, "The Proposed Anglo-French-American Treaty of 1852 to Guarantee Cuba to Spain." *Transactions of the Royal Historical Society,* 4th series, XIII, 154.

[34] A. A. E., St. Domingue, 1.

The view of the French Government that the Dominican Republic should assume a proportionate share of the debt of Haiti proved to be a serious obstacle to a *rapprochement* of that republic with France. On March 16, 1845, Saint-Denis wrote to Guizot to declare that he had declined on behalf of his government the proposal for the establishment of a French protectorate over the new republic. Further, he had suggested that, in their own political interest, the Dominicans should assume a proportionate share of the Haitian debt.[35] In response to this overture, President Santana declared that the Dominicans did not consider themselves bound to assume even a small part of the debt which the Haitians had agreed to pay France; for Spain was the only nation that could properly assert a claim to the eastern portion of the island.[36]

In August, 1847, the Dominican Secretary of Foreign Relations empowered three agents headed by Báez to enter into negotiations with the King of France to secure the recognition of the Dominican Republic and to negotiate a treaty of amity, commerce, and navigation.[37] Early in the following year these commissioners declared that, after spending several months in soliciting Guizot, they had not obtained from him anything more than vague and doubtful promises which scarcely held any hope of a good outcome.[38] On June 9 Minister Bastide assured the commissioners that, as soon as circumstances permitted, the French Republic would employ its good offices " to assure the consolidation and prosperity of the Dominican Republic." [39] In the

[35] *Ibid.*

[36] Santana to Saint-Denis, April 25, 1845 (copy), *ibid.*

[37] Miura to Guizot, August 14, 1847, *ibid.*, 2.

[38] March 30, 1848, *ibid.*   [39] *Ibid.*

summer of 1848, French officials actually prepared the draft of a treaty which not only acknowledged the independence of the new Spanish-American state but also made reciprocal arrangements concerning commerce patterned after provisions in the Franco-Venezuelan treaty.[40]

In a note sent from London on September 14, 1848, complaining that nothing had yet developed from the French offer to mediate between the Dominican Republic and Haiti, the Dominican commissioners renewed their request for the acknowledgment of their independence by France.[41] On September 23, 1848, Minister of Foreign Affairs Bedeau acknowledged the receipt of this plea and responded to the commissioners in decisive fashion:

As this independence has been for several years an accomplished fact, the French Government can only be disposed to take full account of it and to furnish a new proof of its sympathy for the Dominican Republic by acquiescing in the wish which you express to me. The French Government has, accordingly, no objection to the formal recognition of that republic. It is ready to sanction this recognition by the conclusion of a treaty destined to regulate on the principle of reciprocity the relations of amity, commerce, and navigation between the two states. If you are furnished with sufficient power to carry on this negotiation, it can be initiated upon your return from London.[42]

In this manner the French Government made known its decision to acknowledge the independence of the insular Spanish-American republic. On November 15, 1848, the Minister of Foreign Affairs informed Place, who was now

[40] " Traité d'amité, de commerce et de navigation entre les Républiques Française et Dominicaine," *ibid*.

[41] By Báez and others, *ibid*.

[42] To Báez and others, *ibid*.

in charge of the consulate at Santo Domingo City, that his government had not only recognized the new republic but had also signed a treaty with her commissioners.[43] An official review of Franco-Dominican relations which reposes in the French archives contains the following interpretative statement concerning the acknowledgment of Dominican independence: "This recognition has been sanctioned by the treaty of amity and commerce concluded at Paris on October 22, 1848." [44] However, the Haitian Government objected to the Franco-Dominican Treaty of October 22, 1848, and the French National Assembly refused to ratify it.[45]

Because of the rejection of this convention the policy to be adopted by France toward the insular Spanish-American republic was left unsettled at a critical time. A new leader had emerged in Haiti. As the chief magistracy had fallen vacant, on March 1, 1847, the Haitian Senate elected General Faustin Soulouque, a vindictive negro who had risen from the ranks, president of the republic. In the spring of 1849, President Soulouque ordered his troops to invade the territory of the neighboring state. Haitian soldiers defeated the Dominicans at Azua and marched upon Santo Domingo City, but because of disturbances in Haiti they were recalled before they could hoist their red and blue standard over that capital.[46]

Soon after the battle of Azua, a new appeal was made to

[43] *Ibid.*
[44] "Note pour le Ministre," June, 1849, *ibid.*
[45] "Note sur la Répque. Dominicaine," November, 1852, *ibid.,* 6.
[46] Manning, *Diplomatic Correspondence of the United States; Inter-American Affairs, 1831-1860,* VI, 48. See also Dhormoys, *Une visite chez Soulouque,* pp. 13-27.

France. In a dispatch to his government dated April 12, 1849, Place reported that a commission composed of the President of Congress and two of its most influential members had paid him a visit to inquire whether he would allow them to hoist the French flag over the government buildings. On April 19, in a session attended by the President and four secretaries of state, the legislators decided to request that, as they had received proofs of French sympathy, the Dominican Republic should be placed under the protection of France. They reserved for another occasion the framing of a treaty concerning " the conditions of the protectorate." [47]

Yet, even before this proposition came to hand, the Minister of Foreign Affairs had sent a dispatch to Place to inform him in unmistakable terms that, despite the supposed designs of England and Spain upon the Dominican Republic, France did not intend to interfere in the internal affairs of that distracted country.[48] Emphatic refusals by French ministers to protect the new republic did not still the appeals of frightened Dominicans. In December, 1849, Báez addressed a plea for the establishment of a protectorate over the republic to President Napoleon, but in vain.[49] The reasons which restrained one minister of France after another from attempting to establish a protectorate over the insular Spanish-American republic were clearly stated in an official précis on " Santo Domingo " composed in 1849, the very year when the pleas of the Dominicans

[47] Caminero to Place, April 19, 1849, A. A. E., St. Domingue, 2; Manning, *op. cit.,* VI, 47 n.

[48] Drouyn de Lhuys to Place, May 19, 1849, A. A. E., St. Domingue, 2.

[49] Báez to Napoleon, December 20, 1849 (copy), *ibid.*

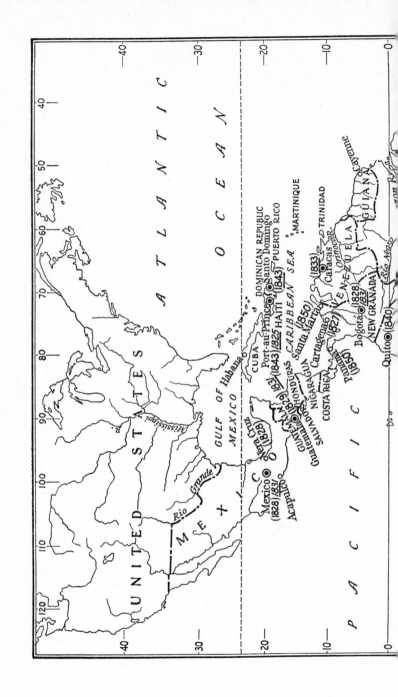

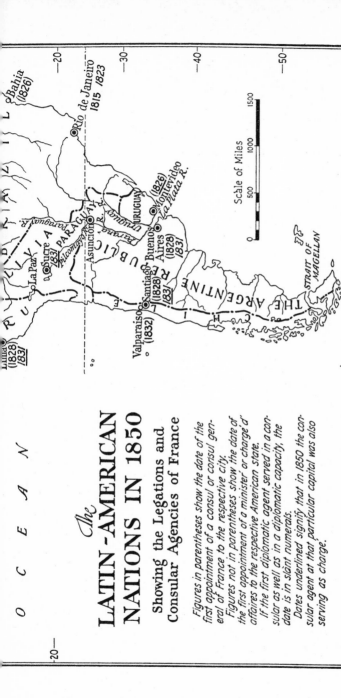

The
LATIN-AMERICAN
NATIONS IN 1850

Showing the Legations and
Consular Agencies of France

*Figures in parentheses show the date of the
first appointment of a consul or consul general of France to the respective city.*

*Figures not in parentheses show the date of
the first appointment of a minister or chargé d'
affaires to the respective American state.*

*If the first diplomatic agent served in a con-
sular as well as in a diplomatic capacity, the
date is in slant numerals.*

*Dates underlined signify that in 1850 the con-
sular agent at that particular capital was also
serving as chargé.*

Scale of Miles

0   500   1000   1500

reached a climax. This memorandum summarized the consequences of the establishment of a French protectorate over the Dominican Republic or of the acceptance by France of the proffered sovereignty. In addition to fearing hostilities with the Black Republic and the displeasure of both Spain and England at intervention by France in the island of Santo Domingo, French statesmen were apprehensive that the United States would consider such interposition as an infringement of American policy. Although the Monroe Doctrine was not mentioned by name, the last sentence in this memorandum could scarcely allude to anything else, for it declared that the United States would " always view with extreme distrust the attempts of European governments to regain a footing in America." [50]

On May 6, 1852, the new consul general of France in the Dominican Republic and three representatives of that republic signed a commercial treaty which aimed at the same time " to sanction the formal recognition by France of the independence of the Dominican Republic." This convention contained several provisions similar to those in French treaties with continental Spanish-American nations.[51]

The acknowledgment of the independence of Paraguay by France was accomplished in a somewhat different fashion from the recognition of former continental colonies of Spain in America. In accordance with the desire of the odd tyrant, Carlos A. López, the commissioner of France ostentatiously recognized Paraguay's independence by a

---

[50] " Copie (1849) Santo Domingo," *ibid.* On the attitude of Spain toward the Dominican Republic, see Manning, *Diplomatic Correspondence of the United States; Inter-American Affairs, 1831-1860,* VI, 65-66, 116.

[51] Clercq, *Recueil des traités,* VI, 185-95.

special act. The negotiation of a treaty with Paraguay was regarded by the French Government as placing the seal of approval upon the last concrete measure resulting from the recognition policy adopted in principle by the Bourgeois King toward the Spanish nations of the New World. In addition to securing commercial privileges for French merchants, this treaty conceded to French captains the privilege of navigating important Paraguayan rivers.

Dissatisfied with the solution of their relations with France which was formulated in the Ordinance of 1825, and without a satisfactory arrangement concerning commercial intercourse, the Haitians strove for years to secure a readjustment. Not until 1838, however, were Franco-Haitian treaties signed which greatly reduced the amount of the indemnity due to France, acknowledged Haiti as a sovereign state, and provided that commerce between the two countries should be upon the most-favored-nation basis.

Of the treaties negotiated by France with Spanish-American nations after 1848, the Franco-Dominican Treaty was perhaps the most comprehensive. Obviously the inhabitants of the Spanish portion of Santo Domingo had been encouraged to rise against their Haitian taskmasters by French officials in the West Indies. Dominican leaders evidently hoped that the rankling differences which still persisted between France and Haiti would encourage the French Government to aid them in their struggles for an autonomous political life. As soon as they realized that the very existence of their nation was menaced by the Black Republic, the Dominicans, relying upon assurances which had been held out by French officials, offered to transfer the sovereignty of their nation to France. Time and again they pleaded with French consular and diplomatic agents for the establishment of a protectorate over their country. Certain French agents in Latin America were, indeed, sorely tempted by pleas that their government protect weak but aspiring communties or, at least, lend them money and furnish them with arms and ammunition. Neverthless, the Chancellery of France refrained from measures that would have lent color to the view that it had schemed to establish a protectorate in the New World.

Recognition by France of the independence of the republics of Spanish origin scarcely holds such a distinctive place in the annals of the Latin-American nations as that occupied by her recognition of Brazil. Yet the adoption by a European power which had regular relations with the Vatican of a recognition policy resembling that pursued by England, Holland, and the United States was not without influence. The policy of the Bourgeois King eliminated a factor which had somewhat restrained the policies of minor European states. South of the Pyrenees a change of monarchs encouraged leaders. Long before certain American treaties contingent upon French recognition were framed, Castilian statesmen had reconsidered the status of their former colonies. In accordance with the wishes of Regent Christina, on December 3, 1836, the Spanish Cortes unanimously approved the report of a committee which recommended that the government be authorized to conclude treaties with the new American states on the basis of the acknowledgment of their independence and the renunciation by the motherland of her sovereign rights. Accordingly by a series of treaties negotiated between 1836 and 1895 Spain acknowledged the independence of her former colonies lying between the Rio Grande and the Strait of

Magellan. The end of the nineteenth century had thus been reached before both parties to the Bourbon Family Compact recognized the republics which had arisen within the former dominions of Charles III.

SELECTED BIBLIOGRAPHY

A. SOURCES

Many of the secondary accounts contain source material.
The abbreviations used for manuscript sources in footnotes of the present work are given below.

a. MANUSCRIPTS

A. A. E.   Archives du Ministère des Affaires Étrangères, Paris. The volumes in the series styled Correspondance Politique are cited in the footnotes simply by the names of the respective countries, while the volumes in the series known as Mémoires et Documents are preceded by that designation and followed by a specific title. The numbers which follow these titles refer to the volumes in the respective series.

A. C.   Archives Coloniales, Paris.

A. G. I.   Archivo General de Indias, Seville.

A. G. M.   Archivo General y Público de la Nación, Mexico City.

A. H. C   Archivo Historico Colonial, Lisbon.

A. H. N   Archivo Histórico Nacional, Madrid.

A. N.   Archives Nationales, Paris.

A. R. V. P.   Arkhiv Revoliutsii i Vneshnei Politiki, Moscow.

D. S.   Department of State, National Archives, Washington.

F. O.   Foreign Office, Public Record Office, London.

H. H. u. S.   Haus-, Hof- und Staats-Archiv, Vienna.

MSS. B. N. P.   Manuscriptos, Bibliotheca Nacional de Portugal, Lisbon.

MSS. F.   Manuscrits Français, Bibliothèque Nationale, Paris.

W. O.   War Office, Public Record Office, London.

b. PUBLISHED MATERIAL

I. Books, Pamphlets, and Broadsides

Abarca, Roque, and others, *Manifiesto,* October 30, 1808, Guadalajara, 1808.

Actas de la diputación general de Españoles que se junto en Bayona el 15 de Junio de 1808, Bayonne, 1808.

Adams, J. Q., *Memoirs of John Quincy Adams, Comprising Portions of His Diary from 1795 to 1848,* edited by C. F. Adams, vols. IV-VI, Philadelphia, 1875-77.

——, *Writings of John Quincy Adams,* edited by W. C. Ford, vol. VII, New York, 1917.

Almanach royal, Paris, 1826-58.

Aranda, Ricardo, editor, . . . *Colección de los tratados, convenciones, capitulaciones, armisticios y otros actos diplomáticos y políticos celebrados desde la independencia hasta el día,* vol. VII, Lima, 1901.

Archives parlementaires de 1787 à 1860. Recueil complet des débats legislatifs et politiques des chambres françaises, 127 vols., Paris, 1879-1913.

Bagot, Josceline, editor, *George Canning and His Friends, Containing Hitherto Unpublished Letters, Jeux d'esprit, etc.,* 2 vols., London, 1909.

Barante, A. G. P. B., *Souvenirs du Baron de Barante,* edited by C. de Barante, vol. III, Paris, 1893.

Beauchamp, Alphonse de, *L'Indépendance de l'Empire du Brésil présentée au monarques européens,* Paris, 1824.

Blanco, J. F., editor, *Documentos para la historia de la vida pública del Libertador de Colombia, Perú y Bolivia,* vols. I-III, Caracas, 1875-76.

Bolívar, Simón, *Cartas del Libertador,* edited by V. Lecuna, vols. IV, V, VIII, Caracas, 1929-30.

Bonaparte, Joseph, *Mémoires et correspondance politique et militaire du Roi Joseph,* edited by A. du Casse, 10 vols., Paris, 1853-54.

British and Foreign State Papers, London, 1841—.

Brossard, Alfred de, *Considérations historiques et politiques sur les républiques de la Plata dans leurs rapports avec la France et l'Angleterre,* Paris, 1850.

Bustamante, C. M., *Campañas del General D. Félix María Calleja, comandante en gefe del ejercito real de operaciones llamado del centro,* Mexico, 1828.

C. . . . de S. . . . , *Les Provinces de la Plata érigées en monarchie. Considérations politiques,* Paris, 1820.

Cadena, P. I., editor, *Anales diplomáticos de Colombia,* Bogotá, 1878.

Canning, George, *Some Official Correspondence of George Canning,* edited by E. J. Stapleton, 2 vols., London, 1887.

Carlota Joaquina, Princeza, *Justa reclamación que los representantes de la casa real de España . . . hacen á su Alteza Real el Principe Real de Portugal,* Rio de Janeiro, 1808.

——, *Manifiesto dirigido á los fieles vasallos de Su Magestad Católica,* Rio de Janeiro, 1808.

Centenario da independencia do Brasil: acclamação e côroação do Principe D. Pedro, Primeiro Imperador Constitucional do Brasil: "fac-similes" dos documentos do senado da camera do Rio de Janeiro, vol. I, Rio de Janeiro, 1922.

Centeno, F., editor, *Virutas históricas (1810-1928)*, 3 vols., Buenos Aires, 1929-35.

Cevallos, Pedro de, *Exposición de los hechos y maquinaciones que han preparado la usurpación de la corona de España y los medios que el Emperador do los Franceses ha puesto en obra para realizarla,* Madrid, 1808.

Chateaubriand, F. R., Vicomte de, *Congrès de Vérone. Guerre d'Espagne. Négociations. Colonies espagnoles,* 2 vols., Paris, 1838.

——, *Correspondance générale de Chateaubriand,* edited by L. Thomas, vols. III-V, Paris, 1913-24.

——, *Mémoires d'outre-tombe,* 6 vols., Paris, 1898-1900.

——, *Œuvres complètes,* edited by C. A. Sainte-Beuve, 12 vols., Paris, 1859-61.

Clark, J. R., . . . *Memorandum on the Monroe Doctrine,* Washington, 1930.

Clercq, A. J. H. de, editor *Recueil des traités de la France,* 17 vols., Paris, 1864-91.

Collecção das leis do Brazil, 1814, 1815, Rio de Janeiro, 1890.

Colección oficial de leyes, decretos, ordenes y resoluciones &c. que se han expedido para el régimen de la república boliviana, 1829-1831, La Paz, 1934.

Comisión de Bernardino Rivadavia ante España y otras potencias de Europa (1814-1820), 2 vols., Buenos Aires, 1933-36.

Communications with France and Spain, relating to the Spanish American Provinces, presented to both Houses of Parliament by Command of His Majesty, March, 1824, London, 1824.

Considérations sur l'état présent de l'Amérique du Sud et sur l'arrivée à Paris de M. Hurtado, Paris, 1824.

Constitución política de la República Dominicana, Santo Domingo, 1844.

Contestación del reyno de Nueva España al oficio, Mexico, 1808.

Convención preliminar acordada entre el gobierno de Buenos Aires y los comisionados de S. M. C., Buenos Aires, 1823.

Correspondencia entre el gobierno de Buenos Aires y el Sr. Visconde de Venancourt, comandante de las fuerzas navales de S. M. Cma. en el Río de la Plata, relativo al apresamiento que el expresado Sr. Vizconde hizo de los buques de guerra de la república en la noche del 21 al 22 de Mayo, Buenos Aires, 1829

Correspondencias generales de la provincia de Buenos Aires rela-

tivas á relaciones exteriores, 1820-1824 (*Documentos para la historia argentina*, vol. XIV), Buenos Aires, 1921.

D'Alaux, Gustave, *L'Empereur Soulouque et son empire*, Paris, 1856.

Damas, A. H. M., Baron de, *Mémoires du Baron de Damas* (*1785-1862*), edited by Count Pierre Damas, 2 vols., Paris, 1922-23.

Decretos del Rey Don Fernando VII, vol. I, Madrid, 1818.

Deffaudis, A. L., Baron, *Questions diplomatiques et particulièrement des travaux et de l'organization du ministère des affaires étrangères*, Paris, 1849.

Dhormoys, Paul, *Une visite chez Soulouque; souvenirs d'un voyage dans l'île d'Haïti*, Paris, 1859.

. . . *La diplomacia mexicana*, 3 vols., Mexico, 1910-13.

Documentos oficiales canjeados entre el gobierno de la República Oriental y el Sr. Vice-Almirante Baron de Mackau: publicados de orden del gobierno para ilustrar la opinión, Montevideo, 1840.

Documentos para la historia argentina, vol. XIV, Buenos Aires, 1921.

. . . *Documentos relativos á los antecedentes de la independencia de la república argentina*, Buenos Aires, 1912.

Errázuriz, Fernando, *Discurso*, June 1, 1831, Santiago de Chile [1831].

Esmangart, Charles, *La vérité sur les affaires d'Haïti*, Paris, 1833.

Estrada, Genaro, *Un siglo de relaciones internacionales de México á través de los mensajes presidenciales* (*Archivo histórico diplomático mexicano*, no. 39), Mexico, 1935.

Funes, Gregorio, *Proclama al clero del obispado de Córdoba de Tucumán por su provisor gobernador*, Buenos Aires [1808].

Gallatin, Albert, *The Writings of Albert Gallatin*, edited by Henry Adams, 3 vols., Philadelphia, 1879.

García, Genaro, editor, *Documentos históricos mexicanos, obra conmemorativa del primer centenario de la independencia de México*, vol. II, Mexico, 1910.

García de León y Pizarro, José, *Memorias de la vida del Exmo. Señor D. José García de León y Pizarro, escritas por el mismo*, 3 vols., Madrid, 1894-97.

El General Andrés de Santa-Cruz, Gran Mariscal de Zepita y el Gran Perú, edited by O. de Santa-Cruz, La Paz, 1924.

Gentz, Friedrich von, *Dépêches inédites du Chevalier de Gentz aux hospodars de Valachie*, edited by Count Prokesch-Osten, 3 vols., Paris, 1876-77.

——, *Schriften von Friedrich von Gentz. Ein Denkmal*, vol. III, Mannheim, 1839.

George IV, *The Letters of King George IV, 1812-1830,* edited by A. Aspinwall, vol. III, Cambridge, 1938.

Guizot, F. P. G., *Mémoires pour servir à l'histoire de mon temps,* vol. II, Paris, 1859.

Hansard, T. C., editor, *The Parliamentary Debates from the Year 1803 to the Present Time,* vol. XXXII, London, 1816.

Historia de la vida y reinado de Fernando VII de España, 3 vols., Madrid, 1842.

Hyde de Neuville, J. G., Baron, *Mémoires et souvenirs du Baron Hyde de Neuville,* vols. II and III, Paris, 1912.

Janvier, L. J., editor, *Les Constitutions d'Haïti (1801-1885),* Paris, 1886.

João, Regente, *Respuesta de S. A. R. el Príncipe Regente de Portugal á la reclamación hecha por Ss. Aa. Rr. la Princesa del Brazil y el Infante de España Don Pedro Carlos,* Rio de Janeiro, 1808.

La junta central gubernativa al presidente de la República Haïtiana, Santo Domingo, 1844.

Jurien de la Gravière, J. P. E., *Souvenirs d'un amiral,* 2 vols., Paris, 1860.

Lacroix, F. J. P., Vicomte de, *Mémoires pour servir à l'histoire de la révolution de Saint-Domingue,* 2 vols., Paris, 1819.

La Forest, A. R. C., Comte de, *Correspondance du Comte de la Forest, Ambassadeur de France en Espagne, 1808-1813,* edited by Geoffroy de Grandmaison (*Societé d'histoire contemporaine,* vols. XLII, XLV), vols. II and III, Paris, 1908-09.

Léger, J. N., editor, *Recueil des traités et conventions de la République d'Haïti,* Port-au-Prince, 1891.

Le Long, John, *Révélations à la France. Les Négociations au Río de la Plata,* Paris, 1851.

Le Moyne, Auguste, Chevalier, *La Nouvelle-Grenade, Santiago de Cuba, la Jamique et l'Isthme de Panama,* 2 vols., Paris, 1880.

Loi et ordonnances relatives à la République d'Haïti, et aux indemnités stipulées en faveur des anciens colons de Saint-Domingue, Paris, 1826.

López, C. A. [Broadside], Asunción, February 28, 1853, Asunción, 1853.

Mabragaña, Heraclio, editor, *Los mensajes: historia del desenvolvimiento de la Nación Argentina redactada cronológicamente por sus gobernantes, 1810-1910,* vols. I and II, Buenos Aires, 1910.

Manifestación de los pueblos de la parte del este de la isla antes Española, ó de Santo Domingo, sobre las causas de su separación de la República Haytiana, Santo Domingo, 1844.

Manifiesto del gobierno español á las potencias extrangeras sobre la independencia de las Américas, Mexico, 1822.

Manning, W. R., editor, *Diplomatic Correspondence of the United States concerning the Independence of the Latin-American Nations,* 3 vols., New York, 1925.

——, *Diplomatic Correspondence of the United States; Inter-American Affairs, 1831-1860,* vols. I-X, Washington, 1932-38.

Marcellus, M. L. J. A. C. de Martin du Tyra, Comte de, *Chateaubriand et son temps,* Paris, 1859.

——, *Politique de la restauration en 1822 et 1823 (correspondance intime de M. le Vte. de Chateaubriand),* Paris, 1853.

Martens, F. F., *Recueil des traités et conventions conclus par la Russie avec les puissances étrangères,* vols. IV, VII, XIV, XV, St. Petersburg, 1878, 1885, 1905, 1909.

Masterman, G. F., *Seven Eventful Years in Paraguay. A Narrative of Personal Experiences amongst the Paraguayans,* London, 1869.

Memorandum upon the Power to Recognize the Independence of a New Foreign State, Senate Documents, 54th Congress, 2d. session, no. 56, Washington, 1897.

Memoria del ministerio de relaciones exteriores presentada al congresso constitucional del año de 1829, Santiago de Chile, 1829.

Memoria que el ministro de estado en el departamento de relaciones esteriores presenta al congreso nacional año de 1834, Santiago de Chile, 1834.

Memoria que el ministro de estado en el departamento de relaciones exteriores presenta al congreso nacional en 1849, Santiago de Chile, 1849.

Memoria que el ministro del despacho en el departamento de relaciones exteriores presenta al congreso nacional de 1846, Santiago de Chile, 1846.

Memoria que el ministro de estado en el departamento de relaciones exteriores presenta al congreso nacional convocado extraordinariamente para el mes de Octubre de 1858, Lima, 1858.

Mensage á la decimatercia legislatura, Buenos Aires, 1836.

Mensage del poder executivo á la tercera legislatura constitutional á la apertura de las sesiones ordinarias de 1838, Montevideo, 1838.

Metternich, C. L. W., Fürst von, *Aus Metternich's nachgelassenen Papieren,* edited by Prince Richard Metternich, 4 vols., Vienna, 1880-84.

Métral, A. M. T., *Histoire de l'expédition des français à Saint-Domingue sous le consulat de Napoléon Bonaparte,* Paris, 1825.

Mollien, F. N., Comte, *Mémoires d'une ministre du trésor public,*

1780-1815, avec une notice par M. C. Gomel, vol. II, Paris, 1898.

Mollien, G. T., *Voyage dans la République de Columbia en 1823,* 2 vols., Paris, 1825.

Monarchical Projects or a Plan to place a Bourbon King on the Throne of Buenos Aires, in Opposition to British Interests, being the Proceedings Instituted against the late Congress and Directory, for the Crime of High Treason, London, 1820.

Monroe, James, *The Writings of James Monroe,* edited by S. M. Hamilton, vol. V, New York, 1901.

Moore, J. B., editor, *A Digest of International Law,* 8 vols., Washington, 1906.

Morel-Fatio, Alfred, editor, *Recueil des instructions données aux ambassadeurs et ministres de France depuis les traités de Westphalie jusqu'à la révolution française,* vol. VII *bis,* Paris, 1899.

Murat, J. B. A., Comte, *Murat, lieutenant de l'empereur en Espagne, 1808, d'après sa correspondance inédite et des documents originaux,* Paris, 1897.

Napoléon I, *Correspondance de Napoléon 1er, publiée par ordre de l'Empereur Napoléon III,* vols. XVI-XX, Paris, 1864-66.

Nesselrode, C. R., Comte de, *Lettres et papiers du Chancelier Comte de Nesselrode, 1760-1850, extraits de ses archives,* vols. V, VI, VII, Paris, 1907-09.

Neves, J. A. das, *Reflexões sobre a invasão dos Franceses em Portugal,* Lisbon, 1809.

Noailles, H. G. H., Marquis de, *Le Comte Molé, 1781-1855. Sa vie, ses mémoires,* vol. III, Paris, 1924.

9a, 10a, 11a y 12a sesiones de la junta española, Bayonne, 1808.

Núñez, Ignacio, *Noticias históricas, políticas y estadísticas de las Provincias Unidas del Río de la Plata,* London, 1825.

Ofalia (Narcisco de Hereida), Conde, de, *Escritos del Conde de Ofalia,* edited by the Marquis of Hereida, Bilbao, 1894.

Oficio del excmo. cabildo de Lima al excmo. señor virey, Lima, 1808.

O'Leary, D. F., editor, *Memorias del General O'Leary, publicados por su hijo Simón B. O'Leary,* vol. XVIII, Caracas, 1882.

Páez, J. A., *Autobiografía del General José Antonio Páez,* 2 vols., New York, 1869.

Parish, Woodbine, *Buenos Ayres and the Provinces of the Río de la Plata,* London, 1852.

Pasquier, E. D., Duc de, . . . *Mémoires du Chancelier Pasquier,* edited by the Duc d'Audiffret-Pasquier, vol. V, Paris, 1894.

Pièces officielles relatives aux négociations du gouvernement français avec le gouvernement haïtien pour traiter de la formalité de la reconnaissance de l'indépendance d'Haïti, Port-au-Prince, 1824.

Pièces relatives aux communications faites au nom du gouvernement français au président d'Hayti par M. le Général Dauxion-Lavaysse, New York, 1816.

Pièces relatives à la correspondance de mm. les commissaires de S. M. Très-Chrétienne et du président d'Haïti, précédées d'une proclamation au peuple et à l'armée, Port-au-Prince, 1816.

Polovstoff, A. A., editor, *Correspondance diplomatique des ambassadeurs et ministres de Russie en France et de France en Russie avec leurs gouvernements de 1814 à 1830*, 3 vols., St. Petersburg, 1902-1907.

Proceso original justificativo contra los reos acusados de alta traición en el congreso y directorio mandados juzgar por el artículo séptimo del tratado de paz firmado por este gobierno con los gefes de las fuerzas federales de Santa Fé y la Banda Oriental en veintitres de Febrero del corriente año de 1820, Buenos Aires, 1820.

Pueyrredón, J. M. de, . . . *Documentos del archivo de Pueyrredón*, vol. II, Buenos Aires, 1912.

Recopilación de leyes del Ecuador, edited by A. Noboa, vol. II, Guayaquil, 1900.

Recueil général des lois et des arrêts en matière civil, criminelle, commerciale et de droit public depuis l'avènement de Napoléon, edited by J. B. Sirey, vols. I—, Paris, n. d.

Registro de documentos del gobierno, no. 44, Santiago de Chile, 1826.

Registro oficial de la república argentina que comprende los documentos espedidos desde 1810 hasta 1873, vols. I and II, Buenos Aires, 1879-80.

República Dominicana: la junta central gubernativa, conservador y representante de los derechos de los pueblos, Santo Domingo, 1844.

Ríos, J. M. de los, editor, *Código español del reinado intruso de José Napoleón Bonaparte, ó sea colección de sus mas importantes leyes, decretos é instituciones*, Madrid, 1845.

Robertson, J. P., and W. P., *Letters on Paraguay, Comprising an Account of a Four Years' Residence in that Republic under the Government of the Dictator Francia*, 2 vols., London, 1838.

Roussin, A. R., *Le Pilote du Brésil, ou description des côtes de l'Amérique meridionale, comprisés entre l'îsle Sta. Catarina et celle de Maranão*, Paris, 1826.

Rovigo, A. M. R. S., Duc de, *Mémoires du Duc de Rovigo, pour servir à l'histoire de l'Empereur Napoléon*, edited by D. Lacroix, vol. II, Paris, 1900.

Rush, Richard, *A Residence at the Court of London, Comprising Incidents, Official and Personal, from 1819 to 1825,* 2 vols., London, 1845.

Saldías, A., *Historia de la Confederación Argentina, Rosas y su época,* 5 vols., Buenos Aires, 1892.

Santander, F. de P., *Archivo Santander,* edited by E. Restrepo Tirado, vol. XII, Bogotá, 1917.

Sesión primera de la junta española, Bayonne, 1808.

Sesión quinta de la junta española, Bayonne, 1808.

Statistique de la France, publiée par le ministre des travaux publics, de l'agriculture et du commerce, Paris, 1838.

. . . , *Tableau générale du commerce de la France avec les colonies et les puissances étrangères,* Paris, 1851.

Tratados y convenciones celebrados y no ratificados por la república mexicana, Mexico, 1878.

Turgot, A. R. J., *Œuvres de Turgot,* edited by E. Daire, vol. II, Paris, 1844.

Uribe, A. J., editor, *Anales diplomáticos y consulares de Colombia,* vol. III, Bogotá, 1914.

Villèle, J. B. S. J., Comte de, *Mémoires et correspondance du Comte de Villèle,* 5 vols., Paris, 1888-90.

Wallez, J. B. G., *Précis historique des négociations entre la France et Saint-Domingue,* Paris, 1826.

Walton, William, *An Exposé on the Dissensions of Spanish America,* London, 1814.

Webster, C. K., editor, *Britain and the Independence of Latin America, 1812-1830: Select Documents from the Foreign Office Archives,* 2 vols., London, 1938.

Wellington, Arthur Wellesley, Duke of, *Despatches, Correspondence, and Memoranda of Field Marshal Arthur, Duke of Wellington,* edited by his son, the Duke of Wellington, 2 vols., London, 1867.

——, *Supplementary Despatches, Correspondence, and Memoranda of Field Marshal Arthur, Duke of Wellington,* edited by his son, the Duke of Wellington, vols. XI, XII, London, 1864-65.

II. NEWSPAPERS, PERIODICALS, AND PUBLICATIONS OF LEARNED SOCIETIES

1. Newspapers

Rare numbers of Spanish-American journals in some years were found in the Archives du ministère des affaires étrangères.

El Araucano, Santiago de Chile, 1833.
British Packet and Argentine News, Buenos Aires, 1836.
El conciliador, Lima, 1830.
El constitucional, periódico oficial del gobierno, San Salvador, 1865.
Le Constitutionnel, journal du commerce, politique et littéraire, Paris, 1819-66.
Correo de Carácas, Caracas, 1839.
Correo político y mercantil de las Provincias Unidas del Río de la Plata, Buenos Aires, 1828.
The Courier, London, 1817—.
Le Courrier français, Paris, 1820-51.
Daily National Intelligencer, Washington, 1819.
Diario de la tarde, comercial, político y literario, Buenos Aires, 1840-41.
Le Drapeau blanc, Paris, 1825.
L'Étoile, journal du soir, Paris, 1820-27.
Feuille du commerce, Port-au-Prince, 1833-60.
Gaceta de Madrid, Madrid, 1824, 1830.
La gaceta mercantil, diario comercial, político y literario, Buenos Aires, 1840.
Gazeta de Guatemala, Santiago de Guatemala, 1808, 1849.
Gazeta de México, Mexico, 1808.
Gazeta ministerial de Sevilla, Seville, 1808.
Gazette de France, Paris, 1820-48.
El indicador, Santiago de Chile, 1827.
El iris de la Paz, La Paz, 1831.
Journal des débats, politiques et littéraires, Paris, 1814-64.
Journal de Paris, politique, commercial et littéraire, Paris, 1817-27.
Journal du commerce, Paris, 1820-30.
El liberal, Santiago de Chile, 1824.
El monitor peruano, Lima, 1831.
Le Moniteur universel, Paris, 1814-65.
The Morning Chronicle, London, 1822-25.
El Paraguayo independiente, Asunción, 1850.
La Quotidienne, Paris, 1820-47.
Supplemento al Peruano, Lima, 1826.
Le Télégraphe, Port-au-Prince, 1813-43.
The Times, London, 1817—.

2. Periodicals; Publications of Learned Societies

D'Alaux, Gustave, "La République Dominicaine et l'Empereur Soulouque," *Revue des deux mondes,* 1st series, LXXXII, 193-224, 459-502, Paris, 1851.

The Annual Register, or a View of the History, Politics, and Literature . . . , 1808—, London, 1810—.

"El aventurero Conde Octaviano d'Alvimar, espía de Napoleón," *Boletín del archivo general de la nación,* VII, 161-75, Mexico, 1936.

C. L. B., "Des Rapports de la France et de l'Europe avec l'Amérique du Sud," *Revue des deux mondes,* 4th series, XXXI, 54-69, Paris, 1838.

Cané, Miguel, editor, "La diplomacia de la revolución; el Director Pueyrredón y el emisario Le Moyne (nuevos documentos)," *La biblioteca,* IV, 206-21, 397-425; V, 94-121, 257-76, 409-32, Buenos Aires, 1897.

Carra de Vaux, Bernard, Baron, "Documents sobre la perte et la rétrocession de la Guyane française (1809-1817)," *Revue de l'histoire des colonies françaises,* I, 333-68, Paris, 1913.

"Clark-Genét Correspondence," *American Historical Association Report,* 1896, I, 930-1107, Washington, 1897.

Coiscou Henríquez, Máximo, editor, "Correspondencia diplomática de Levasseur, de Moges, Barrot, etc. Años 1843 y 1844," *Clío,* IV, 2-6, 39-45, 87-98, 120-23, 144-150; V, 23-28, 45-50, 91-92, Ciudad Trujillo, 1936-37.

Correio braziliense ou armazem literario, vols. I and II, London, 1808-09.

"Correspondence of the Russian Ministers in Washington, 1818-1825," *American Historical Review,* XVIII, 309-45, 537-62, New York, 1913.

Lesur, C. L., editor, *Annuaire historique, ou histoire politique et littéraire,* 1818-55, Paris, 1819-56.

Lokke, C. L., editor, "French Designs on Paraguay in 1803," *Hispanic American Historical Review,* VIII, 392-405, Durham, 1928.

"Napoleón Bonaparte assume la dirección del movimiento de independencia en México," *El movimiento histórico en México,* no. 1, pp. 1 ff., Mexico, 1937.

Niles' Weekly Register, vols. X-XLVIII, Baltimore, 1816-35.

The Pamphleteer, vol. XVIII, London, 1821.

"Papeles de Ugarte: Documentos para la historia de Fernando VII," *Boletín de la biblioteca de Menéndez Pelayo,* vol. XVI, no. 3, pp. 217-45, Santander, 1934.

"Protocols of Conferences of Representatives of the Allied Powers respecting Spanish America, 1824-1825," *American Historical Review*, XXII, 595-616, New York, 1917.

Sbornik Imperatorskago Russkago Istoricheskago Obschestvo, vol. CXIX, St. Petersburg, 1879.

Temperley, Harold, editor, "Documents Illustrating the Reception and Interpretation of the Monroe Doctrine in Europe, 1823-4," *English Historical Review*, XXXIX, 590-93, London, 1924.

——, editor, "The Instructions to Donzelot, Governor of Martinique, 17 December 1823," *English Historical Review*, XLI, 585-87, London, 1926.

B. SECONDARY ACCOUNTS

a. BOOKS AND PAMPHLETS

Accioly, H. P. P., *O reconhecimiento da independencia do Brasil*, Rio de Janeiro, 1927.

Alamán, Lucas, *Historia de Méjico*, vol. I, Mexico, 1849.

Amunátegui, M. L., *Vida de Don Andrés Bello*, Santiago de Chile, 1882.

Arona, Juan de (pseudonym, ascribed to Paz Soldán y Unanue), *Páginas diplomáticas del Perú*, Lima, 1891.

Auchmuty, J. J., *The United States Government and Latin American Independence, 1810-1830*, London, 1937.

Báez, Cecilio, *Historia diplomática del Paraguay*, 2 vols., Asunción, 1931-32.

Bancroft, H. H., *History of Mexico*, vol. V, New York, n. d.

Barros Arana, Diego, *Historia jeneral de Chile*, vols. XV and XVI, Santiago de Chile, 1897, 1902.

Barros Borgoño, Luis, *La missión del vicario apostólico Don Juan Muzi*, Santiago de Chile, 1886.

Baudrillart, Alfred, *Philippe V et la cour de France, 1700 à 1715*, 5 vols., Paris, 1890-1901.

Baumgarten, Fritz, and others, *Ibero-Amerika und die Hansestädte. Die Entwickelung ihrer wirtschaftlichen und kulturellen Beziehungen*, Hamburg, 1937.

Bealer, L. W., . . . , *Los corsarios de Buenos Aires: sus actividades en las guerras hispano-americanas de la independencia, 1815-1821*, Buenos Aires, 1937.

Beau de Loménie, Emmanuel, . . . *La carrière politique de Chateaubriand de 1814 à 1830*, 2 vols., Paris, 1829.

Becker, Jerónimo, *Acción de la diplomacia española durante la guerra de la independencia, 1808-1814*, Saragossa, 1909.

——, *Historia de les relaciones exteriores de España durante el siglo XIX (Apuntes para una historia diplomática)*, vol. I, Madrid, 1924.

——, *Relaciones comerciales entre España y Francia durante el siglo XIX*, Madrid, 1910.

——, *Relaciones diplomáticas entre España y la Santa Sede durante el siglo XIX*, Madrid, 1908.

Belaunde, V. A., *Bolívar and the Political Thought of the Spanish-American Revolution*, Baltimore, 1938.

Belgrano, Mario, *La Francia y la monarquía en el Plata (1818-1820)*, Buenos Aires, 1933.

——, *Rivadavia y sus gestiones diplomáticas con España (1815-1820)*, Buenos Aires, 1934.

Bourgeois, Émile, *Manuel historique de politique étrangère*, vols. I-III, Paris, 1922-24.

Cady, J. F., *Foreign Intervention in the Río de la Plata, 1838-50*, Philadelphia, 1929.

Calogeras, J. P., *A politica exterior do imperio*, vol. II, Rio de Janeiro, 1928.

Cambronero, Carlos, *El rey intruso*, Madrid, 1909.

Campos, R. A. de, *Relações diplomaticas do Brasil*, Rio de Janeiro, 1913.

Capefigue, J. B. H. R., *Diplomatie de la France et de l'Espagne depuis l'avénement de la maison de Bourbon*, Paris, 1846.

——, *Histoire de la restauration et des causes qui ont amené la chute de la branche ainée des Bourbons*, vol. I, Paris, 1845.

Castonnet des Fosses, H. L., *La perte d'une colonie: La révolution de Saint-Domingue*, Paris, 1893.

Chancy, Emmanuel, *L'Indépendance nationale d'Haïti*, Paris, 1884.

Chase, M. K., *Négociations de la République de Texas en Europe, 1837-1845*, Paris 1932.

Cisternes, Raoul de, *Le Duc de Richelieu, son action aux conférences d'Aix-la-Chapelle, sa retraite du pouvoir. Documents originaux recueillis et annotés*, Paris, 1898.

Clercq, A. J. H. de, and Vallet, C. de, *Guide pratique des consulats publié sous les auspices du ministère des affaires étrangères*, 2 vols., Paris, 1858.

Conard, P., . . . *La Constitution de Bayonne (1808), essai d'édition critique*, Paris, 1910.

Cox, I. J., *The West Florida Controversy, 1798-1813*, Baltimore, 1918.

Cresson, W. P., *The Holy Alliance*, New York, 1922.

Dahlgren, E. W., *Les relations commerciales et maritimes entre la France et les côtes de l'Océan Pacifique*, vol. I, Paris, 1909.

Dunn, W. E., *Spanish and French Rivalry in the Gulf Region of the United States, 1678-1702: the Beginnings of Texas and*

Pensacola (University of Texas Bulletin, no. 1705), Austin, 1917.

État sommaire des versements faits aux archives nationales par les ministères et les administrations qui en dépendent (série F, B B *Justice et A D XIX*), vol. II, Paris, 1927.

Fabela, Isidro, *Los precursores de la diplomacia mexicana* (*Archivo histórico diplomático mexicano,* no. 20), Mexico, 1926.

Flammeront, Jules, *Le Chancelier Maupeou et les parlements,* Paris, 1883.

Flassan, J. B. G. de R., *Histoire générale et raisonnée de la diplomatie française ou de la politique de la France depuis la fondation de la monarchie jusqu'à la fin du règne de Louis XVI,* 7 vols., Paris, 1811.

Ford, W. C., and Adams, C. F., *John Quincy Adams; His Connection with the Monroe Doctrine (1823), and with Emancipation under Martial Law (1819-1842),* Cambridge, 1902.

Fugier, André, *Napoléon et Espagne, 1799-1808,* 2 vols., Paris, 1930.

Garrett, M. B., *The French Colonial Question, 1789-1791. Dealings of the Constituent Assembly with Problems Arising from the Revolution in the West Indies,* Ann Arbor, 1918.

Geoffroy de Grandmaison, C. A., *L'Ambassade française en Espagne pendant la révolution (1789-1804),* Paris, 1892.

——, *L'Espagne et Napoléon, 1804-1809,* Paris, 1908.

——, *L'Espagne et Napoléon, 1809-1811,* Paris, 1925.

——, *L'Espagne et Napoléon, 1812-1814,* Paris, 1931.

Gervain, Baronne, *Un ministre de la marine et son ministère sous la restauration, le Baron Portal,* Paris, 1898.

Gibbs, F. W., *Recognition: A Chapter from the History of the North and South American States,* London, 1863.

Gil Fortoul, José, *Historia constitucional de Venezuela,* 2 vols., Berlin, 1907-09.

Goepp, Edouard and Cordiér, E. L., *Les grandes hommes de la France, navigateurs,* Paris, 1882.

Griffin, C. C., *The United States and the Disruption of the Spanish Empire, 1810-1822,* New York, 1937.

Groussac, Paul, . . . *Santiago de Liniers, conde de Buenos Aires, 1753-1810,* Buenos Aires, 1907.

Hatin, Eugène, *Bibliographie historique et critique de la presse periodique française,* Paris, 1866.

Haussonville, J. O. B. de C., Comte d', *Histoire de la politique extérieure du gouvernement français, 1830-1848,* 2 vols., Paris, 1850.

Indice de los papeles de la junta central suprema gubernativa del reino y del consejo de regencia, Madrid, 1904.

Inventaire sommaire des archives du département des affaires étrangères, correspondance politique, vols. I and II, Paris, 1903-19.

Inventaire sommaire des archives du département des affaires étrangères, mémoires et documents, France, Paris, 1883.

Inventaire sommaire des archives du département des affaires étrangères, mémoires et documents, fonds divers, Paris, 1892.

Inventaire sommaire des archives modernes de la marine, série B B⁴, service général (campagnes), part 1, Paris, 1914.

Inventaire sommaire des archives du département des affaires étrangères, mémoires et documents, fonds France et fonds divers, supplément, Paris, 1896.

Leconte, V., *Henri Christophe dans l'histoire d'Haïti,* Paris, 1931.

Leland, W. G., *Guide to Materials for American History in the Libraries and Archives of Paris,* vol. I, Washington, 1932.

Leturia, Pedro, . . . *Bolívar y León XII,* Caracas, 1931.

——, . . . *La acción diplomática de Bolivar ante Pío VII (1820-1823) á la luz del archivo vaticano,* Madrid, 1925.

López, V. F., *Historia de la república argentina, su origen, su revolución, y su desarrollo político hasta 1852,* vols. VIII-X, Buenos Aires, 1911.

Maggiolo, Adrien, Vicomte, . . . *Pozzo di Borgo, 1764-1842,* Paris, 1890.

Manchester, A. K., *British Preëminence in Brazil: Its Rise and Decline,* Chapel Hill, 1933.

Martínez Silva, Carlos, *Biografía de D. José Fernández Madrid,* Bogotá, 1889.

Mitre, Bartolomé, *Historia de Belgrano y de la independencia argentina,* 3 vols., Buenos Aires, 1887.

——, *Historia de San Martín y de la emancipación sud-americana,* 3 vols., Buenos Aires, 1887-88.

Moore, J. B., *The Principles of American Diplomacy,* New York, 1918.

Muhlenbeck, E., *Étude sur les origines de la Sainte-Alliance,* Paris, n. d.

Nettement, Alfred, *Histoire de la restauration,* 8 vols., Paris, 1860-72.

Newton, A. P., *The European Nations in the West Indies, 1493-1688,* London, 1933.

Oliveira Lima, Manoel de, *Dom João VI no Brazil, 1808-1821,* 2 vols., Rio de Janeiro, 1908.

——, *Historia diplomatica do Brazil: o reconhecimento do imperio,* Rio de Janeiro, 1902.

Oman, C. W. C., *A History of the Peninsular War,* vol. I, Oxford, 1902.

Otero, J. P., *Historia del Libertador Don José de San Martín*, 4 vols., Brussels, 1832.

Paxson, F. L., *The Independence of the South-American Republics. A Study in Recognition and Foreign Policy*, Philadelphia, 1903.

Pereira da Silva, J. M., *Historia da fundação do imperio brazileiro*, 3 vols., Rio de Janeiro, 1870, 1871.

Pérez de Guzmán, Juan, *El dos de Mayo de 1808 en Madrid*, Madrid, 1908.

Perkins, Dexter, *The Monroe Doctrine, 1823-1826*, Cambridge, 1927.

——, *The Monroe Doctrine, 1826-1867*, Baltimore, 1933.

Personas que han tenido á su cargo la secretaría de relaciones exteriores desde 1821 hasta 1824 (*Archivo histórico diplomático mexicano*, no. 6), Mexico, 1924.

Phillips, W. A., *The Confederation of Europe, a Study of the European Alliance, 1813-1823, as an Experiment in the International Organization of Peace*, London, 1914.

Posada, Eduardo, *Apostillas á la historia colombiana*, Madrid, 1918.

René-Moreno, Gabriel, *Ultimos días coloniales en el Alto-Perú*, 2 vols., Santiago de Chile, 1896, 1901.

Rippy, J. F., *Rivalry of the United States and Great Britain over Latin America (1808-1830)*, Baltimore, 1929.

Robertson, W. S., "The Beginnings of Spanish-American Diplomacy," *Turner Essays in American History*, pp. 231-67, New York, 1910.

——, "Francisco de Miranda and the Revolutionizing of Spanish America," *American Historical Association Report*, 1907, I, 195-539, Washington, 1908.

——, *Hispanic-American Relations with the United States*, New York, 1923.

——, *The Life of Miranda*, 2 vols., Chapel Hill, 1929.

——, *Rise of the Spanish-American Republics as Told in the Lives of their Liberators*, New York, 1918.

Rubío, J. M., . . . *La Infanta Carlota Joaquina y la política de España en América (1808-1812)*, Madrid, 1920.

Ruíz Guiñazú, Enrique, *La magistratura indiana*, Buenos Aires, 1916.

——, *Lord Strangford y la revolución de Mayo*, Buenos Aires, 1937.

Rydjord, John, *Foreign Interest in the Independence of New Spain*, Durham, 1935.

Santarem, M. F. de Barros, Visconde de, *Quadro elementar das relações politicas e diplomaticas de Portugal com as diversas potencias do mundo desde o principio da monarchia portugueza até nossos dias*, vol. XVIII, Paris, 1876.

Sarrailh, Jean, . . . *Un homme d'état espagnol: Martínez de la Rosa* (*1787-1862*), Bordeaux, 1930.

Sassenay, C. H. E., Marquis de, *Napoléon Ier et la fondation de la République Argentine* . . . , Paris, 1892.

Schiemann, Theodor, *Geschichte Russlands unter Kaiser Nikolaus I,* vols. I and II, Berlin, 1904, 1908.

Schœlcher, Victor, *Vie de Toussaint-Louverture,* Paris, 1889.

Smyth, W. H., *The Life and Services of Captain Philip Beaver,* London, 1829.

Snow, Freeman, *Treaties and Topics in American Diplomacy,* Boston, 1894.

Sorel, Albert, *L'Europe et la révolution française,* vol. VII, Paris, 1904.

Sosa, Luis de, *Don Francisco de la Rosa, político y poeta,* Madrid, 1930.

Stern, Alfred, *Geschichte Europas seit den Verträgen von 1815 bis zum Frankfurter Frieden von 1871,* vols. I-VII, Berlin, 1894-1911.

Tansill, C. C., *The United States and Santo Domingo, 1798-1873,* Baltimore, 1938.

Temperley, Harold, *The Foreign Policy of Canning, 1822-1827,* London, 1925.

——, *Life of Canning,* London, 1905.

Thiers, Adolphe, *Histoire du consulat et de l'empire,* vols. VIII and IX, Leipzig, 1849.

Torres Lanzas, Pedro, *Independencia de América, fuentes para su estudio. Catálogo de documentos conservados en el archivo general de Indies de Sevilla,* 1st series, vols. I-VI, Madrid, 1912; 2d series, vol. I, Seville, 1924.

Villanueva, C. A., *Historia de la república argentina,* 2 vols., Paris, 1914.

——, *Historia y diplomacia: Napoleón y la independencia de América,* Paris, 1911.

——, *La monarquía en América: Bolívar y el General San Martín,* Paris, 1911.

——, *La monarquía en América: Fernando VII y los nuevos estados,* Paris, n. d.

——, *La monarquía en América: el imperio de los Andes,* Paris, 1914.

——, *La monarquía en América: la Santa Alianza,* Paris, n. d.

Villiers du Terrage, Marc, Baron de, *Les dernières années de la Louisiane française,* Paris, 1903.

Ward, A. W., and Gooch, G. P., *The Cambridge History of British Foreign Policy, 1783-1919,* vol. II, London, 1923.

Webster, C. K., *The Foreign Policy of Castlereagh, 1815-1822,* London, 1925.

Williams, J. F., *La doctrine de la reconnaissance en droit international et ses développements récents,* Paris, 1934.
Wilson, A. M., *French Foreign Policy during the Administration of Cardinal Fleury, 1726-1743,* Cambridge, 1936.
Yonge, C. D., *The Life and Administration of Robert Banks, Second Earl of Liverpool,* vol. II, London, 1868.
Zubieta, P. A., . . . *Apuntaciones sobre las primeras misiones diplomáticas de Colombia,* Bogotá, 1924.

b. ARTICLES IN NEWSPAPERS AND PERIODICALS

Adams, Henry, " Napoléon I et Saint Domingue," *Revue historique,* XXIV, 92-130, Paris, 1884.
Belgrano, Mario, " La Francia y la monarquía en el Plata: actitud de Inglaterra, 1818-1820," *Boletín del instituto de investigaciones históricas,* XVIII, 80-113, Buenos Aires, 1935.
Blue, G. V., " French Interest in Pacific America in the Eighteenth Century," *Pacific Historical Review,* IV, 246-66, Glendale, 1935.
Caillet Bois, R. R., " La misión de Antonini en 1808," *Boletín del instituto de investigaciones históricas,* XV, 199-204, Buenos Aires, 1932.
Colmache, G., " How Cuba Might Have Belonged to France," *Fortnightly Review,* new series, LVIII, 747-52, London, 1895.
Cresson, E. P., " Chateaubriand and the Monroe Doctrine," *North American Review,* CCXVII, 475-87, New York, 1923.
Desdevises du Dézert, Georges, " De Trafalgar á Aranjuez (1805-1808). Notas de historia diplomática," *Cultura española,* 1906, no. 4, pp. 943-68; 1907, no. 5, pp. 7-19, Madrid, 1906-07.
Ettinger, A. A., " The Proposed Anglo-Franco-American Treaty of 1852 to Guarantee Cuba to Spain," *Transactions of the Royal Historical Society,* 4th series, XIII, 149-85.
" Francia; relaciones diplomáticas," *La nación,* July 9, 1916, Buenos Aires, 1916.
Gil Fortoul, José, " Relaciones exteriores de Venezuela," *El cojo ilustrado,* XII, 234-35, 264-68, Caracas, 1903.
Green, J. E. S., " Wellington, Boislecomte, and the Congress of Verona, 1822," *Transactions of the Royal Historical Society,* 4th series, I, 59-76, London, 1918.
Key-Ayala, Santiago, " Bolívar y el Almirante Jurien de la Gravière," *El cojo ilustrado,* XXII, 634-36; 662-65, Caracas, 1913.
Leturia, Pedro, " El reconocimiento de la emancipación hispanoamericana en la ' Sacra Congregazione degli affari ecclesi-

astici straordinari,' " . . II⁰ congreso internacional de historia de América, IV, 230-49, Buenos Aires, 1938.

Loreto, Baron de, " Reconnaissance de l'Empire du Brésil par les puissances européennes (1823-1828)," Revue d'histoire diplomatique, III, 502-522, Paris, 1889.

Molinari, D. L., " Mito Canning y Doctrina Monroe, á proposito de una manía," Nosotros, XVII, 86-94, Buenos Aires, 1915.

——, " Fernando VII y la emancipación de América (1814-1819)," . . . II⁰ congreso internacional de historia de América, IV, 256-319, Buenos Aires, 1938.

Mouy, Charles, Comte de, " L'ambassade du général Junot à Lisbonne d'après des documents inédits," Revue des deux mondes, series 4, CXXI, 124-61, Paris, 1894.

Muret, Pierre, " Les papiers de l'abbé Béliardi et les relations commerciales de la France et de l'Espagne au milieu du XVIII⁰ siècle (1757-1770)," Revue d'histoire moderne et contemporaine, IV, 657-72, Paris, 1903.

Perkins, Dexter, " Russia and the Spanish Colonies, 1817-1818," American Historical Review, XXVIII, 656-72, New York, 1923.

——, " Europe, Spanish America, and the Monroe Doctrine," ibid., XXVII, 207-18, New York, 1922.

Robertson, W. S., " The Juntas of 1808 and the Spanish Colonies," English Historical Review, XXXI, 573-85, London, 1916.

——, " The Monroe Doctrine Abroad in 1823-24," American Political Science Review, VI, 546-63, Baltimore, 1912.

——, " The Policy of Spain toward Its Revolted Colonies, 1820-1823," Hispanic American Historical Review, VI, 21-46, Durham, 1926.

——, " The Recognition of the Hispanic American Nations by the United States," ibid., I, 239-69, Baltimore, 1918.

——, " South America and the Monroe Doctrine, 1824-1828," Political Science Quarterly, XXX, 82-105, New York, 1915.

——, " The United States and Spain in 1822," American Historical Review, XX, 781-800, New York, 1915.

Rousseau, François, " L'Ambassade du Marquis de Talaru en Espagne, Juillet, 1823—Août, 1824," Revue des questions historiques, XC, 86-116, Paris, 1911.

Rydjord, John, " Napoleon and the Independence of New Spain," in New Spain and the Anglo-American West, edited by G. P. Hammond, I, 289-312, Lancaster, 1932.

Schaumann, A. F. H., " Geschichte des Congresses von Verona," Historisches Taschenbuch, 3rd series, VII, 1-101, Leipzig, 1855.

Schellenberg, T. R., " The Secret Treaty of Verona: A Newspaper Forgery," Journal of Modern History, VII, 280-91, Chicago, 1935.

Sciout, Ludovic, "La révolution à Saint-Domingue: les commissaires Sonthonax et Polverel," *Revue des questions historiques,* LXIV, 399-470, Paris, 1898.

Sée, Henri, "Esquisse de l'histoire du commerce française à Cadix et dans l'Amérique espagnole au XVIIIᵉ siècle," *Revue d'histoire moderne,* III, 13-31, Paris, 1928.

Sloane, W. M., "Napoleon's Plans for a Colonial System," *American Historical Review,* IV, 439-55, New York, 1899.

Temperley, Harold, "Canning and the Conferences of the Four Allied Governments at Paris, 1823-1826," *ibid.,* XXX, 16-31, New York, 1924.

——, "French Designs on Spanish America in 1820-5," *English Historical Review,* XL, 34-53, London, 1925.

Tessier, G., "Canning et Chateaubriand, L'Angleterre et la France pendant la guerre d'Espagne," *Revue d'histoire diplomatique,* XXII, 569-617, Paris, 1908.

Thomas, Louis, "Supplément au Congrès de Vérone. Correspondance avec le Prince de Polignac," *Revue politique et littéraire; revue bleu,* vol. L, pt. 2, pp. 513-18, 454-51, Paris, 1912.

Thompson, Valentin, "Napoléon et l'Amérique," *Franco-American Review,* I, 208-14, New Haven, 1937.

Turner, F. J., "The Origin of Genêt's Projected Attack on Louisiana and the Floridas," *American Historical Review,* III, 650-71, New York, 1898.

Villanueva, C. A., "La Diplomatie française dans l'Amérique latine," *Bulletin de la bibliothèque américaine,* October, 1916, January-February, 1918, Paris, 1916, 1918.

——, "La Diplomatie française et la reconnaissance de l'indépendance de Buenos Aires, de la Colombie et du Mexique par l'Angleterre (1825)," *ibid.,* October, 1912, Paris, 1912.

——, "French Diplomacy in Latin America," *Inter-America,* I, 157-68, New York, 1917.

——, "Napoléon et les députés de l'Amérique aux cortès de Bayonne (1808)," *Bulletin de la bibliothèque américaine,* Paris, 1911.

Villa-Urrutia, W. R. de, "España en el congreso de Viena, según la correspondencia oficial de D. Pedro Gómez Labrador, Marqués de Labrador," *Revista de archivos, bibliotecas y museos,* XV, 1-27, 177-211, 337-73; XVI, 165-83, 319-44; XVII, 41-58, 181-95, Madrid, 1906-07.

Webster, C. K., "Castlereagh and the Spanish Colonies, I, 1815-1818," *English Historical Review,* XXVII, 78-95, London, 1912.

——, "Castlereagh and the Spanish Colonies, II, 1818-1822," *ibid.,* XXX, 631-45, London, 1915.

INDEX

607